ESSENTIALS OF
CONTEMPORARY
MANAGEMENT

SECOND
CANADIAN
EDITION

Gareth R. Jones
Texas A & M University

Jennifer M. George
Texas A & M University

Michael Rock, Ed.D.
Seneca College of Applied Arts and Technology

Contributor

Jane Haddad
Seneca College of Applied Arts and Technology

Toronto   Montréal   Boston   Burr Ridge, IL   Dubuque, IA   Madison, WI   New York
San Francisco   St. Louis   Bangkok   Bogotá   Caracas   Kuala Lumpur   Lisbon   London
Madrid   Mexico City   Milan   New Delhi   Santiago   Seoul   Singapore   Sydney   Taipei

Dedication

UIOGD

The McGraw·Hill Companies

McGraw-Hill Ryerson

Essentials of Contemporary Management
Second Canadian Edition

ISBN-13: 978-0-07-095184-6
ISBN-10: 0-07-095184-5

1 2 3 4 5 6 7 8 9 10 FR 0 9 8 7

Printed and bound in Canada

Care has been taken to trace ownership of copyright material contained in this text; however, the publisher will welcome any information that enables them to rectify any reference or credit for subsequent editions.

Editorial Director: Joanna Cotton
Sponsoring Editor: Kim Brewster
Marketing Manager: Joy Armitage-Taylor
Developmental Editor: Lori McLellan
Senior Editorial Associate: Christine Lomas
Senior Supervising Editor: Margaret Henderson
Copy Editor: Erin Moore
Production Coordinator: Zonia Strynatka
Cover Design: Greg Devitt Design
Cover Image: © John Sylvester/First Light
Interior Design: Dave Murphy/Valid Design & Layout
Typesetting Page Layout: S R Nova Pvt Ltd, Bangalore, India
Printer: Friesens

Library and Archives Canada Cataloguing in Publication

Essentials of contemporary management / Gareth R. Jones ... [et al.]. — 2nd Canadian ed.

Includes bibliographical references and index.

ISBN 0-07-095184-5

1. Management–Textbooks.   I. Jones, Gareth R. Essentials of Contemporary Management.

HD31.E865 2007   658.4   C2006-905776-1

About The Authors

Michael Rock holds a doctorate in Adult Education from Indiana University (1974) and teaches emotional intelligence and leadership skills at the university and college levels. He has consulted to the World Bank, Bendix Corp., IBM Canada, Esso Resources, American Chiropractic Association, United Financial Investments, and Financial Post. He is the author/editor of 11 books, such as *EQ Goes to Work*, co-author of *The 7 Pillars of Visionary Leadership*, and *Ethics: To Live By, To Work By* as well as authoring over 150 articles on human relations in trade journals and magazines. Professor Rock is a licensed EQ coach and facilitator.

Professor Rock has been a full-time professor at Seneca College, Toronto, Ontario, since 1980, a winner of the Seneca College NISOD Excellence Achievement Award for Teaching, and designed and teaches the ever-popular "Business Ethics" and "EQ and the New Workplace" courses. For a number of years, Michael has also been teaching distance learning courses such as "Organization Theory & Design," "Leadership of Organizational Change," and "Ethics of Leadership" in the MBA Hospitality & Tourism Management and MA Faculty of Management, Graduate Programs, at the University of Guelph, Ontario. In 2006, he designed and taught "Emotional Intelligence & Facilitation Skills" in the Human Sciences Department, Saint Paul University, Ottawa, Ontario. Currently, Dr. Rock is completing the Ph.D. and D.Th. degrees in Theology and Spirituality (in the workplace) at Saint Paul University.

Gareth R. Jones is a Professor of Management in the Lowry Mays College and Graduate School of Business at Texas A&M University. He received his B.A. in Economics/Psychology and his Ph.D. in Management from the University of Lancaster, U.K. He previously held teaching and research appointments at the University Warwick, Michigan State University, and the University of Illinois at Urbana–Champaign.

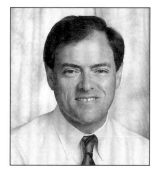

He specializes in strategic management and organizational theory and is well-known for his research that applies transaction cost analysis to explain many forms of strategic and organizational behaviour. He is currently interested in strategy process, competitive advantage, and information technology issues. He is also investigating the relationships between ethics, trust, and organizational culture and studying the role of affect in the strategic decision-making process.

He has published many articles in leading journals of the field and his recent work has appeared in the *Academy of Management Review, Journal of International Business Studies,* and *Human Relations.* He is or has served on the editorial boards of the *Academy of Management Review,* the *Journal of Management,* and *Management Inquiry.*

Jennifer M. George is the Mary Gibbs Jones Professor of Management and Professor of Psychology in the Jesse H. Jones Graduate School of Management at Rice University. She received her B.A. in Psychology/Sociology from Wesleyan University, her M.B.A. in Finance from New York University, and her Ph.D. in Management and Organizational Behavior from New York University. Prior to joining the faculty at Rice University, she was a Professor in the Department of Management at Texas A&M University.

She specializes in Organizational Behavior and is well known for her research on mood and emotion in the workplace, their determinants, and their effects on various individual- and group-level work outcomes. Currently, she is exploring how individual and contextual characteristics interact to promote or inhibit creativity in organizations. She is the author of many articles in leading peer-reviewed journals such as the *Academy of Management Journal, Academy of Management Review, Journal of Applied Psychology, Organizational Behavior and Human Decision Processes, Journal of Personality and Social Psychology,* and *Psychological Bulletin.* She is a Fellow in the American Psychological Association, the American Psychological Society, and the Society for Industrial and Organizational Psychology and a member of the Society for Organizational Behavior. Professor George is currently an Associate Editor for the *Journal of Applied Psychology.*

Brief Contents

Contents

Preface

Many changes have taken place in the world of business management in the three years since the first edition of this text was published. The fast-changing domestic and global environment increased the need for organizations and their managers to find new ways to respond in order to maintain and increase their performance. One of these new strategies has been the growing use of global outsourcing of information technology, services, and manufacturing jobs to countries overseas to reduce operating costs that has led to the loss of many jobs in Canada. Also, to increase their global competitiveness, there has been mounting pressure on managers to integrate new information technology into all aspects of organizations' operations to improve efficiency and customer responsiveness. Finally, the increasing diversity of the global workforce has made it imperative for managers to understand how and why people differ so that they can effectively manage and reap the benefits of diversity. The tasks that managers must perform efficiently and effectively have become more complex and challenging than ever before.

Essentials of Contemporary Management, Second Canadian Edition, has been significantly revised to reflect and address these challenges to managers and their organizations. Encouraged by the reactions and suggestions of both users and reviewers, we have reorganized content, revised and updated all the book's chapters to respond to the many changes that have been taking place.

We set out to write and revise this text to distill new and classic theorizing and research into a contemporary framework that is compatible with the traditional focus on management of planning, leading, organizing, and controlling, but which also transcends this approach. We also set out to present management in a way that makes its relevance obvious even to students who might lack exposure to a "real-life" management context. Our continuing goal has been to relate management theory to real-life examples to drive home the message that management matters both because it determines how well organizations perform and because managers and organizations affect the lives of people who work inside them and people outside the organization, such as customers, communities, and shareholders.

Organization of this Edition

The contemporary nature of our approach can be seen most clearly by examining our table of contents and by perusing our treatment of management issues, especially with reference to the kinds of issues and organizations we discuss in our opening cases and the many real-life examples throughout the book. Such updated and expanded topics as diversity, technology, knowledge management, baby bosses and baby boomers, EQ, and global environment round out this current and relevant new edition.

Essentials of Contemporary Management, Second Canadian Edition, is divided into six parts:

1. Management
2. The Environment of Management
3. Planning and Decision Making
4. Organizing
5. Leading Individuals and Groups
6. Controlling

Each chapter in these parts (13 chapters in total) is interspersed with and followed by additional material provided to supplement the chapter's contents and provide both context and relevance.

Guided Tour

Learning Tools

> **Learning Outcomes** have been highlighted at the beginning of each chapter, and the **Summary and Review** relating to these learning outcomes is included at the end of the chapter.

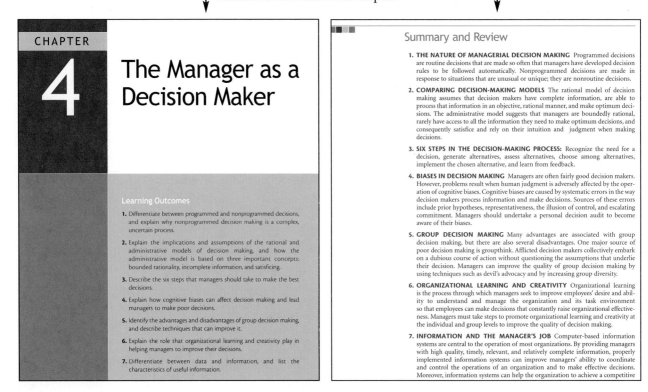

CHAPTER

4

The Manager as a Decision Maker

Learning Outcomes

1. Differentiate between programmed and nonprogrammed decisions, and explain why nonprogrammed decision making is a complex, uncertain process.

2. Explain the implications and assumptions of the rational and administrative models of decision making, and how the administrative model is based on three important concepts: bounded rationality, incomplete information, and satisficing.

3. Describe the six steps that managers should take to make the best decisions.

4. Explain how cognitive biases can affect decision making and lead managers to make poor decisions.

5. Identify the advantages and disadvantages of group decision making, and describe techniques that can improve it.

6. Explain the role that organizational learning and creativity play in helping managers to improve their decisions.

7. Differentiate between data and information, and list the characteristics of useful information.

Summary and Review

1. **THE NATURE OF MANAGERIAL DECISION MAKING** Programmed decisions are routine decisions that are made so often that managers have developed decision rules to be followed automatically. Nonprogrammed decisions are made in response to situations that are unusual or unique; they are nonroutine decisions.

2. **COMPARING DECISION-MAKING MODELS** The rational model of decision making assumes that decision makers have complete information, are able to process that information in an objective, rational manner, and make optimum decisions. The administrative model suggests that managers are boundedly rational, rarely have access to all the information they need to make optimum decisions, and consequently satisfice and rely on their intuition and judgment when making decisions.

3. **SIX STEPS IN THE DECISION-MAKING PROCESS:** Recognize the need for a decision, generate alternatives, assess alternatives, choose among alternatives, implement the chosen alternative, and learn from feedback.

4. **BIASES IN DECISION MAKING** Managers are often fairly good decision makers. However, problems result when human judgment is adversely affected by the operation of cognitive biases. Cognitive biases are caused by systematic errors in the way decision makers process information and make decisions. Sources of these errors include prior hypotheses, representativeness, the illusion of control, and escalating commitment. Managers should undertake a personal decision audit to become aware of their biases.

5. **GROUP DECISION MAKING** Many advantages are associated with group decision making, but there are also several disadvantages. One major source of poor decision making is groupthink. Afflicted decision makers collectively embark on a dubious course of action without questioning the assumptions that underlie their decision. Managers can improve the quality of group decision making by using techniques such as devil's advocacy and by increasing group diversity.

6. **ORGANIZATIONAL LEARNING AND CREATIVITY** Organizational learning is the process through which managers seek to improve employees' desire and ability to understand and manage the organization and its task environment so that employees can make decisions that constantly raise organizational effectiveness. Managers must take steps to promote organizational learning and creativity at the individual and group levels to improve the quality of decision making.

7. **INFORMATION AND THE MANAGER'S JOB** Computer-based information systems are central to the operation of most organizations. By providing managers with high quality, timely, relevant, and relatively complete information, properly implemented information systems can improve managers' ability to coordinate and control the operations of an organization and to make effective decisions. Moreover, information systems can help the organization to achieve a competitive

Command Groups

Subordinates who report to the same supervisor form a **command group**. When top managers design an organization's structure and establish reporting relationships and a chain of command, they are essentially creating command groups. Command groups, often called *departments* or *units*, perform a significant amount of the work in many organizations. In order to have command groups that help an organization gain a competitive advantage, managers need to motivate group members to perform at a high level, and managers need to be effective leaders. Examples of command groups include the salespeople at The Bay who report to the same supervisor, the employees of a small swimming pool sales and maintenance company who report to a general manager, the telephone operators at the Manulife Financial insurance company who report to the same supervisor, and workers on an automobile assembly line at Ford Canada who report to the same first-line manager.

command group
A group composed of subordinates who report to the same supervisor; also called a department or unit.

Task Forces

Managers form **task forces** to accomplish specific goals or solve problems in a certain time period; task forces are sometimes called *ad hoc committees.* When Vancouver Island–based Myra Falls copper and zinc mine was purchased in 1998 by Swedish-controlled Boliden AB, the mine had been facing labour strife for years.[12] Boliden sent over a new mine manager to help get things in order. His first job was to set up five task forces geared to key problem areas. For instance, the ground support task force found that the previous owners had neglected a number of safety problems. The task forces' recommendations were followed, and $15 million worth of improvements were done. This sent a strong signal to employees that the new management team was concerned about its employees. Task forces can be a valuable tool for busy managers who do not

task force
A committee of managers or nonmanagerial employees from various departments or divisions who meet to solve a specific, mutual problem; also called an ad hoc committee.

Definitions of Key Terms are highlighted in each chapter and provided in the margins, and a list of these terms with page references is provided at the end of the chapter.

Exhibits are interspersed throughout the text to illustrate concepts and provide a visual framework for students.

Rich and Relevant Examples

An important feature of our book is the way we use real-world examples and stories about managers and companies to drive home the applied lessons to students. Moreover, unlike boxed material in other books, we integrate more applied and fewer types of boxes seamlessly into the text; they are an integral part of the learning experience, and not tacked on or isolated from the text itself. This is central to our pedagogical approach.

Each chapter opens with a **Management Snapshot**, all of which are new to this edition. These Snapshots pose a chapter-related challenge and then discuss how companies or managers responded to that challenge, bringing to light the many issues surrounding the management process. At the end of the chapter, **So Where Do You Stand?** wraps up the opening in light of the new information gleaned from the chapter.

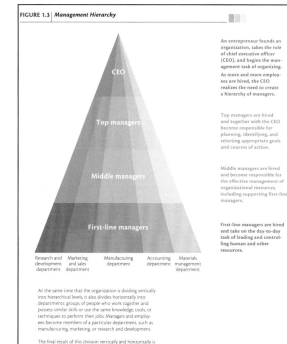

FIGURE 1.3 | *Management Hierarchy*

CEO

Top managers

Middle managers

First-line managers

Research and development department | Marketing and sales department | Manufacturing department | Accounting department | Materials management department

An entrepreneur founds an organization, takes the role of chief executive officer (CEO), and begins the management task of organizing. As more and more employees are hired, the CEO realizes the need to create a hierarchy of managers.

Top managers are hired and together with the CEO become responsible for planning, identifying, and selecting appropriate goals and courses of action.

Middle managers are hired and become responsible for the effective management of organizational resources, including supporting first-line managers.

First-line managers are hired and take on the day-to-day task of leading and controlling human and other resources.

At the same time that the organization is dividing vertically into hierarchical levels, it also divides horizontally into departments: groups of people who work together and possess similar skills or use the same knowledge, tools, or techniques to perform their jobs. Managers and employees become members of a particular department, such as manufacturing, marketing, or research and development.

The final result of this division vertically and horizontally is an organizational structure.

MANAGEMENT SNAPSHOT

To the Beat of the Same Drummer[1]

The idea is to learn to make music as an organization

Drum Café has a tag line on its website: "Building Teams.......One Beat at a Time......"[2]

Successful managers encourage their employees to drum to the same beat. At least, that's what Danny Aaron believes, and he travels the country to spread the word.

Mr. Aaron, who once ran a chain of impotence clinics in Australia and coached skiers in British Columbia, now teaches Canadian executives how to make their companies pulsate. His method: He brings their employees together in a big room and entices them to bang away on African drums. By the end of the hour, even the most timid or pessimistic of the bunch is in the groove, with values such as teamwork and collaboration coming across loud and clear.

"Companies, like music, are made up of a variety of different rhythms," says Mr. Aaron, president of Vancouver-based Drum Café. "You can have sales, marketing, accounting. You can have Vancouver, Calgary, and Toronto. But as long as those different rhythms can play to that same beat—the foundation—and can listen to each other—the communication—then as an organization they can make music."

Jim Patterson, president and chief executive of the Television Bureau of Canada in Toronto, agrees. Earlier this year, Mr. Patterson joined fellow senior executives and 120 people from media outlets across the country at Toronto's Four Seasons Hotel in a drumming circle led

In the 10 years since he led his first corporate drumming circle, Adam Rudolph, a Los Angeles-based composer and percussionist, has had high-level clients such as Texas Instruments, Cognos, and Stanford Business School. Now, his Rhythms of Collaboration drum workshops are bringing the benefits of at-work drumming to the Canadian market.

"With more and more mergers, companies have divisions that are sometimes quite separate from one another. Not only are they in different locales but they have very little to do with each other on an ongoing basis. The drum circle provides them with an opportunity to have a very fun, yet profound, teamwork and bonding experience," he says.

The drumming circle can be tailored to groups from 10 to 2000. Participants enter the room and find an assortment of drums at the ready, from African djembe drums

SO WHERE DO YOU STAND?

Wrap-Up to Opening Case

We began this chapter with a discussion of Danny Aaron, president of Vancouver-based Drum Café Canada. We remarked that successful managers encourage their employees to drum to the same beat. Says Aaron, "Companies, like music, are made up of a variety of different rhythms. You can have sales, marketing,

accounting. You can have Vancouver, Calgary, and Toronto. But as long as those different rhythms can play to that same beat— the foundation—and can listen to each other— the communication—then as an organization they can make music."

Think About It with **You Be the Manager** questions are exercises that present a realistic scenario in which a manager or organization faces some kind of challenge, problem, or opportunity and the student plays the role of a management consultant offering advice and recommending a course of action based on the chapter content.

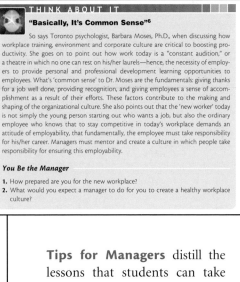

THINK ABOUT IT

"Basically, It's Common Sense"[6]

So says Toronto psychologist, Barbara Moses, Ph.D., when discussing how workplace training, environment and corporate culture are critical to boosting productivity. She goes on to point out how work today is a "constant audition," or a theatre in which no one can rest on his/her laurels—hence, the necessity of employers to provide personal and professional development learning opportunities to employees. What's 'common sense' to Dr. Moses are the fundamentals: giving thanks for a job well done, providing recognition, and giving employees a sense of accomplishment as a result of their efforts. These factors contribute to the making and shaping of the organizational culture. She also points out that the 'new worker' today is not simply the young person starting out who wants a job, but also the ordinary employee who knows that to stay competitive in today's workplace demands an attitude of employability, that fundamentally, the employee must take responsibility for his/her career. Managers must mentor and create a culture in which people take responsibility for ensuring this employability.

You Be the Manager

1. How prepared are you for the new workplace?
2. What would you expect a manager to do for you to create a healthy workplace culture?

✓ Tips for Managers
BUILDING TEAMS FOR HIGH PERFORMANCE[40]

1. Build and manage teams that live up to their promise of higher productivity and greater problem-solving ability.
2. Clarify roles and responsibilities for team members so they work together effectively.
3. Manage interpersonal conflicts among team members.
4. Maximize team productivity by encouraging group discussion and problem-solving.
5. Overcome organizational, management and employee barriers to teamwork through the focus on enhancing the emotional intelligence of team members.
6. Identify and manage team rewards effectively.

Tips for Managers distill the lessons that students can take from the chapter and apply to develop their management skills.

Management in Action

Topics for Discussion and Action

1. What is organizational culture, and how does it affect the way employees behave?
2. Interview some employees of an organization, and ask them about the organization's values, norms, socialization practices, ceremonies and rites, and special language and stories. Referring to this information, describe the organization's culture.
3. What are the main obstacles to change?
4. Interview a manager about a change effort that he or she was involved in. What issues were involved? What problems were encountered? What was the outcome of the change process?
5. What difficulties do managers face when trying to introduce organizational change? How might they overcome some of these difficulties?

Building Management Skills
UNDERSTANDING CHANGE

Choose an organization you know—one that you have worked in or patronized, or one that has received extensive coverage in the popular press. The organization should be involved in only one industry or business. Answer these questions about the organization.

1. What is the output of the organization?
2. Is the organization producing its output efficiently?
3. Try to identify improvements that might be made to boost the organization's responsiveness to customers, quality, and efficiency.
4. How difficult would these changes be?

Management for You

Think of something that you would like to change in your personal life. It could be your study habits, your fitness and nutrition, the way you interact with others, or anything else that is of interest to you. What values and assumptions have encouraged the behaviour that currently exists (i.e., the one you want to change)?

What driving and restraining forces can you address in order to make the desired change?

Small Group Breakout Exercise
REDUCING RESISTANCE TO ADVANCES IN INFORMATION TECHNOLOGY

Form groups of three or four people, and appoint one member as the spokesperson who will communicate your findings to the whole class when called on by the instructor. Then discuss the following scenario.

You are a team of managers in charge of information and communications in a large consumer products corporation. Your company has already introduced many advances in information technology. Managers and employees have access to voice mail, email, the Internet, your company's own intranet, and groupware.

Many employees use the new technology, but the resistance of some is causing communication problems. For example, all managers have email addresses and computers in their offices, but some refuse to turn their computers on, let alone send and receive email. These managers feel that they should be able to communicate as they have always done—in person, over the phone, or in writing. Thus, when managers who are unaware of their preferences send them email messages, those messages are never retrieved.

Experiential Learning Features

We have given considerable time and attention to developing state-of-the-art experiential end-of-chapter learning exercises that drive home the meaning of management to students. These exercises are grouped together at the end of each chapter in the section called **Management in Action**:

Topics for Discussion and Action are a set of chapter-related questions and points for reflection, some of which ask students to research actual management issues and learn firsthand from practising managers.

Building Management Skills are self-development exercises that ask students to apply what they have learned to their own experience of organizations and managers or to the experiences of others.

Management for You is a unique exercise that asks students to internalize concepts from the chapter and apply them to their personal lives and situations at this moment, helping them to grasp the relevance of key chapter ideas and concepts.

Small Group Breakout Exercise is uniquely designed to allow instructors in large classes to utilize interactive experiential exercises in groups of three to four students. The instructor calls on students to form into small groups simply by turning to people around them. All students participate in the exercise in class, and a mechanism is provided for the different groups to share what they have learned with one another.

Managing Ethically is an exercise that presents students with an ethical scenario or dilemma and asks them, either individually or in a group, to think about the issue from an ethical perspective to understand the issues facing practicing managers.

Exploring the World Wide Web are two assignments related to chapter content—one is "Specific," directing students to a specific url with related questions. The second is a more "General" assignment, asking students to find a relevant site to perform research.

Managing Ethically

Strana Corporation uses self-managed teams to develop and produce new greeting cards. Some of the members of the team are engaged in social loafing, and other members of the team are reluctant to say anything. Team members are supposed to provide performance evaluations of each other at the end of each project, but some rate everyone equally, to avoid conflict. This practice has caused low morale on the team, because hard work results in the same pay as loafing. Some team members are complaining that it's unethical to rate everyone the same way when individual performance differs so much. One team member has come to you for advice, because you are an expert in team performance and ethics. What would you advise this team member to do? How could the team's performance be improved?

Exploring the World Wide Web

SPECIFIC ASSIGNMENT

Many companies are committed to the use of teams, including Sears Canada. Scan Sears' website to learn more about this company (www.sears.ca). Then click on "Corporate Information," "Careers at Sears," and "Mission, Vision & Values."

1. What principles or values underlie Sears' use of teams?
2. How does Sears use teams to build employee commitment?

GENERAL ASSIGNMENT

Find the website of a company that relies heavily on teams to accomplish its goals. What kinds of teams does this company use? What steps do managers take to ensure that team members are motivated to perform at a high level?

Be the Manager

BUILDING TEAM SPIRIT[42]

Jim Clemmer is a Kitchener, Ontario-based professional speaker, workshop/retreat leader, and author of *Growing the Distance* and *The Leader's Digest*. He says that "team spirit is the catalyst every organization needs to achieve outstanding performance." Indeed, he goes to say that the "emotional commitment of the people using the tools and executing the plans is what determines whether companies sink or soar." He further explains how companies can kill or build spirit. Because of your knowledge and skill in team-based performance, you have been called into discussions with the two founding partners and 10 employees of a new specialty tire company about to open its doors in Winnipeg, Manitoba. Many of these people have been friends to this point, but the owners want to get the company going on the right footing, especially in view of the fact that, in the planning stage, they have tolerated the use of wireless devices in their meetings. They notice now that some are beginning to resent this "extra presence" while people are doing their best to communicate. They discovered that, when bored, some staff are simply emailing one another "under the table," literally.

Questions

1. What do you think is the problem here?
2. What is your best advice regarding team-building for this group?

Management Case

Greatest Corporate Success: Teams He's Built[43]

When Grant Rasmussen was a teenager he knew he wanted to run his own business. The thing was, he wanted to be an entrepreneur without the risk and without having to back a venture with his own money.
　Childhood naivete? Don't be so sure.

Rasmussen says, no one will ever be going in the same direction.
　Today, Rasmussen's company manages just under $4 billion of Canada's wealth. His company provides investment counselling services to Canada's wealthy—

Be the Manager exercises present a realistic scenario in which a manager/organization faces some kind of challenge, problem, or opportunity and the student plays the role of a management consultant offering advice and recommending a course of action based on the chapter content.

Each chapter contains a **Management Case** dealing with current companies and engaging personalities, one to two pages in length, ending with questions for students to consider.

A **Video Management Case** and questions are included with every chapter to help students make the connections from chapter concepts to real-world applications.

Video Management Case　　CBC ⊛

The Big Chill (Hollywood North)

In recent years, the incentive for Hollywood to go to Canada to produce films has dissolved due to the rising Canadian dollar and the patriotic urgency to make big budget films in Hollywood, transforming the Canadian film production industry drastically. Canadian companies are now relocating south of the border to accommodate for the revenue lost but are still struggling with this seeming overnight change in business.

Questions to Consider

1. How have changes in viewing habits affected the business of film production?
2. What incentives could Canada create to draw Hollywood business back north, and thus reclaim income from large production costs? How might changes to the heavy restrictions on Canadian films affect the situation?

Source: *Venture*, show number 915, "The Big Chill," February 22, 2004, running time 10:11.

Integrated Cases help instructors and students alike apply a broad range of theory to the organizational and managerial problems of various companies including NAV Canada air traffic control and Bombardier. These include discussion questions and occur at the end of Parts Two to Six—after Chapters 3, 5, 7, 12, and 13.

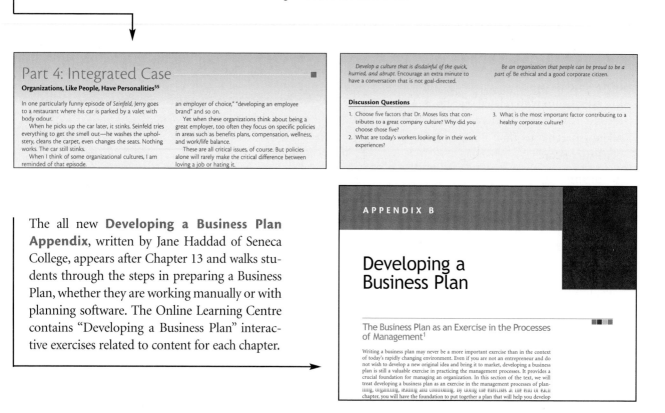

The all new **Developing a Business Plan Appendix**, written by Jane Haddad of Seneca College, appears after Chapter 13 and walks students through the steps in preparing a Business Plan, whether they are working manually or with planning software. The Online Learning Centre contains "Developing a Business Plan" interactive exercises related to content for each chapter.

Integrated Learning System for Students

Students have access to valuable and interactive learning material in addition to the text. They may choose to test their knowledge and comprehension on the Online Learning Centre, or register to go the extra mile with our *i*Study package.

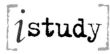

*i***Study**—Available 24/7: Instant feedback so you can study when you want, how you want, and where you want.

This online *i*Study space, authored by Laurel Donaldson of Douglas College, was developed to help you master the concepts and achieve better grades with all the learning tools you've come to expect in addition to new and improved elements—key study aids, summaries and chapter outlines, and self-testing modules with both multiple-choice and true/false application questions. *i*Study offers the best, most convenient way to Interact, Learn, and Succeed.

Instructors: Contact your *i*Learning Sales Specialist for more information on how to make *i*Study part of your students' success.

Student Online Learning Centre
www.mcgrawhill.ca/olc/jones

Essentials of Contemporary Management includes a robust study site for students that follows the text chapter by chapter, with additional quizzes and material to enhance the learning and classroom experience.

Instructor and Student Support

Integrated Learning System for Instructors: Great care was used in the creation of the supplemental materials to accompany *Essentials of Contemporary Management*, Second Canadian Edition. Whether you are a seasoned faculty member or a newly minted instructor, you will find the support materials to be comprehensive and practical.

Instructor's CD-ROM

Instructors can use this resource to access many of the supplements associated with the text and create custom presentations. Most of these supplements are also available for download in the Instructor's Resource Centre of the Online Learning Centre, located at www.mcgrawhill.ca/olc/jones.

The Instructor's CD-ROM includes electronic versions of:

- the Instructor's Manual
- the Computerized Test Bank, and
- the Microsoft® PowerPoint® Presentations

Essentials of Contemporary Management Video Presentations

The video package contains carefully selected segments of various CBC programs and the MHHE Management Video Library, chosen by the author. Every chapter has an associated video with a case and accompanying questions appearing in the text. Videos are available on VHS or DVD, or through online streaming on the Online Learning Centre.

CBC ◉

Instructor Online Learning Centre
www.mcgrawhill.ca/olc/jones

Essentials of Contemporary Management includes a password-protected website for instructors. This site offers downloadable supplements, including most of those found on the Instructor's CD-ROM, and a series of other useful resources. Contact your *i*Learning Sales Specialist for access.

Manager's Hot Seat

In today's workplace, managers are confronted daily with issues such as diversity, working in teams, and the virtual workplace. The Manager's Hot Seat is an interactive, online resource (available as an instructor supplement or for packaging with texts) that allows students to watch as 15 real managers apply their years of experience to confront these issues.

Team Learning Assistant (TLA)

TLA is an interactive, online resource that monitors team members' participation in a peer-review format. The program is designed to maximize the team learning experience and to save professors and students valuable time (available as an optional package).

PageOut

Create a custom course Website with **PageOut**, free with every McGraw-Hill Ryerson textbook.

To learn more, contact your McGraw-Hill Ryerson publisher's representative or visit www.mhhe.com/solutions

McGraw-Hill's unique point-and-click course website tool enables users to create a full-featured, professional quality course website without knowing HTML coding. PageOut is free for instructors, and lets you post your syllabus online, assign McGraw-Hill OLC content, add web links, and maintain an online grade book. (And if you're short on time, we even have a team ready to help you create your site.)

Primis Online

You can customize this text and save your students money off bookstore prices by using McGraw-Hill's Primis Online digital database, the largest online collection of texts, readings, and cases. Contact your McGraw-Hill *i*Learning Sales Specialist for more information.

WebCT/BlackBoard

www.blackboard.com

This text is available in two of the most popular course-delivery platforms—WebCT and BlackBoard—for more user-friendly and enhanced features. Contact your local McGraw-Hill *i*Learning Sales Specialist for more information.

*i*Learning Sales Specialist

ADVANTAGE
McGraw-Hill Ryerson

Your Integrated Learning Sales Specialist is a McGraw-Hill Ryerson representative who has the experience, product knowledge, training, and support to help you assess and integrate any of the above-noted products, technology, and services into your course for optimum teaching and learning performance. Whether it's how to use our test bank software, helping your students improve their grades, or how to put your entire course online, your *i*Learning Sales Specialist is there to help. Contact your local *i*Learning Sales Specialist today to learn how to maximize all McGraw-Hill Ryerson resources!

*i*Learning Services Program

McGraw-Hill Ryerson offers a unique *i*Services package designed for Canadian faculty. Our mission is to equip providers of higher education with superior tools and resources required for excellence in teaching. For additional information, visit www.mcgrawhill.ca/highereducation/iservices/

Acknowledgements

One never writes a book alone. This is especially true when it comes to acknowledging the contribution of **Jane Haddad**, Professor in the School of Business, Seneca College, Toronto, Ontario. In addition to making very insightful comments to improve earlier drafts of this second edition, she also did an outstanding job with the Developing a Business Plan Appendix and accompanying online exercises as well as with the Instructor's Test Bank. Thank you, Jane; I deeply appreciate your involvement and input.

Two other very special people need acknowledgement as well: **Amanda Rappak**, a wonderful assistant who, while completing her Master's degree in Environmental Studies at York University, did an amazing piece of work with the Video Cases and unselfishly offered to help at critical times in the writing of the text; and **Bonita Slunder**, a most proud, new grandmother, award-winning filmmaker and author, and a nature and animal lover, who is completing her Master's degree in Pastoral Counselling at Saint Paul University, for her encouragement and reviews of my early drafts, and for the many wonderful meals with her husband, Daniel, and family, over this past year. Both Amanda and Bonita contributed immensely to designing and testing key exercises, and co-facilitating with me in my "Emotional Intelligence & Facilitation Skills" course in the Human Sciences Deptartment, Saint Paul University, Spring 2006. Thank you, Amanda and Bonita.

I'd also like to extend thanks to my team at McGraw-Hill Ryerson for keeping both me and this project and track, treading through some new and interesting waters, and having fun along the way: **Kim Brewster**, Sponsoring Editor; **Lori McLellan**, Developmental Editor; **Margaret Henderson**, Senior Supervising Editor, and **Erin Moore**, Copy Editor.

In the preparation of this edition, we have benefited greatly from the helpful critiques and suggestions of numerous professors across the country. They helped us identify new topics, as well as clarify information, rearrange and delete material, and suggested examples that students would identify with. Their assistance was invaluable, and we extend our many thanks to:

Robert Bagg	*Mount Saint Vincent University*
Lewie Callahan	*Lethbridge College*
Terri Champion	*Niagara College*
Brooke Dobni	*University of Saskatchewan*
John Fakouri	*Algonquin College*
Steve Fanjoy	*Grant MacEwan College*
Burt Fraughton	*Nova Scotia Community College*
Anne Harper	*Humber College Institute of Technology & Advanced Learning*
Sarah Holding	*Malaspina University-College*
Donnalu Macdonald	*George Brown College*
Garth Maguire	*Okanagan College*
Jody Merritt	*St. Clair College*
Carson Rappell	*Dawson College*
Shirley Rose	*Mount Royal College*
Debra Warren	*Centennial College*
Heather White	*Georgian College*

PART 1

Management

CHAPTER 1

1

Managers and Managing

Learning Outcomes

1. Describe what management is, what managers do, what organizations are for, and how managers use the resources of their organization efficiently and effectively to achieve organizational goals.

2. Explain how planning, organizing, leading, and controlling (the four principal managerial functions) differ, and how managers' ability to handle each one can affect an organization's performance.

3. Differentiate among the three levels of management, and understand the responsibilities of managers at different levels in the organizational hierarchy.

4. Identify the roles managers perform and the skills they need to carry out those roles effectively.

5. Explain the key challenges managers face in the Canadian environment.

6. Discuss the principal challenges managers face in today's increasingly competitive global environment.

Trying Out Managing[1]

Have you ever wondered what it would be like to be a manager? What if you could "try it on," that is, "be manager for a day"?

Wendy Durward, a 13-year employee, and 10 other middle managers, were part of Nissan Canada Inc.'s "acceleration pool" and involved in a day-in-the-life simulation assessment centre exercise where they could practise their management skills. She and the other managers were assessed on their performance and personality attributes, factors that could help or hinder them as Nissan Canada prepared them for more senior management roles to come.

What was the experience like? According to Durward, it was "exhausting and exhilarating" at the same time. The management simulation assessment itself lasted 10 hours. During this time, the following factors were assessed—typical of a manager's role and responsibilities:

- *The positive aspects:* the ability to adapt to new situations, inquisitiveness, learning agility, sensitivity to others and self-awareness—of one's own strengths and development needs, as well as an awareness of the impact of one's behaviour on others.

- *The negative aspects* or "**potential derailers**": awareness of arrogance, self-promotion, insensitivity, argumentativeness, impulsiveness, and a tendency to micro-manage.

During the 10 hours of assessment, Durward endured a "typical" day for any manager: being bombarded with phone calls, deluged with e-mails from dissatisfied customers, colleagues seeking advice and similar kinds of day-to-day activities. "A steady stream of people poured through her office door—from feuding employees to colleagues coming in to consult on a strategic plan. There was an analysis to be done on whether a merger

Nissan's acceleration pool employees deserve applause after taking part in manager-for-a day exercises at Nissan: steady streams of phone calls, e-mails from dissatisfied customers, and colleagues seeking advice are par for the course.

proposal made sense and a presentation to prepare." During all this, "Ms. Durward's every move was analyzed: How sound were her business decisions, was she able to satisfy that customer, coach those employees, make a compelling presentation?"

Today, organizations must plan for the future. This need is especially critical in industries and companies with aging managers. This is true also even in an era when forced retirement at age 65 is on its way out.[2]

Nissan Canada's efforts with this type of simulation is to provide as real-to-life a context as possible so they can determine which managers will be able to lead the organization into its future by bringing up its next generation of leaders.

Jocelyn Bérard, an organizational psychologist and managing director of DDI Canada, says, "The ideal executive candidate in the coming years will need a broader range of job experiences. For example, many organizations will insist on candidates having experience with a start-up, merger or acquisition; a fast-growth organization; a unionized environment; implementing a change or a new technology; or leading and living outside of their home country." William Byham, Audrey Smith, and Matthew Paese, authors of *Grow Your Own Leaders: How to Identify, Develop and Retain Leadership Talent*, point out in their book that this kind of "walking the talk" management development learning, before taking on the role, is critical because people can't be adaptable, agile, and comfortable with the unfamiliar if they have been confined to a functional silo or have only a one-country or regional perspective.[3]

Ms. Durward has worked in a cross-border team arrangement with Nissan Canada in the United States and Mexico as well. "The idea is not just to think Canadian; it's to look at it more globally."

How would you behave under such pressure?

Now It's Your Turn

Development Dimensions International (DDI) management consultants have identified 11 "career derailers" that hinder managers from progressing in their organization.

A few are listed in this opening case. List three additional derailers that you feel you would have to resolve in order to be a better manager.

◼◼◻◼ Overview

The opening case illustrates quite vividly the importance being placed on the quality of managers needed for today's organizations. Managing a company is a complex undertaking, and managers must possess the many kinds of skills and knowledge needed to be effective. With today's emphasis, not only on threshold skills—often called the "hard skills," like accounting, finance, marketing, operations management, managers must also excel in the "soft skills," or the human relations skills. Managers are paid to make decisions, and this is not always easy; even effective managers make mistakes. However, the most effective managers do succeed because they are able to adapt and adjust to new organizational context.

In this chapter, we look at what managers do and what skills and abilities they must develop if they are to manage their organizations successfully over time. We also identify the different kinds of managers that organizations need, and the skills and abilities they must develop if they are to be successful. Finally, we identify some of the challenges that Canadian managers must address if their organizations are to grow and prosper.

What Is Management?

When you think of a manager, what kind of person comes to mind? Do you see someone who can determine the future prosperity of a large for-profit company? Or do you see the administrator of a not-for-profit organization such as a school, library, health care organization or charity? Or do you think of the person in charge of your local McDonald's restaurant or Wal-Mart store? Do you realize that even employees are being asked to assume some managerial functions, and that management occurs even in informal groups? In other words, these days almost everyone is called upon to manage, although the scope of that responsibility will vary. What, then, does management mean?

Management takes place in **organizations**, which are collections of people who work together and coordinate their actions to achieve a wide variety of goals.[4] **Management** is the planning, organizing, leading, and controlling of resources to achieve goals effectively and efficiently. **Resources** are assets such as people, machinery, raw materials, information, skills, and financial capital. A **manager** is a person responsible for supervising the use of a group or organization's resources to achieve its goals.

Achieving High Performance: A Manager's Goal

Organizational performance is a measure of how efficiently and effectively managers use resources to satisfy customers and achieve organizational goals. For instance, the principal goal of Steve Jobs is to manage Apple Computer so that it produces personal computers that customers are willing to buy; the principal goal of doctors, nurses, and hospital administrators is to increase their hospital's ability to make sick people well; the principal goal of each McDonald's restaurant manager is to produce burgers, fries, and shakes that people want to eat and pay for. Organizational performance increases in direct proportion to increases in efficiency and effectiveness (see Figure 1.1).

Efficiency is a measure of how well or how productively resources are used to achieve a goal.[5] Organizations are efficient when managers minimize the amount of input resources (such as labour, raw materials, and component parts) or the amount of time needed to produce a given output of goods or services. For example, McDonald's developed a more efficient fat fryer that not only reduces (by 30 percent) the amount of oil used in cooking but also speeds up the cooking of french fries. A manager's responsibility is to ensure that an organization and its members perform, as efficiently as possible, all the activities that are needed to provide goods and services to customers.

Effectiveness is a measure of the appropriateness of the goals that managers have selected for the organization to pursue, and of the degree to which the organization achieves those goals. Management expert Peter Drucker compared the two this way: Efficiency is doing things right; effectiveness is doing the right thing.[6] Organizations are effective when managers choose appropriate goals and then achieve them. Some years

organizations
Collections of people who work together and coordinate their actions to achieve goals.

management
The planning, organizing, leading, and controlling of resources to achieve organizational goals effectively and efficiently.

resources
Assets such as people, machinery, raw materials, information, skills, and financial capital.

manager
A person who is responsible for supervising the use of an organization's resources to achieve its goals.

organizational performance
A measure of how efficiently and effectively a manager uses resources to satisfy customers and achieve organizational goals.

efficiency
A measure of how well or productively resources are used to achieve a goal.

effectiveness
A measure of the appropriateness of the goals an organization is pursuing and of the degree to which the organization achieves those goals.

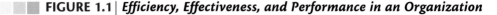

FIGURE 1.1 | *Efficiency, Effectiveness, and Performance in an Organization*

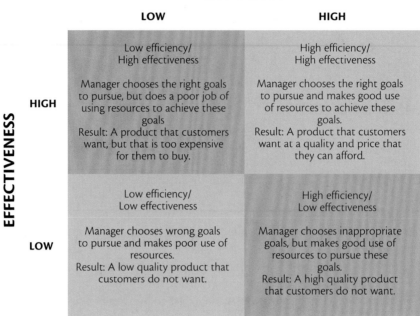

High-performing organizations are efficient *and* effective.

ago, for example, managers at McDonald's decided on the goal of providing breakfast service to attract more customers. This goal was a smart choice, because sales of breakfast food now account for more than 30 percent of McDonald's revenues. High-performing organizations such as Campbell Soup, McDonald's, Wal-Mart, Intel, Home Depot, IKEA, and the March of Dimes are simultaneously efficient and effective, as shown in Figure 1.1.

Managers who are effective are those who choose the right organizational goals to pursue and have the skills to use resources efficiently. Consider, for example, the way that Ed Clark is admired for his management excellence as well as the transparency in his actions.

Managerial Functions

THINK ABOUT IT

The Banker Who Walks on Water[7]

Ed Clark, who has a Ph.D. in economics from Harvard University is currently chief executive officer of Toronto-Dominion Bank. He is greatly admired for turning around his company in 2½ years, and is also greatly respected for speaking plainly and truthfully. Brian Levitt, a lawyer with Osler, Hoskin & Harcourt LLP in Toronto, says, "Ed was the best manager of anyone in our age cohort. He had a knack for taking a group of people and getting everybody to do the most they could do. He's a challenging guy to work for because he's on top of the file, so you can't slide by him with generalizations. It's a standard of: Do you know what you're talking about?"

Clark is willing to lay out the ground rules, resolutely and unapologetically. This was good news for the investment community: a bit of certainty, since they could count on Clark to deal with them straight. "It was an amazing presentation," recalls one analyst, who could almost quote the speech verbatim three years after the fact. "He's the first one to tell you when there's a problem—not the last one. That sets him apart from the other bank CEOs. When you talk to Ed, there's not a lot of spin."

You Be the Manager

1. What are Ed Clark's management strengths?
2. Why is Clark's transparency so important in today's business world?

The job of management is to help an organization make the best use of its resources to achieve its goals. How do managers accomplish this objective? They do so by performing four essential managerial functions: planning, organizing, leading, and controlling (see Figure 1.2). French manager Henri Fayol first outlined the nature of these managerial activities around the start of the 20th century in *General and Industrial Management*, a book that remains the classic statement of what managers must do to create a high-performing organization.[8]

Henri Fayol
www.lib.uwo.ca/business/
fayol.html

Managers at all levels and in all departments—whether in small or large organizations, for-profit or not-for-profit organizations, or organizations that operate in one country or throughout the world—are responsible for performing these four functions, and we will look at each in turn. How well managers perform them determines how efficient and effective their organization is. Individuals who are not managers can also be involved in planning, organizing, leading, and controlling, so understanding these processes is important for everyone.

FIGURE 1.2 | *Four Functions of Management*

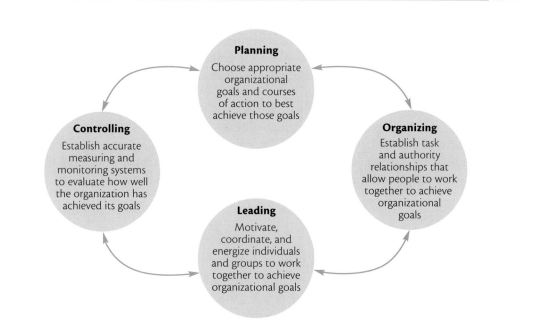

Planning
Choose appropriate organizational goals and courses of action to best achieve those goals

Controlling
Establish accurate measuring and monitoring systems to evaluate how well the organization has achieved its goals

Organizing
Establish task and authority relationships that allow people to work together to achieve organizational goals

Leading
Motivate, coordinate, and energize individuals and groups to work together to achieve organizational goals

Planning

planning
Identifying and selecting appropriate goals and courses of action; one of the four principal functions of management.

Planning is a process used to identify and select appropriate goals and courses of action. There are three steps in the planning process: (1) deciding which goals the organization will pursue, (2) deciding what courses of action to adopt to attain those goals, and (3) deciding how to allocate organizational resources to attain the goals. How well managers plan determines how effective and efficient their organization is—its performance level.[9] For managers who work for Ed Clark, they know, by observing the way he manages, that preparedness, planning, and candidness are critical in their dealings and management of the bank.

strategy
A cluster of decisions about what goals to pursue, what actions to take, and how to use resources to achieve goals.

The outcome of planning is a **strategy**, a cluster of decisions concerning what organizational goals to pursue, what actions to take, and how to use resources to achieve goals. For instance, WestJet's strategy is to be a low-cost provider in the Canadian discount airline market. Planning is a difficult activity because, normally, it's not immediately clear which goals an organization should pursue or how best to pursue them. Choosing the right strategy is risky because managers commit organizational resources for activities that could either succeed or fail. The failure of many of the dot-coms is attributable to managers trying to make money quickly, without business plans or long-term vision. In Chapter 5, we focus on the planning process and on the strategies organizations can select to respond to opportunities or threats.

Organizing

organizing
Structuring workplace relationships in a way that allows members of an organization to work together to achieve organizational goals; one of the four principal functions of management.

Organizing is a process used to structure workplace relationships in a way that allows members of an organization to work together to achieve organizational goals. Organizing involves grouping people into departments according to the kinds of job-specific tasks they perform. In organizing, managers also lay out the lines of authority and responsibility between different individuals and groups, and they decide how best to coordinate organizational resources, and in particular, human resources. When Ed Clark worked in the private sector in Ottawa in the mid-1970s before eventually landing the top job at what is now TD Canada Trust, he realized that he needed a very different set of organizing skills. Says Clark, "Can you imagine running a large organization where you can't fire, you can't hire and you can't reward people, and yet you have to motivate them to work extraordinarily long hours?"

organizational structure
A formal system of task and reporting relationships that coordinates and motivates organizational members so that they work together to achieve organizational goals.

The outcome of organizing is the creation of an **organizational structure**, a formal system of task and reporting relationships that coordinates and motivates organizational members so that they work together to achieve organizational goals. Organizational structure determines how an organization's resources can best be used to create goods and services.

We examine the organizing process in Chapters 6 and 7. In Chapter 6, we consider the organizational structures that managers can use to coordinate and motivate people and other resources. In Chapter 7, we look at the important roles that an organization's culture, values, and norms play in binding people and departments together so that they work toward organizational goals.

Leading

leading
Articulating a clear vision and energizing and empowering organizational members so that everyone understands their individual roles in achieving organizational goals; one of the four principal functions of management.

In **leading**, managers articulate a clear vision, and make sure that organizational members understand their individual roles in achieving organizational goals. Leadership depends on the use of power, influence, vision, persuasion, and communication skills for two important tasks: to coordinate the behaviours of individuals and groups so that their activities and efforts are in harmony, and to encourage employees to perform at a high level. The outcome of good leadership is a high level of motivation and commitment among organizational members. Before becoming CEO of Toronto-Dominion Bank, Ed Clark took the job as CEO of Financial Trustco, a struggling conglomerate run by the flamboyant (and now deceased) entrepreneur, Gerry Pencer. Although Financial Trustco was widely viewed as a mess, and a career-wrecker in the making, Clark's ability to lead a turnaround made the difference. Previously in Ottawa he had earned a reputation "as a consensus-builder, and relied on both that experience and his connections to bring regulators to the bargaining table and buy enough time to unwind Financial Trustco methodically. At the same time, he struck deft agreements with lenders and managed to sell off scattered bits of the company's holdings." He was successful in leading that risky and challenging work.

We discuss the issues involved in managing and leading individuals and groups in Chapters 8 through 12. In Chapters 8 and 9, we examine the best ways to encourage high motivation and commitment among employees. In Chapter 10, we look at the way groups and teams achieve organizational goals, and the coordination problems that can arise when people work together in groups and teams. In Chapter 11, we consider how to manage employees through human resource practices. In Chapter 12, we consider how communication and coordination problems can arise between people and functions, and how managers can try to manage these problems through bargaining and negotiation. Understanding how to manage and lead effectively is an important skill. You might be interested to know that CEOs have just a few short months to prove to investors that they are able to communicate a vision and carry it out. Recent studies suggest that investors and analysts give CEOs only 14 to 18 months to show results.[10]

Controlling

In **controlling**, managers evaluate how well an organization is achieving its goals and take action to maintain or improve performance. For example, managers monitor the performance of individuals, departments, and the organization as a whole to see whether they are all meeting desired performance standards. If standards are not being met, managers take action to improve performance. Individuals working in groups also have the responsibility of controlling, because they have to make sure the group achieves its goals and completes its actions. For Ed Clark of TD Canada Trust, controlling involves working closely with his senior managers; he also has very little patience for poor results.

The outcome of the control process is the ability to measure performance accurately and regulate organizational efficiency and effectiveness. In order to exercise control, managers must decide which goals to measure—perhaps goals pertaining to productivity, quality, or responsiveness to customers—and then they must design information and control systems that will provide the data they need to assess performance. These mechanisms provide feedback to the manager, and the manager provides feedback to employees. The controlling function also allows managers to evaluate how well they themselves are performing the other three functions of management—planning, organizing, and leading—and to take corrective action.

We cover the most important aspects of the control function in Chapter 13, where we outline the basic process of control and examine some control systems that managers can use to monitor and measure organizational performance.

The four managerial functions—planning, organizing, leading, and controlling—are essential to a manager's job. At all levels in a managerial hierarchy, and across all departments in an organization, effective management means making decisions and managing these four activities successfully.

controlling
Evaluating how well an organization is achieving its goals and taking action to maintain or improve performance; one of the four principal functions of management.

Types of Managers

Hannes Blum, Successful Book Merchant, Abebooks of Victoria, B.C.[11]

Jeans-clad 20 and 30-somethings work in what could be called a rabbit's warren of offices, where desks bristle with computer screens and lots of talk of global expansion. How is this for moxy: Abebooks Inc. is going head-to-head with the giants of the Web, using lessons gleaned from the dot-com boom. Making money from the first day it was formed in the very early 1990s, today, it is one of the largest second-hand booksellers in the world and, having recently expanded into new books, is now competing head-to-head with such giants as Amazon.com, Barnes & Noble Inc., and Indigo Books & Music Inc. Hannes Blum's goal is to be the top site worldwide for book-buying.

How does Abebooks work? Interestingly, it doesn't own any books but lists inventory for other booksellers in more than 50 countries on its website. It charges for this service, of course. But think of what they do for the customer and the types of managers they need: "The company allows customers to search its database of books and it also handles transactions, all of which has proved an appealing proposition. It now lists an astounding 70 million books from 13 000 sellers all over the world, with inventory increasing by more than 200 000 books every day." Every minute 17 sales occur. In 2004, book sales were US$130 million. From a management perspective, Blum is leveraging perception: many customers see his company as an alliance of independent booksellers struggling against corporate giants, which, in many ways is true. But it's also a perception Blum would like to nurture as well.

You Be the Manager

1. What types of management skills does Abebooks Inc. require?

2. What's the significance of the "underdog" image Blum is nurturing in his management of Abebooks Inc.?

Abebooks
www.abebooks.com

To perform efficiently and effectively, larger organizations traditionally employ three types of managers—first-line managers, middle managers, and top managers—arranged in a hierarchy (see Figure 1.3). Typically, first-line managers report to middle managers, and middle managers report to top managers. Managers at each level have different but related types of responsibilities for using organizational resources to increase efficiency and effectiveness.

These three types of managers are grouped into departments according to their specific job responsibilities. A **department**—such as manufacturing, accounting, or engineering—is a group of people who work together and possess similar skills or use the same kind of knowledge, tools, or techniques to perform their jobs. As Figure 1.3 indicates, first-line, middle, and top managers, who differ from one another by virtue of their job-specific responsibilities, are found in each of an organization's major departments. Below, we examine the reasons why organizations use a hierarchy of managers and group them into departments. We then examine some recent changes that have been taking place in managerial hierarchies.

department
A group of people who work together and possess similar skills or use the same knowledge, tools, or techniques to perform their jobs.

FIGURE 1.3 | *Management Hierarchy*

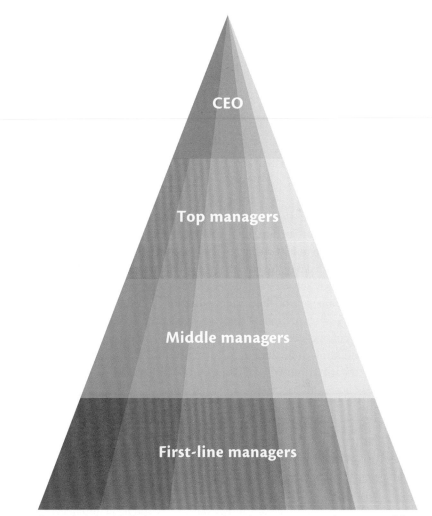

CEO

Top managers

Middle managers

First-line managers

| Research and development department | Marketing and sales department | Manufacturing department | Accounting department | Materials management department |

An entrepreneur founds an organization, takes the role of chief executive officer (CEO), and begins the management task of organizing.

As more and more employees are hired, the CEO realizes the need to create a hierarchy of managers.

Top managers are hired and together with the CEO become responsible for planning, identifying, and selecting appropriate goals and courses of action.

Middle managers are hired and become responsible for the effective management of organizational resources, including supporting first-line managers.

First-line managers are hired and take on the day-to-day task of leading and controlling human and other resources.

At the same time that the organization is dividing vertically into hierarchical levels, it also divides horizontally into departments: groups of people who work together and possess similar skills or use the same knowledge, tools, or techniques to perform their jobs. Managers and employees become members of a particular department, such as manufacturing, marketing, or research and development.

The final result of this division vertically and horizontally is an organizational structure.

Levels of Management

First-Line Managers

At the base of the managerial hierarchy are **first-line managers** (often called supervisors). They are responsible for the daily supervision and coordination of the nonmanagerial employees who perform many of the specific activities necessary to produce goods and services. First-line managers may be found in all departments of an organization.

Examples of first-line managers include the supervisor of a work team in the manufacturing department of a car plant, the head nurse in the obstetrics department of a hospital, and the chief mechanic overseeing a crew of mechanics in the service department of a new-car dealership.

Middle Managers

Middle managers supervise the first-line managers, and have the responsibility of finding the best way to organize human and other resources to achieve organizational goals. To increase efficiency, middle managers try to find ways to help first-line managers and nonmanagerial employees make better use of resources in order to reduce manufacturing costs or improve the way services are provided to customers. To increase effectiveness, middle managers are responsible for evaluating whether the goals that the organization is pursuing are appropriate and for suggesting to top managers ways in which goals should be changed. A major part of the middle manager's job is to develop and fine-tune skills and know-how—manufacturing or marketing expertise, for example—that allow the organization to be efficient and effective. Middle managers also coordinate resources across departments and divisions. Middle managers make the thousands of specific decisions that go into the production of goods and services: Which first-line supervisors should be chosen for this particular project? Where can we find the highest quality resources? How should employees be organized to allow them to make the best use of resources?

Middle managers perform an important role in organizations. For instance, behind a first-class sales force, look for the sales manager responsible for training, motivating, and rewarding salespeople. Behind a committed staff of secondary school teachers, look for the principal who energizes them to look for ways to obtain the resources they need to do an outstanding and innovative job in the classroom.

Top Managers

In contrast to middle managers, **top managers** are responsible for the performance of all departments.[12] They have cross-departmental responsibility and they're responsible for connecting the parts of the organization together. Top managers help carry out the organizational vision; they establish organizational goals, such as which goods and services the company should produce; they decide how the different departments should interact; and they monitor how well middle managers in each department use resources to achieve goals.[13] Top managers are ultimately responsible for the success or failure of an organization, and their performance is continually scrutinized by people inside and outside the organization, such as employees and investors.[14]

Top managers report to a company's chief executive officer— such as WestJet CEO Clive Beddoe, Shaw Communications CEO Jim Shaw, and Quebecor CEO Pierre Karl Péladeau—or to the president of the organization, who is second-in-command. In some organizations one person holds the title of both CEO and president, such as Lee McDonald at Southmedic and Paul Godfrey, president and CEO of the Toronto Blue Jays. The CEO and president are responsible for developing good working relationships among the top managers who head the various departments (manufacturing and marketing, e.g.), and who usually have the title vice-president. A central concern of the CEO is the creation of a smoothly functioning **top-management team**, a group composed of the CEO, the president, and the department heads most responsible for helping to achieve organizational goals.[15] The CEO also has the responsibility of setting the vision for the organization.

The relative importance of each of the four managerial functions—planning, organizing, leading, and controlling—to any particular manager depends on the manager's position in the managerial hierarchy.[16] As managers move up the hierarchy, they spend more time planning and organizing resources to maintain and improve organizational performance (see Figure 1.4). Top managers devote most of their time to planning and organizing, the functions that are so crucial to determining an organization's long-term performance. The lower a manager's position in the hierarchy, the more time he or she spends leading and controlling first-line managers or nonmanagerial employees.

Erica Van Kamp, senior product manager at Mattel Canada, rose to her position after starting out as a marketing brand manager at Good Humor-Breyers in 1997.

top-management team
A group composed of the CEO, the president, and the heads of the most important departments.

FIGURE 1.4 | *Relative Amount of Time That Managers Spend on the Four Managerial Functions*

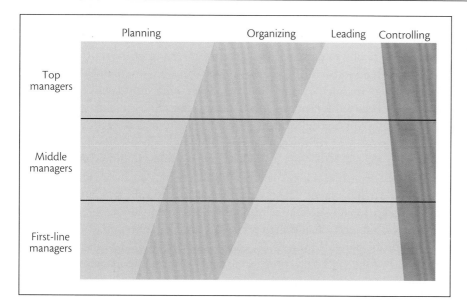

Recent Changes in Managerial Hierarchies

THINK ABOUT IT

Team Players and Scotiabank[17]

Does your boss encourage you to use his office when he is not there? Brian Toda, vice-president of human resources for Scotiabank's compensation group, does. He "invites his employees to use his office when he's not there. They take turns making conference calls from his comfortable, black leather chair or holding small meetings at a round table." Sharing office space reflects Scotiabank's team-oriented culture. Roles have certainly changed! Toda explains, "It's not like employees are coming into my space. It's their space, too." He wants to "deliver the best employment experience."

You Be the Manager

1. What is your experience in sharing office space?
2. As a manager, could you easily shift to the role that Toda works from?

The tasks and responsibilities of managers at different levels have been changing dramatically in recent years. Increasingly, top managers are encouraging lower-level managers to look beyond the goals of their own departments and take a cross-departmental view to find new opportunities to improve organizational performance. Stiff competition for resources—both at home and abroad—has put increased pressure on all managers to improve efficiency, effectiveness, and organizational performance. To respond to these pressures, many organizations have been changing the managerial hierarchy.[18]

Restructuring

restructuring
Downsizing an organization by eliminating the jobs of large numbers of top, middle, and first-line managers and nonmanagerial employees.

To decrease costs, CEOs and their top-management teams have been **restructuring** organizations to reduce the number of employees on the payroll. Restructuring can involve flattening the organization by cutting out some hierarchical layers, reducing the number of departments or the number or types of product lines, selling off parts of the business, closing plants, or even deciding to outsource some of the functions within the organization. Often, restructuring involves downsizing, or eliminating the jobs of large numbers of top, middle, or first-line managers and nonmanagerial employees. Downsizing has been a frequent event in Canada recently. Restructuring promotes efficiency by reducing costs and allowing the organization to make better use of its remaining resources. Large for-profit organizations today typically employ 10-percent fewer managers than they did 10 years ago. Canadian National Railway, Nortel Networks Corporation, General Motors, and many other organizations have eliminated several layers of middle management. The middle managers who still have jobs at these companies have had to assume additional responsibilities and are under increasing pressure to perform. For instance, when Indigo Books & Music Inc. removed a layer of management from all its stores in May 2000, each store's general manager had to handle responsibilities of the marketing, purchasing, and operations managers who had previously reported to the general manager.

Not everyone agrees that restructuring has a positive impact on society at large. For instance, when he was industry minister, federal politician John Manley said, "It's part of my job to push the corporate sector and urge them to take into account the enormous damage it does when you cast people aside instead of retraining them."[19] Moreover, when polled, 58 percent of Canadians did not find it acceptable for profitable corporations to lay off employees.[20] Len Brooks, executive director of the Clarkson Centre for Business Ethics & Board Effectiveness at the University of Toronto, says laying off employees to maximize profit and improve cash flow "is really a dumb idea. Only a third of its practitioners achieve their financial objectives while paying a huge price as employee morale craters."[21] Many studies show that "surviving employees become narrow-minded, self-absorbed, and risk averse [after downsizing]. Morale sinks, productivity drops, and survivors distrust management."[22] For instance,

Professor Terry Wagar, of the Department of Management at Saint Mary's University in Halifax, surveyed almost 2000 firms across Canada and found that companies that downsized during the 1990s suffered a variety of negative consequences. These included less favourable employer-employee relations, and decreases in efficiency and employee satisfaction.[23]

Empowerment and Self-Managed Teams

Another major change in management has taken place at the level of first-line managers, who typically supervise the employees engaged in producing goods and services. Many organizations have taken two steps to reduce costs and improve quality. One is the **empowerment** of the workforce, expanding employees' tasks and responsibilities so that they have more authority and accountability. The other is the creation of **self-managed teams**—groups of employees who are given responsibility for supervising their own activities and for monitoring the quality of the goods and services they provide. At WestJet, CEO Clive Beddoe has created an empowered workforce. He believes that his management from the bottom gives employees pride in what they do. "They are the ones making the decisions about what they're doing and how they're doing it," says Beddoe.

Under both empowerment and self-managed teams, employees assume many of the responsibilities and duties previously performed by first-line managers.[24] What is the role of the first-line manager in this new work context? First-line managers act as coaches or mentors whose job is not to tell employees what to do, but to provide advice and guidance and help teams find new ways to perform their tasks more efficiently.[25] Kathleen Dore is president of television and radio at CanWest MediaWorks. In a speech she gave to the Verity Women's Club in Toronto as part of the Canadian Women in Communications series, she said, "In terms of leadership, one of the problems is that women have very few historical role models, so we tend to imitate the traditional male approach, what I call the 'command and control' model." Further, "In a corporate environment, command and control focuses on you, and how far and how fast you can push people." A good leader, however, according to Dore, empowers people rather than controls them. Borrowing a military term, she calls this the "force multiplier."[26] Similarly, WestJet's employees are encouraged to perform their jobs in ways that meet the company's overall objectives without interference from supervisors.

empowerment
Expanding employees' tasks and responsibilities.

self-managed teams
Groups of employees who supervise their own activities and monitor the quality of the goods and services they provide.

Tips for Managers
MANAGING RESOURCES

1. Develop a list of skills that you need to develop now to become, not only a good manager, but a great one.[27]
2. Review your list of "potential derailers" that you completed after the opening case. Add any new ones that have occurred to this point.
3. Make a list of the "hard skills" you still need to develop.
4. Make a list of the "soft skills" you still need to develop.
5. Write down your description of what "high performance" is.
6. Take a poll of customer needs and expectations and make suggestions so that they could be met and addressed.
7. Identify the different levels of managers in an organization you know. Describe why the organization looks as it does.

Managerial Roles and Skills

Henry Mintzberg
www.henrymintzberg.com

Though we might like to think that a manager's job is highly structured and that management is a logical, orderly process in which managers try hard to make rational decisions, being a manager often involves acting emotionally and relying on gut feelings. Quick, immediate reactions to situations rather than deliberate thought and reflection are an important aspect of managerial action.[29] Often, managers are overloaded with responsibilities, do not have time to analyze every nuance of a situation, and therefore make decisions in uncertain conditions without being sure which outcomes will be best.[30] Moreover, for top managers in particular, the current situation is constantly changing, and a decision that seems right today may prove to be wrong tomorrow.

Despite all this flux, however, it is important to note that the roles managers need to play and the skills they need to use have changed little since the early 1970s, when McGill University Professor Henry Mintzberg detailed 10 specific roles that effective managers undertake. A **role** is a set of specific tasks that a person is expected to perform because of the position he or she holds in an organization. Although the roles that Mintzberg described overlap with Fayol's model, they are useful because they focus on what managers do in a typical hour, day, or week.[31] Below, we discuss these roles and then examine the skills effective managers need to develop.

role
The specific tasks that a person is expected to perform because of the position he or she holds in an organization.

Managerial Roles Identified by Mintzberg

Mintzberg examined all the specific tasks that managers need to perform as they plan, organize, lead, and control organizational resources, and he reduced them to 10 roles.[32] Managers assume each of these roles in order to influence the behaviour of individuals and groups inside and outside the organization. People inside the organization include other managers and employees. People outside the organization include shareholders, customers, suppliers, the local community in which an organization is located, and any local or government agency that has an interest in the organization and what it does.[33] Mintzberg grouped the 10 roles into three broad categories: *interpersonal*, *informational*, and *decisional* (see Table 1.1). Managers often perform several of these roles simultaneously.

Interpersonal Roles

Managers assume interpersonal roles in order to coordinate and interact with organizational members and provide direction and supervision for employees and for the organization as a whole. A manager's first interpersonal role is to act as a *figurehead*—the person who symbolizes an organization or a department. Assuming the figurehead role, the chief executive officer determines the direction or mission of the organization and informs employees and other interested parties about what the

TABLE 1.1 | *Managerial Roles Identified by Mintzberg*

Type of Role	Specific Role	Examples of Role Activities
INTERPERSONAL	**Figurehead**	Outline future organizational goals to employees at company meetings; open a new corporate headquarters building; state the organization's ethical guidelines and the principles of behaviour employees are to follow in their dealings with customers and suppliers
	Leader	Provide an example for employees to follow; give direct commands and orders to subordinates; make decisions concerning the use of human and technical resources; mobilize employee support for specific organizational goals.
	Liaison	Coordinate the work of managers in different departments; establish alliances between different organizations to share resources to produce new goods and services.
INFORMATIONAL	**Monitor**	Evaluate the performance of managers in different functions and take corrective action to improve their performance; watch for changes occurring in the external and internal environment that may affect the organization in the future.
	Disseminator	Inform employees about changes taking place in the external and internal environment that will affect them and the organization; communicate to employees the organization's vision and purpose.
	Spokesperson	Launch a national advertising campaign to promote new goods and services; give a speech to inform the local community about the organization's future intentions.
DECISIONAL	**Entrepreneur**	Commit organizational resources to develop innovative goods and services; decide to expand internationally to obtain new customers for the organization's products.
	Disturbance handler	Move quickly to take corrective action to deal with unexpected problems facing the organization from the external environment, such as a crisis like an oil spill, or from the internal environment, such as producing faulty goods or services.
	Resource allocator	Allocate organizational resources among different functions and departments of the organization; set budgets and salaries of middle and first-level managers.
	Negotiator	Work with suppliers, distributors, and labour unions to reach agreements about the quality and price of input, technical, and human resources; work with other organizations to establish agreements to pool resources to work on joint projects.

organization is seeking to achieve. Managers at all levels act as figureheads and role models who establish the appropriate and inappropriate ways to behave in the organization. Hannes Blum, President of ABE.com (p. 10), is the figurehead who leverages perception, the little person taking on the giant booksellers. In fact, Blum has worked hard, in a hands-on way, at showcasing a worldwide network of finding and selling books on the Internet. After all, when he was a Ph.D. student, he knew the difficulty of finding textbooks.

A manager's role as a *leader* is to encourage subordinates to perform at a high level and to take steps to train, counsel, and mentor subordinates to help them reach their full potential. A manager's power to lead comes both from formal authority, due to his or her position in the organization's hierarchy, and from his or her personal qualities, including reputation, skills, and personality. The personal behaviour of a leader affects employee attitudes and behaviour; indeed, subordinates' desire to perform at a high level—and even whether they desire to arrive at work on time and not to be absent often—depends on how satisfied they are with working for the organization. With her small staff of carpenters, electricians, interior decorators, and maintenance workers, Patsos Stanley acts like a leader, energizing them to provide the quick service that guests expect.

In performing as a *liaison,* managers link and coordinate the activities of people and groups both inside and outside the organization. Inside the organization, managers are responsible for coordinating the activities of people in different departments to improve their ability to cooperate. Outside the organization, managers are responsible for forming linkages with suppliers, customers, or the organization's local community in order to obtain scarce resources. People outside an organization often come to equate the organization with the manager they are dealing with, or with the person they see on television or read about in the newspaper. Patsos Stanley takes on the liaison role when she links her guests to organizations that provide services they may need such as dry cleaning, catering, or hairdressing.

Informational Roles

Informational roles are closely associated with the tasks necessary to obtain and transmit information. First, a manager acts as a *monitor* and analyzes information from inside and outside the organization. With this information, a manager can effectively organize and control people and other resources. Hannes Blum, for example, must use a very sophisticated computer system to identify, find, track, and locate books for customers involving key search engines and his networked 8,000 members.

Acting as a *disseminator,* the manager transmits information to other members of the organization to influence their work attitudes and behaviour. For example, Hannes Blum uses information technology (IT) as an integral part of making his business successful to compete with the giant booksellers. In the role of spokesperson, a manager uses information to promote the organization so that people both inside and outside the organization respond positively. For instance, Hannes Blum also keeps correct information flowing with his 12,000 booksellers who, in total, list 55 million books.

Decisional Roles

Decisional roles are closely associated with the methods that managers use to plan strategy and utilize resources. In the role of *entrepreneur,* a manager must decide which projects or programs to initiate and how to invest resources to increase organizational performance. As a *disturbance handler,* a manager assumes responsibility for handling an unexpected event or crisis that threatens the organization's access to resources. In this situation, a manager must also assume the roles of figurehead and leader to rally employees so they can help secure the resources needed to avert the problem. Patsos Stanley engages in the disturbance handler role when she deals with unexpected problems such as plumbing breakdowns in the middle of the night.

Under typical conditions, *resource allocator* is one of the important roles a manager plays—deciding how best to use people and other resources to increase organizational performance. For instance, Patsos Stanley decides how much money to spend to refurbish and upgrade the apartments to maintain their luxury appeal. While engaged as a resource allocator, the manager must also be a *negotiator,* reaching agreements with other managers or groups claiming the first right to resources, or with the organization and outside groups such as shareholders or customers. For instance, Patsos Stanely contracts with other organizations, such as cleaning or painting companies, to obtain the most economical services her business requires.

Managerial Skills

To successfully perform their roles, managers must have certain skills. Research has shown that formal education, training, and experience help managers to acquire three principal types of skills: *conceptual, human,* and *technical.*[34] As you might expect, the level of these skills that a manager needs depends on his or her level in the managerial hierarchy (see Figure 1.5).

Conceptual Skills

Conceptual skills are demonstrated by the ability to analyze and diagnose a situation and to distinguish between cause and effect. Planning and organizing require a high level of conceptual skill, as does performing the managerial roles discussed above. Top managers require the best conceptual skills, because their primary responsibilities are planning and organizing.[35] Conceptual skills allow managers to understand the big picture confronting an organization. The ability to focus on the big picture lets the manager see beyond the situation immediately at hand and consider choices while keeping the organization's long-term goals in mind.

conceptual skills
The ability to analyze and diagnose a situation and to distinguish between cause and effect.

FIGURE 1.5 | *Conceptual, Human, and Technical Skills Needed by Three Levels of Management*

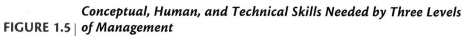

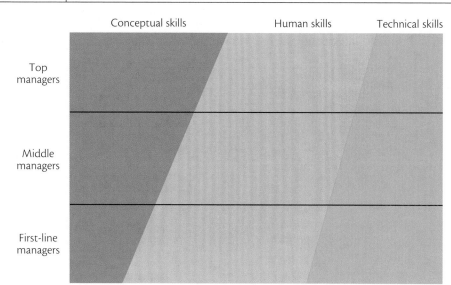

Human Skills

Human skills include the ability to understand, alter, lead, and control the behaviour of other individuals and groups. The ability to communicate and give feedback, to coordinate and motivate people, to give recognition, to mould individuals into a cohesive team, and to play politics effectively distinguishes effective from ineffective managers. By all accounts, Ed Clark of TD Canada Trust and Brian Toda of Scotiabank possess human skills.

To manage interpersonal interactions effectively, each person in an organization needs to learn how to empathize with other people—to understand their viewpoints and the problems they face. One way to help managers understand their personal strengths and weaknesses is to have their superiors, peers, and subordinates provide feedback about their performance in the roles that Mintzberg identified. Managers also need to be able to manage politics effectively so that they can deal with resistance from those who disagree with their goals. Effective managers use political strategies to influence others and gain support for their goals, while overcoming resistance or opposition.

Technical Skills

Technical skills are the job-specific knowledge and techniques that are required to perform an organizational role. Examples include a manager's specific manufacturing, accounting, or marketing skills. Managers need a range of technical skills to be effective. The array of technical skills a person needs depends on his or her position in the organization. The manager of a restaurant, for example, may need cooking skills to fill in for an absent cook, accounting and bookkeeping skills to keep track of receipts and costs and to administer the payroll, and aesthetic skills to keep the restaurant looking attractive for customers.

Crystal Decisions
www.crystaldecisons.com

Effective managers need all three kinds of skills—conceptual, human, and technical. The absence of even one type can lead to failure. Michael Kavanagh, human resources director for Vancouver-based Crystal Decisions, highlights this point. He says that at Crystal, a large computer software company, "We place a lot of emphasis on behavioural [human] skills. It's the difference between who gets hired and who doesn't. Your technical skills get you in the door, but your behavioural skills are increasingly criteria in enhancing your employment opportunities." Management skills, roles, and functions are closely related, and wise managers or prospective managers are constantly in search of the latest educational contributions to help them develop the conceptual, human, and technical skills they need to function in today's changing and increasingly competitive environment.

☑ Tips for Managers

TASKS AND ROLES

1. Think of a manager you know. Estimate what percentage of his/her day is devoted to each of the four tasks just outlined: planning, reorganizing, leading, and controlling. Decide if the balance of these four is appropriate.

2. From your experience, make a list of Mintzberg's roles that managers perform the best.

3. From your experience, make a list of Mintzberg's roles that managers perform the worst.

4. Assume that you are in charge of management education at your local college, identify the necessary steps for managers to have the correct levels of conceptual, technical, and human skills.

Challenges for Management in the Canadian Environment

Two Images, Two Different Realities

Canada is known for its multicultural mosaic as opposed to the melting pot idea that the United States has long held. U.S. president Richard Nixon told Canadians in a 1972 address to our House of Commons, "Mature partners must have autonomous, independent policies: Each nation must define the nature of its own interests, decide the requirements of its own security, the path of its own progress. The soundest unity is that which respects diversity, and the strongest cohesion is that which rejects coercion."[36]

Canada has different management challenges to face as it proceeds into this 21st century. Toronto, for example, may be the only city in the country that can claim a "visible majority" rather than "visible minorities."[37] Gordon Nixon, who is CEO of RBC Financial Group, points out that since Canada has such a small population, in order to grow and prosper, it must attract new immigrants, and they must also be better integrated into our communities, workforce, and economy. Says Nixon, "Canada's standard of living has lagged behind that of the United States for the last 25 years. Our competitive advantage is no longer driven by the resource industry, or by capital assets like plants, equipment and machinery. It is being driven by our ability to tap human capital so we can develop technology, improve productivity and develop creatively."

For businesses, diversity represents both a great opportunity and the right thing to do. Senior managers must exhibit a strong commitment to such diversity. In that way, all employees get a chance to unleash their potential. Finally, says Nixon, "In so doing, we'll provide our country with both a competitive advantage and a source of national pride."

You Be the Manager

1. What has been your experience of diversity in the workplace?
2. Why does managing diversity matter in an organization?
3. In your experience, what makes Canada unique?

Managing in Canada presents a number of unique challenges and opportunities. Though these will be addressed throughout the textbook, we will identify them briefly here.

Organizational Size

It is important to recognize that managers don't manage only in large organizations. There are management responsibilities in organizations of every size. You may think managers primarily manage large manufacturing operations, but you may not realize that only 14.5 percent of Canadians work in manufacturing organizations. This is fewer than the 19 percent of Canadians who work in public sector jobs (those in the local, provincial, or federal government). Most Canadians (around 75 percent) work in the service sector of the economy.[38] You may also think that most people work in large **publicly held organizations** such as Ford Motor Company of Canada, or Nortel Networks.

publicly held organizations
Companies whose shares are available on the stock exchange for public trading by brokers or dealers.

However, large organizations represent only 3 percent of the organizations in Canada. Of the almost 438 000 organizations in Canada in 2000 that had five or more employees, nearly 87 percent employed fewer than 50 people.[39] Big business hires just over 40 percent of all employees in Canada, while small businesses hire about 34 percent of all employees.[40] In 2003, about 15 percent of the labour force was self-employed, meaning that these people were managing themselves.[41]

The Types of Organizations

privately held organizations
Companies whose shares are not available on the stock exchange but are privately held.

Large organizations are often publicly held, so that the managers report to boards of directors that are responsible to shareholders. This represents one form of organization in Canada. There are also numerous **privately held organizations**, both large and small. Privately held organizations, whose shares are not available on the stock exchange, can be individually owned, family owned, or owned by some other group of individuals. Other organizational forms, such as partnerships and cooperatives, also require managers.

Many managers work in the *public sector* as civil servants, for municipal, provincial, or federal governments. The challenges of managing within government departments can be quite different from the challenges of managing in publicly held organizations. Critics argue that governments have no measurable performance objectives, and therefore employees feel less accountable for their actions. Public sector organizations also come under greater scrutiny for how they deal with diversity issues.

In addition to working directly for the government, some managers and employees work for Crown corporations. These are structured like private sector corporations, with boards of directors, CEOs, and so on. Rather than being owned by shareholders, however, they are owned by governments. The employees of a Crown corporation are not civil servants. Managers in Crown corporations are more independent than the senior bureaucrats who manage government departments.

Many of Canada's larger organizations are actually subsidiaries of American parent organizations—including Sears, Safeway, General Motors and Ford Motor Company. This means that managers in these companies often report to American top managers, and are not always free to set their own goals and targets. Conflicts can arise between Canadian managers and the American managers to whom they report about how things should be done.

The Political and Legal Climate

About 30 percent of Canadian employees are unionized, and this presents an additional challenge to management. In unionized organizations, managers must learn to work with unions and union leaders to create a positive work climate. Organizations with unionized employees are governed by the collective agreements negotiated between management and the union(s).

Canadian organizations are affected by Canadian law at a number of levels. The Competition Bureau determines whether there is too little competition in an industry, and rules on what companies must do to increase competition. For instance, the Competition Bureau ruled that Chapters Inc. and Indigo Books & Music Inc. would have to sell 13 superstores and refrain from opening new stores for two years if they were to merge, which they did on June 13, 2001 under the Chapters Inc. name. This ruling affected the plans that the managers of Chapters Inc. could make until mid-2003.

Canadian companies are also affected by interprovincial trade rules, marketing boards, and whether they are in the regulated sector (which includes agriculture, telecommunications, utilities, and transportation, e.g.). Canada has greater regulation of firms than does either the United States or the United Kingdom.[42] These rules and regulations can affect the products that firms are able to provide, or the prices at which goods must be sold. Thus regulations impact managers' abilities to make decisions freely.

Canadian organizations are also affected by trade barriers from other countries. These are discussed more fully in Chapter 2. Many organizations are also affected by the Human Rights Act and the Employment Equity Act, which have an impact on how they manage diversity in the workplace, a topic we cover in Chapter 3. We briefly illustrate all of these challenges below.

Managing a Diverse Workforce

The face of Canada has changed considerably in the past 20 years, and thus another challenge for managers is to recognize the need to treat human resources in a fair and equitable manner. In the past, white male employees dominated the ranks of management, but today the workplace also includes, for example, women, First Nations peoples, Asian Canadians, African Canadians, and Indo-Canadians. Moreover, today's workplace is much more likely to include gays and lesbians, the elderly, and people with disabilities. Managers must recognize the value of a diverse workforce, such as the ability to take advantage of the skills and experiences of different kinds of people.[43] When managers fail to understand how diversity might affect the workplace, they can encounter difficulties such as those experienced by the Canadian Armed Forces.

Even though some managers resist diversity initiatives, managers who value their diverse employees are the managers who best succeed in promoting performance over the long run.[44] Today, more and more organizations are realizing that people are their most important resource and that developing and protecting human resources is an important challenge for management in a competitive global environment. Introducing cultural sensitivity into the workplace is one of the many tasks managers have to face. We discuss many of the issues surrounding the management of a diverse Canadian workforce in Chapter 3.

Challenges for Management in a Global Environment

THINK ABOUT IT

The Talent Challenge: A Globalization Issue[45]

Neil Camarta lies awake at night—counting. He is chief executive officer of Shell Canada Ltd. What is he counting? The 10 000 construction tradespeople— welders, pipe fitters, electricians, and skilled workers of all kinds—whom Shell will need to more than triple its oil sands output over the next decade. The skilled-trades shortage is alive and well in Canada. Human resources recruiting has become a top-level CEO priority, a key piece of the strategy puzzle, particularly for energy, pipeline, and mining companies, but also in manufacturing. To make matters worse, the demographic bulge of baby boomers who are getting closer to retirement simply compounds this globalization challenge. There is also a paucity of trades and engineering talent coming out of universities, colleges, and apprenticeships. Jiri Maly, a Toronto-based principal with McKinsey & Co., the strategy consulting firm, says, "It has become a CEO-level issue and a national productivity issue. You're not just competing with Labrador and Northern Ontario. You are competing with Singapore, Dubai or a whole lot of other places which will do whatever it takes to get the best people to move there." Finally, Cheryl Knight, the executive director of the Petroleum Human Resources Council of Canada, says short-term thinking has aggravated the current people shortage in the oil patch. Massive early retirement and limits on hiring stripped out a generation of potential workers with 10 to 15 years experience.

You Be the Manager

1. How can companies make sure they are doing enough to recruit local Canadian people for their companies?

2. Is Canada better off "going where the talent is" rather than trying to "grow talent at home"?

global organizations
Organizations that operate and compete in more than one country.

Canadian firms are less likely to operate only within their own borders these days. Not only do firms face competition domestically, but they also face global competition. The rise of **global organizations**—organizations that operate and compete in more than one country—has put severe pressure on many organizations to improve their performance and to identify better ways to use their resources. The successes of German chemical companies Schering and Hoescht, Italian furniture manufacturer Natuzzi, Korean electronics companies Samsung and Lucky Goldstar, and Brazilian plane maker Empresa Brasileira de Aeronautica SA (Embraer)—all global companies—are putting pressure on organizations in other countries to raise their level of performance in order to compete successfully.

Canada has been slow historically to face the global challenge. The list of the Top 100 Global Companies of 1998 does not include any Canadian firms. The majority are American, but there are several entries from Switzerland, as well as the United Kingdom, France, and Sweden. Today, managers who make no attempt to learn and adapt to changes in the global environment find themselves reacting rather than innovating, and their organizations often become uncompetitive and fail.[46] Three major challenges stand out for Canadian managers in today's global economy: building a competitive advantage, maintaining ethical standards, and utilizing new kinds of information systems and technologies.

Mountain Equipment
Co-op
www.mec.ca

Building a Competitive Advantage

competitive advantage
The ability of one organization to outperform other organizations because it produces desired goods or services more efficiently and effectively than competitors do.

If Canadian managers and organizations are to reach and remain at the top of the competitive environment, they must build a **Competitive advantage** is the ability of one organization to outperform other organizations because it produces desired goods or services more efficiently and effectively than its competitors. The four building blocks of competitive advantage are superior *efficiency, quality, innovation,* and *responsiveness to customers* (see Figure 1.6).

Increasing Efficiency

Organizations increase their efficiency when they reduce the quantity of resources (such as people and raw materials) they use to produce goods or services. In today's competitive environment, organizations are constantly seeking new ways to use their resources to improve efficiency. Many organizations are training their workers in new

FIGURE 1.6 | *Building Blocks of Competitive Advantage*

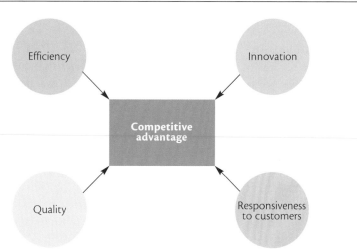

skills and techniques to increase their ability to perform many new and different tasks. Canada could do more on the training front, however. Japanese and German companies invest far more in training employees than do Canadian companies.

In addition to training employees, organizations sometimes work together to increase efficiency. For instance, Montreal-based Radio-Canada and *La Presse* signed a partnership agreement in early 2001 to combine their efforts in such areas as the internet, special events, and marketing. Guy Crevier, president and publisher of *La Presse*, noted that the agreement would "increase the efficiency of the partners." They also planned to share the infrastructure costs for foreign bureaus and the cost and results of public opinion polls.[47]

Managers must improve efficiency if their organizations are to compete successfully with companies operating in Mexico, Malaysia, and other countries where employees are paid comparatively low wages. New methods must be devised either to increase efficiency or to gain some other competitive advantage—higher quality goods, for example—if the loss of jobs to low-cost countries is to be prevented.

Globalization does not necessarily mean that companies are abandoning superior conditions at home in order to save money in low-cost countries. MEC ended contracts with three Vancouver factories because of labour or technological conditions. Nevertheless, globalization does force companies to wrestle with the challenge of being politically correct while providing affordable merchandise to their customers.

Increasing Quality

The challenge from global organizations such as Korean electronics manufacturers, Mexican agricultural producers, and European marketing and financial firms has also increased pressure on companies to improve the quality of goods and services delivered. One major thrust to improve quality has been to introduce the quality-enhancing techniques known as *total quality management* (TQM). Employees involved in TQM are often organized into quality control teams and are given the responsibility of

Today's steel rolling mills are almost all under the control of highly skilled employees who use state-of-the-art, computer-controlled production systems to increase operating efficiency.

continually finding new and better ways to perform their jobs; they also are given the responsibility for monitoring and evaluating the quality of the goods they produce.

Increasing Innovation

innovation

The process of creating new goods and services or developing better ways to produce or provide goods and services.

Innovation—the process of creating new goods and services that customers want, or developing better ways to produce or provide goods and services—poses a special challenge. Managers must create an organizational setting in which people are encouraged to be innovative. Typically, innovation takes place in small groups or teams; management passes on control of work activities to team members and creates an organizational culture that rewards risk-taking. Understanding and managing innovation and creating a work setting that encourages risk-taking are among the most difficult managerial tasks. Dr. Michael Rachlis, an associate professor at the University of Toronto's department of health care policy, and author of *Prescription for Excellence: How Innovation is Saving Canada's Health Care System*, points out how a few years ago, the innovative Sault Ste Marie Group Health Centre in Ontario assigned a home-care nurse to see every heart-failure patient, a practice that reduced readmissions by 70 percent. In another case, the Northwest Territories' diabetic program ensures comprehensive follow-up and, at least partly as a result, no one with diabetes has suffered the loss of kidneys due to complications from the disease.[48]

Increasing Responsiveness to Customers

Organizations use their products and services to compete for customers, so training employees to be responsive to customers' needs is vital for all organizations, but particularly for service organizations. Retail stores, banks, and restaurants, for example, depend entirely on their employees to give high quality service at a reasonable cost.[49] As Canada and other countries move toward a more service-based economy (in part because of the loss of manufacturing jobs to China, Malaysia, and other countries with low labour costs), managing behaviour in service organizations is becoming increasingly important.

Maintaining Ethical Standards

While mobilizing organizational resources, all managers are under considerable pressure to increase the level at which their organizations perform. For example, top managers receive pressure from shareholders to increase the performance of the entire organization in order to boost the stock price, improve profits, or raise dividends. In turn, top managers may then pressure middle managers to find new ways to use organizational resources to increase efficiency or quality in order to attract new customers and earn more revenues.

Pressure to increase performance can be healthy for an organization because it causes managers to question the organization's operations and encourages them to find new and better ways to plan, organize, lead, and control. However, too much pressure to perform can be harmful.[50] It may induce managers to behave unethically in dealings with individuals and groups both inside and outside the organization.[51] For example, a purchasing manager for a large retail chain might buy inferior clothing as a cost-cutting measure, or, to secure a large foreign contract, a sales manager in a large defence company might offer bribes to foreign officials. As another example, in early 2001, supervisory procedures at BMO Nesbitt Burns were investigated by the Manitoba Securities Commission and the Investment Dealers Association after a number of client complaints against brokers in the Winnipeg office. Among other charges, brokers were alleged to have churned client accounts to increase their own personal commissions.[52] The resulting settlement called for the biggest penalty of its kind to the commission.

When managers act unethically, some individuals or groups may obtain short-term gains, but in the long run the organization and people inside and outside the organization will pay. In Chapter 3, we discuss the nature of ethics and the importance of managers and all members of an organization behaving ethically as they pursue organizational goals.

Utilizing New Information Systems and Technologies

Another important challenge facing Canadian managers is the pressure to increase performance through new information systems and technologies.[53] Canadian companies have been slower to adopt new technologies than their American counterparts, lagging behind the United States by two decades when it comes to corporate and government spending on information technology, a recent Conference Board of Canada report found. As a result, the United States enjoys higher productivity and economic growth rates.[54] The importance of information systems and technologies is discussed in greater detail in Chapter 4.

Summary and Review

1. **WHAT IS MANAGEMENT?** A manager is a person responsible for supervising the use of an organization's resources to meet its goals. An organization is a collection of people who work together and coordinate their actions to achieve a wide variety of goals. Management is the process of using organizational resources to achieve organizational goals effectively and efficiently through planning, organizing, leading, and controlling. An efficient organization makes the most productive use of its resources. An effective organization pursues appropriate goals and achieves these goals by using its resources to create the goods or services that customers want.

2. **MANAGERIAL FUNCTIONS** According to Fayol, the four principal managerial functions are planning, organizing, leading, and controlling. Managers at all levels of the organization and in all departments perform these functions. Effective management means managing these activities successfully.

3. **TYPES OF MANAGERS** Organizations typically have three levels of management. First-line managers are responsible for the day-to-day supervision of nonmanagerial employees. Middle managers are responsible for developing and utilizing organizational resources efficiently and effectively. Top managers have cross-departmental responsibility. The top managers' job is to establish appropriate goals for the entire organization and to verify that department managers are using resources to achieve those goals. To increase efficiency and effectiveness, some organizations have altered their managerial hierarchies by restructuring, by empowering their workforces, and by using self-managed teams.

4. **RECENT CHANGES IN MANAGERIAL HIERARCHIES** Managers' tasks and responsibilities have been changing dramatically in recent years. Organizations have become flatter, and large numbers of top, middle, and first-line managers have been cut, increasing the managerial responsibilities of those remaining. Some organizations are empowering more employees at all levels, giving them more authority and accountability. Organizations have also introduced self-managed teams, which are responsible for supervising their own activities.

5. **MANAGERIAL ROLES AND SKILLS** According to Mintzberg, managers play 10 different roles: figurehead, leader, liaison, monitor, disseminator, spokesperson, entrepreneur, disturbance handler, resource allocator, and negotiator. Three types of skills help managers perform these roles effectively: conceptual, human, and technical skills.

6. **CHALLENGES FOR MANAGEMENT IN THE CANADIAN ENVIRONMENT** Canada's environment presents many interesting challenges to managers: different types and sizes of organizations; a number of national and international laws; labour unions; and a diverse workforce.

7. **CHALLENGES FOR MANAGEMENT IN A GLOBAL ENVIRONMENT** Today's competitive global environment presents three main challenges to managers: building a competitive advantage by increasing efficiency, quality, innovation, and responsiveness to customers; behaving ethically toward people inside and outside the organization; and utilizing new information systems and technologies.

Key Terms

competitive advantage, p. 24	**organizational performance, p. 5**
conceptual skills, p. 19	**organizational structure, p. 8**
controlling, p. 9	**organizations, p. 5**
department, p. 10	**organizing, p. 8**
effectiveness, p. 5	**planning, p. 8**
efficiency, p. 5	**privately held organizations, p. 22**
empowerment, p. 15	**publicly held organizations, p. 21**
first-line managers, p. 12	**resources, p. 5**
global organizations, p. 24	**restructuring, p. 14**
human skills, p. 20	**role, p. 16**
innovation, p. 26	**self-managed teams, p. 15**
leading, p. 8	**strategy, p. 8**
management, p. 5	**technical skills, p. 20**
manager, p. 5	**top-management team, p. 13**
middle managers, p. 12	**top managers, p. 12**

SO WHERE DO YOU STAND?

Wrap-Up To Opening Case

So, how did you do listing the potential derailers that could sabotage your career plans? As pointed out, Development Dimensions International (DDI) management consultants refer to these blocks as "potential derailers," that is, if we are not careful or aware of them, we could end up minimizing our chances for success.[55] DDI has identified 11 career derailers. Put a check mark beside the trait(s) that best describe you and the challenges you face in overcoming them.

Career Derailers

Trait	Description	Describes Me
Volatile	Moody, easily irritated and hard to please. Dealing with stress by quitting or ending relationships.	
Argumentative	Mistrusting others' intentions, being alert for signs of mistreatment, then challenging or blaming others when it seems to occur.	
Risk averse	Being overly concerned about making mistakes or being embarrassed, and becoming defensive and conservative when stressed.	
Imperceptive	Seeming independent, uncaring, aloof, uncomfortable with strangers and dealing with stress by withdrawing and being uncommunicative.	
Avoidant	Wanting to work according to one's own pace and standards and feeling put upon when asked to work faster or differently.	
Arrogant	Tendency to over-evaluate one's talents, to not admit mistakes or take advice, and to bluster or bluff when under pressure.	
Impulsive	Taking risks, testing limits, making hasty decisions, not learning from experience and demanding to move on when confronted with mistakes.	
Attention-seeking	Expecting to be seen as talented and interesting, ignoring others' requests and becoming very busy when under pressure.	
Eccentric	Being eccentric—acting and thinking in creative and sometimes unusual ways—and becoming unpredictable when stressed.	
Perfectionistic	Having high standards of performance for self and others, being meticulous, precise, picky, critical, and stubborn when under pressure.	
Approval dependent	Being cordial, agreeable and eager to please, reluctant to take independent action and conforming when under pressure.	

Online **Learning**Centre

After studying the preceding material, be sure to check out our Online Learning Centre at
www.mcgrawhill.ca/olc/jones
for more in-depth information and interactivities that correspond to this chapter.

Management in Action

Topics for Discussion and Action

1. Describe the difference between efficiency and effectiveness, and identify real organizations that you think are, or are not, efficient and effective.

2. In what ways can managers at each of the three levels of management contribute to organizational efficiency and effectiveness?

3. Identify an organization that you believe is high performing and one that you believe is low performing, using the criteria of effectiveness and efficiency. Give 10 reasons why you think the performance levels of the two organizations differ so much.

4. Choose an organization such as a school or a bank, visit it, and then list the different kinds of organizational resources it uses.

5. Visit an organization, and talk to first-line, middle, and top managers about their respective management roles in the organization. What do they do to help the organization be efficient and effective?

6. Ask a middle or top manager, perhaps someone you already know, to give examples of how he or she performs the managerial functions of planning, organizing, leading, and controlling. How much time does he or she spend in performing each function?

7. Mintzberg followed managers for his research on what they do. Try to find a cooperative manager who will allow you to follow him or her around for a day. List the types of roles the manager plays, and indicate how much time he or she spends performing them.

8. What are the building blocks of competitive advantage? Why is obtaining a competitive advantage important to managers?

9. What are some of the challenges that Canadian managers face? To what extent are these challenges specific to Canada?

10. In what ways do you think managers' jobs have changed the most over the past 15 years? Why have these changes occurred?

Building Management Skills

THINKING ABOUT MANAGERS AND MANAGEMENT

Think of an organization that has provided you with work experience, and the manager to whom you reported (or talk to someone who has had extensive work experience); then answer these questions.

1. Think of your direct supervisor. If he or she belongs to a department, what department is it? At what level of management is this person?

2. How do you characterize your supervisor's approach to management? For example, which particular management functions and roles does this person perform most often? What kinds of management skills does this manager have?

3. Do you think the functions, roles, and skills of your supervisor are appropriate for the particular job he or she performs? How could this manager improve his or her task performance?

4. How did your supervisor's approach to management affect your attitudes and behaviour? For example, how well did you perform as a subordinate, and how motivated were you?

5. Think of the organization and its resources. Do its managers use organizational resources effectively? Which resources contribute most to the organization's performance?

6. Describe how the organization treats its human resources. How does this treatment affect the attitudes and behaviours of the workforce?

7. If you could give your manager one piece of advice or change one management practice in the organization, what would it be?

8. How aware are the managers in the organization of the need to increase efficiency, quality, innovation, or responsiveness to customers? How well do you think the organization performs its prime goals of providing the goods or services that customers want or need the most?

Management for You

In each chapter you will find the Management for You *feature, which gives you ideas on how to apply this material to your personal life. We do this to help reinforce the idea that management isn't just for managers—all of us manage our lives and can apply many of the concepts in this book.*

Think about where you hope to be in you life five years from now (i.e., your major goal). What is your competitive advantage for achieving your goal? What do you need to plan, organize, lead and control to make sure that you reach your goal? Looking over Mintzberg's managerial roles (Table 1.1), which roles seem comfortable for you? What areas need improvement?

Small Group Breakout Exercise

OPENING A NEW RESTAURANT

Form groups of three or four people, and appoint one group member as the spokesperson who will communicate your findings to the entire class when called on by the instructor. Then discuss the following scenario.

You and two partners have decided to open a large restaurant in your local community that will serve breakfast, lunch, and dinner between 7 a.m. and 10 p.m. Each of you is investing $75 000 in the venture, and together you have secured a bank loan for $450 000 more to begin operations. You and your partners have little experience in the food industry beyond serving meals or eating in restaurants, and you now face the task of deciding how you will manage the restaurant and what your respective roles will be.

1. Decide what your respective managerial roles in the restaurant will be. For example, who will be responsible for the necessary departments and specific activities? Describe your managerial hierarchy.
2. Which building blocks of competitive advantage do you need to establish to help your restaurant succeed? What criteria will you use to evaluate how successfully you are managing the restaurant?
3. Discuss the most important decisions that must be made about (a) planning, (b) organizing, (c) leading, and (d) controlling, to allow you and your partners to use organizational resources effectively and build a competitive advantage.
4. For each managerial function, list the issue that will contribute the most to your restaurant's success.

Managing Ethically

Recently, six global pharmaceutical companies admitted that they conspired to artificially raise the price of vitamins on a global basis. This involved a Swiss firm, a German firm, and four others. The decision to inflate the prices came from senior managers in each company through a joint decision. This unethical action resulted in passing on unfair expenses to the customers. In several meetings around the world they worked out the details that went undiscovered for many years. Once they were caught, there was jail for some and continuing prosecution for others; all were fired.

The result of this situation was that each company agreed to create a special position of ethics officer to oversee behaviour in the organization. Why are some people unethical while others would not even consider doing what is described above? Is ethics an internal force in each individual, or can you educate people in ethics, or can people be made to be ethical? How do you define "unethical" in this case? Do you think it is possible for businesses to be ethical? What was the gain for the managers?

Exploring the World Wide Web

SPECIFIC ASSIGNMENT
What Makes a Great Manager

Go to the website and print out Gerard M. Blair's article on "What Makes a Great Manager" (www.see.ed.ac.uk/~gerard/Management/art9.html). It's a very down-to-earth article and provides "some common-sense ideas on the subject of great management."

1. What are Blair's specific notions of being a "great manager"?
2. Using Blair's ideas, do a personal write-up of how well you match up to being a "great manager"? Identify your strengths and also your challenges.

GENERAL ASSIGNMENT

Do a search on the Internet and identify a company that you think generally matches up to Blair's ideas of "great management." Be prepared to defend your choice.

1. Why did you choose the company you did?
2. What are the "great manager" strengths that you identified?
3. In what areas would you recommend that they improve?

Developing a Business Plan

(APPENDIX B, PAGE 405)

Go to www.mcgrawhill.ca/olc/jones/1 for online exercises.

Be the Manager

PLANNING FOR THE UNTHINKABLE[56]

By now, many people have seen the movie *Titanic* and know what an incredible tragedy it all turned out to be.[57] "On April 15, 1912, at 2:10 AM, the mighty ship of dreams, The *R.M.S. Titanic* foundered, bringing with it some 1523 souls into the cold sea."[58] The sinking of the *Titanic* turned out to be the "most infamous disaster of the 20th century." Each of us ask, "But how could that be? This was a time of optimism, of new materials, of adventure, of safety."

But could the disaster be attributed to bad management practices? According to Mark Kozak-Holland in "Plan for the Unthinkable," he writes, "…prestige overtook safety as the primary principle in *Titanic*'s design, the ship many thought invincible had a fate that was inevitable. Worse still, the bad guys got away with it."

The business case put forward at the time was that the building of such a ship as the *Titanic* would be a two-year payback project, quite a feat in those days. However, there was a very serious glitch: a competitive frenzy to get the ship out on the water. Executives overrode the architects' plans for "safety, performance, stability, security, maintainability, and the environment to ensure the ship delivered its functions." In practice this meant that operating the *Titanic* put everyone at risk. The ship's performance, therefore, was severely compromised. Pride got in the way as well. The architects gave in to the executive's demands to get the ship afloat and have the "ultimate passenger experience" because of their overconfidence in the ship's design.

"The lifeboats were viewed as an added safety feature, useful if *Titanic* had to rescue another ship in distress." Planning for testing was also compromised because of time and investment pressures. The net result was the perception that the *Titanic* was invincible. Reputations, corporate and personal, were at stake. Testing was sporadic and inadequate at best. However, management philosophy literally was "full-steam ahead"!

Think now what kind of a manager you would be as the planning was being done to get the *Titanic* ready to sail.

Questions

1. What additional suggestions for planning would you have offered?
2. Given the pressures to get the *Titanic* to set sail, what would you have done to make sure that plans for a safe operating ship were in place? Research more information by going to: www.gma.org/space1/titanic.html

Management Case

The Challenges of Heading the CBC

In the summer of 2005 CBC locked out their full-time employees. Robert Rabinovitch is president and CEO of the Canadian Broadcasting Corporation. What is his argument for a lockout of employees? Several management realities bear on his decision:

- The public broadcaster needs the right people to tell the right stories at the right time—or it will lose its relevance.

- The CBC is the "connecting link" for Canadians or, in Rabinovitch's words, "The CBC's radio services must host the Canadian conversation. CBC Television must be the home of Canadian drama in prime time, the deepest, most complete news service, and a place where our children find fun, commercial-free education." This connecting would also include specialized programming, even though it might attract only dedicated but smaller audiences. "But there must also be space for those nation-sharing moments that bring us together and remind us of who we are as Canadians—be it a major news event, a prestigious documentary series, a big-ticket drama, or a must-watch hockey game."

- For Rabinovitch, the CBC's disagreement with its union is over means, not ends. Unlike the BBC with its $7-billion budget, CBC must work with less than

a billion dollars: $950-million in public funding. CBC has exhausted its "external efficiencies" in managing the public corporation (through generating $102 million in one-time funds, and an additional $65 million per year through efficiencies and new revenues), it must now focus on "internal efficiencies" (through generating income from existing assets and by entering into new entrepreneurial partnerships). Without these management efficiencies, the CBC will have to cut jobs and services at a rate of about $12 million every year, just to keep up with inflation.

- To maintain quality, variety of programming and new technologies (e.g., personal video recorders, satellite radio, podcasting), the CBC will have to continually rethink how it does its job and delivers its mandate.

- In examining the skillsets needed by employees, some are more critical and essential than other skillsets.

- The implication of this skillset reality and subsequent strategy is that some jobs will be permanent (e.g., the news-gathering skills of a reporter), others not so (e.g., specialized subject matter that goes out of vogue).

- Hence, competency, relevance and merit, not seniority, should be the basis for hiring which provides a needed flexibility. In this way, "the CBC can employ the right people for the right jobs at the right time" for Canadians.

- "Jobs for life" could lead to the demise of the institution. "The right people for the right jobs" could save it.

Questions

1. How might Robert Rabinovitch's approach to management be affected by conditions at the CBC?
2. What can Rabinovitch do to build a competitive advantage at the CBC?

Source: Robert Rabinovitch, "The CBC's Boss Speaks: The Fight's Over Means, Not Ends," *The Globe and Mail*, Tuesday, August 30, 2005, p. A15.

Part 1: Integrated Case

Canadians as Collateral Damage

Arnold Amber is president of the CBC branch of the Canadian Media Guild. He takes exception, of course, to Robert Rabinovitch's understanding of the CBC labour dispute and lockout. Here is a synopsis of Amber's argument:

- Robert Rabinovitch: what could he have been thinking?

- Rabinovitch "threw 5500 employees onto the streets, creating a major crisis for the CBC and delivering our loyal audiences into the arms of competing broadcasters."

- The lockout didn't have to happen.

- Until August 15, 2005, the Canadian Media Guild has been at the CBC for 53 years without a work stoppage. Compare this to four different unions and their five work stoppages in 6½ years with the loss of more than 250 000 person-days because of these disputes.

- When the Guild didn't accept the contract worker aspect in the negotiations, Rabinovitch simply shut down the CBC—a timing issue. "Apparently, it's better to deny Canadians their public broadcaster in August [2005] than to risk missing coverage of a federal election or of the Olympics."

- The CBC already has provision under its present labour agreement to hire non-permanent employees. The lockout was unnecessary.

- "If CBC gets its way, there will be less hope for real careers in public broadcasting."

- Fallout from the lockout is the integrity of programming and reputation of the CBC with people phoning in and calling an end to public funding to the CBC.

- "What we've always requested is that management respect and form a real partnership with employees and bargain a fair collective agreement for the future. … It's time to stop the war between senior management and CBC employees."

Questions

1. How does the management style affect employer-employee relationships at the CBC?
2. What can managers do to make sure this kind of lockout does not occur again?

Source: Arnold Amber, "Cutting Off CBC Spites Us All," *The Globe and Mail*, Wednesday, August 31, 2005, p. A19.

Video Management Case

Made in Japan

This video traces the history of Sony's production of consumer products by examining the philosophy and vision of the CEO of Sony. The clip describes the CEO as a man with certainty whose managerial success grew out of being a marketing genius and not an engineer to uphold the Sony standard.

Questions to Consider

1. How did the marketing of the "Sony Walkman" product as a cultural icon generate such huge sales?
2. Why does Carla Hills, a consultant and former trade representative in the first Bush administration, speak of CEO Moreta as an "economic nationalist"? How did he navigate a business relationship with the US?

PART 2

The Environment of Management

CHAPTER

2

Managing the Organizational Environment

Learning Outcomes

1. Explain why being able to perceive, interpret, and respond appropriately to the organizational environment is crucial for managers' success.

2. Identify the main forces in an organization's *task* environment and the challenges that these forces present to managers.

3. Identify the main forces in an organization's *general* environment and the challenges that these forces present to managers.

4. Discuss the main ways in which managers can manage the external environment.

Reinventing the Firm

We live and work in a global economy; that is the new reality. Organizations share this same reality as well: the global organization is the new organizational environment. Authors Don Tapscott, David Ticoll, and Alex Lowy of the Alliance For Converging Technologies (Toronto), now called Digital 4Sight (Toronto), have described the fundamental transformation that is affecting all organizations as the digital revolution. Internetworked technologies are completely changing how organizations do business.[1]

What was once historically referred to as intellectual capital, and consisting of three elements—people's brains or "human capital," organizational knowledge, and customer, brand and market share capital—have now become fundamentally transformed and are now called **digital capital.**

According to these authors, digital capital is now the basis for wealth creation. Tapscott says, "When you link those kinds of knowledge assets or intellectual capital over the Internet—we call it Internetworking—they become transformed fundamentally and you create something new, which we call "digital capital." And in the hundreds of cases that we've done, we are convinced that digital capital is now the main foundation of wealth creation." Internetworking is a global reality today and occurs in the world of business webs. According to Ticoll, these business webs are "networks of suppliers, distributors, commerce service providers and customers that communicate and do business over the Internet or by other electronic means. Sometimes participants in these webs are collaborating, sometimes they're competing, sometimes they're just independent and sometimes they're doing all three simultaneously."

The management student today will readily see that while the "corporation was the universal vessel for wealth and value creation in the 20th century," so now "business webs will be the universal vessel in the 21st century." As with any initiative, of course, many shapes and forms will emerge, with some being more successful than others; and success will often depend upon the leadership provided by managers. The business and leadership challenge for managers will be to provide greater value at a more efficient rate. In some cases, a company will be both online integrated and also a bricks-and-mortar reality as well; such as the successful case of Office Depot.

According to Tapscott, if companies ignore this kind of value proposition—paying deliberate and increased attention to the customer and providing significant value in a competitive way—they will be "Eatonized"—a clear reference to the demise of the Eaton stores in Canada that went bankrupt in 1999.[2]

The message for today's management student? Tapscott remarks,

> The key to competing in the new economy is not the good use of information, agility, quality, re-engineering, innovative marketing or sound management. All that has become good housekeeping. Everybody's got to do that. The key to competing is business model innovation. Fundamentally new corporate models are emerging and obliterating the old ones and punishment is proving to be very swift for those who don't understand that. Your challenge is not to build a great website, but to create a great business web, a new organizational model of how partners can work together on the Internet to create value. If you do that, then you have a chance of succeeding.

Finally, the authors illustrate their argument by highlighting eBay, the online auction on the Web. eBay has changed the business model. The one-on-one haggling of the garage sale or flea market has now been supplanted by the new reality: a global marketplace where a global auction takes place 24/7 involving thousands of people. For what purpose? Possibly for a $5 Beanie Baby!

Don Tapscott (right), author of the book *Growing Up Digital*, his daughter Niki (left) and her friends Michael Furdyk, 15, and Renee Crosbie, 11, pose around a computer. Newer generations are quite comfortable with the global e-reality.

digital capital
Intellectual capital consisting of three elements: people's brains or "human capital," organizational knowledge, and customer, brand and market share capital.

Anything can be bought and sold on eBay; welcome to the new global e-reality. From a business perspective, eBay is financially successful, and yet most of the business activity is done by buyers and sellers themselves!

Now It's Your Turn

Operating in a global environment is uncertain and unpredictable because it is complex and consistently changing. Identify three forces from your own experience that contribute to this complexity and change.

◼◼◼◼ Overview

The global digital economy has profoundly changed how we do business. No longer can managers ignore the forces operating in their environments; otherwise, they will simply go out of business. Perhaps the main challenging characteristic of this shift from the Industrial Age model of doing business to the new global model is the shift from a world where business was vertically integrated to one now where business web integration is horizontal. This new reality has profound impact not only on how business does business (its internal processes), but also the effects this shift has on customers, distributors, competitors, and suppliers. Survival of the organization is at stake here and most managers know this and are learning to shift as well.

organizational environment
The set of forces and conditions that can affect the way an organization operates.

In this chapter, we examine the organization's external environment in detail. We describe it and identify the principal forces—both task and general—that create pressure and influence managers and thus affect the way organizations operate. We conclude with a study of several methods that managers can use to help organizations adjust and respond to forces in the organization's environment. By the end of the chapter, you will understand the steps managers must take to ensure that organizations adequately address and appropriately respond to their external environment.

◼◼◼◼ What Is the Organizational Environment?

internal environment
The forces operating within an organization and stemming from the organization's structure and culture.

external environment
The forces operating outside an organization that affect how the organization functions.

task environment
The set of forces and conditions that start with suppliers, distributors, customers, and competitors and affect an organization's ability to obtain inputs and dispose of its outputs, because they influence managers on a daily basis.

The **organizational environment** is a set of forces and conditions, such as technology and competition, that can affect the way the organization operates, and the way managers engage in planning and organizing.[3] These forces change over time and thus present managers with *opportunities* and *threats*. The organizational environment can be divided into the internal environment and the external environment. The **internal environment** consists of forces operating within an organization and stemming from the organization's structure and culture. The **external environment** consists of forces operating outside an organization that affect how an organization functions. We generally divide the organization's external environment into two major categories: the task environment and the general environment. All three of these environments are shown in Figure 2.1.

The **task environment** is a set of external forces and conditions that start with suppliers, distributors, customers, and competitors, and affect an organization's ability to obtain inputs, or raw materials, and dispose of its outputs, or finished

FIGURE 2.1 | *Forces in the Organizational Environment*

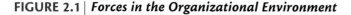

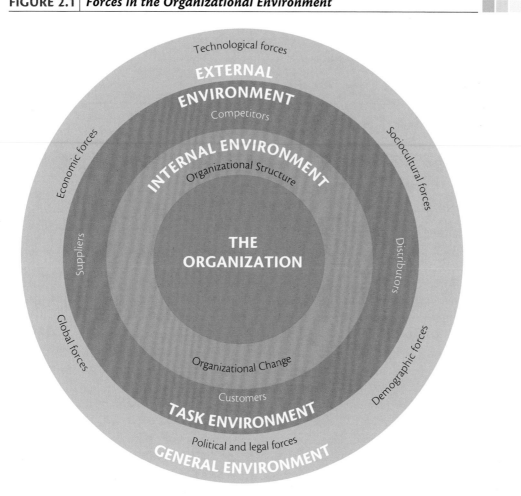

products. When managers turn on the radio or television, arrive at their offices, open their mail, or look at their computer screens, they are likely to learn about problems facing them because of changing conditions in their organization's task environment.

The **general environment** is a wide-ranging set of external factors—including economic, technological, socio-cultural, demographic, political and legal, and global forces—that affect the organization and its task environment directly or indirectly. For the individual manager, opportunities and threats resulting from changes in the general environment are often more difficult to identify and respond to than are events in the task environment. In Chapter 5, we examine how managers analyze their environment, using SWOT (strengths, weaknesses, opportunities, and threats) analysis.

Some changes in the external environment, such as the introduction of new technology or the opening of foreign markets, create opportunities for managers to obtain resources or enter new markets and thereby strengthen their organizations. In contrast, the rise of new competitors, an economic recession, or an oil shortage poses a threat that can devastate an organization if managers are unable to obtain resources or sell the organization's goods and services. The ability of managers to perceive, interpret, and respond to forces in the organizational environment is critical to an organization's performance.

general environment
The economic, technological, socio-cultural, demographic, political and legal, and global forces that affect an organization and its task environment.

Although the task, general, and internal environments influence each other, we leave detailed discussion of how to manage the internal environment until Parts 3 and 4. In this chapter, we explore the nature of the external forces and consider how managers can respond to them.

The Task Environment

THINK ABOUT IT

Globalization Hitting Home[4]

Joan Fisk knows what feeling threatened globally is all about. Tiger Brand Knitting Co., her family's 124-year-old garment factory located in Cambridge, Ontario, on the banks of the Grand River, as of April 2005, is no more. The company was bought by financier Ken Lazar of New York for $15.9 million. Most of this money paid off the company's debt. All manufacturing was moved to China; what was left was a small design and distribution centre in Toronto. Only 178 employees will remain, down from 1450 employees who churned out clothes for such labels as Cotton Ginny, Beaver Canoe, and Gap. The company at the time was even confident it could expand into its own labels. At its peak, it had annual sales of $78 million.

And now, what does Fisk face? An empty, cavernous, and dark warehouse. A false belief in the 1990s, with the low Canadian dollar, slammed her hard; so did the incredible price-lowering power of Wal-Mart Stores Inc., and China's unstinting competition. Larry Kroetsch, a United Steelworkers representative and 16-year Tiger veteran, was quite upset about not receiving a severance package, but deep down he knew what was happening. "You can't compete," he says. "I make $22 an hour and there's a guy in another country who can do it for $7 an hour or 7¢ an hour. The whole world is going somewhere else and it's not Canada."

You Be the Manager

1. Joan Fisk remarked, "From a manufacturing point of view, we did almost everything we could to reduce cycle times." If that's true, what could impact a company from the perspective of global forces?
2. What are the opportunities and threats that suppliers and distributors bring to managers?

Forces in the task environment result from the actions of suppliers, distributors, customers, and competitors (see Figure 2.1). These four groups affect a manager's ability to obtain resources and distribute outputs on a daily, weekly, and monthly basis and thus have a significant impact on short-term decision making. We discuss each of these factors in turn.

suppliers
Individuals and organizations that provide an organization with the input resources that it needs to produce goods and services.

Suppliers

Suppliers are the individuals and organizations that provide an organization with the input resources (such as raw materials, component parts, or employees) that it needs to produce goods and services. In return, the supplier receives compensation for those goods and services. An important aspect of a manager's job is to ensure a reliable supply of input resources. In the digital economy, with networked technologies, organizations can often be picky and choose which suppliers will provide the security and dependence they need. Tapscott and Agnew write, "Around the globe, commercial enterprises are scrambling to avoid not only being left in the dust of the upstarts but also being made irrelevant as suppliers and customers alike embrace new ways of doing business."[5]

Changes in the nature, number, or types of suppliers lead to opportunities and threats that managers must respond to if their organizations are to prosper. Often, when managers do not respond to a threat, they put their organization at a competitive disadvantage. For example, when Joan Fisk was managing the Tiger Brand Knitting Co., she relied too heavily on the strength of the low Canadian dollar at the time. Meanwhile, all this meant was that the dollar was simply buying the company time because "Wal-Mart was demanding price cuts from its suppliers. And all the while China was tooling up to fill the vacuum left by those who couldn't comply."[6]

One major supplier-related threat that confronts managers arises when suppliers have a strong bargaining position with an organization. They can then raise the prices of the inputs they supply to the organization. A supplier's bargaining position is especially strong if (1) the supplier is the sole source of an input and (2) the input is vital to the organization.[7] For example, the Canadian gift store chain Bowrings, operated by Tereve Holdings Ltd., known to many Canadians because it had 64 stores across Canada operating for the past 50 years, filed for bankruptcy protection in August 2005. The reason? They faced tremendous increased competition and were not perceived as the preferred choice for many people any longer. "Chains like Winners' Home Sense, Hudson's Bay Co.'s Home Outfitters, Linens N' Things, Caban, and Pottery Barn have opened in Canada to capitalize on a boom in the home-renovation and housing markets." In addition, non-traditional merchants, such as Loblaw Cos. and Costco, started competing with Bowrings as well.[8]

Distributors

Distributors are organizations that help other organizations sell their goods or services to customers. The decisions that managers make about how to distribute products to customers can have important effects on organizational performance. For many years, Apple Computer refused to let others sell its computers, which meant that customers had to buy directly from Apple. Thus, potential customers who shopped at large computer stores with a variety of products were less likely to buy an Apple computer, since it would not be sold there.

The changing nature of distributors and distribution methods can also bring opportunities and threats for managers. If distributors are so large and powerful that they can control customers' access to a particular organization's goods and services, they can threaten the organization by demanding that it reduce the prices of its goods and services.[9] For example, before Chapters was taken over by Indigo Books & Music, publishers complained that Chapters had used its market share to force them into dropping their wholesale prices to the book retailer. Because Chapters was the largest distributor of books to customers in Canada, publishers felt compelled to comply with Chapters' demands.

In contrast, the power of a distributor may be weakened if there are many options. Demand for service from regional phone companies has declined greatly with the advent of cellphones and the larger number of service providers.

distributors
Organizations that help other organizations sell their goods or services to customers.

Customers

customers

Individuals and groups that buy the goods and services that an organization produces.

Customers are the individuals and groups that buy the goods and services that an organization produces. Dell Canada's customers can be divided into several distinct groups: (1) individuals who purchase personal computers, or PCs, for home use, (2) small companies, (3) large companies, (4) government agencies, and (5) educational institutions. Changes in the numbers and types of customers or changes in customers' tastes and needs result in opportunities and threats. An organization's success depends on its response to customers. When Eaton's failed in the late 1990s, much of the reason for its failure was its lack of responsiveness to changing customer needs. Managers' abilities to identify an organization's main customers and produce the goods and services they want are a crucial factor affecting organizational and managerial success.

Competitors

competitors

Organizations that produce goods and services that are similar to a particular organization's goods and services.

One of the most important forces that an organization confronts in its task environment is competitors. **Competitors** are organizations that produce goods and services that are similar to a particular organization's goods and services. In other words, competitors are organizations that are vying for the same customers. Pollard Banknote has only two competitors, both in the United States.

Rivalry between competitors can be the most threatening force that managers must deal with. A high level of rivalry often results in price competition, and falling prices reduce access to resources and cause profits to decrease. Today, competition in the personal computer industry is intense as all the major players battle to increase their market share by offering customers better-equipped machines at lower prices.

Barriers to Entry

barriers to entry

Factors that make it difficult and costly for an organization to enter a particular task environment or industry.

Although the rivalry between existing competitors is a major threat, so is the possibility that new competitors will enter the task environment. In general, the potential for new competitors to enter a task environment (and thus boost the level of competition) depends on barriers to entry.[10] **Barriers to entry** are factors that make it difficult and costly for an organization to enter a particular task environment or industry.[11] The higher the barriers to entry, the smaller the number of competitors in an organization's task environment and thus the lower the threat of competition. With fewer competitors, it is easier to obtain customers and keep prices high. Airlines are the classic example of barriers to entry. Montreal-based Air Canada operates as a near monopoly because of the high cost of establishing an airline. In 2001 alone, Royal Airlines and CanJet were swallowed up by Canada 3000, and Roots Air was bought out by Air Canada after only one month of operation. Canada 3000 then went out of operation at the end of 2001. In mid-March 2005, Jetsgo also met its demise. "High fuel prices, brutal fare wars and safety concerns all weighed on Jetsgo."[12] Competitors such as Tango, Zip, and a revitalized CanJet Airlines have since appeared, and have also struggled to gain market share. Air Canada's near monopoly has not resulted in the airline being successful in recent years, however.

Barriers to entry result from two main sources: economies of scale and brand loyalty (see Figure 2.2). **Economies of scale** are the cost advantages associated with large operations. Economies of scale result from factors such as being able to manufacture products in large quantities, buy inputs in bulk, or be more effective than competitors at making use of organizational resources by fully utilizing employees' skills and knowledge. If organizations already in the task environment are large and enjoy significant economies of scale, then their costs are lower than the costs of potential

Air Canada
www.aircanada.ca

economies of scale

Cost advantages associated with large operations.

entrants will be, and newcomers will find it very expensive to enter the industry. In the *Management Case* at the end of this chapter, we discuss Sleeman Breweries, where the production of premium beers does not allow for the economies of scale faced by Molson and Labatt.

Brand loyalty is customers' preference for the products of organizations that currently exist in the task environment. If established organizations enjoy significant brand loyalty, then a new entrant will find it extremely difficult and costly to obtain a share of the market. Newcomers must bear the huge advertising costs of building customer awareness of the good or service they intend to provide.[13] Western Glove Works Ltd. of Winnipeg, Manitoba, is a company that fosters brand loyalty. It's considered "a powerhouse in blue jeans."[14] When in 1977 it came out with Ziggy, which became a very successful fashion line, Loblaw Cos. in 1982–83 objected because they had prior rights to the name "Ziggy," its specialty delicatessen products. Western then took their own family name, "Silver," and used it as a brand: the Silver Jeans line. Said Bob Silver, the company president, "What we learned from all this was the value of brand loyalty. It is a very tough business indeed to create a brand and then establish brand loyalty among consumers, but we knew it as something we had to do if we were going to continue to prosper."

In some cases, government regulations function as a barrier to entry. For example, until the late 1980s, government regulations prohibited third parties from reselling long-distance service in Canada. This prevented competition with the established long-distance companies—Bell Canada, SaskTel, and NBTel. When the regulations were amended to allow other companies to compete, the opportunities and threats facing companies in the telephone industry changed. Even more competition opened up when the Canadian Radio-television and Telecommunications Commission (CRTC) allowed for competition in long-distance calls to areas outside of Canada. The government has also established regulations that make it difficult to establish private hospitals.

In summary, high barriers to entry create a task environment that is highly threatening and causes difficulty for managers trying to gain access to the customers and other resources an organization needs. Conversely, low barriers to entry result in a task environment where competitive pressures are more moderate and managers have greater opportunities to acquire the customers and other resources they need for their organizations to be effective.

Bob Silver, president of Western Glove Works makers of Silver and 1921 jeans, in his Winnipeg company's sewing room looking over some new lines with sewing machine operator Adelaida Ebreo.

brand loyalty
Customers' preference for the products of organizations that currently exist in the task environment.

FIGURE 2.2 | *Barriers to Entry and Competition*

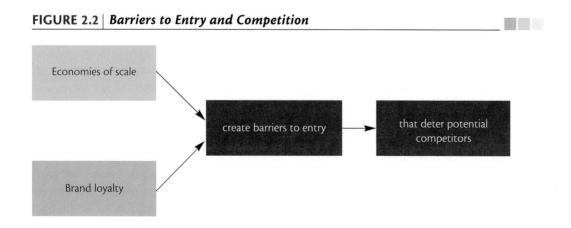

The General Environment

The Coordinated Design: Collaborate or Die[15]

Massive, radical, consistent commoditization is happening across every industry. Peter Keen, founder, Keen Innovations, the Herndon, Virginia-based expert who has spent 40 years in the industry and authored more than 20 books on IT and business, says, "With deregulation and globalization, you get overcapacity, price-erosion and standardization of components. Look at what is happening with car manufacturing—it's all standardized parts. The real challenge is how do you innovate in a commodity world. In the past, you innovated by having something different and proprietary, but look how a standard interface like the USB port created the digital camera market. There is absolutely no way to make money."

Two companies that have taken advantage of deregulated markets and standardization of components are Toyota and Dell. Toyota has standardized all its systems so that it can move production to Mexico, for example, in a week. Dell puts the same product out that others do but does it better.

The key to all this competitive advantage, however, in the global economy is what Keen calls "the enterprise coordination design." Pharmaceutical giant Eli Lilly is a good example of this coordinated design. For example, they have a Web portal where they post research problems; solutions can come from anywhere. Says Keen, "Once you have coordinated design, you push to the next big thing, which is value-add."

In a globally competitive world, collaboration is the only way to work. Multiple ways of doing the same thing in a company—such as the 150 ledger systems that former IBM CEO Louis Gertsner discovered when he took over in the 1990s—will simply not work any more. Coordination of design through successful collaboration processes will decide the winners in the new economy. Again, says Keen, "It's process innovation, it's production innovation and it's relationship innovation."

You Be the Manager

1. What does Keen mean by "process," "production," and "relationship" innovation?

Managers must concern themselves not only with finding suppliers and customers. They must also pay attention to the larger environment around them. Economic, technological, demographic, political, and legal forces in an organization's general environment can have profound effects on the organization's task environment, effects that may be ignored by some managers. For example, technology in the telecommunications industry has made it possible for companies to offer their customers a variety of products. In the past, consumers simply chose the cheapest long-distance package or the best telephone system, but now they're looking at enhanced communication products—such as local calling, cellphone options, long distance, internet access, and videoconferencing—that are offered as part of the package. Telephone providers who failed to expand their range of offerings quickly have had difficulty keeping customers.

If organizations have for years had a monopoly environment to work in—such as the phone companies until recently (e.g., Bell Canada), and the electrical companies (e.g., New Brunswick Power and Ontario Hydro)—and then find themselves facing the reality of operating in a deregulated environment, their managers will have to constantly analyze the forces impacting the new environment in order to manage effectively. Their decisions and planning will have long-term effects. Below we examine each of the major forces in the general environment in turn, exploring their impact on managers and on the organization's task environment, and examining how managers can deal with them. In Chapter 5, we examine one of the major tasks involved in planning—the careful and thorough analysis of forces in the general environment.

Economic Forces

Economic forces affect the general health and well-being of a nation or the regional economy of an organization. They include interest rates, inflation, unemployment, and economic growth. Economic forces produce many opportunities and threats for managers. Low levels of unemployment and falling interest rates mean a change in the customer base: More people have more money to spend, and as a result organizations have an opportunity to sell more goods and services. Good economic times affect supplies: Resources become easier to acquire, and organizations have an opportunity to flourish.

In contrast, worsening macroeconomic conditions pose a threat because they limit managers' ability to gain access to the resources their organization needs. Profit-oriented organizations such as retail stores and hotels have fewer customers for their goods and services during economic downturns. Not-for-profit organizations such as charities and colleges receive fewer donations during economic downturns. Even a moderate deterioration in national or regional economic conditions can seriously affect performance.

Poor economic conditions make the environment more complex and managers' jobs more difficult and demanding. Managers may need to reduce the number of individuals in their departments and increase the motivation of remaining employees, and managers and workers alike may need to identify ways to gain and use resources more efficiently. Successful managers realize the important effects that economic forces have on their organizations and they pay close attention to changes in the national and regional economy in order to respond appropriately.

economic forces
Interest rates, inflation, unemployment, economic growth, and other factors that affect the general health and well-being of a nation or the regional economy of an organization.

Technological Forces

Technology is the combination of skills and equipment that managers use in the design, production, and distribution of goods and services. **Technological forces** are outcomes of changes in the technology that managers use to design, produce, or distribute goods and services. Technological forces have increased greatly since the Second World War because the overall pace of technological change has sped up so much.[16] Computers have become increasingly faster and smaller. Transportation speed has increased. Distribution centres are able to track goods in ways that were unthinkable even 10 years ago.

Technological forces can have profound implications for managers and organizations. Technological change can make established products obsolete overnight—for example, eight-track tapes and black and white televisions—forcing managers to find new products to make. Although technological change can threaten an organization, it also can create a host of new opportunities for designing, making, or distributing new and better kinds of goods and services. Managers must move quickly to respond to such changes if their organizations are to survive and prosper.

Changes in information technology also are changing the very nature of work itself within organizations, and the manager's job. Telecommuting and teleconferencing are now everyday activities that provide opportunities for managers to supervise and

technology
The combination of skills and equipment that managers use in the design, production, and distribution of goods and services.

technological forces
Outcomes of changes in the technology that managers use to design, produce, or distribute goods and services.

coordinate employees working from home or other locations. Even students engage in telecommuting, communicating with classmates and instructors via email or discussion forums, and completing assignments at home. This has changed the way instructors do their jobs.

Demographic Forces

demographic forces
Outcomes of changes in, or changing attitudes toward, the characteristics of a population, such as age, gender, ethnic origin, race, sexual orientation, and social class.

Demographic forces are outcomes of changes in, or changing attitudes toward, the characteristics of a population, such as age, gender, ethnic origin, race, sexual orientation, and social class. Like the other forces in the general environment, demographic forces present managers with opportunities and threats and can have major implications for organizations. "Over the past 30 years, women have made spectacular inroads in business and all of the professions. They now make up nearly 60 percent of university graduates. They outnumber men in the lower managerial ranks, and they'll soon outnumber men in medicine and law."[17] The dramatic increase in the number of working women has focused public concern on issues such as equal pay for equal work and sexual harassment at work. One issue in particular that managers will have to address more and more is the lack of women in top positions. This concern is important because managers are responsible for attracting and making full use of the talents of female employees. According to Catalyst Canada, women account for only 14.4 percent of corporate officer positions in the top 500 companies. This is about the same percentage as it was in 2002, a "disturbingly low" number, according to Catalyst. At this rate, women ascending to the top ranks will not reach a critical mass of 25 percent until 2025! According to *The Globe and Mail* journalist Margaret Wente, there are reasons to explain this circumstance: the mommy track (having families), sex and hormones (the differences between male and female biology), and the reality of boredom for women in the corporate ranks. "Women are more interested in emotionally fulfilling lives than in being leader of the pack."[18] Needless to say, managers must factor in these kinds of circumstances into their decision making. We discuss the important issue of workforce diversity at length in Chapter 3.

political and legal forces
Outcomes of changes in laws and regulations, such as the deregulation of industries, the privatization of organizations, and increased emphasis on environmental protection.

Changes in the age distribution of a population are another example of a demographic force that affects managers and organizations. Currently, most industrialized nations are experiencing the aging of their populations as a consequence of falling birth and death rates and the aging of the baby boom generation. The aging of the population is increasing opportunities for organizations that cater to older people; the recreation and home health care industries, for example, are seeing an upswing in demand for their services.

The aging of the population also has several implications for the workplace. Most significant are a relative decline in the number of young people joining the workforce and an increase in active employees willing to postpone retirement past the traditional retirement age of 65. These changes suggest that organizations will need to find ways to motivate older employees and use their skills and knowledge, an issue that many Western societies have yet to tackle.

Addressing the problem of the lack of women in top managerial positions is a challenge for today's companies. Women account for only 14.4 percent of corporate officer positions in the top 500 companies.

Political and Legal Forces

Political and legal forces result from political and legal developments within society and significantly affect managers and organizations. Political processes shape a society's laws; for instance, public pressure for corporations to be more environmentally conscious has strengthened pollution laws in

Canada. Laws constrain the operations of organizations and managers and thus create both opportunities and threats.[19] For example, in much of the industrialized world there has been a strong trend toward deregulation of industries previously controlled by the state and privatization of organizations once owned by the state. The *Think About It* features "Globalization Hitting Home" on page 40 discusses deregulation and the need for collaboration in the global workplace and "The Coordinated Design: Collaborate or Die" on page 44 addresses the need for a coordinated design and shows how Toyota Corp., Dell Computer Corp., and Eli Lilly were classic examples of managing in a deregulated world.

Deregulation and privatization are just two examples of political and legal forces that can create challenges for organizations and managers. Others include increased emphasis on safety in the workplace and on environmental protection and the preservation of endangered species. Successful managers carefully monitor changes in laws and regulations in order to take advantage of the opportunities they create and counter the threats they pose in an organization's task environment.

The Competition Act of 1986 provides more legislation that affects how companies may operate. Under this act, the Bureau of Competition Policy acts to maintain and encourage competition in Canada. For example, when companies merge, they face intense scrutiny from the bureau to make sure there is not unfair competitive advantage to customers, employees, and other stakeholders. Even though Ellis Jacob, CEO of Cineplex Galaxy LP, had the "deal of a lifetime" with a $500-million purchase of rival movie theatre exhibition chain Famous Players from Viacom Inc., he had to sell theatres to meet the demands of regulators: "The federal Competition Bureau sought to maintain competition in pricing and choice by making it a condition of the deal that Cineplex sell 35 theatres in 17 cities across Canada, which would have brought in about 11 percent of the companies' combined revenue of $874 million last year."[20] In early 2005 the Competition Bureau declared that Sears Canada Inc. breached federal laws by pitching exaggerated savings on automobile tires in its ads and asked that they pay a $500 000 fine. In the summer of 2004, Forzani Group Ltd., the country's largest sporting goods retailer, agreed to pay a record $1.7 million to settle allegations it misled consumers about prices. And a year earlier, clothier Suzy Shier agreed to pay a $1-million penalty in a similar matter.[21]

The Competition Act
http://laws.justice.gc.ca/
en/C-34

Global Forces

Global forces are outcomes of changes in international relationships, changes in nations' economic, political, and legal systems, and changes in technology. Perhaps the most important global force affecting managers and organizations is the increasing economic integration of countries around the world.[22] Developments such as the North American Free Trade Agreement (NAFTA), the free-trade agreements enforced by the World Treaty Organization (WTO), and the growth of the European Union (EU) have led to a lowering of barriers to the free flow of goods and services between nations.[23]

Falling trade barriers have created enormous opportunities for organizations in one country to sell goods and services in other countries. But by allowing foreign companies to compete for an organization's domestic customers, falling trade barriers also pose a serious threat, because they increase competition in the task environment. After NAFTA was signed, one of the major challenges facing Canadian managers was how to compete successfully against American companies moving into this country. Zellers and the Bay, for instance, faced strong challenges from Wal-Mart as well as smaller boutique operations.

global forces
Outcomes of changes in international relationships; changes in nations' economic, political, and legal systems; and changes in technology, such as falling trade barriers, the growth of representative democracies, and reliable and instantaneous communication.

totalitarian regime
A political system in which a single party, individual, or group holds all political power and neither recognizes nor permits opposition.

representative democracy
A political system in which representatives elected by citizens and legally accountable to the electorate form a government whose function is to make decisions on behalf of the electorate.

command economy
An economic system in which the government owns all businesses and specifies which and how many goods and services are produced and the prices at which they are sold.

mixed economy
An economic system in which some sectors of the economy are left to private ownership and free-market mechanisms, and others are owned by the government and subject to government planning.

Despite evidence that countries are becoming more similar to one another and that the world is on the verge of becoming a "global village," countries still differ across a range of political, legal, economic, and cultural dimensions. When an organization operates in the global environment, it confronts a series of forces that differ from country to country and world region to world region.

The Impact of Political and Economic Forces

In recent years, two large and related shifts in political and economic forces have taken place globally (see Figure 2.3).[24] One is the shift away from **totalitarian regimes**, where those in charge allow no opposition, toward more democratic regimes. This change has been most dramatic in Eastern Europe and the former Soviet Union, where totalitarian communist regimes collapsed during the late 1980s and early 1990s. There is, of course, debate going on as to how authentic these reforms are given how Russian President Vladimir Putin has treated Yukos oil company CEO, Mikhail Khodorkovsky: he had him incarcerated and the wealth of his oil company—billions—now goes into government coffers. "Vladimir Putin is an economically ignorant new Czar who seeks to expropriate these more productive assets so that Russia can frighten people again." The concept and reality of the rule of law is absent in Russia; "In Russia, the ruler is Vladimir Putin."[25] The other shift—toward **representative democracy**, where voters elect a government that makes decisions on their behalf—has occurred from Latin America to Africa.

Accompanying this change in political forces has been a worldwide shift away from **command economies** (where the government owns all businesses) and **mixed economies** (where only some sectors are government-owned) and toward **free-market economies** (where competition determines prices).[26] This economic shift began with the realization that government involvement in economic activity often blocks economic growth. Thus, a wave of privatization and deregulation has swept over the world, from the former communist countries to Latin America, Asia, and Western Europe.

 **FIGURE 2.3** | *Changes in Political and Economic Forces*

free-market economy
An economic system in which private enterprise controls production, and the interaction of supply and demand determines which and how many goods and services are produced and how much consumers pay for them.

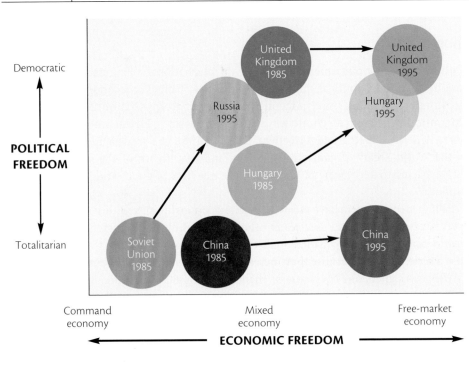

These trends are good news for managers of global organizations because they result in the expansion of opportunities for exporting and investment abroad. The managers of many Western companies have had a lot of trouble establishing business operations in Eastern Europe and China, however. For example, when the Chiquita banana company entered the Czech Republic in 1990, it found that Czech citizens apparently had difficulty understanding why something of better quality should cost more. Chiquita was forced to switch to lower quality bananas after discovering that consumers were unwilling to pay higher prices for superior bananas.[27]

The Impact of National Culture

Differences among national cultures have important implications for managers. First, management practices that are effective in Canada might not work in Japan, Hungary, or Mexico, because of differences in national culture. For example, pay-for-performance systems used in Canada, which emphasize the performance of individuals alone, are less suitable in Japan, where individual performance in pursuit of group goals is the value that receives emphasis.

A culturally diverse management team can be a source of strength in the global marketplace. Organizations that employ managers from a variety of cultures appreciate better how national cultures differ than do organizations with culturally similar management teams, and they tailor their management systems and behaviours to the differences.

✔ Tips for Managers

FORCES IN THE ENVIRONMENT

1. Identify key forces from the environment that act as threats or opportunities for managers today.

2. List the forces that you feel are the most important for managers to work with.

3. Finally, choose the #1 force you believe is affecting most managers today as they grapple with their organizational environment.

Managing The External Environment

THINK ABOUT IT

A Pope's Impact on Free Market Economies[28]

George Bragues who teaches economics, philosophy, and politics at the University of Guelph–Humber and at the Humber College Institute of Technology and Advanced Learning in Toronto, describes the late Pope Paul II as "the capitalist pope." The reason? His influence and impact, from a business perspective, on how business should be conducted. In short, the Pope greatly influenced the external environment, from individual businesses to the market forces themselves. "Here was a pope who recognized the advantages of free market economies and helped consolidate their moral judgment"—in short, connecting free markets with human dignity.

While much can be said about the influence he had around the world because of his travels and especially his decisive role in the fall of the Soviet communist empire, he also influenced and recognized the advantages of free market economies and helped consolidate their moral legitimacy. He believed that capitalism with its adherence to private property and the rights of one's work was best suited to provide people with dignity and the ability of people to make their own choices. Profit, for example, was "a legitimate regulator of commercial life," because it provided businesses with "signals as to what should be produced and how." The Pope also recognized that "businesses succeed only when those involved in them practise such virtues as industriousness, diligence, prudence, honesty, fortitude and courageous risk-taking."

The business world has changed as a result of Pope Paul II. He has greatly impacted everyone's external environment. He insisted that poor nations must "enter the circle of exchange," that they become integral also to the dynamics of the global economy. To fulfill this vision, organizations, he insisted, must design structures that are liberating, life-giving, and truly places of dignity and respect—in short, a "worthplace."[29]

You Be the Manager

1. What are new considerations for managers as they reflect on the external environment in which they work?
2. As a manager, what is your experience of the *worth*place?

As previously discussed, an important task for managers is to understand how forces in the task and general environments create opportunities for, and threats to, their organizations. To analyze the importance of opportunities and threats in the external environment, managers must measure (1) the level of complexity in the environment and (2) the rate at which the environment is changing. With this information, they can plan better and choose the best goals and courses of action.

The complexity of the external environment depends on the number and potential impact of the forces that managers must respond to in the task and general environments. A force that seems likely to have a significant negative impact is a potential threat to which managers must devote a high level of organizational resources. A force likely to have a marginal impact poses little threat to an organization and requires only a minor commitment of managerial time and attention. A force likely to make a significant positive impact warrants a considerable commitment of managerial time and effort to take advantage of the opportunity. When Starbucks went to Vienna, the company had to think carefully about its no-smoking policy, since it would be the only coffee shop in the city to ban smoking.

In general, the larger an organization is, the greater the number of environmental forces that managers must respond to. Consider, for example, the external environment facing the manager of a place like Johnny's Hamburgers on Victoria Park just north of the 401 highway in Toronto. Johnny's has been in its current location for years. This small "burger joint" is known to many people. Their customers cannot stay and eat; they order and receive full portions of food, reasonably priced, and according to many, delicious, and go and eat in their car, or go to the office or home. Johnny's has had regular customers for years; they do the same thing they have done for years; people come and go, but Johnny's remains more or less the same. Now, consider Tim Hortons as it keeps expanding. Now, of course, it is owned by Wendy's International Inc. Each year it must consider, to take just one example, the environment issue of its coffee cups when it announces its 'Roll Up the Rim' contest.

For some people, as in Edmonton, it's a chance to win an SUV; for environmentalists, however, these cups represent a serious biodegradable hazard; they also litter the environment.[30] "I don't think it's socially responsible to have a promotion which creates massive waste," said Ronald Colman, executive director of GPI Atlantic, a non-profit group that researches environmental and quality of life issues.[31] He has a very strong point here: In Nova Scotia, for example, "a government-sponsored study showed Tim Hortons and fast-food rival McDonald's alone account for one-third of all litter in that province. Tim Hortons packaging accounted for 22 percent and McDonald's for 10.1 percent of all identifiable litter."

Thus, in addition to determining how to distribute food supplies to restaurants in the most efficient ways, how to ensure that the organization's practices do not discriminate against any ethnic groups or older workers, how to respond to customers' preferences for different types of foods, for example, here in Canada and then as it expands more aggressively into the United States, and how to deal with other competitors as it expands its business, managers at Tim Hortons will have to deal with a more complex external environment because of complicated forces such as the environmental one just described.

Environmental change is the degree to which forces in the task and general environments change and evolve over time. Change is problematic for an organization and its managers because the consequences of change can be difficult to predict.[32] Managers can try to forecast or simply guess about future conditions in the task environment, such as where and how strong the new competition may be. But, confronted with a complex and changing task environment, managers cannot be sure that decisions and actions taken today will be suitable in the future. This uncertainty makes their jobs especially challenging. It also makes it vitally important for managers to understand the forces that shape the external environment.

environmental change
The degree to which forces in the task and general environments change and evolve over time.

To manage the external environment, managers need to:

1. List the types and relative strengths of the forces that affect their organizations' task and general environments the most.
2. Analyze the way changes in these forces may result in opportunities or threats for their organizations.
3. Draw up a plan indicating how they propose to take advantage of those opportunities or counter those threats, and what kinds of resources they will need to do so.

An understanding of the external environment is necessary so that managers can anticipate how the task environment might look in the future and decide on the actions to pursue if the organization is to prosper. McDonald's is a good example of how adaptive an organization must be to remain successful. With the aging population, plus the emphasis on low-fat foods, McDonald's began changing its menu by including salads and wraps that had less fats and carbohydrates. It is also aware of people with food allergens and other food sensitivities and has adjusted accordingly.[33] The fact that Charlie Bell, McDonald's CEO, died of colorectal cancer in early 2005 at the age of 44, has only heightened awareness of this need for low-fat foods, if no other reason than that of its corporate reputation.[34] However, one commentator put matters this way: "I also know that the human body is designed to live well past 100. To die at any age under 50 requires a sustained poisoning effort: like consuming soft drinks, fried foods, red meat, refined white flour, added sugars, hydrogenated oils and so on. ... I wonder what ingredients are in a Big Mac these days."[35]

FIGURE 2.4 | *How Managers Use Functions to Manage Forces in the Task and General Environments*

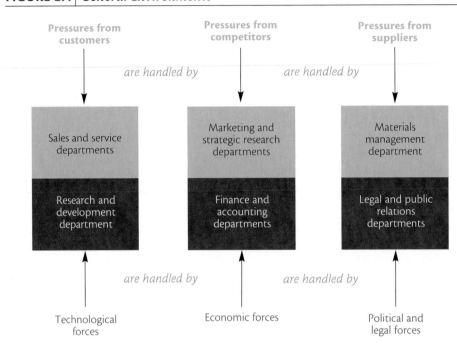

Reducing the Impact of Environmental Forces

Finding ways to reduce the number and potential impact of forces in the external environment is the job of all managers in an organization.

- The principal task of the CEO and top-management team is to devise strategies that will allow an organization to take advantage of opportunities and counter threats in its general and task environments (see Chapter 5 for a discussion of this vital topic).

- Middle managers in an organization's departments collect relevant information about the task environment, such as (1) the future intentions of the organization's competitors, (2) the identity of new customers for the organization's products, and (3) the identity of new suppliers of crucial or low-cost inputs.

- First-line managers find ways to use resources more efficiently to hold costs down or to get close to customers and learn what they want.

Managers are organized in different departments that allow the external environment to be monitored and addressed. Figure 2.4 illustrates different departments and their relationship to the environment.

Managers as Agents of Change

It is important to note that, although much of the change that takes place in the external environment is independent of a particular organization (e.g., basic advances in biotechnology or plastics), a significant amount of environmental change is the direct consequence of actions taken by managers within organizations.[36] As explained in the appendix to Chapter 1, an organization is an open system: It takes in inputs from the environment and converts them into goods and services that are sent back to the environment. Thus, change in the environment is a two-way process (see Figure 2.5). Often, however, the choices that managers make about which products to produce, and even

FIGURE 2.5 | *Change in the Environment as a Two-Way Process*

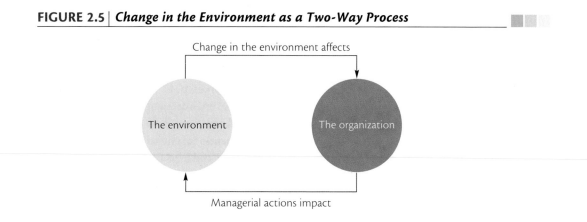

about how to compete with other organizations, affect the environment in many ways. Starbucks' quick success in Vienna may well end up changing the face of all coffee houses in the city.

 Tips for Managers

MANAGING THE EXTERNAL ENVIRONMENT

1. Describe the level of complexity and uncertainty that exists in organizational environments today.

2. Make a list of suggestions you would recommend to managers for their customers, competitors, and suppliers that would be helpful for them to respond to such clients.

3. Itemize your own personal strengths, weaknesses, opportunities, and threats as you prepare to work in this new global environment.

Summary and Review

1. **WHAT IS THE ORGANIZATIONAL ENVIRONMENT?** The organizational environment is the set of forces and conditions that affect a manager's ability to acquire and use resources. The organizational environment has two components: the internal environment and the external environment. The external environment can be divided into the task environment and the general environment.

2. **THE TASK ENVIRONMENT** The task environment is the set of forces and conditions that originate with suppliers, distributors, customers, and competitors and that influence managers on a daily basis.

3. **THE GENERAL ENVIRONMENT** The general environment includes wider-ranging economic, technological, demographic, political and legal, and global forces that affect an organization and its task environment.

4. **MANAGING THE EXTERNAL ENVIRONMENT** Two factors affect the nature of the opportunities and threats that organizations face: (1) the level of complexity in the environment and (2) the rate of change in the environment. Managers must learn how to analyze the forces in the environment in order to respond effectively to opportunities and threats.

Key Terms

barriers to entry, p. 42
brand loyalty, p. 43
command economy, p. 48
competitors, p. 42
customers, p. 42
demographic forces, p. 46
digital capital, p. 38
distributors, p. 41
economic forces, p. 45
economies of scale, p. 42
environmental change, p. 51
external environment, p. 38
free-market economy, p. 48

general environment, p. 39
global forces, p. 47
internal environment, p. 38
mixed economy, p. 48
organizational environment, p. 38
political and legal forces, p. 46
representative democracy, p. 48
suppliers, p. 40
task environment, p. 38
technological forces, p. 45
technology, p. 45
totalitarian regime, p. 48

S O   W H E R E   D O   Y O U   S T A N D ?

Wrap-Up to Opening Case

We began this chapter with a case discussing the digital economy. Authors Don Tapscott, David Ticoll, and Alex Lowy showed us that what was once historically called intellectual capital is, in fact, made up of three elements: human capital, organizational knowledge capital, and customer-brand-market share capital. They referred to this as digital capital.

Listed below are some suggestions that you can experiment with as you align and attune your own experiences to the environmental forces that contribute so much to complexity and change in our world today.

1. **Force #1—Human Capital:** Are you prepared for this new economy? Do you feel you have adequate academic resources, both internally and externally at your disposal to be successful? In short, are you prepared enough? Or, do you need a "career reboot"?[37]

Human capital is an important force to reckon with in today's global environment. We have discussed "brands" in this chapter. Do you have a "personal brand"? What is your value proposition? What do you specifically offer that no one else does? How does this fit in with the global environment and its expectations as far as you are concerned? One branding specialist, William Arruda

of MarketingProfs.com, writes, "If you don't show up in Google, do you exist?"[38] U.S. management expert Tom Peters said in a 2004 interview that there's no big company anywhere in the developed world that's going to guarantee anybody lifetime employment any more. "This is the century of off-shoring, outplacement and self-employment, and it's time to wake up to that reality. The jobs that have gone to places such as India and China are never coming back."[39] It's referred to as Me Inc. and You Inc. That is, you are your own corporation; you are your own brand; you must place your human capital at the doorsteps of the global economy. Are you ready with Force #1? "Tomorrow," writes Daniel Pink, author of *Free Agent Nation*, "and over the next couple of decades [workers] have to look at what they're doing and ask themselves three questions: 'Can someone overseas do it cheaper?' 'Can a computer do it faster?' And 'Is what [I'm] selling in demand in an age of abundance?'"[40]

2. **Force #2—Organizational Knowledge Capital:** How aware are you of the new organizational processes that make today's organizations work in a global environment? For example, we discussed collaboration and coordinated design with such companies as Toyota Corp., Dell Computer Corp.,

and Eli Lilly as classic examples of managing in a deregulated world. As you are starting out on your business career, have you focused on the new technologies, the processes involved in supply chain management, distribution systems, and the "know-how" that organizations possess, not only practically and with skill, but also intuitively and as "this-is-the-way-we-do-things-around-here," often known as the corporate culture. Dell Computer Corp. is not only one of the world's best-run companies; it is also a "smart" company. Kevin Rollins, the 2005 president and chief operating officer of Dell, said, "We [Michael Dell and himself] have been running the company as a team for a number of years now."[41] It is able, like Toyota Corp., to harness the organizational know-how of its staff better than their competitors. The heartbeat for this know-how is its collaborative working model; everyone is literally "on the same page." Such an organizational context demands trust, efficiency, flexibility, being proactive, and aware of global trends so as to be better prepared to meet and be successful in the new global environment.

3. **Force #3—Customer-Brand-Market Share Capital:** What do customers want these days? Of course, the answer depends on the type of business and industry; but there are trends we need to be aware of. Otherwise, we may be trying to selling something—albeit good product or service—but no one is interested! What about your company's brand? Is it fuzzy to today's consumer? Do you know how the average customer feels and thinks about your customer? Do you think they know what your company is all about? Getting "there first" is critical in this global workplace. What about your knowledge of market share in a company where you work? Are you eager? Are you like Ray Kroc, the legendary founder of McDonald's Corp., who once said, "I want your customers. I want your space on the shelves. I want your space of the consumer's stomach."[42] And, as history tells us, he went about making that vision happen. General Motors Corp., as of early 2005, is one such company dealing with structural problems in order to more realistically meet customer expectations, create a clear brand equity, and develop increased market share. What is, therefore, that you know about your customers, your brand(s), and your position and relevance in the marketspace?[43]

After studying the preceding material, be sure to check out our Online Learning Centre at **www.mcgrawhill.ca/olc/jones** for more in-depth information and interactivities that correspond to this chapter.

Management in Action

Topics for Discussion and Action

1. Why is it important for managers to understand the nature of the environmental forces that are acting on them and their organization?

2. Choose an organization, and ask a manager in that organization to list the types and strengths of forces in the organization's task environment. Ask the manager to pay particular attention to identifying opportunities and threats that result from pressures and changes in customers, competitors, and suppliers.

3. Read the business section of your local newspaper, to get an idea of task and general forces that affect the organizations in your community. What local conditions have a major impact on organizations in your area?

4. Which organization is likely to face the most complex task environment: a biotechnology company trying to develop a cure for cancer, or a large retailer such as Zellers or the Bay? Why?

5. The population is aging because of declining birth rates, declining death rates, and the aging of the baby boom generation. What might some of the implications of this demographic trend be for (a) a pharmaceutical company, (b) the home construction industry, and (c) the agenda of political parties?

6. Currently, most households and businesses in Canada, the United Kingdom, the United States, and a number of other countries do not have a choice of electricity supplier. But as a result of deregulation, within a decade the average business and household will be able to choose from among several competing suppliers. How might this development alter the task environment facing a manager in an electric utility?

7. The textile industry has a labour-intensive manufacturing process that uses unskilled and semiskilled workers. What are the implications of the shift to a more open global environment for textile companies whose manufacturing operations are based in high-wage countries such as Australia, Canada, and the United States?

8. After the passage of the North American Free Trade Agreement, some Canadian companies shifted production operations to Mexico to take advantage of lower labour costs and lower standards for environmental and worker protection. As a result, they cut their costs and were better able to survive in an increasingly competitive global environment. Was their behaviour ethical—that is, did the ends justify the means?

9. Go to the library and gather information that allows you to compare and contrast the political, economic, and cultural systems of the United States, Mexico, and Canada. In what ways are the countries similar? How do they differ? How might the similarities and differences influence the activities of managers at an enterprise such as Wal-Mart, which does business in all three countries?

Building Management Skills

ANALYZING AN ORGANIZATION'S TASK AND GENERAL ENVIRONMENTS

Pick an organization that you know. It can be an organization where you have worked or currently work, or it can be an organization that you interact with regularly as a customer (such as the college or university that you are currently attending). Then do the following:

1. Describe the main forces in the task environment that are affecting the organization.

2. Describe the main forces in the general environment that are affecting the organization.

3. Try to determine whether the organization's task and general environments are relatively stable or changing rapidly.

4. Explain how environmental forces affect the job of an individual manager within this organization. How do they determine the opportunities and threats that its managers must confront?

Management for You

You are considering organizing an event to raise funds for a special cause (e.g., children living in poverty, breast cancer research, literacy, or something of your choice). Think about who you might invite to this event (i.e., your "customers"—those who will buy tickets to the event). What type of event might appeal to them? What suppliers might you approach for help in organizing the event? What legal issues might you face in setting up this event? After considering all these issues, how difficult is the environment you face in holding this event?

Small Group Breakout Exercise

HOW TO ENTER THE COPYING BUSINESS

Form groups of three to five people, and appoint one group member as the spokesperson who will communicate your findings to the whole class when called on by the instructor. Then discuss the following scenario.

You and your partners have decided to open a small printing and copying business in a college town of 100 000 people. Your business will compete with companies such as Kinko's. You know that more than 50 percent of small businesses fail in their first year, so to increase your chances of success, you have decided to do a detailed analysis of the task environment of the copying business in order to analyze the opportunities and threats you will encounter. As a group:

1. Decide what you must know about (a) your future customers, (b) your future competitors, and (c) other critical forces in the task environment, if you are to be successful.

2. Evaluate the main barriers to entry into the copying business.

3. Based on this analysis, list some of the steps you will take to help your new copying business succeed.

Managing Ethically

You are a manager for a drug company that has developed a pill to cure river blindness, a common disease in Africa. It was a quick and easy solution, but there were no buyers because the people afflicted or who could be are too poor to buy the pills. Should you shelve the pills and wait until the market can pay the price? What other alternatives might you have?

Exploring the World Wide Web

SPECIFIC ASSIGNMENT

Go to the website for NewAge Consulting in Markham, Ontario: www.newagecanada.com/.[44] Go through the website and read "The New Age Story" and its claim that "NewAge will service our clients better then ANYONE in the market." Click on "Solutions" to read about NewAge's environment.

1. What are the environmental forces that NewAge forces?
2. From your analysis of its website, how well is NewAge managing its opportunities and challenges?

GENERAL ASSIGNMENT

Search for the website of a company that has a complex, rapidly changing environment. What forces in its environment are creating the strongest opportunities and threats? How are managers trying to respond to these opportunities and threats?

Developing a Business Plan

(APPENDIX B, PAGE 405)

Go to www.mcgrawhill.ca/olc/jones/2 for online exercises.

Be the Manager

EMAILING NONVERBAL CUES?[45]

Today's work environment means that a lot of business is carried on "behind-the-scenes," so to speak, that is, electronically. Do you currently work or have you worked in an office where people email one another even though a person could simply walk down the hall or go to the next cubicle and speak with the person? Ron McMillan, vice-president of VitalSmarts LLC, a communication training company, says that up to 90 percent of workplace communication today is fairly routine. He should know: he has 10 000 hours observing people! But what of that other 10 percent where electronic communication does not help in the communications?

McMillan says that three crucial situations in our work environments demand that we meet face-to-face:

- when something really matters
- when there are opinions on a matter
- when strong emotions are at play

Our work environments today with phones, email, and instant messaging make communication must faster than ever before. However …

Questions

1. From your experience, what work environments work best with electronic communications?
2. How would you manage the right balance of electronic and face-to-face communication in the workplace?

Management Case

The Brewing Industry

For many years now, the Canadian brewing industry has effectively been a duopoly, dominated by Labatt Brewing Co. and Molson Inc., which together control some 90 percent of the market.[46] The only other national player in the industry is Guelph, Ontario-based Sleeman Breweries Ltd., which has gained 5 percent of the national market since its 1988 revival, with niche brands such as Stroh, Okanagan Spring, and Upper Canada.

As a new competitor, Sleeman has worked cautiously to build up its market share, working in partnership with more experienced breweries. It started in 1988 with the help of former Detroit-based Stroh Brewery Co., which bought 20 percent of the shares and offered its expertise as one of the biggest US breweries. From that beginning, Sleeman has steadily expanded as a regional maker of premium craft beers.

Sleeman's strategy for growth has been to buy up "craft beer makers that had a reputation for making high-quality natural brews in small quantities."[47] Purchases include Okanagan Spring Brewery in Vernon, BC; Upper Canada Brewing in Toronto; Montreal's La Brasserie Seigneuriale; and the bankrupt Maritime Beer

Co. in Dartmouth, Nova Scotia. With these and other purchases, Sleeman has become a national beer maker.

In 2000, Sleeman started its entrance into the US market, by teaming up with Boston Beer Co. to market its Samuel Adams brand in Canada, in exchange for which Boston would market Sleeman's products in the United States. Sleeman also acquired the Canadian rights to Stroh's low-priced American beers, including Old Milwaukee, Rainier, and Stroh's. Of this move, John Sleeman, chair and CEO, said, "This will counterbalance the premium-priced beers [Sleeman] has specialized in, providing extra volume for the plants and insulating the company from the vagaries of the domestic beer market."[48] Sleeman tries to avoid competing directly with Molson and Labatt: "We compete with them in the value-priced segment, but they don't have strong entries in the premium categories."[49]

With the concentration of sales in the hands of just three major Canadian players, Canada's small brewers looked for help from the federal government. In September 2000, about 70 of them from across the country asked Ottawa for a reduction in the excise tax charged by Ottawa. "This industry is threatened," said Pierre Paquin, general manager of the newly formed Canadian Council of Regional Brewers. "We're not saying give us handouts. We're saying, give us a field where we can play too."[50] The craft-brewing industry employs about 3300 people directly and indirectly in Canada. Industry members see themselves as small business owners who should not have to pay the same rate of excise tax as Canadian beer giants Molson and Labatt. "Canadian brewers, regardless of size, pay about $2.30 in excise tax on a case of beer," said Donald Ross of Granville Island Brewing, chair of the Craft Brewers Association of British Columbia. "But it costs a small brewer as much as $260 to make a hectolitre, about 12 cases of beer, compared with $128 for the big breweries."[51] Craft breweries rely on employees rather than machines to produce their beer, and thus their labour costs are considerably higher. Other countries extract less tax from small brewers. "In the United States, for instance, the big brewers pay about Cdn$1.88 a case in excise taxes while the small brewers pay about 74 cents," said Ross.

John Wiggins, of Creemore Springs Brewery Ltd. and chair of the Ontario Small Brewers Association, said the current excise tax situation "creates an uneven playing field. By dumping us into the same pot as the large brewers and charging us the same amount, it's actually making us non-competitive. It's punitive to our section of the industry."[52] The success of the large brewers resulted from two factors. First, economies of scale allowed them to keep the costs of making beer low and to make higher profits as their market increased. At the same time, their national presence permitted them to engage in large-scale advertising campaigns and develop national brand names for their beers. The smaller brewers have higher costs and mainly regional customers.

A number of forces affect even the Canadian giants in the industry, however. First, sales of beer are flat in Canada because many customers have switched to wine or wine coolers. Second, social attitudes toward drinking, and in particular toward drinking and driving, have changed. Concern over the health effects of drinking alcohol has increased, and organizations such as MADD (Mothers Against Drunk Driving) and SADD (Students Against Destructive Decisions) have lobbied for tighter control over sales of alcohol to minors and for strengthening legal penalties for drunk driving. One of the most interesting forces affecting the large brewers has been an increase in competition from small regional beer makers and import beer makers who are capitalizing on Canadian customers' demands for new tastes and higher beer quality.

Questions

1. What are the principal forces in the external environment facing the major brewers?
2. How has the level of uncertainty changed over time in the brewing industry? What is the source of these changes?

Video Management Case

The Environment of Business

The video, "The Environment of Business," showcases the Trek Bicycle Corporation. The video illustrates how linking quality to managing well creates a high-performance work environment for business. Trek realized that quality and standards would be the new mantra. The company grew 700 percent as a result. Trek's comeback was absolutely amazing. Employees were also empowered to make good judgment calls as they went about their work each day. If something on the line was not right, they could stop production, work with others, and fix the problem. As preparation for watching the video, go to their website and get a "feel" for the company: www.trekbikes.com. Go through the various options at the website as well. Now watch the video, "The Environment of Business."

Questions to Consider

1. What's your sense of the company?
2. Would you want to work for such a company as Trek? Why? Why not?
3. What is Trek's environment for doing business?
4. What are the challenges that managers at Trek face in the global marketplace?
5. How successful do you think Trek will be?

3

Managing Ethics, Social Responsibility, and Diversity

Learning Outcomes

1. Describe the concept of ethics, and the different models of ethics.

2. Describe the concept of social responsibility, and detail the ways in which organizations can encourage both ethical and socially responsible behaviour among their employees.

3. Define diversity, and explain why the effective management of diverse employees is both an ethical issue and a means for an organization to improve its performance.

4. Identify instances of sexual harassment, and discuss how to prevent its occurrence.

Juggling The Juggle[1]

Imagine the following: US$11.7 billion in funds is unaccounted for! Anyone who has trouble balancing his or her chequebook knows what it's like to have the numbers "not add up"! But US$11.7 billion not adding up? That was the amount in the Italian scandal-ridden and disgraced Parmalat Finanziaria SpA case.

Imagine now the following: you are the president of the Canadian subsidiary of this same company. Your company is Parmalat Canada Ltd. Your company has the top four brands: Astro, Beatrice, Lactantia, and Black Diamond; your company employs 2900 people with operating facilities located in Alberta, Manitoba, Ontario, and Quebec.

Parmalat Finanziaria SpA, in 2003 Parmalat the world's 14th leading packaged food manufacturer, was the mother company and was being investigated for scandal and financial mismanagement (US$11.7 billion in unaccounted funds). Parmalat Canada Ltd. was trying not only to survive this financial and ethical landmine, but also, not being involved in such scandal, actually to do well.

Such was the case for Marc Caira, recruited as president of Parmalat Canada Ltd. just a few months before the scandal broke. It is said that he could write the book on crisis management. The following is some of the challenges he faced: nervous lenders, suppliers and customers; bosses arrested on criminal charges; a new boss who wouldn't return his phone calls; speculation that his company may be sold off piecemeal; and 3000 employees worried about their jobs. Throughout all of this, he had to ensure that sales of the company's dairy products didn't slide.

So what did he do? This is the point at which "juggling the juggle" comes into play, said Caira, who goes on to say, "I've seen things and done things and been involved in things that I never would have seen in a regular company. That may sound awkward but, as an individual, I've grown. It's made me a much better manager."

Caira's strategy throughout the scandal was complete transparency. When he picked up news stories on the Internet that there were accounting problems at Parmalat in Italy, and when he got no answers to his phone calls and when customers and lenders in Canada

started asking questions as well, he told them what he knew: nothing. When, in December 2003, regulators in Italy suspended Parmalat's shares and then the company filed for bankruptcy protection after it was unable to account for about US$11.7 billion in funds, the global investing community began referring to Parmalat as "Europe's Enron."

Caira, now left on his own, designed a plan that included:

- Making sure that all employees focused on sales.

- Delegating only a handful of senior executives to work with him on the mess in Italy.

- Communicating with everybody, even though his knowledge of what was going on was basically through the news media! Caira remarked, "Communication

Newly recruited President Marc Caira's vision, transparency, ethics, and business acumen helped him "juggle the juggle" and made Parmalat Canada more successful than it's ever been.

became critical . . . we had to keep repeating it's business as usual, it's not us, we've done nothing wrong and we're fine."

- Hiring forensic accountants who determined that the Canadian operations were clean, thus ensuring that his division was not part of the scandal.

Ken Wong, professor of strategy at Queen's University School of Business in Kingston, Ontario said that Caira deserves full credit for telling his employees, "I don't know, but as soon as I find out, you'll know." According to Wong, honesty in these matters is always the best policy.

Caira's goal was to protect the Canadian operations. His next move, while controversial to some, worked: in spite of the fact that employees were working at full capacity for sales, the operation was not working efficiently; and critical to overall success, these inefficiencies were eating into profits. He hired more staff, restructured and streamlined the entire operation. "Senior management came up with a plan to streamline operations, sell unnecessary assets, trim its work force and put its U.S. operation into bankruptcy protection." Caira also refinanced Parmalat Canada Ltd.'s debt by getting the Ontario Teachers Pension Plan (OTPP) to agree to take over all of Parmalat Canada's debt, which signed a deal to inject $610 million into the dairy company. Caira also made sure OTPP's money was "ring fenced"—meaning every dollar made in Canada, stayed in Canada and didn't flow to Italian bank accounts. For Jim Leech, senior vice-president for Teachers, this aspect of the deal was essential so that OTPP's funds "wouldn't be a cash cow to solve the sins elsewhere."

As a result of Caira's vision, transparency, ethics, and business acumen: "Financially, 2004 was Parmalat Canada's best year ever as sales topped $2 billion and profit was up 60 percent from 2003."

Now It's Your Turn

Assume you were hired by a company under the same circumstances as Marc Caira. Then you discovered you were in the middle of a corporate mess.

1. What would be your initial reaction to your circumstances?

2. What would you do?

3. How would you counsel someone else in your situation?

Overview

It's easy to see that with the best of intentions managers can find themselves in a very awkward and, in Marc Caira's situation, recruited as president of Parmalat Canada Ltd., in a scandal-plagued organization. Some managers refuse to accept responsibility for what happened. In what was labelled the "Aw Shucks" defence, Bernie Ebbers, ex-WorldCom boss, was found guilty of a record-breaking US$11-billion fraud and conspiracy for his role in the biggest corporate blow-up in U.S. corporate history. Ebbers defence was the "Aw-shucks, I'm-not-sophisticated defence," as one prosecutor defined it, also known as the Canadian defence, and also known as the Sgt. Schultz "I know nothing" defence. The jury at his trial in 2005 did not accept that defence.

Journalist Jennifer Wells describes his defence this way: "In the words of that great American cultural icon, Gomer Pyle, 'Well, Golly.'"[2] Ebbers was sentenced to 25 years in prison.

When Caira discovered what was happening, he immediately took steps to rectify matters. He began working on managing what he had to do to protect the Canadian operation. He did this, in spite of the fact that he was not at all involved in the scandal at head office in Italy, a scandal that showed US$11.7 billion in unaccounted funds! Because of his transparency, good management skills, and ethical vision, he saved the Canadian operation from scandal; indeed, he even made it profitable!

The ways in which managers view their responsibilities to the individuals and groups that are affected by their actions are central to the discussion of ethics and social responsibility, and to the discussion of organizational performance as well. In this chapter, we explore what it means to behave ethically. We describe how managers and organizations can behave in a socially responsible way toward the individuals and groups in their organizational environment.

We then focus on one particular aspect of ethical behaviour that is receiving increasing attention today: how to manage diversity to ensure that everyone an organization employs is fairly and equitably treated. Managers' ability and desire to behave ethically and to manage diversity effectively are central concerns in today's complex business environment. Increasingly, if managers ignore these issues or fail to act appropriately, their organizations are unlikely to prosper in the future.

We also discuss sexual harassment, which is both unethical and illegal, and a behaviour that managers and organizations—military as well as civilian—must confront and respond to in a serious manner. By the end of the chapter, you will appreciate why ethics, diversity, and sexual harassment are issues that make a manager's job both more challenging and more complex.

What Are Ethics?

THINK ABOUT IT

Like a Child in a Candy Store?[3]

Paul Coffin, in Montreal, was the first person convicted of 15 counts of fraud in the federal government's sponsorship contracts scandal. He was also the first ad executive to reimburse some of the money improperly paid in federal contracts, by handing back $1 million of the $1.6 million he admitted he owed taxpayers; this agreement was reached as an out-of-court settlement in the civil suit Ottawa filed in spring 2005 against 19 individuals and firms involved in the scandal.

In the courtroom he asked for clemency when being sentenced. The crown attorney said he deserved at least 34 months in prison even though he made amends; Mr. Justice Jean-Guy Boilard of Quebec Superior Court said that the fraud was quite elaborate and that Coffin had truly betrayed the public's trust.

Coffin's defence lawyer said that Coffin was "like a child in a candy store." Raphael Schachter, Coffin's lawyer, said blame should be placed on the federal government's shoulders in Ottawa for tempting his client with the lax way it administered the sponsorship program. This laxness made it virtually impossible for him to avoid the temptation of the fraud, even if it was $1.6 million he admitted he owed taxpayers!

Coffin said that he was an honest man who strayed only once, that he was raised by law-abiding parents, including a mother who told him to return a wallet he had found when he was a boy because "honesty is the best policy." He indicated that he had already contacted Montreal's four universities and offered to give business students lectures on ethics. "My objective is to give back to the community I betrayed," he said.

The crown prosecutor didn't want to accept Coffin's contrition. He said that if Coffin didn't go to jail, it would be like telling the students: "For nearly five years, I sent false invoices, invoices that were paid with your money, I lived well and now I'm before you, a citizen who isn't behind bars—don't do as I did." This, according to the prosecutor, would be sending the wrong message.[4]

Mr. Coffin's intention is to spend the rest of his life, if necessary, in paying off his debts to the people he defrauded. Said Coffin, "I feel very ashamed of what I've done … I want to make restitution. I want to come clean … I want to clear my name and feel better with my family."

You Be the Manager

1. Do you accept Paul Coffin's defence lawyer's claim that his client was really like "a child in a candy store"?

2. What would you recommend as an appropriate sentence for Coffin's fraudulent behaviour?

ethics
Moral principles or beliefs about what is right or wrong.

The questions raised about Paul Coffin's fraudulent role in the sponsorship contracts scandal highlight ethical concerns of which managers need to pay attention. **Ethics** are moral principles or beliefs about what is right or wrong. These beliefs guide individuals in their dealings with other individuals and groups who have a concern in a particular situation (stakeholders), and they provide a basis for deciding if behaviour is right and proper.[5] Ethics help people determine moral responses to situations in which the best course of action is unclear.

Managers often experience an ethical dilemma when they confront a situation that requires them to choose between two courses of action, especially if each decision is likely to serve the interests of one particular stakeholder group to the detriment of the other.[6] To make an appropriate decision, managers must weigh the competing claims or rights of the various stakeholder groups. Sometimes, making a decision is easy because some obvious standard, value, or norm of behaviour applies. In other cases, managers have trouble deciding what to do.

Making Ethical Decisions

Philosophers have debated for centuries about the specific criteria that should be used to determine whether decisions are ethical or unethical. Three models of what determines whether a decision is ethical—the *utilitarian*, *moral rights*, and *justice* models—are summarized in Table 3.1.[7] In theory, each model offers a different and complementary way of determining whether a decision or behaviour is ethical, and all three models should be used to sort out the ethics of a particular course of action. Ethical issues are seldom clear-cut, however, and the interests of different stakeholders often conflict, so it is often extremely difficult for a decision maker to use these models to identify the most ethical course of action. That is why many experts on ethics

TABLE 3.1 | *Utilitarian, Moral Rights, and Justice Models of Ethics*

Model	Managerial Implications	Problems for Managers
Utilitarian Model An ethical decision is a decision that produces the greatest good for the greatest number of people.	Managers should compare and contrast alternative courses of action based on the benefits and costs of those alternatives for different organizational stakeholder groups. They should choose the course of action that provides the most benefits to stakeholders. For example, managers should locate a new manufacturing plant at the place that will most benefit its stakeholders.	How do managers decide on the relative importance of each stakeholder group? How are managers to measure precisely the benefits and harms to each stakeholder group? For example, how do managers choose among the interests of stockholders, employees, and customers?
Moral Rights Model An ethical decision is a decision that best maintains and protects the fundamental rights and privileges of the people affected by it. For example, ethical decisions protect people's rights to freedom, life and safety, privacy, free speech, and freedom of conscience.	Managers should compare and contrast alternative courses of action based on the effect of those alternatives on stakeholders' rights. They should choose the course of action that best protects stakeholders' rights. For example, decisions that would involve significant harm to the safety or health of employees or customers are unethical.	If a decision will protect the rights of some stakeholders and hurt the rights of others, how do managers choose which stakeholder rights to protect? For example, in deciding whether it is ethical to snoop on an employee, does an employee's right to privacy outweigh an organization's right to protect its property or the safety of other employees?
Justice Model An ethical decision is a decision that distributes benefits and harms among stakeholders in a fair, equitable, or impartial way.	Managers should compare and contrast alternative courses of action based on the degree to which the action will promote a fair distribution of outcomes. For example, employees who are similar in their level of skill, performance, or responsibility should receive the same kind of pay. The allocation of outcomes should not be based on arbitrary differences such as gender, race, or religion.	Managers must learn not to discriminate between people because of observable differences in their appearance or behaviour. Managers must also learn how to use fair procedures to determine how to distribute outcomes to organizational members. For example, managers must not give people they like bigger raises than they give to people they do not like or bend the rules to help their favourites.

propose the following practical guide to determine whether a decision or behaviour is ethical.[8] A decision is probably acceptable on ethical grounds if a person can answer "yes" to each of these questions:

1. Does my decision fall within the accepted values or standards that typically apply in the organizational environment?
2. Am I willing to see the decision communicated to all stakeholders affected by it—for example, by having it reported in newspapers or on television?
3. Would the people with whom I have a significant personal relationship, such as family members, friends, or even managers in other organizations, approve of the decision?

From an organizational perspective, an **ethical decision** is a decision that reasonable or typical stakeholders would find acceptable because it aids stakeholders, the organization, or society. By contrast, an **unethical decision** is a decision that a person would prefer to disguise or hide from other people because it enables a company or a particular individual to gain at the expense of society or other stakeholders. The sponsorship contracts scandal incident highlights how easy it can be, even for seasoned managers and executives, to become involved in shady deals and, in Coffin's case, in serious fraudulent behaviour. We saw that even though Paul Coffin demonstrated contrition, agreed to pay back as much as he could, and that he indicated he would spend the rest of his life making amends, he still left it to his lawyer to argue that the temptation to commit fraud was just too great for his client and hence Coffin was at the mercy of the forces, such as a child would be "in a candy store." Ethics and accountability must go hand in hand.

ethical decision
A decision that reasonable or typical stakeholders would find acceptable because it aids stakeholders, the organization, or society.

unethical decision
A decision that a manager would prefer to disguise or hide from other people because it enables a company or a particular individual to gain at the expense of society or other stakeholders.

People will always ask, "Was Paul Coffin really at the mercy of the forces, as his lawyer suggests—like a child in a candy store—or was this defence simply a way to avoid accountability—and prison?" If it was, it also trivialized the seriousness of the charges.

Codes of Ethics

codes of ethics
Formal standards and rules, based on beliefs about right or wrong, that managers can use to help themselves make appropriate decisions with regard to the interests of their stakeholders.

Codes of ethics are formal standards and rules, based on beliefs about right or wrong, that managers can use to help themselves make appropriate decisions with regard to the interests of their stakeholders.[9] Ethical standards embody views about abstractions such as justice, freedom, equity, and equality (see Table 3.1). An organization's code of ethics derives from three main sources in the organizational environment: (1) **societal ethics**, governing how everyone deals with each other on issues such as fairness, justice, poverty, and the rights of the individual; (2) **professional ethics**, governing how members of the profession make decisions when the way they should behave is not clear-cut; and (3) the **individual ethics**, or personal standards for interacting with others, of the organization's top managers (see Figure 3.1).

societal ethics
Standards that govern how members of a society are to deal with each other on issues such as fairness, justice, poverty, and the rights of the individual.

Shell Canada's code of ethics states the following:

Shell Canada's reputation and credibility are based upon its total commitment to ethical business practices. To safeguard the Shell reputation, employees must conduct themselves in accordance with the highest ethical standards and also be perceived to be acting ethically at all times.[10]

professional ethics
Standards that govern how members of a profession are to make decisions when the way they should behave is not clear-cut.

The company's ethics web page (http://66.46.47.14/code/values/commitments/ethics.html) describes in some detail how different stakeholders are to interpret the code of ethics.

individual ethics
Personal standards that govern how individuals interact with other people.

Information is the lifeblood of the new economy and if that gets jeopardized by employees with sloppy ethical standards, the community suffers; serious damage can occur. In 2004, there were some 20 incidents in Canada where the public was affected by IT systems going down. For example, in 2004, three of the big bank's customers

FIGURE 3.1 | *Sources of an Organization's Code of Ethics*

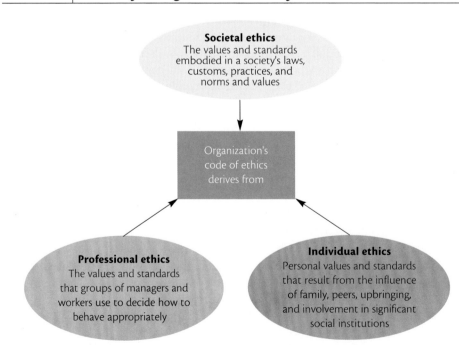

either lost access to their accounts for a period of time or experienced other accounting errors such as being double-charged service fees. In 2005 in British Columbia, Auditor General Wayne Strelioff found security vulnerabilities with the provincial government's Corporate Accounting System that were so serious he withheld his report for fear of tipping off hackers. And in Alberta, the Calgary Health Region experienced a computer error that mixed up 2000 results from blood and urine tests, forcing the region to shut down the database on July 6, 2005. The Canadian Information Processing Society, or CIPS, with its 585 000+ IT workers is trying to address the issue of professionalism, which would include a code of professional ethics. The problem is that only a fraction of these IT workers have their Information Systems Professionals designation, or ISP, which has been offered now for over 16 years. At a conference in Regina, Sask., in 2005, Greg Lane, director of the federal region for Microsoft Canada, said, "We're no longer closet people. We deal with the most valuable commodity: information." Lane said an ISP designation demonstrates an ongoing commitment to education, a code of ethics, and "you're measured by your peers for competency."

Ethics and Stakeholders

The individuals and groups that have an interest, claim, or stake in an organization and in what it does are known as *organizational stakeholders*.[11] **Organizational stakeholders** include shareholders, managers, nonmanagerial employees, customers, suppliers, the local community in which an organization operates, and even citizens of the country in which an organization operates. To survive and prosper, an organization must effectively satisfy its stakeholders.[12] Stockholders want dividends, managers and employees want salaries and stable employment, and customers want high quality products at reasonable prices. If stakeholders do not receive these benefits, they may withdraw their support for the organization: Stockholders will sell their stock, managers and workers will seek jobs in other organizations, and customers will take their business elsewhere.

Managers are the stakeholder group that determines which goals an organization should pursue to benefit stakeholders most, and how to make the most efficient use of resources to achieve those goals. In making such decisions, managers often have to juggle the interests of different stakeholders, including themselves.[13] Managerial decisions that may benefit some stakeholder groups and harm others involve questions of ethics. For example, South Gobi, Mongolia is the exploration site of Ivanhoe Mines Ltd. of Vancouver, which believes it has discovered a gigantic copper and gold deposit there. It is also spending US$10 million a month drilling holes, testing results, and pouring a gigantic concrete shaft in preparation for production to begin in 2007–08. Mongolia is a country without infrastructure. Issues that have to be addressed include power generation, transportation, smelting, water, and dust control. To overcome these obstacles, world-class companies must negotiate who's going to pay for what and when. To meet these challenges is a time-consuming process because all stakeholder concerns must be met. "This is what goes on everywhere," said Ivanhoe chairman Robert Friedland. "It is in everyone's interest that the deal is fair to the government and citizens in order to have a sustainable development franchise."[14]

Ethics and National Culture

Views about what is ethical vary among societies. For example, ethical standards accepted in Canada and the United States are not accepted in all other countries. In many economically poor countries, bribery is standard practice to get things done—such as

organizational stakeholders
Shareholders, employees, customers, suppliers, and others who have an interest, claim, or stake in an organization and in what it does.

Many ethical issues arise for mining companies who do business in countries without infrastructure in South Gobi, Mongolia. Would safety standards compare well with mines in North America?

getting a telephone installed or a contract awarded. In Canada and many other Western countries, bribery as part of doing business in one's home country is considered unethical and often illegal. Bribing foreign public officials is widespread, however. The US government reported that between 1994 and 2001, bribery was uncovered in more than 400 competitions for international contracts.[15] A recent study found that some Asian governments were far more tolerant of corruption than others. Singapore, Japan and Hong Kong scored relatively low on corruption (0.83, 2.5, and 3.77 out of 10, respectively), and Vietnam, Indonesia, India, the Philippines, and Thailand scored as the most corrupt of the 12 Asian countries surveyed.[16]

While Canada has no national laws regarding codes of ethics, in 1997 a coalition of Canadian companies developed a new international code of ethics. The code is voluntary and deals with issues such as the environment, human rights, business conduct, treatment of employees, and health and safety standards. Supporters of the Canadian code include the Alliance of Manufacturers & Exporters Canada, the Conference Board of Canada, and the Business Council on National Issues. Alcan Inc., Komex International Ltd., Shell Canada Ltd., and Talisman Energy Inc. are among the companies that have signed the code. Former foreign affairs minister Lloyd Axworthy hailed the code as a way of putting Canadian values into the international arena.[17] Vern Krishna, CM, QC, FCGA, tax counsel for Borden Ladner Gervais LLP, and executive director of the CGA Tax Research Centre at the University of Ottawa, writes, "But not all bribes are equally offensive in law. Business must go on according to the local culture. In certain Asian societies, 'grease,' 'commissions,' 'facilitation fees,' 'agency fees' and 'baksheesh' are essential to doing business. Many governments in Third World countries control the issuance of licences to produce, manufacture, or distribute products that sometimes assure the recipient of a monopoly or protected market. Civil servants supervise the granting of such licences and, in the process, may supplement their modest income. No bribe, no licence. However, Canadian companies that participate, directly or indirectly, in any such bidding process are open to criminal prosecution and civil sanctions."[18]

What Behaviours Are Ethical?

A key ethical decision for managers is how to divide harms and benefits among stakeholder groups.[19] Suppose a company has a few very good years and makes high profits. Who should receive these profits—managers, employees, stockholders, or customers? For example, as oil prices soared throughout the world in 2000 and 2001, Canadian oil industry profits reached record highs. Customers, whose heating bills rose greatly, thought they should get some of their money back in rebates.

The decision about how to divide profits among managers, employees, stockholders, and even customers might not seem to be an ethical issue, but it is—and in the same manner as how to apportion harms or costs among stakeholders when things go wrong.[20] For instance, it is not unusual for companies to engage in restructurings—resulting in massive layoffs—to improve their bottom line, and perhaps increase returns to stockholders, who are the legal owners of a corporation. Are layoffs of managers and employees ethical? Managers at some companies try to make the layoffs less painful by introducing generous early retirement programs that give employees full pension rights if they retire early. Employees are sometimes paid a month's or several months' salary for each year of service to the company.

Managers also face ethical dilemmas when choosing how to deal with certain stakeholders. For example, suppliers provide an organization with its inputs and expect to be paid within a reasonable amount of time. Some managers, however, consistently delay payment to make the most use of their organization's money. This practice can hurt a supplier's cash flow and threaten its very survival.

An organization that is a powerful customer and buys large amounts of particular suppliers' products is in a position to demand that suppliers reduce their prices. If an organization does this, suppliers earn lower profits and the organization earns more. Is this behaviour just "business as usual," or is it unethical?

In Saint John, N.B., a new order of the day is in progress. The 80-year-old Irving Oil Ltd., Canada's largest refinery, has a reputation for being very tight-lipped about its operation, secrecy in its personnel policies, and with managers who only drive their employees and suppliers for what they can squeeze out of them in order to make more profits. Now the company is in the process of educating managers to shift from being managers to being leaders. They're taking leadership courses, even boss Kenneth Irving, from Forum Corp. of Boston. Even though Irving Oil has a "tough" image from its dealings with the community and suppliers in the past, company executives say that has been a widespread misconception. "Instead, they insist Irving Oil has traditionally focused on corporate values that include a business strategy based on a rewarding working environment that shuns the use of job titles and stresses the importance of relationships with its staff, suppliers and customers."[21] Irving was recently named North American refiner of the year by Hart Publications, a major energy sector publisher based in the United States.[22] Irving is the first Canadian company to receive the annual award, which examines a refiner's environmental performance, ability to produce clean fuel, and investment in facilities and employees.

Sometimes it is suppliers who can take advantage of situations in the market to gain higher profits. After California's energy crisis in 2000 and 2001, a report was filed with the US Federal Energy Regulatory Commission claiming that BC Hydro "reaped US$176 million in 'excessive' profits by price gouging California utilities."[23] BC Hydro was accused of offering "power at a range of high prices and sometimes in large amounts when the state was most desperate."[24] BC Hydro officials "acknowledge they did anticipate periods of severe power shortages and planned for them by letting their reservoirs rise overnight and then opening them to create hydro electricity, which could be produced inexpensively but sold for a premium." But BC Hydro officials say they

BC Hydro
www.bchydro.com

played by the rules of the electricity trade marketplace. "It was the marketplace that determined what the price of electricity would be at any given time," said BC Hydro spokesman Ian Cousins. We can readily raise the question: Was this good business, or was this unethical behaviour?

In addition to suppliers and distributors, customers are a critical stakeholder group because, as noted in Chapter 1, organizations depend on them for their very survival. Customers have the right to expect an organization to provide goods and services that will not harm them. As well, local communities and the general public have an interest or stake in whether the decisions that managers make are ethical. The quality of a city's school system or police department, the economic health of its downtown area, and its general level of prosperity all depend on choices made by managers of organizations.

In sum, managers face many ethical choices as they deal with the different and sometimes conflicting interests of organizational stakeholders. Deciding what behaviour is ethical is often a difficult task that requires managers to make tough choices that will benefit some stakeholders and harm others.

Promoting Ethics

A 2000 ethics survey by KPMG found that nearly two-thirds of Canadian firms promote values and ethical practices. However, more than half of the companies surveyed had not designated a senior manager responsible for ethical issues. Only 14 percent evaluated their employees in terms of ethical performance.[25] Despite a seeming lack of commitment to concrete actions by Canada's companies, there are many ways in which managers can communicate their desire for employees at all levels to behave ethically toward organizational stakeholders. The irony here with this KPMG example is that in August 2005 eight former executives of KPMG LLP were indicted on the largest criminal tax case ever filed, which allowed the firm's clients to avoid $2.5 billion in taxes! To avoid a situation where KPMG might collapse, as did Arthur Anderson, a former Big Four account firm competitor, KPMG agreed to pay US$456 million in penalties and admitted to helping wealthy clients fraudulently avoid billions in taxes.[26]

Establishing Ethical Control Systems

Perhaps the most important step to encourage ethical behaviour is to develop a code of ethics that is given to every employee and published regularly in company newsletters and annual reports. The "Integrity Program" at Calgary-based Nexen Inc. (formerly Canadian Occidental Petroleum Ltd.) covers such issues as business conduct, employee and human rights, and the environment. Each division at Nexen has an integrity leader who is supposed to make sure that the message about the company's commitment to ethics spreads throughout the organization.[27] At UPS Canada, employees must develop an action plan around their codes of conduct. Managers are assessed on matters such as integrity and fair treatment.[28]

The next step is to provide a visible means of support for ethical behaviour. Increasingly, organizations are creating the role of ethics officer, or **ethics ombudsperson**, to monitor their ethical practices and procedures. The ethics ombudsman is responsible for communicating ethical standards to all employees, for designing systems to monitor employees' conformity to those standards, and for teaching managers and nonmanagerial employees at all levels of the organization how to respond to ethical dilemmas appropriately.[29] Because the ethics ombudsperson has organization-wide authority, organizational members in any department can discuss instances of unethical behaviour by their managers or co-workers without fear of retribution. This arrangement makes it easier for everyone to behave ethically. In addition, ethics ombudspeople

Nexen Inc. Integrity Program
www.nexeninc.com/Our_ Commitment/Business_ Practices/

ethics ombudsperson
An ethics officer who monitors an organization's practices and procedures to be sure they are ethical.

can provide guidance when organizational members are uncertain about whether an action is ethical. Some organizations have an organization-wide ethics committee to provide guidance on ethical issues and help write and update the company code of ethics.

Developing an Ethical Culture

An organization can also communicate its position on ethics and social responsibility to employees by making ethical values and norms a central part of its organizational culture. A number of companies try to encourage ethical behaviour through their corporate culture, emphasizing such values as honesty, trust, respect, and fairness. (We discuss organizational culture in depth in Chapter 7.) It is important to note that when organizational members abide by the organization's values and norms, those values and norms become part of each individual's personal code of ethics. Thus, an employee who faces an ethical dilemma automatically responds to the situation in a manner that reflects the ethical standards of the organization. High standards and strong values and norms help individuals resist self-interested action and recognize that they are part of something bigger than themselves.[30]

The manager's role in developing ethical values and standards in other employees is very important. Employees naturally look to those in authority to provide leadership, and managers become ethical role models whose behaviour is scrutinized. If top managers are not ethical, their subordinates are not likely to behave in an ethical manner. They may think that, if it's all right for a top manager to engage in ethically dubious behaviour, it's all right for them too.

Ethical control systems such as codes of ethics and regular training programs help employees learn an organization's ethical values. However, KPMG reported in 2000 that 61 percent of Canadian companies surveyed gave no ethics training at all, and a third of Canadian businesses provide managers with less than one hour of training a year.[31] And in January 2005 "ethical eyebrows" were raised when Nortel Networks Corp., the telephone-equipment maker, known in the past for some "grey-zone" management and compensation practices, announced that it was thinking of paying executive bonuses again, even though it had been struggling financially in recent years. Nortel announced that it was going to pay Susan Shepard, a New York lawyer, its new chief ethics and compliance officer, an annual salary of US$375 000; and if Nortel decided to award bonuses for 2005, she would then be eligible for a bonus of 60 percent of her base salary. Some are questioning the ethics of this situation. David Beatty, managing director of the Canadian Coalition for Good Governance, said, "You've come through a complete exercise where the achievement of financial objectives distorted people's judgments and moral bearings quite considerably by what we read. It seems quite extraordinary to me that such an inbuilt conflict would persist in the compensation plan of a new chief ethics officer."[32]

✔ Tips for Managers

CHAMPIONING ETHICAL BEHAVIOUR

1. Identify the ways that managers can more effectively and with an ethical rationale for their actions make decisions that won't adversely affect stakeholders.

2. Think of an organization you've worked for. Choose one that you know does not have a code of ethics. Design one and make recommendations on how employees can live up to its ideals.

3. List ways to show how managers can help employees develop ways to resolve ethical dilemmas they encounter in their day-to-day work.

4. Make a list of ways to ensure that managers serve as role models for their employees.

Social Responsibility

"C'mon, C'mon, Lemonade for Everybody"[33]

James McDonough is a 10-year-old who was selling lemonade for 25 cents a cup near his backyard in Gordon Head, a Victoria, B.C. suburb. Then, in a blink of an eye, he made $2 a cup for each lemonade. How did this happen? A transit bus driver stopped by the side of the road and bought each of his seven passengers a cup of lemonade just before lunchtime. Lilla, James' mother, said that the bus driver said to everyone on the bus, "'C'mon, c'mon, lemonade for everybody.' I just thought it was the most wonderful thing. He's a very kind and generous man to do that." Of course, James thought the driver's action was very "cool." B.C. Transit spokesperson Ron Drolet was also impressed with what the driver did. The bus driver wanted to remain anonymous.

You Be the Manager

1. What did this bus driver do that made a difference from a social responsibility point of view?
2. What would you have done if you were Ron Drolet, the B.C. Transit spokesperson.

There are many reasons why it is important for managers and organizations to act ethically and to do everything possible to avoid harming stakeholders. However, what about the other side of the coin? What responsibility do managers have to provide benefits to their stakeholders and to adopt courses of action that enhance the well-being of society at large? The term **social responsibility** refers to a manager's duty or obligation to make decisions that nurture, protect, enhance, and promote the welfare and well-being of stakeholders and society as a whole. Many kinds of decisions signal an organization's interest in being socially responsible (see Table 3.2).

Approaches to Social Responsibility

The strength of organizations' commitment to social responsibility ranges from low to high (see Figure 3.2).[34] At the low end of the range is an **obstructionist approach**.

social responsibility
A manager's duty or obligation to make decisions that promote the well-being of stakeholders and society as a whole.

obstructionist approach
Disregard for social responsibility; willingness to engage in and cover up unethical and illegal behaviour.

TABLE 3.2 | *Forms of Socially Responsible Behaviour*

Managers are being socially responsible and showing their support for their stakeholders when they:
- Provide severance payments to help laid-off workers make ends meet until they can find another job;
- Provide workers with opportunities to enhance their skills and acquire additional education so they can remain productive and do not become obsolete because of changes in technology;
- Allow employees to take time off when they need to and provide extended health care and pension benefits for employees;
- Contribute to charities or support various civic-minded activities in the cities or towns in which they are located;
- Decide to keep open a factory whose closure would devastate the local community;
- Decide to keep a company's operations in Canada to protect the jobs of Canadian workers rather than move abroad;
- Decide to spend money to improve a new factory so that it will not pollute the environment;
- Decline to invest in countries that have poor human rights records;
- Choose to help poor countries develop an economic base to improve living standards.

FIGURE 3.2 | *Approaches to Social Responsibility*

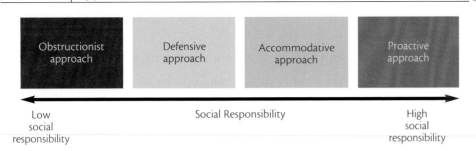

Obstructionist managers choose not to behave in a socially responsible way. Instead, they behave unethically and illegally and do all they can to prevent knowledge of their behaviour from reaching other organizational stakeholders and society at large.

A **defensive approach** indicates at least a commitment to ethical behaviour. Managers adopting this approach do all they can to ensure that their employees behave legally and do not harm others. But when making ethical choices, these managers put the claims and interests of their shareholders first, at the expense of other stakeholders.

Some economists believe that managers in a capitalist society should always put stockholders' claims first. They suggest that if such choices are unacceptable or are considered unethical to other members of society, then society must pass laws and create rules and regulations to govern the choices managers make.[35] From a defensive point of view, it is not managers' responsibility to make socially responsible choices; their job is to abide by the rules that have been legally established.

An **accommodative approach** is an acknowledgment of the need to support social responsibility. Accommodative managers agree that organizational members ought to behave legally and ethically, and they try to balance the interests of different stakeholders against one another so that the claims of stockholders are seen in relation to the claims of other stakeholders. Managers adopting this approach want to make choices that are reasonable in the eyes of society and want to do the right thing when called on to do so. Wal-Mart Canada has been criticized for its policy of doing business with third-party suppliers—such as Hampton Industries, Sutton Creations, Global Gold, Stretch-O-Rama, Cherry Stix, and By Design—that import goods from Myanmar (Burma), which engages in forced labour, including that of children. In defence of the company's actions, Wal-Mart Canada spokesman Andrew Pelletier noted, "We have a policy we are looking at, of monitoring vendors sourcing from other countries."[36] The company started with a defensive approach, focusing on not doing anything illegal, but has moved to a more accommodative style.

Managers taking a **proactive approach** actively embrace the need to behave in socially responsible ways, go out of their way to learn about the needs of different stakeholder groups, and are willing to use organizational resources to promote the interests of stockholders as well as other stakeholders. Taking a proactive approach doesn't seem to be the case when Hardee's introduced its 1420-calorie Monster Thickburger, a move the Center for Science in the Public Interest called likening the burger to a "fast-food pornographic snuff film." Hardee's defended its actions this way when Bruce Frazer, vice-president of marketing, said, "We didn't know how people would react to something that was basically a monument to decadence . . . It turned into a phenomena." The burger has two patties of Angus beef, four strips of bacon, three slices of cheese and mayo on a bun slathered with butter.[37]

On the other hand, a proactive approach is easily demonstrated by Paul Tsaparis, president and chief executive of Hewlett-Packard (Canada) Co. He writes that those who are going to lead our corporations in the decades to come must understand that

defensive approach
Minimal commitment to social responsibility; willingness to do what the law requires and no more.

accommodative approach
Moderate commitment to social responsibility; willingness to do more than the law requires if asked.

proactive approach
Strong commitment to social responsibility; eagerness to do more than the law requires and to use organizational resources to promote the interests of all organizational stakeholders.

there are no substitutes for the fundamentals of business leadership. His recipe for being proactive and socially responsible includes the following:

- A CEO should manage the company, not the share price.

- Managing means balancing short-term returns with long-term investment.

- It is a CEO's job to think about a decade, not just a quarter.

- Real profit and real cash flow and real balance sheets matter.

- Trust, integrity, transparency, accountability, and responsibility matter.[38]

Why Be Socially Responsible?

There are several advantages to social responsibility by managers and organizations. First, employees and society benefit directly because organizations (rather than the government) bear some of the costs of helping employees. Second, it has been said that if all organizations in a society were socially responsible, the quality of life as a whole would be higher.[39] Indeed, several management experts have argued that the way organizations behave toward their employees determines many of a society's values and norms and the ethics of its citizens. Experts point to Japan, Sweden, Germany, the Netherlands, and Switzerland as countries where organizations are very socially responsible and where, as a result, crime and unemployment rates are relatively low, the literacy rate is relatively high, and socio-cultural values promote harmony between different groups of people. Other reasons for being socially responsible are that it is the right thing to do and that companies that act responsibly toward their stakeholders benefit from increasing business and see their profits rise.[40]

Jason Mogus, president of Communicopia.Net, finds that being socially responsible is a competitive advantage: "The times that we are in right now are tough times for a lot of high-tech firms, and the ones that are thriving are the ones that really did build community connections and have strong customer and employee loyalty," says Mogus. "If everyone's just there for the stock price and it goes underwater, then what you have is a staff of not very motivated workers."[41]

Given these advantages, why would anyone quarrel over organizations and their managers pursuing social responsibility? One response is that a commitment to social responsibility could benefit some stakeholders and not others. For instance, some shareholders might think they are being harmed financially when organizational

Communicopia.Net
www.communicopia.net

The antithesis of a proactive approach: burger and fries fly in the face of social responsibility.

resources are used for socially responsible courses of action. Some people argue that business has only one kind of responsibility: to use its resources for activities that increase its profits and thus reward its stockholders.[42]

How should managers decide which social issues they will respond to, and to what extent their organizations should trade profits for social gain? Obviously, illegal behaviour should not be tolerated, and all managers and workers should be alert to its occurrence and report it promptly. The need to behave legally is only one of the criteria managers can use to decide which social actions to undertake. **A social audit** allows managers to consider both the organizational and the social effects of particular decisions. The audit ranks various courses of action according to both their profitability and their social benefits.

Evidence suggests that, in the long run, managers who behave in a socially responsible way will most benefit all organizational stakeholders (including stockholders). It appears that socially responsible companies, in comparison with less responsible competitors, are less risky investments, tend to be somewhat more profitable, have a more loyal and committed workforce, and have better **reputations**; these qualities encourage stakeholders (including customers and suppliers) to establish long-term business relationships with the companies.[43] Socially responsible companies are also sought out by communities, which encourage such organizations to locate in their cities and offer them incentives such as property-tax reductions and the construction of new roads and free utilities for their plants. Thus, there are many reasons to believe that, over time, strong support of social responsibility brings the most benefits to organizational stakeholders (including stockholders) and society at large.

social audit
A tool that allows managers to analyze the profitability and social returns of socially responsible actions.

reputation
The esteem or high repute that individuals or organizations gain when they behave ethically.

Managing an Increasingly Diverse Workforce

THINK ABOUT IT

Business Schmoozing With a Decidedly Indian Flavour[44]

Sanjay Tugnait is the head of Canadian, Caribbean, and Latin American operations for Satyam Computer Services—an international consulting and information technology global sourcing company headquartered in Hyderabad, India. It is listed on the New York Stock Exchange with $1 billion in revenues worldwide and 21 000 employees in 46 countries.

Call it "doing business with an Indian twist" when one meets Tugnait, 38, in his regal silk kurta, who also lectures at the University of Toronto's Rotman School of Management. He set up Satyam's Toronto office in 2003 with a handful of employees. "I feel very proud of my Indian heritage. That's what differentiates us from others, so we shouldn't be shying away from our roots." Satyam employs 130 people in Canada with offices in Calgary and Vancouver as well. In wooing clients, such as General Electric Co. and Citibank, he does what he calls "business schmoozing with a decidedly Indian flavour."

He takes clients or potential clients to top-end Indian restaurants. He helps Western clients understand unfamiliar menu items, with his wife Karishma acting as co-host; clients' spouses are always invited. After dinner, he might take clients to a

Bollywood show featuring megastars Shah Ruk Khan or Hrithik Roshan or to hear new age guru Deepak Chopra, whenever these celebrities are in town. "I don't take them for golf or basketball or any of that. That's left for the competition. . . . They love the food. They love the diversity. They love the culture. It's a total change for them."

You Be the Manager

1. What is Sanjay Tugnait doing in promoting a culture of diversity?
2. Why is diversity so important in today's new workplace?

One of the most important issues in management to emerge over the past 30 years has been the increasing diversity of the workforce. In Chapter 2, we addressed issues of diversity that result from organizations' expansion into the global environment. Here, we address diversity as it occurs closer to home—in an organization's workforce. **Diversity** is dissimilarity—differences—among people due to age, gender, race, ethnicity, religion, sexual orientation, socio-economic background, and capabilities/disabilities (see Figure 3.3). Diversity raises important ethical issues and social responsibility issues as well. It is also a critical issue for organizations, one that if not handled well can bring an organization to its knees, especially in our increasingly global environment.

Canada has become a truly diverse country, although this might not be apparent to everyone. Based on the 2001 census, on average 13 percent of Canada's population are visible minorities.[45] However, this varies widely across the country. In British Columbia, 22 percent of the residents are visible minorities, the highest proportion of any province. Ontario is second, with 19 percent of its population being visible minorities. These concentrations are much higher in Vancouver and Toronto, however—in both of these cities, visible minorities make up about 37 percent of the population. By contrast, only 0.8 percent of the population are visible minorities in Newfoundland

diversity
Differences among people in age, gender, race, ethnicity, religion, sexual orientation, socio-economic background, and capabilities or disabilities.

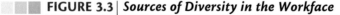

FIGURE 3.3 | *Sources of Diversity in the Workface*

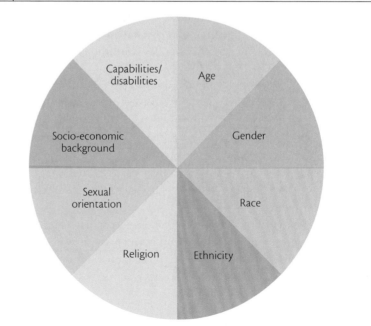

and Labrador and Nunavut, 7.9 percent in Manitoba, and 11 percent in Alberta. There are many more women and minorities—including people with disabilities and gays and lesbians—in the workforce than ever before, and most experts agree that diversity is steadily increasing.

Why is diversity such a pressing issue both in the popular press and for managers and organizations? There are several reasons:

- There is a strong ethical imperative in many societies to see that all people receive equal opportunities and are treated fairly and justly. Unfair treatment is also illegal.

- Effectively managing diversity can improve organizational effectiveness. When managers manage diversity well, they not only encourage other managers to treat diverse members of an organization fairly and justly, but also realize that diversity is an important resource that can help an organization gain a competitive advantage.

- Embracing diversity encourages employee participation, and thus encourages differences of opinions/ideas that are beneficial to the organization.

Canada accepts 300 000 new immigrants each year.[46] In 2017 visible minorities will become the majority in Canada. In addition, Aboriginal entrepreneurs are also growing in number and moving beyond their roots. The Aboriginal birth rate is already 1.5 times that of non-Aboriginals. These fast-changing realities also change the face of business. Orrin Benn is president of the newly formed Canadian Aboriginal and Minority Supplier Council (CAMSC) and wants to help these entrepreneurs succeed in growing their businesses because he doesn't want Canada to lose out on talent. CAMSC offers Aboriginal and minority entrepreneurs the opportunity to enter mainstream business in a way they have never been afforded. For example, John Bernard, president and founder of Donna Cona Inc., Canada's largest Aboriginal-owned technology firm, designed the infrastructure for Nunavut residents to communicate across Canada's largest territory.

In the rest of this section, we examine why effectively managing diversity makes sense. Then we look at the steps that managers can take to manage diversity effectively in their organizations.

The Ethical Need to Manage Diversity Effectively

Effectively managing diversity not only makes good business sense, but is an ethical obligation in Canadian society. Two moral principles provide managers with guidance when they try to meet this obligation: distributive justice and procedural justice.

Distributive Justice

The principle of **distributive justice** dictates that the distribution of pay raises, promotions, job titles, interesting job assignments, office space, and other organizational resources among members of an organization be fair. The distribution of these outcomes should be based on the meaningful contributions that individuals have made to the organization (such as time, effort, education, skills, abilities, and performance levels) and not on irrelevant personal characteristics over which individuals have no control (such as gender, race, or age).[47] Managers have an obligation to ensure that distributive justice exists in their organizations. This does not mean that all members of an organization receive identical or similar outcomes; rather, it means that members who receive more outcomes than others have made much greater or more significant contributions to the organization.

distributive justice
A moral principle calling for the distribution of pay raises, promotions, and other organizational resources to be based on meaningful contributions that individuals have made and not on personal characteristics over which they have no control.

overt discrimination
Knowingly and willingly denying diverse individuals access to opportunities and outcomes in an organization.

Is distributive justice common in organizations in corporate Canada? Probably the best way to answer this question is to say that things are getting better. Fifty years ago, **overt discrimination** (knowingly and willingly denying diverse individuals access to opportunities and outcomes in an organization) against women and minorities was not uncommon; today, organizations are inching closer toward the ideal of distributive justice. Statistics comparing the treatment of women and minorities with the treatment of white men suggest that most managers would need to take a proactive approach in order to achieve distributive justice in their organizations. For instance, Toronto-based Bank of Montreal has worked diligently to advance women through the ranks since 1991, after discovering that, even though 75 percent of its employees were women, only 9 percent of them were in management positions.[48] After bank managers introduced some changes, women held 23 percent of the executive positions at the Bank of Montreal in 1997. The Bank of Montreal continues to monitor its hiring and promotion of women and other diverse groups. Since 2001, senior managers have been given annual hiring and retention goals for members of the four designated groups. A portion of their bonus is tied to success on this front.[49]

In many countries, managers have not only an ethical obligation to strive to achieve distributive justice in their organizations, but also a legal obligation to treat all employees fairly. Managers risk being sued by employees who feel that they are not being fairly treated.

Procedural Justice

procedural justice
A moral principle calling for the use of fair procedures to determine how to distribute outcomes to organizational members.

The principle of **procedural justice** requires managers to use fair procedures to determine how to distribute outcomes to organizational members.[50] This principle applies to typical procedures such as appraising subordinates' performance, deciding who should receive a raise or a promotion, and deciding whom to lay off when an organization is forced to downsize.

Procedural justice exists, for example, when managers (1) carefully appraise a subordinate's performance, (2) take into account any environmental obstacles to high performance beyond the subordinate's control, such as lack of supplies, machine breakdowns, or dwindling customer demand for a product, and (3) ignore irrelevant personal characteristics such as the subordinate's age or ethnicity. Like distributive justice, procedural justice is necessary not only to ensure ethical conduct but also to avoid costly lawsuits.

Effectively Managing Diversity Makes Good Legal Sense

Human Rights Act
http://laws.justice.gc.ca/en/H-6

Employment Equity Act
http://laws.justice.gc.ca/en/E-5.401

A variety of legislative acts affect diversity management in Canada. Under the Canadian Human Rights Act, it is against the law for any employer or provider of service that falls within federal jurisdiction to make unlawful distinctions based on the following prohibited grounds: race, national or ethnic origin, colour, religion, age, sex (including pregnancy and childbirth), marital status, family status, mental or physical disability (including previous or present drug or alcohol dependence), pardoned conviction, or sexual orientation. Employment with the following employers and service providers is covered by the Human Rights Act: federal departments, agencies, and Crown corporations; Canada Post; chartered banks; national airlines; interprovincial communications and telephone companies; interprovincial transportation companies; and other federally regulated industries, including certain mining operations.

In addition to the Human Rights Act, Canada's Employment Equity Act of 1995 lists four protected categories of employees: Aboriginal peoples (whether Indian, Inuit, or Metis); persons with disabilities; members of visible minorities (non-Caucasian in race or nonwhite in colour); and women. The reasoning behind the Employment Equity Act is that individuals should not face employment barriers due to being a woman, a person with a disability, an Aboriginal person, or a member of a visible minority. Thus the federal legislation aims at ensuring that members of these four groups are treated equitably. Employers affected by the Canadian Human Rights Act are also covered by the Employment Equity Act.

A number of provinces have their own legislation, including employment equity acts, governing employers in their provinces. Many companies have difficulty complying with equity acts, as recent audits conducted by the Canadian Human Rights Commission show. In an audit of 180 companies, only Status of Women Canada; Elliot Lake, Ontario-based AJ Bus Lines; the National Parole Board; Canadian Transportation Agency; Les Méchins, Quebec-based Verreault Navigation; and Nortel Networks were compliant on their first try.[51]

Effectively Managing Diversity Makes Good Business Sense

Though organizations are forced to follow the law, the diversity of organizational members can be a source of competitive advantage in more than a legal sense, as it helps an organization to provide customers with better goods and services.[52] The variety of points of view and approaches to problems and opportunities that diverse employees provide can improve managerial decision making. Just as the workforce is becoming increasingly diverse, so too are the customers who buy an organization's goods or services.

Diverse members of an organization are likely to be attuned to what goods and services diverse segments of the market want and do not want. Major car companies, for example, are increasingly assigning women to their design teams to ensure that the needs and desires of female customers (a growing segment of the market) are taken into account in new car design.

Effectively managing diversity makes good business sense for another reason. More and more, consumer and civil rights organizations are demanding that companies think about diversity issues from a variety of angles. For instance, Toronto-based Royal Bank of Canada found its efforts to acquire North Carolina-based Centura Banks Inc. under attack by Inner City Press/Community on the Move (ICP), a US civil rights group. In April 2001, the group asked American and Canadian regulators to delay approval of the acquisition to allow further investigation of alleged abusive lending practices carried out by Centura. "Centura's normal interest rate lending disproportionately denies and excludes credit applications from people of colour," said Matthew Lee, ICP executive director.[53] ICP alleged that, in two American cities, Centura denied applications for home purchase from Black people three times more frequently than applications from White people. The group wanted Royal Bank to guarantee that it would end the alleged unfair lending practices.

Being aware of diversity issues extends beyond employees to include the issues of suppliers, clients, and customers. Nestlé

Women wearing the hajib, the traditional head cover of Muslim women, face discrimination when they look for jobs in Canada. A recent study found that 40 percent of the time when visibly Muslim women asked if jobs were available, they were either told there were not or were not given a chance to apply for a job.

Canada recently announced that it was planning to do away with its nut-free products because trying to keep the production area free of nut products seemed more costly than it was beneficial. Nestlé Canada was soon deluged with protests from Canadian families who had relied upon such products as Kit Kat, Mirage, Coffee Crisp, and Aero chocolate bars; and Smarties. Between 1 and 2 percent of all Canadians, and perhaps as many as 8 percent of children, are allergic to peanuts and/or other nuts, which is why the protest was so vocal. Within a month, Nestlé Canada announced that it would go back to producing these candies in a nut-free facility to appease its consumers with this particular disability. Nestlé's initial decision factored in "a growing public demand for chocolate with nuts, as well as the need to protect jobs at its Toronto plant."[54] Nestlé senior vice-president Graham Lute still wants to expand Nestlé's manufacturing in Canada, but says, "We'll just execute it in a different way, but not as attractive a way as it would have been before, from a sheer business point of view."[55] In other words, the attention to this particular diversity issue has caused the company to rethink part of its business strategy.

Increasing Diversity Awareness

It is natural to see other people from your own point of view, because your feelings, thoughts, attitudes, and experiences guide how you perceive and interact with others. The ability to appreciate diversity, however, requires people to become aware of other perspectives and the various attitudes and experiences of others. Many diversity awareness programs in organizations strive to increase managers' and employees' awareness of (1) their own attitudes, biases, and stereotypes, and (2) the differing perspectives of diverse managers, subordinates, co-workers, and customers. Diversity awareness programs often have these goals:[56]

- Providing organizational members with accurate information about diversity;
- Uncovering personal biases and stereotypes;
- Assessing personal beliefs, attitudes, and values, and learning about other points of view;
- Overturning inaccurate stereotypes and beliefs about different groups;
- Developing an atmosphere in which people feel free to share their differing perspectives;
- Improving understanding of others who are different from oneself.

The Royal Canadian Mounted Police's Canadian Law Enforcement Training Unit in Regina, Sask., has as its mission "to provide the highest quality of training via experienced professionals, as well as state of the art methodology, facilities and technology."[57] The emphasis is on meeting the changing needs of the different communities they serve. In addition, "the Aboriginal Heritage Room, found in D Block, was designed so that Aboriginal candidates at the Academy could attend and experience an area of Aboriginal culture and spiritual significance. The artifacts and photo prints on display are from the RCMP Centennial Museum, and reflect the rich diversity of Aboriginal culture. The room may be used by any candidate in training, as well as members of the RCMP."[58]

Techniques for Increasing Diversity Awareness and Skills

Many managers use a varied approach to increase diversity awareness and skills in their organizations: films and printed materials are supplemented by experiential exercises to uncover any hidden **bias** (the systematic tendency to use information about others in ways that result in inaccurate perceptions) or **stereotype** (simplistic and often inaccurate belief about the typical characteristics of particular groups of people). Sometimes simply providing a forum for people to learn about and discuss their differing attitudes, values, and experiences can be a powerful means for increasing awareness. Also useful are role-playing exercises in which people act out problems that result from lack of awareness, and then indicate the increased understanding that comes from appreciating others' viewpoints. Accurate information and training experiences can debunk stereotypes. Group exercises, role plays, and diversity-related experiences can help organizational members develop the skills they need to work effectively with a variety of people.

RCMP Commander Giuliano Zaccardelli (right) wafts buffalo sage smoke during a smudging ceremony while Timothy Kaiswatum, of the Piapor First Nation, holds the sage. The smudging was part of the opening ceremonies of the Aboriginal Heritage Room at the RCMP training academy in Regina.

Managers sometimes hire outside consultants to provide diversity training. For instance, Trevor Wilson, president of Toronto-based Omnibus Consulting, has presented employment equity programs to such clients as IBM Canada Ltd., Molson Inc., and National Grocers Co. Ltd.[59] Some organizations have their own in-house diversity experts, such as Maureen Geddes at Chatham, Ontario-based Union Gas.

bias
The systematic tendency to use information about others in ways that result in inaccurate perceptions.

stereotype
Simplistic and often inaccurate beliefs about the typical characteristics of particular groups of people.

The Importance of Top-Management Commitment to Diversity

When top management is truly committed to diversity, top managers embrace diversity through their actions and example, spread the message that diversity can be a source of competitive advantage, deal effectively with diverse employees, and are willing to commit organizational resources to managing diversity. That last step alone is not enough. If top managers commit resources to diversity (such as providing money for training programs) but as individuals do not value diversity, any steps they take are likely to fail.

Some organizations recruit and hire women for first-level and middle-management positions, but after being promoted into middle management, some of these female managers quit to start their own businesses. A major reason for their departure is their belief that they will not be promoted into top-management positions because of a lack of commitment to diversity among members of the top-management team. As Professor David Sharp of the Richard Ivey School of Business notes, "It seems that some

Canadian women entrepreneurs are neither born, nor made. They are pushed."[60] The Bank of Montreal is an example of an organization that has been very proactive in making sure women will not leave, through its efforts to aggressively promote women to upper-management positions.

By now, it should be clear that managers can take a variety of steps to manage diversity effectively. Many companies and their managers continue to develop and experiment with new diversity initiatives to meet this ethical and business challenge. Although some steps prove unsuccessful, it is clear that managers must make a long-term commitment to diversity. Training sessions oriented toward the short term are doomed to failure: Participants quickly slip back into their old ways of doing things. The effective management of diversity, like the management of the organization as a whole, is an ongoing process: It never stops and never ends.

Tips for Managers

MANAGING AN INCREASINGLY DIVERSE WORKFORCE

1. Align your decisions with the values of distributive and procedural justice.
2. Pay attention to managers who overtly or indirectly favour certain ethnic groups over others.
3. Make sure your commitment to diversity management is clear and acknowledged by those who work for you.
4. Provide training in diversity management.

Sexual Harassment

THINK ABOUT IT

The Wild West of Gender Relationships[61]

In the 1970s journalist Judith Timson was expected "to show leg" whenever a visitor showed up. "Stand up and show us your legs, there's a good girl," said the assistant editor. Timson was a summer student at the time and "in those days, men—both colleagues and bosses—felt free to comment on any female body part their eyes alighted on."

What about today? Wallace Immen writes, "Incredible as it may seem, sexual harassment still occurs frequently in Canadian workplaces—despite years of effort to eliminate it."[62] Even though policies are available that prohibits sexual harassment, it seems that they are not enough. Sandra Welsh, co-author of the *Workplace Harassment and Violence Report*, organized by the Centre for Research on Violence Against Women and Children at the University of Western Ontario, says, "Only 2 percent of sexual harassment cases filed with the Ontario Human Rights commission involve harassment of men."

The trend in cases has been up in Ontario since 2000, when 213 complaints were received. The number spiked to 292 in 2001. In 2003, the number was up again, to 294. In Alberta, the total number of registered complaints slightly declined, from 224 in 2002 to 206 in 2003. Peter Done, managing director of Peninsula, in the UK, after a massive study that showed 8 out of 10 women claiming sex discrimination, said: "Changes within a company must start from the top down. . . . A simple macho attitude in the workplace could cost a business millions in compensation, so employers must make sure guidelines are drawn up and ensure that these guidelines are followed."[63]

You Be the Manager

1. What would you do to eliminate sexual harassment and discrimination in the workplace?
2. What is a case example of sexual harassment that you are familiar with? Write it out.

There have been several notable cases of sexual harassment in recent years. For instance, the Canadian Armed Forces were subject to intense media scrutiny during 1998 for alleged cover-ups of sexual harassment. University campuses across Canada have seen a dramatic increase in the number of sexual harassment complaints, according to Paddy Stamp, sexual harassment officer at the University of Toronto.[64] Sexual harassment is apparently common in the workplace: A survey conducted by York University in 1999 found that 48 percent of working Canadian women reported that they had experienced some form of sexual harassment in the previous year.

The Supreme Court of Canada defines **sexual harassment** as unwelcome behaviour of a sexual nature in the workplace that negatively affects the work environment or leads to adverse job-related consequences for the employee. In 1987, the court ruled that employers will be held responsible for harassment by their employees. The court also said that the employers should promote a workplace free of harassment. The court recommended that employers have clear guidelines to prevent harassment, including procedures to investigate complaints.

Although women are the most frequent victims of sexual harassment—particularly those in male-dominated occupations, or those who occupy positions stereotypically associated with certain gender relationships (such as a female secretary reporting to a male boss)—men can be victims too. Several male employees at Jenny Craig in the United States said that they were subject to lewd and inappropriate comments from female co-workers and managers.[65] To date, there have been no media reports of women sexually harassing either men or women in Canada.

Sexual harassment seriously damages the victims as well as the reputation of the organization. It is not only unethical, but also illegal. Beyond the negative publicity, sexual harassment can cost organizations large amounts of money. Managers have an ethical obligation to ensure that they, their co-workers, and their subordinates never engage in sexual harassment, even unintentionally.

Forms of Sexual Harassment

There are two basic forms of sexual harassment: *quid pro quo sexual harassment and hostile work environment sexual harassment.* **Quid pro quo sexual harassment** occurs when a harasser asks or forces an employee to perform sexual favours to keep a job, receive a promotion or raise, obtain some other work-related opportunity, or avoid receiving negative consequences such as demotion or dismissal.[66] This "Sleep with me, honey, or you're fired" form of harassment is the more extreme form and leaves no doubt in anyone's mind that sexual harassment has taken place.[67] A study conducted by York University in 1999 found that only 3 percent of working Canadian women reported having experienced quid pro quo sexual harassment.[68]

sexual harassment
Unwelcome behaviour of a sexual nature in the workplace that negatively affects the work environment or leads to adverse job-related consequences for the employee.

quid pro quo sexual harassment
Asking or forcing an employee to perform sexual favours in exchange for some reward or to avoid negative consequences.

hostile work environment sexual harassment
Telling lewd jokes, displaying pornography, making sexually oriented remarks about someone's personal appearance, and other sex-related actions that make the work environment unpleasant.

Hostile work environment sexual harassment is more subtle. It occurs when organizational members are faced with an intimidating, hostile, or offensive work environment because of their gender.[69] Lewd jokes, sexually oriented comments, displays of pornography, displays or distribution of sexually oriented objects, and sexually oriented remarks about someone's physical appearance are examples of hostile work environment sexual harassment. About 45 percent of working Canadian women reported this form of harassment in the recent study at York University. Barbara Orser, a researcher with the Conference Board of Canada, noted that "sexual harassment is more likely to occur in workplace environments that tolerate bullying, intimidation, yelling, innuendo and other forms of discourteous behaviour."[70]

A hostile work environment interferes with organizational members' ability to perform their jobs effectively and has been deemed illegal by the courts. Managers who engage in hostile work environment harassment or allow others to do so risk costly lawsuits for their organizations, as was the experience of Aurora, Ontario-based Magna International Inc. A former saleswoman in the parts maker's Detroit sales office brought a sexual harassment case against the company, alleging that she faced harassment in the office.[71] She also alleged that her male co-workers regularly entertained customers at area strip clubs. That case is still under investigation, though auto industry executives and observers acknowledge that some purchasing executives for the auto makers are entertained at strip clubs.[72]

Steps Managers Can Take to Eradicate Sexual Harassment

Managers have an ethical obligation to eradicate sexual harassment in their organizations. There are many ways to accomplish this objective. Here are four initial steps that managers can take to deal with the problem.[73]

- *Develop and clearly communicate a sexual harassment policy endorsed by top management.* This policy should include prohibitions against both quid pro quo and hostile work environment sexual harassment. It should contain: (1) examples of types of behaviour that are unacceptable, (2) a procedure for employees to use to report instances of harassment, (3) a discussion of the disciplinary actions that will be taken when harassment has taken place, and (4) a commitment to educate and train organizational members about sexual harassment.

- *Use a fair complaint procedure to investigate charges of sexual harassment.* Such a procedure should: (1) be managed by a neutral third party, (2) ensure that complaints are dealt with promptly and thoroughly, (3) protect and fairly treat victims, and (4) ensure that alleged harassers are fairly treated.

- *When it has been determined that sexual harassment has taken place, take corrective actions as soon as possible.* These actions can vary depending on the severity of the harassment. When harassment is extensive, prolonged over a period of time, of a quid pro quo nature, or severely objectionable in some other manner, corrective action may include firing the harasser.

- *Provide sexual harassment education and training to organizational members, including managers.* Managers at DuPont, for example, developed DuPont's "A Matter of Respect" program to help educate employees about sexual harassment and stop it from happening.

Barbara Orser, a researcher with the Conference Board of Canada, noted that most large Canadian organizations have harassment policies on paper. However, many lack a clear resolution process.

Summary and Review

1. **WHAT ARE ETHICS?** Ethics are moral principles or beliefs about what is right or wrong. These beliefs guide people in their dealings with other individuals and groups that have an interest in the situation at hand (stakeholders) and provide a basis for deciding whether behaviour is right and proper. Many organizations have a formal code of ethics derived mainly from societal ethics, professional ethics, and the individual ethics of the organization's top managers. Managers can apply ethical standards to help themselves decide on the proper way to behave toward organizational stakeholders.

2. **SOCIAL RESPONSIBILITY** Social responsibility refers to a manager's duty to make decisions that nurture, protect, enhance, and promote the well-being of stakeholders and society as a whole. Managers generally take one of four approaches to the issue of socially responsible behaviour: obstructionist, defensive, accommodative, or proactive. Promoting ethical and socially responsible behaviour is a major managerial challenge.

3. **MANAGING AN INCREASINGLY DIVERSE WORKFORCE** Diversity refers to differences among people due to age, gender, race, ethnicity, religion, sexual orientation, socio-economic background, and capabilities or disabilities. Effectively managing diversity is an ethical obligation that makes good business sense. Diversity can be managed effectively if top management is committed to principles of distributive and procedural justice, values diversity as a source of competitive advantage, and is willing to devote organizational resources to increasing employees' diversity awareness and diversity skills. Managers need to ensure that they and their subordinates appreciate the value that diversity brings to an organization, understand why diversity should be celebrated rather than ignored, and have the ability to interact and work effectively with men and women who are physically challenged or are of a diverse race, age, gender, ethnicity, nationality, or sexual orientation.

4. **SEXUAL HARASSMENT** Two forms of sexual harassment are quid pro quo sexual harassment and hostile work environment sexual harassment. Steps that managers can take to halt sexual harassment include developing and communicating a sexual harassment policy endorsed by top management, using fair complaint procedures; ensuring prompt corrective action when harassment occurs; and training and educating organizational members on sexual harassment.

Key Terms

accommodative approach, p. 73

bias, p. 81

codes of ethics, p. 66

defensive approach, p. 73

distributive justice, p. 77

diversity, p. 76

ethics, p. 64

ethical decision, p. 65

ethics ombudsperson, p. 70

hostile work environment sexual
   harassment, p. 84

individual ethics, p. 66

obstructionist approach, p. 72

organizational stakeholders, p. 67

overt discrimination, p. 78

proactive approach, p. 73

procedural justice, p. 78

professional ethics, p. 66

quid pro quo sexual harassment, p. 83

reputation, p. 75

sexual harassment, p. 83

social audit, p. 75

social responsibility, p. 72

societal ethics, p. 66

stereotype, p. 81

unethical decision, p. 65

Wrap-Up to Opening Case[74]

Marc Caira took over as president of Parmalat Canada Ltd. at a time when, unknown to him, the Italian parent company, Parmalat Finanziaria SpA, was deep in a US$11.7-billion scandal that threatened the very existence of the Canadian company he was brought in to manage. On Tuesday, June 27, 2005, a judge sentenced Fausto Tonna, a former chief financial officer who has confessed to playing a leading role in the company's spectacular scheme to fake its accounts, to 30 months in jail. He was among 11 defendants including three of the Italian dairy company's former chief financial officers and two members of the founding Tanzi family who consented to plea agreements.

So, what did Caira do that kept things together, saved the Canadian operations, and even made a significant profit? In what Caira called "juggling the juggle," he was able to do the following:

- He chose transparency over secrecy in all his dealings.

- He communicated as honestly as he could, when he had information, to all employees.

- He was courageous enough to say "I don't know," if that was his truth.

- He was ready to make "the tough decisions" about debt reduction, employee layoffs—but only if absolutely necessary.

- He met all challenges head-on; he never gave up.

- He kept employees focused on sales—the major revenue stream.

- He kept a tight group of senior executives to work with himself to untangle the mess.

- He hired professional forensic accountants to examine the books to make sure no fraudulent activity was present in the Canadian operations.

- He worked counterintuitively—he hired more staff when it seemed he should be laying off employees.

- He got the Ontario Teachers Pension Plan (OTPP) to take over the company debt.

- He made a profit.

In short, his managing of the company was a classic textbook example of crisis and ethical management.

Listed below is the Rock-Leduc Model on "How to make an Ethical Decision."[75] It will help you frame your choices in making ethical decisions.

How to Make an Ethical Decision: The Rock-Leduc Model

- Understand the **situation**
- Get all of the **facts** involved
- Identify possible **options**
- Ask the six simple **questions**
  - Is it right? Is it legal?
  - Does it hurt anyone?
  - Can the decision be reported on the front page of the daily newspaper or on TV?
  - Would you counsel your child similarly?
  - Would your mother be proud of you?
  - How does it smell (i.e., your gut reaction)?

- Make the **decision**
- **Evaluate** your decision
  - Is it logical?
  - Is it accurate, relevant, complete?
  - Is it consistent?
  - Can your decision be applied to you as well?

- **Take action**

After studying the preceding material, be sure to check out our Online Learning Centre at **www.mcgrawhill.ca/olc/jones** for more in-depth information and interactivities that correspond to this chapter.

Management in Action

Topics for Discussion and Action

1. Why is it important for people and organizations to behave ethically?
2. Ask a manager to describe an instance of ethical behaviour that she or he observed and an instance of unethical behaviour. What caused these behaviours, and what were the outcomes?
3. Search business magazines such as *Report on Business* or *Canadian Business* for an example of ethical or unethical behaviour, and use the material in this chapter to analyze it.
4. Which stakeholder group should managers be most concerned about when they decide on their approach to social responsibility? Why?
5. Discuss why violations of the principles of distributive and procedural justice continue to occur in modern organizations. What can managers do to support these principles in their organizations?
6. Discuss an occasion when you may have been treated unfairly because of stereotypical thinking. What stereotypes were applied to you? How did they result in your being unfairly treated?
7. Choose a *National Post Business* 500 company not mentioned in the chapter. Conduct library research to determine what steps this organization has taken to effectively manage diversity and eliminate sexual harassment.

Building Management Skills

SOLVING DIVERSITY-RELATED PROBLEMS

Think about the last time that you (1) were treated unfairly because you differed from a decision maker on a particular dimension of diversity, or (2) observed someone else being treated unfairly because that person differed from a decision maker on a particular dimension of diversity. Then answer these questions.

1. Why do you think the decision maker acted unfairly in this situation?
2. In what ways, if any, were biases, stereotypes, or overt discrimination involved in this situation?
3. Was the decision maker aware that he or she was acting unfairly?
4. What could you or the person who was treated unfairly have done to improve matters and rectify the injustice on the spot?
5. Was any sexual harassment involved in this situation? If so, what kind was it?
6. If you had authority over the decision maker (e.g., if you were his or her manager or supervisor), what steps would you take to ensure that the decision maker no longer treated diverse individuals unfairly?

Management for You

Identify an issue that presented an ethical dilemma for you. Analyze the situation and the stakeholder involved using the three models of ethics. How did the decision you made compare to the decisions you might arrive at using these models? The next time you faced an ethical dilemma, would you consider using just one of these models? Why or Why not?

Small Group Breakout Exercise

WHAT IS ETHICAL BEHAVIOUR?

Form groups of three to five people, and appoint one group member as the spokesperson who will communicate your findings to the class when called on by the instructor. Then discuss the following scenario.

You are the managers of the functions of a large hospital, and you have been charged with the responsibility to develop a code of ethics to guide the members of your organization in their dealings with stakeholders. To guide you in creating the ethical code, do the following.

1. Discuss the various kinds of ethical dilemmas that hospital employees—doctors, nurses, pharmacists—may encounter in their dealings with stakeholders such as patients or suppliers.
2. Identify a specific behaviour that the three kinds of hospital employees mentioned in Item 1 might exhibit, and characterize the behaviour as ethical or unethical.
3. Based on this discussion, identify three standards or values that you will incorporate into your personal ethical code to help yourself determine whether a behaviour is ethical or unethical.

Managing Ethically

The state of California is having an energy crisis. You are a manager at BC Hydro. You have discovered that it possible to anticipate periods of severe power shortage and plan for them by letting your reservoirs rise overnight and then opening them to create hydroelectricity. Electricity can thus be produced inexpensively but sold for a premium. Your research of the law suggests that this behaviour would be consistent with what is allowed under the rules of the electricity trade marketplace. Is the good business, or is this unethical behaviour?

Exploring the World Wide Web

SPECIFIC ASSIGNMENT

Go to the Procter & Gamble website (www.pg.com/en_CA/company/index.jhtml). The website states: "Three billion times a day, P&G brands touch the lives of people around the world. Our corporate tradition is rooted in the principles of personal integrity and respect for the individual. Discover how our values guide our business." Review its sections on "Purpose, Values, and Principles" and "Diversity."

1. In what ways does Proctor & Gamble show its support for a diverse workforce?
2. What is the relationship between P&G's policies on diversity and its claims under "Purpose, Values, and Principles"?

GENERAL ASSIGNMENT

Search for a company website that has an explicit statement of the company's approach to workplace diversity. What is its approach, and how does this approach support the company's main goals?

Developing a Business Plan

(APPENDIX B, PAGE 405)

Go to www.mcgrawhill.ca/olc/jones/3 for online exercises.

Be the Manager

EXPENSIVE LESSON IN USING DISCIPLINE[76]

Rather than shrieking with delight, Christine Pynaker's heart sank upon receiving a bouquet of flowers and a gold necklace. Yet again, Wayne Brazeau, 25 years her senior, was after her. For more than three years, Brazeau had showered Pynaker with gifts, including flowers, jewellery—even an airline ticket to visit her parents in Spain—accompanied by romantic cards and emails.

Pynaker's attempts at rebuffing Brazeau, who, like her, was employed as an international representative for the International Brotherhood of Electrical Workers (IBEW), were futile. Although she accepted many of the presents, she also told Brazeau that his conduct was offensive. Finally, after more than three years, Pynaker flatly told Brazeau that he was too old; that no relationship could ever materialize between them; and that she regarded his behaviour as sexual harassment.

Brazeau, properly, immediately ceased directing any attention toward Pynaker. But, improperly, he also ceased being as supportive of her as he had been in the past. Over the next several years, Brazeau was episodically hostile to Pynaker: failing to provide her with the materials and information required to effectively do her work; making disparaging remarks about her sex life; and accusing a male colleague of flirting with her.

Believing that Brazeau was retaliating for her earlier rebuff, Pynaker lodged a complaint of sexual harassment with her employer.

Questions

1. You're the manager. What would you do?
2. What other alternatives could the union have taken?

Management Case

Is It Right to Use Child Labour?

In recent years, the number of Canadian and US companies that buy their inputs from low-cost foreign suppliers has been growing, and concern about the ethics associated with employing young children in factories has been increasing. In Pakistan, children as young as six work long hours in deplorable conditions to make rugs and carpets for export to Western countries. There are children in poor countries throughout Africa, Asia, and South America who work in similar conditions.

Opinions about the ethics of child labour vary widely. Some believe that the practice is totally reprehensible and should be outlawed on a global level. Another view, championed by *The Economist* magazine (www.economist.com), is that, while nobody wants to see children working in factories, citizens of rich countries need to recognize that in poor countries a child is often the family's only breadwinner. Thus, denying children employment would cause whole families to suffer, and correcting one wrong (child labour) might produce a greater wrong (poverty). Instead, *The Economist* favours regulating the conditions under which children are employed and hopes that over time, as poor countries become richer, the need for child employment will disappear.

Many Canadian and US retailers buy their clothing from low-cost foreign suppliers, and managers in these companies have had to take their own ethical stance on child labour. In Chapter 1, we discussed how Mountain Equipment Co-op (www.mec.ca) was facing demands from some of its members to discontinue manufacturing clothing in China. Wal-Mart Canada (www.walmart.com) has been criticized for its policy of doing business with third-party suppliers—such as Hampton Industries, Sutton Creations, Global Gold, Stretch-O-Rama, Cherry Stix and By Design—that import goods from Myanmar (Burma), which engages in forced labour, including that of children. In defence of the company's actions, Wal-Mart Canada spokesman Andrew Pelletier noted, "We have a policy we are looking at, of monitoring vendors sourcing from other countries…. For other corporations, our expectation is that they would take their direction from the Canadian government, that's what we would recommend they would do."

At present, the Canadian government, unlike the US government, does not have regulations governing the use of child labour in foreign countries by Canadian companies.

Questions

1. Should Canada develop regulations governing the use of child labour in foreign countries by Canadian companies?
2. You are the manager of a company considering setting up a factory in a foreign country that allows child labour. What would be the benefits to your company for deciding not to use child labour?
3. You are the manager of a company considering setting up a factory in a foreign country that allows child labour. Should you simply rely on the laws of that country when deciding what to do about child labour? Why or why not?

Video Management Case ■

Working in a Diverse Workplace

Gordon Nixon, CEO of Royal Bank of Canada, made a startling confession in July of 2005: "Governments can attract skilled immigrants to Canada but, once they arrive, businesses have to pick up the ball . . . And to date we have not. In fact, we are dropping it."[77] A new conversation is now apparent in companies; the topic is diversity. Is this talk all altruism? It has more to do with market forces: the increasing numbers and power of the immigrant populations and the diverse workplaces.

Six scenarios are presented in the video, "Working in a Diverse Workplace."

- Jim's retirement party: he is the "old school," but makes sexist remarks that are supposed to be "funny." Standards have changed.

- Jacques' requesting a bereavement leave: he wants time off to go to a funeral, but how will this affect others who don't have time off?

- First Nations and their encounter with Royal Bank: because of how Chief Rivers was treated, he went to the competition. Pride and respect are essential in doing business, especially when cultural differences are evident.

- Chinese customer who wants to do business at the bank *only* with a man: a scenario ripe with prejudice is evident.

- Face time: sometimes employees with the same type of job work differently, each spending different times at the office.

- Accommodating people with different disabilities.

Questions to Consider

1. What's your assessment of Jim's remarks at his retirement party? Did you feel uncomfortable at all when he spoke? Why? Why not? What should the bank policy be when someone acts as Jim did?
2. What is the problem that Jacques is facing? As a manager, would you agree to his request? What is fair?
3. What is your experience when cultural differences are involved?
4. Should the bank accommodate a customer's prejudice?
5. How flexible can workplaces be to accommodate employees' schedules?
6. What are employers expected to do to accommodate disabilities on the job?

Part 2: Integrated Case ■

A "Sellers Market": Workers Calling The Shots[78]

As boomers leave, young people don't want their jobs, new survey suggests.

Aging baby boomers overworked by the federal government for the past 15 years are quitting, retiring, or will be snapped up by competing employers and the young generation of workers who should replace them isn't particularly interested in their jobs.

That's the heart of the recruitment and retention crisis the government knew was coming for years, but a newly released survey of more than 100 000 public servants shows the government simply isn't ready for the "sellers market" of the future in which workers, not bosses, call the shots, says Linda Duxbury, a professor at Carleton University's Sprott School of Business who has studied the workforce for more than 15 years.

The survey shows public servants love what they do, want to make a difference, and generally feel their department is a good place to work. About 90 percent of respondents say they're proud of their work and

96 percent say they are "committed" to making their organization successful.

But the good news ends there.

The survey suggests about a third of public service workers are not content. They're stressed and overworked, can't balance family with their jobs, feel trapped with few career options, and have little trust in senior management.

"You can say three quarters are happy or be realistic and recognize you have a substantial pocket of discontent here," said Ms. Duxbury.

"It's a problem when you're trying to get new people in when there are so many for whom the glass is half empty because young people aren't attracted to an environment like that. And they will have so much choice for work. The public service shines when it comes to pay and benefits, but that isn't going to keep them. You can't buy their love."

The census-like survey, distributed to 180 000 workers, is the third of its kind since 1999 to track public servants' perceptions about a slew of key issues, from career development, promotion opportunities, workload, senior management and harassment. About 60 percent responded to the survey between November 2 and December 22, which the report noted was a period of huge upheaval, coming after the sponsorship scandal and Justice John Gomery's report on how to fix accountability and management in government and in the midst of an election campaign. No margin of error was given for the results.

Although most believe the government hires people who can do the job, one-third say the selection process was unfair, half felt the restrictions in competition blocked their career progress, and nearly half felt departments and supervisors didn't help develop their careers. About one third of respondents said they had three or more supervisors over the past three years and that kind of instability makes it difficult to develop talent, says Ms. Duxbury.

Ms. Duxbury said other worrisome trends for an employer trying to attract and keep top-notch talent are management problems that public servants say are eroding the quality of their work.

More than 40 percent complained about having to do the same or more work with fewer resources, lack of stability in their organizations, constantly changing priorities, and too many approval stages for decisions. About 30 percent complained about unreasonable deadlines.

"What's really troubling is half of your workforce, whom are knowledge workers who contribute ideas, feel there is nowhere to go. That's a really bad sign for retention and recruitment," said Ms. Duxbury.

Ms. Duxbury said many of the problems are the consequences of a government that focused too much on operations and not enough on management. She said the government has to shift from the short-term, bottom-line, and cost-cutting culture of the 1990s to a "people-driven" management that focuses on recruit-

ment, retention, work/life balance, career development, and succession planning.

She argued that cultural shift is the only way the government can keep the aging boomers and Generation Xers, who are between the age of 30 and 42, and attract the young Generation Y workers under the age of 28.

She said the government was able to ignore how it managed people for years because there were so many boomers and dearth of good jobs. As a result, boomers worked long hours to get ahead and distinguish themselves from the pack. But Ms. Duxbury said boomers are sick of working "140 percent and getting paid for 100 percent" and their skills and experience will be in big demand as the labour supply shrinks over the years. She said they are already being recruited by other employers, retiring early to start new businesses or "retiring on the job" and putting in time until they can retire.

But Ms. Duxbury said the biggest question is whether the Generation Xers, the bureaucrats between the ages of 30 and 42, will hang in or not. They are the public service's managers and leaders of tomorrow, and will be in big demand by other employers who didn't hire during the lean years of the 1990s.

"They have to recognize that the market is so different now and will be for a long time to come, and the problem is that public servants are an attractive source of labour especially the older workers and Gen Xers so they will get nabbed and the young ones may go for a year or two to get it on their resume," she said.

Discussion Questions

1. What suggestions would you put forward in terms of planning, organizing, leading, and controlling?

2. What are the main issues in this case that relate to managing a changing and dynamic workplace environment?

3. What are some key ethical challenges in this case?

PART 3   Planning and Decision Making

CHAPTER

4

The Manager as a Decision Maker

Learning Outcomes

1. Differentiate between programmed and nonprogrammed decisions, and explain why nonprogrammed decision making is a complex, uncertain process.

2. Explain the implications and assumptions of the rational and administrative models of decision making, and how the administrative model is based on three important concepts: bounded rationality, incomplete information, and satisficing.

3. Describe the six steps that managers should take to make the best decisions.

4. Explain how cognitive biases can affect decision making and lead managers to make poor decisions.

5. Identify the advantages and disadvantages of group decision making, and describe techniques that can improve it.

6. Explain the role that organizational learning and creativity play in helping managers to improve their decisions.

7. Differentiate between data and information, and list the characteristics of useful information.

Known By Our Commitments[1]

Managers are paid to make decisions, but not just any decisions; they are paid to make good decisions. But what is the difference between "good" decisions and "great" decisions? Great decisions are fundamentally grounded in the commitments that managers make. In other words, ask managers what they are committed to and you will discover the types of decisions they are making. Noble and great commitments rest on operational decision-making moments intimately aligned to such commitments. Irrespective of the type of commitment—capital investments, restructuring, operating processes, partnerships, etc.—the decision making that goes into such commitments is intimately linked to them. We could actually describe such a relationship between commitments and decision making as the relationship between short- and long-range effects and actions on the company itself. When managers get too caught up in the day-to-day decision-making operations and neglect the longer range implications of such decisions, they overlook or forget that all their decision-making efforts are tied to the longer-range commitments they are embracing. It may be less challenging for managers to stick to the here-and-now events they need to attend to than keeping the bigger picture in front of them of *why* they are attending to such events. Such events might be a meeting they set up for 10:00 a.m., or a luncheon engagement with a new client or partner, or a 3:00 p.m. interview with a potential new department head.

When managers realize how their commitments shape the direction, limitations, and opportunities of their departments and organizations, they can make those decision-making choices that will align themselves more deliberately and effectively to fulfilling their commitments. Before making important decisions, a manager needs to ask, "Is this a process or relationship that we can live with in the future? Am I locking us into a course that we'll come to regret?"

Thus, *context* for making decisions is critical, irrespective of the decision. Harvard Business School professors Anthony J. Mayo and Nitin Nohria, in their new book, *In Their Time: The Greatest Business Leaders of the 20th Century*, describe what they call "an immutable attribute that's shared by all of the giants of business: They had an innate ability to read the forces that shaped the times in which they lived—and to seize on the resulting opportunities." This attribute turns out to be "contextual intelligence." For Mayo and Nohria, this is "an acute sensitivity to the social, political, technological, and demographic contexts that came to define their eras." With this sensitivity, they were able to sense their implied business opportunities and make decisions that guided their organizations accordingly.[2]

Managers are always making decisions, if you will, *on behalf of* some viewpoint, goal, commitment that they envision. The clarity of this vision will determine the quality of their here-and-now decisions. An additional reality is the thinking style of managers that influences the kinds of decision making. For example, in a study of IT professions, researchers discovered that contrary to stereotypical perceptions that IT mid-level and senior executives were mainly "analytical" in their processes, they discovered that taken as a whole the analysis showed that a significantly larger percentage of the 339 managers had peaks in the "idealist" and "pragmatist" styles than would be expected,

Commitment makes the difference between "good" decisions and "great" decisions.

and a significantly smaller percentage had peaks in the "analyst" style.[3] The researchers realized that IT managers, therefore, had a perception problem: while people in general expected them to be analytical in their approach to decision making (logical, structured, and prescriptive), many in the study were in fact not that at all, but were idealistic ("big picture" people) and "pragmatic" (having a bias for action, doing "what works"). The point here is that each thinking style (or combination of styles) would necessarily focus on commitments that would be in alignment with such a style or styles.

Hence, for managers who want to fulfill their managerial commitments, they need to ask, "Are the decisions I am making right now going to lead to fulfilling the commitments I envision, have made, and about to make?" In addition, they need to examine themselves as to the *kind* of decisions they are most likely to make; this self-inventory is a reflection on their preferred thinking style. Managers are truly known by their commitments and the decisions that lead to fulfilling such commitments.

Now It's Your Turn

Think of a time in your life when you had to make some important decisions.

1. *Why* were you making these decisions? (This question speaks to the *context* you had in mind.)

2. Were you clear as to *why* you were making the decision(s)?

3. What was the result of your decision(s)?

4. Depending on whether you felt successful in your decision-making efforts, to what extent was knowing *why* (the context) you were making the decision helpful?

▪▪▪▪ Overview

The open scenario to this chapter allows us to see that a manager's job basically is to make decisions. But we kept asking the question, "Making decisions in view of what end?" Such a question introduced the idea that managers make decisions in view of the commitments they have agreed to or envisioned as important for their department or organization. Commitments, therefore, frame the *context* within which managers make decisions. To the best of the ability, managers align their decisions with the end-result in mind: their commitments.

The purpose of this chapter is to examine how managers make decisions, and to explore how individual, group, and organizational factors affect the quality of the decisions they make and thus determine organizational performance. We discuss the nature of managerial decision making and examine some models of the decision-making process that help reveal the complexities of successful decision making. Then we outline the main steps of the decision-making process; in addition, we explore the biases that may cause capable managers to make poor decisions both as individuals and as members of a group. Finally, we examine how managers can promote organizational learning and creativity and improve the quality of their decision making. By the end of this chapter, you will understand the crucial role that decision making plays in creating a high-performing organization.

The Nature of Managerial Decision Making

THINK ABOUT IT

Not Taking "Yes" or "No" for an Answer[4]

The late President John F. Kennedy failed with his Bay of Pigs decision on April 17, 1961 to support a U.S.-trained force of about 1500 armed Cuban exiles to land in the Bahía de Cochinos (Bay of Pigs) on the south coast of Cuba. Their intention was to infiltrate Cuba, foment an insurrection and overthrow the Communist regime of Fidel Castro. The Cuban army on April 20 easily defeated and killed or captured most of them.[5]

Soviet commanders, already based in Cuba, were prepared to use nuclear weapons should the island be invaded. The failure of the U.S. Bay of Pigs invasion saw to it that that disaster never happened. However, in 1964, barely 18 months later, President Kennedy was successful in his decision making on how to handle the Cuban missile crisis, a crisis that brought the world the closest ever to the edge of a nuclear disaster.[6] "Ultimately, President Kennedy chose to initiate a naval blockade against Soviet ships carrying missile equipment. His strategy proved successful; the Soviets withdrew the missiles and nuclear war was averted."[7]

What happened to make the outcome successful this time? It was in the quality of the decision making. President Kennedy had listened uncritically to the arguments put forward by the CIA in relation to the Bay of Pigs invasion. This time he set up a decision-making process that protected him from folly. Candid discussion in meetings was now in versus the established rules of protocol, rank, and deference before. In other words, the *process* of decision was seen as absolutely critical not just "making the decision and getting on with things." To make for a fuller discussion of the matter, President Kennedy had military officials don the hat of the "skeptical generalist"; he also invited lower level personnel to the discussions because he wanted a more well-rounded discussion. In essence, Kennedy was asking for a specific kind of devil's advocate dissent in the meetings. According to Prof. Robert in his book, *Why Great Leaders Don't Take Yes For An Answer: Managing for Conflict and Consensus*, this kind of dissent is a cognitive, or task-oriented, disagreement, in which individuals engage in substantive debate over issues and ideas so that risks and weaknesses and challenges to the validity of key assumptions can be brought to light. What must be avoided, however, is "affective conflict," in which participants in a discussion take matters personally causing personality clashes to erupt. The inability to distinguish cognitive, or task-oriented, dissent from affective, or defensive dissent, can lead to "pernicious consequences."

You Be the Manager

1. What situation have you been in when participants failed to distinguish the difference between "cognitive" and "affective" dissent? Describe the situation.
2. What were the negative or "pernicious consequences" as a result of this failure to distinguish the different kinds of dissent?
3. As a manager how would you establish the positive or cognitive rules of dissent?

Every time a manager acts to plan, organize, direct, or control organizational activities, he or she makes a stream of decisions. In opening a new restaurant, for example, managers have to decide where to locate it, what kinds of food to provide to customers, what kinds of people to employ, and so on. In Chapter 1, where we considered Mintzberg's managerial roles, we described four decision-making roles managers have. We also noted in Chapter 1 the importance of managers having conceptual skills. Decision making is a basic part of every task in which a manager is involved, and in this chapter we study how decisions are made.

decision making
The process by which managers analyze the options facing them and make decisions about specific organizational goals and courses of action.

Decision making is the process by which managers analyze the options facing them and make determinations, or decisions, about specific organizational goals and courses of action. Good decisions result in the selection of suitable goals and courses of action that increase organizational performance; bad decisions result in lower performance.

Programmed and Nonprogrammed Decision Making

Regardless of the specific decision that a manager is responsible for, the decision-making process is either programmed or nonprogrammed.[8]

Programmed Decision Making

programmed decision making
Routine, virtually automatic decision making that follows established rules or guidelines.

Programmed decision making is a routine, virtually automatic process. Programmed decisions are decisions that have been made so many times in the past that managers have been able to develop rules or guidelines to be applied when certain situations inevitably occur. Programmed decision making takes place for much of the day-to-day running of an organization, for example when the office manager needs to order supplies. He or she can rely on long-established decision rules such as these:

- *Rule 1.* When the storage shelves are three-quarters empty, order more copy paper.

- *Rule 2.* When ordering paper, order enough to fill the shelves.

This decision making is called "programmed" because the office manager does not need to make judgments constantly about what should be done. Managers can develop rules and guidelines to regulate all kinds of routine organizational activities.

Nonprogrammed Decision Making

nonprogrammed decision making
Nonroutine decision making that occurs in response to unusual, unpredictable opportunities and threats.

Nonprogrammed decision making occurs when there are no ready-made decision rules that managers can apply to a situation. Why are there no rules? The situation is unexpected, and managers lack the information they would need to develop rules to cover it. Examples of nonprogrammed decision making include decisions to invest in a new kind of technology, to develop a new kind of product, to launch a new promotional campaign, to enter a new market, or to expand internationally. In the remainder of this chapter, when we talk about decision making, we are referring to nonprogrammed decision making because it is the kind that causes the most problems for managers.

Comparing Decision-Making Models

THINK ABOUT IT

"Head" and "Heart" Decisions

French artist, Joseph Roux (1725–1793) once remarked, "We distrust our heart too much and our head not enough."[9]

For companies that manage, not only with "head" but also with "heart," dividends are readily apparent. "Among many tangible and intangible benefits, they claim that opening the purse strings, or giving their employees time to volunteer for a good cause, increases worker satisfaction and reduces turnover."[10] Seventy-nine percent of employees in a 2002 GlobeScan survey said that "the more socially responsible my company becomes, the more motivated/loyal an employee I become." "Head" decision making is not, therefore, the only way to run a business; "heart" must also be involved. For example, when the pharmaceutical company GlaxoSmithKline allowed employees the option to determine where some of the money for social responsibilities causes should go, they noticed an increase in motivation, productivity, and loyalty. Similarly at Bank of Montreal (or BMO) which, in 2003, donated about $25 million to different charities. Said BMO spokesperson Michael Edmonds, "And one of the reasons why employees have shown loyalty to us is they see us as a good corporate citizen." Because employees buy into the vision of the company, said Mark Federman, a consultant and University of Toronto lecturer on new approaches to business strategy, it's important, as we noted in our opening case scenario, that employees know *why* managers are making the decisions they are making. In other words, employees are asking of managers, "What are you committed to? When we notice that you base your decisions not only on 'head' choices but also on 'heart' choices, we can support you, and this kind of employee support will show up in terms of increased loyalty and bottom line profits."

You Be the Manager

1. What are your feelings about working for an organization that has both "head" and "heart"?
2. What was your experience of working for an organization that didn't make "head" and "heart" decisions?

The rational and the administrative decision-making models reveal many of the assumptions, complexities, and pitfalls that affect decision making. We compare and contrast them below.

The Rational Model

One of the earliest models of decision making, the **rational model** (also referred to as the *classical model*), is prescriptive, which means that it specifies how decisions *should* be made. Managers using the rational model make a series of simplifying assumptions about the nature of the decision-making process (see Figure 4.1). The idea behind the rational model is that once managers recognize the need to make a decision, they should be able to make a complete list of *all* alternatives. For each alternative they should be able to list all consequences, and they can then make the best choice. In other words, the rational model assumes that managers have access to *all* the information they need to make the **optimum decision**, which is the best decision possible in light of what they believe to be the most desirable future consequences for their organization. Furthermore, the rational model assumes that managers can easily list their own preferences for each alternative and rank them from least to most preferred in order to make the optimum decision. While we can agree

rational decision-making model
A prescriptive approach to decision making based on the idea that the decision maker can identify and evaluate all possible alternatives and their consequences and rationally choose the most suitable course of action.

optimum decision
The best decision in light of what managers believe to be the most desirable future consequences for their organization.

"Corporate fool" Guy Laliberté receives a leadership award for his achievements at the World Leaders Awards.

FIGURE 4.1 | *The Rational Model of Decision Making*

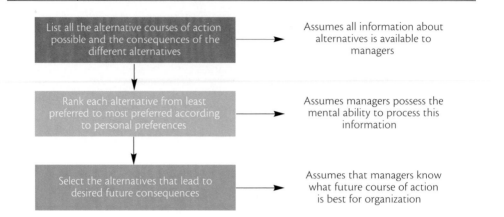

with making decisions rationally is an important task for managers, we can also agree with the Scottish poet, Robert Burns (1759–1796), in his poem "To a Mouse," that "the best laid plans of mice and men" will often go off the tracks precisely because managers do not have all the information they need at the time to make a totally and fully informed rational decision.[11] Because managers don't always have all the information at their fingertips, additional tools such as "social software" are now starting to show up in organizations. For example, Jon Husband is a Vancouver-based social software and blogging guru who has coined his own word: "wirearchy." He says, "Instead of having a few people up at the top make the decisions for all of us, the concept of wirearchy is a two-way flow of power and authority based on knowledge, credibility, trust and results enabled by interconnected people and technology."[12]

The Administrative Model

James March and Herbert Simon were aware that many managers do not have access to all the information they need to make a decision. Moreover, they pointed out that even if all information were readily available, many managers would lack the mental or psychological ability to absorb and evaluate it correctly. As a result, March and Simon developed the **administrative model** of decision making to explain why decision making is always basically an uncertain and risky process—and why managers can rarely make decisions in the manner prescribed by the rational model. The administrative model is based on three important concepts: *bounded rationality*, *incomplete information*, and *satisficing*.

Bounded Rationality

March and Simon pointed out that human decision-making capabilities are bounded by people's limitations in their ability to interpret, process, and act on information.[13] **Bounded rationality** thus describes the situation in which the number of alternatives and the amount of information are so great that it is difficult for the manager to evaluate everything before making a decision.[14]

Incomplete Information

Even if managers did have an unlimited ability to evaluate information, they still would have incomplete information. Information is incomplete because the full range of decision-making alternatives is unknowable in most situations, and the consequences are uncertain.[15] Because of **uncertainty**, the probabilities of alternative outcomes cannot be determined, and future outcomes are *unknown*. Another reason

administrative model
An approach to decision making that explains why decision making is basically uncertain and risky and why managers usually make satisficing rather than optimum decisions.

bounded rationality
Cognitive limitations that constrain one's ability to interpret, process, and act on information.

uncertainty
Unpredictability.

why information may be incomplete is that much of the information that managers have at their disposal is **ambiguous information**. Its meaning is not clear—it can be interpreted in multiple and often conflicting ways.[16]

Satisficing

Faced with bounded rationality and incomplete information, March and Simon argue, managers do not try to discover every alternative. Rather, they use a strategy known as **satisficing**, exploring a limited sample of possible alternatives.[17] In 1978, Herbert Alexander Simon (1901–1985) won the Nobel Prize for this concept called "satisfice"— finding results that are very good instead of looking for the perfect option, which would take longer and might bankrupt firms. Simon, who trained as a political scientist, questioned the mainstream economists' view of the economic manager as "a lightning-quick calculator of costs and benefits."[18] Instead the manager had to also deal with constraints, such as not knowing all the details before making a decision. When managers satisfice, they search for and choose acceptable, or satisfactory, ways to respond to problems and opportunities, rather than trying to make the best decision.[19] For instance, the purchasing manager for Ford Canada would likely engage in a limited search to identify supplies. This might involve asking a limited number of suppliers for their terms, trusting that they are representative of suppliers in general, and making a choice from that set. Although this course of action is reasonable from the point of view of the purchasing manager, it may mean that a potentially superior supplier is overlooked.

March and Simon pointed out that managerial decision making is often more art than science. In the real world, managers must rely on their intuition and judgment to make what seems to them to be the best decision in the face of uncertainty and ambiguity.[20] **Intuition** is a person's ability to make sound decisions based on past experience and immediate feelings about the information at hand. **Judgment** is a person's ability to develop a sound opinion because of the way he or she evaluates the importance of the information available in a particular context. For reasons that we examine later in this chapter, both intuition and judgment are often flawed and can result in poor decision making.

ambiguous information
Information that can be interpreted in multiple and often conflicting ways.

satisficing
Searching for and choosing acceptable, or satisfactory, ways to respond to problems and opportunities, rather than trying to make the best decision.

intuition
Ability to make sound decisions based on past experience and immediate feelings about the information at hand.

judgment
Ability to develop a sound opinion based on one's evaluation of the importance of the information at hand.

Steps in the Decision-Making Process

The conditions for an optimum decision rarely exist. To help managers make the best decision possible, researchers have developed a step-by-step model of the decision-making process and the issues and problems that managers confront at each step. There are six steps that managers should consciously follow to make a good decision (see Figure 4.2).[21] We review them in the remainder of this section.

Recognize the Need for a Decision

The first step in the decision-making process is to recognize the need for a decision. Managers face decisions that arise both internally and as a consequence of changes in the external environment.[22] Once a decision maker recognizes the need to make a decision, the person will need to diagnose the issue or problem, in order to determine all the factors underlying the problem. In the Chumbleys' case, the downturn in the economy prompted the need to evaluate whether they should continue operating both an East Coast and a West Coast facility.

FIGURE 4.2 | *Six Steps in Decision Making*

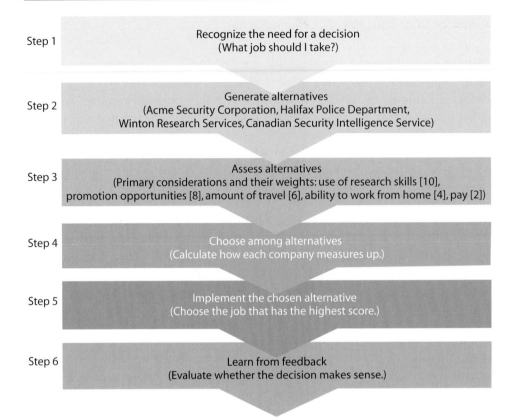

Step 1 — Recognize the need for a decision
(What job should I take?)

Step 2 — Generate alternatives
(Acme Security Corporation, Halifax Police Department,
Winton Research Services, Canadian Security Intelligence Service)

Step 3 — Assess alternatives
(Primary considerations and their weights: use of research skills [10],
promotion opportunities [8], amount of travel [6], ability to work from home [4], pay [2])

Step 4 — Choose among alternatives
(Calculate how each company measures up.)

Step 5 — Implement the chosen alternative
(Choose the job that has the highest score.)

Step 6 — Learn from feedback
(Evaluate whether the decision makes sense.)

Generate Alternatives

Having recognized the need to make a decision, a manager must generate a set of feasible alternative courses of action to take in response to the opportunity or threat. The failure to properly generate and consider different alternatives is one reason why managers sometimes make bad decisions.[23] Paul Sherman is a technology worker and Dallas area manager for Perceptive Sciences Corp. who makes good use of his intuition to generate alternatives to today's use of the personal computer.[24] Most of us have said one time or another when using a computer, "Why don't they make these things more user-friendly?" Sherman is a "usability professional." His job is to make technology more intuitive and less intimidating. Interestingly, to work in this field, one is best prepared with a combination of psychology, marketing, and computer science, as well as a liberal arts background. It is this wide appreciation of interests that allows for the "thinking out of the box" and the generation of alternatives that are necessary in business decision making.[25]

Assess Alternatives

Once managers have listed a set of alternatives, they must evaluate the advantages and disadvantages of each one.[26] The key to a good assessment of the alternatives is being able to define the opportunity or threat exactly, and then specifying the criteria that *should* influence the selection of alternative ways of responding to the problem or opportunity.

One reason for bad decisions is that managers often fail to specify the criteria that are important in reaching a decision.[27] In general, successful managers use four criteria to evaluate the pros and cons of alternative courses of action (see Figure 4.3):

1. *Practicality.* Managers must decide whether they have the capabilities and resources to implement the alternative, and they must be sure that the alternative will not threaten the ability to reach other organizational goals.
2. *Economic feasibility.* Managers must decide whether the alternatives make sense economically and fit the organization's performance goals. Typically, managers perform a cost-benefit analysis of the various alternatives to determine which one is likely to have the best financial payoff.
3. *Ethicality.* Managers must ensure that a possible course of action is ethical and that it will not unnecessarily harm any stakeholder group. Many of the decisions that managers make may help some organizational stakeholders and harm others (see Chapter 3).
4. *Legality.* Managers must ensure that a possible course of action is legal and will not violate any domestic and international laws or government regulations.

Many times managers must apply these four criteria to their decision making. "Ambiguity, inconsistency, uncertainty, insecurity, arbitrariness, bad decision-making, self-centredness, rewarding the wrong things in the office, the fostering of office politics and rewarding political behaviours—that's the earmark of weak leadership," says Bill Wilkerson, president of the Global Business and Economic Roundtable on Addiction and Mental Health.[28] Some alternatives would have seemed more practical or economical, and they might not have been aware of any ethical problems with their decision.

Choose Among Alternatives

Once the set of alternative solutions has been carefully evaluated, the next task is to rank the various alternatives (using the criteria discussed in the previous section) and make a decision. When ranking alternatives, managers must be sure that all of the available information is brought to bear on the problem or issue at hand. Identifying all relevant information for a decision does not mean that the manager has complete information, however; in most instances, information is incomplete.

FIGURE 4.3 | *General Criteria for Evaluating Possible Courses of Action*

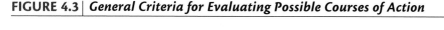

Is the possible course of action:

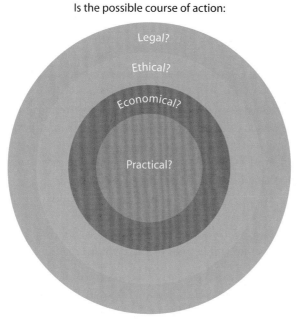

The disastrous breakup of the Columbia space shuttle illustrates the importance of bringing all available information to bear on the decision-making process and making sure the alternative courses of action are evaluated using all relevant criteria.

To go back to the issue of thinking styles in the opening scenario: the researchers had a client, a CIO of a major health care company. She indicated that she had never been able to figure out her Chief Operating Officer (COO). She made a decision to approach him with the learning she had picked up in her own training regarding the synthesist thinking style. "This time, I theorized that he was a synthesist and went into the meeting with alternatives, instead of my usual single recommendation. The results were amazing," she said. "It was the best call I have ever had with the guy."[29]

Implement the Chosen Alternative

Once a decision has been made and an alternative has been selected, the alternative must be implemented and many subsequent and related decisions must be made. Although the need to make further decisions may seem obvious, many managers make the initial decision and then fail to act on it.[30] This is the same as not making a decision at all.

Managers often fail to get buy-in from those around them before making a decision. However, successful implementation requires participation. One study found that participation was used in only 20 percent of decisions, even though broad participation in decisions led to success 80 percent of the time. By contrast, the most common form of decision-making tactics, power or persuasion, used in 60 percent of decisions, are successful in only one of three decisions.[31]

To ensure that a decision is implemented, top managers must let middle managers participate in decisions, and then give them the responsibility to make the follow-up decisions necessary to achieve the goal. They must give middle managers enough resources to achieve the goal, and they must hold the middle managers accountable for their performance. If the middle managers succeed in implementing the decision, they should be rewarded; if they fail, they should be subject to sanctions.

Learn from Feedback

The final step in the decision-making process is learning from feedback. Managers who do not evaluate the results of their decisions do not learn from experience; instead, they stagnate and are likely to make the same mistakes again and again.[32] To avoid this problem, managers must establish a formal procedure for learning from the results of past decisions. The procedure should include these steps:

1. Compare what actually happened to what was expected to happen as a result of the decision.
2. Explore why any expectations for the decision were not met.
3. Develop guidelines that will help in future decision making.

Individuals who always strive to learn from past mistakes and successes are likely to continuously improve the decisions they make. It is known that managers and executives at Hewlett-Packard, for example, "manage by wandering around, gathering feedback in hallways and cafeterias."[33] Their focus is on continually making better decisions. Daniel Goleman, Richard Boyatzis, and Annie McKee, in their book, *Primal Leadership: Realizing the Power of Emotional Intelligence*, use the term "CEO disease" for those executives and managers who are unaware of or don't want feedback about their performance. The opposite of that is the emotionally intelligent executive or manager who actively seeks out feedback.[34]

Tips for Managers

MANAGING THE DECISION-MAKING PROCESS

1. Be the best you can be with the information you have at hand. If you wait for the "best timing" for your decisions, the opportunity will probably be gone.

2. Be at the "top of your game" by continually scanning your environment, being proactive, identifying the key trends and opportunities, and knowing when best to make decisions.

3. Know your audience and the purpose of the decision you are about to make. This is the context discussed earlier. As seen with the example of the executive at the health care company, once she determined or "figured out" the thinking style of her COO (Chief Operating Officer), she was able to get a most successful hearing of her ideas. To reach her objective, she had determined that a very good alternative in the decision-making process was to understand the COO's thinking style.

4. Learn to treat successes and failures as stepping stones in your decision-making practice.

Biases in Decision Making

THINK ABOUT IT

Ignoring the Handwriting on the Wall?

What is known as our cognitive biases—preferences for a decision to be one way or another—can often create great stress and problems for us.[35] For example, have you ever been involved in a business situation or company where, on the surface, everything seems fine. If a friend or family member of co-worker says, "Think it over," we sometimes feel offended by this advice and ignore it . . . sometimes to our own detriment. We can bias our decision making by inflating in our own mind the potential benefits that will happen if we get involved with the project or the new company. This may have been the case when in March 2005 Gary Daichendt quit Nortel Networks Corp. after being involved for just a short time—actually, just three months. His track record as a senior executive at Cisco Systems Inc. showed him to be a very strong operations person, dedicated, and a person who could get the job done. People wondered why he would leave the U.S. and join a floundering Canadian company like Nortel. Was he oversold on the benefits? Did he ignore the proverbial "writing on the wall"? He claimed that there were simply business differences with CEO Bill Owens, not because he had made a boardroom play to oust the Nortel boss.[36]

Cognitive biases and organizational pressures to play up the positive mar our decision making. For example, we exaggerate our project's potential benefits—and downplay its risks. We then cling to our initial forecasts—refusing to adjust them to account for subsequent (and more negative) market and financial analysis. The project flounders because no one anticipated the full range of likely problems. We also tend to seek only the information that supports our points of view. And we exaggerate our abilities and control over events.

You Be the Manager

1. What biases do people typically have when they "really" want a job they find interesting?
2. How do biases affect the way people make decisions?

heristics
Rules of thumb that simplify decision making.

In the 1970s, two psychologists, Daniel Kahneman and Amos Tversky, suggested that because all decision makers are subject to bounded rationality, they tend to use **heuristics**, rules of thumb that simplify the process of making decisions.[37] Kahneman and Tversky argued that rules of thumb are often useful because they help decision makers make sense of complex, uncertain, and ambiguous information. Sometimes, however, the use of heuristics can lead to systematic errors in the way decision makers process information about alternatives and make decisions. **Systematic errors** are errors that people make over and over and that result in poor decision making. Because of cognitive biases, which are caused by systematic errors, otherwise capable managers may end up making bad decisions.[38] Four sources of bias that can negatively affect the way managers make decisions are prior hypotheses, representativeness, the illusion of control, and escalating commitment (see Figure 4.4).

systematic errors
Errors that people make over and over again and that result in poor decision making.

Prior Hypothesis Bias

prior hypothesis bias
A cognitive bias resulting from the tendency to base decisions on strong prior beliefs even if evidence shows that those beliefs are wrong.

Decision makers who have strong prior beliefs about the relationship between two variables tend to make decisions based on those beliefs *even when presented with evidence that their beliefs are wrong*. In doing so, they are falling victim to **prior hypothesis bias**. Moreover, decision makers tend to seek and use information that is consistent with their prior beliefs and to ignore information that contradicts those beliefs. Is it possible that Gary Daichendt was seen as a direct challenge to the vision of Nortel's CEO Bill Owens? Daichendt claimed it wasn't so, that they simply had "differences" of business philosophy? Many did not believe him when he stated that as his reason for leaving Nortel. People recognized that Mr. Owens, meanwhile, was a career naval officer who rose to vice-chairman of the U.S. Joint Chiefs of Staff, which made him the second-ranked U.S. military officer. Such a background would suggest a military-style commitment to hierarchy and proper channels. Was the parting a "parting of the mindsets," a clash of egos, because there was no way Owens' prior hypothesis bias about how Nortel should be run was going to fall victim to Daichendt's way of doing things?[39]

FIGURE 4.4 | *Sources of Cognitive Bias at the Individual and Group Levels*

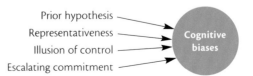

Representativeness Bias

Many decision makers inappropriately generalize from a small sample or even from a single vivid case or episode. An interesting example of the **representativeness bias** occurred as more and more investors perceived that Amazon.com was going to be the next great business model and invested in dot-com companies that had no serious business plan. The investors made the mistake of thinking that marketing on the internet would be good for any new company.

representativeness bias
A cognitive bias resulting from the tendency to generalize inappropriately from a small sample or from a single vivid case or episode.

Illusion of Control

Other errors in decision making result from the **illusion of control**, the tendency of decision makers to overestimate their ability to control activities and events. Top-level managers seem to be particularly prone to this bias. Having worked their way to the top of an organization, they tend to have an exaggerated sense of their own worth and are overconfident about their ability to succeed and to control events.[40] The illusion of control causes managers to overestimate the odds of a favourable outcome and, consequently, to make inappropriate decisions. For example, in the 1980s, Nissan was run by Katsuji Kawamata, an autocratic manager who thought he had the skills to run the car company alone. He made all the decisions—decisions that resulted in a series of spectacular mistakes, including changing the company's name from Datsun to Nissan—and Nissan's share of the North American market fell dramatically.

illusion of control
A source of cognitive bias resulting from the tendency to overestimate one's own ability to control activities and events.

Escalating Commitment

Having already committed significant resources to a course of action, some managers commit more resources to the project *even if they receive feedback that the project is failing*.[41] Feelings of personal responsibility for a project apparently bias the analysis of decision makers and lead to **escalating commitment**. They decide to increase their investment of time and money in a course of action and ignore evidence that it is illegal, unethical, uneconomical, or impractical (see Figure 4.3). Often, the more appropriate decision would be to "cut and run."

A tragic example of where escalating commitment can lead is the Columbia shuttle disaster. Apparently, managers were so anxious to keep the shuttle program on schedule that they ignored or discounted any evidence that falling debris might seriously compromise the shell of the shuttle. Thus, information about potential disaster was downplayed, even during the flight of the doomed shuttle.

escalating commitment
A source of cognitive bias resulting from the tendency to commit additional resources to a project even if evidence shows that the project is failing.

Be Aware of Your Biases

How can managers avoid the negative effects of cognitive biases and improve their decision-making and problem-solving abilities? Managers must become aware of biases and their effects, and they must identify their own personal style of making decisions.[42] One useful way for managers to analyze their decision-making style is to review two decisions that they made recently—one that turned out well and one that turned out poorly. Problem-solving experts recommend that a manager start by determining how much time he or she spent on each of the decision-making steps, such as gathering information to identify the pros and cons of alternatives or ranking the alternatives, to make sure that sufficient time is being spent on each step.[43]

Another recommended technique for examining decision-making style is for managers to list the criteria they typically use to assess and evaluate alternatives—the heuristics (rules of thumb) they typically employ, their personal biases, and so on—and then critically evaluate the appropriateness of these different factors.

Many individual managers are likely to have difficulty identifying their own biases, so it is often advisable for managers to study their own assumptions by working with other managers to help expose weaknesses in their decision-making style. In this context, the issue of group decision making becomes important.

Group Decision Making

THINK ABOUT IT

Emotional Intelligence and Teams[44]

Can we say that groups make better decisions than individuals? We can if that group is an emotionally intelligent one. What does that mean? In 1988 psychologists Williams and Sternberg defined group intelligence as "the functional intelligence of a group of people working as a unit."[45] In their research study, interpersonal skills of group members and compatibility were found to be the key to group performance. While the traditional marker known as IQ was there, the more important marker called "EQ" or emotional intelligence, was more critical. EQ referred to such social skills as empathy, motivation, the ability to resolve differences, and effective communication. The noted author Steven Covey said "when teams achieve synergy, gain momentum, and 'get on a roll,' they become virtually unstoppable."[46] The net result is that teams that are competent in personal and interpersonal skills are more effective. They simply have high problem-solving abilities and better performance.

You Be the Manager

1. What are the differences you have experienced when you were in an emotionally intelligent group?
2. What are the differences you have experienced when you were in a group with low emotional intelligence?

Many, perhaps most, important organizational decisions are made by groups of managers rather than by individuals. Group decision making is superior to individual decision making in several respects. When managers work as a team to make decisions and solve problems, their choices of alternatives are less likely to fall victim to the biases and errors discussed previously. They are able to draw on the combined skills, competencies, and accumulated knowledge of group members, and thereby improve their ability to generate feasible alternatives and make good decisions. Group decision making also allows managers to process more information and to correct each other's errors. In the implementation phase, all managers affected by the decisions agree to cooperate. When a group of managers makes a decision, as opposed to one top manager making a decision and imposing it on subordinate managers, it's more probable that the decision will be implemented successfully.

Nevertheless, some disadvantages are associated with group decision making. Groups often take much longer than individuals to make decisions. Getting two or more managers to agree to the same solution can be difficult because managers' interests and preferences are often different. In addition, just like decision making by individual managers, group decision making can be undermined by biases. A major source of group bias is groupthink.

The Perils of Groupthink

Groupthink is a pattern of faulty and biased decision making that occurs in groups whose members strive for agreement among themselves at the expense of accurately assessing information relevant to a decision.[47] When individuals are subject to groupthink, they collectively embark on a course of action without developing appropriate criteria to evaluate alternatives. Typically, a group rallies around a strong individual and the course of action that the individual supports. Group members become blindly committed to that course of action without evaluating its merits. Commitment is often based on an emotional—rather than objective—assessment of the best course of action.

We have all seen the symptoms of the groupthink phenomenon:[48]

- *Illusion of invulnerability.* Group members become overconfident, and this enables them to take extraordinary risks.

- *Assumption of morality.* Group members believe that the group's objectives are morally right, and so they don't debate the ethics of their actions.

- *Rationalized resistance.* No matter how strongly the evidence may contradict their basic assumptions, group members rationalize that their assumptions are correct and the negative evidence is faulty.

- *Peer pressure.* Members who express doubts about any of the group's shared views are pressured to ignore their concerns and to support the group.

- *Minimized doubts.* Members who have doubts or hold differing points of view may keep silent about their misgivings and even minimize to themselves the importance of their doubts.

- *Illusion of unanimity.* If someone doesn't speak, it's assumed that he or she agrees with the group. In other words, silence becomes viewed as a "Yes" vote.

Pressures for agreement and harmony within a group have the unintended effect of discouraging individuals from raising issues that run counter to majority opinion. For example, a colourful character named Sherman Kent, known as "Buffalo Bill, the Cultured Cowboy," a onetime history professor at Yale, who wore red suspenders, could tell bawdy jokes and use barnyard language, had also previously taught C.I.A. personnel for 17 years how important it was for intelligence analysts to challenge their assumptions, to acknowledge uncertainty and ambiguity, to watch for their own biases, and to meet the needs of policymakers without being seduced by them. When the U.S. Senate Select Committee on Intelligence brought out its paper in July 2004, it cited Professor Kent as the person whose admonitions had been ignored, so much so that "intelligence officials did not explain the uncertainties behind their judgment that Iraq was pursuing biological, chemical and nuclear weapons." Instead, intelligence analysts fell into "group think."[49]

There is considerable anecdotal evidence to suggest the negative implications of groupthink in organizational settings, but very little empirical work has been conducted in organizations on the subject of groupthink.[50] In fact, more recently, groupthink has been criticized for overestimating the link between the decision-making process and its outcome[51] and for suggesting that its effect is uniformly negative.[52] A study of groupthink in five large corporations reported that elements of groupthink may affect decision making differently. For instance, the illusion of vulnerability, the belief in inherent group morality, and the illusion of unanimity often led to greater team performance, counter to what the original groupthink proposals suggest.[53]

groupthink
A pattern of faulty and biased decision making that occurs in groups whose members strive for agreement among themselves at the expense of accurately assessing information relevant to a decision.

■ ■ ■ **FIGURE 4.5 |** *Devil's Advocacy*

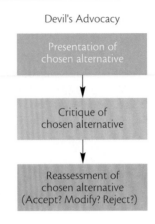

Devil's Advocacy

Presentation of
chosen alternative

↓

Critique of
chosen alternative

↓

Reassessment of
chosen alternative
(Accept? Modify? Reject?)

Improving Group Decision Making

A variety of steps can be taken to improve group decision making.[54] Managers should encourage group leaders to be impartial in their leadership, and actively seek input from all group members. Leaders should avoid expressing their own opinions in the early stages of discussion.

Another strategy to improve group decision making is to encourage one group member to play the role of devil's advocate. **Devil's advocacy** is a critical analysis of a preferred alternative to pinpoint its strengths and weaknesses before it is implemented (see Figure 4.5).[55] Typically, one member of the decision-making group plays the role of devil's advocate. The devil's advocate critiques and challenges the way the group evaluated alternatives and chose one over the others. The purpose of devil's advocacy is to identify all the reasons that might make the preferred alternative unacceptable after all. In this way, decision makers can be made aware of the possible perils of recommended courses of action.

Another way to improve group decision making is to promote diversity in decision-making groups.[56] Bringing together male *and* female managers, from various ethnic, national, and functional backgrounds, broadens the range of life experiences and opinions that group members can draw from as they generate, assess, and choose among alternatives. Moreover, diverse groups are sometimes less prone to groupthink because group members already differ from each other and thus are less subject to pressures for uniformity. The Swiss firm The BrainStore takes advantage of diversity to improve decision making by mixing children and managers together, as we saw earlier.

devil's advocacy
Critical analysis of a preferred alternative, made by a group member who plays the role of devil's advocate to defend unpopular or opposing alternatives for the sake of argument.

■■■■ # Organizational Learning and Creativity

THINK ABOUT IT ■■■■

How to Think About the Problem

"When asked what single event was most helpful in developing the theory of relativity, Albert Einstein is reported to have answered, 'Figuring out how to think about the problem'."[57] Thomas Jefferson stated, "If nature has made any one thing less susceptible than all others of exclusive property, it is the action of the thinking power called an idea, which an individual may exclusively possess as long as he [sic] keeps it to himself [sic]."[58] Today, more than ever, organizations desperately want to have their employees share their ideas and be engaged in what they are doing. They look for creativity among employees. For example, "Modern teams are typically made up of knowledge workers whose competitive advantage lies in their combined ability to out-know other groups. Therefore, the knowledge resources of the team must be supported and protected by the team leader."[59]

For some organizations, the issue of young people in particular downloading music files or sharing music files across the Internet is cause for litigation. One author sees things differently and uses the notion that if these same organizations used more creativity, a new vision would be possible. "The lesson the music industry should be taking from iTunes is not that selling MP3s is viable, it's that the digital music file is the perfect loss leader. Its marginal cost of production is zero. Use it to sell something that cannot be copied (fan merchandise, live performances, endorsements, collectibles). The media (an MP3 file) is not the product. The gold lies in the emotional connection between performer and audience."[60] At the internationally renowned Montreal-based Cirque du Soleil, boss Guy Laliberté told François Gourd, known as a 'corporate fool,' to inject this kind of energy into his employees as a way to get them to be more creative. Gourd said Laliberté used the following exact words, "Contaminate my company. You have carte blanche. Surprise me."[61]

You Be the Manager

1. What would you do to develop more creativity in your company?

The quality of managerial decision making ultimately depends on innovative responses to opportunities and threats. How can managers increase their ability to make nonprogrammed decisions—decisions that will allow them to adapt to, modify, and even drastically alter their task environments so that they can continually increase organizational performance? The answer: by encouraging organizational learning.[62]

Organizational learning is the process through which managers seek to improve employees' desire and ability to understand and manage the organization and its task environment so that employees can make decisions that constantly raise organizational effectiveness.[63] A **learning organization** is one in which managers do everything possible to maximize the ability of individuals and groups to think and behave creatively and thus maximize the potential for organizational learning to take place. At the heart of organizational learning is **creativity**, the ability of a decision maker to discover original ideas that lead to feasible alternative courses of action. Encouraging creativity among managers is such a pressing organizational concern that many organizations hire outside experts to help them develop programs to train their managers in the art of creative thinking and problem solving.

Promoting Individual Creativity

Research suggests that individuals are most likely to be creative when certain conditions are met. First, people must be given the opportunity and freedom to generate new ideas. Creativity declines when managers look over the shoulders of talented employees and try to "hurry up" a creative solution. How would you feel if your boss said you had one week to come up with a new product idea to beat the competition? Creativity results when individuals have an opportunity to experiment, to take risks, and to make mistakes and learn from them. Companies that have a lot of innovation foster that through their formal structure and expectations. For instance, in one recent year, 3M launched more than 200 new

organizational learning
The process through which managers seek to improve employees' desire and ability to understand and manage the organization and its task environment.

learning organization
An organization in which managers try to maximize the ability of individuals and groups to think and behave creatively and thus maximize the potential for organizational learning to take place.

creativity
A decision maker's ability to discover original and novel ideas that lead to feasible alternative courses of action.

products. To encourage this level of development, managers are told that 30 percent of sales are expected to come from products less than four years old.[64]

Once managers have generated alternatives, creativity can be encouraged by providing employees with constructive feedback so that they know how well they are doing. Ideas that seem to be going nowhere can be eliminated and creative energies refocused in other directions. Ideas that seem promising can be promoted, and help from other managers can be obtained as well.[65]

It is also important for top managers to stress the importance of looking for alternative solutions and to visibly reward employees who come up with creative ideas. Being creative can be demanding and stressful. Employees who believe that they are working on important, vital issues will be motivated to put forth the high levels of effort that creativity demands.

Despite the importance of fostering creativity in organizations, in a recent survey of 500 CEOs, only 6 percent felt that they were doing a great job at managing their creative people. John MacDonald, co-founder of Richmond, BC-based MacDonald Dettwiler & Associates Ltd. (MDA), suggests that "managing creative people is a bit like riding herd on a thousand prima donnas. They are all highly individual people who don't follow the herd, so managing them is a challenge."[66]

Promoting Group Creativity

To encourage creativity at the group level, organizations can make use of group problem-solving techniques that promote creative ideas and innovative solutions. These techniques can also be used to prevent groupthink and to help managers and employees uncover biases. Here, we look at three group decision-making techniques: *brainstorming*, the *nominal group technique*, and the *Delphi technique*.

Brainstorming

brainstorming
A group problem-solving technique in which individuals meet face to face to generate and debate a wide variety of alternatives from which to make a decision.

Brainstorming is a group problem-solving technique in which individuals meet face to face to generate and debate a wide variety of alternatives from which to make a decision.[67] Generally, from 5 to 15 individuals meet in a closed-door session and proceed like this:

- One person describes in broad outline the problem the group is to address.

- Group members then share their ideas and generate alternative courses of action.

- As each alternative is described, group members are not allowed to criticize it, and everyone withholds judgment until all alternatives have been heard. One member of the group records the alternatives on a flip chart.

- Group members are encouraged to be as innovative and radical as possible. Anything goes; and the greater the number of ideas put forth, the better. Moreover, group members are encouraged to "piggyback"—that is, to build on each other's suggestions.

- When all alternatives have been generated, group members debate the pros and cons of each and develop a short list of the best alternatives.

production blocking
A loss of productivity in brainstorming sessions due to the unstructured nature of brainstorming.

Brainstorming is very useful in some problem-solving situations—for example, when trying to find a new name for a perfume or for a model of car. But sometimes individuals working alone can generate more alternatives. The main reason, it seems, is the **production blocking** that occurs in groups because members cannot always simultaneously make sense of all the alternatives being generated, think up additional alternatives, and remember what they were thinking.[68]

Nominal Group Technique

To avoid production blocking, the **nominal group technique** is often used. It provides a more structured way of generating alternatives in writing and gives each individual more time and opportunity to generate alternative solutions. The nominal group technique is especially useful when an issue is controversial and when different people might be expected to champion different courses of action. Generally, a small group of people meets in a closed-door session and adopts the following procedures:

- One person outlines the problem to be addressed, and 30 or 40 minutes are allocated for each group member to write down ideas and solutions. Group members are encouraged to be innovative.

- Individuals take turns reading their suggestions to the group. One person writes the alternatives on a flip chart. No criticism or evaluation of alternatives is allowed until all alternatives have been read.

- The alternatives are then discussed, one by one, in the sequence in which they were first proposed. Group members can ask for clarifying information and critique each alternative to identify its pros and cons.

- When all alternatives have been discussed, each group member ranks all the alternatives from most preferred to least preferred, and the alternative that receives the highest ranking is chosen.[69]

nominal group technique
A decision-making technique in which group members write down ideas and solutions, read their suggestions to the whole group, and discuss and then rank the alternatives.

Delphi Technique

Both nominal group technique and brainstorming require people to meet together to generate creative ideas and engage in joint problem solving. What happens if people are in different cities or in different parts of the world and cannot meet face to face? Videoconferencing is one way to bring distant people together to brainstorm. Another way is to use the **Delphi technique**, a written approach to creative problem solving.[70] The Delphi technique works like this:

- The group leader writes a statement of the problem and a series of questions to which participating individuals are to respond.

- The questions are sent to the managers and departmental experts who are most knowledgeable about the problem; they are asked to generate solutions and mail the questionnaire back to the group leader.

- The group leader records and summarizes the responses. The results are then sent back to the participants, with additional questions to be answered before a decision can be made.

- The process is repeated until a consensus is reached and the most suitable course of action is clear.

Delphi technique
www.learn-usa.com/
acf001.htm

Delphi technique
A decision-making technique in which group members do not meet face to face but respond in writing to questions posed by the group leader.

Tips for Managers

IMPROVING DECISION MAKING

1. Make sure you know what biases you bring to your decision making.
2. Identify your strongest bias when you have to make an important decision.
3. Cite two examples of your experience with group think.
4. Describe how important creativity is for you on the job.
5. List ways that creativity could be improved in your workplace.

Information and the Manager's Job

"Men Are From Canon, Women Are From Kodak"[71]

Managers need information to make decisions. The question is: what types of information? "In an age of hyperchange, seeing our way to the future is harder and harder."[72] If you're the Eastman Kodak Co., having the right information at the right time to make decisions is absolutely essential. Kodak got its information correctly: women had traditionally bought film from the company; they were the targeted audience for decades. When the digital camera came along, men jumped on the bandwagon and film met a hasty death. Rather than die, Kodak gathered information that its cameras should be "female-friendly" if it wanted to be and stay competitive. "The company's research showed that women wanted digital photography to be simple, and they desired high-quality prints to share with family and friends." So, what did Kodak do with this new information? "Kodak revamped its digital cameras, stressing simple controls and larger display screens. It invented a new product category, the compact, stand-alone photo printer, which could be used to easily make prints without a computer. And it pushed to make digital-image printing simpler through retail kiosks and an online service." And the result, "Today, Kodak is clawing its way to the top of the digital world by bringing its best customers into that world with it."

You Be the Manager

1. How important is information in the work you do?

In order for managers to generate and assess their alternatives in making a decision, they need access to data and information both from inside the organization and from external stakeholders. When deciding how to price a seat sale, for example, the WestJet marketing manager needs information about how consumers will react to different prices. She needs information about unit costs because she does not want to set the price below the costs of flying. She also needs data about how many people (and what class of flyer—business or vacation) are likely to fly on any given day. WestJet also needs information about competitors' prices, since its pricing strategy should be consistent with its competitive strategy. Some of this information can come from outside the organization (e.g., from consumer surveys) and some from inside the organization (information about flight costs comes from operations). As this example suggests, managers' ability to make effective decisions rests on their ability to acquire and process information.

Information is not the same as data.[73] **Data** are raw, unsummarized, and unanalyzed facts such as volume of sales, level of costs, or number of customers. **Information** is data that are organized in a meaningful fashion, such as in a graph showing the change in sales volume or costs over time. The distinction between data and information is important because one of the uses of information technology is to help managers transform data into information in order to make better managerial decisions. **Information technology** is the means by which information is acquired, organized, stored, manipulated, and transmitted. Rapid advances in the power of information technology—specifically, through the use of computers—are having a fundamental impact on information systems and on managers and their organizations.[74]

data
Raw, unsummarized, and unanalyzed facts.

information
Data that are organized in a meaningful fashion.

information technology
The means by which information is acquired, organized, stored, manipulated, and transmitted.

FIGURE 4.6 | *Factors Affecting the Usefulness of Information*

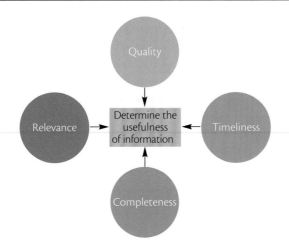

Attributes of Useful Information

When we evaluated the rational decision-making process earlier in this chapter, we noted that it is often difficult for individuals to have access to all possible information needed to make a decision. While information is still collected from individuals, much information is now accessed through information technology (websites, databases, and the like). Regardless of how it is acquired, individuals need to decide whether the information is useful. Four factors determine the usefulness of information: quality, timeliness, completeness, and relevance (see Figure 4.6).

Quality

Accuracy and reliability determine the quality of information.[75] The greater the accuracy and reliability are, the higher is the quality of information. For an information system to work well, the information that it provides must be of high quality. If managers conclude that the quality of information provided by their information system is low, they are likely to lose confidence in the system and stop using it. Alternatively, if managers base decisions on low quality information, poor and even disastrous decision making can result. For example, the partial meltdown of the nuclear reactor at Three Mile Island in Pennsylvania during the 1970s was the result of poor information caused by an information system malfunction. The information system indicated to engineers controlling the reactor that there was enough water in the reactor core to cool the nuclear pile, although this was in fact not the case. The consequences included the partial meltdown of the reactor and the release of radioactive gas into the atmosphere.

Timeliness

Information that is timely is available when it is needed for managerial action, not after the decision has been made. In today's rapidly changing world, the need for timely information often means that information must be available on a real-time basis.[76] **Real-time information** is information that reflects current conditions. In an industry that experiences rapid changes, real-time information may need to be updated frequently. Airlines use real-time information on the number of flight bookings and competitors' prices to adjust their prices on an hour-to-hour basis to maximize their revenues.

real-time information
Frequently updated information that reflects current conditions.

Completeness

Information that is complete gives managers all the information they need to exercise control, achieve coordination, or make an effective decision. We have already noted that because of uncertainty, ambiguity, and bounded rationality, managers have to make do with incomplete information.[77] One of the functions of information systems is to increase the completeness of the information that managers have at their disposal.

Relevance

Information that is relevant is useful and suits a manager's particular needs and circumstances. Irrelevant information is useless and may actually hurt the performance of a busy manager who has to spend valuable time determining whether information is relevant. Given the massive amounts of information that managers are now exposed to and humans' limited information-processing capabilities, the people who design information systems need to make sure that managers receive only relevant information.

Summary and Review

1. **THE NATURE OF MANAGERIAL DECISION MAKING** Programmed decisions are routine decisions that are made so often that managers have developed decision rules to be followed automatically. Nonprogrammed decisions are made in response to situations that are unusual or unique; they are nonroutine decisions.

2. **COMPARING DECISION-MAKING MODELS** The rational model of decision making assumes that decision makers have complete information, are able to process that information in an objective, rational manner, and make optimum decisions. The administrative model suggests that managers are boundedly rational, rarely have access to all the information they need to make optimum decisions, and consequently satisfice and rely on their intuition and judgment when making decisions.

3. **SIX STEPS IN THE DECISION-MAKING PROCESS:** Recognize the need for a decision, generate alternatives, assess alternatives, choose among alternatives, implement the chosen alternative, and learn from feedback.

4. **BIASES IN DECISION MAKING** Managers are often fairly good decision makers. However, problems result when human judgment is adversely affected by the operation of cognitive biases. Cognitive biases are caused by systematic errors in the way decision makers process information and make decisions. Sources of these errors include prior hypotheses, representativeness, the illusion of control, and escalating commitment. Managers should undertake a personal decision audit to become aware of their biases.

5. **GROUP DECISION MAKING** Many advantages are associated with group decision making, but there are also several disadvantages. One major source of poor decision making is groupthink. Afflicted decision makers collectively embark on a dubious course of action without questioning the assumptions that underlie their decision. Managers can improve the quality of group decision making by using techniques such as devil's advocacy and by increasing group diversity.

6. **ORGANIZATIONAL LEARNING AND CREATIVITY** Organizational learning is the process through which managers seek to improve employees' desire and ability to understand and manage the organization and its task environment so that employees can make decisions that constantly raise organizational effectiveness. Managers must take steps to promote organizational learning and creativity at the individual and group levels to improve the quality of decision making.

7. **INFORMATION AND THE MANAGER'S JOB** Computer-based information systems are central to the operation of most organizations. By providing managers with high quality, timely, relevant, and relatively complete information, properly implemented information systems can improve managers' ability to coordinate and control the operations of an organization and to make effective decisions. Moreover, information systems can help the organization to achieve a competitive advantage through their beneficial impact on productivity, quality, innovation, and responsiveness to customers.

Key Terms

administrative model, p. 98
ambiguous information, p. 99
bounded rationality, p. 98
brainstorming, p. 110
creativity, p. 109
data, p. 112
decision making, p. 96
Delphi technique, p. 111
devil's advocacy, p. 108
escalating commitment, p. 105
groupthink, p. 107
heuristics, p. 104
illusion of control, p. 105
information, p. 112
information technology, p. 112
intuition, p. 99

judgment, p. 99
learning organization, p. 109
nominal group technique, p. 111
nonprogrammed decision making, p. 96
optimum decision, p. 97
organizational learning, p. 109
prior hypothesis bias, p. 104
production blocking, p. 110
programmed decision making, p. 96
rational decision-making model, p. 97
real-time information, p. 113
representativeness bias, p. 105
satisficing, p. 99
systematic errors, p. 104
uncertainty, p. 98

S O   W H E R E   D O   Y O U   S T A N D ?

Wrap-Up to Opening Case[78]

We are known by the commitments we make. In the opening case scenario, we showed how decisions must be tied to commitments to be in alignment. Commitment focuses the decision maker on what, how, and why to decide.

Fernando Flores was Chile's minister of finance at one time—and, later, a political prisoner under president and dictator of Chile, Augusto Pinochet Ugarte (1973–1990). His three years in solitary confinement transformed him. Now he teaches companies how to use assessments and commitments to transform the way they do business. The outcome: executives who speak and act with intention. In 1984, Flores founded Action Technologies to develop software that can track the fulfillment of promises and commitments in day-to-day work operations. Flores says that he wants to open up people's moral imagination. By doing this, they will have a strategic advantage in business, in politics, and in their personal lives.

It was while doing his Ph.D. after he got out of prison in Chile that he studied the German philosopher, Martin Heidegger. "From Heidegger, Flores learned that language conveys not only information but also commitment, and that people act by expressing assessments and promises."

Talk all you want to, Flores says, but if you want to act powerfully, you need to master "speech acts": language rituals that build trust between colleagues and customers, word practices that open your eyes to new possibilities. Speech acts are powerful because most of the actions that people engage in—in business, in marriage, in parenting—are carried out through conversation. But most people speak without intention; they simply say whatever comes to mind. Speak with intention, and your actions take on new purpose. Speak with power, and you act with power.

Ask Yourself

1. When I'm making decisions, do I see the "big picture" and the commitment I must first make that will shape my process of decision-making steps?
2. How do people know that when you give your word, you mean it?
3. What are you committed to in your business practice?

After studying the preceding material, be sure to check out our Online Learning Centre at
www.mcgrawhill.ca/olc/jones
for more in-depth information and interactivities that correspond to this chapter.

Management in Action

Topics for Discussion and Action

1. What are the main differences between programmed decision making and nonprogrammed decision making?
2. In what ways do the rational and administrative models of decision making help managers appreciate the complexities of real-world decision making?
3. Ask a manager to recall the best and the worst decisions he or she ever made. Try to determine why these decisions were so good or so bad.
4. Why do capable managers sometimes make bad decisions? What can individual managers do to improve their decision-making skills?
5. In what kinds of groups is groupthink most likely to be a problem? When is it least likely to be a problem?

What steps can group members take to ward off groupthink?
6. What is organizational learning, and how can managers promote it?
7. To be useful, information must be timely, relevant, of high quality, and as complete as possible. Describe the negative impact that a tall management hierarchy, when used as an information system, can have on these desirable attributes.
8. Ask a manager to describe the main kinds of information systems that he or she uses on a routine basis at work.

Building Management Skills

HOW DO YOU MAKE DECISIONS?

Pick a decision you made recently that has had important consequences for you. This decision could be about which college or university to attend, which major to select, whether to take a part-time job, or which part-time job to take. Using the material in this chapter, analyze the way in which you made the decision.

1. Identify the criteria you used, either consciously or unconsciously, to guide your decision making.
2. List the alternatives you considered. Were these all possible alternatives? Did you unconsciously (or consciously) ignore some important alternatives?
3. How much information did you have about each alternative? Did you base the decision on complete or incomplete information?
4. Try to remember how you reached the decision. Did you sit down and consciously think through the

implications of each alternative, or did you make the decision on the basis of intuition? Did you use any rules of thumb to help you make the decision?
5. In retrospect, do you think that your choice of alternative was shaped by any of the cognitive biases discussed in this chapter?
6. Having answered those five questions, do you think in retrospect that you made a reasonable decision? What, if anything, might you do to improve your ability to make good decisions in the future?

Management for You

Suppose your uncle said that he would help you purchase an existing business. How would you go about making a decision on which business you might purchase, and whether you should take him up on his offer?

Small Group Breakout Exercise

BRAINSTORMING

Form groups of three or four people, and appoint one member as the spokesperson who will communicate your findings to the whole class when called on by the instructor. Then discuss the following scenario.

You and your partners are trying to decide which kind of restaurant to open in a centrally located shopping centre that has just been built in your city. The problem confronting you is that the city already has many restaurants that provide different kinds of food in all price ranges. You have the resources to open any type of restaurant. Your challenge is to decide which type is most likely to succeed.

Use the brainstorming technique to decide which type of restaurant to open. Follow these steps.

1. As a group, spend 5 or 10 minutes generating ideas about the alternative kinds of restaurants that you think will be most likely to succeed. Each group member should be as innovative and creative as possible, and no suggestion should be criticized.
2. Appoint one group member to write down the alternatives as they are identified.
3. Spend the next 10 or 15 minutes debating the pros and cons of the alternatives. As a group, try to reach a consensus on which alternative is most likely to succeed.
4. After making your decision, discuss the pros and cons of the brainstorming method, and decide whether any production blocking occurred.
5. When called on by the instructor, the spokesperson should be prepared to share your group's decision with the class, as well as the reasons why you made your decision.

Managing Ethically

In the late 1990s, IBM announced that it had fired the three top managers of its Argentine division because of their involvement in a scheme to secure a $340-million contract for IBM to provide and service the computers of one of Argentina's largest state-owned banks. The three executives paid $19 million of the contract money to a third company, CCR, which paid about $8 million to fake companies. This $8 million was then used to bribe the bank executives who agreed to give IBM the contract.

The bribes were not necessarily illegal under Argentine law. Moreover, the three managers argued that all companies have to pay bribes to get new business contracts in Argentina and that they were doing nothing that managers in other companies were not also doing. Is paying bribes ethical or unethical under these circumstances? If bribery is common in a particular country, what effect would this likely have on the country's economy and culture?

Exploring the World Wide Web

SPECIFIC ASSIGNMENT

Go to the website for Nortel Networks Canada (www.nortel.com/corporate/global/namerica/canada/index.html). Go through the different options available. Check out the section "Latest News." A June 22, 2006 announcement lists John Roese as the new Chief Technology Officer (CTO). While Nortel has had some very difficult times, especially in the plummeting stock prices of 2001 and 2002, Roese believes things can change for the better: ". . . if a company has a strong foundation and the people are good, it can get back its focus."[79] In announcing the appointment, Mike Zafirovski, president and CEO said, "Nortel has a rich and powerful heritage in innovation. As CTO, John will represent the heart and soul of that innovation engine and become the spiritual leader for our more than 12 000 engineers and developers."[80] Roese will be leading Nortel's innovation engine.
1. What opportunities and threats does Nortel currently face?
2. What kinds of decisions does Roese currently need to make?

GENERAL ASSIGNMENT

Search for a website that describes a company whose managers have just made a major decision. What was the decision? Why did they make it? How successful has it been?

Developing a Business Plan

(APPENDIX B, PAGE 405)

Go to www.mcgrawhill.ca/olc/jones/4 for online exercises.

Be the Manager

RATIONAL INVESTING[81]

James O'Shaughnessy, a fund manager who oversees about US$2.4 billion in assets for Bear Stearns Asset Management Inc., including three U.S. and Canadian equity funds on behalf of RBC Asset Management Inc., sees what he does as "Vulcan investing." For example, the RBC O'Shaughnessy Canadian Equity Fund reported a 17-percent return for the 12 months ended August 31. The Cdn$769-million fund has posted an average annual return of 10 percent since its inception in 1997. His sense of making decisions is that emotions pave the road to financial ruin. For him, the key to his success is "cold, hard data" and to offer growth "without the hangover." He has a computer-driver quantitative model for picking stocks. Says O'Shaughnessy,

> There are four horsemen of the investment apocalypse. And they are fear, greed, hope and ignorance. Think about that. Only one of them is not an emotion—ignorance. Fear, greed and hope have lost people more money than any recession, any bear market. We are trying to take a more scientific approach; this is a hypothesis we can test . . . and we are going to be emotionless. Emotions are the biggest bugaboo for investing.

Questions

1. What suggestions would you give O'Shaughnessy based on information from this chapter?
2. What additional decision-making ideas would you include if you were a fund manager?

Management Case

Real-Time Decisions . . . At a Distance[82]

Schlumberger Information Solutions (SIS), an operating unit of Schlumberger Oilfield Services, is the global industry leader for the supply of integrated business solutions comprised of GeoQuest software, information management services, information technology and a complete range of expert services. SIS enables petroleum companies to drive their business performance and enter into the iEconomy.

Schlumberger [NYSE:SLB] is a global leader in technical services spanning the oil and gas, utility, semiconductor, smart cards, network and Internet solutions industries. Schlumberger revenue was $14.3 billion in 2001.

Headquartered in Calgary, Alberta, Husky Energy Inc. is one of Canada's largest energy and energy-related companies. The company has almost $16 billion in assets and employs approximately 4000 employees.[83]

Husky Energy accelerates drilling decision making with real-time data access and interpretation—at a distance.

Situation Analysis

In May 2002, Husky Energy was drilling a new well in southeastern Saskatchewan. The decision to case the well or to continue drilling was approaching. The team responsible for the project was convinced that additional drilling was justified, but needed management approval to proceed.

Challenge

The project team knew that in such a situation, accuracy and speed were critical. To ensure they were making the best decision, the team eliminated the shortcut of interpreting faxes of the data. At the same time, they wanted to minimize the costs that can escalate as a result of holding a rig and crew on the site while data is transported on tape from the field, analyzed in the office, and management approval obtained.

Solution

Husky Energy chose to use a variety of Schlumberger software applications and data services to: deliver the data—in real time—to the right people; facilitate rapid interpretation to management; and enable the ultimate decision. Using the Schlumberger TransACT™ communication system for delivery of oilfield data, the wireline data was transmitted via satellite in real time directly from the drill hole to the Schlumberger Information Solutions (SIS) Data Management Centre (DMC) in Calgary.

SIS data communications staff monitoring the project notified Husky Energy's geologist that the data had been received at 5 a.m. on Sunday. Using the SIS LiveQuest™ application service provider (ASP) solution, the geologist logged in from home and, using his laptop, completed the interpretation of the new log data using Geology Office™ geological workflow tools. On Monday morning, little more than 24 hours after receiving the data, management was presented with—and approved—recommendations to continue drilling.

Results

Data collection and delivery hurdles are no longer factors impeding decision making. Quality data can be transmitted 24/7 in real time from a remote location to an analyst's home, or to a team of experts distributed around the world. Husky Energy's staff and contractors no longer need to travel to the office to complete their work, making off-hour work more convenient and less stressful. And, using the ASP technology, there is no need for installation and maintenance of multiple versions of software on workstations and laptops. Staff simply sign on to the SIS ASP server and always use the most up-to-date software. Finally, at the corporate planning level, Husky Energy senior management is afforded the opportunity for quick decision making based on quality data and interpretations, saving precious exploration time and money.

Questions

1. What were the factors impeding decision making for Husky Energy?
2. What elements contributed to more effective decision making?

Video Management Case

Shuttle Commission Blames NASA and Rocket Builders for Challenger Explosion

In the investigation of Challenger's explosion, the report identified technical failure as well as human errors as responsible for the tragic crash of the NASA rocket. The contributing errors were identified as flaws in decision making due to the managing team reporting falsely on mechanical issues and ignoring documented warnings.

Questions to Consider

1. What changes in decision making would result from following the report's recommendations to reorganize NASA managers?
2. What kinds of decision-making procedures could change to facilitate better communication of concerns?

CHAPTER 5

The Manager as a Planner and Strategist

Learning Outcomes

1. Describe the three steps of the planning process.

2. Explain the relationship between planning and strategy.

3. Explain the role of planning in predicting the future and in mobilizing organizational resources to meet future contingencies.

4. Outline the main steps in SWOT analysis.

5. Differentiate among corporate-, business-, and functional-level strategies.

6. Describe the vital role that strategy implementation plays in determining managers' ability to achieve an organization's mission and goals.

On a Wing and Hard Work[1]

One of the most important lessons Barry Lapointe has learned in his 35 years as chief executive of Kelowna Flightcraft Ltd. is how to stay off the radar screens of giants like Air Canada. That partly explains how Mr. Lapointe's company has grown to become the country's third-biggest airline, even though few outside its home base in British Columbia have heard of it.

Given the fate of companies that over the years have tried to compete with the big guys, Mr. Lapointe's strategy is hardly surprising.

But recently Mr. Lapointe charted a new course that has put his privately held company in direct competition with one of the industry's major players, just the kind of thing he has been trying to avoid. In March [2005], the federal government awarded a whopping $1.77-billion military flight-training contract to a consortium led by Kelowna Flightcraft, a lucrative piece of business that had been held by Montreal-based Bombardier Inc. since the early 1990s.

Under the 22-year agreement, Kelowna Flightcraft and its subcontractors will operate Canadian Forces flight training and support services at Portage La Prairie, Manitoba.

Until now, by choosing niches that are less glamorous than full-fledged passenger service, Kelowna Flightcraft has stayed out of the headlines—and stayed profitable.

"We pioneered the courier business as it's known in Canada today," said Mr. Lapointe, a burly, outspoken man of 60 who has frequently criticized the way the industry is regulated.

Kelowna Flightcraft operates in a number of sectors, including aircraft maintenance and manufacturing, but its core business is leasing its fleet of 19 Boeing 727s and 21 Convair turbo prop planes to other companies.

One of its most important clients is Purolator Courier Ltd., for which it provides freight service to most Canadian cities.

The decision to hand the military flight-training contract to a new player drew angry comments from Bombardier executives, who complained that the move was politically motivated and that the rightful winner was actually the Quebec company.

Mr. Lapointe bristles at such suggestions. He insists his firm won because it had the better bid.

"Nobody should talk about political influence," he said, sitting back in company headquarters at the Kelowna airport. He argues that Bombardier and other industry giants have benefited from hundreds of millions of dollars of federal contracts over the years for which taxpayers received dubious value.

"It seemed to me when we first looked at bidding that only the big guys, the CAE [Inc.]s and the Bombardiers of this world, would get these kinds of contracts. You can see how it happens. Big companies have big entertainment budgets; they give great lunches; they have great lobbyists."

The military contract is a coup for Mr. Lapointe, who has spent most of his career scrambling to avoid getting stepped on by the mostly Eastern-based companies that historically have dominated aerospace in Canada.

Although parts of the contract will be farmed out, Kelowna Flightcraft is the primary contractor and will perform more than 60 percent of the work.

It's the biggest deal the company, which is wholly owned by Mr. Lapointe, has done. He predicts it will increase annual sales by about 50 percent, to $225 million.

For all its growing clout, Kelowna Flightcraft came from humble beginnings. The company began life in 1970 as

President of Kelowna Flight Craft, Barry Lapointe (far right) poses for a photo with Jim Rodgers, (left to right) GM of Kelowna Flight Craft, Industry Minister David Emerson, and Defence Minister Bill Graham after holding a press conference in Kelowna, B.C.

an aircraft maintenance service run out of the back of Mr. Lapointe's Chevy van. Backed by little more than a love of aviation and a strong desire to work for himself, Mr. Lapointe travelled around B.C.'s Okanagan region, fixing small private planes, sometimes in exchange for nothing more than a side of beef from grateful clients.

As the business grew he became acquainted with some of the basic realities of the industry.

"In the early days, it was a pretty cozy relationship with the Canadian Transportation Agency and the big boys," he recalls. "There was no competition."

All the rules seemed to have been drawn up to favour the entrenched players, the national carriers such as Air Canada and others that have since met their demise, he said.

"The government knew it was wrong, but nobody would fix it because it was kind of a good old boy's club; it was all about who you knew and how many people you employed."

But for a brief, ill-fated partnership with Greyhound Air, which operated for a short time in the late 1990s before going out of business, Mr. Lapointe has steered clear of the glitzy passenger side of the business, figuring the big players had all the advantages.

Instead, he focused on the boring but remunerative air-freight sector, striking up a relationship with Purolator in the mid-1970s and, later, leading U.S. couriers.

But even in the freight business, the ugly duckling of the industry as far as the major carriers were concerned, there were rules on everything from who could carry big packages to which companies could move cargo out of which airport.

So Mr. Lapointe took what business he could and lobbied Ottawa to level the playing field.

It was an uphill battle at first. "They would shut you down at first and you couldn't ask any more questions. Back then, if you were told to shut up and leave the office, you did it. They can't do that any more."

The concentration on freight has proved a wise move. The industry has grown rapidly over the past three decades, now providing generous margins to the leading competitors at a time when passenger carriers are still recovering from one of the worst downturns in the history of the sector.

Kelowna Flightcraft has always been profitable, but Mr. Lapointe won't talk about earnings, nor has he plans to hand over control soon. "I've thought about taking it public," he said. "But I'm not really motivated by money."

What that means is that Mr. Lapointe will probably remain at the helm for the foreseeable future, continuing to expand the company, grabbing as much market share as he can from the big guys while he's at it.

Now It's Your Turn

Think of a time in your life when you were involved in a work situation that meant "getting the business" was critical to the future success of the department or company.

1. What kinds of discussions did you have with the personnel involved?

2. What were some of the obstacles the team had to overcome?

3. What was the most important factor "in turning the corner" and realizing that the future could look bright?

4. What was the final outcome?

■■■■ Overview

The open scenario to this chapter allows us to see that there is more than one way to compete in an industry. To find a workable way to enter and compete in an industry, managers must study the way other organizations behave and identify their strategies. This is exactly the strategy Barry Lapointe would have taken with his company, Kelowna Flightcraft Ltd., in their bid for the $1.77-billion military flight-training contract with the federal government. He had taken this contract from under the nose of Montreal-based Bombardier Inc. who had held it since the early 1990s. As it was, Bombardier complained anyways: that the awarding of the contract was politically motivated and that the rightful winner was actually the Quebec company. Lapointe, of course, rejected such a complaint by Bombardier and his firm won because it had the better bid.

In an uncertain competitive environment, managers must engage in thorough planning to find a strategy that will allow them to compete effectively. This chapter explores the manager's role both as planner and as strategist. We discuss the different elements involved in the planning process, including its three major steps: (1) determining an organization's mission and major goals, (2) choosing strategies to realize the mission and goals, and (3) selecting the appropriate way of organizing resources to put the strategies into practice. We also discuss scenario planning and SWOT analysis, important techniques that managers use to analyze their current situation. By the end of this chapter, you will understand the role managers play in the planning and strategy-making process to create high-performing organizations.

An Overview of the Planning Process

THINK ABOUT IT

Business Plan Competitions and Real-World Experience[2]

Rob Warren, director of the Centre for Entrepreneurship at the University of Manitoba's Asper School of Business says, "We put a lot of emphasis on business plan competitions and have worked to make it our signature piece." What's interesting about what he says is that in the past seven years, six businesses have been started as a result of entering business plans into competitions. This is truly real-world experience. Students in Professor Warren's business planning class put strategy and planning together and, as has been shown, come out with winning business plans that create viable businesses. At this Manitoba school the students are responsible for writing, editing, and constantly revising their own plans—with a little guidance from their professor.

An example of a winning competition was the one by Kevin Michaluk and Dr. Michal Miller, both of whom met at a conference months earlier and then met in Professor Warren's class. They formed PlasiaTEK, a startup medical technology enterprise that has already won $75 000 in business plan competitions across Canada and the United States, has gone on to raise more than US$200 000 in investment capital, and whose product is just months away from hitting the U.S. market.

Professor Warren comments, "With a business plan, you have to come up with a real concept, develop the technology, and then write up a plan so someone would want to invest in it. To win, it can't just be an academic exercise. You have to go out and recruit key executive members, develop a sales and marketing plan and prove that the market will pay for your product."

You Be the Manager

1. Why is planning so important?

2. When it comes to developing a successful business, what role does a business plan play?

planning
Identifying and selecting suitable goals and courses of action; one of the four principal functions of management.

strategy
A cluster of decisions about what goals to pursue, what actions to take, and how to use resources to achieve goals.

vision statement
A broad declaration of the big picture of the organization and/or a statement of its dreams for the future.

mission statement
A broad declaration of an organization's purpose that identifies the organization's products and customers, and distinguishes the organization from its competitors.

goal
A desired future outcome that an organization strives to achieve.

Planning, as we noted in Chapter 1, is a process that managers use to identify and select suitable goals and courses of action for an organization.[3] It is also one of the four managerial functions identified by French manager Henri Fayol. The organizational plan that results from the planning process details the goals of the organization and specifies how managers intend to attain those goals. The cluster of decisions and actions that managers take to help an organization attain its goals is its **strategy**. Thus, planning is both a goal-making and a strategy-making process.

In most organizations, planning is a three-step activity (see Figure 5.1). The first step is *determining the organization's vision, mission, and goals.*

- A **vision statement** reveals the big picture of the organization, its dream for the future. When Bill Gates founded Microsoft, his vision was "a computer on every desk, in every home and in every office." Steve Ballmer, Microsoft's current CEO, sees this vision as insufficient in today's high-tech world, and has developed a new vision: "Empower people anytime, anywhere, on any device."[4]

- A **mission statement** is a broad declaration of an organization's overriding purpose; this statement is intended to identify an organization's products and customers, as well as to distinguish the organization in some way from its competitors.

- A **goal** is a desired future outcome that an organization strives to achieve. Generally the goals are set based on the vision and mission of the organization.

The second step is *formulating strategy.* Managers analyze the organization's current situation and then conceive and develop the strategies necessary to attain the organization's mission and goals.

The third step is *implementing strategy.* Managers decide how to allocate the resources and responsibilities required to implement the chosen strategies among individuals and groups within the organization.[5] In subsequent sections of this chapter, we look in detail at the specifics of each of these steps.

FIGURE 5.1 | *Three Steps in Planning*

Before going on to learn more about planning, you might want to consider the words of Ron Zambonini, CEO of Ottawa-based Cognos, who noted that planning went out of fashion during the dot-com years. Speaking of dot-com founders, he said: "You see them in California, and, to a certain extent, here too. They work…90 hours a week, but the whole goal they have is not to build a business or a company. [All they really want is] someone to buy them out."[6] Unfortunately, many of those companies folded, and were not bought out. Planning may have helped them be more successful.

Who Plans?

In large organizations, planning usually takes place at three levels of management: corporate, business or division, and department or func-

Even non-profit organizations have vision and mission statements. For instance, the vision statement of the Girl Guides of Canada is "Every girl in Canada wants to be and can be a member of Girl Guides of Canada–Guides du Canada: a vibrant, dynamic movement for girls, shaping a finer world." Their mission statement is "Girl Guides of Canada–Guides du Canada is a movement for girls, led by women. It challenges girls to reach their potential and empowers them to give leadership and service as responsible citizens of the world."

tional. Figure 5.2 shows the link between the three steps in the planning process and these three levels. To understand this model, consider how General Electric (GE), a large organization that competes in many different businesses, operates.[7] GE has three main levels of management: corporate level, business level, and functional level (see Figure 5.2). At the corporate level are CEO and Chairman Jeffrey Immelt, three other top managers, and their corporate support staff. Below the corporate level is the business

General Electric Company (GE) www.ge.com.

FIGURE 5.2 | *Levels of Planning at General Electric*

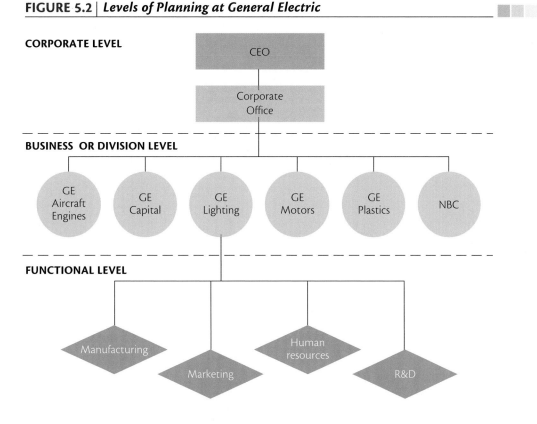

division
A business unit that has its own set of managers and functions or departments and competes in a distinct industry.

divisional managers
Managers who control the various divisions of an organization.

corporate-level plan
Top management's decisions relating to the organization's mission, overall strategy, and structure.

corporate-level strategy
A plan that indicates the industries and national markets in which an organization intends to compete.

level. At the business level are the different divisions of the company. A **division** is a business unit that competes in a distinct industry; GE has more than 150 divisions, including GE Capital, GE Aircraft Engines, GE Lighting, GE Motors and Industrial Systems, GE Plastics, and NBC. Each division has its own set of **divisional managers**. In turn, each division has its own set of functions or departments—manufacturing, marketing, human resources, R&D, and so on. Thus, GE Aircraft Engines has its own marketing function, as do GE Lighting, GE Motors, and NBC.

Corporate-Level Planning

At GE, as at other large organizations, planning takes place at each level. In general, corporate-level planning is the primary responsibility of top managers.[8] The **corporate-level plan** contains decisions relating to the organization's mission and goals, overall (corporate-level) strategy, and structure (see Figure 5.3). **Corporate-level strategy** indicates the industries and national markets in which an organization intends to compete. One of the goals stated in GE's corporate-level plan is that GE should be first or second in market share in every industry in which it competes. A division that cannot attain this goal may be sold to another company. Another GE goal is the acquisition of other companies to help build market share. Over the past decade, GE has acquired several financial services companies and has transformed the GE Capital into one of the largest financial service operations in the world.

At General Electric, the corporate-level goal that GE be first or second in every industry in which it competes was first articulated by former CEO Jack Welch, who stepped down in September 2001. Now, Welch's hand-selected successor, Jeffrey Immelt, and his top-management team decide in which industries GE should compete.

Even though corporate-level planning is the responsibility of top managers, lower-level managers can be and usually are given the opportunity to become involved in the process. At General Electric and many other companies, divisional and functional managers are encouraged to submit proposals for new business ventures to the CEO and top managers, who evaluate the proposals and decide whether to fund them.[9]

FIGURE 5.3 | *Levels and Types of Planning*

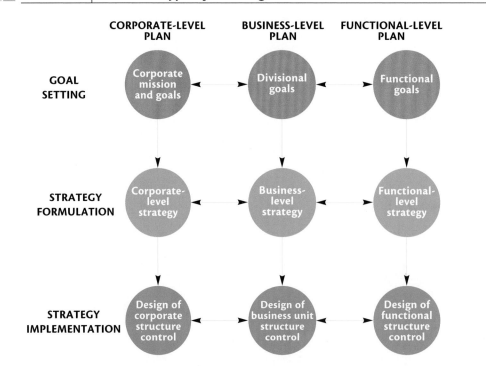

Corporate-level managers are also responsible for approving business- and functional-level plans to ensure that they are consistent with the corporate plan.

Business-Level Planning

The corporate-level plan provides the framework within which divisional managers create their business-level plans. At the business level, the managers of each division create a **business-level plan** that details (1) long-term goals that will allow the division to meet corporate goals, and (2) the division's business-level strategy and structure. **Business-level strategy** states the methods a division or business intends to use to compete against its rivals in an industry. Managers at GE Lighting (currently number two in the global lighting industry behind the Dutch company Philips Electronics N.V.) develop strategies designed to help the division take over the number-one spot and better contribute to GE's corporate goals. The lighting division's competitive strategy might emphasize, for example, trying to reduce costs in all departments in order to lower prices and gain market share from Philips. GE is currently planning to expand its European lighting operations, which are based in Hungary.[10]

Functional-Level Planning

A **function** is a unit or department in which people have the same skills or use the same resources to perform their jobs. Examples include manufacturing, accounting, and sales. The business-level plan provides the framework within which **functional managers** devise their plans. A **functional-level plan** states the goals that functional managers propose to pursue to help the division attain its business-level goals, which, in turn, will allow the organization to achieve its corporate goals. A **functional-level strategy** sets forth the actions that managers intend to take at the level of departments such as manufacturing, marketing, and R&D to allow the organization to reach its goals. Thus, for example, consistent with GE Lighting's strategy of driving down costs, the manufacturing function might adopt the goal "To reduce production costs by 20 percent over three years," and its functional strategy to achieve this goal might include (1) investing in state-of-the-art European production facilities, and (2) developing an electronic global business-to-business network to reduce the cost of inputs and inventory-holding costs.

An important issue in planning is ensuring *consistency* in planning across the three different levels. Functional goals and strategies should be consistent with divisional goals and strategies, which in turn should be consistent with corporate goals and strategies, and vice versa. Once complete, each function's plan is normally linked to its division's business-level plan, which, in turn, is linked to the corporate plan. Although many organizations are smaller and less complex than GE, most do their planning as GE does and have written plans to guide managerial decision making.

Time Horizons of Plans

Plans differ in their **time horizon,** or intended duration. Managers usually distinguish among long-term plans with a horizon of five years or more, intermediate-term plans with a horizon between one and five years, and short-term plans with a horizon of one year or less.[11] Typically, corporate- and business-level goals and strategies require long- and intermediate-term plans, and functional-level goals and strategies require intermediate- and short-term plans.

Although most organizations operate with planning horizons of five years or more, it would be inaccurate to infer from this that they undertake major planning exercises only once every five years and then "lock in" a specific set of goals and strategies for that time period. Most organizations have an annual planning cycle, which is usually linked to their annual financial budget (even though a major planning effort may be undertaken only every few years).

business-level plan
Divisional managers' decisions relating to divisions' long-term goals, overall strategy, and structure.

business-level strategy
A plan that indicates how a division intends to compete against its rivals in an industry.

function
A unit or department in which people have the same skills or use the same resources to perform their jobs.

functional managers
Managers who supervise the various functions—such as manufacturing, accounting, and sales— within a division.

functional-level plan
Functional managers' decisions relating to the goals that functional managers propose to pursue to help the division reach its business-level goals.

functional-level strategy
A plan that indicates how a function intends to achieve its goals.

time horizon
The intended duration of a plan.

Although a corporate- or business-level plan may extend over five years (or more), it is typically treated as a *rolling plan,* a plan that is updated and amended every year to take into account changing conditions in the external environment. Thus, the time horizon for an organization's 2004 corporate-level plan might be 2009; for the 2005 plan it might be 2010; and so on. The use of rolling plans is essential because of the high rate of change in the environment and the difficulty of predicting competitive conditions five years in the future. Rolling plans allow managers to make any mid-course corrections that environmental changes warrant, or to change the thrust of the plan altogether if it no longer seems appropriate. The use of rolling plans allows managers to plan flexibly, without losing sight of the need to plan for the long term.

Standing Plans and Single-Use Plans

Another distinction often made between plans is whether they are standing or single-use plans. Managers create standing and single-use plans to help achieve an organization's specific goals. *Standing plans* are used in situations where programmed decision making is appropriate. When the same situations occur repeatedly, managers develop policies, rules, and standard operating procedures (SOPs) to control the way employees perform their tasks. A **policy** is a general guide to action; as outlined in Appendix A, to a *rule* is a formal, written guide to action, and an *SOP* is a written instruction describing the exact series of actions that should be followed in a specific situation. For example, an organization may have a standing plan about ethical behaviour by employees. This plan includes a policy that all employees are expected to behave ethically in their dealings with suppliers and customers; a rule that requires employees to report any gift worth more than $10 that is received from a supplier or customer; and an SOP that obliges the recipient of the gift to make the disclosure in writing within 30 days.

In contrast, *single-use plans* are developed to handle nonprogrammed decision making in unusual or one-of-a-kind situations. Examples of single-use plans include *programs* (integrated sets of plans for achieving certain goals), and *projects* (specific action plans created to complete various aspects of a program). One of NASA's major programs was to reach the moon, and one project in this program was to develop a lunar module capable of landing on the moon and returning to Earth.

policy
A general guide to action.

Why Planning Is Important

Essentially, planning is determining where an organization is at the present time and deciding where it should be in the future and how to move it forward. When managers plan, they must consider the future and forecast what may happen in order to take action in the present, and gather organizational resources to deal with future opportunities and threats. As we have discussed in previous chapters, however, the external environment is uncertain and complex, and managers typically must deal with incomplete information and bounded rationality. This is one reason why planning is so complex.

Almost all managers engage in planning, and all *should* do so because planning helps to predict future opportunities and threats. The absence of a plan often results in hesitation, false steps, and mistaken changes of direction that can hurt an organization or even lead to disaster. Planning is important for four main reasons:

1. It's a useful way of getting managers to take part in decision making about the appropriate goals and strategies for an organization.
2. It's necessary to give the organization a sense of direction and purpose.[12] By stating which organizational goals and strategies are important, a plan keeps managers on track so that they use the resources under their control effectively.

3. A plan helps coordinate managers of the different functions and divisions of an organization to ensure that they all pull in the same direction. Without a good plan, it is possible that the members of the manufacturing function will produce more products than the members of the sales function can sell, resulting in a mass of unsold inventory.

4. A plan can be used as a device for controlling managers within an organization. A good plan specifies not only which goals and strategies the organization is committed to, but also who is responsible for putting the strategies into action to attain the goals. When managers know that they will be held accountable for attaining a goal, they are motivated to do their best to make sure the goal is achieved.

Effective Plans
Effective plans have four qualities:[13]

- *Unity.* At any one time only one central guiding plan should be put into operation.

- *Continuity.* Planning does not just happen once. Rather, plans are built, refined, and modified so that at all levels—corporate, business, and functional—fit together into one broad framework.

- *Accuracy.* Managers need to make every attempt to collect and use all available information at their disposal in the planning process.

- *Flexibility.* Plans should be altered if the situation changes.

By making sure that plans have these characteristics, planners ensure that multiple goals and plans do not cause confusion and disorder. Managers must recognize that it's important not to be bound to a static plan, because situations change. They must also recognize that uncertainty exists and that information is almost always incomplete, so that one does the best planning possible, and then reviews the plans as situations change or more information becomes available.

Scenario Planning

One of the most difficult aspects of making plans is predicting the future, which can be very uncertain. In the face of uncertainty, one of the most widely used planning techniques is scenario planning. **Scenario planning** (also known as *contingency planning*) is the generation of multiple forecasts of future conditions followed by an analysis of how to respond effectively to each of those conditions.

Scenario planning generates "multiple futures"—or scenarios of the future—based on different assumptions about conditions that *might prevail* in the future, and then develops different plans that detail what a company *should do* in the event that any of these scenarios actually occur. Managers use scenario planning to generate different future scenarios of conditions in the environment. They then develop responses to the opportunities and threats facing the different scenarios, and then develop a set of plans based on these responses. The great strength of scenario planning is its ability not only to anticipate the challenges of an uncertain future but also to educate managers to think about the future—to think strategically.[14]

When former Barrick Gold Corp., Randall Oliphant, was fired, he had no contingency plan to fall back on.[15] While painful at first, not having a contingency plan eventually forced Oliphant to come to his true feelings about what was important in life. Barrick is the world's third-largest gold producer. One can say that "it happens to the best of us." But there was Oliphant one evening "with nothing to do—no bulging briefcase, no travel plans, no pressing files to keep him awake until 1 a.m." the

scenario planning
The generation of multiple forecasts of future conditions followed by an analysis of how to respond effectively to each of those conditions; also called *contingency planning.*

"boy wonder," as he was known in the trade, had come to a complete halt. He was terminated by Barrick chairman and founder Peter Munk in 2003 after 16 years at the company, the final four as president and CEO.

What he realized as he sat alone this one particular night was that he had lost touch with the common experiences of living. Two years later he was back in what he referred to as the real world. "Having reached the top of the greasy pole by his 40s, Mr. Oliphant saw his brilliant career pulled out from under him." In his case, not having a contingency plan—his Achilles' heel—was in fact to become a stepping stone for him to get reconnected with his wife and 10-year-old daughter and to play a regular game of squash with his buddies. Of course, unlike many others who have very little when they are "dumped" from the company payroll, he left with a hefty severance package, worth $9.5 million! This allowed him to buy time and perspective to think about the rest of his life. "But he now appreciates the unreality of life at the top, with its perks and handlers. 'It's like being locked inside a Four Seasons Hotel,' he says. The surroundings are very nice, but it can be a delicious trap." His wife's reaction to him being fired? "Thank goodness!" There is a silver lining at times to having no contingency plan!

Tips for Managers

PLANNING

1. Question yourself as to whether you have a contingency plan or not. Ask yourself: Would I be able to bounce back—even if it took years—from a dramatic fall from grace in a similar way to Randall Oliphant at Barrick Gold Corp.?

2. Don't allow yourself to suffer from what is called "paralysis by analysis," that is, you take too much time mulling over your plans and not coming to a decision.

3. Do remember that plans were made to assist you; do not become a slave to the plans.

4. Plans serve as guides, and give you parameters on how you should be engaged and take action with your projects.

5. It has been said that "those who fail to plan, plan to fail." There is much wisdom in that expression.

Determining the Organization's Vision, Mission, and Goals

THINK ABOUT IT

Planning for the Unthinkable: The *Titanic* Disaster[16]

The *Titanic* disaster of April 15, 1912, can serve as a tremendous business lesson. Terrible mistakes were made in the planning and the ignoring of safety features in order to "win at any cost." The result? Some 1523 passengers and crew lost their lives on that terrible night when the "unsinkable" *Titanic* hit an iceberg and sank.

What went so terribly wrong? Recent research has shown that while bad luck and incompetence played their parts in the disaster, the desire for "prestige," of being the fastest to sail across the Atlantic *at any cost* to the plans and safety of the passengers was the main cause of the disaster. Researchers went back to the planning stages of

1909 and realized that the planners at the company, White Star—mainly with director, Bruce Ismay, who pushed for the ultimate passenger experience—wanted a ship to be a winner for competitive reasons and *at any cost* it seems to the plans and safety. White Star had been losing ground to the competition and so Ismay believed that "sacrificing" certain features would even the playing field, so to speak. In his mind, and those around him, they saw their plans as clearly indicating the *Titanic* would be "unsinkable," no matter what. "Customer experience" became the mantra. No expenses were spared to reach that goal. The mission: construct the fastest luxury liner possible, even if the original plans calling for safety and certain architectural features were ignored or even not implemented. Ismay was blinded by the vision, this mission, and the goal of winning, of beating the competition. "By the construction stage, although the ship's nonfunctional requirements had been severely compromised, there was little acknowledgement that anything was seriously wrong." Hubris and blind spots on the management team led by Ismay ruled the day. Ismay wanted the *Titanic* pushed to her operational limits, even with all the safety compromises and planning issues that had been jeopardized. The result: some 1523 lives lost.

You Be the Manager

1. How did Ismay's vision, mission, and goals collide with effective planning for the *Titanic*?
2. What advice would you give Ismay?

Determining the organization's vision, mission, and goals is the first step of the planning process. Once these are agreed upon and formally stated in the corporate plan, they guide the next steps by defining which strategies are appropriate and which are inappropriate.[17]

Defining the Vision

Vision differs from other forms of organizational direction setting in several ways:

> *A vision has clear and compelling imagery that offers an innovative way to improve, which recognizes and draws on traditions, and connects to actions that people can take to realize change. Vision taps people's emotions and energy. Properly articulated, a vision creates the enthusiasm that people have for sporting events and other leisure time activities, bringing that energy and commitment to the workplace.*[18]

The organization's vision is generally set by the CEO.

Setting the Mission

The organization's mission is supposed to flow from the vision for the organization. To determine an organization's mission, managers must first define its business so that they can identify what kind of value they will provide to customers. To define the business, managers must ask three questions:[19] (1) Who are our customers? (2) What customer needs are being satisfied? (3) How are we satisfying customer needs? These questions identify the customer needs that the organization satisfies and the way the organization satisfies those needs. Answering these questions helps managers to identify not only what customer needs they are satisfying now but what needs they should try to satisfy in the future and who their true competitors are. All of this information helps managers determine the mission and then establish appropriate

FIGURE 5.4 | *Three Mission Statements*

COMPANY	MISSION STATEMENT
Bombardier	Bombardier's mission is to be the leader in all the markets in which it operates. This objective will be achieved through excellence in the fields of aerospace, rail transportation equipment, recreational products, financial services, and services related to its products and core businesses.
Nortel Networks	Delivering greater value for customers worldwide through integrated network solutions spanning data and telephony.
Gildan Activewear	Gildan Activewear is dedicated to being the lowest-cost manufacturer and leading marketer of branded basic activewear to wholesale channels of distribution both in North America and internationally. To attain this goal, we will deliver the best in quality, service, and price to our customers and, ultimately, to the end-users of our activewear products.

goals. The mission statements of Montreal-based Gildan Activewear Inc.; Brampton, Ontario-based Nortel Networks; and Montreal-based Bombardier Inc. are presented in Figure 5.4.

Establishing Major Goals

Workers' compensation
Board of British Columbia
www.worksafebc.com

Once the business is defined, managers must establish a set of primary goals to which the organization is committed. Developing these goals gives the organization a sense of direction or purpose. For example, the mission of the Workers' Compensation Board (WCB) of British Columbia is the safety, protection, and health of workers. Based on this mission, the WCB has established the following goals:[20]

- Creation of workplaces that are safe and secure from injury and disease;

- Successful rehabilitation and return to work of injured workers;

- Fair compensation for workers suffering injury or illness on the job;

- Sound financial management to ensure a viable WCB system;

- Protection of the public interest.

Effective goals have three characteristics: They are ambitious, they are realistic, and they are stated in terms of time period for accomplishment. The best statements of organizational goals are ambitious—that is, they stretch the organization and require managers to improve organizational performance capabilities.[21] Although goals should be challenging, they should be realistic. Challenging goals give managers an incentive to look for ways to improve an organization's operation, but a goal that is unrealistic and impossible to attain may prompt managers to give up.[22] The time period in which a goal is expected to be achieved should be stated. Time constraints are important because they emphasize that a goal must be reached within a reasonable period; they inject a sense of urgency into goal attainment and act as a motivator.

management by objectives
A system of evaluating subordinates for their ability to achieve specific organizational goals or performance standards.

Communicating Goals: Management by Objectives

To allow managers to monitor progress toward achieving goals, many organizations use some version of management by objectives (MBO). **Management by objectives** is a system of evaluating subordinates for their ability to achieve specific organizational goals or performance standards.[23] Most organizations make some use of management by objectives because it is pointless to establish goals and then fail to communicate the goals and their measurement to employees. Management by objectives involves three specific steps:

- Step 1. *Specific goals and objectives are established at each level of the organization.*

Management by objectives starts when top managers establish overall organizational objectives, such as specific financial performance targets. Objective setting then cascades down throughout the organization as managers at the divisional and functional levels set their own objectives to achieve the corporate objectives.[24] Finally, first-line managers and workers jointly set objectives that will contribute to achieving functional goals.

- Step 2. *Managers and their subordinates together determine the subordinates' goals.*

An important characteristic of management by objectives is its participatory nature. Managers at every level sit down with the subordinate managers who report directly to them, and together they determine appropriate and feasible goals for the subordinate and bargain over the budget that the subordinate will need so as to achieve his or her goals. The participation of subordinates in the objective- setting process is a way of strengthening their commitment to achieve their goals.[25] Another reason why it is so important for subordinates (both individuals and teams) to participate in goal setting is so they can tell managers what they think they can realistically achieve.[26]

- Step 3. *Managers and their subordinates periodically review the subordinates' progress toward meeting goals.*

Once specific objectives have been agreed upon for managers at each level, managers are accountable for meeting those objectives. Periodically, they sit down with their subordinates to evaluate their progress. Normally, salary raises and promotions are linked to the goal-setting process. (The issue of how to design reward systems to motivate managers and other organizational employees is discussed in Chapter 8.) The evaluation of whether goals were achieved is part of the control process, which we discuss in Chapter 13.

Formulating Strategy

THINK ABOUT IT

Phoning and the New Playing Field[27]

Although it's a big company and has been around a long time, Bell Canada is currently under fire. New phone companies are posing threats to Bell in a high-stakes market showdown.

Take Vidéotron Ltée of Montréal, Québec, a division of Quebecor Inc. On January 24, 2005, it became the first of the major cable television company to launch residential Internet-based telephone service. This is a serious threat to traditional phone companies because the stakes are so high: markets worth billions of dollars. "We feel that this will radically transform traditional phone service, both local and long distance," Robert Dépatie, president and chief executive officer of Vidéotron, said on a conference call for analysts. Vidéotron has already begun its service to about 300 000 customers on Montreal's South Shore and hopes to roll out the service across its territory of 2.5 million people by the end of 2005. The other big cable companies—Rogers Communications Inc., Shaw Communications Inc., and Cogeco Inc.—are expected to follow with their own services over the coming months.

The opportunity with voice over Internet protocol, or VoIP, for customers and Vidéotron? It offers big discounts on traditional phone service, especially to existing customers. When sold in a bundle with Vidéotron's cable and Internet offerings, VoIP is 30 percent cheaper than a similar bundle marketed by BCE Inc.'s Bell Canada. Iain Grant, managing director of SeaBoard Group in Montreal, said Vidéotron's service offers significant discounts to regular telephone service from Bell. Brahm Eiley of Convergence Consulting Group Ltd. said Vidéotron's pricing is "pretty well what we anticipated. Based on this type of pricing we think Vidéotron will do very well." He predicts Vidéotron will win over about 10 percent of its customer base of 1.5 million subscribers—or 150 000—within 18 months. "We think this will hurt Bell. Vidéotron undercuts what Bell offers on both price and features, unless Bell comes back and tries to underprice them."

And Bell Canada's response both to the threat and the opportunity? "I think Vidéotron's entry is further evidence of the fact the environment we're operating in is dynamic. This is just further proof that the industry is transforming rapidly" and that a new regulatory framework must quickly be put in place, said Mirko Bibic, head of regulatory affairs at Bell Canada.

You Be the Manager

1. What strategy is Vidéotron using?
2. What are the strengths, weaknesses, opportunities, and threats (SWOT) in this short case scenario?

strategy formulation
Analysis of an organization's current situation followed by the development of strategies to accomplish the organization's mission and achieve its goals

Strategy formulation includes analyzing an organization's current situation and then developing strategies to accomplish the organization's mission and achieve its goals.[28] Strategy formulation begins with managers analyzing the factors within an organization and outside—in the task and general environments—that affect or may affect the organization's ability to meet its current and future goals. *SWOT analysis* and the *Five Forces Model* are two techniques managers use to analyze these factors.

SWOT Analysis

SWOT analysis
A planning exercise in which managers identify organizational strengths (S) and weaknesses (W), and environmental opportunities (O) and threats (T).

SWOT analysis is the first step in strategy formulation at any level. It is a planning exercise in which managers identify organizational strengths (S) and weaknesses (W), and environmental opportunities (O) and threats (T). Based on a SWOT analysis, managers at the different levels of the organization select corporate-, business-, and functional-level strategies to best position the organization to achieve its mission and goals (see Figure 5.5).

The first step in SWOT analysis is to identify an organization's strengths and weaknesses that characterize the present state of their organization, and then consider how the strengths will be maintained and the weaknesses overcome.

On October 8 and 9, 2003 a workshop was held in Ingonish, Cape Breton, for example, to do a SWOT analysis on the relationship between sustainable tourism and ecotourism. Sustainable tourism is described as "development that meets the needs of present tourists and hosts regions while protecting and enhancing opportunities for the future. It is envisaged as leading to management of all resources in such a way that

FIGURE 5.5 | *Planning and Strategy Formulation*

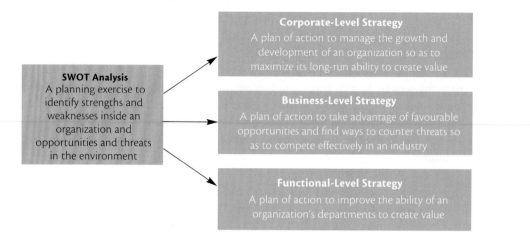

economic, social and aesthetic needs can be fulfilled while maintaining cultural integrity, essential ecological processes, biological diversity and life support systems" (World Tourism Organization). Ecotourism (first coined by Hector Caballos-Lascurian in 1983) is described as "tourism that consists in travelling to relatively undisturbed or uncontaminated areas with the specific objective of studying, admiring, and enjoying the scenery and its wild plants and animals as well as any existent cultural manifestations found in these areas."

Northern Cape Breton is a beautiful part of Canada; tourists have always been welcome; yet, how does an area as beautiful as Northern Cape Breton still be open and maintain the balance? Hence, the topic: sustainable tourism and ecotourism.[29] Listed below in Figure 5.6 is the SWOT analysis that was produced at the workshop in relation to this topic.

FIGURE 5.6 | *SWOT Analysis*

Strengths	Weaknesses
Physical beauty and variety Intact natural systems Proximity to U.S. market (northeast) Picturesque houses and boats Low Canadian dollar value Cultural distinctness Friendliness of community Presence of formally protected land	Short summer season Position at "end of line" Lack of some infrastructure/services Image as drive-by destination High turnover rate/retention of staff For ecotourism, lack of longer, more challenging, hiking trails Lack of directed tourism management plans
Opportunities	**Threats**
Integrated marketing of sustainable product(s) Better coordination of planning, marketing, product development Lengthening of the season and length of stay of visitors Coordinated protection of key assets to mutual benefit	Uncontrolled influx of more tourists or tourists seeking inappropriate experiences Damage to ecosystem from misuse Resentment from communities due to lack of benefits or due to impact on key community values Deterioration of key infrastructure

As can be seen, some of the major strengths are: Northern Cape Breton's physical beauty and variety; its intact natural systems; its proximity to US market (northeast); its picturesque houses and boats; its cultural distinctness, and the friendliness of its community. Some of Northern Cape Breton's weaknesses are: its short summer season; its lack of some infrastructure/services; its image that Northern Cape Breton is simply a drive-by destination; the high turnover rate/retention of staff in the tourism industry; the lack of longer, more challenging, hiking trails; and the lack of directed tourism management plans. When managers view these strengths and weaknesses, using a SWOT analysis, they will then want to assess these forces and anticipate future opportunities and threats that will impact on their planning initiatives and decision making for the future.

In this case with Northern Cape Breton, opportunities were itemized (such as lengthening the season and stay of visitors) and so were the threats (such as damage to the ecosystem from misuse). With the SWOT analysis completed, and strengths, weaknesses, opportunities, and threats identified, managers can begin the planning process and determine strategies for achieving the organization's mission and goals. The resulting strategies should enable the organization to attain its goals by taking advantage of opportunities, countering threats, building strengths, and correcting organizational weaknesses. Using the information gained from the SWOT analysis, as a result of the workshop, some key planning initiatives that resulted from this SWOT analysis for Northern Cape Breton were as follows:

1. Control of environmental impacts, by doing some of the following:
    a. Surveying tourists and locals' for their perception of beach contamination; and
    b. Doing laboratory analysis by sampling the quality of the water in beach/river/stream areas.
2. Economic benefits to the region, by measuring, by means of exit questionnaires, the amount spent per day person.
3. Marketing the region, by measuring, with a survey, tourists opinions of the quality and pricing of their accommodation.
4. Impact on the community, by surveying local attitudes and perception of tourism benefits and non-benefits.
5. Infrastructure, by examining road conditions, percentage of pull-offs per km of highway, and the length of maintained trail systems.

Thus, when managers are to identify potential opportunities and threats in their environments that affect the organization at the present or may affect it in the future, they can then consider how to take advantage of opportunities and overcome any threats to their organization.

P&G Canada
www.pg.com

Tim Penner, CEO of Toronto-based Procter & Gamble Canada, used SWOT analysis to save the jobs of employees at P&G's Brockville, Ontario plant.[30] Penner knew that the Cincinnati, Ohio-based parent company was planning to consolidate the production of laundry detergent in the United States. This threatened the jobs of the Brockville employees. Penner searched for new opportunities, suggesting to head office that P&G centralize the manufacturing of fabric softener sheets and electrostatic cleaning sheets for the Swiffer sweeper in Brockville. Penner convinced his American bosses that the strengths of the Ontario plant included a highly educated workforce that was also known for its commitment and productivity. As a result, Brockville's loss of laundry detergent production turned into a victory for Canadian jobs. Penner defines his mandate to include "aggressively selling Canada as a possible site for new products and reorganized operations." Penner's strategy has paid off. When he became CEO in 1999, P&G Canada was the seventh-largest revenue generator in the world for the US multinational. Three years later, he had taken his company to third place.

The Five Forces Model

Michael Porter's Five Forces Model is a well-known model that helps managers isolate particular forces in the external environment that are potential threats. Porter identified five factors (the first four are also discussed in Chapter 2) that are major threats because they affect how much profit organizations that compete within the same industry can expect to make:

- *The level of rivalry among organizations in an industry.* The more that companies compete against one another for customers—for example, by lowering the prices of their products or by increasing advertising—the lower is the level of industry profits (low prices mean less profit).

- *The potential for entry into an industry.* The easier it is for companies to enter an industry—because, for example, barriers to entry are low (see Chapter 2)—the more likely it is for industry prices and therefore industry profits to be low.

- *The power of suppliers.* If there are only a few suppliers of an important input, then (as discussed in Chapter 2) suppliers can drive up the price of that input, and expensive inputs result in lower profits for the producer.

- *The power of customers.* If only a few large customers are available to buy an industry's output, they can bargain to drive down the price of that output. As a result, producers make lower profits.

- *The threat of substitute products.* Often, the output of one industry is a substitute for the output of another industry (e.g., plastic may be a substitute for steel in some applications). Companies that produce a product with a known substitute cannot demand high prices for their products, and this constraint keeps their profits low.

Porter argued that when managers analyze opportunities and threats, they should pay particular attention to these five forces because they are the major threats that an organization will encounter. It is the job of managers at the corporate, business, and functional levels to formulate strategies to counter these threats so that an organization can respond to both its task and general environments, perform at a high level, and generate high profits.

Formulating Corporate-Level Strategies

THINK ABOUT IT

Less and More Strategy: Both Head *and* Heart[31]

When people hear the word "strategy," they often associate it with another word: "boring." The noted Professor Henry Mintzberg and his colleagues don't think things have to be that way. Strategy can be "novel, creative, inspiring, sometimes even playful." In their book, *Strategy Bites Back: It Is Far More, And Less, Than You Ever Imagined ...*, the authors take a serious look at the idea of strategy and then conclude that it's time for strategy to "bite back." In what they call "bytes" (interesting, educative ideas) and "bites" (stimulating jabs at traditional thinking on strategy), the authors have produced a book that offers "heart" in a field of study—strategy—that has so much "head." Head and heart need to go together. It's a conclusion that Harvard's John Kotter realized also:

Our main finding, put simply, is that the central issue is never strategy, structure, culture, or systems. All those elements, and others, are important. But the core of the matter is always about changing the behaviour of people, and behaviour change happens in highly successful situations by speaking to people's feelings. This is true even in organizations that are very focused on analysis and quantitative measurement, even among people who think of themselves as smart in an M.B.A. sense. In highly successful change efforts, people find ways to help others see the problems or solutions in ways that influence emotions, not just thought. Feelings then alter behaviour sufficiently to overcome all the many barriers to sensible large-scale change. Conversely, in less successful cases, this seeing-feeling-changing pattern is found less often, if at all.[32]

Some key nuggets from the book:

- Jeanne Liedtka of the University of Virginia, "No strategy is ever 'true'—all strategies are inventions. They are man-made designs. Business is not governed by natural laws—our strategies are not 'discovered' truths, like $e = mc^2$."

- Strategy helps everyone shape—not delude or manipulate—an image of a shared corporate future.

- The five Ps of strategy include the following:
  - Strategy is a plan—a consciously intended course of action and guideline to deal with the situation facing an organization
  - Strategy can be a ploy—a manoeuvre to outwit a competitor.
  - Strategy is a pattern—a stream of actions, providing consistency in behaviour.
  - Strategy is a position—a means of locating an organization in its environment, such as a market niche.
  - Strategy is perspective—an ingrained way of perceiving the world by the organization. "Strategy in this respect is to the organization what personality is to the individual," he says.

Strategy, therefore, can act as a flexible guide or like blinders on horses, such that the organization keeps going in a straight line but does not have access to its peripheral vision and, as a result, does not see the whole picture.

You Be the Manager

1. What does Jeanne Liedtka of the University of Virginia, mean when she says, "No strategy is ever 'true'—all strategies are inventions. They are man-made designs. Business is not governed by natural laws—our strategies are not 'discovered' truths, like $e = mc^2$"?

2. What's an example of an organization that has "blinders" for its strategy?

Corporate-level strategy is a plan of action concerning which industries and countries an organization should invest its resources in to achieve its mission and goals. In developing a corporate-level strategy, managers ask: How should the growth and development of the company be managed in order to increase its ability to create value for its customers (and thus increase performance) over the long run? Managers of most organizations have the goal to grow their companies and actively seek out new opportunities to use the organization's resources to create more goods and services for customers. This is precisely what Mintzberg et al. described in their book *Strategy Bites Back: It Is Far More, And Less,*

Than You Ever Imagined. Seeking out new opportunities occurs when companies and their strategies are able to adapt to changing circumstances.

In addition, some managers must help their organizations respond to threats due to changing forces in the task or general environment. For example, customers may no longer be buying the kinds of goods and services a company is producing (manual typewriters, eight-track tapes, black and white televisions), or other organizations may have entered the market and attracted customers away (this happened to Xerox when its patents expired and many companies rushed into the market to sell photocopiers). Or the markets may become saturated, as happened in the telecommunications industry recently, when more high-speed fibre optic networks were built than the market demanded. Top managers aim to find the best strategies to help the organization respond to these changes and improve performance.

The principal corporate-level strategies that managers use to help a company grow, to keep it on top of its industry, and to help it retrench and reorganize in order to stop its decline are: concentration on a single business; diversification; international expansion; and vertical integration.

These four strategies are all based on one idea: An organization benefits from pursuing a strategy only when it helps *further increase the value of the organization's goods and services for customers.* To increase the value of goods and services, a corporatelevel strategy must help an organization, or one of its divisions, differentiate and add value to its products either by making them unique or special or by lowering the costs of value creation. Sometimes formulation of a corporate-level strategy presents difficult challenges. This is what Mintzberg et al. are suggesting when they discuss how some companies and their strategies are more like "blinders" on horses; they keep charging straight head, and are prevented from seeing what's going on around them. This rigid singleness of purpose can be detrimental to a company.

Concentration on a Single Business

Most organizations begin their growth and development with a corporate-level strategy aimed at concentrating resources in one business or industry in order to develop a strong competitive position within that industry. For example, Winnipeg-based Peak of the Market bought Winnipeg-based Stella Produce because it would allow the cooperative to increase its packaging capacity while adding another recognized brand name.[33] This decision by Peak of the Market's president and CEO, Larry McIntosh, continued the company's concentration on a single business while bringing it new growth opportunities. Similarly, even a well established company like BCE Inc. is attempting to consolidate many loose threads with its strategy. Chief Michael Sabia says BCE has to first engage in what he calls "self-inflicted creative destruction" by "blowing up the culture and structures of its Bell Canada unit to prepare for a world when technological boundaries between landline, TV and wireless networks will disappear." He believes this is necessary because if Bell doesn't do its own creative destruction around its torn-worn strategy, "somebody else will"—meaning Rogers Communications Inc. Sabia explains his singleness of purpose and strategy this way: "If we've changed anything, the perspective is now don't diversify away from Bell—reposition Bell, fix Bell, transform Bell, add to Bell, strengthen those capabilities because that is what you know as an organization, that is what you are good at." Call this a vision "to build one of the world's greatest telecommunications companies" with "an image of convergence that carries echoes of his predecessor's dreams, although without the grandiose and expensive scale."[34]

Sometimes, concentration on a single business becomes an appropriate corporate-level strategy when managers see the need to reduce the size of their organizations in order to increase performance. Managers may decide to get out of certain industries, for example, when particular divisions lose their competitive advantage. Managers may sell off those divisions, lay off workers, and concentrate remaining organizational resources in another market or business to try to improve performance. In contrast, when organizations are performing effectively, they often decide to enter new industries in which they can use their resources to create more value.

Diversification

diversification
Expanding operations into a new business or industry and producing new goods or services.

Diversification is the strategy of expanding operations into a new business or industry and producing new goods or services.[35] Examples of diversification include PepsiCo's diversification into the snack-food business with the purchase of Frito-Lay, Time-Warner's diversification into internet services with the acquisition of AOL, and Quebecor Media Inc.'s move into broadcasting with its acquisition of Vidéotron ltée. There are two main kinds of diversification: related and unrelated.

Related Diversification

related diversification
Entering a new business or industry to create a competitive advantage in one or more of an organization's existing divisions or businesses.

synergy
Performance gains that result when individuals and departments coordinate their actions.

Related diversification is the strategy of entering a new business or industry to create a competitive advantage in one or more of an organization's existing divisions or businesses. Related diversification can add value to an organization's products if managers can find ways for its various divisions or business units to share their valuable skills or resources so that synergy is created.[36] **Synergy** is obtained when the value created by two divisions cooperating is greater than the value that would be created if the two divisions operated separately.

In pursuing related diversification, managers often seek to find new businesses where they can use the existing skills and resources in their departments to create synergies, add value to the new business, and hence improve the competitive position of the company. Alternatively, managers may acquire a company in a new industry because they believe that some of the skills and resources of the *acquired* company might improve the efficiency of one or more of their existing divisions. If successful, such skill transfers can help an organization to lower its costs or better differentiate its products, because they create synergies between divisions.

One way to achieve diversification is by forming partnerships, something *The Toronto Star* recently announced it would do with the CBC. The two companies intend to maintain editorial independence while pooling some editorial, promotions, and internet activity.

Unrelated Diversification

unrelated diversification
Entering a new industry or buying a company in a new industry that is not related in any way to an organization's current businesses or industries.

Managers pursue **unrelated diversification** when they enter new industries or buy companies in new industries that are not related in any way to their current businesses or industries. One of the main reasons for pursuing unrelated diversification is that, sometimes, managers can buy a poorly performing company, transfer their management skills to that company, turn its business around, and increase its performance, all of which creates value.

Another reason for pursuing unrelated diversification is that buying businesses in different industries lets managers use a *portfolio strategy*, which is dividing financial resources among divisions to increase financial returns or spread risks among different businesses, much as individual investors do with their own portfolios. For instance, managers may transfer funds from a rich division (a "cash cow") to a new and promising division (a "star") and, by allocating money appropriately between divisions, create value. After the start of the Second World War, E.D. Smith & Sons Ltd. acquired the Canadian rights to H.P. Sauce Ltd. of Britain and in 1948 the latter's subsidiary Lea & Perrins Ltd. On October 15, 1948, E.D. Smith died. The private company bearing his name was sold to Imperial Capital in 2001.[37] In this specific example, when Imperial Capital bought E.D. Smith & Sons Ltd. in 2001, it was following what it describes as "an acquisition strategy that identifies recession-resistant niche businesses in profitable, low-risk industries poised for consolidation."[38] Toronto-based Brascan Corp. is one of the last large Canadian conglomerates that continues to pursue this diversified strategy. As an asset management company, it focuses on the real estate and power generation sectors. Brascan owns over 70 office properties in North America and owns nearly 130 power generating plants in Europe.[39] Under CEO Bruce Flatt, previously president and CEO of Brookfield Properties Corporation,[40] it has focused its development on three of its multiple lines: real estate (Toronto-based Brookfield Properties), financial services (Toronto-based Brascan Financial), and power generation (Masson-Angers, Quebec-based Brascan Power).[41] Nevertheless, the company also owns Toronto-based Noranda Inc., a mining subsidiary, and Toronto-based Nexfor Inc., a paperboard company. Though used as a popular explanation in the 1980s for unrelated diversification, portfolio strategy started running into increasing criticism in the 1990s.[42] Today, many companies and their managers are abandoning the strategy of unrelated diversification because there is evidence that too much diversification can cause managers to lose control of their organizations' core business so that they end up reducing value rather than creating it.[43] Since the 1990s, there has been a trend among many diversified companies to sell off unrelated divisions and concentrate organizational resources on their core business and related diversification.[44] For instance, Toronto-based George Weston Ltd., the food processing and supermarket giant, announced in February 2001 that it would sell Blacks Harbour, New Brunswick-based Connors Bros., a fish processing operation, so that it could acquire Bestfoods Baking Co. Chairman Galen Weston explained that the move would allow the company "to go forward in the baking and the supermarket business."[45] The company did not feel that it held a competitive advantage in the fish processing industry. With the acquisition of Bestfoods Baking, George Weston inherited one of the nation's largest and most efficient DSD (direct-store-delivery) systems, distributing fresh bakery products to more than 60 000 customers on almost 5000 delivery routes. The company's product line includes such grain-based food products as sweet baked goods, doughnuts, soft cookies, breakfast bars, soft breadsticks, pizza crusts, English muffins, rolls, pan bread, pita bread, and pasta.[46]

International Expansion

As if planning the appropriate level of diversification were not a difficult enough decision, corporate-level managers also must decide on the appropriate way to compete internationally. When E.D. Smith & Sons decided to move into the American market, it was partnered with Toronto-based Loblaw Cos. Ltd., which was intending to sell E.D. Smith jams to Wal-Mart. Unfortunately Loblaw's was not successful in getting a contract from Wal-Mart, and E.D. Smith's expansion to the United States did not pay off.

A basic question confronts the managers of any organization that competes in more than one national market: To what extent should the organization customize features of its products and marketing campaign to different national conditions?[47] If managers decide that their organization should sell the same standardized product in each national market in which it competes, and use the same basic marketing approach, they adopt a **global strategy**.[48] Such companies undertake very little, if any, customization to suit the specific needs of customers in different countries. But if managers decide to

global strategy
Selling the same standardized product and using the same basic marketing approach in each national market.

Mars, Incorporated, the candy maker, previously used a multidomestic strategy and sold its candy under different brand names in the different countries in which it operated. Now it has changed to a global strategy to reduce costs and sells the candy under the same name throughout the world, as this billboard in Russia suggests.

multidomestic strategy
Customizing products and marketing strategies to specific national conditions.

customize products and marketing strategies to specific national conditions, they adopt a **multidomestic strategy**. Japan's Matsushita Electric has traditionally pursued a global strategy, selling the same basic TVs and VCRs in every market in which it does business and often using the same basic marketing approach. However, even McDonald's has had to customize its food products for the global market. When McDonald's went to India, it had to sell chicken burgers and mutton burgers rather than beef burgers.

Both global and multidomestic strategies have advantages and disadvantages. The major advantage of a global strategy is the significant cost savings associated with not having to customize products and marketing approaches to different national conditions. The major disadvantage of pursuing a global strategy is that, by ignoring national differences, managers may leave themselves vulnerable to local competitors that do differentiate their products to suit local tastes.

The advantages and disadvantages of a multidomestic strategy are the opposite of those of a global strategy. The major advantage of a multidomestic strategy is that, by customizing product offerings and marketing approaches to local conditions, managers may be able to gain market share or charge higher prices for their products. The major disadvantage is that customization raises production costs and puts the multidomestic company at a price disadvantage because the company often has to charge prices higher than the prices charged by competitors pursuing a global strategy. Obviously, the choice between these two strategies calls for trade-offs.

Vertical Integration

When an organization is doing well in its business, managers often see new opportunities to create value by either producing their own inputs or distributing their own outputs. Managers at E.&J. Gallo Winery, for example, realized that they could lower Gallo's costs if they produced their own wine bottles rather than buying them from a glass company. As a result, Gallo established a new division to produce glass bottles.

CHAPTER 5 The Manager as a Planner and Strategist **143**

FIGURE 5.7 | *Stages in a Vertical Value Chain*

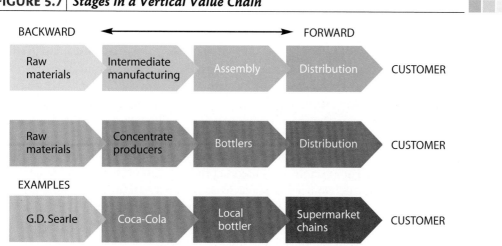

BACKWARD ⟷ FORWARD

Raw materials → Intermediate manufacturing → Assembly → Distribution → CUSTOMER

Raw materials → Concentrate producers → Bottlers → Distribution → CUSTOMER

EXAMPLES

G.D. Searle → Coca-Cola → Local bottler → Supermarket chains → CUSTOMER

Vertical integration is the corporate-level strategy through which an organization becomes involved in producing its own inputs (backward vertical integration) or distributing and selling its own outputs (forward vertical integration).[49] A steel company that supplies its iron ore needs from company-owned iron ore mines is using backward vertical integration. When Steve Jobs announced in 2001 that Apple Computer would open 25 retail stores to sell Macintosh machines directly to consumers, he showed that Apple was engaging in forward vertical integration.

Figure 5.7 illustrates the four main stages in a typical raw-materials-to-consumer value chain; value is added at each stage. Typically, the primary operations of an organization take place in one of these stages. For a company based in the assembly stage, backward integration would involve establishing a new division in intermediate manufacturing or raw-material production, and forward integration would involve establishing a new division to distribute its products to wholesalers or to sell directly to customers. A division at one stage receives the product made by the division in the previous stage, transforms it in some way—adding value—and then transfers the output at a higher price to the division at the next stage in the chain.

Consider how Cisco Systems, for example, makes only a small proportion of the computer networking products that are its stock-in-trade. Instead it coordinates the efforts of other distributors, manufacturers, and suppliers in its business web while applying its own special expertise in marketing and managing customer relationships. "Guided by a primary company, the aim of this type of business web is to manage the contributions of the different members to create a product or service that has a greater value than the sum of its parts."[50]

A major reason why managers pursue vertical integration is that it allows them either to add value to their products, by making them special or unique, or to lower the costs of value creation. For example, SunOpta Inc.'s headquarters is located in a red brick farmhouse north of Toronto, Ontario. It also has a nice, folksy tradition: Executives plant a tree each time they complete an acquisition. If you look around the property, you'll notice a "mall forest" of samplings that illustrates the company's acquisitions. SunOpta had a stated goal of reaching US$1 billion in sales by the end of 2007; to do so, it had to execute 30 acquisitions during 2005–2007. "We plant trees to symbolize growth for the company," says chief executive Jeremy Kendall. "Look around, you'll see trees everywhere." He then goes on to say that he wanted to created a "vertically integrated" food producer offering products "from the field to the table." For example, Coca-Cola and

vertical integration
A strategy that allows an organization to create value by producing its own inputs or distributing and selling its own outputs.

PepsiCo, in a case of forward vertical integration to build brand loyalty and enhance the differentiated appeal of their colas, decided to buy up their major bottlers to increase control over marketing and promotion efforts—which the bottlers had been handling.[51] An example of using forward vertical integration to lower costs is Matsushita Electric's decision to open company-owned stores to sell its own products and thus keep the profit that independent retailers otherwise would earn.[52]

Even though vertical integration can help an organization to grow rapidly, it can be a problem when forces in the organizational environment conflict with the strategies of the organization and make it necessary for managers to reorganize or retrench. Vertical integration can make an organization less flexible in responding to changing environmental conditions. For example, IBM used to produce most of its own components for mainframe computers. Doing this made sense in the 1960s, but it became a major handicap for the company in the fast-changing computer industry of the 1990s. The rise of organization-wide networks of personal computers has meant slumping demand for mainframes. As demand fell, IBM found itself with an excess-capacity problem, not only in its mainframe assembly operations but also in component operations. Closing down this capacity cost IBM more than $7.75 billion in 1993 and clearly limited the company's ability to pursue other opportunities.[53] When considering vertical integration as a strategy to add value, managers must be careful because sometimes vertical integration will actually reduce an organization's ability to create value when the environment changes.

Something managers need to consider when deciding on possible expansion strategies is the human costs of consolidating operations. While Air Canada initially projected $880 million in "synergies" from merging with Canadian Airlines, that figure was at least $150 million less because of the difficulty of bringing the two employee groups together. CEO Robert Milton noted that it was "an emotionally charged process . . . perceived to create winners and losers."[54] Management from the two merged companies can also clash, creating political struggles, as was seen in the public battling between the management of Montreal-based Abitibi-Consolidated Inc., a pulp and paper giant, and Montreal-based Quebecor.

Formulating Business-Level Strategies

THINK ABOUT IT

Concentrating on What We Do Best![55]

In July 2005 grocer Quebec-based Metro Inc. bought the assets of A&P Canada in a $1.7-billion deal, and beat out larger rival Sobeys Inc. to clinch the winning bid. This deal transformed the company into the country's third-largest supermarket chain with 579 stores. This strategic acquisition could place Metro Inc. eventually into the #2 spot in Canada. Sobeys' 2004 sales were $12.2 billion; Metro and A&P's combined were $10.6 billion. Metro chief executive Pierre Lessard said, "It could happen, surely. We would like to be number two (behind Loblaw Cos.). We have the volume to be competitive. But our goal now is to be the best food retailer in Canada and be a very profitable food retailer."

When A&P decided to sell, Metro Inc. saw this opportunity to acquire the company as a very important strategic move for them. Metro Inc. understood the A&P company and found their goals and culture to be quite similar to Metro's. Further, when they met A&P's management team they felt more at ease because they realized that the nature of such a large deal ($1.7 billion) rested on how well the management teams got along. Metro Inc. also felt that their offer was the best one. Said Lessard, "We managed to convince them that a dollar of Metro shares was worth more than a dollar of cash, and if you look at the result of the transaction the stock went up about $5. A&P has about 18 million shares so on top of the offer we made, they have already made about $90 million."

Lessard hopes to cut out $60 million in annual costs at the end of 2007, with a good part coming from procurement synergies as well as distribution efficiencies and some additional administrative costs.

You Be the Manager

1. What kinds of factors went into Metro Inc.'s strategy?

Michael Porter, the researcher who developed the Five Forces Model discussed earlier, also formulated a theory of how managers can select a business-level strategy, a plan to gain a competitive advantage in a particular market or industry.[56] According to Porter, managers must choose between the two basic ways of increasing the value of an organization's products: higher quality or lower costs. Porter also argues that managers must choose between serving the whole market or serving just one segment or part of a market. Given those choices, managers choose to pursue one of four business-level strategies: cost-leadership, differentiation, focused low-cost, or focused differentiation (see Table 5.1).

Cost-Leadership Strategy

With a **cost-leadership strategy**, managers try to gain a competitive advantage by focusing the energy of all the organization's departments or functions on driving the organization's costs down below the costs of its rivals. This strategy means manufacturing managers must search for new ways to reduce production costs, R&D managers must focus on developing new products that can be manufactured more cheaply, and marketing managers must find ways to lower the costs of attracting customers. According to Porter, organizations following a low-cost strategy can sell a product for less than their rivals sell it and yet still make a profit because of their lower costs. Thus, organizations that pursue a low-cost strategy hope to enjoy a competitive advantage based on their low prices.

cost-leadership strategy
Driving the organization's costs down below the costs of its rivals.

Differentiation Strategy

With a **differentiation strategy**, managers try to gain a competitive advantage by focusing all the energies of the organization's departments or functions on distinguishing the

differentiation strategy
Distinguishing an organization's products from the products of competitors in dimensions such as product design, quality, or after-sales service.

TABLE 5.1 | Porter's Business-Level Strategies

Strategy	Number of Market Segments Served	
	Many	Few
Cost-leadership	✓	
Focused low-cost		✓
Differentiation	✓	
Focused differentiation		✓

organization's products from those of competitors in one or more important dimensions, such as product design, quality, or after-sales service and support. For instance, St. Stephen, New Brunswick-based Ganong Bros. Ltd. is a small player in the chocolate market in Canada. It differentiates itself from bigger boxed-chocolate makers by focusing on the assorted chocolates market, where it ranks second in Canada. It's Fruitfull brand, made with real fruit purée and packaged like chocolates, has a 43-per-cent share of fruit jelly sales.[57]

Often, the process of making products unique and different is expensive. This strategy, for example, often requires managers to increase spending on product design or R&D to make the product stand out, and costs rise as a result. However, organizations that successfully pursue a differentiation strategy may be able to charge a *premium price* for their products, a price usually much higher than the price charged by a low-cost organization. The premium price allows organizations pursuing a differentiation strategy to recoup their higher costs.

Don Watt is known as one of the smartest retail brand designers in the country. In terms of differentiation strategies, he was the brains behind Loblaw's President's Choice and No Name labels, designed many of its supermarkets, and has helped behemoth Wal-Mart develop its superstores and private labels. Watts says, "It really isn't rocket science. This is remarkably simple stuff. I've often been amazed that people would pay me for this because it's so simple . . . It's not just a package at a time—it's taking a broad approach to a category and how you differentiate one category from another in a store."[58] Dave Nichol, a former president of two Loblaw divisions and a private label guru in his own right, says of Watt, "He understands the big idea, something that really hits consumers between the eyes, something they can't ignore. The way that Michael Jordan shoots a basketball, the way that Tiger Woods hits a golf ball—that's the way that Don deals with design. He's just an intuitive genius."

"Stuck in the Middle"

According to Porter's theory, managers cannot simultaneously pursue both a cost-leadership strategy and a differentiation strategy. Porter identified a simple correlation: Differentiation raises costs and thus necessitates premium pricing to recoup those high costs. What Best Buy Co. Inc. does to offset these costs—or not incur them— is to focus on customer service and it does this with their employees. "Service," believe it or not, turned out to be their bold new strategy, and it worked! This strategy aligns itself with the new "customer centricity" stores,[59] which aim to woo shoppers with more personalized service. Brian Postol of AG Edwards, a full-service brokerage firm, in St. Louis, Missouri, said that Best Buy's strategy allowed them to differentiate its offerings from those of gargantuan Wal-Mart Stores Inc., as well as rivals Target, Dell, and Amazon. According to Porter, managers must choose between a cost-leadership strategy and a differentiation strategy. He says that managers and organizations that have not made this choice are "stuck in the middle." According to Porter, organizations stuck in the middle tend to have lower levels of performance than do those that pursue a low-cost or a differentiation strategy. To avoid being stuck in the middle, top managers must instruct departmental managers to take actions that will result in either low cost or differentiation.

However, exceptions to this rule can be found. In many organizations, managers have been able to drive costs down below those of rivals and simultaneously differentiate their products from those offered by rivals.[60] For example, Toyota's production system is reportedly the most efficient in the world. This efficiency gives Toyota a low-cost strategy vis-à-vis its rivals in the global car industry. At the same time, Toyota has differentiated its cars from those of rivals on the basis of superior design and quality. This superiority allows the company to charge a premium price for many of its popular models.[61] Thus, Toyota seems to be simultaneously pursuing both a low-cost and a differentiated business-level strategy. This example suggests that although Porter's ideas may be valid in most cases, very well-managed companies such as Toyota, McDonald's, and Compaq may have both low costs and differentiated products.

Focused Low-Cost and Focused Differentiation Strategies

Both the differentiation strategy and the cost-leadership strategy are aimed at serving most or all segments of the market. Porter identified two other business-level strategies that aim to serve the needs of customers in only one or a few market segments.[62] A company pursuing a **focused low-cost strategy** serves one or a few segments of the overall market and aims to be the lowest-cost company serving that segment. This is the strategy that Cott Corporation adopted. Cott focuses on large retail chains and strives to be the lowest-cost company serving that segment of the market. A major reason for Cott's low costs is the fact that the company does not advertise, which allows Cott to underprice both Coke and Pepsi.

By contrast, a company pursuing a **focused differentiation** strategy serves just one or a few segments of the market and aims to be the most differentiated company serving that segment. BMW pursues a focused strategy, producing cars exclusively for higher-income customers. Sleeman has followed this strategy in producing its premium beers.

As these examples suggest, companies pursuing either of these focused strategies have chosen to specialize in some way—by directing their efforts at a particular kind of customer (such as serving the needs of babies or affluent customers) or even the needs of customers in a specific geographical region (customers on the East or West Coast).

focused low-cost strategy
Serving only one segment of the overall market and being the lowest-cost organization serving that segment.

focused differentiation strategy
Serving only one segment of the overall market and trying to be the most differentiated organization serving that segment.

Formulating Functional-Level Strategies

As discussed earlier in the chapter, a *functional-level strategy* is a plan of action to improve the ability of an organization's departments to create value. It is concerned with the actions that managers of individual departments (such as manufacturing or marketing) can take to add value to an organization's goods and services and thereby increase the value customers receive.

There are two ways in which departments can add value to an organization's products:

1. Departmental managers can lower the costs of creating value so that an organization can attract customers by keeping its prices lower than its competitors' prices.
2. Departmental managers can add value to a product by finding ways to differentiate it from the products of other companies.

TABLE 5.2   *How Functions Can Lower Costs and Create Value or Add Value to Create a Competitive Advantage*

Value-creating Function	Ways to Lower the Cost of Creating Value (Low-cost Advantage)	Ways to Add Value (Differentiation Advantage)
Sales and marketing	• Find new customers • Find low-cost advertising methods	• Promote brand-name awareness and loyalty • Tailor products to suit customers' needs
Materials management	• Use just-in-time inventory system/computerized warehousing • Develop long-term relationships with suppliers and customers	• Develop long-term relationships with suppliers to provide high quality inputs • Reduce shipping time to customers
Research and development	• Improve efficiency of machinery and equipment • Design products that can be made more cheaply	• Create new products • Improve existing products
Manufacturing	• Develop skills in low-cost manufacturing	• Increase product quality and reliability
Human resource management	• Reduce turnover and absenteeism • Raise employee skills	• Hire highly skilled employees • Develop innovative training programs

For instance, the marketing and sales departments at Molson and Labatt add value by building brand loyalty and finding more effective ways to attract customers. Each organizational function has an important role to play in lowering costs or adding value to a product (see Table 5.2).

In trying to add value or lower the costs of creating value, all functional managers should pay attention to these four goals:[63]

1. *To attain superior efficiency.* Efficiency is a measure of the amount of inputs required to produce a given amount of outputs. The fewer the inputs required to produce a given output, the higher is the efficiency and the lower the cost of outputs.
2. *To attain superior quality.* Here, quality means producing goods and services that are reliable—they do the job they were designed for and do it well.[64] Providing high quality products creates a brand-name reputation for an organization's products. In turn, this enhanced reputation allows the organization to charge a higher price.
3. *To attain superior innovation.* Anything new or unusual about the way in which an organization operates or the goods and services it produces is the result of innovation. Innovation leads to advances in the kinds of products, production processes, management systems, organizational structures, and strategies that an organization develops. Successful innovation gives an organization something unique that its rivals lack. This uniqueness may enhance the value added and thereby allow the organization to differentiate itself from its rivals and attract customers who will pay a premium price for its product.
4. *To attain superior responsiveness to customers.* An organization that is responsive to customers tries to satisfy their needs and give them exactly what they want. An organization that treats customers better than its rivals treats them provides a valuable service for which customers may be willing to pay a higher price.

The important issue to remember here is that all of these techniques can help an organization achieve a competitive advantage by lowering the costs of creating value or by adding value above and beyond that offered by rivals.

Planning and Implementing Strategy

THINK ABOUT IT

Mergers, Differentiations, Success![65]

The Centre for Addiction and Mental Health (CAMH) in Toronto was created in 1998 through the successful merger of the former Addiction Research Foundation, the Clarke Institute of Psychiatry, the Donwood Institute, and the Queen Street Mental Health Centre. With its 2003/2006 Strategic Plan, CAMH plans to continue being successful in implementing its strategy around the following four mandates: client-centred care, education, health promotion/prevention, and research. They will also update their mission and vision statements to reflect CAMH's increased emphasis on health promotion and the determinants of health as an essential part of their work, and to be more clearly and actively focused on improving the lives of people and building healthy communities.

How has their strategy been practically implemented? They have been able to

- Launch a multi-year public education strategy;
- Establish provincial priorities in the areas of youth, concurrent disorders, and diversity; and
- Acquire a new Positron Emission Tomography (PET) scanner—one of only two in Canada.

Additional highlights include:

- Average length of stay decreased from 87 days to 47 days;
- Professional education has increased by over 30 percent, to 9000 providers/year;
- Over 30 percent increase in volunteers;
- Research funding has increased by close to 60 percent to $28 million per year; and
- The Foundation increased its fundraising from $3 million to $6 million per year, and its donor base from 2280 donors to 4964 donors.

You Be the Manager

1. How does strategy relate to implementation?

After conducting a SWOT analysis and identifying appropriate strategies to attain an organization's mission and goals, managers confront the challenge of putting those strategies into action. Strategy implementation is a five-step process:

1. Allocating responsibility for implementation to the appropriate individuals or groups;
2. Drafting detailed action plans that specify how a strategy is to be implemented;
3. Establishing a timetable for implementation that includes precise, measurable goals linked to the attainment of the action plan;
4. Allocating appropriate resources to the responsible individuals or groups;
5. Holding specific individuals or groups responsible for reaching corporate, divisional, and functional goals.

As the case of CAMH illustrates, the planning process goes beyond the mere identification of strategies; it also includes actions taken to ensure that the organization actually implements its strategies. One of the difficulties Air Canada has faced in recent years is that it has not articulated a clear strategy, particularly in creating Tango to operate alongside the parent airline. Customers face stressed airline employees who are not clear on the real priorities of the airline. By contrast, Southwest Airlines has communicated a very clear strategy to its employees: Flights are to be an enjoyable, affordable experience for travellers, and employees are to make sure that happens while keeping costs down and improving turnaround time. Armed with this strategy, all Southwest Airlines employees know what is expected of them in a crisis, and pilots and fight attendants pitch in to help in whatever ways are necessary to meet this strategy.

It should be noted that the plan for implementing a strategy may require radical redesign of the structure of the organization, the adoption of a program for changing the culture of the organization and the development of new control systems. We address the first two issues in the next two chapters. The issues of control we discuss in Chapter 13.

Tips for Managers
STRATEGY

1. Take time for reviewing your corporate strategy.
2. Ask yourself if you have a strategy with "blinders" or do you also include "peripheral vision" and see what's occurring around you as well?
3. Make sure you clearly see the link between your strategy and how it is implemented.
4. Ask yourself if your strategy will be incurring costs that will negate the bold dream you have for the company.

Summary and Review

1. **PLANNING AS A THREE-STEP PROCESS** Planning is a three-step process involving the following:

   a. Determining an organization's mission and goals;
   b. Formulating strategy; and
   c. Implementing strategy.

2. **RELATIONSHIP BETWEEN PLANNING AND STRATEGY** Managers use planning to identify and select appropriate goals and courses of action for an organization and to decide how to allocate the resources their need to attain those goals and carry out those actions.

3. **ROLE OF PLANNING TO PREDICT AND MEET FUTURE CONTINGENCIES** Managers determine where an organization is currently and decide where and how to take it forward. Because of planning, managers are therefore able to forecast what may happen in the future and then to anticipate and gather resources to meet these anticipated needs, opportunities, and threats.

4. **DETERMINING THE ORGANIZATION'S VISION, MISSION, AND GOALS** Determining the organization's vision and mission requires managers to define the business of the organization and establish major goals. Strategy formulation requires managers to perform a SWOT analysis and then choose appropriate strategies at the corporate, business, and functional levels.

5. **FORMULATING STRATEGY** At the corporate level, organizations use strategies such as concentration on a single business; diversification; international expansion;

and vertical integration to help increase the value of the goods and services provided to customers. At the business level, managers are responsible for developing a successful low-cost or differentiation strategy, either for the whole market or for a particular segment of it. At the functional level, departmental managers strive to develop and use their skills to help the organization either add value to its products by differentiating them or lower the costs of value creation.

6. **PLANNING AND IMPLEMENTING STRATEGY** Strategy implementation requires managers to allocate responsibilities to suitable individuals or groups; draft detailed action plans that specify how a strategy is to be implemented; establish a timetable for implementation that includes precise, measurable goals linked to the attainment of the action plan; allocate appropriate resources to the responsible individuals or groups; and hold individuals or groups accountable for reaching goals.

Key Terms

business-level plan, p. 127
business-level strategy, p. 127
corporate-level plan, p. 126
corporate-level strategy, p. 126
cost-leadership strategy, p. 145
differentiation strategy, p. 145
diversification, p. 140
division, p. 126
divisional managers, p. 126
focused differentiation strategy, p. 147
focused low-cost strategy, p. 147
function, p. 127
functional-level plan, p. 127
functional-level strategy, p. 127
functional managers, p. 127
global strategy, p. 141

goal, p. 124
management by objectives, p. 132
mission statement, p. 124
multidomestic strategy, p. 142
planning, p. 124
policy, p. 128
related diversification, p. 140
scenario planning, p. 129
strategy, p. 124
strategy formulation, p. 134
SWOT analysis, p. 134
synergy, p. 140
time horizon, p. 127
unrelated diversification, p. 140
vertical integration, p. 143
vision statement, p. 124

S O   W H E R E   D O   Y O U   S T A N D ?

Wrap-Up to Opening Case[66]

Barry Lapointe in his 35 years as chief executive of Kelowna Flightcraft Ltd. in British Columbia, kept to a simple strategy for much of those years: do an outstanding job, but stay off the radar screens of the "big guys." That meant mainly not being noticed by Air Canada. "For the worst-kept secret we got a lot of applause," said Defence Minister Bill Graham after making the announcement in Kelowna on March 30, 2005. Allied Wings, the ad hoc consortium of companies spearheaded by Kelowna Flightcraft, had bid and won the project—a whopping $1.77-billion dollar deal over 22 years with the federal government—in the process beating out

Montreal-based Bombardier Inc., which had held the contract since the early 1990s. Bombardier's response, as was noted in the opening case, was defensive, with management claiming that the win was politically motivated. However, Industry Minister David Emerson addressed such concerns at the contract announcement ceremony in Kelowna. "The awarding of the contract to Allied Wings had nothing to do with politics," he said. "It was not a bid to gain favour in Western Canada. It was an open, transparent competition, and Allied Wings was selected on merit and merit alone."

This win for Lapointe was a huge upset for Bombardier because Allied Wings had beaten the aerospace giant Bombardier at its own game. It was a particular sweet win for Lapointe since he just loved planes ever since he was a young boy building model airplanes. In the 1960s he worked as an aircraft mechanic in British Columbia's Okanagan Valley. He realized during those years that he also had business acumen. "So in 1970 Lapointe started his own aircraft maintenance depot that he called Kelowna Flightcraft Ltd. He teamed up with another mechanic, Jim Rogers, and the two set out to see if they could make the new enterprise fly. Says Lapointe: "It was touch and go with the banks. [They'd] say, 'You're overextended without secure contracts.'" Kelowna Flightcraft is no longer overextended!

What were factors involved in Flightcraft's strategy to go after such a contract? Lapointe's partner, Jim Rogers, said that some Ottawa contacts made mention of such a contract five years earlier. Flightcraft didn't think it had a chance, or in Rogers' own words—"It was to me a bit of a long shot," he admits. Here is what they did:

Knowing that Flightcraft alone couldn't challenge the much larger, politically connected Bombardier, Rogers drew together a partnership of small to mid-size companies from across the country. He approached each on its ability to deliver one or more of the stipulated services: Bell Helicopters for flight training; CAE for flight simulators; Canadian Base Operators/Black and McDonald Ltd. for facilities management; Coastal Pacific Aviation to help develop the courses. Flightcraft's role was to administer the operations as well as to buy and maintain additional aircraft.

Barry Lapointe is clear also about another piece of his strategy in saying that his aviation company's success was been built on two things: people and assets. "I don't believe you can make money leasing other people's equity," he says. Kelowna Flightcraft owns all of its planes. And its capital isn't in its buildings: the linoleum is worn and patched, the ceiling water-stained. "How you talk to people and deal with them determines the success of your business," says Lapointe.

Ask Yourself

1. Why would Mr. Lapointe want to stay off the radar screen of giant Air Canada as he built his business?

2. What elements are critical in Kelowna Flightcraft's strategy and implementation plans?

Online Learning Centre

After studying the preceding material, be sure to check out our Online Learning Centre at **www.mcgrawhill.ca/olc/jones** for more in-depth information and interactivities that correspond to this chapter.

Management in Action

Topics for Discussion and Action

1. Describe the three steps of planning. Explain how they are related.
2. How can scenario planning help managers predict the future?
3. Ask a manager about the kinds of planning exercises he or she regularly uses. What are the purposes of these exercises, and what are their advantages or disadvantages?
4. What is the role of divisional and functional managers in the formulation of strategy?
5. Why is it important for functional managers to have a clear grasp of the organization's mission when developing strategies within their departments?
6. What is the relationship among corporate-, business-, and functional-level strategies, and how do they create value for an organization?
7. Ask a manager to identify the corporate-, business-, and functional-level strategies used by his or her organization.

Building Management Skills

HOW TO ANALYZE A COMPANY'S STRATEGY

Pick a well-known business organization that has received recent media coverage and for which you can get a number of years' annual reports from your school library or on the Internet. For this organization, do the following.

1. From the annual reports, identify the main strategies pursued by the company over a 10-year period.
2. Try to identify why the company pursued these strategies. What reason was given in the annual reports, press reports, and elsewhere? What goals and objectives did the company say it had?
3. Document whether and when any major changes in the strategy of the organization occurred. If changes did occur, try to identify the reason for them.
4. If changes in strategy occurred, try to determine the extent to which they were the result of long-term plans and the extent to which they were responses to unforeseen changes in the company's task environment.
5. What is the main industry that the company competes in?
6. What business-level strategy does the company seem to be pursuing in this industry?
7. What is the company's reputation with regard to productivity, quality, innovation, and responsiveness to customers in this industry? If the company has attained an advantage in any of these areas, how has it done so?
8. What is the current corporate-level strategy of the company? What is the company's stated reason for pursuing this strategy?
9. Has the company expanded internationally? If it has, identify its largest international market. How did the company enter this market? Did its mode of entry change over time?

Management for You

Think ahead to five years from now, to consider what it is that you might like to be doing with your life. Develop your own vision and mission statements. Establish a set of goals that will help you achieve your vision and mission.

Develop a SWOT analysis for considering what you want to be doing in five years. What are your strengths and weaknesses? What are the opportunities and threats in carrying out this plan?

Develop a five-year plan that maps out the steps you need to take in order to get to where you want to be with your life at that time.

Small Group Breakout Exercise

PLANNING FOR NEW DEVELOPMENT

Form groups of three or four people, and appoint one member as the spokesperson who will communicate your findings to the class when called on by the instructor. Then discuss the following scenario.

You are a team of city planners for the City of Vancouver. Vancouver's east side is known as the poorest postal code in the country. Recently the city bought the old Woodward's building, and is trying to decide what to do with it. It is considering a mix of social housing, artists' lofts, and retail areas. Can the city create a heart in this poverty-stricken area? You have been asked to come up with a plan of action to determine what to do.

1. Describe the new building project's purpose.
2. Identify the short-term and long-term objectives for the project and how these will be evaluated.
3. Using scenario planning, analyze the pros and cons of each alternative.

Managing Ethically

A major department store has received repeated criticism for selling clothes that are produced in low-cost developing world countries. The CEO of the department store knows that suppliers are paying 5-percent better than the going rate of wages in these countries, and feels that this is fair enough. Working conditions at suppliers' factories are no worse than at other factories in those countries. The CEO has come to you to check her assumptions that as long as the suppliers are buying from manufacturing plants that have better-than-average working conditions for the country where the company is located, nothing further needs to be done. What would you advise her? How would you justify your advice?

Exploring the World Wide Web

SPECIFIC ASSIGNMENT

This exercise follows up on the activities of McDonald's Corporation (www.mcdonalds.com), which is vertically integrating on a global level. Research McDonald's website to get a feel for this global giant. In particular, focus on McDonald's most recent annual report and its descriptions of the company's goals and objectives.

1. What are the main elements of McDonald's strategy at the corporate, business, and functional levels?
2. How successful has the company been recently?
3. Has the strategy of McDonald's Canada been any different than its parent operation's?

GENERAL ASSIGNMENT

Search for a website that contains a good description of a company's strategy. What is the company's mission? Use the concepts and terminology of this chapter to describe the company's strategy to achieve its mission.

Developing a Business Plan

(APPENDIX B, PAGE 405)

Go to www.mcgrawhill.ca/olc/jones/5 for online exercises.

Be the Manager

BEYOND THE GREEN DOOR

The Green Door restaurant is a vegetarian restaurant in Ottawa, Canada, with an "eye and palette . . . focused on nourishment drawn from the local, organic, seasonal, natural, wholesome, comforting and colourful."[67] The restaurant is situated directly across from Saint Paul University[68] (part of the University of Ottawa and home to about 1000 undergraduate and graduate students in such disciplines as spirituality, philosophy, human sciences, pastoral counselling, and conflict studies). OttawaPlus.ca considers the Green Door "heaven for vegetarians" and an Ottawa institution.[69]

Questions

1. What are the vegetarian restaurants in the city where you live? Do a SWOT analysis as to their strengths and weaknesses.
2. Look up reviews on the Green Door on the Internet. If the Green Door wanted to expand, what kind of business-level strategy should it pursue?

Management Case

Creating a Critical Information Service[70]

From having $10 in her pocket to creating critical information service

Jim Blake divides the 37 years he has spent practising law in Toronto into two distinct periods: BRA (before Rani Advani) and ARA (after Rani Advani). The reason is simple: Advani's expertise with search engines and her intuitive grasp of the needs of the legal profession have revolutionized the way Mr. Blake and thousands like him do business.

Research chores that once took days, if not weeks, now can be handled by Mr. Blake or his legal clerks in minutes thanks to Advani, he says. Corporations can be incorporated electronically in less time than it takes to softboil an egg. Searching for and filing liens against personal property once had to be done on a county-by-county basis. Today, Mr. Blake simply enters a name and clicks the mouse; software created by Rani Advani does the rest.

"Rani is absolutely brilliant with search engines," Mr. Blake, a partner at McLean & Kerr LLP in Toronto, says. "I think she has an intuitive understanding of what her clients need. She has also become a trusted gatekeeper for the province, the federal government and dozens of other organizations and agencies."

Advani's company is OnCorp Direct Inc. of Toronto. Its services focus on online search engines and electronic filing of documents at both the federal and provincial government levels. Customers cover a wide range of corporate and individual users. Banks and lending institutions go to OnCorp to register or search for liens when making personal loans. Individuals who want to register a business name can pay a one-time fee for what is known as a nuance search. Federal and Ontario corporations large and small can use OnCorp to update company information.

"It is an absolutely wonderful service," says Helen Nicholls, a law clerk at Fraser Milner Casgrain LLP in Toronto. "I have been doing this for about 30 years and before Rani's service, it was all an onerous chore. Everything had to be done manually and in person." That meant going to the office of the province's Ministry of Consumer and Corporate Affairs to incorporate or make any changes to provincial companies or off to the Ontario Securities Commission to do the same with publicly traded companies. "You had to have agents in or near each of the county seats right across the province," Mr. Blake says. "What once took days, today takes us minutes."

Turning days into minutes has been a passion, Advani says.

"What I love to do is look at something that takes 10 processes and bring that down to two or three," she says. "I thrive on taking the complicated and making it transparent." While her success with search engines and as electronic gatekeeper for government departments is worthy of note, the story of how she got there is even more remarkable. Rani Advani, who was born and raised in Mumbai, India, landed in Canada in 1969 with $10 in her pocket and a bursary to pursue a master's degree in French at the University of Waterloo. She arrived at the university residence on a Saturday and everything was closed. "I couldn't even work the vending machines," she says.

After graduation, she was unhappy about her prospects: She could become a teacher or a translator, but neither appealed. She embarked on a string of what she describes as "not very satisfactory jobs", until, on a whim, she attended a seminar on entrepreneurship at what is now Ryerson University.

"I got hooked," she says. "I wanted more than anything to work for myself. The challenge was finding something I could do with the few resources at my disposal."

A friend came up with an idea. The federal government was about to enter the e-commerce age. During 1977 and 1978, it would make nuance searches available electronically. Nuance search is the fanciful title given to corporate name searches. Anyone considering registering a company or trade name must first conduct a nuance search to make sure the name chosen does not infringe on names already in use.

"I thought this was something I could do, so in 1978 I started my own little one-person company," Ms. Advani says. It was known as National Corporate Name Clearance Co. From Bell Canada, she leased a dumb terminal [without processing capabilities] connected directly to a federal government computer. Then she began looking for clients.

"I started by leasing an IBM Selectric typewriter—I still have it—and sent out 1000 letters to everyone in the legal directory offering my services," she says. "I got a surprisingly good response and I was suddenly in business." Advani very quickly saw the potential of the new information technology and its powerful ability to automate repetitive tasks. While her dumb terminal connected her to the federal database, her ability to earn money rested on the number of hours she spent repeating the same instructions on the keyboard.

"I wanted to automate the process right from order-taking to invoices," she explains. "I wanted to differentiate myself from the others through value-added services for clients. To do that, she hired a software engineer to create soup-to-nuts search applications, and hired a friend of the engineer to build a personal computer for her from scratch.

"It cost me $10 000 and was as big as a desk, but it worked and worked well," she says," As the technology expanded exponentially, Advani tapdanced on what she calls "the bleeding edge."

"I always tried to stay ahead of the curve. We added more and more services, and by the 1980s I had 15 people working for me."

By the early 1990s, she had created what amounted to a precursor to the Internet. She sold clients proprietary software that enabled them to enter the terms of a search. Their computers connected with hers, and her computer connected with government databases. "We did the search for them and returned the information in an easy-to-understand format," she explains. "That is when business really started to grow."

As Jim Blake says: "Rani was one of the very few people with an almost immediate grasp of what the new technology could do. She was absolutely brilliant when it came to search engines."

As one of the few established names in the fast-developing e-search industry, Advani was a natural choice when the Ontario government decided to put a range of business services online in 1997 through the newly created Ontario Business Information System (ONBIS).

"We had enjoyed a long working relationship and had proven software. The government chose two companies to effectively be the gatekeeper for ONBIS and we were one of them," she says.

The idea was sound but the execution lacking, at least in its early days, Advani says. Right up to 2000, the fibre backbone of the Internet was not robust enough to ensure uninterrupted service. Internet service providers would have technical problems, the Web would crash and OnCorp Direct would get the blame. Besides only about five to 10 of every 100 clients had Internet access.

"By 2000, everything had changed," she says. "What kept us going was that we worked hard to keep clients happy. The problems corrected themselves as more and more people flocked to the Internet."

Today, at age 58, Rani Advani is about to set out in a new direction. Her operations manager, Eric Tong, will keep the day-today business humming along while she focuses on the next direction. The company is in the midst of introducing the ability to search government and corporate databanks previously closed to Internet users, such as patent searches.

"We have won approvals and permissions and will slowly roll that out," she says. She is also intent on exploring business opportunities in her native India. She is heading there soon for the 40th anniversary of her high school graduating class. "I think there is enormous potential in India," she says. "What I want to do is meet people, see things, explore possibilities. Eric will handle the grass-roots level. It will be my job to grow the business at a higher level."

Questions

1. How would you analyze the nature of competition in OnCorp Direct Inc.'s industry by using Porter's Five Forces Model?
2. What types of business strategies is Rani Advani using to stay competitive in her industry?

Video Management Case

EBay: Report on the World of Online Auctions

This video reports on EBay's phenomenal growth into a company facilitating online auctions of products in over 4300 different categories. Due to recent auction frauds, EBay is under question for being liable for dealing in fakes. They claim it is the seller's responsibility and that they are merely making a platform for Internet exchanges to happen. Regardless of responsibility, the company has had to adapt by hiring a number of full-time legal staff to resolve buying disputes occurring regularly.

Questions to Consider

1. Will a consultation with professional EBay sellers give directions for the company's future plans to improve on servicing the new industry of buying and selling they helped to create?
2. Should the company intervene when purchases are at the discretion of the consumer? What steps can EBay take to prevent fraudulent auctions from happening?

Part 3: Integrated Case

Window of Opportunity[71]

Well-designed portals provide essential information to clients and employees

If you think your website is simply a window into your company's information, think again. Portal technology can breathe new life into back-end applications—if only companies can learn to build them properly.

NAV Canada, which provides air traffic control information to airlines travelling over Canadian airspace, is saving its clients thousands of dollars with a Web portal designed to supply up-to-the-minute information. The company decided to create a portal—

a personalized Web-based window providing access to multiple online resources simultaneously—after realizing it was obstructing information flowing from NAV Canada's internal departments.

"My group was the bottleneck for that information because every document had to be tagged and published," says Don Kelly, director of information management and enterprise security technology for the company. Building a portal allowed internal departments to manage and publish their content online themselves rather than submitting it to the IT department for processing.

Ten years ago, many companies began producing intranets, which are internal websites with information for employees. Some also allowed suppliers and customers to access parts of those internal websites, creating what is known as an extranet.

Intranets and extranets were often interactive, enabling people to access software services delivered in a browser, but portals make information more relevant to the viewer. They store information about people who use the portals, presenting them with personalized information and services when they log in.

A portal also can offer different software applications in a single browser window. This creates a kind of business dashboard, making it easier to carry out lots of tasks by putting them all in one place rather than making the employee visit different Web pages for each task.

"From an employee perspective, a mechanism that integrates this and creates an experience for them is what a portal does," says Shem Asefaw, principal of human resources consulting firm Mercer, which builds HR portals for clients. "It brings these services together and puts them in a context that the employee understands."

To make access even easier, many portals provide single sign-on technology, enabling an employee to log in using one username and password. The portal then automatically logs into multiple back-end software applications for the user, even though they may all require different login credentials.

Alongside traditional company directories often found on intranets and accessible by everyone, portals might let employees book their vacation time and training courses, while managers would be able to review employees' salaries or evaluate key performance indicators for their departments—all on one screen.

NAV Canada's portal provides personalized information to its airline clients, letting them access different kinds of information including flight times and schedules. It is developing the ability to report on flight delays several hundred miles out.

"If a dispatcher sees that delays in Toronto are going to mean another 10 minutes waiting time before boarding, they can wait another 10 minutes before they start the airplane's jets," he says. With fuel prices so high, such information can add up to substantial savings.

Despite today's successes, Asefaw says portals got off to a shaky start. "In the old days, the idea was that if you built your portal, people would come. But guess what? They didn't." Many portals would vacuum up thousands of dollars from the IT department's budget, and would then go unused by personnel.

Early portal developers got ahead of themselves by building the portal first and deciding what to put into it afterward, says John Sloan, senior research analyst at Info-Tech Research in London, Ontario.

"Five years ago, a portal was just a cool idea, and you built it and then moved backwards from there," he recalls. "These days, you focus on the business process and the portal comes later."

NAV Canada suffered from this problem at first. "When the portal came along, we went through a period where the technology guys didn't know how to manage a portal and the customers didn't understand how to use it. There was some information that went out of date very quickly," Mr. Kelly says. "Over the past year or so, the flavour of that has changed."

Working out what you want to accomplish and then building a portal around it has helped the concept evolve. Portals moved from enterprise data browsing applications to community systems enabling employees to collaborate with each other, says Paul Ciandrini, president of Plumtree Software, which provided NAV Canada's portal.

"The third evolution is integrated activity management," Mr. Ciandrini says. In this model, the portal becomes more than just a collaboration tool for tasks such as scheduling meetings and working on business documents. It becomes a software application in its own right, offering interfaces personalized for employees to carry out specific tasks. These might use data and services from different back-end systems such as sales-lead tracking, customer support and supply chain management, but instead of having to access each individually in the portal, the employee uses a personalized Web form.

NAV Canada's Mr. Kelly might not be quite there yet, but he is extending his portal's functions both internally and externally. The internal portal brings together various departmental applications, including a set of business reporting products. "In the past, they would have been printed reports or distributed e-mails, but by combining the portal environment and the business intelligence, it gives us a more interactive delivery," he says.

"Managers go in whenever they want and pick it up." He is now developing the ability to deliver relevant documents to employees in different departments, such as manuals for engineers.

If your intranet or extranet doesn't include a personalized portal that brings information and services from different systems together into a single place, you could be missing out on an excellent way to increase their usefulness. Failure to make computing resources more accessible could ground the productivity of your back-end software. Get it right, and return on investment from your existing applications could really take off.

Discussion Questions

1. What types of decision making biases may have been at work in this case situation?
2. What was the new vision established by NAV Canada in regard to portal technology?

PART 4 Organizing

CHAPTER 6

Managing Organizational Structure

Learning Outcomes

1. Identify the factors that influence managers' choice of an organizational structure.

2. Explain how managers group tasks into jobs that are motivating and satisfying for employees.

3. Describe the organization structures managers can design and explain why they choose one structure over another.

4. Explain how to coordinate functions and divisions and how authority must be distributed.

5. Describe overall structures of organizations, whether they be flexible or formal, and how each is determined by conditions of the environment.

6. Explain why managers who see new ways to increase efficiency and effectiveness are using strategic alliances and network strategies.

Hierarchies and Chaords

Heaven is purpose, principle, and people. Purgatory is paper and procedure. Hell is rules and regulations. — Dee Hock, founder of Visa International[1]

To Dr. [Elliott] Jaques [1917–2003], the management hierarchy—in its pure form, almost never fully achieved in practice—evolved as a natural vehicle for expressing the capabilities and limits that are innate in each of us as Homo sapiens.—Art Kleiner, co-author (with Peter Senge et al.) of the bestselling *Fifth Discipline Fieldbook* (1994), *The Dance of Change* (1999), and *Schools That Learn* (2000).[2]

Two different visions of structure emerge with the above quotes. And yet, when we read what Dee Hock and Elliott Jaques attempted to do, their visions were noble. The issue of structure and design matters to people, and it matters to organizations. Organizational structure lays out the framework for how the organization will exist and work. Different structures will cause different consequences to emerge.

Let's listen to Dr. Elliott Jaques' case for organizational structure[3]

He claims to have uncovered the predominant form of successful human organizations that existed at the dawn of recorded or "post-tribal" history, as he puts it. Contrary to contemporary people's stereotypical images of organizational structure, what we call the "hierarchy" or "bureaucracy" is not, by nature, a repressive entity. When he has presented this vision in his talks and when someone objects to this claim, he asks the person, "Let me guess. You never had a job in a large organization which used your talents effectively."

Do you work in heaven, purgatory, or hell? It all depends on how your organization is structured.

And that's the key for Jaques. While he is both accepted and rejected for his claims, Jaques insists that properly conceived and implemented, a hierarchical structure allows people to perform at their optimum. He refers to his vision of organizational structure as the "requisite organization" that lays out the best way—at least, according to Jaques' view and research—of what is best for each employee. As such, employees will be drawn into positions that fit them well—that are neither too simple nor too challenging. This possibility allows measurement of their human potential. While his theory, for some, smacks of "ability profiling" with certain employees capable of "x" position in an organization, the theory also explains why one person might become CEO while relegating another to the factory floor. People who have followed through with Jaques' ideas for their organization include Betsy Watson, formerly the chief of police in Austin, Texas and then in Houston, Texas[4]; Shell Oil[5] internal consultant Bill Brenneman; and Tom Helton, a former Whirlpool human resources executive who is now a vice-president at a $4-billion Fortune 500 company called United Stationers Inc.[6] For each of these people, the requisite approach gave them a way to deal with the frustrations and futility of the conventional organizations where they had worked. In Canada, the Bank of Montreal[7] and Hydro One Inc.[8] have begun implementing Jaques' ideas.

Jaques' thesis and research shows that the true fit between a person and a job, depends on the match between the "time span" of the job and the potential capabilities of the person (people's ability to handle cognitive complexity). One's ability, then, prescribes the amount of time a job will take. This time span could be for a job that requires three months, a year, two years, five years, or more. The controversial piece comes in when Jaques claims that a person's "time horizon" is more or less predetermined or hardwired into them, into who they are and break into eight levels or "strata." While one can progress to the next level of complexity, it can take 15 years for a "leap" to occur. For many, we reach our maximum complexity contribution, if you will, and in taking responsibility for our place in this "hierarchy" of organizational structure, we fulfill our potential and are best at work in the organization. In working with unionized employees in the late 1940s, when he worked with the Tavistock Institute in London, England, he realized the issue of what he came to call "felt-fair pay," a compensation concept that said pay should be correlated with the length of time it took to carry out the longest-running assignment for a job. That's when the idea of "strata" came to him. "The fit between time-horizon levels and strata determines how comfortable we will feel at various positions in a hierarchy." See Table 6.1 below for a visual explanation.

While there are pros and cons to this system, Dr. Elliott Jaques' claim to fame is that this design and organizational structure allows for managerial accountability since every manager has to account for his/her subordinates and provide the tools and opportunities for them to succeed.

Let's listen to Dee Hock's case for organizational structure[9]

Dee Hock, founder of the now very famous Visa International symbol and organization believes that "an invisible organization" is best. Says Hock, "It's the results, not the structure or management that should be apparent."

In 1968, with the credit card industry in its infancy and out of control, Dee Hock, then a 38-year-old vice-president at a licensee bank in Seattle, was made chairperson of a committee in Columbus, Ohio to find a solution. He grabbed the opportunity.

TABLE 6.1 |

Strata	Explanation
I	These jobs might include shop floor operator, salesclerk, or general police officer; most work is routine, and supervision is commonplace for new tasks. Such jobs are good fits for "level one" people, who can cope with thinking about a time horizon of one day to three months.
II	First-line managers, shop-floor supervisors, forepersons, proprietors of some small businesses, and police lieutenant positions have a felt-fair pay level of one-and-one-half times what a Stratum I employee might get. This job fits people with a three-month to one-year time horizon (who can handle assignments that take that long to fulfill).
III	Department heads, workshop managers, owners of multistore franchises, and police captains would make felt-fair pay that was three times that of a Stratum I employee. Stratum III managers typically know personally all the people below them in a hierarchy. Many professionals with high technical skill levels operate at this level, managing just a few people. People with a time horizon of one to two years can handle this.
IV	A plant manager, editor of a large media operation, lab manager, or any line leader with responsibility for diverse constituencies would earn felt-fair pay six times that of Stratum I. Appropriate time horizon: two to five years.
V	Positions at this level include large-company divisional executives, business-unit heads (at the vice-presidential level), production directors, and CEOs of 5000-employee organizations. Most "zealot" jobs are probably Stratum V positions. Felt-fair pay: 12 times Stratum I. Time horizon: five to 10 years.
VI	From here on out, the air gets rarefied. Positions include CEOs of companies with 20 000 people, or executive vice-presidents and business-unit leaders of larger companies. Felt-fair pay: 24 times Stratum I. Time horizon: 10 to 20 years.
VII	Positions include CEOs of most Fortune 500 companies, high-level civil servants (like the Sir Humphrey character in "Yes Minister"), and other leaders whose decisions might (or should) be sweeping enough to take decades to fully realize. Felt-fair pay: 48 times Stratum I. Time horizon: 20 to 50 years.
VIII	The CEOs of General Electric Company, the General Motors Corporation, and other super-corporations have Stratum VIII jobs, with a felt-fair pay level 96 times that of Stratum I. If you are chosen for such a job, you'd better be one of those rare people (like Jack Welch) with an innate time horizon of 50 to 100 years, or your corporation will probably decline.
IX	Stratum IX and higher: Now we move beyond the mere CEO level, to the geniuses who operate on behalf of society's far future, or whose work embodies extraordinary complexity . . . for example, Christ, Buddha, Confucius, Mozart, Galileo, Einstein, Gandhi, Winston Churchill, and a few business leaders like Konosuke Matsushita and Alfred Sloan, who graduate from running Stratum VIII companies to looking out for society's development. As for how felt-fair pay fits these people, consider the writer James Joyce: he spent his life in poverty!

Before taking over the Seattle bank, he had already turned down fast-track jobs at three separate financial companies, claiming that hierarchical, rule-based, control-everything organizations were stifling creativity and initiative at the grass roots. The result? An organization too rigid to respond to new challenges and opportunities. What's interesting about Hock is his broad interest in many areas. He quit community college after only two years, but he read voraciously in many areas and didn't worry about disciplinary boundaries. These areas included history, economics, politics, science, philosophy, and poetry. This is an important clue because today's success in the new economy depends both on the rational but also on the intuitive side of the organization: right brain, left brain. Some even claim that managers need an MFA (Master of Fine Arts) more than an MBA (Master of Business Administration)![10] Former editor of The *Globe and Mail*, William Thorsell, writes, "Liberal arts degrees were considered a waste of time for years, but no longer." And, in another editorial column, writes, "Do students of international relations realize how important personal feelings are in colouring the course of events? Probably not. They believe the old saw that nations have no friends, only interests, and they therefore underestimate the personal factor in international relations. Ideas make the world; emotions make the world go "round"; management schools should teach more Shakespeare."[11]

Dee Hock had a deep conviction that if he were ever to design and structure an organization, he would conceive of it based on biological concepts and metaphors. In June 1970, after nearly two years of brainstorming, planning, arguing, and consensus-building, this new organization did emerge, later to be called Visa International. Dee W. Hock was its new CEO.

Hock designed the structure to be highly decentralized and highly collaborative. Authority, initiative, decision making, wealth—everything possible is pushed out to the periphery of the organization, to the members. The result? These other member banks had to cooperate and work together intensely, even though they also competed fiercely. The system could only work that way for any of the banks in the system to honour and accept another bank's Visa card—anywhere! Cooperation meant that these merchant-member banks had to participate in a common clearinghouse operation, reconcile all the accounts, make sure merchants got paid for each purchase, clear the transactions between banks, and bill customers appropriately.

The organizational structure for all this? Hock said, "It was beyond the power of reason to design an organization to deal with such complexity and beyond the reach of the imagination to perceive all the conditions it would encounter." Instead, "the organization had to be based on biological concepts to evolve, in effect, to invent and organize itself." So, the structure was an organic organizational structure! Visa has been called "a corporation whose product is coordination." Hock calls it "an enabling organization."

> Hock eventually saw that his system for design and structure took in both the "edge of chaos" and "order." Hence, his term "chaordic."[12] This design would encourage as much competition and initiative as possible throughout the organization—"chaos"—while building in mechanisms for cooperation—"order."

According to Linda Rising, Ph.D., whose research is in the area of object-based design metrics, she outlines the chaordic characteristic of the projects she has studied:[13]

1. Power and functionality need to be distributed to the lowest level possible, that is, don't hand off responsibility for something to higher levels in an organization when it can be done by those on a lower level.

2. Instead of a chain of command, create a framework for dialogue, deliberation, and coordination among equals, that is, authority comes from the bottom up, not the top down.

3. Take a minimalist approach to rules, that is, minimize the use of rules because people will tend to follow them, even to points of absurdity!

The final word goes to Dee Hock:

> All organizations are merely conceptual embodiments of a very old, very basic idea—the idea of community. "They can be no more or less than the sum of the beliefs of the people drawn to them; of their character, judgments, acts, and efforts," Hock says. "An organization's success has enormously more to do with clarity of a shared purpose, common principles and strength of belief in them than to assets, expertise, operating ability, or management competence, important as they may be."[14]

Now It's Your Turn

Think of the two visions of organizational structure presented in the opening case scenario.

1. What structure would best fit you personally? Why?

2. What are employees looking for today in terms of organizational structure?

3. What are pros and cons to Dr. Elliott Jaques' vision of "strata"?

4. What do you think Dee Hock means by the "invisible organization"?

5. What does Hock mean by organic design for an organization?

■■■■ Overview

The opening scenario to this chapter allows us to see two different visions of organizational structure: hierarchical and chaordic. For Dr. Elliot Jaques, the hierarchy, when set up and managed the way it's supposed to be, brings out the best in employees and produces the most effective results for the organization. For Dee Hock, the chaordic organization design is best because "the better an organization is, the less obvious it is." Two very different visions, two very different consequences for employees and the organization.

In Part 4, we examine how managers can organize human and other resources to create high performing organizations. To organize, managers must design an organization that makes the best use of resources to produce the goods and services customers want.

By the end of this chapter, you will be familiar not only with various organizational structures but also with various factors that determine the organizational design choices that managers make. Then in Chapter 7, we examine issues surrounding the organization's culture and what it takes for an organization to achieve change.

Designing Organizational Structure

THINK ABOUT IT

FarmFolk/CityFolk Society[15]

The FarmFolk/CityFolk Society in Vancouver, B.C. is a non-profit society that wants one simple thing: for people to eat local, fresh, seasonal foods grown using farming practices that contribute to the health of the planet, and is an example of a Canadian organization that has embraced the chaordic design. Their extensive website covers their projects, their vision, their supporters, and their outreach. When they talk about contribution "to the health of the planet," it is easy to see that they do, in fact, "walk the talk," and that a chaordic structure is quite fitting to what they do and hope to accomplish. According to FarmFolk/CityFolk,

> We are evolving a way of work and an organizational model that we feel is appropriate for community action in the 21st century. We are consciously creating a learning organization with a "chaordic" model . . . an organization that

embodies as much diversity as possible (chaos) with strong mechanisms for cooperation (order). FarmFolk/CityFolk has all the characteristics of a chaordic organization: it is highly decentralized and highly collaborative and (like a living organism) is complex, adaptive and self-organizing. It constantly spins off new projects and new organizations or coalitions.[16]

You Be the Manager

1. How does FarmFolk/CityFolk embrace the chaordic design for their organizational structure?

organizational structure
A formal system of both task and reporting relationships that coordinates and motivates organizational members so that they work together to reach organizational goals.

organizational design
The process by which managers make specific organizing choices that result in a particular kind of organizational structure.

Organizing is the process by which managers establish the structure of working relationships among employees to allow them to achieve organizational goals efficiently and effectively. **Organizational structure** is the formal system of task and reporting relationships that determines how employees use resources to reach organizational goals.[17] **Organizational design** is the process by which managers make specific organizing choices that result in the construction of a particular organizational structure.[18]

How do managers design a structure? The way an organization's structure works depends on the organizing choices managers make about four issues:

• how to group tasks into individual jobs;

• how to group jobs into functions and divisions;

• how to coordinate and allocate authority in the organization among jobs, functions, and divisions;

• whether to pursue a more formal or flexible structure.

Grouping Tasks into Jobs: Job Design

THINK ABOUT IT

Design: Competitive Weapon, Innovation Driver[19]

Dr. Roger Martin, dean of the University of Toronto's Rotman School of Management, says that design "has emerged as a new competitive weapon and key driver of innovation for organizations." He goes on to say that "leveraging the power of design across all aspects of a business can establish and sustain an organization's unique competitive advantage."

According to *Fast Company* magazine, in the real world of design, designers frequently cross disciplines, from architecture to graphic arts to industrial design to film to animation. The purpose of this interrelationship of disciplines is to reflect its sense of boundarylessness and from this perspective to embrace and reframe it in a new way. Design is like business and must be in the service of solving problems. That is why Martin says that "design skills and business skills are converging." Design, therefore, matters to all employees because of its impact beyond the organization. For example, think of an organization's design efforts as they impact sales and marketing efforts. The implications are huge.

You Be the Manager ————————————————————————

1. What are some additional implications of the organization design?

2. Can you think of an example where poor organization had disastrous consequences?

The first step in organizational design is **job design**, the process by which managers decide how to divide tasks into specific jobs. Managers at McDonald's, for example, have decided how best to divide the tasks required to provide customers with fast, cheap food in each McDonald's restaurant. After experimenting with different job arrangements, McDonald's managers decided on a basic division of labour among chefs and food servers. Managers allocated all the tasks involved in actually cooking the food (putting oil in the fat fryers, opening packages of frozen french fries, putting beef patties on the grill, making salads, and so on) to the job of chef. They allocated all the tasks involved in giving the food to customers (such as greeting customers; taking orders; putting fries and burgers into bags; adding salt, pepper, and serviettes; and taking money) to food servers. They also created other jobs—the job of dealing with drive-through customers, the job of keeping the restaurant clean, and the job of shift manager responsible for overseeing employees and responding to unexpected events. The result of the job design process is a *division of labour* among employees, one that McDonald's and other managers have discovered through experience is most efficient.

Establishing an appropriate division of labour among employees is a critical part of the organizing process, one that is vital to increasing efficiency and effectiveness. At McDonald's, the tasks associated with chef and food server were split into different jobs because managers found that, for the kind of food McDonald's serves, this approach was most efficient. When employees are given fewer tasks to perform (so that their jobs become more specialized), they become more productive at performing the tasks that constitute their job.

A strict division of labour is not the only way to organize jobs in a fast food restaurant, however. At Subway sandwich shops, there is no division of labour among the people who make the sandwiches, wrap the sandwiches, give them to customers,

job design
The process by which managers decide how to divide tasks into specific jobs.

Workers in assembly lines follow carefully designed work procedures. Too much job simplification may reduce efficiency if boredom sets in.

and take the money. The roles of chef and food server are combined into one role. This different division of tasks and jobs is efficient for Subway and not for McDonald's because Subway serves a limited menu of mostly submarine-style sandwiches that are prepared to order. Subway's production system is far simpler than McDonald's, because McDonald's menu is much more varied and its chefs must cook many different kinds of foods.

Managers of every organization must analyze the range of tasks to be performed and then create jobs that best allow the organization to give customers the goods and services they want. In deciding how to assign tasks to individual jobs, however, managers must be careful not to go too far with **job simplification**—the process of reducing the number of tasks that each employee performs.[20] Too much job simplification may reduce efficiency rather than increase it if workers find their simplified jobs boring and monotonous, become demotivated and unhappy, and as a result perform at a low level.

Job Enlargement and Job Enrichment

Researchers have looked at ways to create a division of labour and design individual jobs to encourage employees to perform at a higher level and be more satisfied with their work. Based on this research, they have proposed job enlargement and job enrichment as better ways than job simplification to group tasks into jobs.

Job enlargement increases the *number of different tasks* in a given job by changing the division of labour.[21] For example, because Subway food servers make the food as well as serve it, their jobs are "larger" than the jobs of McDonald's food servers. The idea behind job enlargement is that increasing the range of tasks performed by an employee will reduce boredom and fatigue and may increase motivation to perform at a high level—increasing both the quantity and the quality of goods and services provided.

Job enrichment increases the *degree of responsibility* a worker has over his or her job by, for example, (1) empowering employees to experiment to find new or better ways of doing the job, (2) encouraging employees to develop new skills, (3) allowing employees to decide how to do the work and giving them the responsibility for deciding

job simplification

Reducing the number of tasks that each worker performs.

job enlargement

Increasing the number of different tasks in a given job by changing the division of labour.

job enrichment

Increasing the degree of responsibility a worker has over his or her job.

Mario Coculuzzi, senior producer of the Xbox 360 version of the game *King Kong*, shows off a scene from the game at the Ubisoft studios in Montreal.

how to respond to unexpected situations, and (4) allowing employees to monitor and measure their own performance.[22] The idea behind job enrichment is that increasing employees' responsibility increases their involvement in their jobs and thus increases their interest in the quality of the goods they make or the services they provide.

In general, managers who make design choices that increase job enrichment and job involvement are likely to increase the degree to which workers behave flexibly rather than rigidly or mechanically. Narrow, specialized jobs are likely to lead people to behave in predictable ways; employees who perform a variety of tasks and who are allowed and encouraged to discover new and better ways to perform their jobs are likely to act flexibly and creatively. Thus, managers who enlarge and enrich jobs create a flexible organizational structure, and those who simplify jobs create a more formal structure. If employees are also grouped into self-managed work teams, the organization is likely to be flexible because team members provide support for each other and can learn from one another.

For example, the video-game development industry has earned a reputation as a sweatshop. However, the design of how work gets done is beginning to change, says Cédric Orvoine, Canadian spokesperson for Ubisoft, whose largest studio is in Montreal, Québec. For him, "It's all a matter of doing your planning and your milestones efficiently so you can get your game done in time without burning out people." Trevor Fencott, president of Toronto games publisher Groove Games, says that although a passion for video games drives many workers to put in long hours voluntarily, two years ago Ubisoft Montreal established a *bureau de project*, a workplace design involving a team of 60 people dedicated to planning and streamlining game production. Instead of a single producer being responsible for each project, now each management team also includes a human resources staffer and a planner. "We're working really hard to make sure that the crunch periods are as short as possible," Orvoine says. In addition, he says, the company offers bonuses and time off at the end of the project to compensate for crunch time.[23]

Grouping Jobs into Functions and Divisions

THINK ABOUT IT

Becoming More Like Design Shops[24]

Design skills and business skills are converging. To be successful in the future, business people will have to become more like designers—more "masters of heuristics" than "managers of algorithms."—Dr. Roger Martin, Dean of the University of Toronto's Rotman School of Management

A heuristic is the ability to visualize and invent; it is both an art and a science. We could say that Wayne Gretzky in playing hockey did so heuristically. The science was in his ability to understand the game of hockey and to play it well; the art was in his ability to know where the puck would be, not where it was at.

Roger Martin (dean of the Rotman School at the University of Toronto) is once again reminding us that we need more heuristics —a way of understanding the world and the people in it—than algorithms—packaging or routinizing a solution in a certain way; we need a greater sense of discovery than simply to solve what is right in front of us. Key companies that succeeded with these kinds of solution-driven algorithms were McDonald's (mass-produced hamburgers), Procter & Gambling (brand management success) and Wal-Mart stores (superior processes). We could say that these companies 'took the mystery' out of hamburgers, brands, and processes, and developed very efficient formulae (algorithms).

Today, in designing organizations, developing *perspective* is more important than "Is this your final answer?" In a world that is constantly changing, the older "formula-producing" design (or code) for company success is now too static. In an effort to get customers back into their stores, for example, they have had to try different approaches with different menus precisely because the old formula or algorithm is running out of steam. As for our future designs, Roger Martin says, "I believe we are transitioning into a 21st century world in which value creation is moving back to the world of taking mysteries and turning them into heuristics. . . . The 21st century presents us with an opportunity to delve into mysteries and come up with new heuristics."

Some of the "mysteries" that organizations are now facing include such questions as: What do customers really want? How do we as an organization enable our employees to become "masters of heuristics" more than "masters of algorithms"? These question harken back to what William Thorsell, former editor of The *Globe and Mail*, who reminded us that we need "more Shakespeare" (mysteries/heuristics) and "less Adam Smith" (algorithms/code). Table 6.2 shows how this shift will look.[25]

You Be the Manager

1. What are some "design" conclusions you can make from what Roger Martin says?
2. Review Table 6.2. What are some implications of grouping jobs into functions and divisions?

TABLE 6.2 | ***Modern Firms Must Become More Like Design Shops***

Feature	From "Traditional Firm . . ."	. . . To "Design Shop"
Flow of Work	Ongoing tasks	Projects
Life	Permanent assignments	Defined Terms
Source of Status	Managing big budgets and large staffs	Solving "wicked problems"
Style of Work	Defined roles	Collaborative
	Wait until it is "right"	Iterative
Mode of Thinking	Deductive	Deductive
	Inductive	Inductive Abductive
Dominant Attitude	We can only do what we have budget to do Constraints are the enemy	Nothing can't be done Constraints increase the challenge and excitement

Once managers have decided which tasks to allocate to which jobs, they face the next organizing decision: how to group jobs together to best match the needs of the organization's environment, strategy, technology, and human resources. Most top-management teams decide to group jobs into departments and develop a functional structure to use organizational resources. As the organization grows, managers design a divisional structure or a more complex matrix or product team structure.

Choosing a structure and then designing it so that it works as intended is a significant challenge. As noted in Chapter 5, managers reap the rewards of a well-thought-out strategy only if they choose a suitable type of structure initially and then execute the strategy. The ability to make the right kinds of organizing choices is often what sets effective and ineffective managers apart.

Functional Structure

A function is a group of people, working together, who possess similar skills or use the same kind of knowledge, tools, or techniques to perform their jobs. Manufacturing, sales, and research and development are often organized into functional departments. A **functional structure** is an organizational structure composed of all the departments that an organization requires to produce its goods or services. Pier 1 Imports, a home furnishings company, uses a functional structure to supply its customers with a range of goods from around the world to satisfy their desires for new and innovative products.

Pier 1's main functions are finance and administration, merchandising (purchasing the goods), stores (managing the retail outlets), logistics (managing product distribution), marketing, human resources, and real estate. Each job inside a function exists because it helps the function perform the activities necessary for high organizational performance. Thus, within the logistics department are all the jobs necessary to distribute and transport products efficiently to stores. Inside the marketing department are all the jobs (such as promotion, photography, and visual communication) that are necessary to increase the appeal of Pier 1's products to customers.

There are several advantages to grouping jobs according to function. First, when people who perform similar jobs are grouped together, they can learn from watching one another. Thus they become more specialized and can perform at a higher level. The tasks associated with one job often are related to the tasks associated with another job, which encourages cooperation within a function. Second, when people who perform similar jobs are grouped together, managers can monitor and evaluate their performance more easily.[26] Finally, as we saw in Chapter 2, managers like functional structure because it allows them to create the set of functions they need for scanning and monitoring the task and general environments.[27]

As an organization grows, and its strategy changes to produce a wider range of goods and services for different kinds of customers, several problems can make a functional structure less efficient and effective.[28] First, managers in different functions may find it more difficult to communicate and coordinate with one another when they are responsible for several different kinds of products, especially as the organization grows both domestically and internationally. Second, functional managers may become so preoccupied with supervising their own specific departments and achieving their departmental goals that they lose sight of organizational goals. If that happens, organizational effectiveness will suffer because managers will be viewing issues and problems facing the organization only from their own, relatively narrow, departmental perspectives.[29] Both of these problems can reduce efficiency and effectiveness.

Divisional Structures: Product, Geographic, and Market

As the problems associated with growth and diversification increase over time, managers must search for new ways to organize their activities to overcome the problems linked with a functional structure. Most managers of large organizations choose a **divisional structure** and create a series of business units to produce a specific kind of product for a specific kind of customer. Each division is a collection of functions or departments that work together to produce the product. The goal behind the change to a divisional structure is to create smaller, more manageable units within the organization. There are three forms of divisional structure (see Figure 6.1).[30]

When managers organize divisions according to the type of good or service they provide, they adopt a *product* structure. When managers organize divisions according to the area of the country or world they operate in, they adopt a *geographic* structure. When managers organize divisions according to the types of customers they focus on, they adopt a *market* structure.

functional structure
An organizational structure composed of all the departments that an organization requires to produce its goods or services.

divisional structure
An organizational structure composed of separate business units within which are the functions that work together to produce a specific product for a specific customer.

FIGURE 6.1 | *Product, Market, and Geographic Structures*

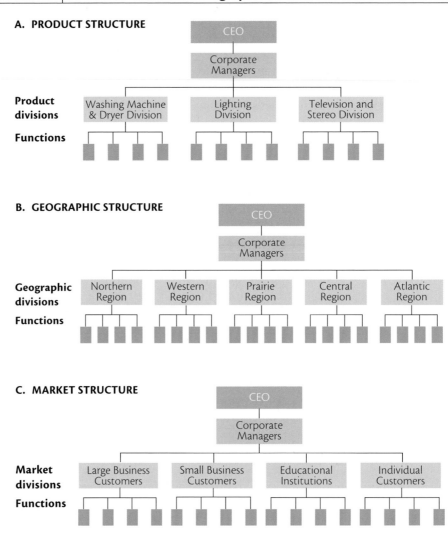

A. PRODUCT STRUCTURE

CEO

Corporate Managers

Product divisions

Washing Machine & Dryer Division | Lighting Division | Television and Stereo Division

Functions

B. GEOGRAPHIC STRUCTURE

CEO

Corporate Managers

Geographic divisions

Northern Region | Western Region | Prairie Region | Central Region | Atlantic Region

Functions

C. MARKET STRUCTURE

CEO

Corporate Managers

Market divisions

Large Business Customers | Small Business Customers | Educational Institutions | Individual Customers

Functions

Product Structure

product structure

An organizational structure in which each product line or business is handled by a self-contained division.

Using a **product structure** (see Figure 6.1A), managers place each distinct product line or business in its own self-contained division and give divisional managers the responsibility for devising an appropriate business-level strategy to allow the division to compete effectively in its industry or market.[31] Each division is self-contained because it has a complete set of all the functions—marketing, R&D, finance, and so on—that it needs to produce or provide goods or services efficiently and effectively. Functional managers report to divisional managers, and divisional managers report to top or corporate managers.

Grouping functions into divisions focused on particular products has several advantages for managers at all levels in the organization. First, a product structure allows functional managers to specialize in only one product area, so they are able to build expertise and fine-tune their skills in this particular area. Second, each division's managers can become experts in their industry; this expertise helps them choose and develop a business-level strategy to differentiate their products or lower their costs while meeting the needs of customers. Third, a product structure frees corporate managers from the need to supervise each division's day-to-day operations directly; this latitude allows corporate managers to create the best corporate-level strategy to maximize the organization's future growth and ability to create value. Corporate managers are likely to make fewer mistakes about which businesses to diversify into or how best to expand internationally, for example, because they are able to take an organization-wide view.[32] Corporate managers also are likely to better evaluate how well divisional managers are doing, and they can intervene and take corrective action as needed.

The extra layer of management, the divisional management layer, can improve the use of organizational resources. Moreover, a product structure puts divisional managers close to their customers and lets them respond quickly and appropriately to the changing task environment. Organizations sometimes change their divisional strategy because of market changes. Even though organizations in the past were generally organized as functional bureaucracies of manufacturing, sales, and R&D, which were coordinated and controlled at the top, today organizations use a complex mix of these structures. For example, AT&T is split into three companies on the basis of product, but continues to use the mix of markets, products, regions, and functions and processes. Its The Network Services Division is structured according to processes such as provisioning, maintenance, leadership, and human resource management.[33] As well, the City of Toronto and its Water Supply and Water Pollution Control Sections, in response to its challenges from new technologies, operations and maintenance practices, and to its business-oriented organizational structures, established the Works Best Practices Program (WBPP) in 2002. The City designed, restructured, and implemented a unique Performance and Operations Management System (POMS) that now consolidates information at all levels, including unit processes, complete plant facilities, and the entire Water Supply and Water Pollution Control Sections. The result: $36 million annual savings.[34]

Geographic Structure

When organizations expand rapidly both at home and abroad, functional structures can create special problems, because managers in one central location may find it increasingly difficult to deal with the different problems and issues that may arise in each region of a country or area of the world. In these cases, a **geographic structure**, in which divisions are broken down by geographical location, is often chosen (see Figure 6.1B). To achieve the corporate mission of providing next-day mail service, Fred Smith, chair, president, and CEO of Federal Express, chose a geographic structure and divided up operations by creating a division in each region. Large retailers often use a geographic structure. Since the needs of retail customers differ by region—for example, umbrellas in Vancouver and down-filled parkas in the Prairies and the East—a geographic structure gives regional retail managers the flexibility they need to choose products that best meet the needs of regional customers.

geographic structure
An organizational structure in which each region of a country or area of the world is served by a self-contained division.

Market Structure

Sometimes, the pressing issue managers face is how to group functions according to the type of customer buying the product, in order to tailor the organization's products to each customer's unique demands. Burnaby, BC-based Telus is structured around six customer-focused business units: Consumer Solutions, focused on households and individuals; Business Solutions, focused on small- to medium-sized businesses and entrepreneurs; Client Solutions, focused on large organizations in Canada; Partner Solutions, focused on Canadian and global carriers into and within Canada; Wireless Solutions, focused on people and businesses on the go; and Telus Québec, a Telus company for the Quebec marketplace.

Telus Communications Inc.
www.telus.com

market structure
An organizational structure in which each kind of customer is served by a self-contained division; also called customer structure.

To satisfy the needs of diverse customers, Telus adopts a **market structure** (also called a *customer structure*), which groups divisions according to the particular kinds of customers they serve (see Figure 6.1C). A market structure allows managers to be both responsive to the needs of their customers and able to act flexibly to make decisions in response to customers' changing needs.

Matrix and Product Team Designs

Moving to a product, market, or geographic divisional structure means managers can respond more quickly and flexibly to the particular set of circumstances they confront. However, when the environment is dynamic and rapidly changing, and uncertainty is high, even a divisional structure may not provide managers with enough flexibility to respond to the environment quickly enough. When technology or customer needs are changing rapidly and the environment is very uncertain, managers must design the most flexible organizational structure available: a matrix structure or a *product team structure* (see Figure 6.2).

FIGURE 6.2 | *Matrix and Product Team Structures*

A. MATRIX STRUCTURE

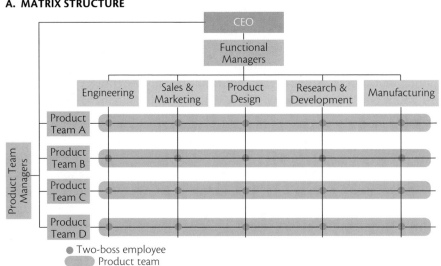

B. PRODUCT TEAM STRUCTURE

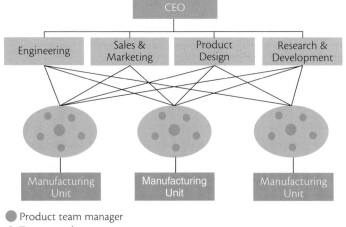

Matrix Structure

In a **matrix structure**, managers group people and resources in two ways simultaneously: by function and by product.[35] Employees are grouped into *functions* to allow them to learn from one another and become more skilled and productive. Employees are also grouped into *product teams*, in which members of different functions work together to develop a specific product. The result is a complex network of reporting relationships among product teams and functions that makes the matrix structure very flexible (see Figure 6.2A). Each person in a product team reports to two managers: (1) a functional manager, who assigns individuals to a team and evaluates their performance from a functional point of view, and (2) the manager of the product team, who evaluates their performance on the team.

The functional employees assigned to product teams change over time as the specific skills that the team needs change. At the beginning of the product development process, for example, engineers and R&D specialists are assigned to a product team because their skills are needed to develop new products. When a provisional design has been established, marketing experts are assigned to the team to gauge how customers will respond to the new product. Manufacturing personnel join when it is time to find the most efficient way to produce the product. As their specific jobs are completed, team members leave and are reassigned to new teams. In this way, the matrix structure makes the most use of human resources.

To keep the matrix structure flexible, product teams are empowered and team members are responsible for making most of the important decisions involved in product development.[36] The product team manager acts as a facilitator, controlling the financial resources and trying to keep the project on time and within budget. The functional managers try to ensure that the product is the best that it can be in order to make the most of its differentiated appeal.

High-tech companies have been using matrix structures successfully for many years. These companies operate in environments where new product developments happen monthly or yearly and the need to innovate quickly is vital to the organization's survival. The matrix structure provides enough flexibility for managers to keep pace with a changing and increasingly complex environment. For this reason, matrixes also have been designed by managers who want to control international operations as they move abroad and face problems of coordinating their domestic and foreign divisions.[37] Motorola, for example, operates a global matrix structure because it hopes to obtain synergies from cooperation among its worldwide divisions.

A global matrix structure allows an organization's domestic divisions to supply its foreign divisions quickly with knowledge about new R&D advances in order to help the foreign divisions gain a competitive advantage in their local markets. Likewise, the foreign divisions can transmit new product marketing ideas to domestic divisions that may give the domestic divisions an advantage in the domestic market. The expression "Think locally but act globally" describes the way managers in global matrix structures should behave.[38]

Product Team Structure

The dual reporting relationships that are at the heart of a matrix structure have always been difficult for managers and employees to deal with. Often, the functional manager and the product manager make conflicting demands on team members, who do not know which manager to satisfy first. Also, functional and product team managers may come into conflict over precisely who is in charge of which team members and for how long. To avoid these problems, managers have devised a way of organizing people and resources that still allows an organization to be flexible but makes its structure easier to operate: a product team structure.

matrix structure
An organizational structure that simultaneously groups people and resources by function and by product.

product team structure
An organizational structure in which employees are permanently assigned to a cross-functional team and report only to the product team manager or to one of his or her direct subordinates.

cross-functional team
A group of individuals from different departments brought together to perform organizational tasks.

The **product team structure** differs from a matrix structure in two ways: (1) It does away with dual reporting relationships for employees, and (2) functional employees are permanently assigned to a cross-functional team that is empowered to bring a new or redesigned product to market. A **cross-functional team** is a group of individuals brought together from different departments to perform organizational tasks. When individuals are grouped into cross-departmental teams, the artificial boundaries between departments disappear, and a narrow focus on departmental goals is replaced with a general interest in working together to achieve organizational goals. The results of such changes have been dramatic: For example, Chrysler Canada's use of cross-functional teams has reduced the time it takes to retool for a new product from months to just weeks.

Members of a cross-functional team report only to the product team manager or to one of his or her direct subordinates. The functional managers have only an informal, advisory relationship with members of the product teams. These managers counsel and help cross-functional team members, share knowledge among teams, and provide new technological developments that can help improve each team's performance (see Figure 6.2B).[39]

Coordinating Functions and Divisions

THINK ABOUT IT

Bureaucracy's Radical Reno[40]

Is it possible that Canada's federal government can act more like businesses on Bay Street? That seems to be what's now taking place—at least when it comes to its procurement policy: public-sector employees behaving more like their private-sector brethren. In practice this will mean that the government, similar to what Wal-Mart does, will attempt to flex its purchasing power muscle in order to get the best deal from suppliers. Scott Brison, Minister of Public Works, whose department is in charge of procurement reform, said, "What we are doing as a government is what large companies did 20 years ago. We can't defend antiquated, expensive, inefficient practices to our neighbours and friends outside of government."

The way the bureaucracy has gone about its business is now being challenged with this initiative. Mike Murphy, senior vice-president at the Canadian Chamber of Commerce, said, "You can't help to agree that this is the right philosophy. These initiatives reflect that the way Ottawa has been doing things needs change. They have to do things much smarter." Obviously a new management culture will result from these changes to the organization structure. The challenges will be immense, of course: reducing the amount of paperwork businesses, large and small, file with bureaucrats; maximizing the value of its real estate properties; and overhauling a regulatory system to ensure harmonization among departments, provinces, and trading partners, most notably the United States.

Up until now, individual government departments or agencies—and there are close to 100 of them—purchased supplies required for its employees. But under the changes envisaged, Public Works would be responsible for a coordinated purchase of goods. Supplies needed would be grouped into roughly 40 commodity buckets, with each bucket managed by a council composed of relevant industry groups and federal procurement specialists.

You Be the Manager

1. Why is the federal government seeking to make changes to its organization structure?

2. What are some of the challenges that these changes will evoke?

In organizing, managers' first task is to group functions and divisions and create the organizational structure best suited to the contingencies they face. Managers' next task is to ensure that there is sufficient coordination among functions and divisions so that organizational resources are used efficiently and effectively. Having discussed how managers divide organizational activities into jobs, functions, and divisions to increase efficiency and effectiveness, we now look at how they put the parts back together.

Allocating Authority

As organizations grow and produce a wider range of goods and services, the size and number of their functions and divisions increase. To coordinate the activities of people, functions, and divisions, and to allow them to work together effectively, managers must develop a clear hierarchy of authority.[41] **Authority** is the power vested in a manager to make decisions and use resources to achieve organizational goals by virtue of his or her position in an organization. The **hierarchy of authority** is an organization's chain of command—the relative authority that each manager has—extending from the CEO at the top, down through the middle managers and first-line managers, to the nonmanagerial employees who actually make goods or provide services. Every manager, at every level of the hierarchy, supervises one or more subordinates. The term **span of control** refers to the number of subordinates who report directly to a manager.

authority
The power to hold people accountable for their actions and to make decisions concerning the use of organizational resources.

hierarchy of authority
An organization's chain of command, specifying the relative authority of each manager.

span of control
The number of subordinates who report directly to a manager.

Tall and Flat Organizations

As an organization grows in size (normally measured by the number of its managers and employees), its hierarchy of authority normally lengthens, making the organizational structure taller. A *tall* organization has many levels of authority relative to company size; a *flat* organization has fewer levels relative to company size (see Figure 6.3).[42] As a hierarchy becomes taller, problems may result that make the organization's structure less flexible and that slow managers' response to changes in the organizational environment.

For instance, communication problems may arise. When an organization has many levels in the hierarchy, it can take a long time for the decisions and orders of upper-level managers to reach managers further down in the hierarchy, and it can take a long time for top managers to learn how well their decisions worked out. Feeling out of touch, top managers may want to verify that lower-level managers are following orders and may require written confirmation from them. Middle managers, who know they will be held strictly accountable for their actions, start devoting more time to the process of making decisions in order to improve their chances of being right. They might even try to avoid responsibility by making top managers decide what actions to take.

Another communication problem that can result is the distortion of commands and orders being transmitted up and down the hierarchy, which causes managers at different levels to interpret differently what is happening. Distortion of orders and messages can be accidental, occurring because different managers interpret messages from their own narrow functional perspectives. Or it can be intentional, occurring because managers low in the hierarchy decide to interpret information to increase their own personal advantage.

FIGURE 6.3 | *Tall and Flat Organizations*

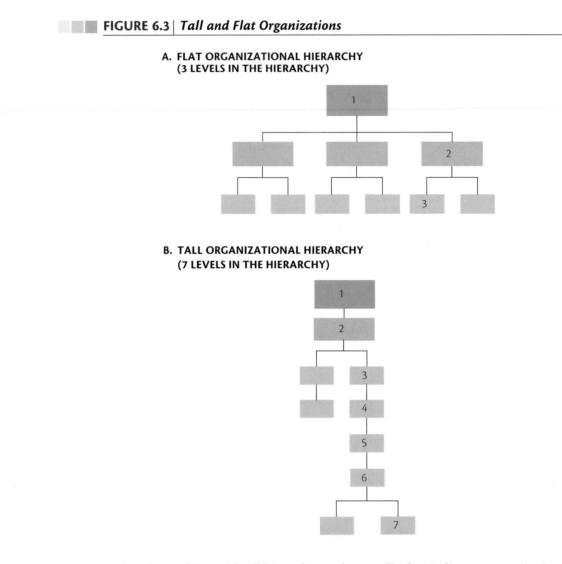

A. FLAT ORGANIZATIONAL HIERARCHY
(3 LEVELS IN THE HIERARCHY)

B. TALL ORGANIZATIONAL HIERARCHY
(7 LEVELS IN THE HIERARCHY)

Another problem with tall hierarchies is that usually they indicate an organization is employing many managers, and managers are expensive. Managerial salaries, benefits, offices, and secretaries are a huge expense for organizations. Large companies such as IBM and General Motors pay their managers billions of dollars a year. Throughout the 1990s, hundreds of thousands of middle managers were laid off as companies tried to reduce costs by restructuring and downsizing their workforces.

The Minimum Chain of Command

To ward off the problems that result when an organization becomes too tall and employs too many managers, top managers need to work out whether they are employing the right number of middle and first-line managers, and to see whether they can redesign their organizational structure to reduce the number of managers. Top managers might well follow a basic organizing principle—the principle of the minimum chain of command—which states that top managers should always construct a hierarchy with the fewest levels of authority necessary to use organizational resources efficiently and effectively.

Effective managers constantly scrutinize their hierarchies to see whether the number of levels can be reduced—for example, by eliminating one level and giving the responsibilities of managers at that level to managers above and empowering employees below. This practice has become more common in Canada and the United States as companies that are battling low-cost foreign competitors search for new ways to reduce costs.

One organization that is trying to empower staff is Ducks Unlimited Canada of Stonewall, Manitoba, a private nonprofit charitable organization, founded by sportsmen, that is devoted to preserving wetlands and associated waterfowl habitats.[43] The company recently went through a reorganization, flattening its management structure. The 330 staff members have been divided into groups to focus on different areas critical to the future of the organization. They are examining such issues as performance, development, and job classification.

Ducks Unlimited Canada
www.ducks.ca

Gary Goodwin, director of human resources, explains that "the reorganization was essentially to help empower employees, making it easier for people working in the field to make decisions quickly without having to go up and down the proverbial power ladder."

Centralization and Decentralization of Authority

Another way in which managers can keep the organizational hierarchy flat is to decentralize authority to lower-level managers and nonmanagerial employees.[44] If managers at higher levels give lower-level employees the responsibility to make important decisions and only manage by exception, then the problems of slow and distorted communication noted previously are kept to a minimum. Moreover, fewer managers are needed because their role is not to make decisions but to act as coach and facilitator and to help other employees make the best decisions. In addition, when decision making is low in the organization and near the customer, employees are better able to recognize and respond to customer needs.

Decentralizing authority allows an organization and its employees to behave flexibly even as the organization grows and becomes taller. This is why managers are so interested in empowering employees, creating self-managed work teams, establishing cross-functional teams, and even moving to a product team structure. These design innovations help keep the organizational structure flexible and responsive to complex task and general environments, complex technologies, and complex strategies.

While more organizations are taking steps to decentralize authority, too much decentralization has certain disadvantages. If divisions, functions, or teams are given too much decision-making authority, they may begin to pursue their own goals at the expense of organizational goals. Managers in engineering design or R&D, for example, may become so focused on making the best possible product that they fail to realize that the best product may be so expensive that few people will be willing or able to buy it. Also, with too much decentralization, lack of communication among functions or among divisions may prevent possible synergies among them from ever materializing, and organizational performance suffers.

Top managers have to look for the balance between centralization and decentralization of authority that best meets the organization's needs. If managers are in a stable environment, using well-understood technology, and producing staple kinds of products (such as cereal, canned soup, books, or televisions), there is no pressing need to decentralize authority, and managers at the top can maintain control of much of the organizational decision making.[45] However, in uncertain, changing environments where high-tech companies are producing state-of-the-art products, top managers must empower employees and allow teams to make important strategic decisions so that the organization can keep up with the changes taking place.

Procter & Gamble chose to centralize rather than decentralize its management structure. Global operations were divided into four main areas—North America, Europe, the Middle East and Africa, and Asia. In each area, P&G created a new position—global executive vice-president—and made the person in that position responsible for overseeing the operation of all the divisions within his or her world region. Each global executive vice-president is responsible for getting the various divisions within his or her area to cooperate and to share information and knowledge that will lead to synergies; thus, authority is centralized at the world area level. All of these new executive vice-presidents report directly to the president of Procter & Gamble, further centralizing authority.

Tips for Managers

CHOOSING A DIVISIONAL STRUCTURE

1. Describe what appeals to you more as a consumer: a product structure or a geographical structure.
2. In today's new economy, evaluate which structure (product or geographic) will allow the organization to be more competitive.
3. Describe what, for you, are the advantages of a divisional structure.
4. Keep track of organizations as they wrestle with *hierarchy* and *chaordic* challenges to their ability to stay competitive.

Overall Structure: Formal or Flexible?

THINK ABOUT IT

Flexible Structures or Business-as-Usual?[46]

The study, called *Beyond a Reasonable Doubt: Building the Business Case for Flexibility*, was sponsored by 10 Canadian law firms. While the average Canadian works 1300 hours per year, the average lawyer works, and is expected to work, at least 2100 hours. Catalyst Canada estimates that it cost $315 000 every time a lawyer leaves his/her firm. Is it a gender issue? "This is a generational issue versus a gender issue," said Kirby Chown, partner at McCarthy Tetrault LLP (Toronto).

The top two reasons cited for leaving their current law firms? (1) To be "in an environment more supportive of my family and personal commitments" and (2) "more control over my work schedule." Hatty Reisman is a case in point. A former Bay Street lawyer, she left the hectic law-firm lifestyle when she was pregnant with her first child. "I worked seven days per week, and I thought there had to be a better way (to raise my family)," she said. "I think the firm would have loved for me to stay." If an alternate work arrangement had been offered, Reisman said, she isn't sure she would have accepted. "I don't think I would have felt comfortable if I wasn't pulling my weight."

You Be the Manager

1. How would you respond to the Hatty Reismans in today's organizations?
2. In what ways is the "generational issue" creating new challenges to the flexible vs. business-as-usual organizational structure?

Overworked and underpaid? Most lawyers work, and are expected to work, at least 2100 hours per year compared to the 1300 hours of the average Canadian.

FIGURE 6.4 | *Mechanistic vs. Organic Organizations*

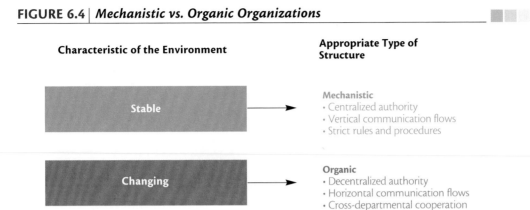

Earlier in this chapter, we discussed the choices managers make in deciding how tasks should be organized into jobs and jobs should be grouped into departments. Managers also need to determine how formal or flexible they want the organization to be.

Burns and Stalker proposed two basic ways in which managers can organize and control an organization's activities to respond to characteristics of its external environment: They can use a formal *mechanistic structure* or a flexible *organic structure*.[47] Figure 6.4 illustrates the differences between these two types of structures. After describing these two structures, we discuss what factors managers consider when choosing between them.

Mechanistic Structures

When the environment around an organization is stable, managers tend to choose a mechanistic structure to organize and control activities and make employee behaviour predictable. In a **mechanistic structure**, authority is centralized at the top of the managerial hierarchy, and the vertical hierarchy of authority is the main means used to control subordinates' behaviour. Tasks and roles are clearly specified, subordinates are closely supervised, and the emphasis is on strict discipline and order. Everyone knows his or her place, and there is a place for everyone. A mechanistic structure provides the most efficient way to operate in a stable environment because it allows managers to obtain inputs at the lowest cost, giving an organization the most control over its conversion processes and enabling the most efficient production of goods and services with the smallest expenditure of resources. This explains McDonald's mechanistic structure.

mechanistic structure
An organizational structure in which authority is centralized at the top of the hierarchy, tasks and roles are clearly specified, and employees are closely supervised.

Organic Structures

In contrast, when the environment is changing rapidly, it is difficult to obtain access to resources. Managers need to organize their activities in a way that allows them to cooperate, to act quickly to obtain resources (such as new types of wood to produce new kinds of furniture), and to respond effectively to the unexpected. In an **organic structure**, authority is decentralized to middle and first-line managers to encourage them to take responsibility and act quickly to pursue scarce resources. Departments are encouraged to take a cross-departmental or functional perspective, and authority rests with the individuals and departments best positioned to control the current problems the organization is facing. Control in an organic structure is much looser than it is in a mechanistic structure, and reliance on shared norms to guide organizational activities is greater. This is somewhat representative of Blue Water Café, where restaurant staff are dependent on what is fresh and available each day to create their menus.

organic structure
An organizational structure in which authority is decentralized to middle and first-line managers and tasks and roles are left ambiguous to encourage employees to cooperate and respond quickly to the unexpected.

FIGURE 6.5 | *Factors Affecting Organizational Structure*

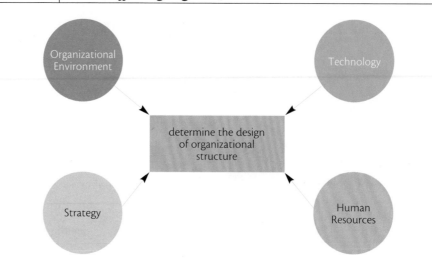

Managers in an organic structure can react more quickly to a changing environment than can managers in a mechanistic structure. However, an organic structure is generally more expensive to operate, so it is used only when needed—when the organizational environment is unstable and rapidly changing. Organic structures may also work more effectively if managers establish semistructures that govern "the pace, timing, and rhythm of organizational activities and processes." In other words, introducing a bit of structure while preserving most of the flexibility of the organic structure may reduce operating costs.[48]

Factors Affecting Choice of Organizational Structure

Organizational structures need to fit the factors or circumstances that affect the company the most and cause them the most uncertainty.[49] Thus, there is no "best" way to design an organization: Design reflects each organization's specific situation. Four factors are important determinants of organizational structure: the nature of the organizational environment, the type of strategy the organization pursues, the technology the organization uses, and the characteristics of the organization's human resources (see Figure 6.5).[50]

The Organizational Environment

In general, the more quickly the external environment is changing and the greater the uncertainty within it, the greater are the problems a manager faces in trying to gain access to scarce resources. In this situation, to speed decision making and communication and make it easier to obtain resources, managers typically make organizing choices that bring flexibility to the organizational structure.[51] They are likely to decentralize authority and empower lower-level employees to make important operating decisions. In contrast, if the external environment is stable, if resources are readily available, and if uncertainty is low, then less coordination and communication among people and functions is needed to obtain resources, and managers can make organizing choices that bring more formality to the organizational structure. Managers in this situation prefer to make decisions within a clearly defined hierarchy of authority and use extensive rules and standard operating procedures to govern activities.

As we discussed in Chapter 2, change is rapid in today's marketplace, and increasing competition both at home and abroad is putting greater pressure on managers to attract customers and increase efficiency and effectiveness. Thus, there has been growing interest in finding ways to structure organizations—such as through empowerment and self-managed teams—to allow people and departments to behave flexibly. A case in point is media executive, Kathleen Dore, president of television and radio at CanWest MediaWorks, and her unique empowerment management style. In a world dominated by men, she has become a role model for other women. She uses a term she calls the "force multiplier," which focuses "on using your skills, abilities and experience as a magnet, which pulls others toward you, and makes them want to engage in the undertaking you're about."[52]

Strategy

As discussed in Chapter 5, once managers decide on a strategy, they must choose the right means to implement it. Different strategies often call for the use of different organizational structures. For example, a differentiation strategy aimed at increasing the value customers perceive in an organization's goods and services usually succeeds best in a flexible structure. Flexibility assists a differentiation strategy because managers can develop new or innovative products quickly—an activity that requires extensive cooperation among functions or departments. In contrast, a low-cost strategy that is aimed at driving down costs in all functions usually fares best in a more formal structure, which gives managers greater control over the expenditures and actions of the organization's various departments.[53]

In addition, at the corporate level, when managers decide to expand the scope of organizational activities by, for example, vertical integration or diversification, they need to design a flexible structure to provide sufficient coordination among the different business divisions.[54] As discussed in Chapter 5, many companies have been divesting businesses because managers have been unable to create a competitive advantage to keep them up to speed in fast-changing industries. By moving to a more flexible structure, such as a product division structure, divisional managers gain more control over their different businesses.

Finally, expanding internationally and operating in many different countries challenges managers to create organizational structures that allow organizations to be flexible on a global level.[55] As we discuss later, managers can group their departments or functions and divisions in several ways to allow them to pursue an international strategy effectively.

Technology

Technology is the combination of skills, knowledge, tools, machines, computers, and equipment that are used in the design, production, and distribution of goods and services. As a rule, the more complicated the technology that an organization uses, the more difficult it is for managers and employees to impose strict control on technology or to regulate it efficiently.[56] Thus, the more complicated the technology, the greater is the need for a flexible structure to enhance managers' and employees' ability to respond to unexpected situations and give them the freedom to work out new solutions to the problems they encounter. In contrast, the more routine the technology, the more appropriate a formal structure is, because tasks are simple and the steps needed to produce goods and services have been worked out in advance.

The nature of an organization's technology is an important determinant of its structure. Today, there is a growing use of computer-controlled production, and a movement toward using self-managed teams (groups of employees who are given the responsibility for supervising their own activities and for monitoring the quality of the goods and service they provide) to promote innovation, increase quality, and reduce costs. As a result, many companies are trying to make their structures more flexible to take advantage of the value-creating benefits of complex technology.

Human Resources

A final important factor affecting an organization's choice of structure is the characteristics of the human resources it employs. In general, the more highly skilled an organization's workforce and the more people are required to work together in groups or teams to perform their tasks, the more likely is the organization to use a flexible, decentralized structure. Highly skilled employees or employees who have internalized strong professional values and norms of behaviour as part of their training usually desire freedom and autonomy and dislike close supervision. Accountants, for example, have learned the need to report company accounts honestly and impartially, and doctors and nurses have absorbed the obligation to give patients the best care possible.

Flexible structures, characterized by decentralized authority and empowered employees, are well suited to the needs of highly skilled people. Similarly, when people work in teams, they must be allowed to interact freely, which also is possible in a flexible organizational structure. Thus, when designing an organizational structure, managers must pay close attention to the workforce and to the work itself.

In summary, an *organization's external environment, strategy, technology,* and human resources are the factors to be considered by managers seeking to design the best structure for an organization. The greater the level of uncertainty in an organization's environment, the more complex its strategy and technology, and the more highly qualified and skilled its workforce, the more likely managers will design a structure that is flexible. The more stable an organization's environment, the less complex and better understood its strategy or technology, and the less skilled its workforce, the more likely managers will design an organizational structure that is formal and controlling.

 ## Tips for Managers
DESIGNING STRUCTURE AND JOBS

1. Monitor the challenges an organization faces as it structures its design to meet those challenges.
2. When new structures are implemented, new roles and responsibilities as well as job descriptions will occur.
3. Flexible structures need enriched jobs and a corporate culture that sees value in its organizational flexibility.
4. When managers rethink jobs, roles, and responsibilities, there is always room to build in a sense of empowerment.

Strategic Alliances and Network Structure

 THINK ABOUT IT

Native Communities With Cash; Big Banks Seeking Alliances[57]

Anticipated and unprecedented economic development is in the air as a result of native communities, flush with cash from land claim deals—almost $1.2 billion in the hands of First Nations groups, says Margot Geduld, a spokesperson for Indian and

Northern Affairs Canada. Perhaps it's not the best motivation in the world, but the big banks know about this and are seeking to make alliances with them. The only bank branch on the Wikwemikong native reserve—located on a picturesque island in Lake Huron, a six-hour drive north of Toronto—closed in 1999. When its 3000 permanent residents left to do banking elsewhere, they also did their shopping away from the reserve as well. For Walter Manitowabi and his family, this spelled trouble since they ran the supermarket, hardware store, gas station, and a handful of other businesses. Finding another bank became a priority. In 2001, an "agency" bank arrangement with Royal Bank became a reality. Residents then started using Walter's services again.

Canada's biggest banks all took an interest in developing business relationships with Aboriginal groups in the mid-1990s when the prospect of land claim settlements and self-government promised large pools of money for First Nations groups, located on 2900 reserve lands, that would be spent on business and infrastructure development. RBC's Ms. Carla Woodward, national manager of Aboriginal banking at Royal Bank who is herself Métis, says these initiatives are integral to relationship building. "It's beyond corporate citizenship," she says. "It's a smart business decision."

You Be the Manager

1. What's so smart about the decision Royal Bank made?

Recently, innovations in organizational structure—strategic alliances, joint ventures, and network structures—have been sweeping through Canadian, American, and European businesses. These structures allow for considerably more flexibility by creating links outside the organization. We cover each of these in turn.

Strategic Alliances and Joint Ventures

Many people use the terms *strategic alliance* and *joint venture* interchangeably, but technically they are different. A **strategic alliance** is a formal agreement that commits two or more companies to exchange or share their resources in order to produce and market a product.[58] A **joint venture** is a strategic alliance among two or more companies that agree to establish jointly and share the ownership of a new business.

Japanese car companies such as Toyota and Honda have formed a series of strategic alliances with suppliers of inputs such as car axles, gearboxes, and air-conditioning systems. More and more Canadian, American, and European organizations are relying on strategic alliances to gain access to low-cost foreign sources of inputs. This approach allows managers to keep costs low.

Network Structure

A **network structure** is a series of strategic alliances that an organization creates with suppliers, manufacturers, and distributors to produce and market a product. For instance, Handspring, which is known for its PDAs (personal digital assistants), doesn't actually make them. A network of partner companies manufacture, design, ship and support Handspring's products. Handspring's role is to manage the network. Network structures allow an organization to bring resources (workers especially) together on a long-term basis in order to find new ways to reduce costs and increase the quality of products—without experiencing the high costs of operating a complex organizational structure (such as the costs of employing many managers).

strategic alliance
An agreement in which managers pool or share their organization's resources and know-how with a foreign company, and the two organizations share the rewards and risks of starting a new venture.

joint venture
A strategic alliance among two or more companies that agree to establish jointly and share the ownership of a new business.

network structure
A series of strategic alliances that an organization creates with suppliers, manufacturers, and distributors to produce and market a product.

boundaryless organization

An organization whose members are linked by computers, faxes, computer-aided design systems, and video teleconferencing, and who rarely, if ever, see one another face to face.

iGen Knowledge Solutions Inc.
www.igeninc.com

The ability of managers to develop networks to produce or provide the goods and services customers want, rather than creating a complex organizational structure to do so, has led many researchers and consultants to popularize the idea of a **boundaryless organization** composed of people who are linked by computers, faxes, computer-aided design systems, and video teleconferencing, and who rarely, if ever, see one another face to face. This structure is also referred to as *network organizations, learning organizations,* or *virtual corporations.*[59] People are used when their services are needed, much as in a matrix structure, but they are not formal members of an organization. They are functional experts who form an alliance with an organization, fulfill their contractual obligations, and then move on to the next project.

New Westminster, BC-based iGEN Knowledge Solutions Inc. operates as a virtual organization to bring technical solutions to its business clients. Associates work from home offices connected by wireless technologies and the internet, and collaborate to solve client problems. The virtual model allows fast cycle times for idea implementation, service delivery, and product development. The model also makes it easy to set up operations in different regions of the country without large overhead costs.

Leadership in virtual organizations may be more important and more difficult than in conventional organizations. A study of a number of successful virtual organizations found that the most important factor was a leader organization with a strategically important core competence.[60] The leader organization manages and inspires the other organizational relationships. Because virtual organizations have similar characteristics to voluntary organizations, leaders need to be able to build trust while recognizing that they do not have authority or full control over partners.

business-to-business (B2B) networks

A group of organizations that join together and use software to link themselves to potential global suppliers to increase efficiency and effectiveness.

The push to lower costs has also led to the development of electronic **business-to-business (B2B) networks** in which most or all of the companies in an industry (e.g., car makers) use the same software platform to link to each other and establish industry specifications and standards. Then, these companies jointly list the quantity and specifications of the inputs they require and invite bids from the thousands of potential suppliers around the world. Suppliers also use the same software platform so electronic bidding, auctions, and transactions are possible between buyers and sellers around the world. The idea is that high-volume standardized transactions can help drive down costs at the industry level.

Outsourcing

outsourcing

Using outside suppliers and manufacturers to produce goods and services.

The use of **outsourcing** is increasing rapidly as organizations recognize the many opportunities that the approaches offer to reduce costs and increase organizational flexibility. Canadian companies spent almost $49 billion on outsourcing in 1999.[61] Canadian Pacific Railway (CPR) outsources the maintenance of applications that it doesn't need to develop the expertise for in-house. For example, it has outsourced the maintenance of some of its legacy applications to RIS and also outsources its mainframe infrastructure to IBM. When CPR did the work itself in-house everything wasn't running smoothly. Allen Borak, vice-president for information services at CPR in Calgary, said, "I would say that part of our business wasn't well managed." The decision to outsource has left CPR free to concentrate on what it does best.[62] Stephen Libman, president of Libman Chimo Travel in Montreal, has a similar story. He has gained 90 percent of his time back after he outsourced with another Montreal company, Eternitee Systems Inc., that now looks after Libman's desktop hardware and software, and its network for a fixed monthly fee. Libman says he spends about the same amount of money on technology as before, but he gained his time back.[63]

Companies that specialize in outsourced work, such as EDS Corporation—which manages the information systems of large organizations like Xerox and Eastman Kodak—are major beneficiaries of this new approach. While many companies use outsourcing, not all have been successful at implementing it. Managers should be aware of the following concerns when considering its use: (1) choosing the wrong activities to outsource, (2) choosing the wrong vendor, (3) writing a poor contract, (4) failing to consider personnel issues, (5) losing control over the activity, (6) ignoring the hidden costs, and (7) failing to develop an exit strategy (for either moving to another vendor or deciding to bring the activity back in-house.)[64] A review of 91 outsourcing activities found that writing a poor contract and losing control of the activity were the most likely reasons for an outsourcing venture to fail. Designing organizational structure is becoming an increasingly complex management function. To maximize efficiency and effectiveness, managers must carefully assess the relative benefits of having their own organization perform a functional activity versus forming an alliance with another organization to perform the activity. It is still not clear how B2B networks and other forms of electronic alliances between companies will develop in the future.

Summary and Review

1. **DESIGNING ORGANIZATIONAL STRUCTURE** Organizational structure is the formal system of both task and reporting relationships that determines how employees use resources to achieve organizational goals. The way an organization's structure works depends on how tasks are grouped into individual jobs; how jobs are grouped into functions and divisions; how coordination and allocating authority are accomplished; and whether the structure is formal or flexible.

2. **GROUPING TASKS INTO JOBS: JOB DESIGN** Job design is the process by which managers group tasks into jobs. To create more interesting jobs, and to get workers to act flexibly, managers can enlarge and enrich jobs.

3. **GROUPING JOBS INTO FUNCTIONS AND DIVISIONS** Managers can choose from many kinds of organizational structures to make the best use of organizational resources. Depending on the specific organizing problems they face, managers can choose from functional, product, geographic, market, matrix, and product team structures.

4. **COORDINATING FUNCTIONS AND DIVISIONS** No matter which structure managers choose, they must decide how to distribute authority in the organization, how many levels to have in the hierarchy of authority, and what balance to strike between centralization and decentralization to keep the number of levels in the hierarchy to a minimum. As organizations grow, managers must increase integration and coordination among functions and divisions.

5. **OVERALL STRUCTURE: FORMAL OR FLEXIBLE?** Overall organizational structure is determined by conditions of the environment. When the environment is stable, a mechanistic structure is appropriate. When the environment is changing rapidly, an organic structure is more appropriate. An organic structure is more flexible. To avoid many of the communication and coordination problems that emerge as organizations grow, managers are adopting more flexible structures. The four main determinants of organizational structure are the external environment, strategy, technology, and human resources. In general, the higher the level of uncertainty associated with these factors, the more appropriate is a flexible, adaptable structure as opposed to a formal, rigid one.

6. STRATEGIC ALLIANCES AND NETWORK STRUCTURE   In a strategic alliance, managers enter into a contract with another organization to provide inputs or to perform a functional activity. If managers enter into a series of these contracts and a substantial number of activities are performed outside their organization, they have created a network structure.

Key Terms

authority, p.177
boundaryless organization, p.186
business-to-business (B2B)
    networks, p.186
cross-functional team, p.176
divisional structure, p.171
functional structure, p.171
geographic structure, p.173
hierarchy of authority, p.177
job design, p.167
job enlargement, p.168
job enrichment, p.168
job simplification, p.168

joint venture, p.185
market structure, p.174
matrix structure, p.175
mechanistic structure, p.181
network structure, p.185
organic structure, p.181
organizational design, p.166
organizational structure, p.166
outsourcing, p.186
product structure, p.172
product team structure, p.176
span of control, p.177
strategic alliance, p.185

SO WHERE DO YOU STAND?

Wrap-Up to Opening Case[65]

We began this chapter with a discussion on the notion of hierarchical and the chaordic organization designs. While this approach to organizational structure may at first seem surprising, the discussion captures much of what the corporate tension is all about these days. In a time of rapid change, such as ours, managers and employees "fall back" on to trusted structures that worked in the past and, in so doing, miss the competitive opportunities in the current situation. On the other hand, there are companies that not only feel relieved but indeed, liberated, with the new thinking that allows for its flexibility and growth in the new economy.

On the one hand, Dr. Elliot Jaques is asking us to consider the hierarchy, but not in its repressive form that so many employees have experienced. His claim to fame, as we noted, is that this type of organizational structure allows each employee to contribute to his/her fullest potential. In his explanation of the different "strata," he has

organized jobs and competencies and time frames that will embrace many different types of employees with their different skill sets and interests.

On the other hand, we discussed Dee Hock, founder of Visa International, whose product, he says, is "coordination." With this vision, we begin to see a new type of organizational structure, more akin to an organic structure, where the whole is always greater than the sum of its parts. There is much merit to Hock's observations and experience since much of what has happened since he first started envisioning Visa in the early 1970s has come to pass. Today there is increasing emphasis on making alliances, networking, and outsourcing, all of which bear a resemblance to Hock's coordination vision. As a result, organizational structures are being realigned; new responsibilities and roles are being assigned to employees; and the work of being and staying competitive becomes a constant work in process.

To reinforce this vision of "the coordinated organization," we discussed the insights from Dr. Roger Martin, dean of the Rotman School of Management at the University of Toronto, who points out that the real challenge for organizations today is to develop a greater sense of *heuristics*, of embracing questions, and minimizing the trained need that companies have been expert in to turn a question into a quick answer, or *algorithm*, and produce a product or service. These questions, or "mysteries," as he calls them, means that managers will need to wrestle more and more with questions the marketplace is asking, questions such as: What do customers really want? How do we find the best possible people to do what needs to be done? What's the "next new thing"?

The more traditional structural elements of organizations will certainly continue, such elements as product and geographic structures, matrix organizational and team-based designs, tall vs. flat organizations, issues of authority, and chain of command.

The immediate future for business is not going to see a reduction of these issues. Indeed, organizational design and structure will be in the forefront of managers' thinking as they attempt to stay current, hire and maintain the best employees, and remain competitive.

Ask Yourself

1. Which organizational structure is more appealing to you: one with more or one with less structure?
2. What will happen to organizations that will not adapt to changing circumstances?

Online **Learning Centre**   After studying the preceding material, be sure to check out our Online Learning Centre at **www.mcgrawhill.ca/olc/jones** for more in-depth information and interactivities that correspond to this chapter.

Management in Action

Topics for Discussion and Action

1. Would a flexible or a more formal structure be appropriate for these organizations: (a) a large department store, (b) one of the big accounting firms, (c) a biotechnology company? Explain your reasoning. Using the job characteristics model as a guide, discuss how a manager can enrich or enlarge subordinates' jobs.

2. How might a salesperson's or secretary's job be enlarged or enriched to make it more motivating?

3. When and under what conditions might managers change from a functional structure to (a) a product, (b) a geographic, or (c) a market structure?

4. How do matrix structure and product team structure differ? Why is product team structure more widely used?

5. Find a manager and identify the kind of organizational structure that his or her organization uses to coordinate its people and resources. Why is the organization using that structure? Do you think a different structure would be more appropriate? Which one?

6. With the same or another manager, discuss the distribution of authority in the organization. Does the manager think that decentralizing authority and empowering employees is appropriate?

7. Compare the pros and cons of using a network structure to perform organizational activities, and performing all activities in-house or within one organizational hierarchy.

Building Management Skills

UNDERSTANDING ORGANIZING

Think of an organization you know—perhaps one you have worked in—such as a store, restaurant, office, club, or school. Then answer the following questions.

1. Which contingencies are most important in explaining how the organization is organized? Do you think it is organized in the best way?

2. Can you think of any ways in which a typical job could be enlarged or enriched?

3. What kind of organizational structure does the organization use? If it is part of a chain, what kind of structure does the entire organization use? What other structures discussed in the chapter might allow the organization to operate more effectively? For example, would the move to a product team structure lead to greater efficiency or effectiveness? Why or why not?

4. How many levels are there in the organization's hierarchy? Is authority centralized or decentralized?

Describe the span of control of the top manager and of middle or first-line managers.

5. Is the distribution of authority appropriate for the organization and its activities? Would it be possible to flatten the hierarchy by decentralizing authority and empowering employees?

6. What are the main integrating mechanisms used in the organization? Do they provide sufficient coordination among individuals and functions? How might they be improved?

7. Now that you have analyzed the way in which this organization is organized, what advice would you give its managers to help them improve the way it operates?

Management for You

Choose an organization for which you have worked. How did the structure of your job and the organization affect your job satisfaction? Did the tasks within your job make sense? In what ways could they be better organized? What structural changes would you make to this organization? Would you consider making this a taller or flatter organization? How would the changes you have proposed improve responsiveness to customers and your job satisfaction?

Small Group Breakout Exercise

BOB'S APPLIANCES

Form groups of three or four people, and appoint one member as the spokesperson who will communicate your findings to the whole class when called on by the instructor. Then discuss the following scenario.

Bob's Appliances sells and services household appliances such as washing machines, dishwashers, stoves, and refrigerators. Over the years, the company has developed a good reputation for the quality of its customer service, and many local builders are customers at the store. Recently, some new appliance retailers, including Circuit City and Future Shop, have opened stores that also provide numerous appliances. In addition to appliances, however, to attract more customers these stores carry a complete range of consumer electronics products, including television sets, stereos, and computers. Bob Lange, the owner of Bob's Appliances, has decided that if he is to stay in business he must widen his product range and compete directly with the chains.

In 2006, he decided to build a new 1800-square-metre store and service centre, and he is now hiring new employees to sell and service the new line of consumer electronics. Because of his company's increased size, Lange is not sure of the best way to organize the employees. Currently, he uses a functional structure; employees are divided into sales, purchasing and accounting, and repair.[66]

You are a team of local consultants that Bob has called in to advise him as he makes this crucial choice. Which structure do you recommend? Why?

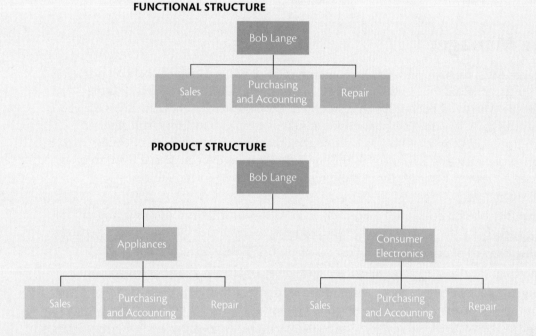

FUNCTIONAL STRUCTURE

PRODUCT STRUCTURE

Managing Ethically

In many businesses—such as chicken-processing plants, small engineering companies, furniture makers, warehouses, and offices—unskilled workers perform the same repetitive task for many hours a day, day in and day out, and often for years if they stay at the same job. Boredom is common, as is the development of bodily ailments such as skin conditions, muscle fatigue, and carpal tunnel syndrome. Is it ethical for managers to allow workers to perform repetitive tasks for long periods of time? What kinds of standards would you use to decide this issue? To what degree should job redesign be used to change such a situation and enrich jobs if it also would raise costs and make a company less competitive? How could organizational structure be redesigned to make this problem less prevalent?

Exploring the World Wide Web

SPECIFIC ASSIGNMENT

Go to the website for Onex Corp. (www.onex.com). Onex is one of Canada's largest companies that acquires attractive businesses and builds them in partnership with management. "Since 1983, we acquire attractive companies at fair prices and, in partnership with operating managers, we grow them and ultimately realize on the value we've created through a variety of strategies."[67] Review the Onex Corp. website.

1. What are Onex Corp.'s mission and corporate goals?
2. What kind of organizational structure does Onex Corp. have?
3. What is Onex Corp.'s approach to managing its structure (its approach to decentralization, delegation, etc.).

GENERAL ASSIGNMENT

Search for a website that tells the story of how an organization changed its structure in some way to increase its efficiency and effectiveness.

Developing a Business Plan

(APPENDIX B, PAGE 405)

Go to www.mcgrawhill.ca/olc/jones/6 for online exercises.

Be the Manager

As a management consultant you try to keep up with some of the best current books on managing and strategy. Recently you read *Peripheral Vision*[68] and were quite excited about the ideas the authors (of the Wharton School of Business) presented. Their research has shown that less than 20 percent of firms have developed peripheral vision in sufficient capacity to remain competitive.[69] They claim that while companies need to focus on their planned strategic growth, often they may be unaware of a competitor "lurking" off to the side. Hence, the need for peripheral vision to avoid any surprises. To raise managers' vigilance, they propose the following solution to developing peripheral vision:

- **Scoping:** the skill of determining how broadly to look. "If your scope is too narrow, you can still be blindsided, but if the scope is too wide you risk being overwhelmed by unimportant signals."[70]
- **Scanning:** the skill of practising more active searching, being more "detective-like."
- **Interpreting:** the skill of making sense of the puzzle that emerges as you go about your work.
- **Probing:** the skill of exploring more closely what seems to be occurring in the patterns emerging, an activity that will often involve experimenting and testing the market perhaps in unique ways.
- **Acting:** the skill of exploiting any new possibilities uncovered or avoiding any imminent threats determined.

Question

1. Your new business client has asked you to show how the idea of peripheral vision could enhance the business of developing strategic alliances for her. What would you say?

Management Case

The Core Group[71]

What purpose are most organizations seeking to fulfill? ... Art Kleiner asserts that the primary purpose is not—as many of us believe—meeting customers' needs, fostering innovation, or making a better world. Rather, organizations are set up, first and foremost, to fulfill the perceived desires and priorities of a "core group" of people. As such, *the success or failure of the organization is determined by the behaviour of this key set of individuals.[72]*

[Author Art Kleiner] ... asserts that core groups exist in every organization, large or small, for-profit or not-for-profit, private or public sector. Members of this elite set take their power not from their position in the hierarchy, but from the way they influence decisions at every level of the hierarchy. Every organization, at any given moment in time, has its own unique core group pattern; the most influential people might be high-profile shareholders, critical technology specialists, key suppliers, major customers, or members of the company's founding family. Core groups often include "bottlenecks," people who control or manage essential parts of operations, such as the graphic design and production staff of a publishing company, or the veteran school bus administrator of a local school system. In other words, the core group doesn't necessarily comprise just people with hierarchical authority but those who are, for whatever reason, perceived as central to the enterprise by the people who work there.

Managing Organizational Complexity

According to Kleiner, core groups are not inherently bad or good; they are simply part of the nature of organizational systems. Without them, it would be impossible for organizations to exist, simply because the complexity of most organizational environments would be too great to manage effectively. Art says that, just as a baby instinctively recognizes human faces, most of us in organizations are instinctively attuned to the people whom we have come to believe are important. Instead of making decisions based on the balance of customer and shareholder priorities, we say to ourselves, "I don't want to be the one to walk into Cheryl's office and say we can't do that." We let Cheryl, whom we probably know only slightly, represent the full range of factors affecting the decision we have to make.

For those who resist the idea of a core group, Art asks us to examine our thinking when faced with a complex decision. Do we consider how it will sit with our boss, our boss's boss, or someone else entirely? If so, then we're basing our choices on the needs of the core group. The reason that the influence of these key people "trumps all other concerns," the author explains, "is not because of some mystical resonance, but simply because of the cumulative effect of the decisions made throughout the organization. If people believe the core group needs and wants some-

thing to happen, they assume that making it happen is a part of their job." As such, those who do make it happen often get rewarded and recognized, while those who act based on other criteria usually get left behind.

Creating Great Core Groups

One of the reasons that Art developed the core group theory was his awareness of the rapid proliferation of organizations in the world. "If we are going to act effectively in a society of organizations," he says, "we need a theory that helps us see organizations clearly, as they are." Organizations in which core groups behave in self-serving and exploitative ways, such as Enron, are dismal places to work and often end in failure. Organizations in which decision makers expand the core group by creating structures that take into account the welfare and development of everyone in the enterprise, such as Springfield Remanufacturing Corporation and Southwest Airlines, are typically high-performing work environments with deeply committed workforces. In other words, behind every great organization is a great core group.

By understanding the characteristics and principles of the core group in their organizations, people can act far more effectively. Employees, for example, can decide if they're interested in building a career in an organization even if they never get into the core group. People trying to change the organization from within can increase their chances of success by seeking sponsorship from core group members. And those at the top of the organization can consider how to galvanize spirit and effectiveness among employees by creating the conditions for the core group to expand to a larger group of people. When leaders guide core groups to work in the best interests of everyone in the organization, they can amplify the capabilities of their enterprise and create a legacy of which they can be proud.

Questions

1. What are the main elements in Kleiner's approach to organizational design?
2. What organizational problems might emerge from his approach?

Video Management Case

CBC

Designing Organizational Structure: Richard Branson of Virgin Airlines

Richard Branson, chairman of Virgin, is an individual of tremendous flexibility and entrepreneurial foresight. Branson describes his work as managing a "total-life company," targeting various industries to become their greatest competitor in terms of price, quality, and selection. He discusses the benefits of living his vision as a private company and the times he learned from changing that structure.

Questions to Consider

1. How has Branson's decision to have the Virgin name on dozens of little companies enabled much of the success of his company?
2. What does Branson cite as the most important difference that defines his products and reflects the structure of the company?

Source: *Venture*, show number 613, "Richard Branson," October 20, 1996, running time 7:58.

Organizational Culture and Change

Learning Outcomes

1. Explain what organizational culture is and its role in guiding behaviour in organizations.

2. Explain how culture is learned by members of an organization.

3. Identify what is involved in managing organizational change.

4. Explain how managers could help to overcome resistance to change.

5. Explain why managing change in a unionized environment is important.

Walking the Talk

Corporate culture involves people. A healthy corporate culture means that managers and employees act congruently with a shared sense of values and perspectives. They meet what Samy Chong calls their "internal challenges":

As leaders, we must be examples of the new model that honours the lives of our employees. We can never teach what we do not possess. Actions that honour our employees include asking for and listening to their input and allowing them the opportunity to speak their truth without fear of reprisals. If we treat others as we wish to be treated, we will lead an organization that is empowered by the example we set. Corporate cultures that don't reflect this awareness will find themselves in a challenging place. They will spend more time on internal issues—dealing with disagreements, decreased output, low staff morale and high turnover. The energy that is needed to drive the company forward in this new world market will be diverted to clean up the internal challenges. The more we begin to channel that energy to the compelling vision we all want of ourselves and our organization, the faster we will achieve our desired results.[1]

A very compelling movie that brought home the point of *who* we are inside and *what* we do, and how we affect the world around us, was vividly portrayed in the March 15, 2005 release of *What the Bleep Do We Know?*[2] While the movie provided incredible insights into the world of subatomic physics—quantum reality, or how matter interacts with other matter at the particle level—what was stunning for the viewer—and hence for a manager—is how we are integral to shaping reality. The implications for the workplace and organizational cultures are enormous. Revolutionary research by Dr. Masaru Emoto described how thoughts and feelings affect physical reality. These and other insights from the quantum world should make managers and employees stop and realize how important their words, interactions, and decisions are to the heart and soul of their organization—in other words, to the organizational culture. Corporate culture, therefore, reflects not only *what* managers do, but especially *who* they are; it is also life-giving oxygen for the workplace.

Two case examples will illustrate this point: in June 2005 two very senior seasoned executives from Cisco Systems Inc.—Chief Operating Officer Gary Daichendt and Chief Technology Officer Gary Kunis—walked out from their jobs at embattled Nortel Networks Corp. after only three months working with Nortel CEO Bill Owens. The reason?

Divergent management styles and different views of the future of the business. Two different realities. "Cisco's strength is speed to market, combined with an aggressive attitude toward technology, which is tightly controlled up to the point of manufacturing, much of which is outsourced. Nortel, on the other hand, has a reputation for slower sales response, but also close attention to the needs of its telecom carrier customers." Steven Levy, an analyst with Lehman Brothers, said, "A traditional telecom company will not ship something to a customer until it's 100-percent-plus ready for the market. Cisco's culture is when it's good enough, let's get it out and we'll fix it when it's out there. Time to market is absolutely critical."[3] In other words: any inner confidence that Daichendt and Kunis might have had when they first joined Nortel quickly evaporated given the cultural

Subatomic physics—quantum reality, or how matter interacts with other matter at the particle level—affects life at a particle level. In turn, we are integral to shaping reality.

context that CEO Owens had established; so they left the company. They felt that working with Owens and the already established culture would not be congruent and sustainable with their own vision and values. In other words, they felt they would not be able to influence events and create the reality that the movie *What the Bleep* says that each of us is responsible for doing.

The second case was the destruction of the space shuttle *Columbia* and the death of its seven astronauts in early 2003.[4] There was a breach in the heat shield on the craft's left wing such that foam insulation peeled from the external fuel tank during launch and struck the wing at high speed. Upon re-entry superheated air penetrated this wing and melted it from the inside, causing the spacecraft to break apart and scatter debris over parts of Texas and Louisiana. After months of investigation, investigators in their 248-page report said the disaster was caused by a NASA culture driven by schedule, starved for funds, and burdened with an eroded, insufficient safety program. A corporate culture and attitude that bred a sense of complacency with dangerous possibilities should anything go wrong also became part of the established corporate culture at NASA. NASA was simply allowing too much risk-taking in its attitudes and decision making. But most of all, the report noted, there was "ineffective leadership" that "failed to fulfill the implicit contract to do whatever is possible to ensure the safety of the crew." Management techniques in NASA, the report said, discouraged dissenting views on safety issues and ultimately created "blind spots'" about the risk to the space shuttle of the foam insulation impact. In short, as the movie *What the Bleep* illustrates so vividly: in the context or organizational culture, managers create the reality they envision; the corporate culture is a major reflection of that reality.

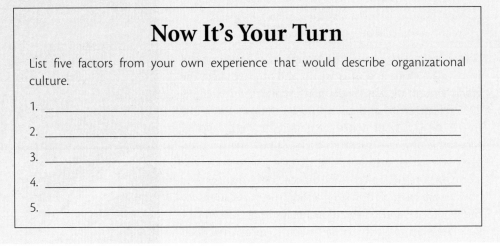

Now It's Your Turn

List five factors from your own experience that would describe organizational culture.

1. _____

2. _____

3. _____

4. _____

5. _____

■■■■ Overview

As our opening case scenarios show, the culture of an organization can affect so much of what the company stands for and does. Over a decade ago Harvard professors John Kotter and James Heskett showed through empirical research at more than 200 companies such as Hewlett-Packard, Xerox, and Nissan, how the culture of a corporation powerfully influences its economic performance, for better or for worse. Their thesis is that adaptive cultures—not necessarily strong ones on certain dimensions—are more likely to survive. For example, K-Mart's lack of a customer-service ethos cost it dearly when they had to compete with Wal-Mart.[5] Different cultures in organizations will be shaped by the different ways that managers interact with their employees. That is why the power of words is so important—a reality brought forth so vividly by the movie *What the Bleep Do We Know?* in its presentation of positive vs. negative words. If, as we saw in Chapter 6, organizational structure provides an organization with a skeleton, organizational culture provides the muscles, sinews, nerves, and sensations that allow managers to regulate and govern the organization's activities. Organizational culture also affects the ability of the organization to engage in change and adapt to new environments when necessary. K-Mart was ineffective at doing precisely this in relation to Wal-Mart.

In this chapter, we look at how culture works, and how it is taught to organizational members. This continues our discussion from the previous chapter about how managers organize human and other resources to create high-performing organizations We will examine why culture can inspire employees to achieve great goals, and why it can also lead to organizational failure. We will look at how to manage change successfully, in the face of strong culture, and how to overcome resistance to change. By the end of this chapter, you will understand how culture helps convey meaning and purpose to employees. You will also understand the vital role that change plays in building competitive advantage and creating a high-performing organization.

Organizational Culture

THINK ABOUT IT

"Basically, It's Common Sense"[6]

So says Toronto psychologist, Barbara Moses, Ph.D., when discussing how workplace training, environment and corporate culture are critical to boosting productivity. She goes on to point out how work today is a "constant audition," or a theatre in which no one can rest on his/her laurels—hence, the necessity of employers to provide personal and professional development learning opportunities to employees. What's 'common sense' to Dr. Moses are the fundamentals: giving thanks for a job well done, providing recognition, and giving employees a sense of accomplishment as a result of their efforts. These factors contribute to the making and shaping of the organizational culture. She also points out that the 'new worker' today is not simply the young person starting out who wants a job, but also the ordinary employee who knows that to stay competitive in today's workplace demands an attitude of employability, that fundamentally, the employee must take responsibility for his/her career. Managers must mentor and create a culture in which people take responsibility for ensuring this employability.

You Be the Manager

1. How prepared are you for the new workplace?
2. What would you expect a manager to do for you to create a healthy workplace culture?

Organizational culture refers to a system of shared meaning, held by organization members, that distinguishes the organization from other organizations.[7] Culture is the "glue" that keeps organizational members together, and guides their behaviour. New employees learn the organizational culture from their managers and other employees.

organizational culture
A system of shared meaning, held by organization members, that distinguishes the organization from other organizations.

Culture can be viewed as something that both helps employees make sense of the organization and guides employee behaviour. In essence, culture defines the rules of the game:

> Culture by definition is elusive, intangible, implicit, and taken for granted. But every organization develops a core set of assumptions, understandings, and implicit rules that govern day-to-day behaviour in the workplace. Until newcomers learn the rules, they are not accepted as full-fledged members of the organization. Transgressions of the rules on the part of high-level executives or front-line employees result in universal disapproval and powerful penalties. Conformity to the rules becomes the primary basis for reward and upward mobility.[8]

Organizational culture can control individuals and groups in an organization through shared values, norms, standards of behaviour, and expectations. **Values** are the stable, long-lasting beliefs about what is important. **Norms** are unwritten rules or guidelines that prescribe appropriate behaviour in particular situations. Norms emerge from values.[9]

Organizational culture is not an externally imposed system of constraints, such as direct supervision or rules and procedures. Rather, employees internalize organizational values and norms and then let those values and norms guide their decisions and actions. Just as people in society at large generally behave in accordance with socially acceptable values and norms, such as the norm that people should line up at the checkout counters in supermarkets, so are individuals in an organizational setting mindful of the force of organizational values and norms.

Levels of Culture

Culture exists at two levels in an organization: the visible level and the invisible level. We see culture through its **artifacts**. These are what you see, hear, and feel when you are within an organization. For instance, organizations have different dress policies, have different ways of organizing office space, and have different ideas of what should be displayed on company walls. The things you see reveal the organization's culture.

At the invisible level of culture are the values, beliefs, and assumptions that make up the organizational culture. **Beliefs** are the understandings of how objects and ideas relate to each other. **Assumptions** are the taken-for-granted notions of how something should be. Because of basic assumptions that are held by organizational members, it can be difficult to introduce change. Darren Entwistle, CEO of Burnaby, BC-based Telus, struggled through negotiations with employees during 2003 because of basic assumptions of employees. Those based in Alberta, who had merged into Telus, were quite happy with a variable-pay program that Entwistle proposed, and they assumed they would be rewarded for good performance. Those based in British Columbia, where management-employee relations were more antagonistic, assumed the program would end up lowering their pay by expecting them to work harder than they were currently working.[10] These differing assumptions made it difficult for Telus management to reach agreement with BC employees about having a variable-pay program.

During the summer of 2005 Telus Corp. experienced this same dynamic when its 11 000 employees went on strike. While some Alberta employees eventually crossed the picket line—Telus claiming up to 50 percent, the Telecommunications Workers Union (TWU) saying 25 percent—none of the Vancouver employees did so. Telus also gave out MP3 players worth between $60 and $100 to workers who crossed the picket line in Alberta.[11]

values

The stable, long-lasting beliefs about what is important.

norms

Unwritten rules or guidelines for appropriate behaviour in particular situations.

artifacts

Aspects of an organization's culture that one sees, hears, and feels.

beliefs

The understandings of how objects and ideas relate to each other.

assumptions

The taken-for-granted notions of how something should be in an organization.

Telus workers walk the picket line out in front of the Telus building in Edmonton.

The values and assumptions of an organization are not easily observed. Thus, we look to organizational artifacts (i.e., the things we can observe) to help us uncover the values and assumptions. For instance, managers' and employees' behaviour often reveals the organization's values and assumptions. When employees continue talking to each other in front of a waiting customer, they signal that employees are more important than customers to this organization.

Creating a Strong Organizational Culture

Culture is created and sustained in three ways:[12]

1. The founders and/or senior managers of the organization hire and keep only employees who think and feel the way they do.
2. The management indoctrinates and socializes these employees to their way of thinking and feeling.
3. Top managers serve as role models. By observing their behaviour, employees identify with them and internalize their beliefs, values, and assumptions.

In an organization, values and norms make it clear to organizational members what goals they should pursue and how they should behave to reach those goals. Thus, values and norms perform the same function as formal goals, written rules, or direct supervision. Research shows that having a strong culture usually pays off, except in times of a changing environment.[13] Those companies with stronger cultures tend to have better returns on investment, higher net income growth, and larger increases in share price than firms with weaker cultures. However, strong culture can be a liability when the environment is changing. Organizations with strong cultures have greater difficulty adapting to change.

Managers can influence the kinds of values and norms that develop in an organization. Some managers might cultivate values and norms that let subordinates know they are welcome to perform their roles in innovative and creative ways. Employees are thus encouraged to be entrepreneurial and willing to experiment and go out on a limb even if there is a significant chance of failure. At organizations such as Nortel Networks, Lucent Technologies, and 3M Canada, top managers encourage employees to adopt such values in order to support organizational commitment to innovation as a source of competitive advantage.

Other managers, however, might cultivate values and norms that let employees know that they should always be conservative and cautious in their dealings with others. Thus, these employees should always consult with their superiors before making important decisions, and should always put their actions in writing so they can be held accountable for whatever happens. In any setting where caution is needed—nuclear power stations, large oil refineries, chemical plants, financial institutions, insurance companies—a conservative, cautious approach to making decisions might be highly appropriate.[14] Caution when used inappropriately, however, may stifle employees' ability to innovate or communicate. One interesting merger to watch over the coming years is the one between Molson Inc. of Montreal with Colorado's Adolph Coors Co. Some are asking if this is a culture shock already in the brewing stages.[15] Chairman Pete Coors said, "We've known each other for a long time, we respect them as brewers, they respect us as brewers, we respect each other from a marketing perspective. You can't put two people together and expect perfect harmony but this is as harmonic as I think you can possibly get putting two companies together." Is he just putting on a brave face? When three executives each "at random" picked up a bottle of either Coors or Molson to toast the successful conclusion of the merger, the eldest Coors swivelled slowly toward the meeting and said, "I'd stick with Coors Light if I were all of you."

Difficulties arise when two organizations with different cultures merge. For instance, when Calgary-based TransCanada PipeLines Ltd. and Nova Corporation merged in 1998, different cultures led to conflicts in bringing the two companies together. Nova and TransCanada treated their employees very differently. TransCanada had a more traditional, top-down management control structure. Nova relied on its culture of empowering employees to govern their behaviour. One Nova employee described the merger as "GI Joe meets the Care Bears."[16] Three years later the two companies had not completely resolved their cultural differences.

Teaching the Culture to Employees

Managers deliberately cultivate and develop the organizational values and norms that are best suited to their task and general environments, strategy, or technology. Organizational culture is transmitted to and shared with organizational members through the values of the founder; the process of socialization; ceremonies and rites; and stories and language (see Figure 7.1).

Values of the Founder

One manager who has a very important impact on the kind of organizational culture that emerges in an organization is the founder. An organization's founder and his or her personal values and beliefs have a substantial influence on the values, norms, and standards of behaviour that develop over time within the organization.[17] Founders set the stage for the way cultural values and norms develop because they hire other managers to help them run their organizations. It is reasonable to assume that founders select managers who share their vision of the organization's goals and what it should be doing. In any case, new managers quickly learn from the founder what values and norms are appropriate in the organization and thus what is desired of them. Subordinates imitate the style of the founder and, in turn, transmit his or her values and norms to their subordinates. Gradually over time, the founder's values and norms permeate the organization.[18]

A founder who requires a great display of respect from subordinates and insists on things such as formal job titles and formal modes of dress encourages subordinates to act in this way toward their subordinates. Often, a founder's personal values affect an organization's competitive advantage. Frank Stronach, founder of Aurora, Ontario-based Magna Corporation, believes that his employees should show a "strong sense of ownership and entrepreneurial energy." He practises this belief by diverting 10 percent of pre-tax profit to profit-sharing programs for his employees. Similarly, managers' salaries are deliberately set "below industry standards" so that managers will earn more through profit-sharing bonuses. To further emphasize managerial responsibility, Magna's managers are given considerable autonomy over buying, selling, and hiring. Through

FIGURE 7.1 | *Factors Creating a Strong Organizational Culture*

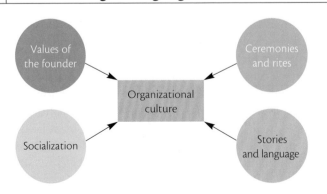

these policies of profit-sharing and empowerment, Stronach has developed a workforce that has made Magna one of the largest and most profitable companies in the country.

Similarly, Richard Branson of the Virgin Group, known for his entrepreneurial style, challenges his managers to act like him. All of his small companies are headed by managing directors who have a stake in the company they run. He wants his managers to operate the companies as if they were their own. Branson's style of management has made Virgin a success in a number of different markets it has entered.

Socialization

Over time, organizational members learn from each other which values are important in an organization and the norms that specify appropriate and inappropriate behaviours. Eventually, organizational members behave in accordance with the organization's values and norms—often without realizing they are doing so. **Organizational socialization** is the process by which newcomers learn an organization's values and norms and acquire the work behaviours necessary to perform jobs effectively.[19] As a result of their socialization experiences, organizational members internalize an organization's values and norms and behave to fit in with them, not only because they think they have to but because they think that these values and norms describe the right and proper way to behave.[20]

Most organizations have some kind of socialization program to help new employees "learn the ropes"—the values, norms, and culture of their organization. The military, for example, is well known for the rigorous socialization process it uses to turn raw recruits into trained soldiers. Many organizations put new recruits through a rigorous training program to provide them with the knowledge they need not only to perform well in their jobs but also to represent the company to its clients. Thus, through the organizational socialization program, the founder and top managers of an organization can transmit to employees the cultural values and norms that shape the behaviour of organizational members.

Ceremonies and Rites

Another way in which managers can try to create or influence an organizational culture is by developing organizational ceremonies and rites—formal events that recognize incidents of importance to the organization as a whole and to specific employees.[21] The most common rites that organizations use to transmit cultural norms and values to their members are rites of passage, of integration, and of enhancement (see Table 7.1).[22]

Rites of passage determine how individuals enter, advance within, or leave the organization. The socialization programs developed by military organizations (such as the Canadian Armed Forces) or by large accountancy firms are rites of passage. Likewise, the ways in which an organization prepares people for promotion or retirement are rites of passage.

Sometimes, rites of passage can get out of hand. Fraternities, sororities, sports teams, and even the military have been known to use hazing to initiate members. Activities can include "sleep deprivation, public nudity and childish pranks or, at worst, extreme drunkenness, gross racial slurs, even beatings."[23] The videotaped hazing rituals at CFB

Richard Branson, Virgin Group
www.virgin.com/aboutus/autobiography/

organizational socialization
The process by which newcomers learn an organization's values and norms and acquire the work behaviours necessary to perform jobs effectively.

TABLE 7.1 | *Organizational Rites*

Type of Rite	Example of Rite	Purpose of Rite
Rite of passage	Induction and basic training	Learn and internalize norms and values
Rite of integration	Office Christmas party	Build common norms and values
Rite of enhancement	Presentation of annual award	Motivate commitment to norms

Petawawa caused the Airborne Regiment to be disbanded in 1995. While the goal of the hazing might have been to desensitize new recruits to the brutality of war, many Canadians felt that the practice had gone too far. In Australia a court held an organization liable for assault after a teenager, who was wrapped in cling film during a hazing ritual, prosecuted a company and two of its directors for assault under workplace safety laws.

> *His shoes and bag were then filled with sawdust and he was placed on a work trolley. He was covered with sawdust, and his co-workers squirted wood glue in his shoes, over his body and into his mouth. "Doyle, an asthmatic, coughed, choked and was unable to breathe," said New South Wales Chief Industrial Magistrate George Miller. "What started out as a simple episode of bullying got out of control, leading to a serious physical threat to Doyle's health and safety." Employees were not disciplined, and a company director knew in advance the hazing would take place.[24]*

Rites of integration, such as office parties, company cookouts, and shared announcements of organizational successes, both build and reinforce common bonds among organizational members. Southwest Airlines is well known for its efforts to develop ceremonies and rituals to bond employees to the organization by showing them that they are valued members. Southwest holds cookouts in the parking lot of its Dallas headquarters, and Herb Kelleher, the founder and chair, personally attends each employee Christmas party throughout the country. Because there are so many Christmas parties to attend, Kelleher often finds himself attending parties in July!

Rites of enhancement, such as awards dinners, newspaper releases, and employee promotions, let organizations publicly recognize and reward employees' contributions and thus strengthen their commitment to organizational values. By bonding members within the organization, rites of enhancement help promote group cohesiveness.

Stories and Language

Stories and language also communicate organizational culture. Stories (whether fact or fiction) about organizational heroes and villains and their actions provide important clues about values and norms. Such stories can reveal the kinds of behaviours that are valued by the organization and the kinds of practices that are frowned on.[25] Stories about Ted Rogers, the person (hero) who made Rogers Communications the company it is today, shed light on many aspects of Rogers Communications' corporate culture. Stories also about Bill Newnham, founder of Seneca College in Toronto, speak volumes about his spirit and how this spirit lives on in the organizational culture of the college.[26]

Language—through slogans, symbols, and jargon—is used to help employees come to know expectations while bonding with one another. Toronto-based Lucent Technologies Canada uses two acronyms to convey a set of expectations to employees. GROWS summarizes the behaviours expected for high performance: *G* is for global growth mind set; *R* is for results focus; *O* is for obsession with customers and competitors; *W* is for a workplace that is open, supportive, and diverse; and *S* is for speed to market. Similarly, employees are evaluated for paying attention to Lucent Canada's TOUCH: *T* is for teamwork; *O* is for obsession with customers; *U* is for uncompromising quality; *C* is for cost effectiveness; and *H* is for helping others excel.[27]

Material Symbols

The organization's layout is a material symbol, and so are the size of offices; whether individuals wear uniforms or have a dress code; and the kinds of cars that top executives are given.[28] Material symbols convey to employees who is important, how much distance there is between top management and employees, and what kinds of behaviour are appropriate. For example, at Toronto-based Willow Manufacturing, everyone from the CEO down wears a uniform to convey the message that everyone in the company is part of a team.

Lucent Technologies
Canada & GROWS
www.innoversity.org/
lucent_technologies.asp

Similarly, Alain Batty, the current director, European Sales Staffs, Ford of Europe, when he was president and CEO of Ford Motor Company of Canada, Limited from 2001–2005, had the same kind of huge desk in his office in Toronto as William Clay Ford Jr., chair and CEO of Ford Motor Company, and every other Ford divisional head. The office buildings for all of Ford's operations are also similar. Founder Henry Ford believed it was more efficient to organize office space this way.[29] At Bolton, Ontario-based Husky Injection Molding Systems, employees and management share the parking lot, dining room, and even washrooms, conveying the sense of an egalitarian workplace.

The concept of organizational language encompasses not only spoken language but how people dress, the offices they occupy, the cars they drive, and the degree of formality they use when they address one another. IBM Canada, long known for its dark-blue suits, introduced less formal clothing in 1993 so that customers would feel more comfortable when interacting with the company.[30] When employees "speak" and understand the language of their organization's culture, they know how to behave in the organization and what attitudes are expected of them.

Organizational Culture and Change

 THINK ABOUT IT

The Archetypes of "Man-Child CEO" and "Mother-Wife Secretary"[31]

Has the stereotyped secretary job category changed since the 1950s? It might seem so on first glance as one looks at professional women going about their workday.

Globe and Mail reporter, Susan Bourette, set out to find out precisely, in other words, to find a job a as 21st-century administrative worker. "It was the late '80s. Wide-eyed and freshly armed with an utterly useless philosophy degree, I hit the Bay Street temp circuit. For eight dreary months, I shuffled from tower to tower, into banks, brokerage houses and insurance companies. I spent my days stuffing envelopes, answering phones, typing form letters. And, above all, biting my tongue."

Writing in the September 2005 issue of *Report on Business Magazine*, here is what she discovered—her 10 "dirty secrets"—laid out with plenty of examples to support her observations:

1. You need to know only two words: "No problem."
2. Secretaries are idiots.
3. Hundred-million-dollar losses are just part of business—it's your typo that will bring the company down.
4. Fashion is the new apartheid.
5. It's like a marriage—without the upside.
6. Like the aquarium and the oil painting in the lobby, you are there to be stared at.
7. When not stared at, you are invisible.
8. There are actually some nice bosses out there.
9. "Wrong" is a relative concept.
10. Bay Street is one big daycare.

You Be the Manager

1. How would you make sure that an administrative assistant at your company was treated with dignity and respect?

To understand how widespread the need for change in Canadian organizations is, consider the findings of a 1999 study of 309 human resource executives across a variety of industries. All of them reported that they were going through at least one of the following changes: mergers, acquisitions, divestitures, global competition, management, and/or organizational structure.[32]

A variety of organizational factors can be changed, such as the structure, the technology, or the people. Often, however, it is not possible to change any of these without changing culture, because culture signals to employees what behaviour is appropriate and what is not inappropriate. In 2003 chief executive Jeff Casselman of furniture maker Shermag Inc., with offices in Sherbrooke, Quebec, and New Brunswick, faced not only how to manufacture differently but also to change the culture to continue to be successful.[33] The company was very successful because it sold much of its inventory to the United States market. But that didn't hold when the US dollar fell. In 2005 the company had its first loss. His solution was to shift 25 percent of its production to China. He realized that choice and speed were critical for survival; hence, his nine remaining Canadian facilities would have to change in order to be sustainable. Changes, however, did not come without pain; he even had to endure some strikes. He said the workers now realize that this is the only way to compete with China.

Organizations that want to move in a new direction must alter policies, structures, behaviours, and beliefs in order to get from how "we've always done it" to how things will be done in the future. Thus even the changes in the production system need to be carried out within the context of examining and changing an organization's culture. Managers play a crucial role in changing culture because employees watch their behaviour to assess what is and is not important.

Edgar Schein identifies five mechanisms that alert employees to what management finds important in the culture.[34] These mechanisms are:

- *Attention.* Those things to which the leader directs employee attention (i.e., what is criticized, praised, or asked about). These things communicate what the leader and the employee value.

- *Reactions to crises.* The reaction of the leader and managers to crisis conveys to employees the core values of the organization. For instance, when companies face financial difficulties, employees receive the message from downsizing that people do not matter in this organization.

- *Role modelling.* Leaders communicate to employees strong messages about their values through their actions. In other words, actions speak louder than words when employees are trying to determine what the culture of the organization is. For example, when entrepreneur Tom Monaghan started in the pizza business in 1960 and in 1965 renamed his business Domino's Pizza, he created an innovative pizza culture. "Domino's Pizza's 30-minute guarantee forged an identity that reaped huge rewards—and is a role model for every business."[35]

- *Allocation of rewards.* Rewards such as pay increases or promotions signal to employees how one succeeds in the organization.

- *Criteria for selection and dismissal.* The leader's decisions about what kinds of employees to recruit or dismiss send a signal to all about what kinds of employees are valued.

In order to change the culture of the organization, managers need to consider these mechanisms and the messages they are sending to employees. Thus, they need to look at how they recruit and dismiss, how they reward, how they act, and what things they bring to employees' attention. Changes in these activities may well result in resistance, but successful change will require the consistent application of new procedures and rewards. We discuss how to deal with resistance to change below.

Managing Organizational Change

THINK ABOUT IT

The Pope's Running Shoes![36]

Endorsements are important for companies, especially those companies selling running shoes. Michael Jordan gets behind the Nike brand; Allen Iverson does the same thing with Reebok. Adidas hit it big with David Beckham. But what about the Converse Chuck Taylor brand—also known as "Chucks"? Believe it or not, there have been 750 000 pairs of Chucks sold during the last 100 years.

Never heard of it? Pope Paul II certainly did when he was still a bishop. He was wearing a pair and photographed in them! Mick Jagger often performs in them; Jim Belushi wore them in the movie *Animal House*. But, more important, Chucks have *soul*, because "what better celebrity endorsement could a running shoe have than a pope." Glen Lynch, owner of Baggins Shoes in downtown Victoria, B.C., which has one of the world's largest collection of Chucks, said, "Chucks have always been good at placement with pop icons which is why they've become more fashionable the last couple of years."

Change hit Converse hard. In 2001 the company declared bankruptcy, closed its U.S. factories and shifted production to Asia. Two important factors have allowed it to continue: (a) pop culture, and (b) an acquisition by Nike. But, in terms of corporate culture and change, Chucks are still available as they are known in the public's mind. Like the "New Coke" debacle of 1985,[37] lovers of Chucks running shoes will not switch because of new corporate owners; there is unequivocal resistance to any change to the brand. Lynch is convinced that with Chucks it's "easier for people to express their individuality—more than with other shoes."

Elizabeth Semmelhack, curator for the Bata Shoe Museum in Toronto, believes the shoe's recent popularity is the result of a backlash against the sort of $165 biomechanical space boots that Nike pushes. "People embrace their low-tech aspect," says Semmelhack. "I think anytime something becomes too complex, there will be a backlash, and people will want to go back to basics." Perhaps that will always be the Chuck's secret weapon—its stubborn refusal to change. For a product that is 82-years-old, the question is: Why look for followers when they always keep finding you? "I've got an 84-year-old customer who won't wear anything else," says Lynch, grabbing a pair of classic black-and whites off the shelf. "It's the tradition. There aren't many companies who've used the same design since their beginning. But the best reason is, it's just a good shoe. That's why you'll still be able to get Chucks 30 years from now."

Organizational change and brand loyalty: Converse's unequivocal resistance to any change to the Chuck brand contributes to the shoe's success.

You Be the Manager

1. Why do some managers feel compelled to make changes?
2. What are some reasons that Chucks have "staying power"?

Deciding how to change an organization is a complex matter, not least because change disrupts the status quo and poses a threat, prompting employees to resist attempts to alter work relationships and procedures. Several experts have proposed a model that managers can follow to introduce change successfully while effectively managing conflict and politics.[38] Figure 7.2 outlines the steps that managers must take to manage change effectively. In the rest of this section we examine each one.

Assessing the Need for Change

Assessing the need for change calls for two important activities: recognizing that there is a problem and identifying its source. This is not always easy. NASA generally has been reluctant to address management failures after problems arise, and more willing to look for and address mechanical failures. When the Columbia Accident Investigation Board issued its report in the summer of 2003, it listed many of the same management failures that were identified after the Challenger disaster of 1983. NASA is not unique in this approach. Sometimes the need for change is obvious, such as when an organization's performance is suffering. Often, however, managers have trouble determining that something is going wrong because problems develop gradually; organizational performance may slip for a number of years before it becomes obvious. This is what happened at NASA. Thus, during the first step in the change process, managers need to recognize that there is a problem that requires change.

Often, a gap between desired and actual performance signals that there is a problem. By looking at performance measures—such as falling market share or profits, rising costs, or employees' failure to meet their established goals or stay within budgets—managers can see whether change is needed. These measures are provided by organizational control systems (discussed in Chapter 13). When chief executive Jeff Casselman of furniture maker Shermag Inc. saw that in the year ended April 1, 2005, the company had lost $9.9 million (74¢ per share) on revenue of $242 million compared with a record $17.1 million ($1.27 per share) profit on $252 million revenue a year earlier and that this was its first loss in 12 years, he knew he had a serious problem with the company.[39]

If there is a gap between desired and actual performance, managers need to discover the source of the problem. They do this by looking both inside and outside the organization. Outside the organization, they must examine how changes in environmental forces may be creating opportunities and threats that are affecting internal work relationships. Perhaps the emergence of low-cost foreign competitors has led to conflict among different departments that are trying to find new ways to gain a competitive advantage. In Shermag Inc.'s case, even though revenues were up 18 percent in 2003 and the company was debt-free, the company had really become a victim of its own success: the US dollar fell sharply and, because the company got 70 percent of its sales from the United States, some of its profits were floating with the value of the Canadian dollar. As well, competition from Chinese manufacturers was getting stronger and stronger.

FIGURE 7.2 | *Four Steps in the Organizational Change Process*

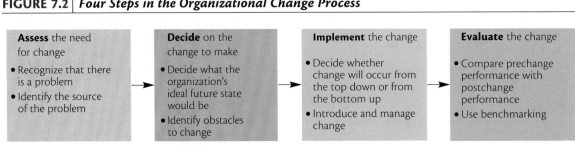

Assess the need for change	**Decide** on the change to make	**Implement** the change	**Evaluate** the change
• Recognize that there is a problem • Identify the source of the problem	• Decide what the organization's ideal future state would be • Identify obstacles to change	• Decide whether change will occur from the top down or from the bottom up • Introduce and manage change	• Compare prechange performance with postchange performance • Use benchmarking

Managers also need to look within the organization to see whether its structure and culture are causing problems between departments. Perhaps a company does not have the integrating mechanisms in place to allow different departments to respond to low-cost competition (see Chapter 6).

Deciding on the Change to Make

Once managers have identified the source of the problem, they must decide what they think the organization's ideal future state would be. In other words, they must decide where they would like their organization to be in the future—what kinds of goods and services it should be offering, what its business-level strategy should be, how the organizational structure should be changed, and so on. During this step, managers also must engage in planning how they are going to attain the organization's ideal future state. McDonald's is at a crossroads because consumers are starting to move away from a constant diet of Cokes and Big Macs, and looking for something a bit healthier. McDonald's can see this in its bottom line, but managers don't know how to meet the challenge. In part, their continued success over the past 30 years makes it difficult to determine a new strategy.

This step in the change process also includes identifying obstacles or sources of resistance to change. Managers must analyze the factors that may prevent the company from reaching its ideal future state. Obstacles to change are found at the corporate, divisional, departmental, and individual levels of the organization.

Corporate-level changes in an organization's strategy or structure—even seemingly trivial changes—may significantly affect how divisional and departmental managers behave. Suppose that to compete with low-cost foreign competitors, top managers decide to increase the resources spent on state-of-the-art machinery and reduce the resources spent on marketing or R&D. The power of manufacturing managers would increase, and the power of marketing and R&D managers would fall. This decision would alter the balance of power among departments and might lead to increased politics and conflict as departments start fighting to retain their status in the organization. An organization's present strategy and structure are powerful obstacles to change.

Organizational culture also can make change easier or harder. Organizations with entrepreneurial, flexible cultures, such as high-tech companies, are much easier to change than are organizations with more rigid cultures such as those sometimes found in large bureaucratic organizations like the military or General Motors.

The same obstacles to change exist at the divisional and departmental levels as well. Division managers may differ in their attitudes toward the changes that top managers propose and will resist those changes if their interests and power seem threatened. Managers at all levels usually fight to protect their power and control over resources. Given that departments have different goals and time horizons, they may also react differently to the changes that other managers propose. When top managers are trying to reduce costs, for example, sales managers may resist attempts to cut back on sales expenditures if they believe that problems stem from manufacturing managers' inefficiencies.

At the individual level, too, people are often resistant to change because change brings uncertainty and uncertainty brings stress. For example, individuals may resist the introduction of a new technology because they are uncertain about their abilities to learn it and effectively use it.

These obstacles make organizational change a slow process. Managers must recognize these potential obstacles to change and take them into consideration. Some obstacles can be overcome by improving communication so all organizational members are aware of both the need for change and the nature of the changes being made. Empowering employees and inviting them to take part in the planning for change also can help overcome resistance and reduce employees' fears. Emphasizing big-picture goals, such as organizational effectiveness and gaining a competitive advantage, can make organizational members who resist a change realize that the change is ultimately in everyone's best interests because it will increase organizational performance. The larger and more complex an organization is, the more complex is the change process.

Introducing the Change

top-down change
Change that is introduced quickly throughout an organization by upper-level managers.

Generally, managers can introduce and manage change from the top down or from the bottom up.[40] **Top-down change** is implemented quickly: Top managers identify the need for change, decide what to do, and then move quickly to introduce the changes throughout the organization. For example, top managers may decide to restructure and downsize the organization and then give divisional and departmental managers specific goals to achieve. With top-down change, the emphasis is on making the changes quickly and dealing with problems as they arise.

bottom-up change
Change that is introduced gradually and involves managers and employees at all levels of an organization.

Bottom-up change is typically more gradual. Top managers consult with middle and first-line managers about the need for change. Then, over time, these low-level managers work with nonmanagerial employees to develop a detailed plan for change. A major advantage of bottom-up change is that it can reduce uncertainty and resistance to change. The emphasis in bottom-up change is on participation and on keeping people informed about what is going on.

Lewin's Three-Stage Model of Change

Kurt Lewin identified a three-step process that organizations could use to manage change successfully: *unfreeze* the status quo, *move* to a new state, and *refreeze* the new change to make it permanent.[41]

driving forces
Forces that direct behaviour away from the status quo.

Organizations in their ordinary state reflect the status quo. To move toward a new state, unfreezing is necessary. Unfreezing, the process by which an organization overcomes the resistance to change, can occur in one of three ways, as shown in Figure 7.3. **Driving forces**, which direct behaviour away from the status quo, can be increased.

restraining forces
Forces that prevent movement away from the status quo.

Restraining forces, which hinder movement from the existing equilibrium, can be decreased. One can also combine the first two approaches.

FIGURE 7.3 | *Unfreezing the Status Quo*

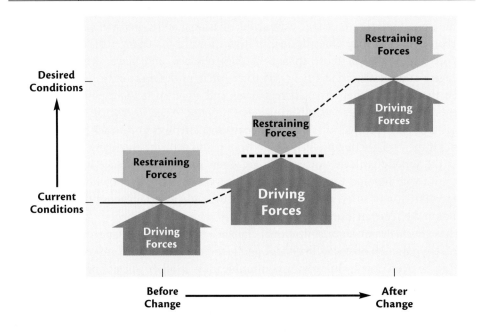

Individuals generally resist change, and therefore managers must take steps to break down that resistance. They can increase the driving forces by promising new rewards or benefits if employees work toward the change. Managers can also remove some of the restraining forces. For instance, if employees fear change because they don't know how to use the new technology, training could be given to reduce that fear. When resistance to change is extremely high, managers may have to work on both the driving and the restraining forces for unfreezing to be successful.

Moving involves getting the change process itself underway. Once change has been implemented, the behaviours have to be refrozen so that they can be sustained over time. Otherwise, change is likely to be short-lived, and employees are likely to go back to the previous state. Refreezing balances the driving and restraining forces to prevent the old state from arising again.

To refreeze the change, managers need to put permanent driving forces into place. For instance, the new bonus system could reinforce specific new changes. Over time, the norms of the employee work groups and managers will also help solidify the change if senior managers have sufficiently reinforced the new behaviour.

Evaluating the Change

The last step in the change process is to evaluate how successful the change effort has been in improving organizational performance.[42] Using measures such as changes in market share, profits, or the ability of managers to meet their goals, managers compare how well an organization is performing after the change with how well it was performing before. After chief executive Jeff Casselman of Sherbrooke, Quebec's Shermag Inc. made the necessary changes, set up outsourcing arrangements with China, he gained the two options that would be critical to success in the marketplace: customization and choice.

> *For example, Mr. Casselman pointed to three night tables on display. Each was a different colour and style, but "the basic frame of each is the same," he said. "Historically, we had to make 400 at a time. Now the consumer can come in and pick this one or that one." Shermag's newly retooled Bishopton, Que. plant can get an order Monday and be ready to ship Wednesday. The turnaround used to take eight weeks. Other plants are being similarly retooled, and a new centre in Sherbrooke will develop products at a faster rate than before.*[43]

Managers also can use **benchmarking**, comparing their performance on specific dimensions with the performance of high-performing organizations to decide how successful the change effort has been. For example, when Xerox was doing poorly in the 1980s, it benchmarked the efficiency of its distribution operations against those of L.L. Bean, the efficiency of its central computer operations against those of John Deere, and its marketing abilities against those of Procter & Gamble. Those companies are renowned for their skills in those different areas, and by studying how they performed, Xerox was able to dramatically increase its own performance.

benchmarking
Comparing performance on specific dimensions with the performance of high-performing organizations.

Tips for Managers

INTRODUCING CHANGE

1. No one likes change forced on them. However, sometimes change is the only alternative. Think through why change is necessary in the work you do and the people you manage.

2. Ponder the following statement: "Change is the only constant."

3. Ponder the following statement: "Change changed."

Managing Change in a Unionized Environment

THINK ABOUT IT

Featherbedding and All That![44]

The British created a civil service job in 1803 calling for a man to stand on the Cliffs of Dover with a spyglass. He was supposed to ring a bell if he saw Napoleon coming. The job was abolished in 1945.

Featherbedding refers to "the practice of requiring an employer to hire more workers than are needed or to limit their production in keeping with a safety regulation or union rule."[45] Can that same requirement be justified or tolerated in an age such as ours with so much rapid change, downsizings, and outsourcings? That is the question facing both managers and union officials. Some even ask if there is a future to unions? "But the deep question is whether unions have any chance of regaining power in a world of computerization and globalization. So are unions capable of delivering real value to postmodern workers, or are they just gangs of conspiratorial spongers who smother the occasional business to death as a means of clinging to relevance?"[46]

Statistics Canada shows that Canada's "union density," as it is called, for the year 2004 was 28.6 as a percentage of the Civilian Labour Force and 30.4 as a percentage of Non Agricultural Paid Workers. While the Civilian Labour Force statistics have remained relatively stable over a 14-year period (28.7% for 1990 vs. 28.6% for 2004), the Non Agricultural Paid Workers statistics have shown a decrease (34.8% for 1990 vs. 30.4% for 2004).[47]

It is claimed that the over union density is high because of public service employees. The Canadian union movement is also dominated by the "bloated public sector," according to Colby Cosh, Canadian commentator, writer and editor, and "since the Canadian union movement is dominated by the public sector, most of its leaders are decades away from perceiving this as a problem."

University of Ottawa economics professor Gilles Paquet, paints an unflattering economic portrait of Canada, depicting it as a risk-averse nation on the brink of becoming an ageing society. Canada, he wrote in *Policy Options* magazine, is "plagued by social rigidities that prevent it from adapting smoothly and quickly to meet the new [economic] challenges. . . . Such an ageing economy is marred by a decline in risk-taking, clinging to old techniques when new and more economical ones are available, resistance to rationalization, [and] a propensity to featherbedding."[48]

You Be the Manager

1. How will managers engage unions in meaningful ways that involve changes for the future of the workplace?

When managers work in a unionized environment, they may have some other considerations to face. Two consultants who have worked with a number of Canadian organizations in recent years note four essential elements for managing change in a unionized environment.[49]

- *An effective system for resolving day-to-day issues.* Employees should have alternatives to the formal grievance process so that they feel they can be heard easily. If the workplace is open to hearing workers' issues, this will underscore a commitment to participation and empowerment.

- *A jointly administered business education process.* Because union leaders and their members become uneasy about the effects of change on jobs, education can help employees understand the need for change. Making them more aware of company performance helps them better understand the decisions the company makes.

- *A jointly developed strategic vision for the organization.* Giving union members the opportunity to be involved in setting the vision lets them focus on how change can be made, rather than whether it should be made. The vision "should describe performance expectations, work design, organizational structure, the supply chain, governance, pay and rewards, technology, education and training, operating processes, employee involvement, employment security, and union-management roles and relations."[50]

- *A nontraditional, problem-solving method of negotiating collective agreements.* Managers need to create an atmosphere of tolerance and willingness to listen. Expanding the traditional scope of bargaining to include complex issues such as strategic plans is also helpful. Management resists bargaining over these issues, but when managers do bargain, it communicates a commitment to working jointly with unionized employees.

Summary and Review

1. **ORGANIZATIONAL CULTURE** Organizational culture is the set of values, norms, standards of behaviour, and common expectations that guide how individuals and groups in an organization interact with each other and work to achieve organizational goals. Culture guides individuals and groups through shared values, norms, standards of behaviour, and expectations.

2. **TEACHING CULTURE TO EMPLOYEES** Organizational culture is transmitted to employees through the values of the founder, the process of socialization, organizational ceremonies and rites, and stories and language. The way managers perform their management functions influences the kind of culture that develops in an organization.

3. **ORGANIZATIONAL CULTURE AND CHANGE** Changing the culture of an organization is difficult, and managers need to be aware of the signals they send to employees about change. If managers do not support the change themselves, it is unlikely that employees will go along with change.

4. **MANAGING ORGANIZATIONAL CHANGE** Managing organizational change is one of managers' most important and difficult tasks. Four steps in the organizational change process are assessing the need for change, deciding on the change to make, introducing the change, and evaluating how successful the change effort has been.

5. **MANAGING CHANGE IN A UNIONIZED ENVIRONMENT** To manage change in a unionized environment it is important to resolve day-to-day issues, provide education about the change, work together on developing a vision for the organization, and establish new problem-solving arrangements.

Key Terms

artifacts, p. 198

assumptions, p. 198

beliefs, p. 198

benchmarking, p. 209

bottom-up change, p. 208

driving forces, p. 208

norms, p. 198

organizational culture, p. 197

organizational socialization, p. 201

restraining forces, p. 208

top-down change, p. 208

values, p. 198

SO WHERE DO YOU STAND?

Wrap-Up to Opening Case

Our opening case began with a reflection on how corporate culture is the net result of how managers and employees envision and create their corporate reality. Reference was made to the movie *What the Bleep Do We Know?* In the movie the viewer is presented with the latest findings of subatomic physics and discussions of what the findings mean philosophically and practically to individuals and organizations. By its very nature, as we saw in this chapter, culture is elusive, it's intangible, and we simply take it for granted. We also take the air we breathe for granted—until we are deprived of it! Culture takes in our assumptions, understandings, and the implicit rules and expectations we have around our lives and our workplace. Words connect us, one to the other. The adage that "sticks and stones may break your bones, but words will never hurt you" is simply untrue. Words can truly hurt; words can truly heal as well.

When managers, therefore, seek to create positive, life-giving corporate cultures, what they say and how they say it became critical to that health. Culture represents the "way we do things around here." In the case of Nortel Networks Corp., we saw how two seasoned executives got up and abruptly left the company after three months. The official line was that there were differences in management style. That translates in the real world as differences in corporate culture approaches to getting the job done.

The final example in our opening case was that of the space shuttle *Columbia*. Because of certain factors in NASA's corporate culture—namely, an attitude of complacency around safety issues that had developed over the years and a failure to see their "blind spots"—a terrible tragedy happened and seven astronauts were killed on re-entry into the atmosphere.

Organizational culture can be the life-blood to an extremely effective workplace, but it can also create incredible harm. So much depends on the how managers go about creating their corporate reality. Most of us are familiar with, or have experienced, bosses whose work habits have created pain and anguish in the workplace. Many administrative assistants can validate how destructive some managers can be in creating the building blocks for the corporate culture. A woman named Lisa shared this story with Susan Bourette, the *Globe and Mail* reporter:

> He'd [manager] lose it if his pickles weren't sliced properly. He'd lose it if the freshly squeezed grapefruit juice she served him had settled. He lost it for 45 minutes the day she replaced a broken coffee maker with one that wasn't in the company colours. And once, when he was left waiting at the airport for 10 minutes, he called the office, shouting: "How dare you keep me waiting here. Don't you know I'm the most important man in the world?"[51]

Luckily, there are also effective managers who do create engaging corporate cultures, such people as Darwin Smith, CEO at paper-products maker Kimberly-Clark.[52] According to Jim Collins, author of *From Good to Great*, he created not only a "good" company, but he created a "great" company, in all aspects of this term. What singles out the "great" leaders are two factors: will and humility. "Out of 1435 Fortune 500 companies that renowned management researcher Jim Collins studied, only 11 achieved and sustained greatness—garnering stock returns at least three times the market's—for 15 years after a major transition period."

Organizational culture matters because people matter. That declaration not only is ethically correct, it is also the only profitable way to do business.

After studying the preceding material, be sure to check out our Online Learning Centre at
www.mcgrawhill.ca/olc/jones
for more in-depth information and interactivities that correspond to this chapter.

Management in Action

Topics for Discussion and Action

1. What is organizational culture, and how does it affect the way employees behave?
2. Interview some employees of an organization, and ask them about the organization's values, norms, socialization practices, ceremonies and rites, and special language and stories. Referring to this information, describe the organization's culture.
3. What are the main obstacles to change?
4. Interview a manager about a change effort that he or she was involved in. What issues were involved? What problems were encountered? What was the outcome of the change process?
5. What difficulties do managers face when trying to introduce organizational change? How might they overcome some of these difficulties?

Building Management Skills

UNDERSTANDING CHANGE

Choose an organization you know—one that you have worked in or patronized, or one that has received extensive coverage in the popular press. The organization should be involved in only one industry or business. Answer these questions about the organization.

1. What is the output of the organization?
2. Is the organization producing its output efficiently?
3. Try to identify improvements that might be made to boost the organization's responsiveness to customers, quality, and efficiency.
4. How difficult would these changes be?

Management for You

Think of something that you would like to change in your personal life. It could be your study habits, your fitness and nutrition, the way you interact with others, or anything else that is of interest to you. What values and assumptions have encouraged the behaviour that currently exists (i.e., the one you want to change)?

What driving and restraining forces can you address in order to make the desired change?

Small Group Breakout Exercise

REDUCING RESISTANCE TO ADVANCES IN INFORMATION TECHNOLOGY

Form groups of three or four people, and appoint one member as the spokesperson who will communicate your findings to the whole class when called on by the instructor. Then discuss the following scenario.

You are a team of managers in charge of information and communications in a large consumer products corporation. Your company has already introduced many advances in information technology. Managers and employees have access to voice mail, email, the Internet, your company's own intranet, and groupware.

Many employees use the new technology, but the resistance of some is causing communication problems. For example, all managers have email addresses and computers in their offices, but some refuse to turn their computers on, let alone send and receive email. These managers feel that they should be able to communicate as they have always done—in person, over the phone, or in writing. Thus, when managers who are unaware of their preferences send them email messages, those messages are never retrieved.

Moreover, the resistant managers never read company news sent by email. Another example of the resistance that your company is encountering concerns the use of groupware. Members of some work groups do not want to share information with others electronically.

Although you do not want to force people to use the technology, you want them at least to try it and give it a chance. You are meeting today to develop strategies for reducing resistance to the new technologies.

1. One resistant group of employees is made up of top managers. Some of them seem computer-phobic. They have never used, and do not want to start using, personal computers for any purpose, including communication. What steps will you take to get these managers to give their PCs a chance?

2. A second group of resistant employees consists of middle managers. Some middle managers resist using your company's intranet. Although these middle managers do not resist the technology per se and use their PCs for multiple purposes, including communication, they seem to distrust the intranet as a viable way to communicate and get things done. What steps will you take to get these middle managers to take advantage of the intranet?

3. A third group of resistant employees is made up of members of groups and teams who do not want to use the groupware that has been provided to them. You think that the groupware could improve their communication and performance, but they seem to think otherwise. What steps will you take to get these members of groups and teams to start using groupware?

Managing Ethically

Some organizations, such as Arthur Andersen, the former accounting firm, and Enron, seem to have developed norms and values that caused their members to behave in unethical ways. When and why might a strong norm that encourages high performance become one that can cause people to act unethically? How can organizations prevent their values and norms becoming "too strong"?

Exploring the World Wide Web

SPECIFIC ASSIGNMENT

Enter Hewlett-Packard's website (www.hp.com). Click on "Company Information"; then click on "About Us" and "Corporate Objectives."

1. What are the main elements of the HP Way?
2. How does the HP Way lead to an organizational culture that helps Hewlett-Packard to achieve its strategies?
3. How easy would it be to institute the HP Way and culture in other companies?

GENERAL ASSIGNMENT

Search for the website of a company that actively uses organizational culture to build competitive advantage. What kind of values and norms is the culture based on? How does it affect employee behaviour?

Developing a Business Plan
(APPENDIX B, PAGE 405)

Go to www.mcgrawhill.ca/olc/jones/7 for online exercises.

Be the Manager

THE PERSONAL TOUCH[53]

You have been called in to help with a five-year-old plastics company. This company has grown enormously since its inception and been very successful financially. It has expanded rapidly and now has over 100 employees. They have come to realize that while they have a very "hands-on" culture as far as technical expertise goes, this approach to working with employees has created a culture that has alienated some of the newer employees. As a matter of fact, the company recently lost three of its best employees. In exit interviews, they said they found the company had become very "impersonal" and they didn't want to work in such an organization.

Questions

1. What would be some suggestions you could make to create a more "personal" corporate culture?
2. How would you go about helping managers develop a team performance culture as well?

Management Case

New Workers, New Employers[54]

Workplace training, environment, and culture are critical to boosting productivity

Companies will be more productive if senior managers respond to the needs of the "new worker," says Barbara Moses, an author and career expert.

Contrary to expectation, this "new worker" is not the young and the restless twentysomething armed with a master's of business administration degree and a Blackberry. Instead, it is the person trying to get ahead in a tough, competitive marketplace while dealing with the stress of trying to achieve balance in work and life.

"The new worker is independent of age," says Moses. . . . "Today, everybody has to take responsibility for their own employability."

Work today is a constant audition, she says, a theatre in which no one can rest on [his/her] laurels. That is why employers who offer personal and professional development and who provide learning opportunities stand to reap rewards.

New workers crave everything from formal training and online learning to cross-departmental movement opportunities, says Moses, who emphasizes that professional development should be provided in good times and bad, not just when staff retention is an issue. "Managers need to give people the tools by which they can take charge of their own careers, so they can identify what they need and want."

Here are some ways to keep new workers motivated —and more productive:

Managers who want to advance productivity would be wise to coach and counsel their employees. "People can benefit from the opportunity to be counselled in everything from career development to how to solve tricky political problems," Moses says. "The best way to ensure that someone feels good about having a career inside this company is to give them the skills so they know that, no matter what happens, they are equipped.

That also means mentoring and creating a culture in which people take responsibility for ensuring their own employability."

Provide a life-friendly environment. "The bar is very high in the workplace but, at the same time, people are overwhelmed in their personal lives," Moses says. "If you are asking people to work 110 percent all the time, they will have nothing left and are not going to be productive. Ironically, if you don't have a culture of overwork, then people are more productive."

Although small and mid-sized companies may not be able to provide the bonanza of benefits—such as on-site daycare or help with elder care—offered by giant corporations, they still can be more sensitive to the needs of all staff, regardless of their age and whether or not they are parents.

Smaller organizations need not wait for policies in order to affect change. A company president with small children may decide that work/life balance is a priority and his attitude can permeate an entire organizational culture. "If anything, the opportunity to leverage things in small to medium-sized companies is there more than in larger organizations," Moses says. "A policy may be unnecessary."

Create a more intimate culture, an environment where people can feel more closely aligned to their work and its results, Moses advises. "If you're running an organization of 65 000 people, there can be a more alienating experience and employees tend to identify more with their work unit," Moses says. A smaller company's personality also can be influenced by the personality of its owner: If that person is motivational, inspiring, and positive, the result can be a terrific work environment.

The opposite is also true in that an egotistical or temperamental leader can wreak havoc and misery. And it is not just a leader's personality that impacts on an organization, but also his or her management style. For instance, if the president controls all aspects of the company and is reluctant to let professional managers do their jobs, the results can be disastrous.

Micro-managers can be a real turn-off, Moses notes, especially since today's workers want opportunities to own a project, to have the same kinds of experiences they might have if they were running their own business.

Managers will get the best from their employees if they recognize the unique needs of each and every one of them.

While we all work for money, Moses observes, we also work to be intellectually engaged, to make a difference, to satisfy our needs for connection to others, to refine our craft, to be appreciated for our contribution, or to satisfy deeply held personal values.

Some of these reasons are more important to some employees than others: Ideally, with input from employees, a manager should be able to understand the unique needs of individuals who report to them.

Senior managers on the lookout for ways to improve productivity in others are themselves often under-nurtured. The result is job apathy—a threat to the productivity of both themselves and those they manage. "Many feel caught in a rut. You can't expect them to be models promoting inspiring behaviour for others if they feel overworked, underappreciated or resentful," Moses says.

She says senior managers should closely examine their own needs and motivations before looking for a new job. "Sometimes you will be able to make minor shifts, to act on the one or two things that are really bothering you within your own organization."

Employees often are motivated by fundamental things such as thanks for a job well done and some recognition. "Give them the opportunity to make a contribution and feel a sense of accomplishment, and provide them with the kind of training they need to manage their career," Barbara Moses says. "Basically, it's common sense."

Questions

1. What are some new factors in the new corporate culture?
2. Of the new norms and values, which ones will make it easy or difficult to create or change an already existing organization culture?

Video Management Case   CBC◉

The Big Chill (Hollywood North)

In recent years, the incentive for Hollywood to go to Canada to produce films has dissolved due to the rising Canadian dollar and the patriotic urgency to make big budget films in Hollywood, transforming the Canadian film production industry drastically. Canadian companies are now relocating south of the border to accommodate for the revenue lost but are still struggling with this seeming overnight change in business.

Questions to Consider

1. How have changes in viewing habits affected the business of film production?
2. What incentives could Canada create to draw Hollywood business back north, and thus reclaim income from large production costs? How might changes to the heavy restrictions on Canadian films affect the situation?

Source: *Venture*, show number 915, "The Big Chill," February 22, 2004, running time 10:11.

Part 4: Integrated Case

Organizations, Like People, Have Personalities[55]

In one particularly funny episode of *Seinfeld*, Jerry goes to a restaurant where his car is parked by a valet with body odour.

When he picks up the car later, it stinks. Seinfeld tries everything to get the smell out—he washes the upholstery, cleans the carpet, even changes the seats. Nothing works. The car still stinks.

When I think of some organizational cultures, I am reminded of that episode.

There are five particularly "stinky" organizations to which I have had repeated exposure over the past 20 years.

Although these organizations have been continuously reengineered, reinvented, reimagined, restructured, redesigned, and every other "re" you can think of, like Jerry Seinfeld's car, they still stink.

Tellingly, when I ask experienced consultants who have had broad corporate exposure about their worst clients, the names of these same companies invariably pop up.

Organizations, like people, have personalities. Go into an organization and, within about 10 minutes, you can get a general sense of what it is like to work there.

At the core, I would describe these "stinky" companies as rigid, arrogant, and cold. People look fed up. They have that determined look you get when you have to catch the commuter train in three minutes and you're late. Their speech is abrupt.

In contrast, when you go into a great work environment, you see and hear people talking as if they really want to be in on the conversation.

There is laughter in the background. People ask their co-workers how projects are going and make offers of help, and some talk about personal life events.

So what makes for a great organization? Obviously people work for and are motivated by different things, whether it be money, career advancement, collegial work relationships, flexibility, or perfecting a craft.

But at the foundation, we all want the same thing: the opportunity to do work in sync with our values, that plays to our strengths, provides a sense of accomplishment, makes us feel valued, and still leaves something left over in time and emotional resources to give to other parts of our lives.

Looming skills shortages have led many organizations to talk about "winning the war for talent," "becoming

an employer of choice," "developing an employee brand" and so on.

Yet when these organizations think about being a great employer, too often they focus on specific policies in areas such as benefits plans, compensation, wellness, and work/life balance.

These are all critical issues, of course. But policies alone will rarely make the critical difference between loving a job or hating it.

Having a work/life balance policy that looks good on paper, for example, is not sufficient.

What makes the difference is whether the organizational culture truly promotes in employees the sense that they can accomplish their work to a level of personal satisfaction and still go home with energy and a sense of well-being.

The glue that binds work attachment is psychological. It is the product of doing work that speaks to the individual at a deep emotional or intellectual level. People need to feel connected, whether to their colleagues or their boss, the challenge, importance or interest of their work.

They should be able to answer the question, "What's in it for you to work here?" with simple responses such as "I really like my boss," "I'm getting great training," "I love the challenges I deal with," or "I'm contributing to something I care about."

As one human resources executive, discussing her company's retention strategy, commented: "You don't want to sell your commodity in terms of price, because there is always someone out there who can pay a talented employee more than you can, so that's a no-win proposition. You have to differentiate yourself in a way that's hard to duplicate. People won't go across the street for a few extra dollars if they think 'I won't be able to replicate the feeling I have now at work, where I can be myself, I like the people I work with, I'm learning, and so on.'"

What is the experience most people have today of their working environment? Sadly, it is not very good, with record levels of employee dissatisfaction and a long line of those just waiting for the right time to quit ("When the economy turns around, I'm out of here" is a comment I hear frequently).

Many workers express a sense of helplessness. As one female client said, "I used to fight for things to be done right. Now it's kind of whatever. I'm too tired to fight. And I don't believe it would accomplish anything."

When speaking to large audiences of managers and professionals, I routinely ask: "Are you accomplishing your work to your level of personal satisfaction?" Only a handful indicate that they are.

This is particularly disturbing given that my research, along with that of many others, shows that the strongest motivator of today's managers/professionals is the opportunity to practise their craft in a way that's personally satisfying and to develop themselves.

People today are hungry—for time, recognition, and appreciation. And when these needs are not met, they are not productive.

Anger ("I'm working too hard for too little reward"), resentment ("my boss gets the best of me, my family gets the dregs") and deprivation ("I have nothing left for me") are not a recipe for employee engagement.

Organizations today talk about the need to promote innovation. But to be creative, people need to feel good about themselves and what they are accomplishing, and an environment that allows them the resources to get their work done. They will not generate innovative ideas when they are exhausted or have a sense of helplessness.

Managers who simultaneously lament looming skills shortages while piling on the work and not providing training, resources, or time are operating as if staff will have collective amnesia when talent again becomes scarce, which it surely will.

Do they think they can come into work one day in 2007 and say, "Hey, guys, the skills shortage is here. We've got to start to be nice to people from today on."

Remember Seinfeld. Once the stink sets in, you can't get it out. People have acute senses of smell—and long memories.

Workplace wisdom

Here are some ways that organizations can promote a positive employee experience:

Recognize the diminishing returns from excessive demands. No one can be effective working at full blast all the time.

Demonstrate understanding of the overcommitted lives of staff both in small ways, such as saying thank you, and larger ones, such as meaningful work/life balance opportunities.

Make every employee feel like a unique and valued human being. The acid test: They should be able to answer the question "What is in it for me to work here?" in a simple and compelling way. Show appreciation for individual differences in psychological motivators, life stage needs, and strengths.

Enable staff to have a sense of accomplishment. This means providing sufficient resources, from being able to get information and support to the time required to finish work to a satisfactory level. When people talk about feeling good about themselves and their work, this is often the major reason; that is also conversely the case when they feel demoralized.

Equally important, allow people time "to experience their experience." Most people are actually accomplishing more than they realize but they have no time to reflect and therefore to digest what they have accomplished. No sooner have they sort of finished something than something else is thrown at them.

Promote learning opportunities. About 70 percent of today's managers and professionals are personal developers, motivated by opportunities to learn, be challenged and improve their professional skills. Learning can come from conferences, on-the-job training, working with a mentor, or participation in a project that stretches skills.

Provide psychologically meaningful rewards. As one thirtysomething woman commented: "Why do they always want us to play golf? It means I have to buy expensive golf clothes and give up time with my kids. How about a nice massage?"

Provide autonomy. For example, let individuals see through a project to experience outcomes associated with their work initiatives, and show trust in their competencies to do it right.

Promote career self-management. Provide staff with tools to enable them to make informed career and life decisions about how they want to spend their time, and design work that plays to their strengths and supports their values and needs. Ask people what they need to feel good about their work experience.

Value all workers regardless of their employment relationship and age. Part-time contract student workers, for example, may become your future full-time employees; older workers, many of whom now are just weighing up how soon they can retire, might also well be a future talent pool, not to mention a valuable mentoring resource, if treated with a degree of respect for their experience, and offered opportunities for phased retirement.

Develop a culture that is disdainful of the quick, hurried, and abrupt. Encourage an extra minute to have a conversation that is not goal-directed.

Be an organization that people can be proud to be a part of. Be ethical and a good corporate citizen.

Discussion Questions

1. Choose five factors that Dr. Moses lists that contributes to a great company culture? Why did you choose those five?

2. What are today's workers looking for in their work experiences?

3. What is the most important factor contributing to a healthy corporate culture?

PART 5

Leading Individuals and Groups

CHAPTER

8

Motivation

Learning Outcomes

1. Explain how the fulfillment of human needs is the basis of motivation and why managers need to be concerned about it.

2. Explain how knowledge of needs theories of motivation helps managers assist employees in achieving organizational goals.

3. Describe how expectancy theory focuses on major factors in motivating employees.

4. Explain how organizational goals determine employees' motivation and subsequent performance.

5. Explain how managers can use reinforcement and behaviour modification to support high performance workplace behaviours.

6. Explain equity theory with its notion of employees' perceptions of *fairness* between what they contribute and what they receive.

7. Explain why and how managers can use pay as a major motivation tool.

Engaging People: The Cognos Way

Each of us at one time or another has asked the following question: "Why do we do the things we do?"

That question is the motivational question.

Cognos Inc. is an Ottawa-based software company that has a program built into their corporate strategy called Global People Strategy.[1] Every manager in all its offices worldwide is required to attend regular workshops on recognizing individual achievements, and keeping employees challenged and motivated to stay.

"The results managers get can sometimes be sobering," says Rod Brandvold, the company's vice-president of organizational development. "People consistently say that more feedback, more recognition and more help in meeting their personal goals make them more likely to stay with the company."

Cognos began this program in 2001. The results thus far? One of the best rates of employee retention in an industry prone to high staff turnover. Retention of good employees is a critical reality facing many companies in the increasingly competitive Canadian job market. But something else is also important: the motivational aspect—how not only to retain talented employees but also keep them committed and working at their peak. Cognos has obviously figured out some solutions to this challenge of an engaged workforce. Experts agree with Cognos also.

"It seems so obvious that we should explore what employees really want and what will keep them on the team and performing at their best. But yet, when managers are stressed and stretched to the max, it is easy to forget to ask," says Beverly Kaye, a California-based author and consultant whose theories are the basis of the Cognos program.[2] "I find managers have to be reminded not once but regularly to ask employees whether their work is meeting their goals," she says.

Kaye also points out that most often the sources of disengagement from a job don't involve salary or benefits, but things that managers do have control over, such as providing challenging, meaningful work and opportunities to learn and gain recognition. As with any relationship, if there is not a full commitment, there may be a temptation to stray. She says managers don't realize how much they themselves can have an impact on such a decision.

Toronto consultant Edmond Mellina, president of Transitus Management Consulting, is blunt in his advice to his clients. "If you don't find ways to engage people, you are dead." Mellina continues, "Regardless of how much power you have, if you don't create the conditions to engage people, you are powerless. The more distance you have between yourself and the people you manage the less power you have. It's hard to do, especially in Canada, where people tend not to talk about their personal lives and define their lives by what they do. It's amazing what you get if you just ask the question, 'What are your passions, what are your long-term goals?' Just ask, then just listen."

Rob Ashe congratulates former Cognos CEO Ron Zambonini.

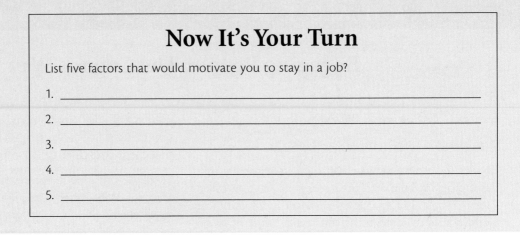

Now It's Your Turn

List five factors that would motivate you to stay in a job?

1. _____

2. _____

3. _____

4. _____

5. _____

▪▪□▪ Overview

Over 200 years ago the Scots poet and writer, Robert Burns (1759–1796) wrote about "the best-laid plans of mice and men." His idea was that people's plans are no more secure than those of the mouse. This same notion can be applied to life in organizations as well. That is, even with the best strategy in place and an appropriate organizational architecture, an organization will be effective only if its members are motivated to perform at a high level. In any organization leadership is critical to ensure that every member is motivated to perform highly and help the organization achieve its goals. Effective leadership ensures that an organization has a highly motivated workforce. The key, however, as we read in the opening Cognos Inc. scenario, is for managers to get to know their employees in order that they perform at a high level.

In this chapter, we describe what motivation is, where it comes from, and why managers need to promote high levels of it for an organization to be effective and achieve its goals. In Figure 8.1 we examine important theories of motivation.

Each of the theories found in Figure 8.1 provides managers with important insights about how to motivate organizational members. The theories are complementary in that each focuses on a somewhat different aspect of motivation. Considering all of the theories together will give managers a rich understanding of the many issues and problems involved in encouraging high levels of motivation throughout an organization. Finally, we consider the use of pay as a motivation tool. The net result of all this discussion is that you will understand what it takes to have a highly motivated workforce.

FIGURE 8.1 | *Important Theories of Motivation*

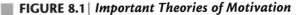

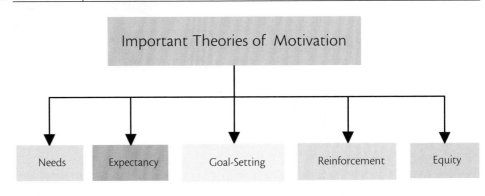

The Nature of Motivation

Spend Time With Your Employees!

Carol Pamasiuk is the executive vice-president and general manager of Cohn & Wolfe Canada,[3] with offices in Toronto and Montreal and more than 50 employees. It is an affiliate of Cohn & Wolfe, a leading marketing and communications firm with clients around the world. Says Pamasiuk, "Maybe you didn't start out in the mailroom and then work your way to the top, but if you truly want to understand your employees, spend some time doing their jobs and working with them. Unless you've done some of these jobs yourself, you'll never truly appreciate what your employees do, how they do it, what motivates them and how they see themselves contributing to the organization. Also, standing in your employees' shoes will help you to gain insights into your customers' experiences in interacting with your company, and you may even get some ideas on how to make your business run more efficiently."[4]

You Be the Manager

1. Identify a situation when you spent some time with someone doing their job. What happened and how did you feel?
2. Why would "standing in your employees' shoes" help you to gain insights into your customers' experiences in interacting with your company?

Motivation is the psychological forces that determine the *direction* of a person's behaviour in an organization, a person's level of *effort*, and a person's level of *persistence* in the face of obstacles.[5] People are motivated to obtain certain outcomes that they desire. An outcome is anything a person gets from a job or organization. Some outcomes, such as autonomy, responsibility, a feeling of accomplishment, and the pleasure of doing interesting or enjoyable work, result in intrinsically motivated behaviour. Other outcomes, such as pay, job security, benefits, and vacation time, result in extrinsically motivated behaviour. **Intrinsically motivated behaviour** is behaviour that is performed for its own sake; the source of motivation is actually to perform the behaviour, and motivation comes from doing the work itself. **Extrinsically motivated behaviour** is behaviour that is performed to acquire material or social rewards or to avoid punishment; the source of motivation is the consequences of the behaviour, not the behaviour itself.

Organizations hire people to obtain important inputs. An input is anything a person contributes to his or her job or organization, such as time, effort, education, experience, skills, knowledge, and actual work behaviours. Inputs such as these are necessary for an organization to achieve its goals. Managers strive to motivate members of an organization to contribute inputs—through their behaviour, effort, and persistence—that help the organization achieve its goals. They do this by making sure that members of an organization obtain the outcomes they desire when they make valuable contributions to the organization.

This alignment between employees and organizational goals as a whole can be described by the motivation equation shown in Figure 8.2. Managers aim to ensure that people are motivated to contribute important inputs to the organization, that these inputs are put to good use or focused in the direction of high performance, and that high performance results in employees obtaining the outcomes they desire.

motivation
Psychological forces that determine the direction of a person's behaviour in an organization, a person's level of effort, and a person's level of persistence.

intrinsically motivated behaviour
Behaviour that is performed for its own sake.

extrinsically motivated behaviour
Behaviour that is performed to acquire material or social rewards or to avoid punishment.

FIGURE 8.2 | *The Motivation Equation*

INPUTS FROM ORGANIZATIONAL MEMBERS	PERFORMANCE	OUTCOMES RECEIVED BY ORGANIZATIONAL MEMBERS
Time Effort Education Experience Skills Knowledge Work behaviours	Contributes to organizational efficiency, organizational effectiveness, and the attainment of organizational goals	Pay Job security Benefits Vacation time Job satisfaction Autonomy Responsibility A feeling of accomplishment The pleasure of doing interesting work

The main theories of motivation that we cover in this chapter fall into one of two categories: needs theories and process theories. *Needs theories* focus on the types of needs individuals have that will lead them to be motivated, while *process theories* explore how one actually motivates someone. Each of the theories of motivation we discuss focuses on one or more aspects of the motivation equation in Figure 8.2. Together, the theories provide a comprehensive set of guidelines for managers to follow to promote high levels of employee motivation. Effective managers such as Rod Brandvold in the opening *Management Snapshot* tend to follow many of these guidelines, whereas ineffective managers often fail to follow them and seem to have trouble motivating organizational members.

Needs Theories

THINK ABOUT IT

"Echo Employees": Coddled, Confident, and Cocky![6]

Managers today have to manage "echo employees"! They may not particularly appreciate these employees precisely because of their demographic identity. The challenge for such managers is to learn how to motivate them.

Echo employees, born since the 1980s, are the children of the baby boomers. So, who are they?

This is the first postwar generation that, on the whole, has not rebelled against their parents' or society's values, nor against a work environment they view as withholding opportunities.... Gen Yers were raised by guilty, work-obsessed, hovering parents who made their kids' feelings and success their hobby. They worshipped at the altar of promoting self-esteem and

Echo employee confidently exhibiting her own style.

tried to make up for the lack of time spent with their kids by lavishing them with travel experiences, clothes, and electronic toys.

As kids, Gen Yers were told they were brilliant because they could program the VCR. They were given the vote on almost everything, from where to go on vacation to the colour of the family car. It's not surprising they believe their feelings matter, that they should feel good about their work, and that they should be able to express themselves. People used to think about work only when it felt bad, if they thought about it at all. Now, as a result of heightened work consciousness, this generation asks, "Does this feel good?" They use a finely nuanced vocabulary to describe their work and are more thoughtful about their careers and work. And when they are not happy, much to management's regret, they are vocal about it.

You Be the Manager

1. What are the two most important concerns for "echo employees"?
2. What advice would you give an older manager on how to motivate "echo employees"?

A **need** is a requirement or necessity for survival and well-being. The basic premise of need theories is that people are motivated to obtain outcomes at work that will satisfy their needs. **Needs theories** suggest that in order to motivate a person to contribute valuable inputs to a job and perform at a high level, a manager must determine what needs the person is trying to satisfy at work and ensure that the person receives outcomes that help to satisfy those needs when the person performs at a high level and helps the organization achieve its goals.

We discuss two needs theories below: Abraham Maslow's *hierarchy of needs* and Frederick Herzberg's *motivator-hygiene theory*. These theories describe needs that people try to satisfy at work. In doing so, the theories provide managers with insights about what outcomes will motivate members of an organization to perform at a high level and contribute inputs to help the organization achieve its goals.

Maslow's Hierarchy of Needs

Psychologist Abraham Maslow proposed that everyone aims to satisfy five basic kinds of needs: physiological needs, safety needs, belongingness needs, esteem needs, and self-actualization needs (see Table 8.1).[7] He suggested that these needs constitute a **hierarchy of needs,** with the most basic or compelling needs—physiological and safety needs—at the bottom. Maslow argued that these lowest-level needs must be met before a person will strive to satisfy needs higher up in the hierarchy, such as self-esteem needs. Once a need is satisfied, he proposed, it no longer is a source of motivation, and needs at the next highest level become motivators.

Although Maslow's theory identifies needs that are likely to be important sources of motivation for many people, research does not support his contention that there is a needs hierarchy or his notion that only one level of needs is motivational at a time.[8] Nevertheless, a key conclusion can be drawn from Maslow's theory: People differ in what needs they are trying to satisfy at work. To have a motivated workforce that achieves goals, managers must determine which needs employees are trying to satisfy in organizations and then make sure that individuals receive outcomes that will satisfy their needs when they perform at a high level and contribute to organizational effectiveness.

need
A requirement or necessity for survival and well-being.

needs theories
Theories of motivation that focus on what needs people are trying to satisfy at work and what outcomes will satisfy those needs.

Abraham Maslow
www.ship.edu/~cgboeree/maslow.html

Maslow's hierarchy of needs
An arrangement of five basic needs that, according to Maslow, motivate behaviour. Maslow proposed that the lowest level of unmet needs is the prime motivator and that only one level of needs is motivational at a time.

TABLE 8.1 | *Maslow's Hierarchy of Needs*

	Needs	Description	Examples of How Managers Can Help People Satisfy These Needs at Work
Highest-level needs	**Self-actualization needs**	The needs to realize one's full potential as a human being	By giving people the opportunity to use their skills and abilities to the fullest extent possible
	Esteem needs	The needs to feel good about oneself and one's capabilities, to be respected by others, and to receive recognition and appreciation	By granting promotions and recognizing accomplishments
	Belongingness needs	Needs for social interaction, friendship, affection, and love	By promoting good interpersonal relations and organizing social functions such as company picnics and holiday parties
Lowest-level needs (most basic or compelling)	**Safety needs**	Needs for security, stability, and a safe environment	By providing job security, adequate medical benefits, and safe working conditions
	Physiological needs	Basic needs for things such as food, water, and shelter that must be met in order for a person to survive	By providing a level of pay that enables a person to buy food and clothing and have adequate housing

The lowest level of unsatisfied needs motivates behaviour; once this level of needs is satisfied, a person tries to satisfy the needs at the next level.

In an increasingly global economy it is also important for managers to realize that citizens of different countries might differ in the needs they try to satisfy through work.[9] Some research suggests, for example, that people in Greece and Japan are especially motivated by safety needs and that people in Sweden, Norway, and Denmark are motivated by belongingness needs.[10] In poor countries with low standards of living, physiological and safety needs are likely to be the prime motivators of behaviour. As countries become wealthier and have higher standards of living, it is likely that needs related to personal growth and accomplishment (such as esteem and self-actualization) become important as motivators of behaviour.

Herzberg's motivator-hygiene theory
A needs theory that distinguishes between motivator needs (related to the nature of the work itself) and hygiene needs (related to the physical and psychological context in which the work is performed). Herzberg proposed that motivator needs must be met in order for motivation and job satisfaction to be high.

Herzberg's Motivator-Hygiene Theory

According to **Herzberg's motivator-hygiene theory**, people have two sets of needs or requirements: motivator needs and hygiene needs.[11] *Motivator needs* are related to the nature of the work itself and how challenging it is. Outcomes such as interesting work, autonomy, responsibility, being able to grow and develop on the job, and a sense of accomplishment and achievement help to satisfy motivator needs. In order to have a highly motivated and satisfied workforce, Herzberg suggested, managers should take steps to ensure that employees' motivator needs are being met.

Hygiene needs are related to the physical and psychological context in which the work is performed. Hygiene needs are satisfied by outcomes such as pleasant and

FIGURE 8.3 | *Herzberg's Motivation-Hygiene Theory*

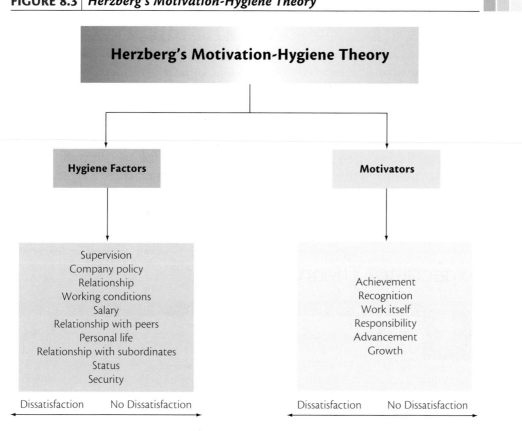

comfortable working conditions, pay, job security, good relationships with co-workers, and effective supervision. According to Herzberg, when hygiene needs are not met, workers will be dissatisfied, and when hygiene needs are met, workers will not be dissatisfied, that is, they will be neutral. For satisfaction to occur, the motivator needs must be met. This is illustrated in Figure 8.3. Pazmac's owner, Steve Scarlett, exhibits his understanding of Herzberg's theory. To satisfy motivator needs, he provides opportunities for his employees to be involved in decision making and ensures good relationships among employees. He also shows concerns about employees' hygiene needs. Usually machine shops are noisy and messy, the floors are covered with oil, and employees wear dirty overalls. Pazmac, however, is spotlessly clean. The lunchroom is tastefully designed, and the men's washroom is plush, with potpourri bowls and paintings on the walls.

Pazmac Enterprises
www.pazmac.com

Many research studies have tested Herzberg's propositions, and, by and large, the theory fails to receive support.[12] Nevertheless, Herzberg's formulations have contributed to our understanding of motivation in at least two ways. First, Herzberg helped to focus researchers' and managers' attention on the important distinction between intrinsic motivation (related to motivator needs) and extrinsic motivation (related to hygiene needs), covered earlier in the chapter. Second, his theory helped to prompt researchers and managers to study how jobs can be designed or redesigned so that they are intrinsically motivating.

Frederick Herzberg
www.lib.uwo.ca/business/
herzberg.html

Other Needs

Clearly more needs motivate employees than the needs described by these theories. For example, more and more employees are feeling the need for work-life balance and time to take care of their loved ones while simultaneously being highly motivated at work. Interestingly enough, recent research suggests that being exposed to nature (even just by being able to see some trees from your office window) has many beneficial effects and a lack of such exposure can actually impair well-being and performance.[13] Thus, having some time during the day when one can at least see nature may be another important need.

Managers of successful companies often strive to ensure that as many of their valued employees' needs as possible are satisfied in the workplace.

Needs theories address the different needs that individuals have that could be used to motivate them. **Process theories**, which we cover below, focus on the more concrete ways of actually motivating someone. Within the process theories, we cover *expectancy theory, goal-setting theory, and reinforcement theory.*

process theories
Theories of motivation that explore how one actually motivates someone.

Expectancy Theory

THINK ABOUT IT

Kid-Glove Managing![14]

Sometimes the expression "touchy-feely" can turn people off. But, as a manager, what if you wanted to attract the best possible candidates to work for you? Then you would certainly want to attract a person such as Nadia Ramos. Ramos not only has an MBA from McGill University in Montreal (2003) but she is also fluent in three languages: English, French, and Portuguese.

The Bank of Nova Scotia came through with flying colours for Ramos. Why? Because of the "touchy-feely" elements that she considered as essential for her new work experience. Consider Herzberg's hygiene factors here: when she went for a panel interview with bank personnel, they did a "walkabout" with her as well. The bank was upfront and clear with her right from the start: she was promised an overseas field assignment within her first two years. Obviously her fluency in three languages but the bank's acknowledgement and rewarding of that was apparent. As for the "touch-feely" elements, Ramos said, "You walk around afterward and see where you are going to be working, not only the boardroom, but the actual cubicles." The small things cemented her decision to begin working with the bank. The Bank of Nova Scotia calls this process that Ramos experienced onboarding. Sylvia Chrominska, executive vice-president of human resources, says that hiring candidates is really only the start of the process. Says Chrominska, "We have to make sure, once they are in the door, that they start having a great experience as an employee—and that we haven't over-promised. . . . Employees have much different expectations of employment now. Gen X and Gen Y need to find work challenging. The really capable ones have much more choice: They have worldwide access to job opportunities. And they ask tough questions: How soon will I be able to make a move, what kind of training am I going to be offered? The bank makes a point of ensuring those kinds of questions get answers."

You Be the Manager

1. What are your expectations when you go for a job interview?
2. What are some additional ways that managers can use to motivate employees?

Expectancy theory, formulated by Victor H. Vroom in the 1960s, states that motivation will be high when employees believe that high levels of effort will lead to high performance, and high performance will lead to receiving desired outcomes. Expectancy theory is one of the most popular theories of work motivation because it focuses on all three parts of the motivation equation: inputs, performance, and outcomes. Expectancy theory identifies three major factors that determine a person's motivation: *expectancy, instrumentality,* and *valence* (see Figure 8.4).[15]

Inco Ltd. has rolled out a front-line planning and scheduling system at its Copper Cliff smelter in Sudbury, Ontario, in which the daily, weekly, and monthly goals for production and maintenance are clearly established every day.

Expectancy

Expectancy is a person's perception about the extent to which effort (an input) will result in a certain level of performance. A person's level of expectancy determines whether he or she believes that a high level of effort will result in a high level of performance. People are motivated to put forth a lot of effort on their jobs only if they think that their effort will pay off in high performance—that is, if they have a high expectancy. Think about how motivated you would be to study for a test if you thought that, no matter how hard you tried, you would get a D. In this case, expectancy is low, so overall motivation is also low.

In trying to influence motivation, managers need to make sure that their subordinates believe that if they do try hard they actually can succeed. For example, excessive criticism, as we know from our own experiences, leads to relatively low levels of expectancy on our part. We begin to doubt our own ability to succeed which then leads to low motivation. In addition to expressing confidence in subordinates, another way for managers to boost subordinates' expectancy levels and motivation is by providing training so that people have all the expertise they need for high performance. At Irving Oil Ltd., of Saint John, New Brunswick, a family-owned company known for its tankers, truck stops, and refinery towers, managers eagerly look forward to leadership training with the workplace learning provider Forum Corp. of Boston, Massachusetts. Kenneth Irving, a senior executive, at Irving Oil, actively promotes the training and the need for more of such training.[16] St. Catherines, Ontario, NuComm International Inc., a privately held company that provides "customer care" services for North American companies in the cable, telecommunications, automotive, entertainment, and retail sectors, is another such company that believes in training. Linda Robichaud, who works as a telephone service representative, remarked that NuComm's training is comprehensive and professional, "I was on the phones for one week, and then I moved up. I'm training to be a trainer." The training increases Robichaud's expectancy by improving her ability to perform well.

Instrumentality

Expectancy captures a person's perceptions about the relationship between effort and performance. **Instrumentality**, the second major concept in expectancy theory, is a person's perception about the extent to which performance at a certain level will result in receiving outcomes or rewards (see Figure 8.4). According to expectancy theory, employees will be motivated to perform at a high level only if they think that high performance will lead to outcomes such as pay, job security, interesting job assignments, bonuses, or a feeling of accomplishment.

expectancy theory
The theory that motivation will be high when employees believe that high levels of effort will lead to high performance, and high performance will lead to the attainment of desired outcomes.

expectancy
In expectancy theory, a perception about the extent to which effort will result in a certain level of performance.

instrumentality
In expectancy theory, a perception about the extent to which performance will result in the attainment of outcomes.

■■■ **FIGURE 8.4** | *Expectancy, Instrumentality, and Valence*

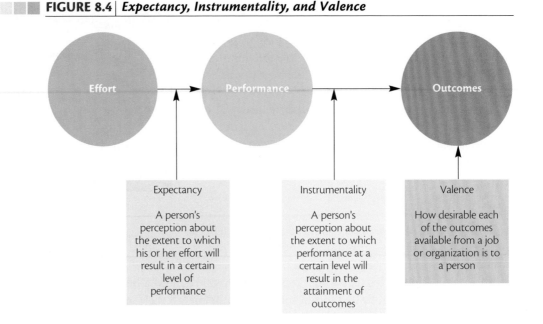

Managers promote high levels of instrumentality when they clearly link performance to desired outcomes and communicate this. By making sure that rewards are given to organizational members based on their performance, managers promote high instrumentality and motivation. When rewards are linked to performance in this way, high performers receive more than low performers. In the case of Cognos Inc., the Ottawa-based software company, when employees realized there would be more feedback, more recognition, and more help in meeting their personal goals, they were more motivated to stay with the company. They see the link between performance and reward.

Valence

Expectancy theory acknowledges that people differ in their preferences for outcomes or rewards. For many people, pay is the most important outcome of working. For others, a feeling of accomplishment or enjoying one's work is more important. At Motorola's Malaysian plant, the rewards to employees reflect things that they value. Salaries are relatively high ($287 a month), as are job security and promotional opportunities, which makes employees feel that they are valued members of Motorola.[17] The term **valence** refers to how desirable each of the outcomes available from a job or organization is to a person. To motivate organizational members, managers need to determine which outcomes have high valence for them—are highly desired—and make sure that those outcomes are provided when members perform at a high level.

valence

In expectancy theory, how desirable each of the outcomes available from a job or organization is to a person.

Bringing It All Together

According to expectancy theory, high motivation results from high levels of expectancy, instrumentality, and valence (see Figure 8.5). If any one of these factors is low, motivation is likely to be low. No matter how tightly desired outcomes are linked to performance, if a person thinks that it is practically impossible for him or her to perform at a high level, then motivation to perform at a high level will be exceedingly low. Similarly,

FIGURE 8.5 | *Expectancy Theory*

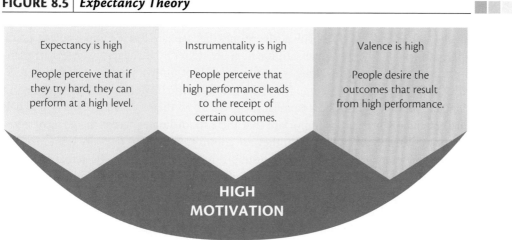

if a person does not think that outcomes are linked to high performance, or if a person does not desire the outcomes that are linked to high performance, then motivation to perform at a high level will be low.

Managers of successful companies try to ensure that employees' levels of expectancy, instrumentality, and valence are high so that they will be highly motivated, as is illustrated by Motorola's efforts at managing globally.

Goal-Setting Theory

"People do not always argue because they misunderstand one another; they argue because they hold different goals."
—William H. Whyte, author of *The Organization Man*[18]

Goal-setting theory, developed by Ed Locke and Gary Latham, suggests that the goals that organizational members strive to achieve determine their motivation and subsequent performance. A *goal* is what a person is trying to accomplish through his or her efforts and behaviours.[19] Just as you may have a goal to get a good grade in this course, so do members of an organization have goals that they strive to meet. If you recall, in our opening scenario, *Management Snapshot*, Rod Brandvold, the company's vice-president of organizational development for Cognos Inc. said, "The results managers get can sometimes be sobering. People consistently say that more feedback, more recognition and more help in meeting their personal goals make them more likely to stay with the company." Psychologist Barbara Moses writes, "Without any goals, we drift. Take one 35-year-old man who has spent the past decade bouncing around among different occupational pursuits. With indulgent and wealthy parents behind him, he has never had any sense of urgency to commit to a particular career path nor has he ever thought through what he wanted to achieve in his occupational pursuits, other than a vague feeling of 'this might be it.' When you talk to him, you get a sense of a lost soul who has no belief in himself or his future."[20]

Goal-setting theory suggests that in order to result in high motivation and performance, goals must be *specific and difficult*.[21] Specific goals are often quantitative—a salesperson's goal to sell $200 worth of merchandise each day, a scientist's goal to finish a project in one year, a CEO's goal to reduce debt by 40 percent and increase revenues by 20 percent,

goal-setting theory
A theory that focuses on identifying the types of goals that are most effective in producing high levels of motivation and performance and explaining why goals have these effects.

a restaurant manager's goal to serve 150 customers per evening. In contrast to specific goals, vague goals such as "doing your best" or "selling as much as you can" do not have much motivational force. Difficult goals are ones that are hard but not impossible to attain.

Regardless of whether specific, difficult goals are set by managers, workers, or managers and workers together, they lead to high levels of motivation and performance. As CEO of Eastman Kodak, George Fisher set specific, difficult goals for his employees but then left decisions about how to meet the goals up to them. When managers set goals for their subordinates, it is important that their subordinates accept the goals or agree to work toward them and also that they are committed to them or really want to attain them. Some managers find that having subordinates participate in the actual setting of goals boosts their acceptance of and commitment to the goals. It is also important for organizational members to receive *feedback* about how they are doing; feedback can often be provided by the performance appraisal and feedback component of an organization's human resource management system (see Chapter 11).

Reinforcement Theory

THINK ABOUT IT

Take This Job and Shove It![22]

There are jobs, and then there are jobs! Have you ever had a job that you would classify as "less-than-perfect"? In fact, you had to "gear up" every day, so to speak, just to get to work. Many of us have had those jobs when first in the workforce. Then, again, we might have such a job in order to pay the bills.

Some would consider night-shift work to be one of those "less-than-perfect" jobs. Take the work that many of us take for granted: taxi drivers, medical personnel at hospitals, emergency service personnel, and police officers. Many of these people do shift work. Abdul Said, a Royal Taxi night-shift taxi driver in Toronto, who works seven days a week at 12-hour shifts that start late in the afternoon, says he needs to work such hours because his wife is only employed sporadically and he wants to give his growing children the advantages their friends have. "I feel guilty that I don't have a lot of time with my family. But I would feel more guilty if I abandoned my kids to the social system or leave them alone. So I prefer to work to provide them with food and shelter," said Said, who has been on the night shift for three years." Somehow he has to find that motivational spark that will provide the energy to do what he has to do.

For Sgt. Jim Adamson, with 26 years as a police officer, he finds it very difficult to get his body "turned around again," as he puts it. "Often tired on the midnight shift, the police officer nonetheless tosses and turns when he has to try to get some sleep during the day—his body rebelling against its natural circadian rhythms. He pays extra attention to his health because he finds his body is more susceptible to illnesses when he is on midnights. The cyclical night-time absences from home have also taken a toll on his personal life. His marriage fell apart after 14 years and he blames the graveyard duty for contributing to the breakup."

You Be the Manager

1. What are the challenges that the following shift workers face in their jobs: police officers, taxi drivers, medical personnel?

2. How would you motivate yourself if you did shift work?

Reinforcement theory is a motivation theory that looks at the relationship between behaviour and its consequences. **Reinforcement** is defined as anything that causes a certain behaviour to be repeated or stopped. Four reinforcements are generally discussed in the theory: *positive reinforcement, negative reinforcement, extinction,* and *punishment.*

Positive Reinforcement

Positive reinforcement gives people outcomes they desire when they perform well. These outcomes, called positive reinforcers, include any outcomes that a person desires, such as pay, praise, or a promotion. Performing well might include producing high quality goods and services, providing high quality customer service, and meeting deadlines. By linking positive reinforcers to the positive performance, managers motivate people to perform the desired behaviours. For instance, managers at Brandon's hog slaughterhouse offer a variety of incentives to encourage workers to show up for their shifts. To be eligible for a truck raffle, held every three months, employees have to show up for every one of their shifts during that period. Employees get bonuses of 75 cents an hour for perfect attendance during shorter periods. Regular wages range from $8.25 to $13 an hour. The incentive program has paid off. Before the rewards, 12 percent of the employees skipped work each day. Since the rewards, absenteeism has dropped to about 7 to 8 percent.

Negative Reinforcement

Negative reinforcement also can be used to encourage members of an organization to perform well. Managers using negative reinforcement actually eliminate or remove undesired outcomes once the desired behaviour is performed. These undesired outcomes, called *negative reinforcers*, can include unpleasant assignments, a manager's constant nagging or criticism, or the ever-present threat of losing one's job. When negative reinforcement is used, people are motivated to perform behaviours because they want to avoid or stop receiving undesired outcomes. Managers who try to encourage salespeople to sell more by threatening them with being fired are using negative reinforcement. In this case, the negative reinforcer is the threat of job loss, which is removed once the functional behaviours are performed.

Whenever possible, managers should try to use positive reinforcement. Negative reinforcement can make for a very unpleasant work environment and even a negative culture in an organization. No one likes to be nagged, threatened, or exposed to other kinds of negative outcomes. The use of negative reinforcement sometimes causes subordinates to resent managers and try to get back at them.

Extinction

Sometimes members of an organization are motivated to engage in poor performance. One way for managers to stop dysfunctional behaviours is to eliminate whatever is reinforcing the behaviours. This process is called **extinction**.

Suppose a manager has a subordinate who frequently stops by the office to chat—sometimes about work-related matters but at other times about various topics ranging from politics to last night's football game. Though the chats are fun, the manager ends up working late to catch up. To extinguish this behaviour, the manager stops acting interested in these nonwork-related conversations and keeps responses polite and friendly but brief. No longer being reinforced with a pleasurable conversation, the subordinate eventually ceases to be motivated to interrupt the manager during working hours to discuss nonwork issues.

reinforcement theory
A motivation theory based on the relationship between a given behaviour and its consequence.

reinforcement
Anything that causes a given behaviour to be repeated or stopped.

positive reinforcement
Giving people outcomes they desire when they perform organizationally functional behaviours well.

negative reinforcement
Eliminating or removing undesired outcomes once people have performed organizationally functional behaviours.

extinction
Stopping the performance of dysfunctional behaviours by eliminating whatever is reinforcing them.

punishment

Administering an undesired or negative consequence when dysfunctional behaviour occurs.

organizational behaviour modification (OB MOD)

The systematic application of operant conditioning techniques to promote the performance of organizationally functional behaviours and discourage the performance of dysfunctional behaviours.

Punishment

When employees are performing dangerous behaviours or behaviours that are illegal or unethical, the behaviour needs to be stopped immediately. Therefore the manager will use **punishment**, administering an undesired or negative consequence to subordinates when they perform the dysfunctional behaviour. Punishments used by organizations range from verbal reprimands to pay cuts, temporary suspensions, demotions, and firings. Punishment, however, can have unintended side effects—resentment, loss of self-respect, a desire for retaliation, etc.—and should be used only when absolutely necessary.

Organizational Behaviour Modification

When managers use reinforcement to encourage positive behaviours and discourage negative behaviours, they are engaging in **organizational behaviour modification (OB MOD)**.[23] OB MOD has been used successfully to improve productivity, efficiency, attendance, punctuality, compliance with safety procedures, and other important behaviours in a wide variety of organizations. The five basic steps in OB MOD are described in Figure 8.6.

FIGURE 8.6 | *Five Steps in OB MOD*

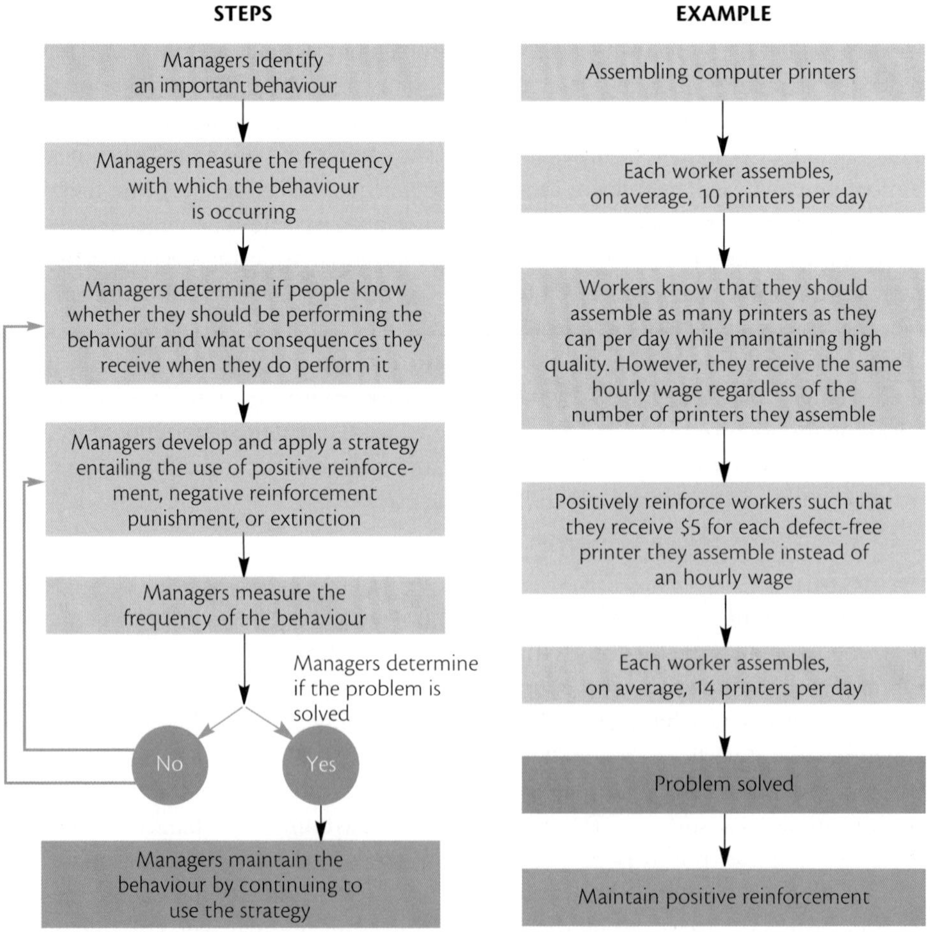

Source: Adapted from F. Luthans and R. Kreitner, Organizational Behavior Modification and Beyond (Glenview, IL: Scott, Foresman, 1985).

OB MOD works best for behaviours that are specific, objective, and countable—such as attendance and punctuality, making sales, or putting telephones together—which lend themselves to careful scrutiny and control. OB MOD may be questioned because of its lack of relevance to certain kinds of work behaviours (e.g., the many work behaviours that are not specific, objective, and countable). Some people also have questioned it on ethical grounds. Critics of OB MOD suggest that it is overly controlling and robs workers of their dignity, individuality, freedom of choice, and even their creativity. Supporters counter that OB MOD is a highly effective means of promoting organizational efficiency. Both sides of this argument have some merit. What is clear, however, is that when used appropriately, OB MOD provides managers with a technique to motivate the performance of at least some positive behaviours.

In trying to understand how all of these theories of motivation fit together, it may be helpful to remember that needs theories suggest that individuals have needs, and that they will be motivated to have these needs met. Expectancy, goal-setting and reinforcement theories show the processes by which individuals can be encouraged to behave in ways that earn rewards. Job design, which we discussed in Chapter 6, can also be a way of motivating individuals. Job rotation, job enlargement, and job enrichment can increase an employee's job satisfaction, and thus lead him or her to be more motivated in performing the job.

Equity Theory

THINK ABOUT IT

Is This Fair?[24]

You are earning $28 822 per annum as your salary. Then you hear of someone making $40 155 for doing the same kind of work as you do. How would you feel about that? Would you think that was fair? Most of us would have very strong feelings about the *inequity* or unfairness of such a circumstance. And who would blame anyone! In Nova Scotia, as in other parts of Canada, people are starting to take notice. Why? Because the lower salary most probably belongs to a woman doing the same type of work as the man! Brigitte Neumann, executive director for the Nova Scotia Advisory Council on the Status of Women points out that while more and more women are breaking through what is called the glass ceiling, many still work in lower paying jobs and only make 71.6 cents for every dollar earned by a man doing comparable work. Being forced to work on the margins of the workforce can lead to a great sense of unfairness.

You Be the Manager

1. Have you ever been paid unfairly compared to others you worked with? How did you feel? What did you do about the situation?
2. How could you "rebalance" the equity scales if you were a manager?

Equity theory is a theory of motivation that concentrates on people's perceptions of the fairness of their work *outcomes* relative to, or in proportion to, their work *inputs*. Equity theory complements need and expectancy theories by focusing on how people perceive the relationship between the outcomes they receive from their jobs and organizations and the inputs they contribute.

equity theory
A theory of motivation that focuses on people's perceptions of the fairness of their work outcomes relative to their work inputs.

TABLE 8.2 | *Equity Theory*

Condition	Person		Referent	Example
Equity	$\frac{Outcomes}{Inputs}$	=	$\frac{Outcomes}{Inputs}$	An engineer perceives that he contributes more inputs (time and effort), and receives proportionally more outcomes (a higher salary and choice job assignments), than his referent.
Underpayment inequity	$\frac{Outcomes}{Inputs}$	< (less than)	$\frac{Outcomes}{Inputs}$	An engineer perceives that he contributes more inputs but receives the same outcomes as his referent.
Overpayment inequity	$\frac{Outcomes}{Inputs}$	> (greater than)	$\frac{Outcomes}{Inputs}$	An engineer perceives that he contributes the same inputs but receives more outcomes than his referent.

Equity

equity
The justice, impartiality, and fairness to which all organizational members are entitled.

Equity exists when a person perceives his or her own outcome/input ratio to be equal to a referent's outcome/input ratio. The *referent* could be another person or a group of people who are perceived to be similar to oneself; the referent also could be oneself in a previous job or one's expectations about what outcome/input ratios should be. Under conditions of equity (see Table 8.2), if a referent receives more outcomes than you receive, the referent contributes proportionally more inputs to the organization, so his or her outcome/input ratio still equals your outcome/input ratio. Similarly, under conditions of equity, if you receive more outcomes than a referent, then your inputs are perceived to be proportionally higher. Maria Lau and Claudia King, for example, both work in a shoe store in a large mall. Lau is paid more per hour than King but also contributes more inputs, including being responsible for some of the store's bookkeeping, closing the store, and periodically depositing cash in the bank. When King compares her outcome/input ratio to Lau's (her referent's), she perceives the ratios to be equitable because Lau's higher level of pay (an outcome) is proportional to her higher level of inputs (bookkeeping, closing the store, and going to the bank). In a comparison of one's own outcome/input ratio to a referent's outcome/input ratio, one's *perceptions* of outcomes and inputs (not any objective indicator of them) are key.

When equity exists, people are motivated to continue contributing their current levels of inputs to their organizations in order to receive their current levels of outcomes. Under conditions of equity, if people wish to increase their outcomes, they are motivated to increase their inputs.

Inequity

inequity
Lack of fairness.

Inequity, lack of fairness, exists when a person's outcome/input ratio is not perceived to be equal to a referent's. Inequity creates pressure or tension inside people and motivates them to restore equity by bringing the two ratios back into balance.

There are two types of inequity: underpayment inequity and overpayment inequity (see Table 8.2). **Underpayment inequity** exists when a person's own outcome/input ratio is perceived to be less than that of a referent: In comparing yourself to a referent, you think that you are not receiving the outcomes you should be, given your inputs. For instance, in international assignments, this notion of fairness is absolutely critical: "Failure to establish a uniform compensation policy in an international alliance that requires high interaction among employees from different partners can lead to

underpayment inequity
Inequity that exists when a person perceives that his or her own outcome/input ratio is less than the ratio of a referent.

predictably adverse effects. Differences in compensation systems, especially for employees doing the same jobs, often lead to feelings of inequity among those receiving lower compensation and benefits. Morale and motivation therefore suffer among group members."[25]

Overpayment inequity exists when a person perceives that his or her own outcome/input ratio is greater than that of a referent: In comparing yourself to a referent, you think that the referent is receiving fewer outcomes than he or she should be, given his or her inputs.

overpayment inequity
Inequity that exists when a person perceives that his or her own outcome/input ratio is greater than the ratio of a referent.

Ways to Restore Equity

According to equity theory, both underpayment inequity and overpayment inequity create tension that motivates most people to restore equity by bringing the ratios back into balance.[26] When people experience *underpayment* inequity, they may be motivated to lower their inputs by reducing their working hours, putting forth less effort on the job, or being absent, or they may be motivated to increase their outcomes by asking for a raise or a promotion. Take an employee like Mary Campbell, a financial analyst at a large corporation: when she noticed that she was working longer hours and getting more work accomplished than a co-worker who had the same position, yet they both received the exact same pay and other outcomes, to restore equity, Campbell decided to stop coming in early and staying late. Alternatively, she could have tried to restore equity by trying to increase her outcomes by, for example, asking her boss for a raise.

When people experience *overpayment* inequity, they may try to restore equity by changing their perceptions of their own or their referents' inputs or outcomes. Equity can be restored when people "realize" that they are contributing more inputs than they originally thought. Equity also can be restored by perceiving the referent's inputs to be lower or the referent's outcomes to be higher than one originally thought. When equity is restored in this way, actual inputs and outcomes are unchanged. What is changed is how people think about or view their own or the referent's inputs and outcomes. For example, employee Susan Martineau experienced overpayment inequity when she realized that she was being paid $2 an hour more than a co-worker who had the same job as hers in a record store and who contributed the same amount of inputs. Martineau restored equity by changing her perceptions of her inputs. She "realized" that she worked harder than her co-worker and solved more problems that came up in the store.

By experiencing either overpayment or underpayment inequity, you might decide that your referent is not appropriate because, for example, the referent is too different from yourself. Choosing a more appropriate referent may bring the ratios back into balance. However, when people experience *underpayment* inequity and other means of equity restoration fail, they may leave the organization.

Motivation is highest when as many people as possible in an organization perceive that they are being equitably treated, that is, their outcomes and inputs are in balance. Top contributors and performers are motivated to continue contributing a high level of inputs because they are receiving the outcomes they deserve. Mediocre contributors and performers realize that if they want to increase their outcomes, they have to increase their inputs. Managers of effective organizations, such as Calgary-based Telvent Canada Inc., which develops information management systems, with its dozens of professional mentoring relationships that benefit both its employees and profit margin,[27] and Regina-based Saskatchewan Power Corp., with its leadership succession planning,[28] realize the importance of equity for motivation and performance and continually strive to ensure that employees feel they are being equitably treated.

Tips for Managers

EXPECTANCY AND EQUITY THEORIES

1. Express sincere confidence in your subordinates' capabilities and let them know that you expect them to succeed.

2. Distribute outcomes based on important inputs and performance levels and clearly communicate to your subordinates that this is the case.

3. Determine which outcomes your subordinates desire and try to gain control over as many of these as possible (i.e., have the authority to distribute or withhold outcomes).

4. Provide clear information to your subordinates about which inputs are most valuable for them to contribute to their jobs and the organization in order to receive desired outcomes.

Pay and Motivation

THINK ABOUT IT

Is Pay the "Be-All and End-All"?[29]

"It's not just about the best pay or the best benefits program anymore because all our peers do that," says Susan O'Dowd, vice-president of human resources at Hoffman-La Roche Ltd., one of the 50 best Canadian employers in 2004. "It's about engaging employees and finding out how engaged they are." O'Dowd continues, "Now CEOs are seeing that the next frontier for productivity enhancement is people. They know the next great $10-million or $100-million computer system isn't where they're going to get the next round of productivity increases. It's by getting their people truly engaged in helping them make the business more successful, whether that's cutting costs, employees helping them to drive more revenue, or whatever the avenue is."

What's also getting increased attention today for motivating employees is the notion of the *healthy workplace*. "Healthy" is not simply a company's occupational health and safety record or access to an employee assistance program (EAP). Bill Wilkerson, president of the Global Business and Economic Roundtable on Addiction and Mental Health, says, "Ambiguity, inconsistency, uncertainty, insecurity, arbitrariness, bad decision-making, self-centredness, rewarding the wrong things in the office, the fostering of office politics and rewarding political behaviours—that's the earmark of weak leadership. And if you're a lousy leader, you're making people sick." What's becoming a real issue with health is minimizing the *say-do gap*, as we saw in the opening *Management Snapshot*. Cognos Inc. recognizes individual achievements, and keeps employees challenged and motivated to stay. Joan Burton, manager of health strategy for the Industrial Accident Prevention Association (IAPA), writes in her report, "A sense of fairness in the workplace is related to trust, which is key to employer-worker relations, high morale, and productivity. Feelings associated with a sense of unfairness are anger, depression, demoralization, and anxiety. These strong negative feelings translate chemically within workers into compromised immune systems, setting the stage for a variety of adverse physical and mental health problems."[30]

You Be the Manager

1. What are the advantages for having a "healthy workplace"?
2. How would you create a healthy motivational work environment?

Once a pay level and structure are in place, managers can use pay to motivate employees to perform at a high level and attain their work goals. Pay is used to motivate entry-level workers, first-line and middle managers, and even top managers such as CEOs. Pay can be used to motivate people to perform behaviours that will help an organization achieve its goals.

How Does Pay Motivate?

Each of the theories described in this chapter alludes to the importance of pay and suggests that pay should be based on performance (see Figure 8.7):

*   *Needs theories.* People should be able to satisfy their needs by performing at a high level; pay can be used to satisfy several different kinds of needs.

*   *Expectancy theory.* Instrumentality, the association between performance and outcomes such as pay, must be high for motivation to be high. Pay is also an outcome that has high valence for many people.

*   *Goal-setting theory.* Outcomes such as pay should be linked to the attainment of goals.

*   *Reinforcement theory.* The distribution of outcomes such as pay should be contingent on the performance of organizationally functional behaviours.

*   *Equity theory.* Outcomes such as pay should be distributed in proportion to inputs (including performance levels).

As these theories suggest, to promote high motivation, managers should base the distribution of pay to organizational members on performance levels so that high performers receive more pay than low performers (other things being equal).[31]

FIGURE 8.7 | *How Pay Motivates*

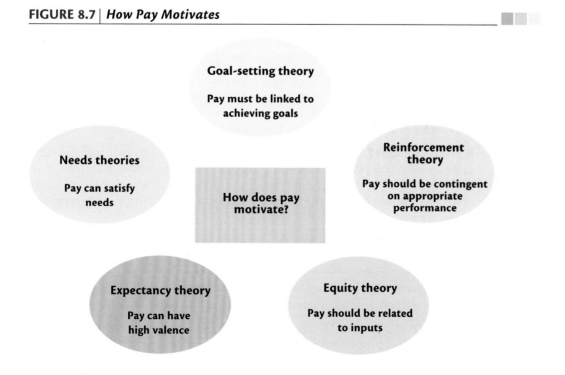

In deciding whether to pay for performance, managers also have to determine whether to use salary increases or bonuses. Thus some pay-for-performance programs (particularly those that use bonuses) are variable-pay programs. With variable pay, earnings go up and down annually based on performance.[32] Thus, there is no guarantee that an individual will earn as much this year as last.

The number of employees affected by variable-pay plans has been rising in Canada. A 2002 survey of 191 firms by Hewitt Associates found that 76 percent of them have variable-pay plans in place, compared to 43 percent in 1994.[33] These programs are more common among nonunionized workers, although more than 30 percent of unionized companies had such plans in 2002.[34] In Canada, pay-for-performance programs are more common for nonunionized workers than unionized ones. Prem Benimadhu from the Conference Board of Canada notes, "Canadian unions have been very allergic to variable compensation."[35] In addition to wage uncertainty, employees may object to pay for performance if they feel that factors out of their control might affect the extent to which bonuses are possible.

Summary and Review

1. **THE NATURE OF MOTIVATION** Motivation encompasses the psychological forces within a person that determine the direction of a person's behaviour in an organization, a person's level of effort, and a person's level of persistence in the face of obstacles. Managers strive to motivate people to contribute their inputs to an organization, to focus these inputs in the direction of high performance, and to ensure that people receive the outcomes they desire when they perform at a high level.

2. **NEEDS THEORIES** Needs theories suggest that in order to have a motivated workforce, managers should determine what needs people are trying to satisfy in organizations and then ensure that people receive outcomes that will satisfy these needs when they perform at a high level and contribute to organizational effectiveness.

3. **EXPECTANCY THEORY** According to expectancy theory, managers can promote high levels of motivation in their organizations by taking steps to ensure that *expectancy* is high (people think that if they try, they can perform at a high level), *instrumentality* is high (people think that if they perform at a high level, they will receive certain outcomes), and *valence* is high (people desire these outcomes).

4. **GOAL-SETTING THEORY** Goal-setting theory suggests that managers can promote high motivation and performance by ensuring that people are striving to achieve specific, difficult goals. It also is important for people to accept the goals, be committed to them, and receive feedback about how they are doing.

5. **REINFORCEMENT THEORY** Reinforcement theory suggests that managers can motivate people to perform highly by using *positive reinforcement* or *negative reinforcement* (positive reinforcement being the preferred strategy). Managers can motivate people to avoid performing dysfunctional behaviours by using *extinction* or *punishment*.

6. **EQUITY THEORY** According to equity theory, managers can promote high levels of motivation by ensuring that people perceive that there is equity in the organization or that outcomes are distributed in proportion to inputs. *Equity* exists when a person perceives that his or her own outcome/input ratio equals the outcome/input ratio of a referent. Inequity motivates people to try to restore equity.

7. **PAY AND MOTIVATION** Each of the motivation theories discussed in this chapter alludes to the importance of pay and suggests that pay should be based on performance.

Key Terms

equity, p. 236

equity theory, p. 235

expectancy, p. 229

expectancy theory, p. 229

extinction, p. 233

extrinsically motivated behaviour, p. 223

goal-setting theory, p. 231

Herzberg's motivator-hygiene
   theory, p. 226

inequity, p. 236

instrumentality, p. 229

intrinsically motivated behaviour, p. 223

Maslow's hierarchy of needs, p. 225

motivation, p. 223

need, p. 225

needs theories, p. 225

negative reinforcement, p. 233

organizational behaviour modification
   (OB MOD), p. 234

overpayment inequity, p. 237

positive reinforcement, p. 233

process theories, p. 228

punishment, p. 234

reinforcement, p. 233

reinforcement theory, p. 233

underpayment inequity, p. 236

valence, p. 230

S O   W H E R E   D O   Y O U   S T A N D ?

Wrap-Up to Opening Case

We left off with Toronto consultant Edmond Mellina, president of Transitus Management Consulting, saying he was quite blunt in his advice to his clients, "If you don't find ways to engage people, you are dead." He says employees should have support in five areas, which can be thought of as legs of a stool. If one or two are missing, the stool will still stand up, but it will be unbalanced. According to Mellina, the following five legs are important in motivating and retaining good staff:

1. The most important leg is the assurance that an employee has a job that meets his/her underlying goals.
2. The second leg is the challenge of the work itself. Even if a person is not fully engaged with the company, he or she can feel passionate about individual projects.
3. The third leg is the feeling of being involved. People feel more committed to the success of the task if they feel they have influence over how it is done.
4. The fourth leg is the team. People can become disengaged or lose motivation if they don't believe the manager makes all people pull their weight.

5. The final leg—and the one that helps balance all the others—is the leadership, i.e., the leader expressing his/her goals and offering praise and feedback.

These areas are also in line with the more than 16 000 respondents to an ongoing online survey conducted by Career Systems International, the consulting firm run by Beverly Kaye, co-author of *Love 'Em or Lose' Em* to the question: "What makes employees stick with an employer?"[36] Here are the top 10 reasons:

1. Exciting work and challenge
2. Career growth, learning, and development
3. Working with great people
4. Fair pay
5. Supportive management or good boss
6. Being recognized, valued, and respected
7. Benefits
8. Meaningful work and making a difference
9. Pride in an organization and its product
10. Great work environment and culture

After studying the preceding material, be sure to check out our Online Learning Centre at
www.mcgrawhill.ca/olc/jones
for more in-depth information and interactivities that correspond to this chapter.

Management in Action

Topics for Discussion and Action

1. Interview four people who have the same kind of job (such as salesperson, waiter, or teacher), and determine what kinds of needs they are trying to satisfy at work.
2. Discuss why two people with similar abilities may have very different expectancies for performing at a high level.
3. Describe why some people have low instrumentalities even when their managers distribute outcomes based on performance.
4. Describe three techniques or procedures that managers can use to determine whether a goal is difficult.
5. Discuss why managers should always try to use positive reinforcement instead of negative reinforcement.
6. Analyze how professors try to promote equity to motivate students.

Building Management Skills

DIAGNOSING MOTIVATION

Think about the ideal job that you would like to obtain upon graduation. Describe this job, the kind of manager you would like to report to, and the kind of organization you would be working in. Then answer the following questions.

1. What would be your levels of expectancy and instrumentality on this job? Which outcomes would have high valence for you on this job? What steps would your manager take to influence your levels of expectancy, instrumentality, and valence?
2. Whom would you choose as a referent on this job? What steps would your manager take to make you feel that you were being equitably treated? What

would you do if, after a year on the job, you experienced underpayment inequity?

3. What goals would you strive to achieve on this job? Why? What role would your manager play in determining your goals?
4. What needs would you strive to satisfy on this job? Why? What role would your manager play in helping you satisfy these needs?

Management for You

The following is a typical situation that students often face. Consider the following: you are in a team with six other management students, and you have a major case analysis due in four weeks. This assignment will count for 25 percent of your course mark. *You are the team's leader.*

The problem: Several of your team members are having difficulty getting motivated to start work on the project.

The task: Identify ways you could motivate your team members by using the following theories of motivation as studied in this chapter:

1. Needs theories;
2. Expectancy theory;
3. Goal setting;
4. Reinforcement theory; and
5. Equity theory.

Small Group Breakout Exercise

INCREASING MOTIVATION

Form groups of three or four people, and appoint one member as the spokesperson who will communicate your findings to the whole class when called on by the instructor. Then discuss the following scenario.

You are a group of partners who own a chain of 15 dry-cleaning stores in a medium-sized town. You are meeting today to discuss a problem in customer service that surfaced recently. When any one of you is spending the day or even part of the day in a particular store, clerks seem to be providing excellent customer service, spotters are making sure all stains are removed from garments, and pressers are doing a good job of pressing difficult items such as silk blouses. Yet during those same visits customers complain to you about such things as stains not being removed and items being poorly pressed in some of their previous orders; indeed, several customers have brought garments in to be redone. Customers also sometimes comment on having waited too long for service on previous visits. You are meeting today to address this problem.

1. Discuss the extent to which you believe that you have a motivation problem in your stores.
2. Given what you have learned in this chapter, design a plan to increase the motivation of clerks to provide prompt service to customers even when they are not being watched by a partner.
3. Design a plan to increase the motivation of spotters to remove as many stains as possible even when they are not being watched by a partner.
4. Design a plan to increase the motivation of pressers to do a top-notch job on all clothes they press, no matter how difficult.

Managing Ethically

You are the new CEO of a pharmaceutical company that has a reputation for compensating managers well but not employees. Top and middle managers get a 15-percent across-the-board increase, while the employees receive a 4-percent increase. The justification is that managers take the risks, make the decisions, and figure out the strategies. But in fact for years the company has been using teams to make many of the most crucial decisions for the company. And everyone has input into strategic planning. Employees also have to work extra-long hours during the busiest seasons with no overtime pay. You find morale very low. While employees seem motivated because they have a passion for the work, developing drugs to help cure major diseases, many are threatening to leave if they are not rewarded more fairly. What would you do?

Exploring the World Wide Web

SPECIFIC ASSIGNMENT

Many companies take active steps to recognize their employees for jobs well done. One such company is DuPont Canada. Scan DuPont Canada's website (ca.dupont.com) to learn more about this company. Then under "Careers in Canada" click on "Compensation & Benefits" and "Personal Development."

1. What kinds of rewards is Dupont Canada using to motivate its employees to perform at a high level?
2. How does Dupont Canada use training to motivate? How might this increase an employee's expectancy?

GENERAL ASSIGNMENT

Find a website of a company that bases pay on performance for some or all of its employees. Describe the pay-for-performance plan in use at this company. Which employees are covered by the plan? Do you think this pay plan will foster high levels of motivation? Why or why not?

Developing a Business Plan

(APPENDIX B, PAGE 405)

Go to www.mcgrawhill.ca/olc/jones/8 for online exercises.

Be the Manager

HANDING OVER THE REINS

Recently a former colleague at a company of 100 employees has called you in where you used to work before becoming a motivational consultant. You know this company very well because you worked there for seven years. It is a family-owned business. Your former colleague is the daughter of the founder who is very reluctant to hand over the reins of management completely to his daughter. He knows he must, but he keeps saying that he needs that "little extra push"! Your former colleague believes that you have the "motivational key" for this transfer of power.

Questions

1. Using the motivational theories from this chapter, what theory or theories would you enlist to try to work this current challenge?
2. What is your motivational plan that you feel reasonably secure with that you can present to your former colleague?

Management Case

Motivating Your Team "Spirits"[37]

Investing in the skills of your people makes smart business sense. If you don't motivate your team, the good people leave and worse still, the poor ones stay!

Profitable bars and contented customers depend upon motivated, enthusiastic people and that takes good management. Are you giving your staff something to smile about?

It is an old but proven fact in running any business that people buy people first. Great decor, good prices, and fine food won't bring in the customers without friendly, efficient people on hand who enjoy what they do. If staff are ill-tempered, ill-equipped, or ill-trained, customers definitely notice and then vote with their feet. So, what steps can astute managers take to ensure that their bar is delivering the positive atmosphere and service that matters to customers?

Recognition

There's a whole lot of skill involved in being a good barperson but how often is that recognized? Ben Reed of IPBartenders in England said, "On the continent, bartenders are seen as professionals and held in high esteem. But that's not always the case in the UK."

Bar work is often seen as a casual, unskilled job, with staff being treated accordingly. Low status leads to low morale, so the effective manager is always looking to encourage staff to develop their skills and take pride in their work. Recognition for a job well done is a key factor in developing staff satisfaction.

Information

Ben Reed also said that to have happy, successful staff they need to be empowered and inspired. That goes beyond telling staff what to do and how to do it, it is also explaining why things are done in a particular way. For example, demonstrating the perfect serve will make far more sense to people when they know why it's important to customers and how it helps to encourage repeat orders. Empowerment is also about giving people reasonable control over how they do their job and how they respond to customers. But if you want them to make good decisions, then you need to invest in your people.

Training

"A good bartender will have four main areas of expertise," says Ben. "Knowledge, speed, style, and etiquette. Each requires training to develop."

Ben feels that bar owners and managers should look at training as a sound business investment. Staff who understand wines, for example, are in a much stronger position to influence customer choice, and customers will appreciate that knowledge. Upselling is a great profit opportunity but it requires staff who understand the products. You can't sell an expensive cocktail if you don't know how to mix it and serve it with style and without keeping your other customers waiting for their orders.

There are always difficult customers but how serious a problem they will be also depends on the people skills of barstaff. Staff need to recognize and know how to refuse to serve someone who is at their limit or possibly underage. Training can play a vital role in helping staff become confident and capable of dealing with tricky situations.

Equipment

Good quality service also depends on having the right materials on hand, the right glasses, the ice, the lemons, and so on. Making sure your bar area is sensibly organized and uncluttered will also help your staff work more effectively.

Teamwork

Job satisfaction is closely related to the success of working relationships. Smart managers should be on the lookout for ways of stimulating team working and cooperation. Team incentives and rewards possibly linked to a manufacturer's promotion can be used in this way. Work needs to have an element of fun to it. If your staff don't enjoy their job, your customers won't enjoy your bar or pub.

Questions

1. What are some motivation challenges outlined in this case?
2. What theories of motivation would work more seamlessly to develop a motivating environment?
3. As a manager, what kind of a training program would you set up to get the best out of the employees?

Video Management Case

CBC ⊛

Boom: Drum Room Team Building

This video describes the shift away from earlier team building exercises and the new corporate initiatives being used, like acoustically oriented activities to motivate groups to work better as a team. Many companies have signed on to this kind of team building workshop where fun is built in and participants feel excited about their often new-found "skill."

Questions to Consider

1. How might these activities done in a group setting contribute to motivating individual's sense of interest in promoting a quality work environment?
2. What kinds of obstacles would these activities be challenged with in trying to produce a greater sense of community in the workplace? How could participation and usefulness be measured?

Source: *Venture*, show number 914, "21st Century Drumming," February 15, 2004, running time 3:10.

CHAPTER

9

Leadership

Learning Outcomes

1. Describe what leadership is, when leaders are effective and ineffective, and the sources of power that enable managers to be effective leaders.

2. Identify the traits that show the strongest relationship to leadership, the behaviours leaders engage in, and the limitations of the trait and behaviour models of leadership.

3. Explain how contingency models of leadership enhance our understanding of effective leadership and management in organizations.

4. Describe what transformational leadership is, and explain how managers can engage in it.

5. Characterize how gender and national culture affect leadership.

6. Describe how moods and emotions that leaders experience on the job may affect their leadership effectiveness.

Unto the Seventh Generation[1]

How has it come that we cannot see the value of a forest? And, what does this mean to leaders of our organizations? We live in a time when our corporate leaders manage quarter by quarter and our political leaders tell us they can't be bound by three year plans. Yet, the most pressing problem faced by our planet—the current decline of every living system—requires a multi-generational strategy.
—Gabriel Draven[2]

The opening quote by Gabriel Draven is part of his reflection on leadership as he sits one evening in September 2004 in what he calls "the cathedral of Temagami, an old growth forest of 150 year-old trees in the near north of Ontario." He had been invited by an elder of the Teme-Augama Anishnabai, who is "among the last of his people homesteading on ancestral lands, to visit an area that has served as a gathering place for his people for a thousand years as they seek wisdom and commune with their elders." This area contains the Spirit Forest that lies between Lake Temagami and Lake Obakika. What is deeply troubling Draven is that this land may be no more because plans have been approved to commence clear-cutting of the trees. It is within this context that he asks why it is that we cannot see the value of a forest. And then he asks further, "And, what does this mean to leaders of our organizations?

Draven points out what writers like Dee Hock (founder of Visa International, whom we discussed in Chapter 6 on Managing Organizational Structure)[3] and Thomas Homer-Dixon[4] remind us of: that our institutions are failing us because they are unable to deal, for example, with complex crises like global environmental meltdown, world hunger, peace and conflict, and the gap between the rich and the poor. In Draven's own words:

Our religions have become efficiency and consumption. We fall to the myth of perpetual economic growth while the only organism in nature, which is governed by such an imperative, is the cancer cell that eventually kills its host. We have traded compassion and replaced it with competition. Somewhere along the way we forgot people live in communities and neighborhoods, not marketplaces. In our organizations, I see workplaces that are over-managed and under-led. I see corporations that would rather make decisions for the casino of the stock market than long-term value creation. I see a world where we demand compliance in our people rather than inspiring their commitment and
engaging them in a process of co-creating a positive vision of the future. Is it any wonder most Fortune 500 corporations last no longer than 40 years. Is it any wonder that worker disengagement costs US corporations $350B a year according to Gallop Research? Is it any wonder that disability represents up to 12% of payroll costs in Canada with mental health claims as the fastest growing category of disability, or so according to a major roundtable study completed in 2000 looking at depression in the Canadian workplace?

To be disengaged is to show up physically for work but to be absent mentally.[5] This state of affairs, or disengagement, is known as "presenteeism."[6] When presenteeism is rampant because employees show up for work, even though they may be quite ill, not only is this an organizational health issue, but the Harvard Business School estimates that costs associated with this type of presenteeism to be about US$150 billion/year.[7] Some employees even work at honing their presenteeism! In his book, *Hardly Work*, which he wrote "on company time," author Chris Morran, referred to by www.amazon.ca as "an idol of idleness," claims that overachieving underperformers get all the credit for everyone else's effort.[8]

What is needed are leaders that will do the right thing, as Warren Bennis[9] reminds us. Robert Greenleaf (1904–1990) founded the Center for Applied Ethics, Inc. in 1964, which was then renamed the Robert K. Greenleaf Center in 1985.[10] Today it is known as The Robert K. Greenleaf Center for Servant-Leadership, In 1970 he

According to Gabriel Draven, we can no longer see the forest for the trees: "Our religions have become efficiency and consumption."

published *The Servant as Leader*. Draven writes that the most powerful lessons on leadership do not come from the business schools or from such notables as Donald Trump or former New York City mayor Rudy Giuliani.

> *Rather, it is a piece of wisdom that guided leaders in the Iroquois Confederacy, instructing them to consider the impact of their decisions on the seven generations around them. Our indigenous people knew that one man, one leader, could only hope to know the seven generations around him: the three that preceded him—to his great grandparents—and the three that will follow—to his great grandchildren. The leader was bound by a moral duty to care for the Seven Generations.*

For Draven, in reflecting on this notion of the Seven Generations, he asks the question: "What would Seventh Generation Leadership look like in our organizations?" He lists the following implications of Seventh Generation leadership:

1. Corporations would be principle-based.
2. Leadership would be spiritual, not religious.
3. Leaders would intuitively understand the power of inclusion, the power of conversation.
4. Leadership would be transformed into *stewardship* and leaders' roles would be as keepers of dialogue, the proverbial village elder and sage.
5. Leaders would be earth-affirming.

Draven finishes his reflection this way: "The hallmark of leadership is when old men and old women plant trees they know they will not live long enough to enjoy. Our world needs such leaders. For, one thousand years from now, I want my descendents to be able to worship in a cathedral of trees. It does not look hopeful."

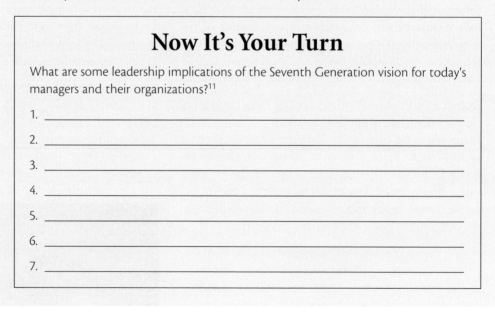

Now It's Your Turn

What are some leadership implications of the Seventh Generation vision for today's managers and their organizations?[11]

1. _____
2. _____
3. _____
4. _____
5. _____
6. _____
7. _____

■■■■ Overview

In the opening scenario we see perhaps a new vision of leadership, one that goes beyond simply the traditional model of leader-follower and looks at the vision a manager or person in authority brings to the organization. Draven reminds us that leadership, from the big picture point of view, is a vision of "seven generations." As such, the implications by and for organizations are immense. In Chapter 1, we explained that one of the four principal tasks of managers is leading. Thus, it should come as no surprise that leadership is a key ingredient in effective management. When leaders are effective, their subordinates or followers are highly motivated, committed, and high-performing. When leaders are ineffective, chances are good that their subordinates do not perform up to their capabilities, are demotivated, and may be dissatisfied as well. Leadership is an important ingredient for managerial success at all levels of an organization: top management, middle management, and first-line management. Moreover, leadership is a key ingredient for managerial success for organizations large and small.

In this chapter, we describe what leadership is and examine the major leadership models that shed light on the factors that help make a manager an effective leader. *Trait and behaviour models* focus on what leaders are like and what they do. *Contingency models*—Fiedler's contingency model, Hersey-Blanchard's situational leadership theory, path-goal theory, and the leader substitutes model—take into account the complexity surrounding leadership and the role of the situation in leader effectiveness. We describe how managers can have dramatic effects in their organizations by means of transformational leadership. We also examine the relationship between gender and leadership. By the end of this chapter, you will have a good appreciation of the many factors and issues that managers face in their quest to be effective leaders.

The Nature of Leadership

THINK ABOUT IT

Finding Our Way: Leadership for an Uncertain Time[12]

We first think in images. One of the most embedded images we have of the organization—since the time of the Industrial Age—is that the organization, to work well, should be like a well-oiled machine. Everything, then, would be in its place; everything would fit; and a manager's job would be making sure that all the parts continue to work well together. That's one image. It's called the "command and control" image.

But what if we were to choose another image of how organizations work? What if we, as Dr. Margaret Wheatley suggests, looked at organizations as "living systems" and as "self-organizing systems"? Such systems would be without command and control and would structure themselves organically, that is, leadership would *emerge* and the best ways to work and organize would become self-evident as people experimented freely through their networks of communication, values and meaning, behaviour and norms. Dr. Wheatley points out that there is a clear correlation between participation and productivity and that in truly self-managed work environments, productivity is at least 35 percent higher than in traditionally managed organizations.

The question is: if this reality of self-managed teams is so obvious, why don't leaders choose to nurture and develop self-organizing systems? The answer, according to Wheatley, is that leaders keep choosing power over productivity and control over trust. The excuses for such behaviour will range from "these are turbulent times" to "somebody has to be in charge." The problem with this kind of thinking, for Wheatley, is that when the risks are high, leaders need everyone's commitment and intelligence, not easily evoked with power and control. The net result is that leaders prevent intelligent work from being accomplished, or in Wheatley's own words, "Guaranteed levels of performance are preferable to surprising breakthroughs. In our machine-like organizations, we try to extinguish individuality in order to reach our goal of compliance. We trade uniqueness for control, and barter our humanness for petty performance measures."

leadership
The process by which an individual exerts influence over other people and inspires, motivates, and directs their activities to help achieve group or organizational goals.

leader
An individual who is able to exert influence over other people to help achieve group or organizational goals.

Leadership is the process by which a person exerts influence over other people and inspires, motivates, and directs their activities to help achieve group or organizational goals.[13] The person who exerts such influence is a **leader**. When leaders are effective, the influence they exert over others helps a group or organization to achieve its performance goals. When leaders are ineffective, their influence does not contribute to, and often detracts from, goal attainment. As the opening scenario in *Management Snapshot* demonstrates (as well as in Chapter 6), Dee Hock was an effective leader. He was able to practise his leadership ability in setting up Visa International, thus enabling a "seventh generation" leadership vision to become real. Or, in Gabriel Draven's words, "The leader was bound by a moral duty to care for the Seven Generations."[14] Visa International continues to exist today all around the world.

Effective leadership increases an organization's ability to meet a variety of challenges, including the need to obtain a competitive advantage, the need to foster ethical behaviour, and the need to manage a diverse workforce fairly and equitably. Leaders who exert influence to help meet these goals increase their organization's chances of success.

In considering the nature of leadership, we first look at leadership styles and how they affect managerial tasks, and at the influence of culture on leadership styles. We then focus on the key to leadership, *power*, which can come from a variety of sources. Finally, we consider the contemporary use of empowerment and how it relates to effective leadership. Table 9.1 illustrates the comments of several Canadians about what it means to be a Canadian leader.

Personal Leadership Style and Managerial Tasks

A manager's *personal leadership style*—that is, the specific ways in which a manager chooses to influence other people—shapes the way that the manager approaches planning, organizing, and controlling (the other principal tasks of managing).

Hock describes leadership this way:

> *Here is the very heart and soul of the matter. If you look to lead, invest at least 40% of your time managing yourself—your ethics, character, principles, purpose, motivation, and conduct. Invest at least 30% managing those with authority over you, and 15% managing your peers. Use the remainder to induce those you "work for" to understand and practice the theory. I use the terms "work for" advisedly, for if you don't understand that you should be working for your mislabeled "subordinates," you haven't understood anything. Lead yourself, lead your superiors, lead your peers, and free your people to do the same. All else is trivia.[15]*

Managers at all levels and in all kinds of organizations have their own personal leadership styles, which determine not only how they lead their subordinates but also how they perform the other management tasks. Recall that Ricardo Semler found it stressful to manage Semco by creating fear in his employees, even though some other traditional Brazilian companies were and still are managed in that fashion.[16]

TABLE 9.1 | *Some Thoughts About What It Means to Be a Canadian Leader*

Canadian ambassador to the United States Raymond Chrétien:	I think our leadership is based upon what we are as a society. We have maintained our cohesion. We have maintained our capacity to build a tolerant, caring society that speaks to all aspects of our human development. This is why we are highly regarded.
Maclean's editor-in-chief Robert Lewis:	Recently, I sat beside an American CEO at a conference and, as the discussion unfolded, he started mumbling, "You Canadians are always trying to get some kind of consensus. Why don't you stop that and make some decisions?"
ABC news anchor Peter Jennings:	I think Canadian leadership, as we've already cited in peacekeeping operations, in international conventions, in international situations, is reflected in the notion that we've had to make our way somewhat more subtly on the world stage than the United States has ever been obliged to do.
Wi-LAN Inc. founder Hatim Zaghloul:	In high-tech, we Canadians often will take longer making a decision, whereas in Silicon Valley, they would advertise their product when it's just a concept, and then they would go and build it if someone bought it. In Canada, we only advertise once it's meeting 99.99 percent of our specifications.
Olympic gold-medal rower Marnie McBean:	Canadians just don't follow the person who's shouting the loudest.... And I think that's where this sense of a style of Canadian leadership comes from—not from being boastful or a braggart. It comes from being able to do the job. Just sort of putting the head down, doing the job and we get our respect from our actions and from our performance.

Source: R. Lewis, "The Canadian Way: There Is a Confident Canadian Style of Leadership, and It Is Making a Global Impact," *Maclean's*, July 1, 2000, p. 26.

Power: The Key to Leadership

No matter what one's leadership style, a key component of effective leadership is found in the *power* the leader has to affect other people's behaviour and get them to act in certain ways.[17] There are several types of power: *legitimate, reward, coercive, expert,* and *referent power* (see Figure 9.1).[18] Effective leaders take steps to ensure that they have sufficient levels of each type and that they use the power they have in beneficial ways.

Legitimate Power

Legitimate power is the authority a manager has by virtue of his or her position in an organization's hierarchy. This is the power, for instance, that allows managers to hire new employees, assign projects to individuals, monitor their work, and appraise their performance.

legitimate power
The authority that a manager has by virtue of his or her position in an organization's hierarchy.

FIGURE 9.1 | *Sources of Managerial Power*

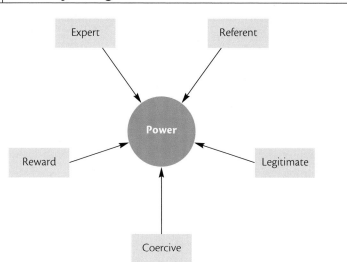

Reward Power

Reward power is the ability of a manager to give or withhold tangible rewards (pay raises, bonuses, choice job assignments) and intangible rewards (verbal praise, a pat on the back, respect). As you learned in Chapter 8, members of an organization are motivated to perform at a high level by a variety of rewards. Being able to give or withhold rewards based on performance is a major source of power that allows managers to have a highly motivated workforce.

Effective managers use their reward power in such a way that subordinates feel that they are doing a good job and their efforts are appreciated. Ineffective managers use rewards in a more controlling manner (wielding the "stick" instead of offering the carrot"), which signals to subordinates that the manager has the upper hand. One example of effective use of reward power was with the New York firefighters who "were heralded as heroes for their acts on 9-11-01."[19] Rewards need to be aligned also with ethics and corporate governance. Craig Johnston of Canada Post was rewarded for his bright idea with a $10 000 cheque, the respect of his bosses, and the admiration of his peers. He developed a time-saving device so that Canada Post could revamp its sorting line by jury-rigging its existing machinery to generate mail barcodes on the fly. Previous to his suggestion, packages without barcodes had to be manually sorted by clerks; this labour-intensive activity contributed to clogging up the machines. The $10 000 was part of Canada Post's employee involvement award program—an initiative designed to encourage and reward innovation on the job.[20] Charles Schwab & Co., the discount broker, is another example. The company

pays its brokers a straight salary, unlike other brokerage firms that offer commissions on the basis of the number of transactions that a client makes—an incentive that can lead to brokers encouraging customers to buy and sell stocks excessively. Moreover, Schwab has no investment banking division and is thus free to offer unbiased ratings of company stocks.[21]

As Wolfe J. Rinke, Ph.D. points out, trust is also very central to creating a leadership and rewarding environment.[22] *Chief Executive Perspectives* magazine has described the key challenge facing CEO leaders of the 21st century: *people* issues in the workplace.[23] They estimate that "people costs" account for some 65 percent of corporate spending, indicating an obvious impact issue for the bottom line. Mark A. Huselid, who is an associate professor in the Department of Human Resource Management at Rutgers University and the editor of *Human Resource Management Journal,* puts things this way: "The ability to execute strategy well is a source of competitive advantage, and 'people' are the linchpin of effective strategy execution." The key skills needed for effective leaders? "Hiring the right people, training them, paying them, rewarding them, supporting them and promoting them appropriately."

Coercive Power

Coercive power is the ability of a manager to punish others. Punishment can include verbal reprimands, reductions in pay or working hours, and actual dismissal. Punishment can have negative side effects such as resentment and retaliation and should be used only when necessary (e.g., to reduce a dangerous behaviour). Managers who rely heavily on coercive power tend to be ineffective as leaders.

Excessive use of coercive power seldom produces high performance and is questionable ethically. Sometimes it amounts to a form of mental abuse, robbing workers of their dignity and causing excessive levels of stress. Better results are obtained with reward power.

Expert Power

Expert power is based in the special knowledge, skills, and expertise that a leader possesses. The nature of expert power varies, depending on the leader's level in the hierarchy. First-line and middle managers often have technical expertise relevant to the tasks that their subordinates perform. Their expert power gives them considerable influence over subordinates.

Some top managers derive expert power from their technical expertise. Dee Hock, described in Chapter 6 and in the opening scenario to this chapter, is one of these, with his experience, strategic intelligence, and his ability to envision what needed to be done to eventually build and lead a dynamic organization such as Visa International. Many top-level managers lack technical expertise, however, and derive their expert power from their abilities as decision makers, planners, and strategists. Expert power tends to be best used in a guiding or coaching manner rather than in an arrogant, high-handed manner.

Referent Power

Referent power is more informal than the other kinds of power. **Referent power** is a function of the personal characteristics of a leader. It is the power that comes from subordinates' and co-workers' respect, admiration, and loyalty. Leaders who are likeable and whom subordinates wish to use as a role model are especially likely to possess referent power.

In addition to being a valuable asset for top managers, referent power can help first-line and middle managers be effective leaders.

> *Referent power is the power that you derive from the trust and commitment given to you by your colleagues because of who you are and how you are perceived. Celebrities are often used in marketing campaigns because they have referent power. You have to be seen as a role model, someone whom others like and admire. This is a precarious power source because if the respect and trust afforded to you falters, you can easily lose it.*[24]

Managers can take steps to increase their referent power—or other powers—by taking time, for example, to get to know their subordinates and showing interest and concern for them, thus demonstrating also emotional intelligence in action. Mario F. Heilmann of the University of California at Los Angeles reminds us that there is also an ethical implication to referent power as well, "Referent power facilitates learning from positive models and therefore enhances inclusive fitness."[25] Prof. Hugh Gunz, professor of organizational behaviour at the Rotman School of Management at the University of Toronto, makes the suggestion that one should look at the different sources of power and ask how they apply to oneself. Where there are gaps, one can then develop a plan to fill what he calls one's "power gap."

Empowerment: An Ingredient in Modern Management

More and more managers today are incorporating in their personal leadership styles an aspect that at first glance seems to be the opposite of being a leader. In Chapter 1, we described how **empowerment**—the process of giving employees at all levels in the organization the authority to make decisions, be responsible for their outcomes, improve quality, and cut

expert power
Power that is based in the special knowledge, skills, and expertise that a leader possesses.

referent power
Power that comes from subordinates' and co-workers' respect, admiration, and loyalty.

empowerment
The process of giving employees the authority to make decisions and be responsible for their outcomes.

Hilary Duff endorses a video game as an example of referent power. How can managers increase their own referent power?

costs—is becoming increasingly popular in organizations. When leaders empower their subordinates, the subordinates typically take over some of the responsibilities and authority that used to reside with the leader or manager, such as the right to reject parts that do not meet quality standards, the right to check one's own work, and the right to schedule work activities. Empowered subordinates are given the power to make some of the decisions that their leaders or supervisors used to make.

At first glance, empowerment might seem to be the opposite of effective leadership because managers allow subordinates to take a more active role in leading themselves. In actuality, however, empowerment can contribute to effective leadership for several reasons:

- Empowerment increases a manager's ability to get things done because the manager has the support and help of subordinates who may have special knowledge of work tasks.

- Empowerment often increases workers' involvement, motivation, and commitment, which helps ensure that they will be working toward organizational goals.

- Empowerment gives managers more time to concentrate on their pressing concerns because they spend less time on day-to-day supervisory activities.

Effective managers realize the benefits of empowerment; ineffective managers try to keep control over all decision making and force agreement from subordinates. The personal leadership style of managers who empower subordinates often includes developing subordinates, so that they can make good decisions, and being subordinates' guide, coach, and source of inspiration. Empowerment is a popular trend in Canada and the United States at companies as diverse as United Parcel Service of America Inc. (a package delivery company), Burnaby, BC-based Dominion Information Services Inc. (which publishes *Super Pages* in BC, Alberta, Ontario, and Quebec), and Langley, BC-based Redwood Plastics Corp. (a manufacturing company), and it is also taking off around the world.[26] Even companies in South Korea (such as Samsung, Hyundai, and Daewoo), in which decision making typically was centralized with the founding families, are empowering managers at lower levels to make decisions.[27]

Not every employee is a good candidate for empowerment, however. A recent study that Professor Jia Lin Xie, of the University of Toronto's Joseph L. Rotman School of Management, conducted with several others found that people who lack confidence can get ill from being put in charge of their own work. The researchers found that "workers who had high levels of control at work, but lacked confidence in their abilities or blamed themselves for workplace problems, were more likely to have lower antibody levels and experienced more colds and flus."[28]

Some of the difficulty with empowerment is that not all companies introduce it properly. Professor Dan Ondrack at the Rotman School of Management notes that for employees to be empowered, four conditions need to be met: (1) There must be a clear definition of the values and mission of the company; (2) the company must help employees acquire the relevant skills; (3) employees need to be supported in their decision making, and not criticized when they try to do something extraordinary; and (4) workers need to be recognized for their efforts.[29]

Models of Leadership

Is there a difference between leadership and management? Harvard Business School Professor John Kotter suggests that "managers promote stability while leaders press for change and only organizations that embrace both sides of the contradiction can survive in turbulent times."[30] Professor Rabindra Kanungo of McGill University reports growing agreement "among management scholars that the concept of 'leadership' must be distinguished from the concept of 'supervision/management.'"[31] Leaders look to the big picture, providing vision and strategy. Managers are charged with implementing vision and strategy; they coordinate and staff the organization, and handle day-to-day problems.

Below we discuss two aspects of leadership: leading as supervision, and leading with vision.

Leadership as Supervision

THINK ABOUT IT

Building a Company to Last[32]

Art Phillips is a retired investment manager and former mayor of Vancouver, British Columbia. He points out that building a company in order to sell it has been a dominant theme and trait among BC entrepreneurs and accounts for the fact that there are so few corporate head offices in Vancouver. Just across the border, in nearby Seattle, such is not the case. The ethos there has bred such companies as Starbucks and Microsoft. However, Jim Pattison, founder of the Pattison Group[33] and "the last great tycoon still standing in British Columbia," is one leader who still oversees a company that grosses $5.7 billion a year, contains $3.3 billion in assets, and employs 28 000 people in total. He is an exception to this entrepreneurial trait of a "cash-out" style of leadership. Pattison's traits are reflected in his instinct for being a long-term leader.

You Be the Manager

1. What would be your suggestions for traits that leaders should have?
2. How do managers act in a company that has a long-term vision?

Leadership theories developed before about 1980 focused on the supervisory nature of leadership. Thus they were concerned with managing the day-to-day functions of employees. These theories took three different approaches to how supervision could be viewed: (1) Do leaders have traits different from nonleaders? (2) Should leaders engage in particular behaviours? (3) Does the situation a leader faces matter? We briefly examine these approaches below.

The Trait Model

The trait model of leadership focused on identifying the personal characteristics that are responsible for effective leadership. Decades of research (beginning in the 1930s) and hundreds of studies indicate that certain personal characteristics do appear to be associated with effective leadership (see Table 9.2 for a list of these).[34] Traits alone, however, are not the key to understanding leader effectiveness. Some effective leaders do not possess all of these traits, and some leaders who do possess them are not effective in their leadership roles. This lack of a consistent relationship between leader traits and leader effectiveness led researchers to search for new explanations for effective leadership. Researchers began to turn their attention to what effective leaders actually do—in

TABLE 9.2 | *Traits and Personal Characteristics Related to Effective Leadership*

TRAIT	DESCRIPTION
Intelligence	Helps managers understand complex issues and solve problems
Knowledge and expertise	Help managers make good decisions and discover ways to increase efficiency and effectiveness
Dominance	Helps managers influence their subordinates to achieve organizational goals
Self-confidence	Contributes to managers' effectively influencing subordinates and persisting when faced with obstacles or difficulties
High energy	Helps managers deal with the many demands they face
Tolerance for stress	Helps managers deal with uncertainty and make difficult decisions
Integrity and honesty	Help managers behave ethically and earn their subordinates' trust and confidence
Maturity	Helps managers avoid acting selfishly, control their feelings, and admit when they have made a mistake

other words, to the behaviours that allow effective leaders to influence their subordinates to achieve group and organizational goals.

The Behavioural Models

There are a variety of behavioural models of leadership, including the Ohio Studies,[35] the Michigan Studies,[36] and Blake and Mouton's Managerial Grid.[37] These models identify two basic kinds of leader behaviours that many leaders in the United States, Germany, and other countries used to influence their subordinates: *employee-centred behaviours* (also called *consideration, concern for people, and supportive behaviours*) and *job-oriented behaviours* (also called *initiating structure, concern for production, and task-oriented behaviours*). All of the behavioural theories suggest that leaders need to consider the nature of their subordinates when trying to determine the extent to which they should perform these two types of behaviours.

Leaders engage in **employee-centred behaviour** when they show subordinates that they trust, respect, and care about them. This behavioural leadership modelling is borne out with enthusiastic employees.[38] According to the company Sirota Survey Intelligence, specialists in attitude research, employees start out with a company by being enthusiastic. What eventually gets in the way is management! For example, when it comes to diversity in the workplace, Nick Starritt, European managing director for Sirota Survey Intelligence says,

> *Although compliance with the relevant diversity laws is obviously a "must" for every organization, what's important to realize is that what people want from their work is essentially the same, the world over. Our data shows overwhelmingly that if employers create an inclusive environment—where everyone feels respected and performance expectations are the same, irrespective of skin colour, gender or ethnicity, then it's more likely that enthusiasm at work will be high.[39]*

In addition, according to Starritt, at the end of the day, employees want three things from their work: equity, or being proud of one's work and employer; achievement, or having an opportunity to have positive, productive relationships at work; and camaraderie, or feeling treated justly in relation to the basic conditions of employment, such as pay benefits and job security. Managers, therefore, who truly look out for the well-being of their subordinates and do what they can to help subordinates feel good and enjoy their work are performing consideration behaviours. With the increasing

employee-centred behaviour
Behaviour indicating that a manager trusts, respects, and cares about subordinates.

focus on the importance of high quality customer service, many managers are realizing that when they are considerate to subordinates, subordinates are more likely to be considerate to customers and vice versa. Leaders engage in **job-oriented behaviours** when they take steps to make sure that work gets done, subordinates perform their jobs acceptably, and the organization is efficient and effective. Assigning tasks to individuals or work groups, letting subordinates know what is expected of them, deciding how work should be done, making schedules, encouraging adherence to rules and regulations, and motivating subordinates to do a good job are all examples of initiating structure.[40]

job-oriented behaviours
Behaviours that managers engage in to ensure that work gets done, subordinates perform their jobs acceptably, and the organization is efficient and effective.

These two behaviours are independent of each other. Leaders can be high on both, low on both, or high on one and low on the other. You might expect that effective leaders and managers would perform both kinds of behaviours, but research has found that this is not necessarily the case. The relationship between performance of employee-oriented and job-oriented behaviours and leader effectiveness is not clear-cut. Some leaders are effective even when they do not perform either type of behaviour, and some leaders are ineffective even when they perform both kinds of behaviours. Like the trait model of leadership, the behaviour model alone cannot explain leader effectiveness. Realizing this, researchers began building more complicated models of leadership, models that focused not only on the leader and what he or she does but also on the situation or context in which leadership occurs.

Contingency Models of Leadership

Managers lead in a wide variety of situations and organizations and have various kinds of subordinates performing diverse tasks in many environmental contexts. Given the wide variety of situations in which leadership occurs, what makes a manager an effective leader in one situation (such as certain traits or certain behaviours) is not necessarily what that manager needs in order to be equally effective in a different situation. An effective army general might not be an effective university president, an effective manager of a restaurant might not be an effective manager of a clothing store, an effective coach of a football team might not be an effective manager of a fitness centre, and an effective first-line manager in a manufacturing company might not be an effective middle manager. The traits or behaviours that may contribute to a manager being an effective leader in one situation might actually result in the same manager being an ineffective leader in another situation.

Contingency models of leadership take into account the situation or context within which leadership occurs. So for instance, while behavioural theories explored whether managers should be more employee-centred or more task-centred, contingency theories answer: It depends (or is contingent) on the situation. According to contingency models, whether or not a manager is an effective leader is the result of the interplay between what the manager is like, what he or she does, and the situation in which leadership takes place. In this section, we discuss four prominent contingency models developed to shed light on what makes managers effective leaders: Fiedler's contingency model, Hersey-Blanchard's situational leadership theory, House's path-goal theory, and the leader substitutes model. As you will see, these leadership models are complementary. Each focuses on a somewhat different aspect of effective leadership in organizations.

Fiedler's Contingency Model

Fred E. Fiedler was among the first leadership researchers to acknowledge that effective leadership is contingent on, or depends on, the characteristics of the leader and of the

Fred Fiedler
www.eou.edu/~blarison/
321afied.html

situation. Fiedler's contingency model helps explain why a manager may be an effective leader in one situation and ineffective in another; it also suggests which kinds of managers are likely to be most effective in which situations.[41]

Drawing from the previous behavioural studies, Fiedler identified two basic leader styles: *relationship-oriented* and *task-oriented*. All managers can be described as having one style or the other.

Relationship-oriented leaders are mainly concerned with developing good relationships with their subordinates and being liked by them. The quality of interpersonal relationships with subordinates is a prime concern for relationship-oriented leaders. Task-oriented leaders are mainly concerned with ensuring that subordinates perform at a high level. Task-oriented managers focus on task accomplishment and making sure the job gets done.

Fiedler identified three situational characteristics that are important determinants of how favourable a situation is for leading:

- *Leader-Member Relations.* The extent to which followers like, trust, and are loyal to their leader. Situations are more favourable for leading when leader-member relations are good.

task structure
The extent to which the work to be performed is clear-cut so that a leader's subordinates know what needs to be accomplished and how to go about doing it; a determinant of how favourable a situation is for leading.

- **Task Structure.** The extent to which the work to be performed is clear-cut so that a leader's subordinates know what needs to be accomplished and how to go about doing it. When task structure is high, situations are favourable for leading. When task structure is low, goals may be vague, subordinates may be unsure of what they should be doing or how they should do it, and the situation is unfavourable for leading.

position power
The amount of legitimate, reward, and coercive power that a leader has by virtue of his or her position in an organization; a determinant of how favourable a situation is for leading.

- **Position Power.** The amount of legitimate, reward, and coercive power a leader has by virtue of his or her position in an organization. Leadership situations are more favourable for leading when position power is strong.

When a situation is favourable for leading, it is relatively easy for a manager to influence subordinates so that they perform at a high level and contribute to organizational efficiency and effectiveness. Therefore it makes the most sense to be task-oriented because the relationship is already going well. In a situation unfavourable for leading, it is much more difficult for a manager to exert influence. This makes being task-oriented the most desirable behaviour for the leader. After extensive research, Fiedler determined that relationship-oriented leaders are most effective in moderately favourable situations (IV, V, VI, and VII in Figure 9.2) and task-oriented leaders are most effective in very favourable situations (I, II, and III) or very unfavourable situations (VIII).

FIGURE 9.2 | *Fiedler's Contingency Theory of Leadership*

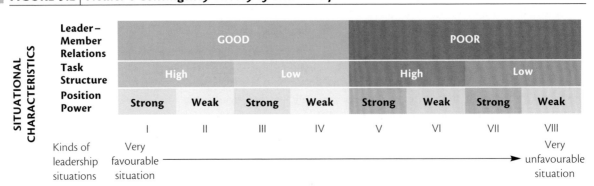

Relationship-oriented leaders are most effective in moderately favourable situations for leading (IV, V, VI, VII).
Task-oriented leaders are most effective in very favourable situations (I, II, III) or very unfavourable situations (VIII) for leading.

According to Fiedler, individuals cannot change their leader style. Therefore, managers need to be placed in leadership situations that fit their style, or situations need to be changed to suit the manager. Situations can be changed, for example, by giving a manager more position power, or by taking steps to increase task structure such as by clarifying goals. Research studies tend to support Fiedler's model but also suggest that, like most theories, it needs to be adjusted.[42] Some researchers also find fault with the model's premise that leaders cannot alter their styles.

Hersey-Blanchard's Situational Leadership Theory

Paul Hersey and Ken Blanchard's **situational leadership theory (SLT)**[43] has been incorporated into leadership training programs at numerous Fortune 500 companies. More than one million managers a year are taught its basic elements.[44]

SLT compares the leader-follower relationship to that between a parent and child. Just as parents needs to give more control to a child as the child becomes more mature and responsible, so too should leaders do this with employees. Hersey and Blanchard identify four specific leader behaviours that managers can use to lead their employees: telling, selling, participating, and delegating. The styles vary in their degree of task-oriented behaviour and relationship-oriented behaviour. The appropriate style depends on the follower's ability and motivation:

- *Telling.* If a follower is *unable* and *unwilling* to do a task, the leader needs to give clear and specific directions (in other words, the leader needs to be highly directive).

- *Selling.* If a follower is *unable* but *willing*, the leader needs to display both high task orientation and high relationship orientation. The high task orientation will compensate for the follower's lack of ability. The high relationship orientation will encourage the follower to "buy into" the leader's desires (in other words, the leader needs to "sell" the task).

- *Participating.* If the follower is *able* but *unwilling*, the leader needs to use a supportive and participative style.

- *Delegating.* If the employee is both *able* and *willing*, the leader doesn't need to do much (in other words, a laissez-faire approach will work).

Figure 9.3 illustrates the relationship of leader behaviours to follower readiness.

Path-Goal Theory

Developed by Rotman School of Management Professor Martin Evans in the late 1960s, and then expanded on by Robert House (formerly at Rotman, but now at the Wharton School of Business at the University of Pennsylvania), **path-goal theory** focuses on what leaders can do to motivate their subordinates to reach group and organizational goals.[45] The premise of path-goal theory is that effective leaders motivate subordinates to achieve goals by (1) clearly identifying the outcomes that subordinates are trying to obtain from the workplace, (2) rewarding subordinates with these outcomes for high performance and the attainment of work goals, and (3) clarifying for subordinates the paths leading to the attainment of work goals. Path-goal theory is a contingency model because it proposes that the steps that managers should take to motivate subordinates depend on both the nature of the subordinates and the type of work they do.

Based on the expectancy theory of motivation (see Chapter 8), path-goal theory provides managers with three guidelines to follow to be effective leaders:

1. *Find out what outcomes your subordinates are trying to obtain from their jobs and the organization.* These outcomes can range from satisfactory pay and job security to reasonable working hours and interesting and challenging job assignments. After

situational leadership theory (SLT)
A contingency model of leadership that focuses on the followers' readiness.

path-goal theory
A contingency model of leadership proposing that leaders can motivate subordinates by identifying their desired outcomes, rewarding them for high performance and the attainment of work goals with these desired outcomes, and clarifying for them the paths leading to the attainment of work goals.

FIGURE 9.3 | *Hersey-Blanchard's Situational Leadership Styles*

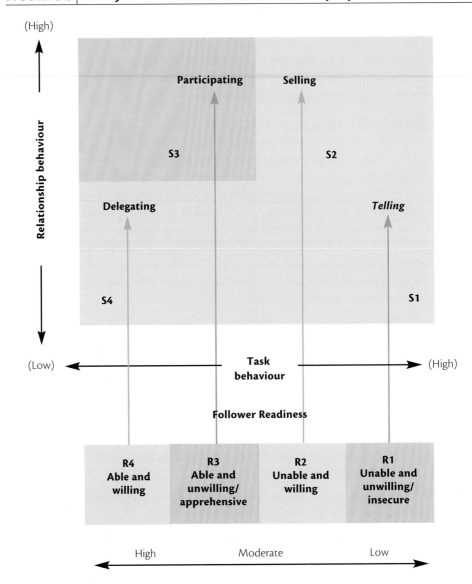

identifying what these outcomes are, the manager should make sure that he or she has the reward power needed to distribute or withhold them.

2. *Reward subordinates for high performance and goal attainment with the outcomes they desire.*

3. *Clarify the paths to goal attainment for subordinates, remove any obstacles to high performance, and express confidence in subordinates' capabilities.* This does not mean that a manager needs to tell his or her subordinates what to do. Rather, it means that a manager needs to make sure that subordinates are clear about what they should be trying to accomplish and have the capabilities, resources, and confidence levels they need to be successful.

Path-goal theory identifies four kinds of behaviours that leaders can use to motivate subordinates:

- *Directive behaviours* include setting goals, assigning tasks, showing subordinates how to complete tasks, and taking concrete steps to improve performance.

- *Supportive behaviours* include expressing concern for subordinates and looking out for their best interests.

- *Participative behaviours* give subordinates a say in matters and decisions that affect them.

- *Achievement-oriented behaviours* motivate subordinates to perform at the highest level possible by, for example, setting very challenging goals, expecting that they be met, and believing in subordinates' capabilities.

Which of these behaviours should managers use to lead effectively? The answer to this question depends, or is contingent, on the nature of the subordinates and the kind of work they do.

Directive behaviours may be beneficial when subordinates are having difficulty completing assigned tasks, but they might be detrimental when subordinates are independent thinkers who work best when left alone. *Supportive* behaviours are often advisable when subordinates are experiencing high levels of stress. *Participative* behaviours can be particularly effective when subordinates' support of a decision is required. *Achievement-oriented* behaviours may increase motivation levels of highly capable subordinates who are bored from having too few challenges, but they might backfire if used with subordinates who are already pushed to their limit.

Effective managers seem to have a knack for determining the kinds of leader behaviours that are likely to work in different situations and result in increased efficiency and effectiveness.

To illustrate the importance of understanding that situations are different, and can require different styles, consider the fate of some of the Americans who have been recruited to run Canadian companies. Retailer Millard Barron was brought north to turn Zellers around, and American Bill Fields was supposed to save Hudson's Bay Co. Neither could replicate their US successes in Canada. Texas oilman J.P. Bryan was given the chance to restore profitability at two Canadian companies—Gulf Canada Resources Ltd. (now ConocoPhillips Company) and Canadian 88 Energy Corp. (now Esprit Exploration Limited)—and failed at both attempts.[46] We also saw in Chapter 7 how chief operating officer Gary Daichendt and chief technology officer Gary Kunis walked away from Nortel Corp. over management differences or "divergent management styles and different views of the future of the business" with CEO Bill Owens. These examples show the importance of understanding that one's leadership style may need to be adjusted for different companies and employees, and perhaps even for different countries.

The Leader Substitutes Model

The leader substitutes model suggests that leadership is sometimes unnecessary because substitutes for leadership are present. A **leader substitute** is something that acts in place of the influence of a leader and makes leadership unnecessary. This model suggests that under certain conditions managers do not have to play a leadership role—that members of an organization sometimes can perform highly without a manager exerting influence over them.[47] The leader substitutes model is a contingency model because it suggests that in some situations leadership is unnecessary.

Both the *characteristics of subordinates*—such as their skills, abilities, experience, knowledge, and motivation—and the *characteristics of the situation or context*—such as the extent to which the work is interesting and enjoyable—can be substitutes for leadership.[48] When work is interesting and enjoyable, job holders do not need to be coaxed into performing because performing is rewarding in its own right. Similarly, when managers empower their subordinates or use *self-managed work teams* (discussed in detail in Chapter 10), the need for leadership influence from a manager is decreased because team members manage themselves.

leader substitute
Characteristics of subordinates or characteristics of a situation or context that act in place of the influence of a leader and make leadership unnecessary.

Substitutes for leadership can increase organizational efficiency and effectiveness because they free up some of managers' valuable time and allow managers to focus their efforts on discovering new ways to improve organizational effectiveness.

Bringing It All Together

Effective leadership in organizations occurs when managers take steps to lead in a way that is appropriate for the situation or context in which leadership occurs and the subordinates who are being led. The four contingency models of leadership just discussed help managers identify the necessary ingredients for effective leadership. They are complementary in that each one looks at the leadership question from a different angle. Fiedler's contingency model explores how a manager's leadership style needs to be matched to the leadership situation that the manager is in for maximum effectiveness. Hersey-Blanchard's situational leadership theory examines the need for leaders to adjust their style to match their followers' ability and motivation. House's path-goal theory focuses on how managers should motivate subordinates and describes the specific kinds of behaviours that managers can engage in to have a highly motivated workforce. The leadership substitutes model alerts managers to the fact that sometimes they do not need to exert influence over subordinates and thus can free up their time for other important activities. Table 9.3 recaps these four contingency models of leadership.

 Tips for Managers

CONTINGENCY MODELS OF LEADERSHIP

1. Examine for yourself the kinds of situation where you feel you will be the most effective as a leader.

2. Know how flexible you can be in choosing a different style to lead when the situation calls for such a difference.

3. Link your leadership style to the outcomes you want your employees to achieve; know how you will reward them; and make clear the paths for employees to follow to be successful.

4. Know when your subordinates can effectively manage and lead themselves.

TABLE 9.3 | *Contingency Models of Leadership*

MODEL	FOCUS	KEY CONTINGENCIES
Fiedler's contingency model	Describes two leader styles, relationship-oriented and task-oriented, and the kinds of situations in which each kind of leader will be most effective	Whether or not a relationship-oriented or a task-oriented leader is effective is contingent on the situation
Hersey-Blanchard's situational leadership theory	Describes how leaders adjust their styles to match their followers' ability and motivation	The styles that managers should use are contingent on the ability and motivation of subordinates
House's path-goal theory	Describes how effective leaders motivate their followers	The behaviours that managers should engage in to be effective leaders are contingent on the nature of the subordinates and the work they do
Leader substitutes model	Describes when leadership is unnecessary	Whether or not leadership is necessary for subordinates to perform highly is contingent on characteristics of the subordinates and the situation

Transformational Leadership: Leading With Vision

THINK ABOUT IT

Seven Transformations of Leadership[49]

The leader's voyage of development is not an easy one. Some people change little in their lifetimes; some change substantially. Despite the undeniably crucial role of genetics, human nature is not fixed. Those who are willing to work at developing themselves and becoming more self-aware can almost certainly evolve over time into truly transformational leaders.

So ends the article, "Seven Transformations of Leadership" by David Rooke, a partner at Harthill Consulting in Hewelsfield, England, and William R. Torbert, a professor at Boston College's Carroll School of Management in Massachusetts.[50] The authors based their research and applications on what they call "action inquiry": the process of transformational learning that individuals (and even whole organizations) can undertake to better assess current dangers and opportunities, act in a timely manner, and make future visions come true. What they discovered is that there is a transformational progression of leadership abilities in organizations: from opportunist to alchemist, with expert and achiever leadership styles being the most predominant. What is significant about their work is the possibility of transforming oneself from one "action logic," or mindset, to a more refined one. For example, if a manager is seen to be an opportunist, he/she demonstrates a style that says: "I win at any cost. I am self-referencing and manipulative. I believe that 'might makes right.'" This is obviously a very undeveloped style and in their research found that only 5 percent of managers were described as such. At the other end of the spectrum is the alchemist who is quite focused on social transformation and the integration of material, spiritual, and societal issues for transformation. This action logic individual accounts for only 1 percent of the managers. The bulk of managers (38 percent and 30 percent) turned out to be experts and achievers respectively. What makes an individual manager transform from one action logic way of seeing and leading is attributed to a variety of reasons: personal changes, loss of faith in the system, external events, changes in the work environment—in other words, factors that challenge the status quo of the leader.

You Be the Manager

1. What are factors that have forced you to shift how you see the world?
2. What are some of the transformations you have experienced?

The trait, behavioural, and contingency theories are transactional leadership theories developed when organizations were more hierarchical, with classic lines of command. **Transactional leadership** occurs when managers guide or motivate their subordinates in the direction of established goals. Some transactional leaders use rewards and recognize appropriate behaviour. Under this kind of leadership, employees will generally meet performance expectations, though rarely will they exceed expectations.[51] Other transactional leaders emphasize correction and possibly punishment rather than rewards and recognition. This style "results in performance below expectations, and discourages innovation and initiative in the workplace."[52] While leaders should not ignore poor performance, effective leaders emphasize how to achieve expectations, rather than dwelling on mistakes.

transactional leadership
Leaders who guide their subordinates toward expected goals with no expectation of exceeding expected behaviour.

Hierarchical organizations still dominate Canada's "Most Respected Corporations,"[53] but some organizations are trying to be more innovative, faster moving, and more responsive to employees. These organizations have turned to a different style of leadership where leaders and managers are not expected to perform only supervisory tasks but also need to focus on vision-setting activities. These theories try to explain how certain leaders can achieve extraordinary performance from their followers, and they emphasize symbolic and emotionally appealing leadership behaviours.[54]

When managers have such dramatic effects on their subordinates and on an organization as a whole, they are engaging in transformational leadership. **Transformational leadership** occurs when managers change (or transform) their subordinates in three important ways:[55]

1. *Transformational managers make subordinates aware of how important their jobs are for the organization and how necessary it is for them to perform those jobs as best they can so that the organization can attain its goals.* At LG Electronics, Hun-Jo Lee opened new paths of communication between nonmanagerial employees and managers, and openly shared the company's problems with employees. He made everyone feel responsible for helping to solve the problems. Decision making was decentralized, and all employees were encouraged to feel responsible for coming up with improvements, ideas for new products, and ways to increase quality.

2. *Transformational managers make their subordinates aware of the subordinates' own needs for personal growth, development, and accomplishment.* One of Lee's important steps at LG Electronics was to improve management relations with the union. He encouraged union members to meet with him whenever they have ideas for improving things at LG Electronics.[56] He wants his employees to reach their full potential and is doing whatever he can think of to help them do that. He also empowers his employees, so they will feel free to consider new ways of doing things at the company.

3. *Transformational managers motivate their subordinates to work for the good of the organization as a whole, not just for their own personal gain or benefit.* In transforming LG Electronics, Lee explained to employees the need for change at the company, and that growth and improvement in productivity would make the company much stronger, thus benefiting everyone.

Many transformational leaders engage in transactional leadership. They reward subordinates for a job well done and notice and respond to substandard performance. But they also have their eyes on the bigger picture of how much better things could be in their organizations, how much more their subordinates are capable of achieving, and how important it is to treat their subordinates with respect and to help them reach their full potential.

Influencing Others

How do managers like Lee transform subordinates and produce dramatic effects in their organizations? There are at least three ways in which managers and other transformational leaders can influence their followers: by being a charismatic leader, by stimulating subordinates intellectually, and by engaging in developmental consideration (see Table 9.4).

Being a Charismatic Leader

Transformational managers are **charismatic leaders**. They have a vision of how good things could be in their work groups and organizations, and it is in contrast with the

transformational leadership
Leadership that makes subordinates aware of the importance of their jobs and performance to the organization and aware of their own needs for personal growth, and that motivates subordinates to work for the good of the organization.

LG Electronics Inc.
www.lg.co.kr/english/

charismatic leader
An enthusiastic, self-confident leader able to communicate clearly his or her vision of how good things could be.

TABLE 9.4 | *Transformational Leadership*

Transformational Managers

- Are charismatic
- Intellectually stimulate subordinates
- Engage in developmental consideration

Subordinates of Transformational Managers

- Have increased awareness of the importance of their jobs and high performance
- Are aware of their own needs for growth, development, and accomplishment
- Work for the good of the organization and not just their own personal benefit

status quo. Their vision usually entails dramatic improvements in group and organizational performance as a result of changes in the organization's structure, culture, strategy, decision making, and other critical processes and factors. This vision paves the way for gaining a competitive advantage.

Charismatic leaders are excited and enthusiastic about their vision and clearly communicate it to their subordinates. The excitement, enthusiasm, and self-confidence of a charismatic leader contribute to the leader's being able to inspire followers to enthusiastically support his or her vision.[57] People often think of charismatic leaders or managers as being "larger than life." The essence of charisma, however, is having a vision and enthusiastically communicating it to others. Thus, managers who appear to be quiet and earnest can also be charismatic.

The most comprehensive analysis of charismatic leadership was conducted by Professor Rabindra Kanungo at McGill University, together with Jay Conger.[58] Based on studies of managers from Canada, the United States, and India, they identified five dimensions that characterize charismatic leadership. These are shown in Table 9.5.

Does charismatic leadership really make a difference? An unpublished study by Robert House and some colleagues looking at 63 American and 49 Canadian companies (including Nortel Networks, Molson, Gulf Canada [now ConocoPhillips], and Manulife Financial) found that "between 15 and 25 percent of the variation in profitability among the companies was accounted for by the leadership qualities of their CEO."[59] Charismatic leaders led more profitable companies.

TABLE 9.5 | *Key Characteristics of a Charismatic Leader*

1. *Vision and articulation.* Has a vision—expressed as an idealized goal—that proposes a future better than the status quo; is able to clarify the importance of the vision in terms that are understandable to others.

2. *Personal risk.* Willing to take on high personal risk, incur high costs, and engage in self-sacrifice to achieve the vision.

3. *Environmental sensitivity.* Able to make realistic assessments of the environmental constraints and resources needed to bring about change.

4. *Sensitivity to follower needs.* Perceptive of others' abilities and responsive to their needs and feelings.

5. *Unconventional behaviour.* Engages in behaviours that are perceived as novel and counter to norms.

Source: Based on J.A. Conger and R.N. Kanungo, *Charismatic Leadership in Organizations* (Thousand Oaks, CA: Sage, 1998), p. 94.

An increasing body of research shows that people who work for charismatic leaders are motivated to exert extra work effort and, because they like their leaders, they express greater satisfaction.[60] One of the most cited studies of the effects of charismatic leadership was done at the University of British Columbia in the early 1980s by Jane Howell (now at the Richard Ivey School of Business, University of Western Ontario) and Peter Frost.[61] The two found that those who worked under a charismatic leader generated more ideas, produced better results, reported higher job satisfaction, and showed stronger bonds of loyalty. Howell, in summarizing these results, says, "Charismatic leaders know how to inspire people to think in new directions."[62]

The recent accounting scandals and high-profile bankruptcies of North American companies, including Enron and WorldCom, suggest some of the dangers of charismatic leadership. WorldCom Inc.'s Bernard Ebbers and Enron Corp.'s Kenneth Lay "seemed almost a breed apart, blessed with unique visionary powers" when their companies were increasing stock prices at phenomenal rates in the 1990s.[63] After the scandals, however, there was some desire for CEOs with less vision and more ethical and corporate responsibility.

Stimulating Subordinates Intellectually

Transformational managers openly share information with their subordinates so that subordinates are aware of problems and the need for change. The manager causes subordinates to view problems in their groups and throughout the organization from a different perspective, consistent with the manager's vision. Whereas in the past subordinates may not have been aware of some problems, may have viewed problems as a "management issue" beyond their concern, or may have viewed problems as insurmountable, the transformational manager's **intellectual stimulation** leads subordinates to view problems as challenges that they can and will meet and conquer. The manager engages and empowers subordinates to take personal responsibility for helping to solve problems.[64]

Engaging in Developmental Consideration

When a manager engages in **developmental consideration**, he or she not only performs the consideration behaviours described earlier, such as demonstrating true concern for the well-being of subordinates, but goes one step further. The manager goes out of his or her way to support and encourage subordinates, giving them opportunities to enhance their skills and capabilities and to grow and excel on the job.[65]

Research Support

The evidence supporting the superiority of transformational leadership is overwhelmingly impressive. For example, studies of Canadian, American, and German military officers found, at every level, that transformational leaders were considered more effective than their transactional counterparts.[66] Professor Jane Howell (at the University of Western Ontario) and her colleagues studied 250 executives and managers at a major financial-services company and found that "transformational leaders had 34 percent higher business unit performance results than other types of leaders."[67] Studies also find that when leaders engage in transformational leadership, their subordinates tend to have higher levels of job satisfaction and performance.[68] Additionally, subordinates of transformational leaders may be more likely to trust their leaders and their organizations and feel that they are being fairly treated, which in turn may positively influence their work motivation (see Chapter 8).[69]

intellectual stimulation
Behaviour a leader engages in to make followers aware of problems and view these problems in new ways, consistent with the leader's vision.

developmental consideration
Behaviour a leader engages in to support and encourage followers and help them develop and grow on the job.

Tips for Managers

TRANSFORMATIONAL LEADERSHIP

1. Facilitate employee development and attainment of goals to ensure commitment and corporate goal attainment.

2. Develop ways for self-understanding so that you can be the very best.

3. Visualize what are ideal states of business operation and develop steps for their completion.

4. Let your employees know that you care for them, their well-being, and their productivity.

Gender, Culture, and Leadership

THINK ABOUT IT

Women and Leadership[70]

It is estimated that women now own 35 percent of all small businesses in Canada. When journalist Mary Teresa Bitti asked Dr. Lance Secretan, international bestselling author of 13 books on leadership, a corporate coach and a business adviser, about gender and leadership, he replied:

The landscape is changing very fast here, but the fact remains men have had a lot of forces working for them—clubs, old boy networks. They are swimming with the tide. Women, until very recently, have not typically had that. As a result, in some ways, they are better problem-solvers. They have had to work around things and create solutions that are innovative in order to get around the system. If a man wants to solve a financial problem, he will go to his pals in the financial world and ask for advice. Women don't have those pals and have to make it up themselves. They are more creative and collaborative.

Key success stories:

- Meg Whitman has transformed eBay Inc. from a trading post for collectors of Pez dispensers into the world's dominant online auctioneer.

- At Xerox Corp., Lucent Technologies Inc., and Avon Products Inc., successful turnaround CEOs Anne Mulcahy, Patricia Russo, and Toronto native Andrea Jung, respectively, have been cleaning up the mess left by ousted male predecessors.

- PepsiCo Inc. veteran Brenda Barnes was named the incoming CEO at food and apparel giant Sara Lee Corp. in early 2005.

- Business writer, David Olive, says that investors in women-led Fortune 500 companies enjoyed a 53.7-percent return on their stock in the past two years, compared with a 37.7-percent gain for the Standard & Poor's 500 index."[71]

You Be the Manager

1. What are the challenges that women face that men do not?

2. *Globe and Mail* journalist, Margaret Wente, writes, "Bye-bye fast track, hello mommy track." What would she imply with that statement in terms of women as leaders?

There are many questions about whether men and women have different leadership styles, or whether observed differences have more to do with personality differences across people, rather than explicit gender differences. Others consider whether leadership is done the same cross-culturally, and whether our North American leadership theories apply in other countries. We consider these issues in the following sections.

Gender and Leadership

The increasing number of women entering the ranks of management as well as the problems some women face in their efforts to be hired as managers or promoted into management positions have prompted researchers to explore the relationship between gender and leadership. Although relatively more women are in management positions today than 10 years ago, relatively few women are in top management in larger organizations, and, in some organizations, even in middle management. Although women make up 45 percent of the labour force in Canada, they fill only 32 percent of managerial roles, and only 12 percent of the senior management roles. Of the *National Post's* Top 150 CEOs of 2000, only two were women, and half of Canada's larger companies have no women in the senior ranks at all.[72] Women are represented better in smaller organizations. Industry Canada reports that in 2000, 45 percent of all small- to medium-sized enterprises reported at least one female owner.[73]

When women do advance to top-management positions, special attention is often focused on the fact that they are women, such as when Bobbi Gaunt was named to head Ford Motor Co. of Canada and Maureen Kempston Darkes was named to head General Motors of Canada.

A widespread stereotype of women is that they are nurturing, supportive, and concerned with interpersonal relations. Men are stereotypically viewed as being directive and focused on task accomplishment. Such stereotypes suggest that women tend to be more relationship-oriented as managers and engage in more consideration behaviours, whereas men are more task-oriented and engage in more initiating structure behaviours. Does the behaviour of actual male and female managers bear out these stereotypes? Do female managers lead in different ways than males? Are male or female managers more effective as leaders?

Research suggests that male managers and female managers who have leadership positions in organizations behave in similar ways.[74] Women do not engage in more consideration than men, and men do not engage in more initiating structure than women. Research does suggest, however, that leadership style may vary between women and men. Women tend to be somewhat more participative as leaders than men, involving subordinates in decision making and seeking their input.[75] Male managers tend to be less participative than female managers, making more decisions on their own and wanting to do things their own way.

There are at least two reasons why female managers may be more participative as leaders than male managers.[76] First, subordinates may try to resist the influence of female managers more than they do the influence of male managers. Some subordinates may never have reported to a woman before, some may inappropriately see management roles as being more appropriate for men than for women, and some may just

Andrea Jung—CEO of Avon, the famous cosmetic producer—advanced to that rank after first serving as the company's president and chief operating officer.

resist being led by a woman. To overcome this resistance and encourage subordinates' trust and respect, female managers may adopt a participative approach.

A second reason why female managers may be more participative is that they sometimes have better interpersonal skills than male managers.[77] A participative approach to leadership requires high levels of interaction and involvement between a manager and his or her subordinates, sensitivity to subordinates' feelings, and the ability to make decisions that may be unpopular with subordinates but necessary for reaching goals. Good interpersonal skills may help female managers have the effective interactions with their subordinates that are crucial to a participative approach.[78] To the extent that male managers have more difficulty managing interpersonal relationships, they may shy away from the high levels of interaction with subordinates that are necessary for true participation.

Perhaps a question even more important than whether male and female managers differ in the leadership behaviours they perform is whether they differ in effectiveness. Consistent with the findings for leader behaviours, research suggests that across different kinds of organizational settings, male and female managers tend to be *equally* effective as leaders.[79] Thus, there is no logical basis for stereotypes favouring male managers and leaders or for the existence of the glass ceiling (an invisible barrier that seems to prevent women from advancing as far as they should in some organizations). Because women and men are equally effective as leaders, the increasing number of women in the workforce should result in a larger pool of highly qualified candidates for management positions in organizations, ultimately enhancing organizational effectiveness.[80]

Leadership Styles Across Cultures

Some evidence suggests that leadership styles vary not only among individuals but also among countries or cultures. Some research suggests that European managers tend to be more humanistic or people-oriented than Japanese and American managers. The collectivistic culture in Japan places prime emphasis on the group rather than the individual, so the importance of individuals' own personalities, needs, and desires is minimized. Organizations in North America tend to be very profit-oriented and thus tend to downplay the importance of individual employees' needs and desires. Many countries in Europe have a more individualistic outlook than Japan and a more humanistic outlook than the United States, which may result in some European managers being more people-oriented than their Japanese or American counterparts. European managers, for example, tend to be reluctant to lay off employees, and when a layoff is absolutely necessary, they take careful steps to make it as painless as possible.[81]

Another cross-cultural difference that has been noted is in time horizons. Managers in any two countries often differ in their time horizons, but there also may be cultural differences. Canadian and US organizations tend to have a short-run profit orientation, which results in a leadership style emphasizing short-run performance. Many of the investors and creators of the dot-com companies that failed in 2000 and 2001 demonstrated very short-term objectives, along the lines of "get rich quick." Many of these companies failed to have a business plan that would guide them in a long-term strategy. By contrast, Japanese organizations tend to have a long-run growth orientation, which results in Japanese managers' personal leadership styles emphasizing long-run performance. Justus Mische, now chair at the European organization Aventis (formerly Hoechst) has suggested that "Europe, at least the big international firms in Europe, have a philosophy between the Japanese, long term, and the United States, short term."[82] Research on these and other global aspects of leadership is in its infancy, but as it continues, more cultural differences in managers' personal leadership styles may be discovered.

Emotional Intelligence and Leadership

Do the moods and emotions leaders experience on the job influence their behaviour and effectiveness as leaders? Preliminary research suggests that this is likely to be the case. For example, one study found that when store managers experienced positive moods at work, salespeople in the stores they led provided high quality customer service and were less likely to quit.[83]

emotional intelligence
The ability to understand and manage one's own moods and emotions and the moods and emotions of other people.

Emotional intelligence is the ability to understand and manage one's own moods and emotions and the moods and emotions of other people. A leader's level of emotional intelligence may play a particularly important role in leadership effectiveness.[84] For example, emotional intelligence may help leaders develop a vision for their organizations, motivate their subordinates to commit to this vision, and energize them to enthusiastically work to achieve this vision. Moreover, emotional intelligence may enable leaders to develop a significant identity for their organization and instill high levels of trust and cooperation throughout the organization while maintaining the flexibility needed to respond to changing conditions.[85]

Summary and Review

1. **THE NATURE OF LEADERSHIP** Leadership is the process by which a person exerts influence over other people and inspires, motivates, and directs their activities to help achieve group or organizational goals. Leaders are able to influence others because they possess power. The five types of power available to managers are *legitimate power, reward power, coercive power, expert power,* and *referent power.* Many managers are using empowerment as a tool to increase their effectiveness as leaders.

2. **LEADERSHIP AS SUPERVISION** The *trait model* of leadership describes personal characteristics or traits that contribute to effective leadership. However, some managers who possess these traits are not effective leaders, and some managers who do not possess all the traits are nevertheless effective leaders. The *behaviour model* of leadership describes two kinds of behaviour that most leaders engage in: consideration and initiating structure.

3. **CONTINGENCY MODELS OF LEADERSHIP** Contingency models take into account the complexity surrounding leadership and the role of the situation in determining whether a manager is an effective or ineffective leader. *Fiedler's contingency model* explains why managers may be effective leaders in one situation and ineffective in another. *Hersey-Blanchard's situational leadership theory* examines the need for leaders to adjust their style to match their followers' ability and motivation. *House's path-goal theory* describes how effective managers motivate their subordinates by determining what outcomes their subordinates want, rewarding subordinates with these outcomes when they achieve their goals and perform at a high level, and clarifying the paths to goal attainment. The *leader substitutes model* suggests that sometimes managers do not have to play a leadership role because their subordinates perform highly without the manager having to exert influence over them.

4. **TRANSFORMATIONAL LEADERSHIP: LEADING WITH VISION** Transactional leaders generally only get their subordinates to meet expectations. Transformational leadership occurs when managers have dramatic effects on their subordinates and on the organization as a whole and inspire and energize

subordinates to solve problems and improve performance. These effects include making subordinates aware of the importance of their own jobs and high performance; making subordinates aware of their own needs for personal growth, development, and accomplishment; and motivating subordinates to work for the good of the organization and not just their own personal gain. Managers can engage in transformational leadership by being charismatic leaders, by stimulating subordinates intellectually, and by engaging in developmental consideration. Transformational managers also often engage in transactional leadership by using their reward and coercive powers to encourage high performance.

5. **GENDER, CULTURE, AND LEADERSHIP** Female and male managers do not differ in the leadership behaviours that they perform, contrary to stereotypes suggesting that women are more relationship-oriented and men more task-oriented. Female managers sometimes are more participative than male managers, however. Research has found that women and men are equally effective as managers and leaders. Studies have found differences in leadership styles across cultures. European leaders tend to be more people-oriented than either American or Japanese leaders. Leaders also differ in their time orientations, with US and Canadian leaders being very oriented toward the short term in their approach.

6. **EMOTIONAL INTELLIGENCE AND LEADERSHIP** The moods and emotions leaders experience on the job may affect their leadership effectiveness. Moreover, emotional intelligence has the potential to contribute to leadership effectiveness in multiple ways.

Key Terms

charismatic leader, p. 264

coercive power, p. 252

developmental consideration, p. 266

emotional intelligence, p. 270

employee-centred behaviour, p. 256

empowerment, p. 253

expert power, p. 253

intellectual stimulation, p. 266

job-oriented behaviours, p. 257

leader, p. 250

leadership, p. 250

leader substitute, p. 261

legitimate power, p. 251

path-goal theory, p. 259

position power, p. 258

referent power, p. 253

reward power, p. 252

situational leadership theory (SLT), p. 259

task structure, p. 258

transactional leadership, p. 263

transformational leadership, p. 264

SO WHERE DO YOU STAND?

Wrap-Up to Opening Case

We began this chapter on leadership with what could be called "the long view" of leadership. That is, we looked at leadership "unto the seventh generation." There is definitely a need among leaders and society at large to build organizations that serve not only shareholders but also stakeholders, or the wider community. The effect of numerous business scandals has drawn attention to the negative effects of short-term leadership decision making. For example, Ivanhoe Mines Ltd. of Vancouver, believes it has discovered a gigantic copper and gold deposit in South Gobi, Mongolia and is spending US$10 million a month drilling holes, testing results, and pouring a gigantic concrete shaft in preparation for production in about two years. Like other companies in similar situations, time and money are being spent because the consequences of not consulting all the stakeholders can simply be too costly in terms of money and corporate reputation.

Dr. Warren Bennis reminded us that true leaders want to do the right thing. One model that was described in our open scenario was that of the Iroquois Confederacy. Leaders in the Confederacy consider the impact of their decisions on the seven generations of people around them: the three that preceded them, the current one, and the three that will follow each leader. In this way, care was a moral duty because of these seventh generation considerations. "Our world is crying—even dying—for such leaders. John Kotter[86] says that the ultimate act of leadership is to create a culture of leadership."[87] In the spirit of Dr. Margaret Wheatley's thoughts on leader, she believes that in tune with such a culture of leadership is the presence of "the leader-as-host," not the hero-leader. The cult of the hero-leader has created much of the corporate malfeasance that the beginning years of the 21st century have experienced from business.[88] Charles Elson, a corporate governance expert at the University of Delaware, puts matters this way: "We're seeing the outcome of a real dramatic shift. It's the destruction of the myth of the imperial CEO."[89]

Much has been researched in the 20th century regarding leadership styles, approaches, traits, etc. What is becoming more and more critical, however, in order to build a future worth going to, is the presence of what Richard Branson, famed British entrepreneur and founder of the Virgin Group, calls "living life to its full."[90] It is this "leadership authenticity" that will decide the new winners and losers in business.

After studying the preceding material, be sure to check out our Online Learning Centre at
www.mcgrawhill.ca/olc/jones
for more in-depth information and interactivities that correspond to this chapter.

Management in Action

Topics for Discussion and Action

1. Describe the steps managers can take to increase their power and ability to be effective leaders.
2. Think of specific situations in which it might be especially important for a manager to engage in consideration and in initiating structure.
3. Interview an actual manager to find out how the three situational characteristics that Fiedler identified are affecting the manager's ability to provide leadership.
4. For you current job or for a failure job that you expect to hold, describe what your supervisor could do to strongly motivate you to be a top performer.
5. Discuss why manager might want to change the behaviours they engage in, given their situation, their subordinates, and the nature of the work being done.

Do you think managers are able to change their leader-ship behaviours readily? Why or why not?
6. Discuss why substitutes for leadership can contribute to organizational effectiveness.
7. Describe what transformational leadership is, and explain how managers can engage in it.
8. Find an example of a company that has dramatically turned its fortunes around and improved its performance. Determine whether a transformational leader was behind the turnaround and, if so, what this leader did.
9. Discuss why some people still think that men make better managers than women even though research indicates that men and women are equally effective as managers and leaders.

Building Management Skills

ANALYZING FAILURES OF LEADERSHIP

Think about a situation you are familiar with in which a leader was very ineffective. Then answer the following questions.

1. What sources of power did this leader have? Did the leader have enough power to influence his or her followers?
2. What kinds of behaviours did this leader engage in? Were they appropriate for the situation? Why or why not?
3. From what you know, do you think this leader was a task-oriented leader or a relationship-oriented leader? How favourable was this leader's situation for leading?
4. What steps did this leader take to motivate his or her followers? Were these steps appropriate or inappropriate? Why?
5. What signs, if any, did this leader show of being a transformational leader?

Management for You

Your school is developing a one-day orientation program for new students majoring in business. You have been asked to consider leading the group of students who will design and implement the orientation program. Develop a two- to three-page "handout" that shows whether the position is a natural fit for you. To do this, (1) identify your strengths and weaknesses in the sources of power you can bring to the project, and (2) discuss whether you would be a transactional or transformation leader and why. Provide a strong concluding statement about whether or not you would be the best leader for this task.

Small Group Breakout Exercise

IMPROVING LEADERSHIP EFFECTIVENESS

Form groups of three to five people, and appoint one member as the spokesperson who will communicate your findings and conclusions to the whole class when called on by the instructor. Then discuss the following scenario.

You are a team of human resource consultants who have been hired by Carla Caruso, an entrepreneur who started her own interior decorating business. At first, she worked on her own as an independent contractor. Then, because of a dramatic increase in the number of new homes being built, she decided to form her own company.

She hired a secretary/bookkeeper and four interior decorators. Caruso still does decorating jobs herself and has adopted a hands-off approach to leading the four decorators because she feels that interior design is a very personal, creative endeavour. Rather than paying the decorators on some kind of commission basis, she pays them a higher-than-average salary so that they are motivated to do what's best for their customers, not what will result in higher billings and commissions.

Caruso thought everything was going smoothly until customer complaints started coming in. These complaints were about the decorators being hard to reach, promising unrealistic delivery times, being late for or failing to keep appointments, and being impatient and rude when customers had trouble making up their minds. Caruso knows that her decorators are competent people and is concerned that she is not effectively leading and managing them. She has asked for your advice.

1. What advice can you give Caruso to either increase her power or use her existing power more effectively?
2. Does Caruso seem to be performing appropriate leader behaviours in this situation? What advice can you give her about the kinds of behaviours she should perform?
3. How can Caruso increase the decorator's motivation to deliver high quality customer service?
4. Would you adviser Caruso to try engage in transformational leadership in this situation? If not, why not? If so, what steps would you advise her to take?

Managing Ethically

One of your subordinates has noticed that your expense account reports have repeatedly overstated your expenses because you always bill for an extra day, at the "daily rate," when you go out of town on company business. Your assistant knows that you have always been in town and working at home on that extra day. He has questioned your reports, as you have now submitted 15 of these for the year. How would you use your knowledge of power to resolve this dilemma? Which use of power would be most ethical, and why?

Exploring the World Wide Web

SPECIFIC ASSIGNMENT

Smed is a Calgary-based construction company that specializes in modular interior office construction. The company's network of offices and showrooms includes Alberta locations in Edmonton, St. Albert, and Grande Prairie. In early 2003, Gary Scitthelm was named president. He has been with Smed for 10 years and was vice-president of sales and marketing. Scan the following website that has an interview with him by *Business Edge* magazine (www.businessedge.ca/article.cfm/newsID/5796.cfm).[91]

1. How would you characterize Gary Scitthelm's personal leadership style?
2. How might Scitthelm's early experiences during the previous 10 years influence his leadership optics?
3. How might Scitthelm be considered a transformational leader?

GENERAL ASSIGNMENT

Find the website of a company that provides information on the company's missions, goals, and values, and on the company's top managers and their personal leadership styles. How might the company's missions, goals, and values impact the process of leadership in this company?

Developing a Business Plan

(APPENDIX B, PAGE 405)

Go to www.mcgrawhill.ca/olc/jones/9 for online exercises.

Be the Manager

NAPOLEON ON LEADERSHIP[92]

Jim Warthin is a friend of yours; he is also CEO of a small plastics firm and has invited you in to discuss a new book he has recently read on leadership and Napoleon Bonaparte.[93] He tells you in an email that the author of this text has identified Napoloeon's six winning leadership principles. Jim wants to discuss these principles in the context of the leadership course that you both took when in business school together. He wants your trusted feedback.

1. **Exactitude:** He sought pinpoint precision through extensive research, continuous planning, and constant awareness of the situation he faced, which included meditating on what might occur—in other words, awareness, research, and continuous planning.
2. **Speed:** He recognized that momentum—mass times velocity—applied to achieving goals with people as well. "He knew that resistance causes momentum to fade. Increasing speed is about reducing resistance, increasing urgency, and providing focus by employing concentration of force and economy of force," Mr. Manas says—in other words, reducing resistance, increasing urgency, and providing focus.
3. **Flexibility:** Napoleon ensured that his armies could react quickly to situations, yet still operate according to a strategic plan. He organized his troops into mobile units; empowered them by providing knowledge of the mission and structuring them to operate independently; yet he also made sure they were operating under a unified doctrine and serving one ultimate leader—in other words, building teams that are adaptable, empowered, and unified.
4. **Simplicity:** He ensured his objectives were simple, his messages were simple, and his processes simple, reducing confusion. "The art of war does not require complicated manoeuvre. The simplest are the best," he declared—in other words, clear simple objectives, messages, and processes.
5. **Character:** While driven by his ambition, Napoleon always maintained honour and integrity, calmness and responsibility, and encouraging respect of other cultures.
6. **Moral Force:** "In war, everything depends upon morale," Napoleon said. People do their best work when they have self-confidence, feel what they are doing is worthwhile, and are recognized for their effort—in other words, providing order, purpose recognition, and rewards.

Management Case

Leadership to the Seventh Generation[94]

'I wish to speak for nature …… for there are enough champions of civilization'
—Henry David Thoreau

In September [2004] I am invited to celebrate the changing of the seasons in the cathedral of Temagami, an old growth forest of 150 year old trees in the near north of Ontario. I am invited by an elder of the Teme-Augama Anishnabai, among the last of his people homesteading on ancestral lands, to visit an area that has served as a gathering place for his people for a thousand years as they seek wisdom and commune with their elders.

This may not be possible in the near future. For anyone. Plans have been approved to commence clear-cutting in the area that contains the Spirit Forest that lies between Lake Temagami and Lake Obakika. It is this area that contains the old growth forest and the Spirit Rock I have been invited to visit.

I sit here late at night, consider this trip and write this article. How has it come that we cannot see the value of a forest? And, what does this mean to leaders of our organizations?

We live in a time when our corporate leaders manage quarter by quarter and our political leaders tell us they can't be bound by three year plans. Yet, the most pressing problem faced by our planet—the current decline of every living system—requires a multi-generational strategy.

Our institutions are failing us. And while writers like Dee Hock and Thomas Homer-Dixon look to the inability of our institutions to deal with complex crises like global environmental meltdown, world hunger, peace and conflict, and the gap between the rich and the poor, I look to more pedestrian signposts.

Our religions have become efficiency and consumption. We fall to the myth of perpetual economic growth while the only organism in nature, which is governed by such an imperative, is the cancer cell that eventually kills its host. We have traded compassion and replaced it with competition. Somewhere along the way we forgot people live in communities and neighbourhoods, not marketplaces.

In our organizations, I see workplaces that are over-managed and underled. I see corporations that would rather make decisions for the casino of the stock market than long-term value creation. I see a world where we demand compliance in our people rather than inspiring their commitment and engaging them in a process of co-creating a positive vision of the future.

Is it any wonder most Fortune 500 corporations last no longer than 40 years. Is it any wonder that worker disengagement costs US corporations $350 billion a year according to Gallop Research? Is it any wonder that disability represents up to 12 percent of payroll costs in Canada with mental health claims as the fastest growing category of disability, or so according to a major round-table study completed in 2000 looking at depression in the Canadian workplace?

Robert Greenleaf, the man who coined the term *servant-leader* admonishes that servant leaders must seek to *do no harm*. Meanwhile Warren Bennis says that managers are people who do things right while leaders do the right thing. Our organizations are crying for leaders who will help us do the right thing.

The most powerful leadership philosophy I know of does not come from our leading business schools, our leading corporations. It is not from celebrity authors like Donald Trump or Rudy Giuliani. Rather, it is a piece of wisdom that guided leaders in the Iroquois Confederacy, instructing them to consider the impact of their decisions on the seven generations around them. Our indigenous people knew that one man, one leader, could only hope to know the seven generations around him: the three that preceded him— to his great grandparents—and the three that will follow—to his great grandchildren. The leader was bound by a moral duty to care for the Seven Generations.

Would that our leaders were servants to the Seven Generations. Our oil companies would cease to deny global climate change. Our utilities would promote conservation. Our car companies would care about fuel efficiency. And no forest would fall to a clear-cut ever again.

And this begs the question. What would Seventh Generation Leadership look like in our organizations? For just as the economy of nature requires long-term perspectives, so too does the economy of men.

First, I believe Seventh Generation leadership in our corporations would be principle-based. Principle-based leaders would create organizations that are aligned with the principles of their people. The challenge is not to align people with the principles of our workplaces but to create workplaces that enable people to live in accordance with their core values and beliefs. This is not mysticism. This is a competitive imperative. Our people and their innate values become our compass in times of great complexity rather than our directives and corporate statements of ethics. Company-destroying malfeasance is simply not possible in organizations where people work in accordance with their core values and beliefs.

I believe Seventh Generation leadership would be spiritual. Not religious, but spiritual. For too long we have viewed spirituality as akin to voodoo. Yet, as people, we are spiritual beings. What's more, we struggle for meaning in times of incredible turbulence. Amid such turbulence and complexity, our natural instinct is to seek control. Yet, chaos cannot be controlled; complexity cannot be controlled. Our science tells us this is the case. Leadership based on spirituality better prepares us to cope with the inevitable question of *why*? Leadership based on trying to control the uncontrollable is doomed to failure. Too much of what is around us is simply beyond our control. Rather than trying to control the uncontrollable, far better that we act paradoxically and relinquish control by enabling our people to act in accordance with the factors that surround them locally. Again, a paradox. By relinquishing control we actually build capacity that enables us to better respond to rapid change. How do we do this? We do so by sharing power and leading through inclusion.

I believe Seventh Generation leaders would intuitively understand the power of inclusion, the power of conversation. Their leadership style would be participative, involving and inclusive, not exclusive. As Margaret Wheatley has said, we no longer need hero-leaders, we need the leader-as-host. The leader-as-hero model is an insult to our people. It confirms our suspicion that they need saving from their own ineptitude. The leader-as-host by comparison would be the person who invites plurality and diversity into the conversation. Such a leader would understand the incredible wisdom that resides in the diversity of our organizations and that the power of such wisdom can be honoured and captured through inclusive dialogue.

This is not some feel-good directive, it is a corporate survival imperative. The research indicating that successful organizations fail to evolve in changing competitive environments is overwhelming. The evidence is that these successful companies fail because they fail to consider new perspectives and new ways of doing things. Their dialogue becomes one-dimensional and exclusive rather than inclusive. Seventh Generation leadership would be about inclusive dialogue that seeks and honours the wisdom in diversity. It is this diversity of opinion that will bring new perspectives to our organizations, thus ensuring our ability to evolve.

I believe Seventh Generation leaders would see themselves, not as being in roles of prestige and privilege but as in roles of burden and responsibility. Such is a principle found in our religious and martial arts traditions where elders are expected to carry the heaviest of loads. As Margaret Wheatley has proposed, this changes the definition of leadership to *stewardship*. Stewards would foster intergenerational collaboration; they would actively grow leaders in their organization; they would create cultures of leadership. Stewards would devolve leadership authority to the next generation of leaders. In such a capacity they would see their role as being the keepers of dialogue, the proverbial village elder and sage.

This is not fuzzyheaded romanticism and misguided egalitarianism. Consider that in a recent HR.com survey of human resources practitioners around the world, 82 percent of respondents—human resources leaders in our top organizations—report that their organizations do not have clear succession plans in place for their top talent. Stewardship is an organizational imperative. Our boards and our stockholders should be demanding the continuity and organizational stability such thinking will ensure.

Finally, I believe Seventh Generation leadership would be earth affirming. As one institutional investor recently said to me, the money she makes her clients is meaningless if the planet fails their children. Pretty much every piece of peer-reviewed research coming out today indicates that every living system on our planet is in a state of decline. We are failing our unborn children. And one day, we will learn that all our money is meaningless if our planet fails them. One day, maybe our leaders will learn that the money you get is not worth the price you pay.

Our world is crying—even dying—for such leaders. John Kotter says that the ultimate act of leadership is to create a culture of leadership. This is one of the best and clearest definitions of the duty of a leader I have come across. But to this, I would suggest an alternative that is more abstract, metaphorical: the hallmark of leadership is when old men and old women plant trees they know they will not live long enough to enjoy.

Our world needs such leaders. For, one thousand years from now, I want my descendents to be able to worship in a cathedral of trees. It does not look hopeful.

Questions

1. How would you describe Gabriel Draven's personal leadership style?
2. What leadership behaviours does Draven engage in?
3. Is Draven a transformational leader? Why or why not?

Video Management Case

Daniel Goleman Interview

Emotional Intelligence (EI) is considered the measure of how well people manage themselves and their relationships. Goleman speaks of his new book, *Working with Emotional Intelligence*, claiming that whereas IQ might help predict abilities and appropriate employment based on skills and knowledge, EI, he proposes, gauges competence in the workplace in its application. EI helps articulate, as Goleman says, what sets apart an outstanding performer from others in work settings.

Questions to Consider

1. What does Goleman mean when he says that EI skills are *learnable* and can be improved upon?
2. How does Goleman differentiate between personality or maturity and specific EI skills?

Managing Teams

Learning Outcomes

1. Explain why groups and teams are key contributors to organizational effectiveness.

2. Identify the different types of groups and teams that help managers and organizations achieve their goals.

3. Explain how different elements of group dynamics influence the functioning and effectiveness of groups and teams.

4. Describe how managers can motivate group members to achieve organizational goals and reduce social loafing in groups and teams.

To the Beat of the Same Drummer[1]

The idea is to learn to make music as an organization

Drum Café has a tag line on its website: "Building Teams...........One Beat at a Time..........."[2]

Successful managers encourage their employees to drum to the same beat. At least, that's what Danny Aaron believes, and he travels the country to spread the word.

Mr. Aaron, who once ran a chain of impotence clinics in Australia and coached skiers in British Columbia, now teaches Canadian executives how to make their companies pulsate. His method: He brings their employees together in a big room and entices them to bang away on African drums. By the end of the hour, even the most timid or pessimistic of the bunch is in the groove, with values such as teamwork and collaboration coming across loud and clear.

"Companies, like music, are made up of a variety of different rhythms," says Mr. Aaron, president of Vancouver-based Drum Café Canada. "You can have sales, marketing, accounting. You can have Vancouver, Calgary, and Toronto. But as long as those different rhythms can play to that same beat—the foundation—and can listen to each other—the communication—then as an organization they can make music."

Jim Patterson, president and chief executive of the Television Bureau of Canada in Toronto, agrees. Earlier this year, Mr. Patterson joined fellow senior executives and 120 people from media outlets across the country at Toronto's Four Seasons Hotel in a drumming circle led by the Drum Café. It was the closing event of the company's three-day annual conference and achieved what Mr. Patterson had hoped it would: The majority of participants realized the significance of working together to achieve common goals.

"[In music] there's a base beat and that's something the whole orchestra has to work with," he says. "It's unchanging through an orchestral piece. But against that orchestral beat there can be a whole bunch of notes and a whole bunch of sub-rhythms. There can be points and counterpoints. What I was hoping to communicate to my members was the importance of a base beat. And I use that word interchangeably: b-a-s-s as in music and b-a-s-e as in basic. Without that, they were merely 120 people making noise."

In the 10 years since he led his first corporate drumming circle, Adam Rudolph, a Los Angeles-based composer and percussionist, has had high-level clients such as Texas Instruments, Cognos, and Stanford Business School. Now, his Rhythms of Collaboration drum workshops are bringing the benefits of at-work drumming to the Canadian market.

"With more and more mergers, companies have divisions that are sometimes quite separate from one another. Not only are they in different locales but they have very little to do with each other on an ongoing basis. The drum circle provides them with an opportunity to have a very fun, yet profound, teamwork and bonding experience," he says.

The drumming circle can be tailored to groups from 10 to 2000. Participants enter the room and find an assortment of drums at the ready, from African djembe drums

Drum circles bridge language and cultural barriers as employees learn how to drum to the same beat.

to handheld buffalo drums and big surdo Brazilian bass drums with mallets. Participants are treated to a spirited performance by a group of professional musicians, during which the facilitator makes a plug about listening, creativity, risk-taking, trust, timing, shared leadership, and other corporate cornerstones, weaving in specific issues related to the participants' company.

Then the fun begins, with participants getting the chance to bang the drums. Mr. Aaron likes to give out tiny bells to infuse a totally different sound into the music, and illustrate this important lesson: "No matter how small or insignificant somebody may feel their department is or their role is in the grand scheme of things, when they come into the group the energy gets manifested and they get back 10 times more than they put in," he says. "Everybody has a role, no matter how small it is."

Sometimes participants break into groups to play; others may decide to drum while moving around the room. The facilitator then ties it all together by reiterating the issues and goals and engaging the participants in dialogue.

Leadership lessons also come into play. For a chief executive or senior manager, "there's a commitment to something greater, like the longevity of the company or the product," Mr. Rudolph says.

"You can function as a leader, devoting yourself to something greater than your own glory. Even if you're the person who has responsibility for something, that doesn't mean you have to function in a top-down style. It has to do with shared responsibility."

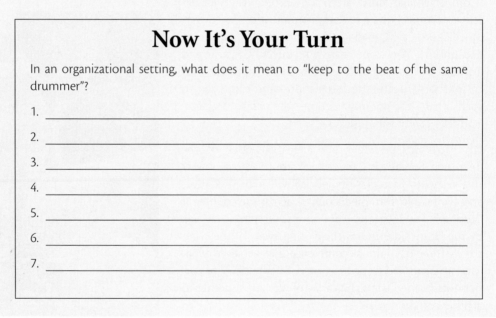

Now It's Your Turn

In an organizational setting, what does it mean to "keep to the beat of the same drummer"?

1. _____
2. _____
3. _____
4. _____
5. _____
6. _____
7. _____

■■■■ Overview

Danny Aaron and Vancouver-based Drum Café Canada are not alone in the shift toward using groups and teams to produce goods and services that better meet customers' needs. Companies such as Zellers, Xerox Canada, Dofasco, Toyota Canada, Westinghouse Canada, and Sears Canada are all relying on teams to help them gain a competitive advantage.[3] In this chapter, we look in detail at how groups and teams can contribute to organizational effectiveness, and at the types of groups and teams used in organizations. We discuss how different elements of group dynamics influence the functioning and effectiveness of groups, and we describe how managers can motivate group members to achieve organizational goals and reduce social loafing in groups and teams. By the end of this chapter, you will appreciate why the effective management of groups and teams is a key ingredient for organizational performance and a source of competitive advantage.

Key Elements That Make a Team Approach Successful

THINK ABOUT IT

Teamwork Tips[4]

Teams are very popular in today's work environment. It's likely you will be asked to work as part of a team to complete a project. Knowing the key elements that make a team approach successful can impress your superiors and lead to recognition.

1. The first thing a team must do is determine and understand the goals of the project. Sit down with management and go over what is expected.
2. Determine the major task requirements as soon as possible. In many cases, these might not be completely ascertainable upfront. This is particularly true when performing duties for the first time.
3. At the very least, the steps required to complete the project should be outlined and tasks added as appropriate.
4. Set up a time limit to complete the project. Try and segment the required tasks into specific periods. Realize that adjustments will occur.
5. Assign tasks based on the expertise of the team members. In some cases, certain team members might not have a lot of time to donate to the project, so they should be brought in at predetermined points to provide guidance.
6. Managers should select a team leader but if they don't, the team should select a leader. In larger projects, sub-leaders might be required.
7. Make sure management is kept abreast of progress.
8. Communication among team members is important. Day-to-day interaction should be encouraged. Face-to-face discussions should be held. The use of email can be helpful but it is not a substitute for conversation. If members are working in subgroups, at frequent intervals the groups should inform each other of their progress.
9. Brainstorming by team members should be encouraged. A smart team leader selects the best ideas, not just their own. Brainstorming should continue periodically throughout the project.
10. Team leaders should lead by example, not just words. Individuals tend to imitate how they see others act on the job.

If leaders work hard, team members tend to work hard. If the leader takes a lot of breaks, others will often to do the same. As work progresses, the team leader can see the types of skills and preferences individual members have. Adjustments might be needed to balance the team. For instance, some individuals prefer to work alone, while others like to work with a partner. Allowing these alterations can speed up the timetable or reduce conflict.

When personal differences arise, the leader should step in and quiet the situation. In some cases, personality conflicts can reach a point that two individuals cannot work together. When this happens, they should be separated or at least one replaced if adjustments within the team can't be easily made.

If things begin to stall, new individuals might need to be brought in to add energy. New personality types or additional expertise can make a big difference sometimes.

Teams should be recognized for successful work. Incentives in the form of bonuses or promotions can be advantageous.

You Be the Manager

1. What has your experience been in working in a teamwork setting?
2. What aspects of teamwork would you emphasize that have not been outlined above?

It's difficult to escape reading about teams if you pick up almost any business magazine. Teams are widely used these days. A Conference Board of Canada report found that more than 80 percent of its 109 respondents used teams in the workplace.[5] In the United States at least half of the employees at 80 percent of Fortune 500 companies work on teams, while 68 percent of small manufacturers use teams in their production areas.[6]

Teams increase an organization's competitive advantage (see Figure 10.1) by:

- *Enhancing its performance.* People working in teams are able to produce more or higher quality outputs than would have been produced if each person had worked separately and all their individual efforts had been combined.

- *Increasing its responsiveness to customers.* Bringing salespeople, research and development experts, and members of other departments together in a group or cross-functional team can enhance responsiveness to customers by increasing the skills and expertise available.

- *Increasing innovation.* Managers can better encourage innovation by creating teams of diverse individuals who together have the knowledge relevant to a particular type of innovation, rather than by relying on individuals working alone.

FIGURE 10.1 *Groups' and Teams' Contributions to Organizational Effectiveness*

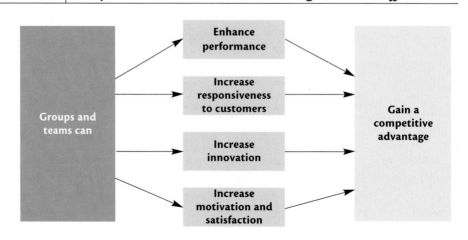

- *Increasing employees' motivation and satisfaction.* Members of teams are likely to be more highly motivated and satisfied than they would have been while working on their own. The experience of working alongside other highly charged and motivated people can be very stimulating.

Types of Groups and Teams

THINK ABOUT IT

Emotionally Intelligent and Self-Managed Teams

Dr. Reuven Bar-On, author and developer of the now-standard *Emotional Quotient-Inventory™ (or EQ-i™)* defined emotional intelligence as an array of personal, emotional, and social competencies and skills that influence one's ability to succeed in coping with environmental demands and pressures.[7] These competencies and skills are critical when it comes to working in a team-based environment, a reality that is ever-increasing in today's workplaces. Emotional intelligence, therefore, becomes the hidden advantage. Groups often know *what* it is they must accomplished. Where the difficulties arise are in *how* the tasks are to be accomplished. This is where the emotional intelligence capability of the team members and the group as a whole play the major part. "Emotions impact everything we do. In an office setting, emotions can lead to team camaraderie and increased productivity. Likewise, emotions can also prove destructive. Not surprisingly, it is an individual's emotional intelligence that dictates interpersonal relationships."[8]

The important difference between effective teams and ineffective ones lies in the emotional intelligence of the group. Teams have an emotional intelligence of their own. It is comprised of the emotional intelligence of individual members, plus a collective competency of the group. Everyone contributes to the overall level of emotional intelligence, and the leader has more influence. The good news is that teams can develop greater emotional intelligence and boost their performance. . . . To be most effective, the team needs to create emotionally intelligent norms—the attitudes and behaviors that eventually become habits—that support behaviors for building trust, group identity and group efficacy. Group identity is described as a feeling among members that they belong to a unique and worthwhile group. A sense of group efficacy is the belief that the team can perform well and that group members are more effective working together than apart.[9]

When we apply these notions to the self-managed team process, we realize each team member must play his/her part. It is important each individual team member assume a sense of responsibility for the team effort, well-being and outcome. This process of working *with* and *for* the team includes:

- Making sure the team stays on topic and keeps its focus;

- Contributes to facilitating input from group members;

- Stays aware of procedures that will help the group function more intelligently and smoothly, such as clarifying questions and summaries of key points; and

- Fostering effective listen skills so that each member has a chance to contribute and gets heard, in short, nurturing a collaborative team norm for working together.

group
Two or more people who interact with each other to reach certain goals or meet certain needs.

team
A group whose members work intensely with each other to achieve a specific common goal or objective.

A **group** may be defined as two or more people who interact with each other to reach certain goals or meet certain needs.[11] A **team** is a group whose members work intensely with each other to achieve a specific common goal or objective. As these definitions imply, all teams are groups but not all groups are teams. The two characteristics that distinguish teams from groups are the *intensity* with which team members work together and the presence of a *specific, overriding team goal or objective*. Organizations use a variety of groups and teams in the workplace. We describe a few of these in the next few pages (see Figure 10.2).

The Top-Management Team

top-management team
A group composed of the CEO, the president, and the heads of the most important departments.

cross-functional team
A group of individuals from different departments brought together to perform organizational tasks.

A central concern of the CEO and president of a company is to form a **top-management team** to help the organization achieve its mission and goals. Top-management teams are responsible for developing the strategies that produce an organization's competitive advantage; most have between five and seven members. In forming their top-management teams, CEOs are well advised to stress diversity—in expertise, skills, knowledge, and experience. Thus, many top-management teams are **cross-functional teams**: They include members of different departments, such as finance, marketing, production, and engineering. Diversity helps ensure that the top-management team will have all the background and resources it needs to make good decisions.

Research and Development Teams

research and development team
A team whose members have the expertise and experience needed to develop new products.

Managers in pharmaceuticals, computers, electronics, electronic imaging, and other high-tech industries often create **research and development teams** to develop new products. Managers select R&D team members on the basis of their expertise and experience in a certain area. Sometimes R&D teams are cross-functional teams with members from departments such as engineering, marketing, and production in addition to members from the research and development department.

FIGURE 10.2│ *Types of Groups and Teams in Organizations*

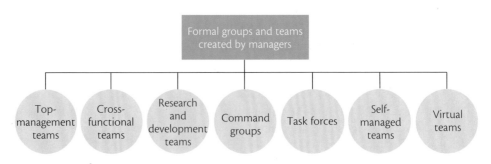

Command Groups

Subordinates who report to the same supervisor form a **command group**. When top managers design an organization's structure and establish reporting relationships and a chain of command, they are essentially creating command groups. Command groups, often called *departments* or *units*, perform a significant amount of the work in many organizations. In order to have command groups that help an organization gain a competitive advantage, managers need to motivate group members to perform at a high level, and managers need to be effective leaders. Examples of command groups include the salespeople at The Bay who report to the same supervisor, the employees of a small swimming pool sales and maintenance company who report to a general manager, the telephone operators at the Manulife Financial insurance company who report to the same supervisor, and workers on an automobile assembly line at Ford Canada who report to the same first-line manager.

command group
A group composed of subordinates who report to the same supervisor; also called a department or unit.

Task Forces

Managers form **task forces** to accomplish specific goals or solve problems in a certain time period; task forces are sometimes called *ad hoc committees*. When Vancouver Island–based Myra Falls copper and zinc mine was purchased in 1998 by Swedish-controlled Boliden AB, the mine had been facing labour strife for years.[12] Boliden sent over a new mine manager to help get things in order. His first job was to set up five task forces geared to key problem areas. For instance, the ground support task force found that the previous owners had neglected a number of safety problems. The task forces' recommendations were followed, and $15 million worth of improvements were done. This sent a strong signal to employees that the new management team was concerned about its employees. Task forces can be a valuable tool for busy managers who do not have the time to explore an important issue in depth on their own.

task force
A committee of managers or nonmanagerial employees from various departments or divisions who meet to solve a specific, mutual problem; also called an ad hoc committee.

Sometimes organizations need to address a long-term or enduring problem or issue facing an organization, such as how to contribute most usefully to the local community or how to make sure that the organization provides opportunities for potential employees with disabilities. Task forces that are relatively permanent are often referred to as *standing committees*. Membership in standing committees changes over time. Members may have, for example, a two- or three-year term on the committee, and memberships expire at varying times so that there are always some members with experience on the committee. Managers often form and maintain standing committees to make sure that important issues continue to be addressed.

Self-Managed Work Teams[13]

Self-managed (or self-directed) work teams, such as that found at Langley Memorial Hospital, are teams whose members are empowered and have the responsibility and autonomy to complete identifiable pieces of work. On a day-to-day basis, team members decide what the team will do, how it will do it, and which team members will perform specific tasks.[14] Managers provide self-managed work teams with their overall goals (such as assembling defect-free computer keyboards) but let team members decide how to meet those goals. Managers usually form self-managed work teams to improve quality, increase motivation and satisfaction, and lower costs. Often, by creating self-managed work teams, they combine tasks that individuals used to perform on their own, so the team is responsible for the whole set of tasks that yield an identifiable output or end product. The Conference Board of Canada found that self-directed work

self-managed (or self-directed) work teams
Groups of employees who supervise their own activities and monitor the quality of the goods and services they provide.

Langley Memorial Hospital
www.city.langley.bc/
commun/hospital.htm

teams are used in a variety of manufacturing environments (e.g., the auto and chemicals industries) and service environments (e.g., hotels, banks, and airlines).[15]

Managers can take a number of steps to ensure that self-managed work teams are effective and help an organization gain a competitive advantage:[16]

- Give teams enough responsibility and autonomy to be truly self-managing. Refrain from telling team members what to do or solving problems for them even if you (as a manager) know what should be done.

- Make sure that a team's work is sufficiently complex so that it entails a number of different steps or procedures that must be performed and results in some kind of finished end product.

- Carefully select members of self-managed work teams. Team members should have the diversity of skills needed to complete the team's work, have the ability to work with others, and want to be part of a team.

- Recognize that self-managed work teams need guidance, coaching, and support, not direct supervision. Managers should be a resource for teams to turn to when needed.

- Analyze what type of training team members need, and provide it. Working in a self-managed work team often requires that employees have more extensive technical and interpersonal skills.

Managers in a wide variety of organizations have found that self-managed work teams help the organization achieve its goals.[17] However, self-managed work teams can run into trouble. Members are often reluctant to discipline one another by withholding bonuses from members who are not performing up to par or by firing members.[18]

They are also reluctant to evaluate each other's performance and determine pay levels. One reason for team members' discomfort may be the close personal relationships they sometimes develop with each other. In addition, sometimes members of self-managed work teams actually take longer to accomplish tasks, such as when team members have difficulties coordinating their efforts.

Virtual Teams

virtual team

A team whose members rarely or never meet face to face and interact by using various forms of information technology such as email, computer networks, telephones, faxes, and video conferences.

Virtual teams are teams whose members rarely or never meet face to face and instead interact by using various forms of information technology such as email, computer networks, telephones, faxes, and video conferences. As organizations become increasingly global and have operations in far-flung regions of the world, and as the need for specialized knowledge increases due to advances in technology, virtual teams allow managers to create teams to solve problems or explore opportunities without being limited by the need for team members to be working in the same geographic location.[19]

Take the case of an organization that has manufacturing facilities in Australia, Canada, the United States, and Mexico, and is encountering a quality problem in a complex manufacturing process. Each of its manufacturing facilities has a quality control team that is headed by a quality control manager. The vice-president for production does not try to solve the problem by forming and leading a team at one of the four manufacturing facilities; instead, she forms and leads a virtual team composed of the quality control managers of the four plants and the plants' general managers. Team members communicate via email and video conferencing, and a wide array of knowledge and experience is brought to bear to solve the problem.

The principal advantage of virtual teams is that they enable managers to disregard geographic distances and form teams whose members have the knowledge, expertise, and experience to tackle a particular problem or take advantage of a specific opportunity.[20] Virtual teams can include members who are not employees of the organization itself. For example, a virtual team might include members of an organization that is used for outsourcing. More and more companies—including Hewlett-Packard, Pricewaterhouse Coopers, and Kodak—are either using or exploring the use of virtual teams.[21]

Beware! Teams Aren't Always the Answer

Though we have given lots of information about how teams are used in the workplace, teams are not always the best way to get work done. Because teams have increased communication demands, have more conflicts to manage, and need more meetings, the benefits of using teams have to exceed the costs.

When trying to determine if a team is appropriate to the situation, consider the following:[22]

- Can the work be performed better by an individual? If so, it is not necessary to form a team.

- Can the team provide more value than the individual? For instance, new-car dealer service departments have introduced teams that link customer service staff, mechanics, parts specialists, and sales representatives. These teams can better manage customer needs.

- Are there interdependent tasks, so that employees have to rely on each other to get work completed? Teamwork often makes interdependent work go more smoothly.

Other situations where organizations would find teams more useful include:

When work processes cut across functional lines; when speed is important (and complex relationships are involved); when the organization mirrors a complex, differentiated and rapidly changing market environment; when innovation and learning have priority; when the tasks that have to be done require online integration of highly interdependent performers.[23]

Group Dynamics

THINK ABOUT IT

Team Operating Agreements (TOAs)

How does professional corporate trainer Claire Sookman build a virtual team that works seamlessly together? After all, she has coached over 1000 project managers across North America. She creates what she calls a "team operating agreement" (or TOA)[24] through brainstorming, clarification, and discussion and knows that in a global work environment, dedicated teams of skilled employees need expert managers who create effective communication channels. An interesting comment she makes is that if such a norm is not created by the project manager, team members will do so on their own, opening up the possibility of potential problems or misunderstanding. What needs to be managed well are geographic, ethnic, and cultural differences especially so that the team can be as effective as possible. Says Sookman, "The more inclusive it is, the less chance for miscommunication, conflict and lost opportunities. Ideally, the TOA should be created at the beginning of a project or when a new team forms." A TOA is also *not* a stagnant document, and will possibly be modified during the course of the project.

Sookman's suggestions for a TOA could include the following categories:

1. **Meeting Protocols:**
   a. Beginning and ending meetings on time;
   b. Scheduling meetings to accommodate people in different time zones;
   c. Taking into consideration holidays of the different cultures;
   d. Respecting and listening to what other people are saying on the call and not holding sidebar conversations; and
   e. Giving one week's notice to the team if a member is unable to attend.

2. **Communication:**
   a. Checking emails twice a day;
   b. Call into the office once a day;
   c. Handling conflict directly with the person concerned and working to resolve it by identifying and communicating possible conflicts clearly and immediately;
   d. Giving feedback in a timely manner, respecting cultural sensitivities; and
   e. Valuing confidentiality.

You Be the Manager

1. What factors are important when virtual teams need to work together?
2. How effective would you be in working on a virtual team?

How groups and teams function and how effective they will ultimately be depends on a number of characteristics and processes known collectively as *group dynamics*. In this section, we discuss five key elements of group dynamics: group size and roles; group leadership; group development; group norms; and group cohesiveness. As we mentioned earlier in the chapter, teams and groups are not the same thing, though some of their processes are similar. Thus, much of what we call group dynamics here also applies to teams.

Group Size and Roles

Managers need to take group size and group roles into account as they create and maintain high-performing groups and teams.

Group Size
The number of members in a group can be an important determinant of members' motivation and commitment and of group performance. There are several advantages to keeping a group relatively small—between two and nine members. Compared with members of large groups, members of small groups tend to

- interact more with each other and find it easier to coordinate their efforts;
- be more motivated, satisfied, and committed;
- find it easier to share information;
- be better able to see the importance of their personal contributions for group success.

Recognizing these advantages, Nathan Myhrvold, former chief technology officer at Microsoft Corporation, found that eight is the ideal size for the types of R&D teams he would form to develop new software.[25] A disadvantage of small rather than large groups is that members of small groups have fewer resources available to accomplish their goals.

Large groups—with 10 or more members—also offer some advantages. They have at their disposal more resources to achieve group goals than do small groups. These resources include the knowledge, experience, skills, and abilities of group members as well as their actual time and effort. Large groups also have advantages stemming from the **division of labour**—splitting the work to be performed into particular tasks and assigning tasks to individuals. Individuals who specialize in particular tasks are likely to become skilled at performing those tasks and contribute significantly to high group performance.

division of labour
Splitting the work to be performed into particular tasks and assigning tasks to individual workers.

Large groups suffer a number of problems, including greater communication and coordination difficulties and lower levels of motivation, satisfaction, and commitment. It is clearly more difficult to share information and coordinate activities when you are dealing with 16 people rather than 8. Moreover, members of large groups might not feel that their efforts are really needed and sometimes might not even feel a part of the group.

As a general rule of thumb, groups should have no more members than necessary to achieve a division of labour and provide the resources needed to achieve group goals. Group size is too large when[26]

- members spend more time communicating what they know to others rather than applying what they know to solve problems and create new products;

- individual productivity decreases;

- group performance suffers.

Group Roles

In forming groups and teams, managers need to communicate clearly the expectations for each group role, what is required of each member, and how the different roles in the group fit together to accomplish group goals. A **group role** is a set of behaviours and

group role
A set of behaviours and tasks that a member of a group is expected to perform because of his or her position in the group.

Smaller groups allow for more interaction, improve motivation, and make it easier for members to share information.

tasks that a member of a group is expected to perform because of his or her position in the group. Members of cross-functional teams, for example, are expected to perform roles relevant to their special areas of expertise. Managers also need to realize that group roles change and evolve as a group's tasks and goals change and as group members gain experience and knowledge. Thus, to get the performance gains that come from experience or "learning by doing," managers should encourage group members to take the initiative to modify their assigned roles by taking on extra responsibilities as they see fit. This process, called **role making**, can enhance individual and group performance.

Beyond the simple roles that each person fulfills in order to complete the task at hand, two major kinds of roles need to be discussed: task-oriented roles and maintenance roles. **Task-oriented roles** are performed by group members to make sure that the group accomplishes its tasks. **Maintenance roles** are carried out to make sure that team members have good relationships. For teams to be effective, there needs to be some balance between task orientation and relationship maintenance. Table 10.1 identifies a number of task-oriented and maintenance roles that you might find in a team.

In self-managed work teams and some other groups, group members themselves are responsible for creating and assigning roles. Many self-managed work teams also pick their own team leaders. When group members create their own roles, managers should be available in an advisory capacity, helping group members effectively settle conflicts

role making
Taking the initiative to modify an assigned role by taking on extra responsibilities.

task-oriented roles
Roles performed by group members to make sure the task gets done.

maintenance roles
Roles performed by group members to make sure there are good relations among group members.

TABLE 10.1 | Roles Required for Effective Group Functioning

	Function	Description	Example
Roles that build task accomplishment	Initiating	Stating the goal or problem, making proposals about how to work on it, setting time limits.	"Let's set up an agenda for discussing each of the problems we have to consider."
	Seeking information and opinions	Asking group members for specific factual information related to the task or problem, or for their opinions about it.	"What do you think would be the best approach to this, Jack?"
	Providing information and opinions	Sharing information or opinions related to the task or problems.	"I worked on a similar problem last year and found . . ."
	Clarifying	Helping one another understand ideas and suggestions that come up in the group.	"What you mean, Sue, is that we could . . .?"
	Elaborating	Building on one another's ideas and suggestions.	"Building on Don's idea, I think we could . . ."
	Summarizing	Reviewing the points covered by the group and the different ideas stated so that decisions can be based on full information.	Appointing a recorder to take notes on a blackboard.
	Consensus testing	Periodic testing about whether the group is nearing a decision or needs to continue discussion.	"Is the group ready to decide about this?"
Roles that build and maintain a group	Harmonizing	Mediating conflict among other members, reconciling disagreements, relieving tensions.	"Don, I don't think you and Sue really see the question that differently."
	Compromising	Admitting error at times of group conflict.	"Well, I'd be willing to change if you provided some help on . . ."
	Gatekeeping	Making sure all members have a chance to express their ideas and feelings and preventing members from being interrupted.	"Sue, we haven't heard from you on this issue."
	Encouraging	Helping a group member make his or her point. Establishing a climate of acceptance in the group.	"I think what you started to say is important, Jack. Please continue."

Source: D. Ancona, T. Kochan, M. Scully, J. Van Maanen, D.E. Westney, "Team Processes," in *Managing for the Future* (Cincinnati, OH: South-Western College Publishing, 1996), p. 9.

and disagreements. At Johnsonville Foods, for example, the position titles of first-line managers were changed to "advisory coach" to reflect the managers' new role vis-à-vis the self-managed work teams they oversee.[27]

Group Leadership

All groups and teams need leadership. Indeed, as we discussed in detail in Chapter 9, effective leadership is a key ingredient for high-performing groups, teams, and organizations. Sometimes managers assume the leadership role, as is the case in many command groups and top-management teams. Or a manager may appoint a member of a group who is not a manager to be group leader or chairperson, as is the case in a task force or standing committee. In other cases, group or team members may choose their own leaders, or a leader may emerge naturally as group members work together to achieve group goals. When managers empower members of self-managed work teams, they often let group members choose their own leaders. Some self-managed work teams find it effective to rotate the leadership role among their members. Whether leaders of groups and teams are managers or not, and whether they are appointed by managers or emerge naturally in a group, they play an important role in ensuring that groups and teams perform up to their potential.

Group Development Over Time

Every group's development over time is somewhat unique. However, researchers have identified five stages of group development that many groups seem to pass through (see Figure 10.3):[28]

- *Forming.* Members try to get to know each other and reach a common understanding of what the group is trying to accomplish and how group members should behave. During this stage, managers should strive to make each member feel like a valued part of the group.

- *Storming.* Group members experience conflict and disagreements because some members do not wish to submit to the demands of other group members. Disputes may arise over who should lead the group. Self-managed work teams can be particularly vulnerable during the storming stage. Managers need to keep an eye on groups at this stage to make sure that conflict does not get out of hand.

- *Norming.* Close ties between group members develop, and feelings of friendship and camaraderie emerge. Group members arrive at a consensus about what goals they should be aiming to achieve and how group members should behave toward one another.

- *Performing.* The real work of the group gets accomplished during this stage. Depending on the type of group in question, managers need to take different steps at this stage to help ensure that groups are effective. Managers of command groups need to make sure that group members are motivated and that they are effectively leading group members. Managers overseeing self-managed work teams have to empower team members and make sure that teams are given enough responsibility and autonomy at the performing stage.

FIGURE 10.3| *Five Stages of Group Development*

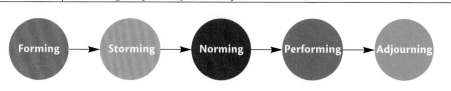

- *Adjourning.* This stage applies only to groups that eventually are disbanded, such as task forces. During adjourning, a group is dispersed. Sometimes, adjourning takes place when a group completes a finished product, such as when a task force evaluating the pros and cons of providing on-site child care produces a report supporting its recommendation.

Managers need a flexible approach to group development and need to keep attuned to the different needs and requirements of groups at the various stages.[29] Above all else, and regardless of the stage of development, managers need to think of themselves as *resources* for groups. Thus, managers always should be trying to find ways to help groups and teams function more effectively.

Group Norms

All groups, whether top-management teams, self-managed work teams, or command groups, need to control their members' behaviour to ensure that the group performs well and meets its goals. Roles as well as group norms control behaviour in groups.[30] **Group norms** are shared guidelines or rules for behaviour that most group members follow. Groups develop norms for a wide variety of behaviours, including working hours, the sharing of information among group members, how certain group tasks should be performed, and even how members of a group should dress.

Managers should encourage members of a group to develop norms that contribute to group performance and the attainment of group goals. These could include group norms that dictate that each member of a cross-functional team should always be available for the rest of the team when his or her input is needed, return phone calls as soon as possible, inform other team members of travel plans, and give team members a phone number at which he or she can be reached when travelling on business. Virtual teams such as those at Ryder System Inc. in Mississauga, Ontario establish such norms as how often to have conference calls and how often they should meet face to face in order to increase their ability to communicate effectively.

Conformity and Deviance

Group members conform to norms for three reasons:[31]

- They want to obtain rewards and avoid punishments.

- They want to imitate group members whom they like and admire.

- They have internalized the norm and believe it is the right and proper way to behave.

Failure to conform, or deviance, occurs when a member of a group violates a group norm. Deviance signals that a group is not controlling one of its members' behaviours. Groups generally respond to members who behave deviantly in one of three ways:[32]

- The group might try to get the member to change his or her deviant ways and conform to the norm. Group members might try to convince the member of the need to conform, or they might ignore or even punish the deviant.

- The group might expel the member.

- The group might change the norm to be consistent with the member's behaviour.

That last alternative suggests some deviant behaviour can be functional for groups. Deviance is functional for a group when it causes group members to stop and evaluate norms that may be dysfunctional but that are taken for granted by the group. Often, group members do not think about why they behave in a certain way or why they follow certain norms. Deviance can cause group members to reflect on their norms and change them when appropriate, such as when a new employee comes up with a new procedure, because she wasn't aware of "the right way" to do something, and everyone realizes it's a better way.

Encouraging a Balance of Conformity and Deviance

In order for groups and teams to be effective and help an organization gain a competitive advantage, they need to have the right balance of conformity and deviance (see Figure 10.4). A group needs a certain level of conformity to ensure that it can control members' behaviour and channel it in the direction of high performance and group goal accomplishment. A group also needs a certain level of deviance to ensure that dysfunctional norms are discarded and replaced with functional ones. Balancing conformity and deviance is a pressing concern for all groups, whether they are top-management teams, R&D teams, command groups, or self-managed work teams.

Managers can take several steps to ensure that there is enough tolerance of deviance in groups so that group members are willing to deviate from dysfunctional norms:

- Be role models by not rigidly insisting on existing norms and procedures.

- Encourage openness to new norms and procedures.

- Encourage the evaluation of existing norms.

Group Cohesiveness

Another important element of group dynamics that affects group performance and effectiveness is **group cohesiveness**, the degree to which members are attracted or loyal to their group or team.[33] When group cohesiveness is high, individuals strongly value

group cohesiveness
The degree to which members are attracted or loyal to a group.

FIGURE 10.4 | *Balancing Conformity and Deviance in Groups*

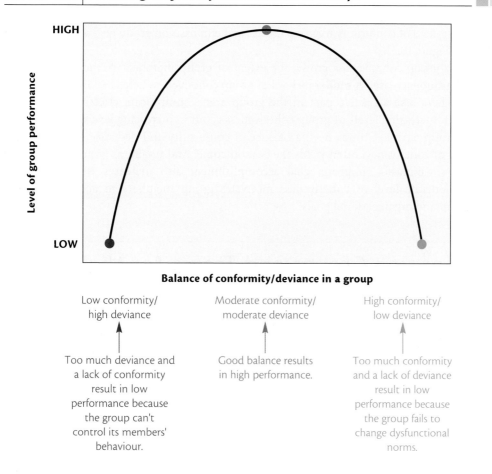

FIGURE 10.5| *Sources and Consequences of Group Cohesiveness*

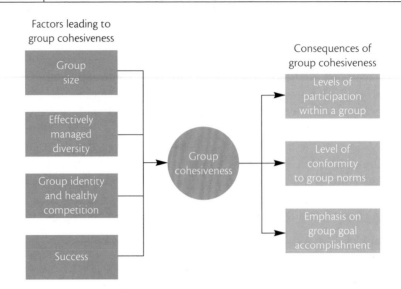

their group membership, find the group very appealing, and have strong desires to remain part of the group. When group cohesiveness is low, group members do not find their group particularly appealing and have little desire to retain their group membership. Research suggests that managers should aim to have a moderate level of cohesiveness in the groups and teams they manage because that is most likely to contribute to an organization's competitive advantage.

Consequences of Group Cohesiveness
There are three major consequences of group cohesiveness: level of participation within a group, level of conformity to group norms, and emphasis on group goal accomplishment (see Figure 10.5).[34]

As group cohesiveness grows, the extent of group members' participation within the group increases. A moderate level of group cohesiveness helps to ensure that group members take an active part in the group and communicate effectively with each other. Increasing levels of group cohesiveness result in increasing levels of conformity to group norms. Groups need a balance of conformity and deviance, so a moderate level of cohesiveness often yields the best outcome. And finally, as group cohesiveness grows, emphasis on group goal accomplishment also increases within a group. A moderate level of cohesiveness motivates group members to accomplish both group and organizational goals.

Managing Groups and Teams for High Performance

 THINK ABOUT IT

Teams and Pre-emptive Crisis Management[35]

For any courier company, the busiest time of the year is the Christmas season. It's also the time of the year when weather can be unpredictable and interfere with the best-laid plans of any manager and team. Federal Express Corp. knows this only too well as it attempts to deliver its 5.5 million daily packages at this time of year;

usually daily volume is 3.3 million packages. Canada Post also faces the same challenge: delivering its 50 million pieces of mail (including courier packages), when normally it would be 38 million pieces per day. It's a similar situation with United Parcel Service Inc., with its 20 million packages, up from a typical 13.5 million.

FedEx Express has to make sure all the logistics for all the teams are working together to get the job done. This means coordinating its 1129 sorting centres in 215 countries around the world, plus its entire workforce that consists of 136 000 employees! Arthur Stanley, president of Federal Express Canada Ltd., says, "We try to 'what if' any type of scenario that most people wouldn't think of. Then we have a contingency plan. . . . Let's face it, the best-laid plans are only as good as what mother nature dishes out." To accomplish this kind of precision, teams draw up "almost an infinite number" of crises that fit into two different categories: predictable and unpredictable.

You Be the Manager

1. What factors impact on whether the teamwork for FedEx works effectively?

Now that you have a good understanding of the reasons why groups and teams are so important for organizations, the types of groups that managers create, and group dynamics, we consider additional steps that managers can take to make sure groups and teams perform highly and contribute to organizational effectiveness. Managers who want top-performing groups and teams need to (1) motivate group members to work toward the achievement of organizational goals, (2) prevent groupthink, (3) reduce social loafing, and (4) help groups to manage conflict effectively.

Motivating Group Members to Achieve Organizational Goals

Managers can motivate members of groups and teams to reach organizational goals and create a competitive advantage by making sure that the members themselves benefit when the group or team performs highly. If members of a self-managed work team know that they will receive a percentage of any cost savings that the team discovers and implements, they probably will try to cut costs. For example, Canadian Tire offers team incentives to employees of its gas bars. "Secret" retail shoppers visit the outlets on a regular basis, and score them on such factors as cleanliness, manner in which the transaction was processed, and the types of products offered, using a 100-point scoring system. Scores above a particular threshold provide extra compensation that is shared by the team. Xerox Canada, through its XTRA program, rewards districts for achieving profit and customer satisfaction targets. Everyone in the district shares equally in the bonuses.

Managers often rely on some combination of individual and group-based incentives to motivate members of groups and teams to work toward reaching organizational goals and a competitive advantage. When individual performance within a group can be assessed, pay is often determined by individual performance or by both individual and group performance. When individual performance within a group cannot be assessed accurately, then group performance should be the key determinant of pay levels.

"Neither rain nor sleet nor snow ...." Canada Post delivers 50 million pieces of mail per day over the Christmas season. What yearly managerial challenges does this present?

Benefits that managers can make available to group members when a group performs highly could also include equipment and computer software, awards and other forms of recognition, and choice future work assignments. For example, members of self-managed work teams that develop new software at companies such as Microsoft often value working on interesting and important projects, and so members of teams that perform highly are rewarded with interesting and important new projects.

Preventing Groupthink

We have been focusing on the steps that managers can take to encourage high levels of performance in groups. Managers, however, need to be aware of an important downside to group and team work: the potentials for groupthink, social loafing, and conflict, all of which can reduce group performance. **Groupthink** occurs when group members become so focused on reaching agreement that they stop examining alternative courses of action and try to prevent the full expression of deviant, minority, or unpopular views within the group. The group pressure to conform causes a deterioration in an individual's mental efficiency, reality testing, and moral judgment.[36]

Groupthink does not affect all groups. It seems to occur most often where there is a clear group identity, where members hold a positive image of their group that they want to protect, and where the group perceives an outside threat to this positive image.[37] Groupthink is less about preventing dissent among group members and more about ways for a group to protect its positive image.

Groupthink can be minimized.[38] Group leaders need to play an impartial role, actively seek input from all members, and avoid expressing their own opinions early on in the discussion. One group member could be appointed to the role of devil's advocate, explicitly challenging the majority position and offering a different perspective. The group should also actively seek out discussion of diverse alternatives, and consider the negative sides of all alternatives. By doing so, the group is less likely to prevent dissenting views and more likely to gain an objective evaluation of each alternative.

Reducing Social Loafing in Groups

Social loafing is the tendency of individuals to put forth less effort when they work in groups than when they work alone.[39] Have you ever watched one or two group members who never seemed to be pulling their weight?

Social loafing can occur in all kinds of groups and teams and in all kinds of organizations. It can result in lower group performance and may even prevent a group from reaching its goals. Fortunately, managers can take steps to reduce social loafing, by making sure that individual contributions are recognizable, emphasizing the valuable contributions of each individual, and making sure that the group size is not too large (see Figure 10.6). Individuals who feel their contributions matter will be less likely to engage in social loafing.

Helping Groups to Manage Conflict Effectively

At some point or other, practically all groups experience conflict either within the group (intragroup conflict) or with other groups (intergroup conflict). In Chapter 12, we discuss conflict in depth and explore ways to manage it effectively. As you will learn there, managers can take several steps to help groups manage conflict and disagreements.

groupthink
A pattern of faulty and biased decision making that occurs in groups whose members strive for agreement among themselves at the expense of accurately assessing information relevant to a decision.

social loafing
The tendency of individuals to put forth less effort when they work in groups than when they work alone.

FIGURE 10.6 | *Three Ways to Reduce Social Loafing*

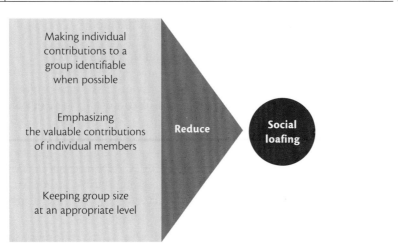

 Tips for Managers

BUILDING TEAMS FOR HIGH PERFORMANCE[40]

1. Build and manage teams that live up to their promise of higher productivity and greater problem-solving ability.

2. Clarify roles and responsibilities for team members so they work together effectively.

3. Manage interpersonal conflicts among team members.

4. Maximize team productivity by encouraging group discussion and problem-solving.

5. Overcome organizational, management and employee barriers to teamwork through the focus on enhancing the emotional intelligence of team members.

6. Identify and manage team rewards effectively.

Summary and Review

1. WHY THE POPULARITY OF GROUPS AND TEAMS IN THE WORKPLACE?
A group is two or more people who interact with each other to reach certain goals or meet certain needs. A team is a group whose members work intensely with each other to achieve a specific common goal or objective. Groups and teams can contribute to organizational effectiveness by enhancing performance, increasing responsiveness to customers, increasing innovation, and being a source of motivation for their members.

2. TYPES OF GROUPS AND TEAMS Managers can establish a variety of groups and teams to reach organizational goals. These include cross-functional teams, top-management teams, research and development teams, command groups, task forces, self-managed work teams, and virtual teams. Teams may not always be the answer for reaching a goal, however.

3. GROUP DYNAMICS Key elements of group dynamics are group size and roles; group leadership; group development; group norms; and group cohesiveness. The advantages and disadvantages of large and small groups suggest that managers should form groups with no more members than are needed to provide the human resources the group needs to reach its goals and use a division of labour. A group role is a set of behaviours and tasks that a member of a group is expected to perform because of his or her position in the group. All groups and teams need leadership.

Five stages of development that many groups pass through are *forming, storming, norming, performing,* and *adjourning.*

Group norms are shared rules for behaviour that most group members follow. To be effective, groups need a balance of conformity and deviance. Conformity allows a group to control its members' behaviour in order to achieve group goals; deviance provides the impetus for needed change.

Group cohesiveness is the attractiveness of a group or team to its members. As group cohesiveness increases, so, too, do the level of participation and communication within a group, the level of conformity to group norms, and the emphasis on group goal accomplishment. Managers should strive to achieve a moderate level of group cohesiveness in the groups and teams they manage.

4. **MANAGING GROUPS AND TEAMS FOR HIGH PERFORMANCE** To make sure that groups and teams perform highly, managers need to motivate group members to work toward the achievement of organizational goals, prevent groupthink, reduce social loafing, and help groups to manage conflict effectively. Managers can motivate members of groups and teams to work toward the achievement of organizational goals by making sure that members personally benefit when their group or team performs highly.

Key Terms

command group, p. 285
cross-functional team, p. 284
division of labour, p. 289
group, p. 284
group cohesiveness, p. 293
group norms, p. 292
group role, p. 289
groupthink, p. 296
maintenance roles, p. 290
research and development team, p. 284

role making, p. 290
self-managed (or self-directed) work teams, p. 285
social loafing, p. 296
task force, p. 285
task-oriented roles, p. 290
team, p. 284
top-management team, p. 284
virtual team, p. 286

S O   W H E R E   D O   Y O U   S T A N D ?

Wrap-Up to Opening Case

We began this chapter with a discussion of Danny Aaron, president of Vancouver-based Drum Café Canada. We remarked that successful managers encourage their employees to drum to the same beat. Says Aaron, "Companies, like music, are made up of a variety of different rhythms. You can have sales, marketing, accounting. You can have Vancouver, Calgary, and Toronto. But as long as those different rhythms can play to that same beat— the foundation—and can listen to each other—the communication—then as an organization they can make music."

The challenge today, especially in the global marketplace, is not only staying in business because of the international trade competition, but making sure employees, most likely working in a team-based culture, also work and "drum to the same beat." For example, in addition to such organizations as the Television Bureau of Canada, Texas Instruments, Cognos, and Stanford Business School using the drum motif for team development learning, other companies such as IBM Canada Ltd., Scotia Bank, and Xerox Canada Ltd., have also resorted to this "primal instinct" tool for their communications as well. In a 1999 article, writer Andy Georgiades wrote, "On the doorstep of the 21st century, big business, in its quest for higher productivity, is turning to a technology almost as primitive as a caveman beating on his chest."[41]

To demonstrate its effectiveness, a conference was held at Georgian College's Kempenfelt Conference Centre, just outside Barrie, Ontario, in 1999, with 100 casually dressed businesspeople. Lance Secretan, former professor, author, leadership guru who lectures to 200 000 people each year, and founder of the Secretan Centre's Higher Ground Community, in Alton, south of Orangeville, Ontario, led the conference. Says Secretan, "Most people will go home and forget 80 percent of the things that have happened here, but they won't forget the drumming." Sue Anderson, director of internal communication at Xerox Canada at the time, had already organized two such sessions. "Doing something like this in a large corporate environment is a risk," she said, because "you don't know how anybody in that room is going to react. But for us it's about getting into an new kind of rhythm, a rhythm that allows you to reach new kinds of heights."

Drumming, therefore, is a metaphor, and a practice for some companies, to synchronize efforts, to get individuals to work together as a team, and to develop a sense of shared responsibility. Doug Sole, drum aficionado, author and co-owner of Toronto's Soul Drums, says, "There's more than 100 of us in this room," Sole warns. "If we all start banging our own thing, it's going to be chaos." He ends by saying that the same goes for companies.

The new reality is that everyone must work together to be effective.

After studying the preceding material, be sure to check out our Online Learning Centre at
www.mcgrawhill.ca/olc/jones
for more in-depth information and interactivities that correspond to this chapter.

Management in Action

Topics for Discussion and Action

1. Why do all organizations need to rely on groups and teams to achieve their goals and gain a competitive advantage?
2. Interview one or more managers in an organization in your local community to identify the types of groups and teams that the organization uses to achieve its goals.
3. Think about a group of which you are a member, and describe your group's current stage of development. Does the development of this group seem to be following the forming-storming-norming-performing-adjourning stages described in the chapter?
4. Discuss the reasons why too much conformity can hurt groups and their organizations.
5. Why do some groups have very low levels of cohesiveness?
6. Imagine that you are the manager of a hotel. What steps will you take to reduce social loafing by members of the cleaning staff who are responsible for keeping all common areas and guest rooms spotless?

Building Management Skills

DIAGNOSING GROUP FAILURES

Think about the last dissatisfying or discouraging experience you had as a member of a group or team. Perhaps the group did not accomplish its goals, perhaps group members could agree about nothing, or perhaps there was too much social loafing. Now answer the following questions.

1. What type of group was this?
2. Were group members motivated to achieve group goals? Why or why not?
3. What were the group's norms? How much conformity and deviance existed in the group?
4. How cohesive was the group? Why do you think the group's cohesiveness was at this level? What consequences did this level of group cohesiveness have for the group and its members?
5. Was social loafing a problem in this group? Why or why not?
6. What could the group's leader or manager have done differently to increase group effectiveness?
7. What could group members have done differently to increase group effectiveness?

Management for You

One of your professors has just informed your class that you will be working on a new major assignment worth 30 percent of your course mark. The assignment is to be done in teams of seven. Realistically you will need to function as a virtual team, because it turns out that each of you has a different work and class schedule, so that there is almost no time when more than three people could meet face to face. As you know, virtual teams have benefits, but they can also face problems. How will you build group cohesiveness of this team? What norms might help the team function, and how should the norms be decided? What will you do to prevent social loafing?

Small Group Breakout Exercise

CREATING A CROSS-FUNCTIONAL TEAM

Form groups of three or four people, and appoint one member as the spokesperson who will communicate your findings to the whole class when called on by the instructor. Then discuss the following scenario.

You are a group of managers in charge of food services for a large university. Recently, a survey of students, faculty, and staff was conducted to evaluate customer satisfaction with the food services provided by the university's eight cafeterias. The results were disappointing, to put it mildly. Complaints ranged from dissatisfaction with the type and range of meals and snacks provided, operating hours, and food temperature, to unresponsiveness to current concerns about the importance of low-carb/high-protein diets and the preferences of vegetarians. You have decided to form a cross-functional team to further evaluate reactions to the food services and to develop a proposal for changes that can be made to increase customer satisfaction.

1. Indicate who should be on this important cross-functional team and why.
2. Describe the goals the team should be trying to achieve.
3. Describe the different roles team members will need to perform.
4. Describe the steps you will take to help ensure that the team has a good balance between conformity and deviance and a moderate level of cohesiveness.

Managing Ethically

Strana Corporation uses self-managed teams to develop and produce new greeting cards. Some of the members of the team are engaged in social loafing, and other members of the team are reluctant to say anything. Team members are supposed to provide performance evaluations of each other at the end of each project, but some rate everyone equally, to avoid conflict. This practice has caused low morale on the team, because hard work results in the same pay as loafing. Some team members are complaining that it's unethical to rate everyone the same way when individual performance differs so much. One team member has come to you for advice, because you are an expert in team performance and ethics. What would you advise this team member to do? How could the team's performance be improved?

Exploring the World Wide Web
SPECIFIC ASSIGNMENT

Many companies are committed to the use of teams, including Sears Canada. Scan Sears' website to learn more about this company (www.sears.ca). Then click on "Corporate Information," "Careers at Sears," and "Mission, Vision & Values."

1. What principles or values underlie Sears' use of teams?
2. How does Sears use teams to build employee commitment?

GENERAL ASSIGNMENT

Find the website of a company that relies heavily on teams to accomplish its goals. What kinds of teams does this company use? What steps do managers take to ensure that team members are motivated to perform at a high level?

Developing a Business Plan
(APPENDIX B, PAGE 405)

Go to www.mcgrawhill.ca/olc/jones/10 for online exercises.

Be the Manager

BUILDING TEAM SPIRIT[42]

Jim Clemmer is a Kitchener, Ontario-based professional speaker, workshop/retreat leader, and author of *Growing the Distance* and *The Leader's Digest*. He says that "team spirit is the catalyst every organization needs to achieve outstanding performance." Indeed, he goes to say that the "emotional commitment of the people using the tools and executing the plans is what determines whether companies sink or soar." He further explains how companies can kill or build spirit. Because of your knowledge and skill in team-based performance, you have been called into discussions with the two founding partners and 10 employees of a new specialty tire company about to open its doors in Winnipeg, Manitoba. Many of these people have been friends to this point, but the owners want to get the company going on the right footing, especially in view of the fact that, in the planning stage, they have tolerated the use of wireless devices in their meetings. They notice now that some are beginning to resent this "extra presence" while people are doing their best to communicate. They discovered that, when bored, some staff are simply emailing one another "under the table," literally.

Questions

1. What do you think is the problem here?
2. What is your best advice regarding team-building for this group?

Management Case

Greatest Corporate Success: Teams He's Built[43]

When Grant Rasmussen was a teenager he knew he wanted to run his own business. The thing was, he wanted to be an entrepreneur without the risk and without having to back a venture with his own money.

Childhood naivete? Don't be so sure.

Rasmussen, now 39, has found a way. Indeed, the CEO and president of UBS Bank (Canada) consistently seems to find a way to make things happen.

"The one thing I heard was: Be careful how much passion you show; be careful how much emotion you show," says Rasmussen. "That's old school.

"(But) I don't think you can have a successful team without emotion and passion."

Rasmussen says that his greatest corporate success has been the teams he's built.

"But companies would say, it's the financial results I deliver." As president and CEO of Royal Bank Action Direct, his team increased profit by 300 percent over 2.5 years.

The other way Rasmussen makes things happen is telling employees everything senior management and the board knows.

"Employees should know the good, bad, and ugly about what happens," he says.

Rasmussen likens transparency to rowing. If the cox knows something that only a few of the rowers do,

Rasmussen says, no one will ever be going in the same direction.

Today, Rasmussen's company manages just under $4 billion of Canada's wealth. His company provides investment counselling services to Canada's wealthy—his average client has a portfolio of between $3 million and $4 million, with a range of about $1 million to just under a billion.

Rasmussen wasn't brought up in such opulence; rather he was raised "solidly middle-class." His dad was in sales and his mother worked as on office administrator.

He remembers his parents giving him $25 every October to help supplement the purchase of a $50 Canada Savings Bond.

His parents "were big believers that children should pay for education themselves," so from a young age, Rasmussen worked part-time.

At age nine, Rasmussen collected and sold stray golf balls at the golf course now called Markham Greens. That job was followed by a four-year stint as a bus boy and then waiter at the Duchess of Markham, a pub near his childhood home.

After graduating from Queen's University in 1987 with a business degree in marketing, Rasmussen had a job interview at the firm now known as Boston Consulting Group. The interviewer concluded by telling

Rasmussen, "good luck with your job hunt"—one of "lots of failures," Rasmussen says he had.

He landed a job at Amex, where he came up with a marketing campaign where clients would fax in information on a form he designed. Unfortunately, the design he chose caused fax transmission of new client information to be unintelligible because the colours used on the form were too dark.

"These were good lessons learned," he says.

"You have to talk to people in all sides of the business. You'll get cool ideas and you'll get stinkers."

In 1994, ready for a new challenge, Rasmussen started looking for a different opportunity. "Then RBC called me."

A favourite childhood teacher, Jim Reid, was working for RBC at the time, and recruited Rasmussen.

"When Mr. Reid called me in 1994 (to discuss the position), he had been there for 17 years," Rasmussen says. That was sufficient incentive for him to join.

Rasmussen stayed with RBC for a decade, and then one day received a call from a headhunter about the UBS position.

"I didn't know what the next thing was," he remembers.

And then, serendipity played a role. In quick succession, his wife received notice that their application to adopt a baby from China was approved, his other daughter won the high-rocket launch contest at summer camp, and Rasmussen received a job offer from UBS.

He decided to take it.

"It sounded like a dream job," he says.

"I'm attached to an incredible brand. It's the world's largest manager of wealth. It's an $800-billion gorilla."

Leading a subsidiary of a large foreign-owned company is often likened to being an order-taker rather than a decision-maker.

But Rasmussen says that's not the case for his Swiss-owned parent company.

"In Switzerland, they get it," Rasmussen insists. "They're a country of seven million. They know they don't have all the answers for those in the rest of the world."

So far at UBS, his greatest challenge has been gaining recognition in the Canadian marketplace. But Rasmussen and his team are working on it.

Rasmussen's proudest accomplishment is his family. He's been married to wife Mona for 16 years. Together they have three children: Alex, aged 12, Nicole, 10, and baby Grace, 2.

His success managing wealth has helped secure his own family's wealth, yet Rasmussen and his wife wonder if this will negatively impact their children.

"We wanted the kids to be grounded," he says. "And we wonder if (our wealth) will take away from the kids's success."

Probably not. Regardless of the challenge, Rasmussen, seems to find a way to succeed.

Questions

1. How would you describe Grant Rasmussen's personal management style?
2. Why does Rasmussen believe that it's the teams he's built that is his greatest success?
3. How have "failures" contributed to Rasmussen's "success"?

Video Management Case

CBC

The Trouble with Teams

In an individualistic culture, it seems unsurprising that teams can struggle to find consensus. This video highlights a group of friends who became colleagues when they developed an IT business partnership together. The group speaks of their experiences avoiding internal conflict and the challenges inherent in managing each other in a team setting.

Questions to Consider

1. How can one remain a leader within a team setting?
2. What might be the likely challenges/benefits in working with people you know on a personal basis outside of work?

Source: *Venture*, show number 703, "The Trouble with Teams," November 10, 1998, running time 6:16.

CHAPTER

11

Managing Human Resources

Learning Outcomes

1. Explain why strategic human resource management can help an organization gain a competitive advantage.

2. Describe the steps managers take to recruit and select organizational members.

3. Discuss the training and development options that ensure organizational members can perform their jobs effectively.

4. Explain the issues managers face in determining levels of pay and benefits.

5. Explain why performance appraisal and feedback is such a crucial activity, and list the choices managers must make in designing effective performance appraisal and feedback procedures.

6. Describe what labour relations are and the purpose that managers engage in them.

Ensuring the Best Value for the Money[1]

The perspective that continuous learning is essential to business growth is now widespread, particularly in the knowledge-based economy. The search for efficient and effective ways of learning has led from traditional classroom-based training to e-learning alternatives. The choices are bewildering. Companies are looking for the right content, delivered at the right time, to the right people, with the right organizational support, all at a reasonable cost.[2]

Canada's Software Human Resource Council (SHRC)[3] is aiming to help Canadian businesses evaluate training investments with a software tool that helps set performance objectives and measure training effectiveness.[4] A Halifax-based designer has created a software program that helps companies ensure they're getting the best value from the money they spend on training.

The Online Performance Evaluation and Learning Support (OPELS)[5] software is an efficient online method that can be used by SMEs (small and medium-sized enterprises) and workgroups in larger organizations to measure the impact of learning and training on performance and business outcomes. This process provides needed assurance that investments in learning can be effectively evaluated in terms in respect to these outcomes. The pilot testing was done with nine SMEs in Nova Scotia. David Sable, the software's Halifax-based designer, said it grew out of work for a multinational corporation. The goal was to develop software to evaluate the impact of e-learning. When the project was shelved after a merger, "we took it home and we said, 'Look, we could use this for small and medium-sized businesses.'" Specifically, OPELS

- Enables SMEs and workgroups in larger organizations to measure the impact of learning (formal and informal, online and traditional) in terms meaningful to management, through an efficient online method;

- Supports various types of informal learning on-the-job; and

- Supports the integration of learning into work processes.

The idea of OPELS is to have both learners and managers identify the results they are seeking from a training program and then measure what the training delivers against those goals. The OPELS process includes the following steps:[6]

- **Actions Plans (for Learners)**—What they will do differently as a result of the training.

- **Performance Targets (for Learners)**—Learners specify performance targets in their action plan. Performance targets are explicitly stated tasks that have measurable outcomes, usually directly related to business outcomes.

- **Expected Business Outcomes (for Managers)**—Managers are concerned with how the learner's performance objectives relate to business outcomes. Managers using OPELS are asked to define the business outcomes they expect from the learning event.

Continuous learning is a goal in many organizations. New software facilitates evaluation of e-learning methods.

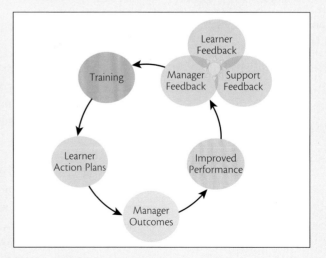

- **Feedback Templates**—Three-minute feedback loops with peers and supervisors (driven by email reminders) to:
  - evaluate each learner's performance according to Action Plans and Expected Business Outcomes; and
  - identify the barriers to accomplishing the desired performance and meeting management expectations (What kind of support does the learner need?)
- **Reports**—Based on the information collected, summary reports can be generated for learners, peers, and managers leading to appropriate action.

Learners "actually set up a little action plan that shows what they're going to do differently" as a result of the training, Sable explained. Their managers set up similar plans indicating what they are expecting the training to do for the business.[7] Amy Lynn Bell, an administrator at Digital Image FX Inc. in Dartmouth, N.S.,[8] said she used OPELS to track her own training on accounting software and found its reminders helped her focus on the goals of the training. "It was helpful in just making it more in-your-face as to what you're doing," she said. "It just makes you more conscious of it." Bell said the software's reminders made her follow through on tracking the results of her training. "I would not have probably done that unless I was put into a system that tracked whether I had done it or not," she said.

John McKinnon, vice-president of operations at Sydney, N.S.-based AG Research, said the 30-employee software developer has used OPELS to assess the benefits of various training courses for its employees. OPELS helped AG Research understand whether its training investments produced enough benefit to pay for themselves, he said. "It helps us understand the exercise of training and better methods or modes of training for our organization."

Now It's Your Turn

Why is training such an important human resource activity in today's organizations?

_____

_____

_____

Overview

Managers are responsible for acquiring, developing, protecting, and using the resources that an organization needs to be efficient and effective. One of the most important resources in all organizations is human resources—the people involved in the production and distribution of goods and services. Human resources include all members of an organization, ranging from top managers to entry-level employees. In our opening scenario, we see that effective managers such as John McKinnon, vice-president of operations at Sydney, N.S.-based AG Research, realize how valuable human resources are and take active steps to make sure that their organizations integrate and make best use of human resource tools such as OPELS to gain a competitive advantage. For McKinnon, the benefits justified the time invested in learning and integrating the training software.

This chapter examines how managers can tailor their human resource management system to their organization's strategy and structure. We discuss in particular the major components of human resource management: recruitment and selection, training and development, pay and benefits, performance appraisal, and labour relations. By the end of this chapter, you will understand the central role that human resource management plays in creating a high-performing organization.

Strategic Human Resource Management

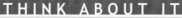

THINK ABOUT IT

Schickedanz Bro. Ltd., Galten Farms, Family, Health, and a Little Faith[9]

Arthur Schickedanz is a 44-year-old Markham, Ontario farmer who takes nothing for granted, loves his family, his Lithuanian roots, and the success he has enjoyed with his 80 hectares (200 acres) at Galten Farms—the name of the town that his father and uncles came from in Europe—and his additional 810 hectares (2000 acres) of rented land in York Region. To keep his 1500-head beef cattle operation going, Mr. Schickedanz needs seven full-time workers, while his equipment includes 10 tractors and two combines, valued at $1.5 million. He also does business in Alberta and Nebraska.

Despite all this, the farmer is quick to point out his father, Gerhard and uncles Kurt, Danny, and Gus Schickedanz shared the same dream in the early 1950s. All farm boys and skilled stone masons, the brothers packed their youth, energy, and determination and left their homeland to come to Canada. Soon after arriving, the brothers put their heads and their muscle together and launched a construction company. Hired by contractors and subcontractors in Toronto and surrounding area, the brothers went on to establish Schickedanz Bro. Ltd., now one of Canada's largest residential and commercial development companies. The brothers have their names on projects across Ontario, Alberta, and Florida.

Arthur Schickedanz graduated from his local Markham District High School, and then went on to study agriculture at the University of Guelph, Ontario. For him, farming is more of a lifestyle than a business: "It's a fine life. It's good to be out on the land. At the end of each day, I can see the fruits of our labour. We work. The cattle have to be fed twice a day, 365 days a year. They never miss a meal." As president of the York Region Cattlemen's Association, he oversees the interest of 45 beef farmers in the region. The local association, a branch of the Ontario Cattlemen's Association, promotes beef cattle production through policy planning, government lobbying, development programs, and research.

Mr. Schickedanz readily acknowledges that life in Canada is good; he is very thankful. Along with other York Region farmers, he is generous in giving to others to combat hunger in the Third World with wheat, soy bean, and corn. As a member of a local Canadian Foodgrains Bank project, Mr. Schickedanz grows and donates 10 hectares (25 acres) of wheat to the project. Together, the few local farmers raise about $400 000 a year to feed the hungry in Africa, India, Ethiopia, Uganda, Haiti, and other locations around the world. For Schickedanz, family, health, and a little faith is all that really matters.

You Be the Manager

1. What fundamental attitudes are present in the story about Arthur Schickedanz that contribute to effective management of human resources?

Farmer Lloyd Crowe watches as the last of a load of winter wheat is loaded into a hopper trailer in Belleville, Ont. The Canadian Foodgrains Bank project raises about $400 000 to feed the hungry around the world.

■■■ **FIGURE 11.1** | *Components of a Human Resource Management System*

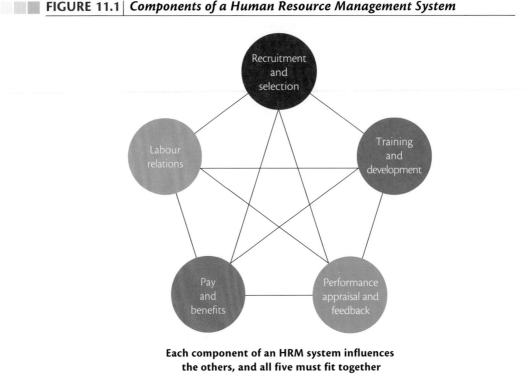

**Each component of an HRM system influences
the others, and all five must fit together**

human resource management (HRM)
Activities that managers engage in to attract and retain employees and to ensure that they perform at a high level and contribute to the accomplishment of organizational goals.

strategic human resource management
The process by which managers design the components of a human resource management system to be consistent with each other, with other elements of organizational architecture, and with the organization's strategy and goals.

Human resource management (HRM) includes all the activities that managers engage in to attract and retain employees and to ensure that they perform at a high level and contribute to the accomplishment of organizational goals. **Strategic human resource management** is the process by which managers design the components of an HRM system to be consistent with each other, with other elements of organizational architecture, and with the organization's strategy and goals.[10] The objective of strategic HRM is the development of an HRM system that enhances an organization's efficiency, quality, innovation, and responsiveness to customers—the four building blocks of competitive advantage, which we discussed in Chapter 1.

Overview of the Components of HRM

An organization's human resource management system has five major components: recruitment and selection, training and development, performance appraisal and feedback, pay and benefits, and labour relations (see Figure 11.1). Managers use *recruitment and selection*, the first component of an HRM system, to attract and hire new employees who have the abilities, skills, and experiences that will help an organization achieve its goals. For instance, Arthur Schickedanz is an obvious example of an owner-manager who puts people first, feels deep gratitude for the kind of work he does and how Canada provides him with such bounty, plus he is also family-focused and believes that "hard work, fresh air, a healthy and loving family, and a little faith translates into a good life."[11]

After recruiting and selecting employees, managers use the second component, *training and development*, to ensure that organizational members develop skills and abilities that will enable them to perform their jobs effectively in the present and the future. Training and development is an ongoing process, because changes in technology and the environment, as well as in an organization's goals and strategies, often require organizational members to learn new techniques and ways of working. The opening

Management Snapshot scenario describing OPELS illustrates that when companies invest in and acquire effective human resource processes, they have the possibility of gaining significant competitive advantage.

The third component, *performance appraisal and feedback*, serves two purposes in HRM. First, performance appraisal can provide managers with the information they need to make good human resources decisions—decisions about how to train, motivate, and reward organizational members.[12] Thus, the performance appraisal and feedback component is a kind of control system that can be used with management by objectives (discussed in Chapter 7). Second, performance feedback from performance appraisal serves a developmental purpose for members of an organization. When managers regularly evaluate their subordinates' performance, they can provide subordinates with valuable information about their strengths and weaknesses and the areas in which they need to concentrate. On the basis of performance appraisals, managers distribute pay to employees.

In the fourth component of HRM, *pay and benefits,* managers distribute pay to employees, first by determining their starting salaries, and then later by determining whether raises or bonuses should be given. By rewarding high-performing organizational members with pay raises, bonuses, and the like, managers increase the likelihood that an organization's most valued human resources are motivated to continue their high levels of contribution to the organization. Moreover, when pay is linked to performance, high-performing employees are more likely to stay with the organization, and managers are more likely to be able to fill open positions with highly talented individuals. Benefits, such as health insurance, are important outcomes that employees receive by virtue of their membership in an organization.

Last but not least, *labour relations* includes the steps that managers take to develop and maintain good working relationships with the labour unions that may represent their employees' interests. For example, an organization's labour relations component can help managers establish safe working conditions and fair labour practices in their offices and plants.

Managers must ensure that all five of these components fit together and complement their companies' structure and control systems.[13] For example, if managers decide to decentralize authority and empower employees, they need to invest in training and development to ensure that lower-level employees have the knowledge and expertise they need to make the decisions that top managers would make in a more centralized structure.

Each of the five components of HRM influences the others (see Figure 11.1).[14] The kinds of people that the organization attracts and hires through recruitment and selection, for example, determine (1) the training and development that are necessary, (2) the appropriate levels of pay and benefits, and (3) the way performance is appraised.

Recruitment and Selection

THINK ABOUT IT

Chain of Knowledge: Boomers Filling the Gaps[15]

"It's a bit of a paradigm shift," says David Lathrop, president of Grey Fox Associates Inc.[16] "The world is slowly coming to realize there is a real need (for senior management expertise) that isn't a full-time need." And so a growing number of baby boomers with senior-level business experience will be recruited to fill a niche created by their retiring colleagues, who are leaving a skills gap in their wake.

David Lathrop and Bob Eccleston, 57-year-old information technology executives, felt the sting of downsizing. They wanted to capitalize on their expertise in a way that gave them the work flexibility they wanted—and could afford—at this stage in life. So they set up a consulting business that allows them to work 40 or 50 hours a month on a contract basis to client companies that need to develop the skills of current, and often much more inexperienced, leaders. "It's about providing very senior level help, but in very small and manageable quantities in a way that a customer can see great value," says Mr. Eccleston, who was downsized three times before deciding to venture in a different direction.

Most human resource experts agree there will be a relatively sudden lack of senior experience in the market once the majority of baby boomers retire, leaving unprepared companies scrambling to find the qualified talent to replace them. Increasingly, firms such as Grey Fox are offering their services by coaching and mentoring up-and-coming leaders while keeping their own hands in the business world, Mr. Eccleston says. "You get so much satisfaction out of taking what you've learned over 35 years and helping these people get through those bumps in their careers." Mr. Lathrop says the goal is to recruit more partners with the same amount of experience and wisdom so the chain of knowledge continues moving along to the next generation of business leaders. The trend has also given rise to the increased use of interim managers, or contract executives who take over the helm of a department or company until a replacement can be groomed or recruited. "What [more junior executives] really need is just a few hours a week of someone with 30-plus years behind them who has kind of seen it all to hold them by the hand and get them through those difficult moments," Mr. Eccleston says.

You Be the Manager

1. Why is the recruitment of older employees important in managing the skills gap?
2. What is the paradigm shift that David Lathrop refers to?

---

recruitment
Activities that managers use to develop a pool of qualified candidates for open positions.

selection
The process that managers use to determine the relative qualifications of job applicants and the individuals' potential for performing well in a particular job.

human resource planning
Activities that managers use to forecast their current and future needs for human resources.

Recruitment includes all the activities that managers use to develop a pool of qualified candidates for open positions.[17] **Selection** is the process by which managers determine the relative qualifications of job applicants and their potential for performing well in a particular job. Before actually recruiting and selecting employees, managers need to make use of two important activities: human resource planning and job analysis (see Figure 11.2).

Human Resource Planning

Human resource planning includes all the activities that managers use to forecast their current and future needs for human resources. Current human resources are the employees an organization needs today to provide high quality goods and services to customers. Future human resources are the employees the organization will need at some later date to achieve its longer-term goals. As part of human resource planning, managers must make both demand forecasts and supply forecasts. *Demand forecasts* estimate the qualifications and numbers of employees an organization will need given its goals and strategies. *Supply forecasts* estimate the availability and qualifications of current employees now and in the future, and the supply of qualified workers in the external labour market. One of the factors facing some amusement parks was that not

FIGURE 11.2 *The Recruitment and Selection System*

enough teenagers are available or willing to work at them. With low supply, they have had to look to senior citizens as an alternative supply of labour.

The assessment of both current and future human resource needs helps managers determine whom they should be trying to recruit and select to achieve organizational goals now and in the future. As we saw in our previous *Think About It* case example, some baby boomers are creating companies to fulfill this leadership talent need. According to Statistics Canada, the average retirement age in Canada is now 62. Older workers are still in demand, of course. Dan Ondrack, academic director of executive programs at the University of Toronto's Joseph L. Rotman School of Management, says that older workers "have a lot of tacit knowledge about the ins and outs of getting a job done, which makes them valuable employees. And many will take jobs that pay less than their earlier careers."[18] However, succession planning is also becoming a critical need as more and more companies actively search for talent that will provide the leadership and direction for future organizational success. In recent years, Montreal-based BCE has created a new position, "chief talent officer," and appointed Léo Houle to the post. Houle reports directly to BCE's CEO, Michael Sabia. He is responsible for executive recruitment, compensation, and succession planning to make sure that BCE's companies have the right leadership and talent as BCE looks toward the future.[19]

As a result of their human resource planning, managers sometimes use **outsourcing** to fill some of their human resource needs. Instead of recruiting and selecting employees to produce goods and services, managers contract with people who are not members of their organization to produce goods and services. Outsourcing can be used for functional activities such as legal work, after-sales service on appliances and equipment, and the management of human resources or information systems. Outsourcing is increasingly being used on a global level. Managers in some Canadian computer software companies are outsourcing some of their programming work to programmers in India who are highly skilled but cost the companies substantially less than if the programming work were done in-house.

There are at least two reasons why human resource planning sometimes leads managers to outsource: flexibility and cost. First, outsourcing provides flexibility, especially if it is difficult to forecast human resource needs accurately or find skilled workers in a particular area, or if human resource needs fluctuate over time. Second, outsourcing can save money. When work is outsourced, the organization does not have to provide benefits to workers, managers are able to contract for work only when the work is needed, and managers do not have to invest in training.

Outsourcing does have disadvantages, however. When work is outsourced, managers may lose some control over the quality of goods and services. Also, individuals performing outsourced work may have less knowledge of organizational practices, procedures, and goals and less commitment to an organization than regular employees. In addition, unions resist outsourcing because it has the potential to eliminate the jobs of some of their members.

BCE Inc.
www.bce.ca

outsourcing
Using outside suppliers and manufacturers to produce goods and services.

With downsized baby boomers filling the gap, senior management expertise can be available on a part-time basis.

Job Analysis

Job analysis is a second important activity that managers need to undertake before recruitment and selection.[20] **Job analysis** is the process of identifying (1) the tasks, duties, and responsibilities that make up a job (the *job description*), and (2) the knowledge, skills, and abilities needed to perform the job (the job specifications).[21] For each job in an organization, a job analysis needs to be done.

A job analysis can be done in a number of ways, including by observing current employees as they perform the job or by interviewing them. Often, managers rely on questionnaires completed by job holders and their managers. The questionnaires ask about the skills and abilities needed to perform the job, job tasks and the amount of time spent on them, responsibilities, supervisory activities, equipment used, reports prepared, and decisions made.[22]

When managers complete human resource planning and job analyses for all jobs in an organization, they know their human resource needs and the jobs they need to fill. They also know what knowledge, skills, and abilities potential employees will need to perform those jobs. At this point, recruitment and selection can begin.

External and Internal Recruitment

As noted earlier, recruitment is what managers use to develop a pool of qualified candidates for open positions.[23] They generally use two types of recruiting: external and internal.

External Recruiting

When managers recruit externally to fill open positions, they look outside the organization for people who have not worked for the organization before. There are many ways in which managers can recruit externally—advertisements in newspapers and magazines, open houses for students, career counsellors at high schools and colleges, career fairs at colleges, recruitment meetings with groups in the local community, and notices on the web.

External recruitment can also take place through informal networks, such as when current employees inform friends about open positions in their companies or recommend people they know to fill vacant spots. Some organizations use employment agencies for external recruitment, and some external recruitment takes place simply through walk-ins, where job hunters come to an organization and inquire about employment possibilities.

External recruiting has both advantages and disadvantages for managers. Advantages include having access to a potentially large applicant pool; being able to hire people who have the skills, knowledge, and abilities the organization needs to achieve its goals; and being able to bring in newcomers who may have a fresh approach to problems and be up to date on the latest technology. These advantages have to be weighed against the disadvantages, however, including lower morale if current employees feel that there are individuals within the company who should be promoted. External recruitment also has high costs. Employees recruited externally lack knowledge about the inner workings of the organization and may need to receive more training than those recruited internally. InSystems uses its website to inform potential employees about its culture and strategic plans. Finally, when employees are recruited externally, there is always uncertainty about whether they actually will be good performers. Vancouver-based Angiotech Pharmaceuticals, Inc. solves this problem by working with potential employees years before they are ready to be hired. The company provides research money to graduate students at the University of British Columbia who are working on projects closely related to Angiotech's needs.

Angiotech
Pharmaceuticals, Inc.
www.angiotech.com

Internal Recruiting

When recruiting is internal, managers turn to existing employees to fill open positions. Employees recruited internally want either **lateral moves** (job changes that entail no major changes in responsibility or authority levels) or promotions. Internal recruiting has several advantages. First, internal applicants are already familiar with the organization (including its goals, structure, culture, rules, and norms). Second, managers already know internal candidates; they have considerable information about their skills and abilities and actual behaviour on the job. Third, internal recruiting can help boost levels of employee motivation and morale, both for the employee who gets the job and for other workers. Those who are not seeking a promotion or who may not be ready for a promotion can see that it is a possibility for the future, or a lateral move can alleviate boredom once a job has been fully mastered and also provide a useful way to learn new skills. Finally, internal recruiting is normally less time-consuming and expensive.

Given the advantages of internal recruiting, why do managers rely on external recruiting as much as they do? The answer is that there are disadvantages to internal recruiting—among them, a limited pool of candidates and a tendency among those candidates to be "set" in the organization's ways. Often, the organization simply does not have suitable internal candidates. Sometimes, even when suitable internal applicants are available, managers may rely on external recruiting to find the very best candidate or to help bring new ideas and approaches into the organization. When organizations are in trouble and performing poorly, external recruiting is often relied on to bring in managerial talent with a fresh approach. Thus, when Nortel Networks announced in October 2001 that it would promote the company's chief financial officer, Frank Dunn, as the replacement for John Roth, some analysts expressed disappointment, because Dunn was a career number cruncher, not a dynamic strategist.

lateral move
A job change that entails no major changes in responsibility or authority levels.

The Selection Process

Once managers develop a pool of applicants for open positions through the recruitment process, they need to find out whether each applicant is qualified for the position and whether he or she is likely to be a good performer. If more than one applicant meets these two conditions, managers must further determine which applicants are likely to be better performers than others. They have several selection tools to help them sort out the relative qualifications of job applicants and to appraise applicants' potential for being good performers in a particular job. Those tools include background information, interviews, tests, and references.[24]

Background Information

To aid in the selection process, managers obtain background information from job applications and from résumés. Such information might include highest levels of education obtained, university or college majors and minors, type of college or university attended, years and type of work experience, and mastery of foreign languages. Background information can be helpful both to screen out applicants who are lacking key qualifications (such as a post-secondary degree) and to determine which qualified applicants are more promising than others (e.g., applicants with a BSc may be acceptable, but those who also have an MBA are preferable).

Interviews

Virtually all organizations use interviews during the selection process. Two general types of interviews are structured and unstructured. In a structured interview, managers ask each applicant the same standard questions (such as "What are your unique qualifications for this position?" and "What characteristics of a job are most important for you?"). Particularly informative questions may be those where the actual answering allows an interviewee to demonstrate skills and abilities needed for the job. Sometimes called *situational interview questions*, these questions present interviewees with a scenario that they would likely encounter on the job and ask them to indicate how they would handle it.[25] For example, applicants for a sales job may be asked to indicate how they would respond to a customer who complains about waiting too long for service, a customer who is indecisive, and a customer whose order is lost.

An *unstructured interview* proceeds more like an ordinary conversation. The interviewer feels free to ask probing questions to discover what the applicant is like and does not ask a fixed set of questions prepared in advance. In general, structured interviews are superior to unstructured interviews because they are more likely to yield information that will help identify qualified candidates and they are less subjective. Also, evaluations based on structured interviews may be less likely to be influenced by the biases of the interviewer than evaluations based on unstructured interviews.

Even when structured interviews are used, however, there is always the potential for the biases of the interviewer to influence his or her judgment. Recall from Chapter 3 how the similar-to-me effect can cause people to perceive others who are similar to themselves more positively than they perceive those who are different and how stereotypes can result in inaccurate perceptions. It is important for interviewers to be trained to avoid these biases and sources of inaccurate perceptions as much as possible. Many of the approaches to increasing diversity awareness and diversity skills described in Chapter 3 can be used to train interviewers to avoid the effects of biases and stereotypes. In addition, using multiple interviewers can be advantageous, for their individual biases and idiosyncrasies may cancel one another out.[26]

When conducting interviews, managers have to be careful not to ask questions that are irrelevant to the job in question, or their organizations run the risk of costly lawsuits. It is inappropriate and illegal, for example, to inquire about an interviewee's spouse or to ask questions about whether an interviewee plans to have children. Questions such as these, which are irrelevant to job performance, may be viewed as discriminatory and as violating human rights legislation. Thus, interviewers also need to be instructed in what is required under the legislation and informed about questions that may be seen as violating those laws.

Testing

Potential employees may be asked to take ability tests, personality tests, physical ability tests, or performance tests. Ability tests assess the extent to which applicants possess skills necessary for job performance, such as verbal comprehension or numerical skills. Keep in mind that all selection techniques must be both valid (predict job performance) and reliable (yield consistent results). Also, giving a realistic job preview (RJP) is a useful technique to prevent the mismatching of employee expectations and the reality of the job, thereby minimizing high turnover.

Personality tests measure personality traits and characteristics relevant to job performance. Some retail organizations, for example, give job applicants honesty tests to determine how trustworthy they are. The use of personality tests (including honesty tests) for hiring purposes is controversial. Some critics maintain that honesty tests do not really measure honesty (i.e., they are not valid) and can be subject to faking by job applicants. For jobs that require physical abilities—such as firefighting, garbage collecting, and package delivery—managers' selection tools include physical ability tests that measure physical strength and stamina.

Performance tests measure job applicants' performance on actual job tasks. Applicants for secretarial positions, for example, are typically required to complete a typing test that measures how quickly and accurately they are able to type. Applicants for middle- and top-management positions are sometimes given short-term projects to complete—projects that mirror the kinds of situations that arise in the job being filled—to assess their knowledge and problem-solving capabilities.[27]

References

Applicants for many jobs are required to provide references from former employers or other knowledgeable sources (such as a college instructor or adviser) who know the applicants' skills, abilities, and other personal characteristics. These individuals are asked to provide candid information about the applicants. References are often used at the end of the selection process to confirm a decision to hire. Yet the fact that many former employers are reluctant to provide negative information in references sometimes makes it difficult to interpret what a reference is really saying about an applicant.

In fact, several recent lawsuits filed by applicants who felt that they were unfairly denigrated or had their privacy invaded by unfavourable references from former employers have caused managers to be increasingly wary of providing any kind of negative information in a reference, even if it is accurate. For jobs in which the job holder is responsible for the safety and lives of other people, however, failing to provide accurate negative information in a reference does not just mean that the wrong person might get hired; it also may mean that other people's lives will be at stake.

✔ Tips for Managers

RECRUITMENT AND SELECTION

1. Use human resource planning and job analysis as the basis to know what your human resource needs are.
2. Be transparent with potential new recruits as to the advantages and disadvantages of a job.
3. Be aware that older workers may be your solution to a skills gap in your company.
4. Think through the leadership talent you will need to build future organizational success.
5. Make sure your selection tools are reliable and valid.

Training and Development

THINK ABOUT IT

Rethinking the Education System for Small Business

Andre Piché, a director for the Canadian Federation of Independent Business, believes the education system needs to be rethought. "There is definitely a gap. There is a distinct lack of training in the skills needed by small business. We really have to rethink the entire education system."[28] After completing a cross-country interviewing process of labour union officials, employers, and educators, Johanne Mennie, director of program policy in the workplace skills branch for Human Resources and Skills Development Canada, realized that for small businesses—75 percent of whom employ 10 or fewer people with small and mid-size enterprises accounting for 45 percent of the gross national product, compared with 25 percent two decades ago—a new strategy is needed: create more generalists who have sound communications, team building, and priority management skills vs. pricey MBAs.

The emphasis on the development of such generalist skills would be better aligned to the needs of small and medium-sized businesses. Ms. Mennie says, "I think we have to change expectations and training right down the line, certainly to undergraduates and community colleges and perhaps even to the high school level." She believes that most educational institutions continue to focus on either technical skills or producing graduates who have so much invested in their education that they demand high salaries that only large organizations can afford. This leaves small business at a disadvantage. She says, "Small business wants people with the skills of an MBA but they simply can't afford to pay for them."

Organizations that are addressing this small business training need are go2 in Vancouver, which acts as an informal human resources department for British Columbia's hospitality industry—with three-quarters of the companies involved in hospitality having 10 or fewer workers—and Advancing Canadian Entrepreneurship (or ACE), based in Toronto, founded by University of Western Ontario undergraduate Ian Aitken in 1987 to encourage university and college students to learn small business skills by doing, which operates chapters at 45 Canadian campuses. For example, at Bishop's University in Lennoxville, Quebec, the ACE chapter set up an on-campus video store. At Ryerson University in Toronto, Bachelor of Commerce students can get a major in Enterprise Resource Planning; other students can also obtain a minor in entrepreneurial studies. Algonquin College in Ottawa also has a Small-to-Medium-Size Business Program.

You Be the Manager

1. What factors are important for small business success in Canada?

training
Teaching organizational members how to perform their current jobs and helping them acquire the knowledge and skills they need to be effective performers.

development
Building the knowledge and skills of organizational members so that they will be prepared to take on new responsibilities and challenges.

needs assessment
An assessment of which employees need training or development and what type of skills or knowledge they need to acquire.

Training and development help to ensure that organizational members have the knowledge and skills they need to perform their jobs effectively, take on new responsibilities, and adapt to changing conditions. **Training** focuses mainly on teaching organizational members how to perform their current jobs and on helping them acquire the knowledge and skills they need to be effective performers.

Development focuses on building the knowledge and skills of organizational members so that they will be prepared to take on new responsibilities and challenges. Training tends to be used more often at lower levels of an organization; development tends to be used more often with professionals and managers. As we saw with our opening case scenario, the Online Performance Evaluation and Learning Support (OPELS) software and process provides the needed training and feedback information both for employee learners and managers. The program aims at ongoing training and development and employee-manager targets, action plans, and check-off points.

Before creating training and development programs, managers should perform a **needs assessment** in which they determine which employees need training or development and what type of skills or knowledge they need to acquire (see Figure 11.3).[29]

FIGURE 11.3 *Training and Development*

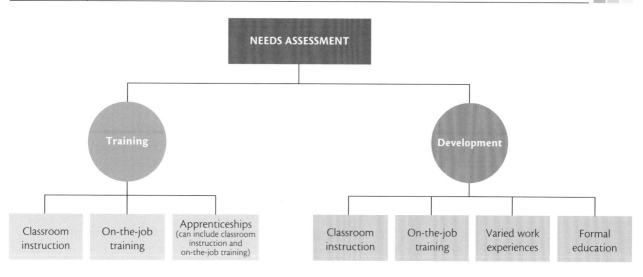

NEEDS ASSESSMENT

Training

Development

| Classroom instruction | On-the-job training | Apprenticeships (can include classroom instruction and on-the-job training) | Classroom instruction | On-the-job training | Varied work experiences | Formal education |

Issues in Career Development

A career is "the evolving sequence of a person's work experiences over time."[30] As individuals progress through their lives, they may get promoted, or they may change employers, or even become self-employed. All of this constitutes one's career. There are benefits to effective career development: It improves satisfaction and self-esteem, reduces stress, and strengthens an individual's psychological and physical health.[31] It also helps the organization, because employees are better suited to meet organizational needs.

The issue of career development, and who is responsible for making sure it happens, has become a national issue. The federal government is predicting "a looming national employment crisis" because of an aging and shrinking labour force.[32] Within 10 to 15 years, there will not be enough young people to replace those who are retiring. There is also concern that employees need to develop more job-related skills due to the increase in technology and the demands of the information economy. There is no single answer as to who should take action to resolve the issue of skills training: the government, employers, or employees.

Human Resources Development Canada (HRDC) proposed in 2001 a plan to increase the skills of Canada's workforce. The plan's main proposals included encouraging individuals to retrain and pursue lifelong learning; giving incentives to private industry to make employee training a top priority; increasing the numbers of skilled immigrants and speeding up their accreditation; and bringing traditionally unemployed groups into the labour force. The HRDC proposal faced serious controversy and is only one way of trying to resolve the skills crisis in Canada.

Organizations benefit when they offer career development programs:[33] They can make sure that the right people will be available for changing staffing needs, they can increase workforce diversity, and they can help employees get a better understanding of what is expected in various positions, that is, to have more realistic job expectations. At SaskPower, the leadership training program was started because management recognized that an aging workforce, and rapid turnover in the executive ranks, would otherwise lead to a lack of leadership experience in the company. The training program also helps individuals see whether they really want to move up the management ranks.

Human Resources Development Canada www.hrdc-drhc.gc.ca

SaskPower Corporation www.saskpower.com

Below, we describe both the organization's and employee's responsibilities for career development today.

The Organization's Responsibilities

What, if any, responsibility does the organization have for career development? Organizations take a variety of positions on this question. At Montreal-based Alcan Inc., employees are assessed annually, and then the individual employee's manager provides feedback regarding the potential for advancement and career prospects.[34] At the same time, employees discuss their career aspirations with their manager. High-potential employees are brought to the attention of senior management so that divisions anywhere within Alcan have knowledge about employees and their skills. Alcan's managers also develop an annual five-year plan to examine their human resource needs so that appropriate individuals can be identified and given training. At Hewlett-Packard Canada, by contrast, employees are expected to develop their own career plans and seek out the development they need. This is done with encouragement by their managers.

Employers that have successful career development programs provide support for employees to continually add to their skills, abilities, and knowledge. This support includes:[35]

1. *Clearly communicating the organization's goals and future strategies.* When people know where the organization is headed, they're better able to develop a personal plan to share in that future.
2. *Creating growth opportunities.* Employees should have the opportunity to get new, interesting, and professionally challenging work experiences.
3. *Offering financial assistance.* The organization should offer tuition reimbursement to help employees keep their skills and knowledge current.
4. *Providing the time for employees to learn.* Organizations should be generous in providing paid time off from work for off-the-job training. Additionally, workloads should not be so demanding that they preclude employees having the time to develop new skills, abilities, and knowledge.

The Employee's Responsibilities

While it is to an organization's advantage to develop its employees, Canada's employers do not have a good reputation for employee training. The country ranks 17th in terms of private sector employers placing a "high priority" on employee training—falling behind Sweden, Japan, Norway, Germany, Australia, and the United States.[36] Therefore, it is wise for individuals to take a more entrepreneurial approach to their careers. By maintaining flexibility and keeping skills and knowledge up to date, individuals will have more job opportunities available to them. Author and consultant Barbara Moses makes the following suggestions for how to be a career activist and take charge of your own career.[37]

Barbara Moses
www.bbmcareerdev.com/
bio.html

1. *Ensure your employability.* Make sure you have alternatives, in case you lose your job. Gain new skills, and pursue opportunities that will stretch you.
2. *Have a fallback position.* Have multiple options for your career, and try to see yourself in multiple roles. This means you could be an employee, a contract worker, or a freelance consultant using a broader set of skills.
3. *Know your key skills.* Know how to package your existing skills and experience in new ways (e.g., an architect who has a hobby as a gardener may start a business designing and building greenhouses). Identify your key talents and skills, and don't limit yourself to a job title.
4. *Market! Market! Market!* Always keep your eyes open for new work assignments, and position yourself for these. Let key people know your skills, and how you can bring value to the organization. Be sure to network. Be sure to treat everyone you meet as a potential client.

5. *Act Type A, be Type B.* While it is important to have the drive and achievement orientation of a Type A personality, it is also important to have the more relaxed Type B attitude of feeling good about yourself, even if you are not producing at a mile a minute. Your sense of self should not be completely tied to your job and the workplace.

6. *Stay culturally current.* Make sure that you are aware of world and cultural events. Being in the know helps you establish relationships with other people, and can help you manage your career effectively.

7. *Be a compelling communicator.* Everyone is busy these days, so it's important to communicate effectively and efficiently. You may be communicating with people halfway around the globe, or individuals who know little about the technical details of what you do. So being clear is important.

8. *Manage your finances.* If you have your finances in order, this will give you greater opportunities to explore new options.

9. *Act like an insider, think like an outsider.* Work as a team player and be self-aware, and able to evaluate your performance with some objectivity. It is important to be able to think independently. Sometimes you will have to make decisions without the help of a group.

10. *Be capable of rewarding yourself.* With increased demands on everyone, you may not receive all of the external feedback you might like. Learn how to give yourself a pat on the back when you do things well. Celebrate your successes, and take time to nourish yourself.

Performance Appraisal and Feedback

THINK ABOUT IT

Performance Review Ritual[38]

"Here we go again! It's that time of year!"

One can almost hear these voices as the time for the annual or semi-annual performance review time comes around.

Ideally this is a time for managers and their direct reports to "agree on what is important, how to measure success or failure in the future, and how to reward it," says Akhil Bhandari, chief information officer at CCL Industries Inc. What often happens instead can be the exact opposite: demotivation, frustration, dread, and cynicism.

To avoid the downsides and the ritualistic feeling often accompanying performance appraisals, here is a checklist to keep them effective:[39]

1. Align objectives specifically to the job and its contribution to corporate value;
2. Provide regular and consistent feedback so that the review should not come as a surprise to the employee;
3. Do your homework so that you know what you're talking about and can provide encouragement and competency;
4. Shorten the review process to a short checklist that shows everyone what they need to do and by what date;
5. Weigh your criticism to keep it balanced, fair, and remotivating;
6. Use flexible rating systems so that employees don't feel they're boxed in;
7. Reward star performers because they're the ones who need recognition;
8. Listen *and* respond so that the review process is simply not one-sided;
9. Don't invent "weaknesses" just because there is an area on the performance review sheet for "improvement";
10. Support transparency by sharing average statistics, similar to what happens when students receive their grades;

11. Be honest, by being appreciative, direct, and constructive; and
12. Follow up, that is, do what you said you would do, no later than a month after the review.

You Be the Manager

1. After reviewing the above performance review checklist, what factors are important to you? Why?

2. What areas would give you the most challenge? Why?

performance appraisal
The evaluation of employees' job performance and contributions to their organization.

performance feedback
The process through which managers share performance appraisal information with subordinates, give subordinates an opportunity to reflect on their own performance, and develop, with subordinates, plans for the future.

The recruitment and selection and the training and development components of a human resource management system ensure that employees have the knowledge and skills they need to be effective now and in the future. Performance appraisal and feedback complement recruitment, selection, training, and development. **Performance appraisal** is the evaluation of employees' job performance and contributions to their organization. **Performance feedback** is the process through which managers share performance appraisal information with their subordinates, give subordinates an opportunity to reflect on their own performance, and develop, with subordinates, plans for the future. In order for there to be performance feedback, performance appraisal must take place. Performance appraisal could take place without providing performance feedback, but wise managers are careful to provide feedback because it can contribute to employee motivation and performance.

Performance appraisal and feedback contribute to the effective management of human resources in two ways. Performance appraisal gives managers important information on which to base human resource decisions.[40] Decisions about pay raises, bonuses, promotions, and job moves all hinge on the accurate appraisal of performance. Performance appraisal also can help managers determine which workers are candidates for training and development, and in what areas. Performance feedback encourages high levels of employee motivation and performance. It lets good performers know that their efforts are valued and appreciated and lets poor performers know that their lacklustre performance needs improvement. Performance feedback can provide both good and poor performers with insight into their strengths and weaknesses and ways in which they can improve their performance in the future.

Who Appraises Performance?

We have been assuming that managers or the supervisors of employees evaluate performance. This is a pretty fair assumption, for supervisors are the most common appraisers of performance. Performance appraisal is an important part of most managers' job duties. It is managers' responsibility to motivate their subordinates to perform at a high level, and managers make many of the decisions that hinge on performance appraisals, such as decisions about pay raises or promotions. Appraisals by managers can, however, be usefully supplemented by appraisals from other sources (see Figure 11.4).

Although appraisals from each of these sources can be useful, managers need to be aware of potential issues that may arise when they are used. Subordinates sometimes may be inclined to inflate self-appraisals, especially if organizations are downsizing and they are worried about their job security. Managers who are appraised by their subordinates may fail to take needed but unpopular actions for fear that their subordinates will appraise them negatively.

FIGURE 11.4 | *Who Appraises Performance?*

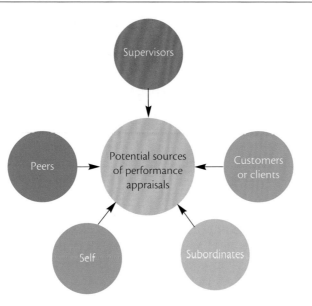

360-Degree Performance Appraisals

To improve motivation and performance, some organizations include **360-degree appraisals** and feedback in their performance appraisal systems, especially for managers. In a 360-degree appraisal, an individual's performance is appraised by a variety of people, such as one's self and one's peers or co-workers, subordinates, superiors, and sometimes even customers or clients. The individual receives feedback based on evaluations from these multiple sources.

The growing number of companies using 360-degree appraisals and feedback includes Toronto-based Celestica; Markham, Ontario-based InSystems; Burnaby, BC-based Dominion Information Services; and Toronto-based Hudson's Bay. A 360-degree appraisal and feedback is not always as clear-cut as it might seem. On the one hand, some subordinates may try to get back at their managers by giving them negative evaluations, especially when evaluations are anonymous (to encourage honesty and openness). On the other hand, some managers may coach subordinates to give—or even threaten punishment if they fail to give—positive evaluations.

Peers often are very knowledgeable about performance but may be reluctant to provide an accurate and negative appraisal of someone they like or a positive appraisal of someone they dislike. In addition, whenever peers, subordinates, or anyone else evaluates an employee's performance, managers must be sure that the evaluators are actually knowledgeable about the performance dimensions being assessed. For example, subordinates should not evaluate their supervisor's decision making if they have little opportunity to observe this dimension of his or her performance.

These potential problems with 360-degree appraisals and feedback do not mean that they are not useful. Rather, they suggest that in order for 360-degree appraisals and feedback to be effective, trust is needed throughout the organization. More generally, trust is a critical ingredient in any performance appraisal and feedback procedure. Managers using 360-degree appraisals and feedback also have to consider carefully the pros and cons of using anonymous evaluations and of using the results of the appraisals for decision making about important issues such as pay raises.[41]

360-degree appraisal
A performance appraisal by peers, subordinates, superiors, and sometimes clients who are in a position to evaluate a manager's performance.

Effective Performance Feedback

formal appraisal
An appraisal conducted at a set time during the year and based on performance dimensions and measures that were specified in advance.

informal appraisal
An unscheduled appraisal of ongoing progress and areas for improvement.

In order for the performance appraisal and feedback component of a human resource management system to encourage and motivate high performance, managers must provide their subordinates with performance feedback. To generate useful information to pass on to subordinates, managers can use both formal and informal appraisals. **Formal appraisals** are conducted at set times during the year and are based on performance dimensions and measures that have been specified in advance. A salesperson, for example, may be evaluated by his or her manager twice a year on the performance dimensions of sales and customer service, sales being measured from sales reports and customer service being measured by the number of complaints received. **Informal appraisals**—unscheduled appraisals of ongoing progress and areas for improvement—may occur at the request of the employee.

An integral part of a formal appraisal is a meeting between the manager and the subordinate in which the subordinate is given feedback on his or her performance. Performance feedback shows subordinates areas in which they are excelling and areas in which they are in need of improvement. It should also provide them with guidance for improving performance. Canadian workers report that the practice of performance appraisals is not carried out well in many workplaces. A survey of 2004 Canadian workers from a variety of industrial sectors by Watson Wyatt Worldwide, an international consulting firm, found the following:[42]

- Only 60 percent said they understood the measures used to evaluate their performance.

- Only 57 percent thought their performance was rated fairly.

- Only 47 percent said their managers clearly expressed goals and assignments.

- Only 42 percent reported regular, timely performance reviews.

- Only 39 percent reported that their performance review was helpful in improving their on-the-job performance.

- Only 19 percent reported a clear, direct, and compelling linkage between their performance and their pay.

Managers often dislike providing performance feedback, especially when the feedback is negative, but doing so is an important managerial activity. Here are some guidelines for effectively giving performance feedback that will contribute to employee motivation and performance:

- Be specific and focus on behaviours or outcomes that are correctable and within a worker's ability to improve. *Example:* Telling a salesperson that he or she is too shy when interacting with customers is likely to do nothing more than lower the person's self-confidence and prompt him or her to become defensive. A more effective approach is to give the salesperson feedback about specific behaviours to engage in—greeting customers as soon as they enter the department, asking customers whether they need help, and volunteering to help customers find items if they seem to be having trouble.

- Approach performance appraisal as an exercise in problem-solving and solution-finding, not criticizing. *Example:* Rather than criticizing a financial analyst for turning reports in late, the manager helps the analyst determine why the reports are late and identify ways to better manage time.

- Express confidence in a subordinate's ability to improve. *Example:* Instead of being skeptical, a first-level manager tells a subordinate of confidence that the subordinate can increase quality levels.

- Provide performance feedback both formally and informally. *Example:* The staff of a preschool receives feedback from formal performance appraisals twice a year. The director of the school also provides frequent informal feedback, such as complimenting staff members on creative ideas for special projects, noticing when they do a particularly good job of handling a difficult child, and pointing out when they provide inadequate supervision.

- Praise instances of high performance and areas of a job in which an employee excels. *Example:* Rather than focusing on just the negative, a manager discusses the areas the subordinate excels in as well as areas in need of improvement.

- Avoid personal criticisms, and treat subordinates with respect. *Example:* An engineering manager acknowledges subordinates' expertise and treats them as professionals. Even when the manager points out performance problems to subordinates, it is important to refrain from criticizing them personally.

- Agree to a timetable for performance improvements. *Example:* A first-level manager and subordinate decide to meet again in one month to determine whether quality has improved.

In following these guidelines, managers need to keep in mind why they are giving performance feedback: to encourage high levels of motivation and performance. Moreover, the information that managers gather through performance appraisal and feedback helps them determine how to distribute pay raises and bonuses.

Tips for Managers
BUILDING TEAMS FOR HIGH PERFORMANCE[43]

1. Do performance appraisals on a more or less frequent basis so that the formal occurrence will not bring up surprises.
2. Make sure you have adequate training in administering a performance appraisal process.
3. Focus on making the performance review process a problem-solution process.
4. Minimize defensiveness to the best of your ability.

Pay and Benefits

THINK ABOUT IT

Strategic Compensation[44]

Canadian organizations are shifting toward a more strategic approach to rewarding employees that focuses on business results, according to a new survey released on Monday, January 11, 2005, by Watson Wyatt Canada. Watson Wyatt's 2004 Survey of Canadian Strategic Rewards and Pay Practices[45] found that 77 percent of organizations have either adopted a total rewards strategy or plan to do so. Total rewards can be defined as an integrated set of monetary and non-monetary rewards, such as base salary—perceived as effective levers in attracting and retaining top performers, cash recognition, health and retirement benefits, training, and work environment.

When asked what they are trying to achieve with respect to total rewards, organizations cited improving competitive position (55 percent), allocating rewards funds more effectively (52 percent), increasing emphasis on variable pay (43 percent), maintaining competitive position (39 percent), and shifting to less costly programs (22 percent).

You Be the Manager

1. What is your personal reaction to strategic compensation?

In Chapter 8, we discussed the ways in which pay can be used to motivate organizational members to perform at a high level. Here we focus on how organizations determine their pay levels and pay structures.

Pay Level

Pay includes employees' base salaries, pay raises, and bonuses and is determined by a number of factors, including characteristics of the organization and of the job and levels of performance. **Pay level** is a broad comparative concept that refers to how an organization's pay incentives compare, in general, to those of other organizations in the same industry employing similar kinds of workers. Managers must decide whether they want to offer relatively high wages, average wages, or relatively low wages. High wages help ensure that an organization is going to be able to recruit, select, and retain high performers, but high wages also raise costs. Low wages give an organization a cost advantage but may undermine the organization's ability to select and recruit high performers and motivate current employees to perform at a high level. Either of these situations may lead to inferior quality or inferior customer service.

In determining pay levels, managers should take their organization's strategy into account. A high pay level may prohibit managers from effectively pursuing a low-cost strategy. But a high pay level may be well worth the added costs in an organization whose competitive advantage lies in superior quality and excellent customer service. As one might expect, hotel and motel chains with a low-cost strategy, such as Days Inn and Hampton Inns, have lower pay levels than chains striving to provide high quality rooms and services, such as Four Seasons and Hyatt Regency.

Pay Structure

After deciding on a pay level, managers have to establish a pay structure for the different jobs in the organization. A **pay structure** clusters jobs into categories that reflect their relative importance to the organization and its goals, levels of skill required, and other characteristics that managers consider to be important. Pay ranges are established for each job category. Individual job holders' pay within job categories is then determined by factors such as performance, seniority, and skill levels.

There is quite a difference between public and private sector pay structures. On average, governments at all three levels (federal, provincial, and local) pay a premium of about 9 percent to their employees, compared with private sector jobs. Public sector employees are also more likely to be covered by pension plans. Despite the seeming differences between public and private sector wages, it is generally women and less-skilled workers who get higher wages for working in the public sector. Managers, especially male managers, do not get paid much more for working in the public sector. Moreover, at the federal level, senior managers are paid less than they might earn in the private sector. There is also far more wage compression in the public sector. In

pay level
The relative position of an organization's pay incentives in comparison with those of other organizations in the same industry employing similar kinds of workers.

pay structure
The arrangement of jobs into categories that reflect their relative importance to the organization and its goals, levels of skill required, and other characteristics.

the private sector, on average, individuals in managerial, administrative, or professional occupations are paid 41-percent more than those in service occupations. In the public sector, it is not uncommon for managers to be paid only 10-percent more than other employees.[46]

Benefits

Employee benefits are based on membership in an organization (and not necessarily on the particular job held) and include sick days, vacation days, and medical and life insurance. Organizations are legally required to provide certain benefits to their employees, including workers' compensation, social insurance, and employment insurance. Workers' compensation provides employees with financial assistance if they become unable to work because of a work-related injury or illness. Social insurance provides financial assistance to retirees and disabled former employees. Employment insurance provides financial assistance to employees who lose their jobs through no fault of their own.

Other benefits—such as extended health insurance, dental insurance, vacation time, pension plans, life insurance, flexible working hours, company-provided daycare, and employee assistance and wellness programs—are provided at the option of employers. Benefits mandated by public policy and benefits provided at the option of employers cost organizations a substantial amount of money.

In some organizations, top managers decide which benefits might best suit the organization and employees, and offer the same benefit package to all employees. Other organizations, realizing that employees' needs and desires for benefits might differ, offer **cafeteria-style benefit plans** that let employees themselves choose the benefits they want, from among such options as flextime, tuition credits, and extended medical and dental plans. Some organizations have success with cafeteria-style plans, while others find them difficult to manage.

cafeteria-style benefit plan
A plan from which employees can choose the benefits that they want.

Labour Relations

THINK ABOUT IT

Unionism in Alberta[47]

In August three powerful unions in the United States—the Teamsters, the Service Employees International Union (SEIU), and the United Food and Commercial Workers—broke away from the AFL-CIO, a labour federation that encompasses 60 unions and represents about 13 million workers and probably the world's most prominent labour federation. "The deep question is whether unions have any chance of regaining power in a world of computerization and globalization. ... So are unions capable of delivering real value to postmodern workers, or are they just gangs of conspiratorial spongers who smother the occasional business to death as a means of clinging to relevance?"[48]

Alberta's labour philosophy was largely imported from the US primarily because of the oil industry, which was kickstarted by Imperial Oil's first big discovery, known as Leduc No. 1, in 1947. The result is that Alberta "is a province with a decidedly American bent when it comes to organized labour, having the lowest number of unionized workers per capita in the country." Some labour lawyers would claim that Alberta is "the wild west" of labour legislation, or "the Alabama of the north in terms of labour standards and worker protection." But other reasons also enter into this discussion: the thriving oil and gas business means that workers are paid higher wages compared with the rest of Canada. Noella Martin, a partner with Merrick Holm in Halifax who specializes in labour law said, "because there is no economic need for a union to protect the workers. Employees in Alberta don't need the same kind of protection that their counterparts in Cape Breton might. There's always another job to go to, but that's not the case in other provinces."

Other factors that enter the picture include those of the nonreplacement of the unionized aging workforce; demographics and the shifting younger generation. The new generation is also on the move much more; stability is not as prevalent; global trade and technology are impacting dramatically; and in Alberta, with its perception by people as the land of opportunity, why let unions interfere with the entrepreneurial spirit?

You Be the Manager

1. What is your opinion: do labour unions have a future in Canada?[49]

labour relations

The activities that managers engage in to ensure that they have effective working relationships with the labour unions that represent their employees' interests.

Labour relations are the activities that managers engage in to ensure that they have effective working relationships with the labour unions that represent their employees' interests. As a way to deal with the potential for unethical organizations and managers to treat workers unfairly, the federal and provincial governments created and enforce the Canada Labour Code, the Canadian Human Rights Act, and provincial Employment Standards laws. However, some employees believe that unions will be more effective than codes and laws in protecting their rights.

Labour Unions

Labour unions exist to represent workers' interests in organizations. Given that managers have more power than rank-and-file employees and that organizations have multiple stakeholders, there is always the potential that managers might take steps that will benefit one set of stakeholders (such as shareholders) while hurting another (such as employees). For example, managers might decide to speed up a production line to lower costs and increase production in the hope of increasing returns to shareholders. This action could, however, hurt employees who are forced to work at a rapid pace, who may have increased risk of injuries as a result of the line speedup, and who receive no additional pay for the extra work they are performing. Unions represent employees' interests in such scenarios. The students working at Montreal's downtown Indigo bookstore were unhappy with their working conditions, for instance, when they voted to join the CSN.

Employees might vote to have a union represent them for any number of reasons.[50] They may feel that their wages and working conditions are in need of improvement. They may feel that managers are not treating them with respect. They may think that their working hours are unfair or that they need more job security or a safer work environment. Or they may be dissatisfied with management and find it difficult to communicate their concerns to their managers. Regardless of the specific reason, one overriding reason is power: A united group inevitably wields more power than an individual, and this type of power may be especially helpful to employees in some organizations.

Although these would seem to be potent forces for unionization, some workers are reluctant to join unions. Sometimes this reluctance is due to the perception that union leaders are corrupt. Some workers may simply feel that belonging to a union might not do them much good or might actually cause more harm than good while costing them money in membership dues. Employees also might not want to be "forced" into doing something they do not want to do (such as striking) because the union thinks it is in their best interest. Moreover, although unions can be a positive force in organizations, they sometimes can be a negative force, impairing organizational effectiveness. For example, when union leaders resist needed changes in an organization or are corrupt, organizational performance can suffer.

About 31 percent of Canadian employees are represented by unions today.[51] Representation has remained fairly consistent for the past 20 years, although it is a decline from 30 years ago, when more than 40 percent of employees were unionized.[52] In the United States, where union representation peaked in the 1950s at about 35 percent, today it stands at about 13 percent.[53]

Union membership and leadership, traditionally dominated by white men, is also becoming increasingly diverse.

Summary and Review

1. **STRATEGIC HUMAN RESOURCE MANAGEMENT** *Human resource management* (HRM) includes all the activities that managers use to ensure that their organizations are able to attract, retain, and utilize human resources effectively. *Strategic HRM* is the process by which managers design the components of a human resource management system to be consistent with each other, with other elements of organizational architecture, and with the organization's strategies and goals.

2. **RECRUITMENT AND SELECTION** Before recruiting and selecting employees, managers must engage in human resource planning and job analysis. *Human resource planning* includes all the activities managers engage in to forecast their current and future needs for human resources. *Job analysis* is the process of identifying (1) the tasks, duties, and responsibilities that make up a job and (2) the knowledge, skills, and abilities needed to perform the job. *Recruitment* includes all the activities that managers engage in to develop a pool of qualified applicants for open positions. *Selection* is the process by which managers determine the relative qualifications of job applicants and their potential for performing well in a particular job.

3. **TRAINING AND DEVELOPMENT** Training focuses on teaching organizational members how to perform effectively in their current jobs. Development focuses on broadening organizational members' knowledge and skills so that employees will be prepared to take on new responsibilities and challenges. As part of the training and development process, organizations and individuals need to consider career development of employees.

4. **PAY AND BENEFITS** *Pay level* is the relative position of an organization's pay incentives in comparison with those of other organizations in the same industry employing similar kinds of employees. A *pay structure* clusters jobs into categories that reflect their relative importance to the organization and its goals, levels of skill required, and other characteristics. Pay ranges are established for each job category. Organizations are legally required to provide certain benefits to their employees; other benefits are provided at the discretion of employers.

5. **PERFORMANCE APPRAISAL AND FEEDBACK** *Performance appraisal* is the evaluation of employees' job performance and contributions to their organization.

Performance feedback is the process through which managers share performance appraisal information with their subordinates; give subordinates an opportunity to reflect on their own performance; and help subordinates develop plans for the future. Performance appraisal provides managers with useful information for decision making. Performance feedback can encourage high levels of motivation and performance.

6. **LABOUR RELATIONS** *Labour relations* are the activities that managers engage in to ensure that they have effective working relationships with the labour unions that may represent their employees' interests.

Key Terms

cafeteria-style benefit plan, p. 325

development, p. 316

formal appraisal, p. 322

human resource management
   (HRM), p. 308

human resource planning, p. 310

informal appraisal, p. 322

job analysis, p. 312

lateral move, p. 313

needs assessment, p. 316

outsourcing, p. 311

pay level, p. 324

pay structure, p. 324

performance appraisal, p. 320

performance feedback, p. 320

recruitment, p. 310

selection, p. 310

strategic human resource
   management, p. 308

360-degree appraisal, p. 321

training, p. 316

SO WHERE DO YOU STAND?

Wrap-Up to Opening Case

We saw in the opening scenario how Canada's Software Human Resource Council (SHRC)—together with David Sable, a Halifax-based designer, who created a software program to evaluate the impact of e-learning in order to help companies ensure they were getting the best value from the money spent on training—was helping Canadian businesses evaluate training investments with a software tool that helps set performance objectives and measure training effectiveness.[54] The result was the Online Performance Evaluation and Learning Support (OPELS) software; the focus was ongoing learning, feedback, and development.

Peter B. Vaill coined the term "permanent white water" to refer to the "complex, turbulent, changing environment in which we are all trying to operate." He writes, "Permanent white water conditions are regularly taking us out of our comfort zones and asking things of us that

we never imagined would be required. Permanent white water means permanent life outside one's comfort zone."[55]

Knowledge is the competitive advantage today. Recruiting the right people, training and developing them, rewarding them appropriately, providing feedback, and building succession plans are the key human resource steps to ensure this competitive advantage. Managers must adopt planned approaches to human resource management. In today's new economy, learning is the basis for ongoing organizational success. Managers need to subscribe, both in theory and in practice, to developing a corporate culture that is deeply embedded in the learning process. Again, Vaill provides us insight:

   Learning as a way of being is a whole mentality. It is a way of being in the world.... More than just a skill, learning as a way of being is a whole posture toward experience, a way of framing or interpreting all experience as a learning opportunity or learning process. 'Why must anyone seek for new ways of acting?' asked the biologist J.Z. Young. "The answer is that in the long run the continuity of life itself depends on the making of new experiments. … [T]he continuous invention of new ways of observing man's [sic] special secret of living."[56]

Authors Daniel H. Kim and Eileen Mullen describe what they call the spirit of the learning organization. "In a 'spirited' learning organization," say these authors, "the energy released with this kind of freedom is infectious. People like to come into this kind of space. When we do not have to censor what we really think and care about, we have more energy to devote to creating something that really matters to us."[57]

One person who translated his thirst for learning when he came from Calcutta, India to Canada over 40 years ago was Gora Aditya.[58] He ended up creating a multimillion dollar laboratory business—Med-Chem Laboratories Ltd. in 1970. He saw at the time that Toronto needed more health clinics, so he helped start one, then many more.

What he had learned at home while growing up was the value of discipline and hard work. By 1987 the private company had grown from its original 400-square-foot space to an operation with 40 locations, 700 employees, a 92 000-square-foot headquarters, and annual sales of $60 million, with 40 000 tests performed each day. When he lost the company over a court battle after taking on a partner several years later when sales were at $100 million, he decided not to let bitterness take over his life. Today he is president and CEO of ACT Health Group Corp., which is a chain of physiotherapy clinics, and is also a director for an Indian condom company.

He still works very hard, but he attributes his overall success to his thirst for learning, such as, when he was 11 years old, he noticed many Nobel Prize winners were German, so he learned the language! He learned early in his career what Brian Stanfield calls *learning a living*: "In the new economy, learning a living is the name of the game."[59]

Learning a living: the heart-and-soul of today's management of human resources.

After studying the preceding material, be sure to check out our Online Learning Centre at
www.mcgrawhill.ca/olc/jones
for more in-depth information and interactivities that correspond to this chapter.

Management in Action

Topics for Discussion and Action

1. Discuss why it is important for the components of the human resource management system to be in sync with an organization's strategy and goals and with each other.
2. Interview a manager in a local organization to determine how that organization recruits and selects employees.
3. Discuss why training and development is an ongoing activity for all organizations.
4. Evaluate the pros and cons of 360-degree performance appraisals and feedback. Would you like your performance to be appraised in this manner? Why or why not?
5. Discuss why two restaurants in the same community might have different pay levels.
6. Explain why union membership is becoming more diverse.

Building Management Skills

ANALYZING HUMAN RESOURCE SYSTEMS

Think about your current job or a job that you had in the past. If you have never had a job, then interview a friend or family member who is currently working. Answer the following questions about the job you have chosen.

1. How are people recruited and selected for this job? Are the recruitment and selection procedures that the organization uses effective or ineffective? Why?
2. What training and development do people who hold this job receive? Is it appropriate? Why or why not?
3. How is performance of this job appraised? Does performance feedback contribute to motivation and high performance on this job?
4. What levels of pay and benefits are provided for this job? Are these levels of pay and benefits appropriate? Why or why not?

Management for You

Your instructor has asked class members to form teams to work on a major class project. You have worked on teams before, and have not always been pleased with the results. This time you are determined to have a good team experience. You have reason to believe that how people are recruited to and selected for teams might make a difference. You also know that evaluating performance and giving feedback are important. You have also heard that training can make a difference. With all of this in mind, write up a plan that indicates how you might recruit an excellent set of team members, and make sure that they perform well throughout.

Small Group Breakout Exercise

BUILDING A HUMAN RESOURCE MANAGEMENT SYSTEM

Form groups of three or four people, and appoint one group member as the spokesperson who will communicate your findings to the whole class when called on by the instructor. Then discuss the following scenario.

You and your two or three partners are engineers with a business minor who have decided to start a consulting business. Your goal is to provide manufacturing-process engineering and other engineering services to large and small organizations. You forecast that there will be an increased use of outsourcing for these activities. You discussed with managers in several large organizations the services you plan to offer, and they expressed considerable interest. You have secured funding to start the business and are now building the HRM system. Your human resource planning suggests that you need to hire between five and eight experienced engineers with good communication skills, two clerical/secretarial workers, and two MBAs who between them will have financial, accounting, and human resource skills. You are striving to develop an in-house approach to building your human resources that will enable your new business to prosper.

1. Describe the steps you will take to recruit and select (a) the engineers, (b) the clerical/secretarial workers, and (c) the MBAs.
2. Describe the training and development the engineers, the clerical/secretarial workers, and the MBAs will receive.
3. Describe how you will appraise the performance of each group of employees and how you will provide feedback.
4. Describe the pay level and pay structure of your consulting firm.

Managing Ethically

Nadia Burowsky has recently been promoted to a managerial position in a large downtown bank. Before her promotion, she was one of a group of bank tellers who got together weekly and complained about their jobs. Burowsky enjoyed these get-togethers, because she is recently divorced and they provided a bit of a social life for her. In Burowsky's new role, she will be conducting performance appraisals and making decisions about pay raises and promotions for these same tellers. Burowsky reports to you, and you are aware of her former weekly get-togethers with the tellers. Is it ethical for her to continue attending these social functions? How might she effectively manage having relationships with co-workers and evaluating them?

Exploring the World Wide Web

SPECIFIC ASSIGNMENT[60]

On Monday, July 10, 2006, Toyota Boshuku Corp. announced plans to build a $65-million parts plant in Woodstock, Ontario, a move that will create 330 jobs. The plant will supply seats, door trim, and carpets for Toyota Motor Manufacturing Canada Inc. (www.toyota.ca/cgi-bin/WebObjects/WWW.woa/wa/vp?vp=Home.TMMC). Scan the Toyota Boshuku Corp. website (www.toyota-boshoku.co.jp/en/index.html) to learn more about this company, including clicking on "Company Profile," and under that, "Social Contributions, Human Resource Training." Now scan the Toyota Motor Manufacturing Canada Inc. website and review the various options available from their dropdown menus, including "Join Our Team" and "Who We Are."

1. What human resources factors are most readily demonstrated?
2. What features will attract new recruits for the Woodstock plant?

GENERAL ASSIGNMENT

Find websites of two companies that try to recruit new employees by means of the World Wide Web. Are their approaches to recruitment on the web similar or different? What are the potential advantages of the approaches of each? What are the potential disadvantages?

Developing a Business Plan
(APPENDIX B, PAGE 405)

Go to www.mcgrawhill.ca/olc/jones/11 for online exercises.

Be the Manager

STRATEGIC HRM[61]

As Canada's economy grew stronger after the dot-com bust, a new power emerged in the executive suite. Many companies began shifting from cutback-survival mode to embracing such enlightened concepts as growth, expansion, and a healthy corporate culture. Canada's human resource specialists finally began getting away from planning layoffs and calculating severance packages to building productive teams, enhancing employee motivation, and creating a winning corporate culture. In some companies, HR's new role is not just evolutionary but revolutionary. A prominent medical products company, for instance, recently appointed its HR vice-president as VP of marketing. One large retailer promoted its former head of HR to country manager. In a recovering economy, it figured its biggest challenge is not merchandising, but improving the quality of customer service and building staff morale. Similarly, a high-tech firm created a senior HR position to forge a new corporate culture. The company knew it had more than enough software engineers on staff (most of them recruited right out of college) but realized it now needed more people who could challenge the culture—develop new markets, build relationships, and foster risk-taking in a company that had always talked things to death. The HR executive's mandate: Find tech-savvy business leaders and hire them now, even if their job doesn't exist yet. Because of your expertise, your advice is now being sought by a well-known mid-sized company in your area on how to make the shift from HRM to SHRM.

Questions

1. How would you begin explaining the difference between HRM and SHRM?
2. What steps would you recommend to make the shift from HRM to SHRM?

Management Case

From the Pages of *Business Week* Job Security, No. Tall Latte, Yes.

When dot-coms started building gourmet coffee bars modeled on Central Perk from the TV show *Friends*—complete with mood lighting, overstuffed sofas, and 14 varieties of premium brews—some wondered if the New Economy frills were getting out of hand. It was one thing to hand out signing bonuses to janitors, and maids to summer interns. If a slowdown occurred, these perks could easily be whacked. But caffeine-addicted employees swarmed the espresso machines like druggies angling for a fix. Yanking this freebie could send them into convulsions of revolt.

Not to worry. The dot-com era may be dead, but, for the most part, connoisseur office coffee is here to stay. In fact, instead of worrying about being cut off from their caffeine supplies, employees can also look forward to mainlining free bottled water and subsidized snacks, both of which are in the offing at many companies—despite the slowdown-induced emphasis on cost-cutting.

Souped Up

What began as a dot-com dividend has "spilled over into a legacy," says Richard Wyckoff, president of corporate America's top coffee supplier, Aramark

Refreshment Services, which reports that sales of souped-up coffee machines tripled in the past year. Many companies such as Philadelphia-based Omicrom say that no matter how bad things get, they wouldn't dare pull the perk. Even managers at MCI Worldcom Inc., who postmerger were told to can the coffee, have resumed re-ordering.

The any-kind-of-coffee-you-want largesse is not the only New Economy legacy. Far from being fads that will evaporate like so many market caps, many of the workplace revolutions developed to coddle employees and warehouse them in offices for as long as possible might very well strengthen during the next 15 years. Part of the reason is economic. Even with the slow-down, companies must still compete for valued knowledge workers. And as employees are forced to clock workaholic hours in the global, 24/7 economy, companies will have to make offices seem more and more like home.

Out Gen Y-ers

Attitudinal shifts about the workplace are also a key factor. Earlier in their lives, many of the boomers now running the show spat on bourgeois values, disdained all things corporate, and fancied themselves as bohemians.

In fact, today's corporate chieftains make up the first generation that didn't serve in the armed forces and wasn't weaned on military models of organization. Thus, some have refashioned offices in the image of their free-wheeling, anti-establishment values. They want to succeed, but they also want to be cool.

In Return of the Suit

Of course, not everything about the loosey-goosey New Economy workplace will stick. Skin-tight spandex and scruffy facial hair at the office are fading as fast as knee-length skirts on the runway. Underscored by a US president who requires crisp, company-man dress, the suit is making a big comeback. Some firms such as recruiter Korn/Ferry have even reinstituted the button-down codes of yore—except in Silicon Valley. Already, retailer Men's Warehouses Inc. and fashion design Joseph Abboud are forming a marketing alliance aimed at the resurgence of professional dress.

Waning, too, is the reign of the unwrinkled. Seasoned, over-40 types bring a level of comfort to employers that post-pubescent wireheads never could. Another casualty: résumé puffery. Gone are the days when employers skipped the background and reference checks, allowing fakers to sail through. And the corporate carpetbaggers who bounced from job to job, collecting fatter paycheques and more options along the way, are no longer laughing at those "loyalist losers." They're asking them for jobs.

Bur for the most part, dot-com style perks will become permanent fixtures of the work landscape. Cultural changes wrought by the New Economy stem from when all those startups were siphoning off Old Economy workers amid the worst labour shortage in modern history. Rather than sit back and take it, Big Five accounting firms, Rust Belt stalwarts, investment banks, and law firms were forced to remake themselves in the image of their worker-snatching rivals. The strategy shifted the balance of power in employees' favour, and companies still haven't been able to completely regain their upper hand. That's why the recent pileup in layoffs isn't going to magically turn everyone back into a gold-watch seeker. Those days have been replaced by the free-agent mentality, in which the most talented workers can still afford to seek better deals within their companies and on the open market.

The smartest companies know this. Instead of ensnaring employees financially with more signing bonuses and huge salaries, they are trying to hook them emotionally with management retreats, specials awards, and assistance with elder and dependent care. And rather than resorting to their old strategy of assembling secret SWAT teams to psychologically pressure would-be defectors into staying, they are rechristening these leave-takers "alumni" and bidding them to boomerang back to the firm—if and when it's still hiring.

That's why Ernst & Young renamed its Office for Retention to the Center for the New Workforce. "People will have nine jobs by the time they are 30," says E&Y job czar Deborah K. Holmes. "We'd be delighted to be two or three of those jobs." And when skilled workers take those jobs, they'll do so with dot-com-style employment contracts in hand that protect them from mergers and downturns. After all, the Nasdaq may be in shreds, but if talented workers learned anything from the boom, it's that their careers—and offices—don't have to be.[62]

Questions

1. Why does it appear that managers are preserving some traditions from the dot-com heyday and eliminating others?

2. How important are job benefits, perks, and work environment factors for organizational effectiveness?

Video Management Case

CBC

Loyalty in the Workplace

This video segment questions whether employee loyalty still exists as a quality in today's workforce. Due to changes in the relationship between employer and worker, the question quickly becomes, however, how much can employees trust their employer to offer them security. In a world of downsizing and dot-com busts, companies are also struggling to make commitments to their workers.

Questions to Consider

1. What do the study's findings suggest; that employees are loyal to their managers; as opposed to the company itself?

2. Do "remote control job transitions" mean disloyalty or is it evidence of a more self-assured workforce?

Source: *Venture*, show number 777, "Loyalty in the Workplace," March 6, 2001, running time 5m 7s.

12

Communication, Conflict, and Negotiation

Learning Outcomes

1. Describe the communication process, and explain the role of perception in communication.

2. Define information richness, and describe the information richness of communication media available to managers.

3. Describe important communication skills that individuals need as senders and as receivers of messages.

4. Explain why conflict arises, and identify the difference between functional and dysfunctional conflict.

5. Describe conflict management strategies that individuals can use to resolve conflict effectively.

6. Describe how integrative bargaining can be used to resolve conflict.

Communicate, Communicate, Communicate[1]

"People do not always argue because they misunderstand one another; they argue because they hold different goals."

—William H. Whyte, author of *The Organization Man*[2]

It appears that communication not only helps get one's message cross, but it also contributes to healthier and more productive workplaces. When executives leave their corner office and venture out to communicate with employees, they must go beyond simply showing up at the cafeteria, checking the menu, and chit-chatting with those around them. They must realize that powerful communications skills are not a warm-and-fuzzy evil but vital to their success. Edward R. Morrow, known as the most distinguished and renowned figure in the history of American broadcast journalism, said, "The newest computer can merely compound, at speed, the oldest problem in the relations between human beings, and in the end the communicator will be confronted with the old problem, of what to say and how to say it."[3]

Regular, effective communication from the top can enhance employee pride, offer inspiration, and directly correlates to employee satisfaction and retention. When US journal *CIO Insight* asked in a 2003 online survey what skills define a strong leader, 65 percent of the 792 information technology senior executives who responded cited effective communication skills as the top choice.

For some, communication is considered a "soft skill." By that they often mean that it is "secondary" to the "harder skills" like accounting and spreadsheet analysis. Today, however, business realizes more and more that "soft is hard." Being able to communicate well in the workplace can lead not only to effective relationships in the office but also to enhanced community relations. Take the case of Andrew Grant, age 34, for example, from Vancouver. Besides having done work for the civil service and the Aboriginal health centre on Vancouver Island, he also speaks fluent Spanish and has a Masters degree in corporate social responsibility from the University of Barcelona. One would think that such a background is not what is required to work in the mining industry. But think again. In early 2005 he was appointed general manager in Ecuador for Arizona-based International Minerals Corp., or, IMC, a junior

resource company trying to make the leap from explorer to producer.[4] Chief executive officer, Stephen Kay, said it made perfect sense to put a non-miner in charge of a mining company's affairs—though he admits it takes some getting used to. Why would that be so? "If someone had asked me three or four years ago, 'Would you ever consider hiring a sociologist to work for you, or an environmental person as a manager?' I would have said, 'You're crazy, we're in the gold exploration business, why do we need that sort of thing?'" Today, however, he readily admits that a sociologist is as important as a geologist! The reason is that in working in other countries, community relations are vital. Says Kay, "But what a lot of companies are realizing is that they need other types of skills, in community engagement, consultation, relationship-building." Vancouver-based Manhattan Minerals Corp., for example, learned this lesson the hard way because it had to write off its entire $60-million investment in Peru in 2003 after a permit was yanked for its

Getting the message across: Effective communication is paramount for successful managers.

Tambogrande copper-gold project, which had run into fierce opposition for its potential impact on an agricultural area. Kay said, "You see it all the time. You go into a village and you see a nice concrete schoolhouse and the villagers are using it to store rice—because nobody thought to ask them where the teachers were going to come from or how they would be paid."

Quality of work specialist Dr. Graham Lowe points out that what is needed in the workplace is "not change management but change leadership." While a workplace may be deemed 'healthy' and 'safe,' that may be only true from a physical environment point of view. What is new is a growing recognition that negative psychological and social conditions at work affect employees' health—and productivity. Poor leadership and an organizational culture that allows managers to overwork and mistreat staff can actually make people ill. Bill Wilkerson, president of the Global Business and Economic Roundtable on Addiction and Mental Health, says, "And if you're a lousy leader, you're making people sick."

Joan Burton, in her report, *Creating Healthy Workplaces*, published in November 2004 by the Industrial Accident Prevention Association, described supportive managers as people who respect employees, who give positive feedback, communicate, and listen well. They also coach and mentor their employees. Dr. Lowe echoes this sentiment as well: "In workshops I often ask people, 'What would make your workplace healthier?' They don't say, put in a fitness centre. They say, ask us for our opinions and take into account what we have to say. Value our input. Communicate better. Acknowledge our contributions."

So, if managers want to be effective communicators with their employees, here are some suggestions that will certainly help:

1. Communication must be an important part of a manager's vision of being an effective leader. Managers must leave their offices and communicate directly with their employees. They must establish clear communication relationships.
2. If there are difficult communications to convey, getting either in-house help or seeking advice from a seasoned manager or executive, can be very helpful.
3. Whatever the message, make sure it's targeted and "packaged" appropriately so that the right people get the right message. There are many ways this can happen: the company newsletter, the intranet, a regular email update or regular employees meetings, personal newsletter designed to share information in a friendly, candid and informative way, face-to-face communication. Some managers enjoy getting together regularly with small groups of employees to share ideas over breakfast. Others eat in the cafeteria everyday to ask for feedback and gauge employee morale.
4. Managers need to seek feedback on how they are communicating. Sometimes this takes courage on the part of the managers; it is also difficult for employees to be candid as well at times, especially if their experiences have been negative up to this point.
5. Finally, good interpersonal communications can build a friendlier workplace which, according to researcher Jeffrey Sanchez-Burks, also creates more productive workplaces. The researchers found that friendly workers pay attention to indirect meanings, work well with other cultures, and are perceived as trustworthy; in other words, they also pick up the nonverbal communication signals as well. "An impersonal style tends to restrict the bandwidth of information a person attends to in the workplace," he said. "What is literally said will be followed closely but information about the context in which the information is conveyed—information often critical for task success and productivity—is lost."[5]

Now It's Your Turn

From your experience, what characteristics do managers have who are effective communicators?

_____

_____

_____

■■■■ Overview

We can see from the opening vignettes that communication is not only important in the office, but also in community relations. In the office, it is an essential component in the fabric of a healthy workplace. It wards off toxic work environments. Ineffective communication is detrimental for managers, employees, and organizations; it can lead to conflict, poor performance, strained interpersonal relations, poor service, and dissatisfied customers. Managers at all levels need to be good communicators in order for an organization to be effective and gain a competitive advantage.

In this chapter, we describe the nature of communication and the communication process and explain why it is so important for all managers and their subordinates to be effective communicators. We describe the communication media available to managers, and the factors that managers need to consider in selecting a communication medium for each message they send. We describe the communication skills that help individuals be effective senders and receivers of messages. We describe conflict, and the strategies that managers can use to resolve it effectively. We discuss one major conflict resolution technique—negotiation—in detail, outlining the steps managers can take to be good negotiators. By the end of this chapter, you will have a good appreciation of the nature of communication and the steps that all organizational members can take to ensure that they are effective communicators. You will also become aware of the skills necessary to manage organizational conflict.

Communication and Organizations

THINK ABOUT IT

Communication and Chief Financial Officers[6]

It might seem that to be an effective chief financial officer (CFO) doesn't involve as much need for communication skills as it does for financial skills. However, a survey of Canadian chief financial officers would tell a different story. According to the survey of 270 CFOs of Canadian companies with more than 20 employees done by Robert Half Management Resources, coming to a job interview ready to prove you can quickly solve problems, can effectively communicate verbally, and show confidence are the keys to getting an executive job in finance these days. The CFOs were asked to name qualities that impressed them most, other than technical expertise, when interviewing senior-level candidates for executive positions. Thirty percent of respondents listed problem-solving as the #1 skill, but 26 percent of respondents chose verbal communication skills as the next most important requirement, followed by such requirements as self-confidence, negotiation skills, personality and character attributes, and teamwork skills. David King, vice-president of Robert Half in Toronto, said hiring issues in today's new workplaces are centred around fast thinking in a changing regulatory environment in the financial sector. For him, the survey results demonstrate the need to show diplomacy, tact, and persuasion, but also enthusiasm to a wide range of audiences as critical to getting hired.

You Be the Manager

1. What additional requirements do you think are needed to be an effective CFO?

communication
The sharing of information between two or more individuals or groups to reach a common understanding.

Communication is the sharing of information between two or more individuals or groups to reach a common understanding.[7] Some organizations are more effective at doing this than others. We saw in Chapter 3 with Toronto-based Parmalat Canada Ltd. how CEO Marc Caira "juggled the juggle" when he wasn't receiving any communication from his parent company in Italy. Even though his knowledge of the parent company's ethical scandal was normally limited to what he could read about in the news media, he put together a plan: ensured all employees remained focused on sales; delegated only a handful of senior executives to work with him on the mess in Italy; and kept communicating with everybody.[8]

Good communication is essential for organizations to function effectively. Managers spend about 85 percent of their time engaged in some form of communication, whether in meetings, in telephone conversations, through email, or in face-to-face interactions. Employees also need to be effective communicators.[9] When all members of an organization are able to communicate effectively with each other and with people outside the organization, the organization is much more likely to perform highly and gain a competitive advantage.

sender
The person or group wishing to share information.

message
The information that a sender wants to share.

encoding
Translating a message into understandable symbols or language.

The Communication Process

The communication process consists of two phases. In the *transmission phase*, information is shared between two or more individuals or groups. In the *feedback phase*, a common understanding is reached. In both phases, a number of distinct stages must occur for communication to take place (see Figure 12.1).[10]

The **sender** (the person or group wishing to share information with some other person or group) starts the transmission phase by deciding on the **message** (the information to communicate). Then the sender translates the message into symbols or language, a process called **encoding**. Often, messages are encoded into words but they could also be symbols, such as :-) or a stop sign. **Noise** is a general term that refers to anything that hampers any stage of the communication process.

noise
Anything that hampers any stage of the communication process.

receiver
The person or group for which a message is intended.

medium
The pathway through which an encoded message is transmitted to a receiver.

decoding
Interpreting and trying to make sense of a message.

Once encoded, a message is transmitted through a medium to the **receiver**, the person or group for which the message is intended. A **medium** is simply the pathway—such as a phone call, a letter, a memo, or face-to-face communication in a meeting—through which an encoded message is transmitted to a receiver. At the next stage, the receiver interprets and tries to make sense of the message, a process called **decoding**. This is a critical point in communication.

FIGURE 12.1 *The Communication Process*

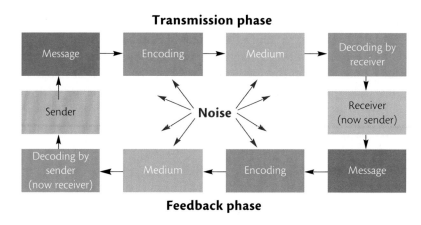

The feedback phase is begun by the receiver (who becomes a sender). The receiver decides what message to send to the original sender (who becomes a receiver), encodes it, and transmits it through a chosen medium (see Figure 12.1). The message might contain a confirmation that the original message was received and understood, a restatement of the original message to make sure that it was correctly interpreted, or a request for more information. The original sender decodes the message and makes sure that a common understanding has been reached. If the original sender determines that a common understanding has not been reached, the sender and receiver go through the whole process as many times as needed to reach a common understanding. Failure to listen to employees prevents many managers from receiving feedback and reaching a common understanding with their employees. Feedback eliminates misunderstandings, ensures that messages are correctly interpreted, and enables senders and receivers to reach a common understanding.

Nonverbal Communication

The encoding of messages into words, written or spoken, is **verbal communication**. We also encode messages without using written or spoken language. **Nonverbal communication** shares information by means of facial expressions (smiling, raising an eyebrow, frowning, dropping one's jaw), body language (posture, gestures, nods, shrugs), and even style of dress (casual, formal, conservative, trendy). "People make judgments about you based on how you look. If you're sloppily dressed or look like you're going to the beach, you'll leave a negative impression on clients and other employees," warns Natasha vandenHoven, senior vice-president, human resources, at Aon Consulting in Toronto.[11]

Nonverbal communication can reinforce verbal communication. Just as a warm and genuine smile can back up words of appreciation for a job well done, a concerned facial expression can back up words of sympathy for a personal problem. In such cases, similarity between verbal and nonverbal communication helps to ensure that a common understanding is reached.

People tend to have less control over nonverbal communication, and often a verbal message that is withheld gets expressed through body language or facial expressions. For instance, studies show that maintaining eye contact while speaking is seen as being more credible and more competent than if eye contact wanders. A manager who agrees to a proposal that she or he actually is not in favour of may unintentionally communicate disfavour by grimacing.

verbal communication
The encoding of messages into words, either written or spoken.

nonverbal communication
The encoding of messages by means of facial expressions, body language, and styles of dress.

It is important to be aware of nonverbal aspects of communication, as well as the literal meaning of the words. You should particularly be aware of contradictions between the messages. A manager may say it's a good time to discuss a raise, but then keep looking at the clock. This nonverbal signal may indicate that this is really *not* a good time to talk. Thus, actions can speak louder (and more accurately) than words. A variety of popular books help one interpret body language. However, do use some care. For instance, while it is often thought that crossing your arms in front of your chest is showing resistance to a message, you might also do this simply because you feel cold.

The Role of Perception in Communication

perception
The process through which people select, organize, and interpret sensory input to give meaning and order to the world around them.

Perception plays a central role in communication and affects both transmission and feedback. **Perception** is the process through which people select, organize, and interpret sensory input to give meaning and order to the world around them. But it is inherently subjective and influenced by people's personalities, values, attitudes, and moods, as well as by their experience and knowledge. Thus, when senders and receivers communicate with each other, they are doing so based on their own subjective perceptions. The encoding and decoding of messages and even the choice of a medium hinge on the perceptions of senders and receivers.

In addition, perceptual biases can hamper effective communication. Recall from Chapter 3 that *biases* are systematic tendencies to use information about others in ways that result in inaccurate perceptions. In Chapter 3, we described a number of biases that can result in diverse members of an organization being treated unfairly. These same biases also can lead to ineffective communication. For example, stereotypes—simplified and often inaccurate beliefs about the characteristics of particular groups of people—can interfere with the encoding and decoding of messages.

One group that has suffered extensively over the years from unwarranted stereotypes has been Canada's Aboriginal population. However, today, Aboriginal entrepreneurs are growing in number and moving beyond their roots.[12] In 2017 visible minorities, for example, will become Canada's majority. It's one of the reasons that Orrin Benn, president of the newly formed Canadian Aboriginal and Minority Supplier Council (CAMSC), is working hard to make sure Aboriginal entrepreneurs succeed in growing their businesses. Otherwise, as he points out, given the stereotypical perceptions, "Canada loses." John Bernard, president and founder, of Donna Cona Inc., Canada's largest Aboriginal-owned technology firm, has experienced first hand the unique challenges facing Aboriginal and minority entrepreneurs. He readily admits that being Aboriginal makes it that much harder gaining access to the supply chains of major corporations. For example,

> *Six months after beating out IBM and CGI to design the infrastructure for Nunavut residents to communicate across the two million-square-kilometre expanse of Canada's largest territory, Mr. Bernard learned the fact he was aboriginal could have cost him the contract. "I was at an event with the CIO of the Nunavut project and he asked if I was aboriginal. I said, 'Yes, isn't that one of the reasons we won.' And he said, 'Oh God, no. You won because you had the best proposal. 'In fact,' he said, 'if we had known you were aboriginal that would have gone against you.' Why? Because of the stereotype aboriginal firms do not deliver. If an aboriginal company makes a mistake, it reflects on the entire community. That is a huge obstacle to overcome."*

Instead of relying on stereotypes, effective communicators strive to perceive other people accurately by focusing on their actual behaviours, knowledge, skills, and abilities. Accurate perceptions, in turn, contribute to effective communication.

Information Richness and Communication Media

Cables, Airwaves Don't Relay Non-Verbal Clues[13]

James Moutsos, president of Dynamix Solutions Inc., a Markham, Ontario-based information technology support company, says that when he meets new prospects, "it's important to get in front of the client to build trust, something that can't always be done by email or on the phone." Ron McMillan, vice-president of VitalSmarts LLC, a communication training company, agrees with this viewpoint and says that with 10 percent of business communication, people need to meet face to face. The other 90 percent can be effectively conducted by electronic means. Says McMillan, "Email is a great way to convey information but not in crucial situations. That's a recipe for disaster." Issues turn from "casual" to "critical" when something really matters and the stakes and emotions are high. These three factors are always present in that 10 percent of critical issues. Master communicators, at this point, don't have what he calls a "meltdown"; rather, they communicate in person; they communicate well; they listen, paraphrase, understand the issue at hand, and state their case in a calm, rational manner. Phones, email, and instant messaging may speed up communication, but what is missing are the nonverbals: eye contact, voice inflection, and body language.

You Be the Manager

1. How do you find yourself using email in your communications?

2. What do you do when you have a communication conflict with a colleague?

To be effective communicators, individuals need to select an appropriate communication medium for *each* message they send. Should a change in procedures be communicated to subordinates in a memo or sent as email? Should a congratulatory message about a major accomplishment be communicated in a letter, in a phone call, or over lunch? Should a layoff announcement be made in a memo or at a plant meeting? Should the members of a purchasing team travel to Europe to finalize a major agreement with a new supplier, or should they do this through faxes?

There is no one best communication medium. In choosing a communication medium for any message, individuals need to consider three factors:

- *The level of information richness that is needed.* **Information richness** is the amount of information a communication medium can carry and the extent to which the medium enables sender and receiver to reach a common understanding.[14] The communication media that managers use vary in their information richness (see Figure 12.2).[15] Media high in information richness are able to carry a lot of information and generally enable receivers and senders to come to a common understanding.

- *The time needed for communication.* Managers' and other organizational members' time is valuable, and this affects the way messages should be sent.

- *The need for a paper or electronic trail.* An individual may want written documentation that a message was sent and received.

In the remainder of this section, we examine four types of communication media that vary along these three dimensions: information richness, time, and need for a paper or electronic trail.[16]

information richness
The amount of information that a communication medium can carry and the extent to which the medium enables sender and receiver to reach a common understanding.

FIGURE 12.2 | *The Information Richness of Communication Media*

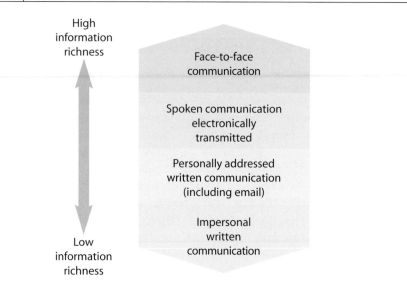

Face-to-Face Communication

Face-to-face communication has the highest information richness. When individuals communicate face to face, they not only can take advantage of verbal communication but also can interpret each other's nonverbal signals, such as facial expressions and body language. A look of concern or puzzlement can sometimes tell more than a thousand words, and individuals can respond to these nonverbal signals on the spot. Face-to-face communication also enables instant feedback. Points of confusion, ambiguity, or misunderstanding can be resolved, and individuals can cycle through the communication process as many times as they need to, to reach a common understanding.

Because face-to-face communication is highest in information richness, you might think that it should always be the medium of choice. This is not the case, however, because of the amount of time it takes and the lack of a paper or electronic trail resulting from it. For messages that are important, personal, or likely to be misunderstood, it is often well worth the time to use face-to-face communication and, if need be, supplement it with some form of written communication documenting the message.

Many organizations are using videoconferences to capture some of the advantages of face-to-face communication (such as access to facial expressions), while saving time and money because individuals in different locations do not have to travel to meet with one another. In addition to saving travel costs, videoconferences can speed up decisions, shorten new product development time, and lead to more efficient meetings. Some managers have found that meetings are 20- to 30-percent shorter when they use videoconferences instead of face-to-face meetings.[17]

Spoken Communication Electronically Transmitted

After face-to-face communication, spoken communication electronically transmitted over the phone is second-highest in information richness (see Figure 12.2). Although individuals communicating over the phone do not have access to body language and facial expressions, they do have access to the tone of voice in which a message is delivered, the parts of the message the sender emphasizes, and the general manner in which the message is spoken, in addition to the actual words themselves. Thus, phone conversations have the capacity to convey extensive amounts of information. Individuals also can ensure that mutual understanding is reached because they can get quick feedback over the phone and can answer questions.

Voice mail systems and answering machines also allow people to send and receive verbal electronic messages. Such systems are obviously a necessity when managers or employees are frequently out of the office, and those on the road are well advised to check their voice mail periodically.

Personally Addressed Written Communication

Lower than electronically transmitted verbal communication in information richness is personally addressed written communication (see Figure 12.2). One of the advantages of face-to-face communication and verbal communication electronically transmitted is that they both tend to demand attention, which helps ensure that receivers pay attention. Personally addressed written communication such as a memo or letter also has this advantage. Because it is addressed to a particular person, the chances are good that the person will actually pay attention to (and read) it. Moreover, the sender can write the message in a way that the receiver is most likely to understand. Like voice mail, written communication does not enable a receiver to have his or her questions answered immediately, but when messages are clearly written and feedback is provided, common understandings can still be reached. Even if managers use face-to-face communication, a follow-up in writing is often needed for messages that are important or complicated and need to be referred to later on.

Email

Email also fits into this category of communication media because senders and receivers are communicating through personally addressed written words. The words are appearing on their personal computer screens, however, rather than on pieces of paper. Email is becoming so widespread in the business world that managers are even developing their own email etiquette. For instance, messages in capital letters are often perceived as being shouted or screamed. Here are some guidelines from polite emailers:

E-Mail Etiquette
www.emailreplies.com

- Always punctuate messages.

- Do not ramble on or say more than you need to.

- Do not act as though you do not understand something when in fact you do understand it.

- Pay attention to spelling and format (put a memo in memo form).

While the growing use of email has enabled better communication within organizations, not all benefits have been positive. Many individuals complain of "email overload," and being unable to keep up with all the email that arrives, even personally addressed messages. In addition, some employees sexually harass co-workers through email, and employees often find their electronic mailboxes clogged with junk mail. In a recent survey, more than half of the organizations surveyed acknowledged some problems with their email systems.[18]

To avoid these and other costly forms of email abuse, managers need to develop a clear policy specifying what company email can and should be used for and what is out of bounds. Managers also should clearly communicate this policy to all members of an organization, as well as describe both the procedures that will be used when email abuse is suspected and the consequences that will result when email abuse is confirmed.

The increasing use of voice mail and email in companies large and small has led to some ethical concerns, as we noted at the beginning of this section. These forms of communication are not necessarily private. The federal Privacy and Access to Information Acts apply to all federal government departments, most federal agencies,

Videoconferencing can effectively facilitate meetings by retaining a personal feeling.

and some federal Crown corporations, but many private sector employees are not covered by privacy legislation. Only Quebec's privacy act applies to the entire private sector.

The ethics of listening to other people's voice mail or reading their email are likely to be a growing concern for many managers. While no comparable Canadian data are available, a recent survey of more than 2000 large American firms found that 38 percent reported that they "store and review" employee email messages. This was up from 27 percent in 1999 and just 15 percent in 1997.[19] The Ontario, Manitoba, and BC governments have told their employees that email will be monitored if abuse is suspected. The governments' positions are that the Internet and email should be used only for business purposes.

Impersonal Written Communication

Impersonal written communication is lowest in information richness and is well suited for messages that need to reach a large number of receivers. Because such messages are not addressed to particular receivers, feedback is unlikely, so managers must make sure that messages sent by this medium are written clearly in language that all receivers will understand.

Managers can use impersonal written communication, including company news letters, for various types of messages, including rules, regulations, policies, newsworthy information, and announcements of changes in procedures or the arrival of new organizational members. Impersonal written communication also can be used to communicate instructions about how to use machinery or how to process work orders or customer requests. For these kinds of messages, the paper trail left by this communication medium can be invaluable for employees. Much of this information is also being posted to company intranets. The danger with impersonal communication, however, is that individuals will not read it, so it is important that employees are made aware of important messages.

 ## Tips for Managers
INFORMATION RICHNESS AND COMMUNICATION MEDIA

1. When you have something to communicate that is important, emotion-based, and personal, use face-to-face communication.

2. Use videoconferencing when distance or weather or cost hinders face-to-face communication.

3. Consider introducing "Email Free Friday," recommended by Sport England, as part of its Everyday Sport campaign. Dr. Dorian Dugmore, an international heart expert in the UK, said: "We need the nation to get behind Email Free Friday as we are losing millions of hours of exercise through the explosion of email."[20]

4. Be clear with employees about the company policy on the use of email in the office.

5. Whether or not privacy is protected by law or contract, foster a workplace culture where privacy is valued and respected, contributes to morale and mutual trust, and makes good business sense.[21]

Developing Communication Skills

THINK ABOUT IT

"C-Suite Coaching" and Executives[22]

Even though he felt he was "a pretty connected, aware and effective leader," Jim Suttie, chief executive officer of Vancouver-based Selkirk Financial Technologies for more than a decade, reached out to a leadership coaching consultant for help. He felt he was losing touch with his staff and needed to re-establish rapport. He enjoyed the experience so much and made changes in his leadership style such that he strongly recommended that all his managers get coaches as well. "C-suite" executives are those with the titles of CEO, COO, and CFO. Executive coaches are able to help even seasoned managers like Jim Suttie update and improve their leadership abilities. This type of learning and coaching is particularly helpful for newly hired CEOs so that they can quickly learn to fit in with the organization. ICON International, in Toronto, specializes in such executive coaching and leadership development. Paul Morse, founder and president of ICON, says that "communication is the heart-and-soul, the lifeblood, of what a manager or executive does. Follow-up coaching after hiring a manager or executive is essential."[23] According to a survey by Booz Allen Hamilton Inc., 31 percent of the CEOs in Canada and the United States who left their jobs in 2003 were asked to resign because they didn't work out as the company had hoped. Learning more effective communication skills allows managers and executives to avoid what Goleman, Boyatzis and McKee call "CEO disease," or the inability or refusal to accept feedback on his/her performance. As a matter of fact, emotionally intelligent managers and executives seek out negative feedback so they grow and not be blinded by things in themselves that interfere with effectively managing and communicating![24] One of the interesting pieces of feedback that Jim Suttie received was how imposing he was as a person. At a height of 6' 1" and weighing 118 kilograms (260 pounds), he was physically intimidating to smaller people. "I could appear to be threatening, even though I think I'm pretty soft and easy," Mr. Suttie says. He made a conscious effort to trim down and become more approachable.

You Be the Manager

1. What factors might interfere with your effectiveness as a communicator?

There are various kinds of barriers to effective communication in organizations. Some barriers have their origins in senders. When messages are unclear, incomplete, or difficult to understand, when they are sent over an inappropriate medium, or when no provision for feedback is made, communication suffers. Other communication barriers have their origins in receivers. When receivers pay no attention to, or do not listen to messages, or when they make no effort to understand the meaning of a message, communication is likely to be ineffective.

To overcome these barriers and effectively communicate with others, managers (as well as other organizational members) must possess or develop certain communication skills. Some of these skills are particularly important when individuals send messages, and others are critical when individuals receive messages. These skills help ensure not only that individuals will be able to share information, but that they will have the information they need to make good decisions and take action, and also that they will be able to reach a common understanding with others.

TABLE 12.1 | *Seven Communication Skills for Managers as Senders of Messages*

- Send messages that are clear and complete
- Encode messages in symbols that the receiver understands
- Select a medium that is appropriate for the message
- Select a medium that the receiver monitors
- Avoid filtering and information distortion
- Ensure that a feedback mechanism is built into messages
- Provide accurate information to ensure that misleading rumours are not spread

Communication Skills for Senders

Individuals can make sure that they consider all of the steps of the communication process when they are engaging in communication. They can also develop their skills in giving feedback. We discuss each of these issues in turn.

Improving the Communication Process

Table 12.1 summarizes seven communication skills that help ensure that when individuals send messages, they are properly understood and the transmission phase of the communication process is effective. Let's see what each skill entails.

SEND CLEAR AND COMPLETE MESSAGES Individuals need to learn how to send a message that is clear and complete. A message is clear when it is easy for the receiver to understand and interpret, and it is complete when it contains all the information that the sender and receiver need to reach a common understanding. In trying to send messages that are both clear and complete, managers must learn to anticipate how receivers will interpret messages, and adjust messages to eliminate sources of misunderstanding or confusion.

ENCODE MESSAGES IN SYMBOLS THE RECEIVER UNDERSTANDS Individuals need to appreciate that when they encode messages, they should use symbols or language that the receiver understands. When sending messages in English to receivers whose native language is not English, for example, it is important to use commonplace vocabulary and to avoid clichés that, when translated, may make little sense and in some cases are unintentionally comical or insulting.

jargon
Specialized language that members of an occupation, group, or organization develop to facilitate communication among themselves.

Jargon, specialized language that members of an occupation, group, or organization develop to facilitate communication among themselves, should never be used to communicate with people outside the occupation, group, or organization. For example, truck drivers refer to compact cars as "roller skates," highway dividing lines as "paints," and orange barrels around road construction areas as "Schneider eggs." Using this jargon among themselves results in effective communication because they know precisely what is being referred to. But if a truck driver used this language to send a message (such as "That roller skate can't stay off the paint") to a receiver who did not drive trucks, the receiver would not know what the message meant.[25]

SELECT A MEDIUM APPROPRIATE FOR THE MESSAGE When choosing among communication media, individuals need to take into account the level of information richness required, time constraints, and the need for a paper or electronic trail. A primary concern in choosing an appropriate medium is the nature of the message. Is it personal, important, nonroutine, and likely to be misunderstood and in need of further clarification? If it is, face-to-face communication is likely to be in order.

SELECT A MEDIUM THAT THE RECEIVER MONITORS Another factor that individuals need to take into account when selecting a communication medium is whether it is one that the receiver uses. Not everyone checks voice mail and email routinely. Many people simply select the medium that they themselves use the most and are most comfortable with, but doing this can often lead to ineffective communication. No matter how much an individual likes email, sending an email message to someone else who never checks his or her email is useless. Learning which individuals like things in writing and which prefer face-to-face interactions and then using the appropriate medium enhances the chance that receivers will actually receive and pay attention to messages.

A related consideration is whether receivers have disabilities that limit their ability to decode certain kinds of messages. A blind receiver, for example, cannot read a written message. Managers should ensure that their employees with disabilities have resources available to communicate effectively with others.

AVOID FILTERING AND INFORMATION DISTORTION Filtering occurs when senders withhold part of a message because they (mistakenly) think that the receiver does not need the information or will not want to receive it. Filtering can occur at all levels in an organization and in both vertical and horizontal communication. Rank-and-file employees may filter messages they send to first-line managers, first-line managers may filter messages to middle managers, and middle managers may filter messages to top managers. Such filtering is most likely to take place when messages contain bad news or problems that subordinates are afraid they will be blamed for.

filtering
Withholding part of a message out of the mistaken belief that the receiver does not need or will not want the information.

Information distortion occurs when the meaning of a message changes as the message passes through a series of senders and receivers. Some information distortion is accidental—due to faulty encoding and decoding or to a lack of feedback. Other information distortion is deliberate. Senders may alter a message to make themselves or their groups look good and to receive special treatment.

information distortion
Changes in the meaning of a message as the message passes through a series of senders and receivers.

Managers themselves should avoid filtering and distorting information. But how can they eliminate these barriers to effective communication throughout their organization? They need to establish trust throughout the organization. Subordinates who trust their managers believe that they will not be blamed for things beyond their control and will be treated fairly. Managers who trust their subordinates provide them with clear and complete information and do not hold things back.

INCLUDE A FEEDBACK MECHANISM IN MESSAGES Because feedback is essential for effective communication, individuals should build a feedback mechanism into the messages they send. They either should include a request for feedback or indicate when and how they will follow up on the message to make sure that it was received and understood. When writing letters and memos or sending faxes, one can request that the receiver respond with comments and suggestions in a letter, memo, or fax; schedule a meeting to discuss the issue; or follow up with a phone call. Building feedback mechanisms such as these into messages ensures that messages are received and understood.

PROVIDE ACCURATE INFORMATION Rumours are unofficial pieces of information of interest to organizational members but with no identifiable source. Rumours spread quickly once they are started, and usually they concern topics that organizational members think are important, interesting, or amusing. Rumours, however, can be misleading and can cause harm to individual employees and to an organization when they are false, malicious, or unfounded. Managers can halt the spread of misleading rumours by providing organizational members with accurate information on matters that concern them.

rumours
Unofficial pieces of information of interest to organizational members but with no identifiable source.

Giving Feedback

We have discussed the importance of feedback in making sure that communication is understood. We can also talk about providing feedback more generally, because communicating feedback is an important task for managers. While positive feedback is easier to give, many individuals do not provide such feedback. Most people find giving negative feedback more difficult. Individuals can learn from feedback, whether it is positive or negative, so providing it in a timely fashion is important. The following suggestions can lead to more effective feedback:

- *Focus on specific behaviours.* Individuals should be told what it was that they did well or poorly, rather than simply being told that they did a good job. They can learn more from comments such as "You were very organized in your presentation," or "You managed your time effectively on this project," than when told simply, "Great job."
- *Keep feedback impersonal.* When giving feedback, you should describe the behaviour, rather than judge or evaluate the person.[26] Particularly when giving negative feedback, it is easy to focus on personal characteristics (rudeness, laziness, incompetence, etc.), but this rarely helps the person learn from mistakes. It is better to explain that the report was late, it contained a number of errors, and was missing an important section.
- *Keep feedback goal-oriented.* Feedback should not be given just because it will make you feel better. Rather, it should have a goal, such as improving performance for next time.
- *Make feedback well-timed.* Feedback should be given shortly after the behaviour occurs. This ensures that the individual remembers the event, and also is more likely to result in change if change is needed. Giving feedback to someone six months later, during a performance review, is usually not helpful. If a situation has provoked an emotional response in you, however, delaying feedback until you have had time to lessen the emotional impact is wise.
- *Direct negative feedback toward behaviour that the receiver can control.* When giving negative feedback, consider which things the individual can fix, and which are out of his or her control. Criticizing someone's writing skills and then suggesting that the person take a writing course focuses on behaviour that can be controlled. Criticizing someone for not sending an important email when the company's network was down is not likely a situation the individual can fix or control.

Communication Skills for Receivers

Senders also receive messages, and thus they must possess or develop communication skills that allow them to be effective receivers of messages. Table 12.2 summarizes three of these important skills, which we examine in greater detail.

Pay Attention

When individuals are overloaded and forced to think about several things at once, they sometimes do not pay sufficient attention to the messages they receive. To be effective, however, individuals should always pay attention to messages they receive, no matter how busy they are. For example, when discussing a project with a subordinate, an effective manager focuses on the project and not on an upcoming meeting with his or her own boss. Similarly, when individuals are reading written forms of communication, they should focus their attention on understanding what they are reading and not be sidetracked into thinking about other issues.

TABLE 12.2 | ***Three Communication Skills for Managers as Receivers of Messages***

- Pay attention
- Be a good listener
- Be empathetic

Be a Good Listener

Part of being a good communicator is being a good listener. This is an essential communication skill for all organizational members. Being a good listener is surprisingly more difficult than you might realize, however. The average person speaks at a rate of 125 to 200 words per minute, but the average listener can effectively process up to 400 words per minute. Therefore listeners are often thinking about other things at the same time that a person is speaking.

It is important to engage in active listening, which requires paying attention, interpreting, and remembering what was said. Active listening requires making a conscious effort to hear what a person is saying, and interpreting it to see that it makes sense. Being a good listener is an essential communication skill in many different kinds of organizations, from small businesses to large corporations.

Organizational members can practise the following behaviours to become active listeners:[27]

1. *Make eye contact.* Eye contact lets the speaker know that you are paying attention, and it also lets you pick up nonverbal cues.
2. *Exhibit affirmative head nods and appropriate facial expressions.* By nodding your head and making appropriate facial expressions, you further show the speaker that you are listening.
3. *Avoid distracting actions or gestures.* Do not look at your watch, shuffle papers, play with your pencil, or engage in similar distractions when you are listening to someone talk. These actions suggest to the speaker that you are bored or uninterested. The actions also mean that you probably are not paying full attention to what is being said.
4. *Ask questions.* The critical listener analyzes what he or she hears, and asks questions. Asking questions provides clarification, and reduces ambiguity, leading to greater understanding. It also assures the speaker that you are listening.
5. *Paraphrase.* Paraphrasing means restating in your own words what the speaker has said. The effective listener uses such phrases as "What I hear you saying is . . ." or "Do you mean . . . ?" Paraphrasing is a check on whether you are listening carefully and accurately.
6. *Avoid interrupting the speaker.* Interruptions can cause the speaker to lose his or her train of thought and cause the listener to jump to wrong conclusions based on incomplete information.
7. *Don't overtalk.* Most of us prefer talking to listening. However, a good listener knows the importance of taking turns in a conversation.
8. *Make smooth transitions between the roles of speaker and listener.* The effective listener knows how to make the transition from listener to speaker roles, and then back to being a listener. It's important to listen rather than plan what you are going to say next.

Be Empathetic

Receivers are empathetic when they try to understand how the sender feels and try to interpret a message from the sender's perspective, rather than viewing a message from only their own point of view.

Understanding Linguistic Styles

Deborah Tannen, who has written a number of books on communication, describes **linguistic style** as a person's characteristic way of speaking. Elements of linguistic style include tone of voice, speed, volume, use of pauses, directness or indirectness, choice of words, credit-taking, and use of questions, jokes, and other manners of speech.[28] When people's linguistic styles differ and these differences are not understood, ineffective

linguistic style
A person's characteristic way of speaking.

communication is likely. Differences in linguistic style can cause problems because linguistic style is often taken for granted. People rarely think about their own linguistic styles and often are unaware of how linguistic styles can differ. Communication between men and women can be affected by differences in linguistic style, as can communication cross-culturally.

Gender Differences

Deborah Tannen
www.georgetown.edu/
faculty/tannend/

Research conducted by Tannen and other linguists indicates that the linguistic styles of men and women differ in practically every culture and language.[29] Men and women take their own linguistic styles for granted and thus do not realize when they are talking with someone of the opposite sex that gender differences in style may lead to ineffective communication.

In Canada and the United States, women tend to downplay differences between people, are not overly concerned about receiving credit for their own accomplishments, and want to make everyone feel more or less on an equal footing so that even poor performers or low-status individuals feel valued. They are less likely to criticize poor performance, as a result. Men, in contrast, tend to emphasize their own superiority and are not reluctant to acknowledge differences in status or differences in performance.[30]

Do some women try to prove that they are better than everyone else, and are some men unconcerned about taking credit for ideas and accomplishments? Of course. The gender differences in linguistic style that Tannen and other linguists have uncovered are general tendencies evident in many women and men but not in all women and men.

Where do gender differences in linguistic style come from? Tannen suggests that they develop from early childhood on. Girls and boys tend to play with children of their own gender, and the ways in which girls and boys play are quite different. Girls play in small groups, engage in a lot of close conversation, emphasize how similar they are to each other, and view boastfulness negatively. Boys play in large groups, emphasize status differences, expect leaders to emerge who boss others around, and give each other challenges to try to meet. These differences in styles of play and interaction result in differences in linguistic styles when boys and girls grow up and communicate as adults. The ways in which men communicate emphasize status differences and play up relative strengths, while the ways in which women communicate emphasize similarities and downplay individual strengths.[31]

Cross-Cultural Differences

Managers from Japan tend to be more formal in their conversations and more deferential toward upper-level managers and people with high status than are managers from Canada. Japanese managers do not mind extensive pauses in conversations when they are thinking things through or when they think that further conversation might be detrimental. Canadian managers, in contrast, find very lengthy pauses disconcerting and feel obligated to talk to fill the silence.[32]

Another cross-cultural difference in linguistic style concerns the appropriate physical distance separating speakers and listeners in business-oriented conversations.[33] The distance between speakers and listeners is greater in Canada, for example, than it is in Brazil or Saudi Arabia. Citizens of different countries also vary in how direct or indirect they are in conversations and in the extent to which they take individual credit for accomplishments. Japanese culture, with its collectivist or group orientation, tends to encourage linguistic styles in which group rather than individual accomplishments are emphasized. The opposite tends to be true in the United States, where Americans proudly reel off their accomplishments.

These and other cross-cultural differences in linguistic style can and often do lead to misunderstandings. Communication misunderstandings and problems can be overcome

Differences in linguistic style may come from early childhood, when girls and boys are inclined to play with members of their own sex. Girls tend to play in small groups, noting how they are similar to each other. Boys tend to emphasize status differences, challenging each other and relying on a leader to emerge.

if managers make themselves familiar with cross-cultural differences in linguistic styles. Before managers communicate with people from abroad, they should try to find out as much as they can about the aspects of linguistic style that are specific to the country or culture in question. Expatriate managers who have lived in the country in question for an extended period of time can be good sources of information about linguistic styles because they are likely to have experienced first-hand some of the differences that citizens of a country are not aware of. Finding out as much as possible about cultural differences also can help managers learn about differences in linguistic styles, for the two are often closely linked.

Managing Differences in Linguistic Styles

Managers should not expect to change people's linguistic styles and should not try to. Instead, to be effective, managers need to understand differences in linguistic styles. Knowing that some individuals are slower to speak up, or that they wait for cues to jump into a conversation, managers can be more proactive about inviting quiet members to speak up. As Tannen points out, "Talk is the lifeblood of managerial work, and understanding that different people have different ways of saying what they mean will make it possible to take advantage of the talents of people with a broad range of linguistic styles."[34]

 Tips for Managers

SENDING AND RECEIVING MESSAGES

1. Symbolically encode your message well so that the other person will be as receptive as possible to the meaning you wish to convey.

2. Create a culture of trust in your organization to foster effective communication.

3. Learn to be a good listener. Effective listeners *attend* to what the other person is communicating.

4. Be sensitive to the various multicultural ways that people in your organization communicate their messages.[35]

Organizational Conflict

THINK ABOUT IT

Conflict, Toxic Organizations, and Morale

Think you have the boss from hell? Consider the American manager who kept goldfish and piranhas in his office—in separate tanks, naturally. Each employee had to pick a goldfish, name it, feed it and generally, be responsible for its welfare. Whenever staff members screwed up, the boss would march all his underlings into his office. In a bizarre ceremony, the bungler would step forward, be directed to remove his or her goldfish, and to feed it to the piranhas. Take that, Donald Trump.[36]

Companies often promote managers who may have technical expertise but whose people skills come from the Saddam Hussein school of management. Screaming matches, tears, sudden heart attacks and other stress-related illnesses are overlooked, blamed on anything but the organization, or written off as the cost of doing business.[37]

Unresolved conflict in the workplace can take a deadly toll on an organization. Gallop Research estimates that US worker disengagement costs US corporations $350B a year.[38] The cost of emotional pain does not show up on the corporate financial statements. If it is mishandled or ignored, it turns toxic, producing a legacy of poor morale and chronic underperformance, says the late Dr. Peter J. Frost (1939–2004), a University of British Columbia commerce professor, who conducted an in-depth study of the phenomenon. The study led to his recently published book, *Toxic Emotions at Work: How Compassionate Managers Handle Pain and Conflict.[39]* His book is an effectively delivered business case for creating compassionate organizations. There is a direct link between "organizational toxicity and red ink on the balance sheet."

According to Dr. Frost, if an organization, with its unresolved conflicts, keeps taking away employee confidence, or self-esteem, then there will be a negative impact over time. "People can't do their best work when they are hurting." The usual entry points for conflict are often downsizings, mergers or a change in leadership, job stress, and real or perceived abuse of employees by employers. As we saw in the previous *Think About It* scenario on "C-Suite Coaching and Executives," when CEO disease is present, there is also the absence of any corrective feedback to leaders. The underlying conflicts that he/she does not want to be aware of, or refuse to have anything to do with, turn office behaviour emotionally toxic. Sadly, but ironically, "when the people around them fail to tell leaders how they affect people, it only reinforces the sense of certainty and control they already feel."

You Be the Manager

1. How can organizations manage conflict more effectively?
2. What is your worst experience of workplace conflict?

---

organizational conflict
The discord that arises when the goals, interest, or values of different individuals or groups are incompatible and those individuals or groups block or thwart each other's attempts to achieve their objectives.

Organizational conflict often arises as the result of communication breakdowns among individuals or units. **Organizational conflict** is the discord that arises when the goals, interests, or values of different individuals or groups are incompatible and those individuals or groups block or thwart each other's attempts to achieve their objectives.[40] Conflict is an inevitable part of organizational life because the goals of different stakeholders such as managers and workers are often incompatible. Organizational conflict also can exist between departments and divisions that compete for resources or even between managers who may be competing for promotion to the next level in the organizational hierarchy.

Though many people dislike conflict, it is not always dysfunctional. Too little conflict can be as bad as too much conflict, but a medium level of conflict can encourage a variety of perspectives that improve organizational functioning and effectiveness and help decision making. Conflict is a force that needs to be managed rather than eliminated.[41] Managers should never try to eliminate all conflict but rather should try to keep conflict at a moderate and functional level to promote change efforts that benefit the organization. To manage conflict, one should understand the types and sources of conflict and to be familiar with certain strategies that can be effective in dealing with it.

Conflict Management Strategies

Organizational conflict can happen between individuals, within a group or department, between groups or departments, or even across organizations. Conflict can arise for a variety of reasons. Within organizations conflict occurs for such reasons as incompatible goals and time horizons, overlapping authority, task interdependencies, incompatible evaluation or reward systems, scarce resources, and status inconsistencies (see Figure 12.3).[42] Regardless of the source of the conflict, knowing how to handle conflict is an important skill.

The behaviours for handling conflict fall along two dimensions: *cooperativeness* (the degree to which one party tries to satisfy the other party's concerns) and *assertiveness* (the degree to which one party tries to satisfy his or her own concerns).[43] This can be seen in Figure 12.4. From these two dimensions emerge five conflict-handling behaviours:

- *Avoiding.* Withdrawing from conflict.

- *Competing.* One person tries to satisfy his or her own interests, without regard to the interests of the other party.

- *Compromising.* Each party is concerned about its own goal accomplishment and the goal accomplishment of the other party and is willing to engage in a give-and-take exchange and to make concessions until a reasonable resolution of the conflict is reached.

FIGURE 12.3 | *Sources of Conflict in Organizations*

FIGURE 12.4 | *Dimensions of Conflict-Handling Behaviours*

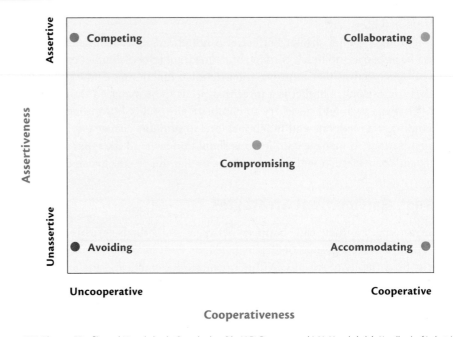

Source: K.W. Thomas, "Conflict and Negotiation in Organizations," in M.D. Dunnette and L.M. Hough (eds.), *Handbook of Industrial Psychology*, 2nd ed., vol. 3 (Palo Alto, CA: Consulting Psychologists Press, 1992), p. 668. Copyright 2001 by Acad. of Mgmt. Reproduced with permission of Acad. of Mgmt. in the format Textbook via Copyright Clearance Center.

- *Accommodating.* One person tries to please the other person by putting the other's interests ahead of his or her own.

- *Collaborating.* The parties to a conflict try to satisfy their goals without making any concessions and instead come up with a way to resolve their differences that leaves them both better off.

When the parties to a conflict are willing to cooperate with each other and devise a solution that each finds acceptable (through compromise or collaboration), an organization is more likely to achieve its goals. One can well imagine, as we saw in the *Think About It* account of the toxic workplace, that employees in such a workplace would end up with a mixture of conflict management strategies, e.g., avoiding, competing, and accommodating.

Conflict management strategies that ensure conflicts are resolved in a functional manner focus on individuals and on the organization as a whole. Below, we describe four strategies that focus on individuals: increasing awareness of the sources of conflict, increasing diversity awareness and skills, practising job rotation or temporary assignments, and using permanent transfers or dismissals when necessary. We also describe two strategies that focus on the organization as a whole: changing an organization's structure or culture, and directly altering the source of conflict.

Strategies Focused on Individuals

INCREASING AWARENESS OF THE SOURCES OF CONFLICT Much conflict arises because individuals are not aware of how differences in linguistic styles, personality, background, and job requirements affect interactions. For example, differences in linguistic styles may lead some men in work teams to talk more, and take more credit for ideas, than women in those teams. These communication differences can result in conflict when the men incorrectly assume that the women are uninterested or less capable because they participate less, and the women incorrectly assume that the men are being bossy and are not interested in their ideas because they seem to do all the talking. Conflict can also arise when co-workers are unaware of the demands of each other's jobs, and place unrealistic expectations on someone to complete a project. When individuals are aware of the source of conflict, they can take steps to interact with each other more effectively. Awareness can be increased through diversity training, open communication, and job rotation or temporary assignments that increase understanding of the work activities and demands that others in an organization face.

USING PERMANENT TRANSFERS OR DISMISSALS Sometimes when other conflict resolution strategies do not work, managers may need to take more drastic steps, including permanent transfers or dismissals.

Suppose two first-line managers who work in the same department are always at each other's throats; frequent bitter conflicts arise between them even though they both seem to get along well with the other people they work with. No matter what their supervisor does to increase their understanding of each other, these conflicts keep occurring. In this case, the supervisor may want to transfer one or both managers so that they do not have to interact as frequently.

When dysfunctionally high levels of conflict occur among top managers who cannot resolve their differences and understand each other, it may be necessary for one of them to leave the company.

Strategies Focused on the Organization

CHANGING STRUCTURE OR CULTURE Conflict can signal the need for changes in an organization's structure or culture. Sometimes, managers can effectively resolve conflict by changing the organizational structure they use to group people and tasks.[44] As an organization grows, for example, the *functional structure* that was effective when the organization was small may no longer be effective, and a shift to a product structure might effectively resolve conflicts (see Chapter 6).

Managers also can effectively resolve conflicts by increasing levels of integration in an organization. When individuals from different departments are assigned to the same team, they can directly resolve issues on the spot, rather than going through departments.

Sometimes managers may need to take steps to change an organization's culture to resolve conflict (see Chapter 7). Norms and values in an organizational culture might inadvertently promote dysfunctionally high levels of conflict that are difficult to resolve. For instance, norms that stress respect for formal authority may create conflict that is difficult to resolve when an organization creates self-managed work teams. Values stressing individual competition may make it difficult to resolve conflicts when organizational members need to put others' interests ahead of their own. In circumstances such as these, taking steps to change norms and values can be an effective conflict resolution strategy.

ALTERING THE SOURCE OF CONFLICT When conflict is due to overlapping authority, status inconsistencies, and incompatible evaluation or reward systems, managers can sometimes effectively resolve the conflict by directly altering the source of conflict—the overlapping authority, the status inconsistency, or the evaluation or reward system. For example, managers can clarify the chain of command and reassign tasks and responsibilities to resolve conflicts due to overlapping authority.

Tips for Managers

HANDLING CONFLICT[45]

1. Use compromise or collaboration as much as you can to resolve conflict.
2. Identify that factors of a conflict that cause you the most difficulty and seek to resolve them.
3. Identify factors that may be contributing to unhealthy workplace conflict.
4. Examine the organizational structure to see if it is causing unnecessary conflict.

Negotiation Strategies

THINK ABOUT IT

Quebec Unions Accused: Taking Public Hostage[46]

In the late summer of 2005, classes were disrupted for 65 000 returning students in 20 junior colleges in Quebec as the province's public-sector unions fired an opening shot in their brewing confrontation over new contracts for 550 000 public and para-public employees with Jean Charest's liberal government. At the time, other strikes were also being planned for grade schools, high schools, daycares, and other public services in Quebec.

In our opening case scenario to this chapter, we read the quote by William H. White, author of *The Organization Man*: "People do not always argue because they misunderstand one another; they argue because they hold different goals."[47] With the Quebec government and the union, the two sides were quite far apart and would have to eventually begin negotiations to settle the matter. The government was offering a 12.6-percent wage hike over six years, including pay equity; the unions were seeking a 12.6-percent increase over three years, without counting pay equity. Turning up the heat, Education Minister Jean-Marc Fournier accused the unions of taking the public "hostage." However, Louis Roy, first vice-president of the Confédération des syndicats nationaux, which had created a common front with the Quebec Federation of Labour, said the government was negotiating in bad faith and trying to get them to accept rollbacks in their working conditions. "Taking the public hostage? They should go to Iraq to see what a hostage taking looks like."

You Be the Manager

1. What negotiation strategies would you propose for the above conflict?

negotiation
A method of conflict resolution in which the parties in conflict consider various alternative ways to allocate resources to each other in order to come up with a solution acceptable to them all.

distributive negotiation
Adversarial negotiation in which the parties in conflict compete to win the most resources while conceding as little as possible.

A particularly important conflict resolution technique for managers and other organizational members to use in situations in which the parties to a conflict have approximately equal levels of power is negotiation. During **negotiation**, the parties to a conflict try to come up with a solution acceptable to themselves by considering various alternative ways to allocate resources to each other.[48]

There are two major types of negotiation—distributive negotiation and integrative bargaining.[49] In **distributive negotiation**, the parties perceive that they have a "fixed pie" of resources that they need to divide up.[50] They take a competitive, adversarial stance. Each party realizes that he or she must concede something but is out to get the lion's share of resources.[51] The parties see no need to interact with each other in the future and do not care if their interpersonal relationship is damaged or destroyed by their competitive negotiations.[52] To some extent, this is the stance that the BC Nurses' Union and hospital administrators have taken with each other.

In **integrative bargaining**, the parties perceive that they might be able to increase the resource pie by trying to come up with a creative solution to the conflict. They do not view the conflict competitively, as a win-or-lose situation; instead, they view it cooperatively, as a win-win situation in which all parties can gain. Integrative bargaining is characterized by trust, information sharing, and the desire of all parties to achieve a good resolution of the conflict.[53] For the BC Nurses' Union and the hospital administrators to show a commitment to integrative bargaining, each side would need to figure out ways to address some of the needs of the other, rather than simply taking an adversarial position.

There are five strategies that individuals can rely on to increase the odds of a win-win solution:[54]

- *Emphasize the big-picture goals.* This reminds individuals that they are working together for a larger purpose or goal despite their disagreements.

- *Focus on the problem, not the people.* All parties to a conflict need to keep focused on the source of the conflict and avoid the temptation to discredit each other by personalizing the conflict.

- *Focus on interests, not demands.* Demands are what a person wants, and interests are why the person wants them. When two people are in conflict, it is unlikely that the demands of both can be met. Their underlying interests often can be met, creating a win-win solution.

- *Create new options for joint gain.* Rather than having a fixed set of alternatives from which to choose, the parties can come up with new alternatives that might even expand the resource pie.

- *Focus on what is fair.* Emphasizing fairness will help the parties come to a mutual agreement about what is the best solution to the problem.

Any and all of these strategies would help the BC Nurses' Union and the hospital administrators negotiate with each other more effectively. When managers pursue these five strategies and encourage other organizational members to do so, they are more likely to resolve their conflicts effectively, through integrative bargaining. In addition, throughout the negotiation process, managers and other organizational members need to be aware of, and on their guard against, the biases that can lead to faulty decision making (see Chapter 4).[55]

Collective Bargaining

Collective bargaining is negotiation between labour unions and managers to resolve conflicts and disputes about important issues such as working hours, wages, benefits, working conditions, and job security. Before sitting down with management to negotiate, union members sometimes go on strike to drive home their concerns to managers. Once an agreement that union members support has been reached (sometimes with the help of a neutral third party called a *mediator*), union leaders and managers sign a contract spelling out the terms of the collective bargaining agreement.

Collective bargaining is an ongoing consideration in labour relations. The signing of a contract, for example, does not bring collective bargaining to a halt. Disagreement and conflicts can arise over the interpretation of the contract. In these cases, a neutral

integrative bargaining
Cooperative negotiation in which the parties in conflict work together to achieve a resolution that is good for them all.

British Columbia Nurses' Union (BCNU)
www.bcnu.org

collective bargaining
Negotiation between labour unions and managers to resolve conflicts and disputes about issues such as working hours, wages, benefits, working conditions, and job security.

third party known as an *arbitrator* is usually called in to resolve the conflict. An important component of a collective bargaining agreement is a *grievance procedure* through which workers who feel they are not being fairly treated are allowed to voice their concerns and have their interests represented by the union. Employees who feel they were unjustly fired in violation of a union contract, for example, may file a grievance, have the union represent them, and get their jobs back if an arbitrator agrees with them.

 Tips for Managers

NEGOTIATION[56]

1. Separate the people in the conflict negotiation from the problem.
2. Negotiate about interests, not positions, which parties cling to.
3. Invent options for mutual gain, and be mutually creative.
4. Insist on objective decision criteria.
5. Know your BATNA (best alternative to a negotiated agreement).

You Be the Manager

1. What do you feel would be your most effective negotiation strategy? Why?
2. When did you use such a negotiation strategy effectively?

Summary and Review

1. **COMMUNICATION IN ORGANIZATIONS** Communication is the sharing of information between two or more individuals or groups to reach a common understanding. Good communication is necessary for an organization to gain a competitive advantage. Communication takes place in a cyclical process that has two phases: *transmission* and *feedback.*

2. **INFORMATION RICHNESS AND COMMUNICATION MEDIA** Information richness is the amount of information a communication medium can carry and the extent to which the medium enables the sender and receiver to reach a common understanding. Four categories of communication media in descending order of information richness are *face-to-face communication* (includes videoconferences), *spoken communication electronically transmitted* (includes voice mail), *personally addressed written communication* (includes email), and *impersonal written communication.*

3. **DEVELOPING COMMUNICATION SKILLS** There are various barriers to effective communication in organizations. To overcome these barriers and effectively communicate with others, individuals must possess or develop certain communication skills. As senders of messages, individuals should send messages that are clear and complete, encode messages in symbols the receiver understands, choose a medium that is appropriate for the message and monitored by the receiver, avoid filtering and information distortion, include a feedback mechanism in the message, and provide accurate information to ensure that misleading rumours are not spread. Communication skills for individuals as receivers of messages include paying *attention*, being a *good listener*, and being *empathetic.* Understanding linguistic styles is also an essential communication skill. Linguistic styles can vary by geographic region, gender, and country or culture. When these differences are not understood, ineffective communication can occur.

4. **ORGANIZATIONAL CONFLICT** Organizational conflict is the discord that arises when the goals, interests, or values of different individuals or groups clash, and those individuals or groups block or thwart each other's attempts to achieve their objectives.

5. **CONFLICT MANAGEMENT STRATEGIES** Conflict management strategies focused on individuals include increasing awareness of the sources of conflict, increasing diversity awareness and skills, practising job rotation or temporary assignments, and using permanent transfers or dismissals when necessary. Strategies focused on the whole organization include changing an organization's structure or culture and altering the source of conflict.

6. **NEGOTIATION STRATEGIES** Negotiation is a conflict resolution technique used when parties to a conflict have approximately equal levels of power and try to come up with an acceptable way to allocate resources to each other. In *distributive negotiation*, the parties perceive that there is a fixed level of resources for them to allocate, and each competes to receive as much as possible at the expense of the others, not caring about their relationship in the future. In *integrative bargaining*, the parties perceive that they may be able to increase the resource pie by coming up with a creative solution to the conflict, trusting each other, and cooperating with each other to achieve a win-win resolution. Five strategies that managers can use to facilitate integrative bargaining are to emphasize big-picture goals; focus on the problem, not the people; focus on interests, not demands; create new options for joint gain; and focus on what is fair. *Collective bargaining* is the process through which labour unions and managers resolve conflicts and disputes and negotiate agreements.

Key Terms

collective bargaining, p. 357

communication, p. 338

decoding, p. 338

distributive negotiation, p. 356

encoding, p. 338

filtering, p. 347

information distortion, p. 347

information richness, p. 341

integrative bargaining, p. 357

jargon, p. 346

linguistic style, p. 349

medium, p. 338

message, p. 338

negotiation, p. 356

noise, p. 338

non-verbal communication, p. 339

organizational conflict, p. 352

perception, p. 340

receiver, p. 338

rumours, p. 347

sender, p. 338

verbal communication, p. 339

SO WHERE DO YOU STAND?

Wrap-Up to Opening Case

We began this chapter with a quote highlighting the fact that people argue because they hold different goals. This obvious and human reality, therefore, means that we must learn how to communicate effectively and use effec-tive negotiation techniques to navigate any goal discrep-ancies. We saw also that senior executives and managers realize more and more that they must interact more dynamically with staff and employees so that a mutuality of trust—a trust culture—can be fostered and developed. It is within such a context of trust and effective communications that employees not only succeed personally, but the organization does as well. The Hudson's Bay Company (HBC) did precisely this when it forced its big technology suppliers to cooperate and collaborate with its Strategic Technology Alliance. The result? More money for them, and better solutions for the retailer. HBC promised the Alliance certain chunks of its business, provided, as CIO Gary Davenport, put it, they "stop trying to fleece the customer, stop competing with each other and start working together—really collaborating—for the good of all."[57]

We saw also that what was considered a "soft skill" is now, more and more, seen as very "hard." Soft is hard, in other words. The example of Andrew Grant working with community relations in South America for his mining company more than proves this point. Community relations and good communication skills are critical in getting the job done well.

Thus, what is needed today, as work specialist Dr. Graham Lowe reminded us, is "not change management but change leadership." It is not the same processes that need to be upgraded, but the whole change vision. Managers today must not only communicate, but be perceived to be communicating effectively. We saw also that there is plenty of professional help with coaches and mentors that can help with this task should the manager need additional help. Sharing information in friendly, candid, and informative ways through personal newsletters as well as in face-to-face communication can strengthen the communication linkages and morale with employees and staff. As well, we learned that managers must seek regular feedback to minimize unanticipated negative consequences to their decision making or communications.

Such positive efforts at communication, negotiations, and conflict resolution will more than pay dividends with more productive workplaces.

After studying the preceding material, be sure to check out our Online Learning Centre at
www.mcgrawhill.ca/olc/jones
for more in-depth information and interactivities that correspond to this chapter.

Management in Action

Topics for Discussion and Action

1. Interview a manager in an organization in your community to determine with whom he or she communicates on a typical day and what communication media he or she use.
2. Which medium (or media) do you think would be appropriate for each of the following kinds of messages that a subordinate could receive from his or her manager: messages about (a) a raise, (b) not receiving a promotion, (c) an error in a report prepared by the subordinate, (d) additional job responsibilities, and (e) the schedule for company holidays for the upcoming year? Explain your choices.
3. Why do some managers find it difficult to be good listeners?
4. Explain why subordinates might filter and distort information about problems and performance shortfalls when communicating with their managers.
5. Explain why differences in linguistic style, when not understood by senders and receivers of messages, can lead to ineffective communication.
6. Discuss why too little conflict in an organization can be just as detrimental as too much conflict.
7. Interview a manager in a local organization to determine the kinds of conflicts that occur in that manager's organization and the strategies that are used to manage them.
8. Why is integrative bargaining a more effective way of resolving conflicts than distributive negotiation?

Building Management Skills

DIAGNOSING INEFFECTIVE COMMUNICATION

Think about the last time you experienced very ineffective communication with another person—someone you work with, a classmate, a friend, or a member of your family. Describe the incident. Then answer the following questions.

1. Why was your communication ineffective in this incident?
2. What stages of the communication process were particularly problematic and why?
3. Describe any filtering or information distortion that occurred.
4. Do you think differences in linguistic styles adversely affected the communication that took place? Why or why not?
5. How could you have handled this situation differently so that communication would have been effective?
6. Are there conflict management strategies or bargaining strategies you could have used to improve the communication?

Management for You

Consider a person with whom you have had difficulty communicating. Using the communication skills for senders as a start, analyze what has gone wrong with the communication process with that person. What can be done to improve communication? To what extent did sender and receiver problems contribute to the communication breakdown?

Small Group Breakout Exercise

NEGOTIATING A SOLUTION

Form groups of three or four people. One member of your group will play the role of Jane Rister, one member will play the role of Michael Schwartz, and one or two members will be observer(s) and spokesperson(s) for your group.

Jane Rister and Michael Schwartz are assistant managers in a large department store. They report directly to the store manager. Today they are meeting to discuss important problems that they need to solve but on which they disagree.

The first problem hinges on the fact that either Rister or Schwartz needs to be on duty whenever the store is open. For the last six months, Rister has taken most of the least desirable hours (nights and weekends). They are planning their schedules for the next six months. Rister hoped Schwartz would take more of the undesirable times, but Schwartz has informed Rister that his wife has just started a nursing job that requires her to work weekends, so he needs to stay home on weekends to take care of their infant daughter.

The second problem concerns a department manager who has had a hard time retaining sales-people in his department. The turnover rate in his department is twice that of the other depart-ments in the store. Rister thinks the manager is ineffective and wants to fire him. Schwartz thinks the high turnover is a fluke and the manager is effective.

The last problem concerns Rister's and Schwartz's vacation schedules. Both managers want to take off the week of July 1, but one of them needs to be in the store whenever it is open.

1. The group members playing Rister and Schwartz assume their roles and negotiate a solution to these three problems.
2. Observers take notes on how Rister and Schwartz negotiate solutions to their problems.
3. Observers determine the extent to which Rister and Schwartz use distributive negotiation or integrative bargaining to resolve their conflicts.

4. When called on by the instructor, observers communicate to the rest of the class how Rister and Schwartz resolved their conflicts, whether they used distributive negotiation or integrative bargaining, and their actual solutions.

Managing Ethically

About 75 percent of medium and large companies that were surveyed engaged in some kind of monitoring of employees' email and Internet activities. Critics say this is an invasion of privacy. Proponents say that Web surfing costs millions of dollars in lost productivity. What is your opinion of Web surfing? To what extent should it be allowed? When does Internet use at work become unethical? To what extent should it be monitored? When does monitoring become unethical?

Exploring the World Wide Web

SPECIFIC ASSIGNMENT

Many companies use the World Wide Web to communicate with prospective employees, including Ford Motor Company of Canada, Ltd. Scan the Ford website (www.ford.ca) to learn more about this company and the kinds of information it communicates to prospective employees through its website. Then click on "More About Ford" and "Career Centre." Click on the various selections in this location of the website, such as "Ford in Canada," "Career Starting Points," "Empowerment, Diversity, Teamwork," and "Sharing in the Rewards."

1. What kinds of information does Ford communicate to prospective employees through its website?
2. How might providing this information on the Web help Ford Canada attract new employees?

GENERAL ASSIGNMENT

Find the website of a company that you know very little about. Scan the website of this company. Do you think it effectively communicates important information about the company? Why or why not?

Can you think of anything that customers or prospective employees might want to see on the website that is not currently there? Is there anything on the website that you think should not be there?

Developing a Business Plan

(APPENDIX B, PAGE 405)

Go to www.mcgrawhill.ca/olc/jones/12 for online exercises.

Be the Manager

THE "PERSONAL TOUCH"[58]

As a communications expert, you have just read that research shows that friendlier workers are more productive. You found this very interesting because you will shortly be consulting to a company that wants to make its workplace a friendlier place to work. Until now this company has felt that it was more professional to stay impersonal at work, but in fact research is showing that friendlier employees are more productive. A comparison of the American work ethic to approaches in other countries shows that keeping an emotional distance may not be the most effective way to get the job done. Friendly workers pay attention to indirect meanings, work well with other cultures, and are perceived as trustworthy, the research found.

An impersonal style tends to restrict the bandwidth of information a person attends to in the workplace. What is literally said will be followed closely but information about the context in which the information is conveyed—information often critical for task success and productivity—is lost. This impersonal attitude at work is rooted in Protestant beliefs of putting emotion aside at the office. The American style of keeping things impersonal at the workplace is virtually confined to the United States. Workers in South Korea, Japan and India and especially Latin American countries place high importance on personal relationships at work. Latin Americans become friends with people they are doing business with first and then move onto the work while Americans work first and then become friends.

Question

1. How will you integrate this research so that you can provide the client the best communications expertise you have?

Video Management Case

Money and Ethics

In terms of business and ethics; the Arthur Anderson tapes of the 90s, which instructed on values and urged companies to be held to a high moral standard demonstrate the value of the ethical message. That this group was later found to be featuring speakers as well as themselves who were guilty of participating in the very activities they preached against, highlights that the cost of being ethical as at odds with companies communicating honestly with their employees.

Questions to Consider

1. How might employees react to the discovery that their "big boss" was using company funds for personal gain?
2. How can ethics be communicated in a format that is not pedagogical; that is, demonstrating a code of moral behaviour instead of instructing it?

Part 5: Integrated Case ▪

On World Stage: CEO in Waiting[59]

[The following is a discussion between Karl Moore, Ph.D., associate professor at McGill University's Desautels Faculty of Management and co-director of McGill's advanced leadership program and Pierre Beaudoin, executive vice-president of Bombardier Inc., president and chief operating officer of Bombardier's aerospace division, and the son and heir apparent of Bombardier chairman and chief executive officer Laurent Beaudoin. In the interview he reflects on the challenges and rewards of leading a family controlled business on the world stage.]

Karl Moore: When did you first realize you are a leader?

Pierre Beaudoin: If you look at how you behave in team sports, I would say you generally tend to lead the pack from the beginning. But I was never somebody who would impose myself. If it was just a game for a half hour, I would let others do that, but if we stayed around for two or three days, I would become the leader.

KM: It would naturally arise over a bit of time.

PB: It would naturally arise and I would feel comfortable in that way, and that is very much the way I lead today.

KM: Have you always seen yourself as a leader and known that you wanted to be in charge of a company at some point?

PB: I grew up in a family that talked about business all the time, so business always interested me. The challenge of creating something and being able to work with people to accomplish a commercial transaction was always interesting for me, and I guess I developed the taste for this through time.

KM: Your dad is a great entrepreneur. Do you see yourself as a great manager or entrepreneur?

PB: Somewhere in-between. My father [Laurent] is a great entrepreneur who has essentially built a business from $10 million in sales to where we are today. I have been part of a large enterprise my entire career, so I think I've got a good understanding of how you start a business. But, I spend more time managing teams and the politics of a large enterprise. I see myself as a manager.

KM: Everybody knows you are a Beaudoin…. How do you deal with the fact that everybody knows who you are and, especially as a younger person, it may have given you an unfair advantage?

PB: That is one of the great heritages of my father. He has never been somebody who takes advantage of that or is pretentious because he is a Beaudoin. He is a very simple guy, very close to the people he works with.

He is himself all the time. I've learned that from him, so I have never felt the disadvantage or advantage.

KM: Has your relationship with your father changed since being at Bombardier?

PB: We have a very good relationship. It's hard for me to appreciate where it would be if I didn't work at Bombardier. But I think I was fortunate that I did not work for him early on. It's actually the first time I've directly worked for him. I'm saying that in a very positive way because, you know, as you grow as a young manager, you are going to do good things and less good things. It's hard for your father to challenge you and it's also hard for the recipient to accept it. So I did not have to deal with large conflicts directly with my father. I have worked with other leaders outside of Bombardier. So having to work for him directly now is fun because I know his strengths and he's seen me in the last 20 years. I can see him as somebody with great experience that I respect and can work with.

KM: One of the criticisms made of Bombardier is that it is family controlled and some people are critical of that. What are the advantages of being a family controlled firm?

PB: I find it interesting because when people are critical of that, I guess they don't spend much time looking at facts because the most profitable companies in the US are generally family controlled. The advantage: a long-term view of the business; the dedication you will have because you have your name on the door; and… you are going to be committed to the long-term success—not only for financial reasons but it is also how you define yourself because your name is on the door.

KM: Why do you enjoy leading a large organization?

PB: What I enjoy is the intellectual challenge of being part of a world leader like Bombardier and making a complex product, making all of this come together to accomplish a transaction, to grow your enterprise, to develop a business where you will be able to play on the planet and make a difference with what you do. You've got to think about it when you are in business, because it can be about just the profit… We play on the planet and I think that is what I enjoy the most.

KM: Why has Bombardier been successful?

PB: I think the spirit you will see at Bombardier. We always thought that everything's possible. With Laurent, we never started with saying it can't be done, we'd say: "why not?" So, when we got in trouble in snowmobiles because the industry went down, we started looking at things and there was a contract to build mass transit, so we bid on it because we said: "Well, it's mechanical, we know how to bend metal, so to say, and I think we can do that." So, we had always a large dream and, when we got into aerospace, a lot of people told us it couldn't be done, but we never allowed ourselves to limit the possibilities that we have, limit our dreams if you want.

KM: Do you see leaders as made or born?

PB: A little bit of both. You have to have some leadership aptitude or trait but they are very different from one person to the other and I think, generally, we sometimes pay too much attention to the person who makes a lot of noise and displaces a lot of air. I don't think leadership is about egos and there are, unfortunately, too many leaders where it is about them and I don't think that is the trait of a good leader. That's why it's not always the obvious person for me who is the leader of the group.

KM: How do you develop leaders at Bombardier?

PB: We talk a lot about our people's strengths and weakness, so we have good detailed reviews of who shows aptitude and then we give them a challenge, a smaller challenge to start, then we enlarge the challenges. We try also to enlarge their ability from engineering to going into marketing or other trades, although I must say that we don't do that as well as we should because it is always challenging to see a good engineer as a guy who has got potential in marketing. If you look at what I would like us to do more, that would be part of that.

KM: Quebec seems to produce more entrepreneurs who have done well compared with the rest of the country. Why is it that Quebec is particularly strong?

PB: In Quebec, we value people like my grandfather [Joseph-Armand Bombardier] who went after putting together a little business… We used to call that *patenteux*—putting things together, people who are very good with their hands.

KM: Tinkerers.

PB: Yes. We value that very much. So there are a lot of tinkerers who ended up turning that tinkering into business.

KM: How has your management style changed over the years?

PB: Now, I spend a lot more time managing people and objectives and challenging them…and, 20 years ago, I was very much hands-on in the day-to-day work. Learning to evolve that way to get involved enough, but not too much, and at the same time giving liberty to people to execute [and] accepting mistakes because they will do it differently than you…. That is the challenging part, which I am continuing to learn.

KM: I remember someone telling me a story of how you were out on a boat not long ago in Florida with a friend and you were going at a really high speed and an anchor fell out and the story is that you are a very calm sort of person and the other person was a bit nervous. What's in you that you like to be a bit on the edge?

PB: It's a little bit part of the character [when] you have to have to deal with what we deal with all the time. There are always many balls in the air, many risks you take, so when you deal with risk in your professional life, you enjoy some kind of risk in your personal life. I wouldn't say that I'm extreme in sports, but I like to take risks.

KM: You like high speed.

PB: I like high speed, yes.

KM: But it's not extreme. It's not bungee jumping.

PB: Right, exactly. I enjoy that, of course. Motorized product is a little more than just "I like speed." I grew up with those types of products. It's not only a professional, personal like; it was a part of my life for so many years.

KM: Do you turn [your BlackBerry] off on weekends?

PB: Yes I turn it off. But I go and take a peek once in a while.

KM: How do you keep the balance with your family life?

PB: I pretend that I keep a balance, but I try to keep weekends for the family and I do a lot of different sports with my kids. Now, I am starting to have a hard time following them as they are teenagers, but we do all those sports together and I think quality time with my family but not much time.

KM: I guess it's tough to be a leader at the level you are at and go home at five o'clock.

PB: Yeah, that's true, although I must say I try to keep a discipline, but maybe if you ask my wife she might have a slightly different answer…. I'm at the office at 8. I want to see my kids in the morning before they go to school, so it's really an 8 to 7 type of day when I'm not travelling.

KM: Some people would see a 14-hour day, as you often experience when you are travelling, as just burdensome. But you don't seem burdened, you seem happy.

PB: We enjoy what we do. If you are in a job like mine and you don't enjoy it, you've got to think of something else because it's your life; it is part of what you do. It never leaves you…. But I don't want to let it take over my life. I'm going to do this until I don't like doing this. If it is not fun any more, I will do something else.

Discussion Questions

1. What are some of the leadership challenges that Pierre Beaudoin faces as he looks to take over Bombardier eventually?

2. Describe Beaudoin's philosophy of teamwork?

3. Why does Beaudoin consider himself so fortunate to have worked with his father?

4. According to Beaudoin, what are some motivating factors in working for a family-controlled business?

CHAPTER

13

Organizational Control

Learning Outcomes

1. Define organizational control, and describe the four steps of the control process.

2. Identify the main output controls, and discuss their advantages and disadvantages as means of coordinating and motivating employees.

3. Identify the main behaviour controls, and discuss their advantages and disadvantages as means of coordinating and motivating employees.

4. Explain how culture can control managerial behaviour.

Control, On-the-Job Massages, and Boardroom Yoga![1]

Paul Madden has an unusual problem. As the owner of The Spa at the Monastery in St. John's,[2] his business has grown by over 350 percent a year over the past four years. He has expanded his facility's space to 25 500 square feet from about 10 000 square feet and he's now contemplating construction of an entirely new spa on the Atlantic coast outside the city.

His dilemma?

"Everyone talks about stress and we've offered stress release spa packages from the start," he explains. "But the thing is no one wants to spend the time. Everyone wants express service, they want to relax in 15 minutes and move on to the next thing."

Eli Bay, founder of the Relaxation Response Institute in Toronto,[3] where he has been teaching stress management skills for 25 years, shares that frustration. "It's a Type A culture focused on performance and doing. People are reluctant to admit that they suffer from stress. It's perceived as weak," he says. "They might accept exercise because it's active and high-octane. But dealing with it through breathing, meditation, or just being aren't really valid."

The two men are part of one of the most dynamic growth sectors in the modern economy: stress. Certainly the costs of the problem are well-documented. According to Statistics Canada the annual cost to the economy is about $12 billion.

Stress as a reason for employee absenteeism has increased 316 percent in the past decade. About 40 percent of job turnover and 60 percent to 80 percent of on-the-job accidents are stress-related. Stress and emotional burnout were cited as among the main reasons for Canada's United Church clergy to form a union under the auspices of the Canadian Autoworker's union. In addition to having a negative impact on productivity and morale, workplace stress carries a hefty tab for benefit costs, specifically prescription drug plans.

"Stress is a very individual thing. People respond very differently to the same external factors," says Gabor Maté, a Vancouver-based physician and author of the book *When The Body Says No: The Hidden Cost of Stress.*[4] "But whatever triggers the stress, it has a real physical effect on the hormonal and nervous systems."

He adds that there are three principal causes of stress: conflict that people can't handle; loss of control; uncertainty and lack of information.

"Work pretty much ignites all three of those causes. But while a strong emotional connection with others can mitigate the impact of the stress response, that's exactly what's missing in our lives," says Dr. Maté. "We deal more and more with machines, we don't have extended families close by, we don't have community. So as stress reducers diminish, the causes increase."

And that's where the business of stress kicks in—sort of.

Companies now offer employees everything from on-the-job chair massages to employee assistance programs (which provide off-site counselling services for troubled staffers) and boardroom yoga sessions. "Because I worked as a manager before I became a massage therapist, I've got a good grip on stress in the workplace," says

Practising yoga encourages stress release among many business people.

Keith Peck of Upper Canada Corporate Massage in Toronto.[5] "I've focused on corporate work from the outset and it has grown phenomenally in the past five years."

Mr. Peck charges $18 for a 15-minute neck and shoulder massage, spending as much as two days a week at the offices of clients such as insurance company, Kingsway Financial. "We can set up in a boardroom, a lunch room. It's very simple. All you need is a mat and some loose clothes," says Lynn Roberts of Pure Yoga Mobile Studio in Vancouver.[6] "It's very popular because it's not disruptive and it's not expensive." She charges $64 for a one-hour session for up to nine people, $80 for an hour with up to 19 attendees.

Eli Bay's relaxation response classes are also popular with corporate clients including Bell Canada, CIBC, Celestica, Motorola, and American Express. "It's still a hard sell for me despite all the data that's available," Mr. Bay says. "They may invite me in the door but they're more interested in a quick fix, a 'lunch and learn' session, than in the real work." (Mr. Bay charges individual clients $550 for five three-hour sessions, including a workbook, three CDs, and a moneyback guarantee.)

"There's still a lot of lip service to the issue of stress management, especially at the most senior levels," notes Wendy Poirier, a consultant with Towers Perrin in Calgary. "But there is more awareness. Especially since the issue of employee engagement has become so hot. It's being seen as the key to improved productivity." She adds that another reason why companies are starting to pay more attention to employee stress is the growing competition to recruit young, educated talent. "For younger employees, for the ones companies have to retain to compete, it's not about benefits and pensions. It's about work/life balance, about control," Ms. Poirier says. "And that's the new challenge. It's not about an easy tweak of the status quo."

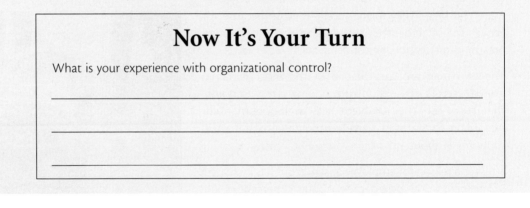

Now It's Your Turn

What is your experience with organizational control?

_____

_____

_____

■■□■ Overview

Organizations are always trying to manage the delicate balance of too much and too little control. As we saw from our opening case, Dr. Gabor Maté reminds us that stress is caused by conflict that people can't handle, loss of control, uncertainty and lack of information. Wendy Poirier, a consultant with Towers Perrin in Calgary, would support Dr. Maté as well, "There's still a lot of lip service to the issue of stress management, especially at the most senior levels. But there is more awareness. Especially since the issue of employee engagement has become so hot. It's being seen as the key to improved productivity."

As discussed in Chapter 6, one major task facing managers is organizing—that is, establishing the structure of task and reporting relationships that allows organizational members to use resources most efficiently and effectively. Structure alone, however, does not provide the incentive or motivation for people to behave in ways that help achieve organizational goals. The purpose of organizational control is to provide managers with a means of motivating subordinates to work toward achieving organizational goals, and to provide managers with specific feedback on how well an organization and its members are performing. Organizational structure provides an organization with a skeleton, for which organizational control and culture provide the muscles, sinews, nerves, and sensations that allow managers to regulate and govern the organization's activities. The managerial functions of organizing and controlling are inseparable, and effective managers must learn to make them work together harmoniously.

In this chapter, we look in detail at the nature of organizational control and describe the steps in the control process. We discuss three types of control available to managers for controlling and influencing organizational members: *output control*, *behaviour control*, and *clan control* (which operates through the values and norms of an organization's culture).[7] By the end of this chapter, you will appreciate the rich variety of control systems available to managers and understand why developing an appropriate control system is vital to increasing the performance of an organization and its members.

What Is Organizational Control?

THINK ABOUT IT

A Husky Solution for Organizational Control[8]

One company that has become a poster child for progressive employee management is Husky Injection Mouldings of Aurora, Ontario. Reflecting the personal values of the company's founder and CEO, Robert Schad, the company has constructed a culture that proactively addresses stress in the workplace. In addition to a 150-child on-site daycare centre, Husky also offers workers a subsidized cafeteria where only healthy foods are served.

Although red meat is not served, chicken, fish, and tofu are available along with a customized salad bar. Herbal teas are free.

Husky also has a wellness centre that employs a naturopath and a full-time massage therapist and a chiropractor. At the fitness centre, tai chi and yoga are among the daily classes on offer.

"We take the view that if it's good for quality of life, it's good for business," says Dirk Schlimm, Husky's director of human resources. "We mean well but we also measure our return on investment."

He says the savings come in the fact that his firm's rate of absenteeism is 40 percent below the national average. Spending on its drug plan, which also covers naturopathic remedies, comes in at half the natural average. Workers' Compensation Board claims are 1.5 percent for every 200 000 hours of operation, compared with the average 7.2 percent. Adds Mr. Schlimm, "We also offer the usual employee assistance programs for those who are in distress—which takes a burden off managers. The paycheque will always be a motivator, but we also want people to feel like they are part of something meaningful. That's a very basic human desire."

You Be the Manager

1. What is Husky doing to create organizational control?

As noted in Chapter 1, *controlling* is the process that managers use to monitor and regulate how efficiently and effectively an organization and its members are performing the activities necessary to achieve organizational goals. As discussed in previous chapters, in *planning* and *organizing*, managers develop the organizational strategy and then create the structure that they hope will allow the organization to use resources most effectively to create value for customers. In *controlling*, managers monitor and evaluate whether their organization's strategy and structure support the plans they have created. Based on this evaluation they determine what could be improved or changed. In the case of Husky the whole company is proactively geared to managing that effective balance of too much/too little control. Managers feel that if they create a healthy corporate culture and minimize, as Dr. Gabor Maté reminded us in the opening scenario, conflict that people can't handle, loss of control, uncertainty and lack of information, Husky will not only have that healthy work culture but also an effective bottom line. If you recall the four managerial functions from Chapter 1—planning, organizing, directing, and controlling—we can now state that with an innovative company like Husky, planning for managers by being proactive and participative are part of their culture; organizing is seen in their flexible structures that can respond effectively to employee well-being and business demands; leading is demonstrated because managers truly support and build an organizational culture that leads by example; and controlling is illustrated in their ability to balance the too much/too little organizational control process. By investing in their employees, managers build self-controls and organizational controls in a mutually satisfying manner.

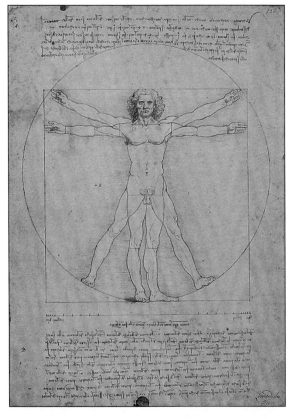

This famous Leonardo da Vinci drawing illustrates the artist's concern for understanding how the human body controls its own movements and how the different parts of the body work together to maintain the body's integrity. The interconnection of the body is similar to the way in which various departments operate in an organization.

The Importance of Organizational Control

Control systems are intended to make organizations more successful. As we see in Figure 13.1, they help managers do the following:[9]

1. *Adapt to change and uncertainty.* We described in Chapter 2 how managers face uncertain task and external environments. New suppliers and customers can appear, as well as new technologies and regulations. Control systems help managers to anticipate these changes and be prepared for them.
2. *Discover irregularities and errors.* There may be problems with quality control, customer service, or even human resource management. Control systems help managers uncover these problems before they become too serious to overcome.
3. *Reduce costs, increase productivity, or add value.* Control systems can be used to reduce labour or production costs, to improve productivity, or to add value to a product, making it more attractive to a customer.
4. *Detect opportunities.* Control systems can help managers identify new markets, demographic changes, new suppliers, and other opportunities.
5. *Deal with complexity.* When organizations become large, it sometimes becomes impossible to know what the different units are doing. This is particularly the case when two companies merge. There may be redundancies in product lines or employees. Control systems help managers deal with these complexities.

FIGURE 13.1 *Six Steps in Decision Making*

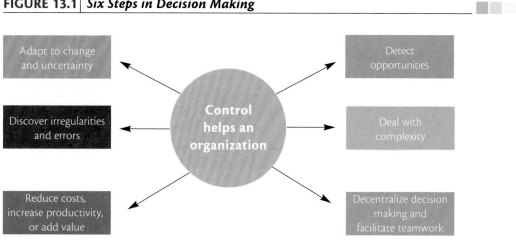

6. *Decentralize decision making and facilitate teamwork.* When control systems are in place, managers can allow employees to make more decisions, and work in teams.

Steps in the Control Process

The control process can be broken down into four steps: establishing standards of performance, then measuring, comparing, and evaluating actual performance (see Figure 13.2).[10]

FIGURE 13.2 *Steps in Organizational Control*

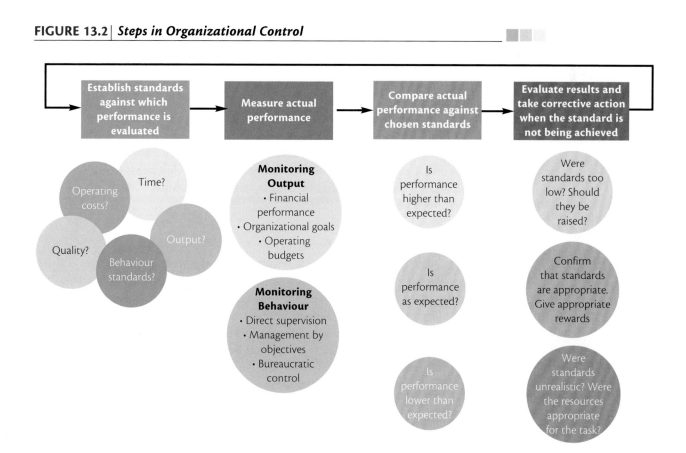

Step 1: *Establish the standards of performance*

At Step 1 in the control process, managers decide on the standards of performance, goals, or targets that they will use to evaluate the performance of either the entire organization or some part of it, such as a division, a function, or an individual. The standards of performance that managers select measure efficiency, quality, responsiveness to customers, and innovation.[11] If managers decide to pursue a low-cost strategy, for example, they need to measure efficiency at all levels in the organization.

At the corporate level, a standard of performance that measures efficiency is *operating costs*—the actual costs associated with producing goods and services, including all employee-related costs. Top managers might set a corporate goal of "reducing operating costs by 10 percent for the next three years" to increase efficiency. Corporate managers might then evaluate divisional managers for their ability to reduce operating costs within their respective divisions, and divisional managers might set cost-savings targets for functional managers. Thus, performance standards selected at one level affect those at the other levels, and ultimately individual managers are evaluated for their ability to reduce costs. For example, S.I. Newhouse, the owner of Condé Nast Publications Inc., which produces magazines such as *GQ, Vanity Fair, Vogue,* and Wired, started an across-the-board attempt to reduce costs so he could reverse the company's losses, and instructed all divisional managers to begin a cost-cutting program. When Newhouse decided to retire he chose Steven T. Florio to replace him. Florio had been the division head who had been most successful in reducing costs and increasing efficiency at *The New Yorker* magazine.

Managers can set a variety of standards, including time, output, quality, and behaviour standards. *Time standards* refer to how long it is supposed to take to complete a task. Some companies, for instance, instruct staff that all emails must be answered within 24 hours. *Output standards* refer to the quantity of the service or product the employee is to produce. *Quality standards* refer to the level of quality expected in the delivery of goods or services. For instance, a company might set what it considers an acceptable level of defects. Or a retail store might set a standard of one complaint per thousand customers served. Finally, a company might set *behaviour standards*, which can govern factors such as hours worked, dress code, or how one interacts with others.

Managers must be careful to choose standards of performance that are not harmful in unintended ways. If managers focus on just one issue (such as efficiency) and ignore others (such as determining what customers really want and innovating a new line of products to satisfy them), managers may end up hurting their organization's performance. Being aware of this threat, managers at Husky take a proactive approach to organizational control and not only emphasize efficiency (what needs to get done), but also effectiveness (how it is done) by creating an organizational culture that supports their employees' well-being.

Step 2: *Measure actual performance*

Once managers have decided which standards or targets they will use to evaluate performance, the next step in the control process is to measure actual performance. In practice, managers can measure or evaluate two things: (1) the actual *outputs* that result from the behaviour of their members and (2) the *behaviours* themselves (hence the terms *output* control and *behaviour control*).[12]

Sometimes both outputs and behaviours can be easily measured. Measuring outputs and evaluating behaviour are relatively easy in a fast-food restaurant, for example, because employees are performing routine tasks. Managers of a fast-food restaurant can measure outputs quite easily by counting how many customers their employees serve and how much money customers spend. Managers can easily observe each employee's behaviour and quickly take action to solve any problems that may arise.

Condé Nast
Publications
Inc.condenast.com

When an organization and its members perform complex, nonroutine activities that are difficult to measure, it is much more difficult for managers to measure outputs or behaviour.[13] It is very difficult, for example, for managers in charge of R&D departments at Merck or Microsoft to measure performance or to evaluate the performance of individual members because it can take 5 or 10 years to determine whether the new products that scientists are developing are going to be profitable. Moreover, it is impossible for a manager to measure how creative a research scientist is by watching his or her actions.

In general, the more nonroutine or complex organizational activities are, the harder it is for managers to measure outputs or behaviours.[14] Outputs, however, are usually easier to measure than behaviours because they are more tangible and objective. Therefore, the first kind of performance measures that managers tend to use are those that measure outputs. Then managers develop performance measures or standards that allow them to evaluate behaviours in order to determine whether employees at all levels are working toward organizational goals. Some simple behaviour measures are: Do employees come to work on time? Do employees consistently follow the established rules for greeting and serving customers? Each type of output and behaviour control and the way it is used at the different organizational levels—corporate, divisional, functional, and individual—is discussed in detail later in the chapter.

Step 3: *Compare actual performance against chosen standards of performance*

During Step 3, managers evaluate whether—and to what extent—performance deviates from the standards of performance chosen in Step 1. If performance is higher than expected, managers might decide that performance standards are too low and may raise them for the next time period to challenge subordinates.[15] Managers at Japanese companies are well known for the way they try to raise performance in manufacturing settings by constantly raising performance standards to motivate managers and employees to find new ways to reduce costs or increase quality.

However, if performance is too low and standards were not reached, or if standards were set so high that employees could not achieve them, managers must decide whether to take corrective action.[16] If managers are to take any form of corrective action, Step 4 is necessary.

Step 4: *Evaluate the result and initiate corrective action if necessary*

The final step in the control process is to evaluate the results. Whether performance standards have been met or not, managers can learn a great deal during this step. If managers decide that the level of performance is unacceptable, they must try to solve the problem. Sometimes, performance problems occur because the standard was too high—for example, a sales target was too optimistic and impossible to achieve. In this case, adopting more realistic standards can reduce the gap between actual performance and desired performance. However, if managers determine that something in the situation is causing the problem, then to raise performance they will need to change the way in which resources are being used.[17] Perhaps the latest technology is not being used, perhaps workers lack the advanced training they need to perform at a higher level, perhaps the organization needs to buy its inputs or assemble its products abroad to compete against low-cost rivals, or perhaps it needs to restructure itself or re-engineer its work processes to increase efficiency. If managers decide that the level has been achieved or exceeded, they can consider whether the standard set was too low. However, they might also consider rewarding employees for a job well done.

Establishing targets and designing measurement systems can be difficult for managers. Because of the high level of uncertainty in the organizational environment, managers rarely know what might happen. Thus, it is vital for managers to design control systems to alert them to problems so that these can be dealt with before they become threatening. Another issue is that managers are not just concerned with bringing the organization's performance up to some predetermined standard; they want to push that standard forward, to encourage employees at all levels to find new ways to raise performance.

Control Systems

As we see from the control process described above, managers need effective control systems to help them evaluate whether they are staying on target with their planned performance. **Control systems** are formal target-setting, monitoring, evaluation, and feedback systems that provide managers with information about whether the organization's strategy and structure are working efficiently and effectively.[18] Effective control systems alert managers when something is going wrong and give them time to respond to opportunities and threats. An effective control system has three characteristics:

- It is flexible enough to allow managers to respond as necessary to unexpected events.

- It provides accurate information and gives managers a true picture of organizational performance.

- It provides managers with the information in a timely manner because making decisions on the basis of outdated information is a recipe for failure.

New forms of information technology have revolutionized control systems because they ease the flow of accurate and timely information up and down the organizational hierarchy and between functions and divisions. Today, employees at all levels of the organization routinely feed information into a company's information system or network and start the chain of events that affect decision making at some other part of the organization. This could be the department-store clerk whose scanning of purchased clothing tells merchandise managers what kinds of clothing need to be reordered; or the salesperson in the field who uses a wireless laptop to send information about customers' changing needs or problems.

Control and information systems are developed to measure performance at each stage in the work process, from gathering inputs to delivering finished goods and services (see Figure 13.3).

Feedforward Control

Before the work begins, managers use **feedforward control** to anticipate possible problems that they can then avoid once the work is underway.[19] For example, by giving stringent product specifications to suppliers in advance (a form of performance target), an organization can control the quality of the inputs it receives from its suppliers and thus avoid potential problems at the conversion stage (see Figure 13.3). Similarly, by screening job applicants and using several interviews to select the most highly skilled people, managers can lessen the chance that they will hire people who lack the skills or experience needed to perform effectively. Another form of feedforward control is the development of management information systems that provide managers with timely information about changes in the task and general environments that may impact their organization later on. Effective managers always monitor trends and changes in the external environment to try to anticipate problems.

Concurrent Control

During the actual production phase, **concurrent control** gives managers immediate feedback on how efficiently inputs are being transformed into outputs so that managers can correct problems as they arise. Concurrent control alerts managers to the need for

---

control systems

Formal target-setting, monitoring, evaluation, and feedback systems that provide managers with information about how well the organization's strategy and structure are working.

---

feedforward control

Control that allows managers to anticipate and deal with potential problems.

---

concurrent control

Control that gives managers immediate feedback on how efficiently inputs are being transformed into outputs so that managers can correct problems as they arise.

FIGURE 13.3 | *Three Types of Control*

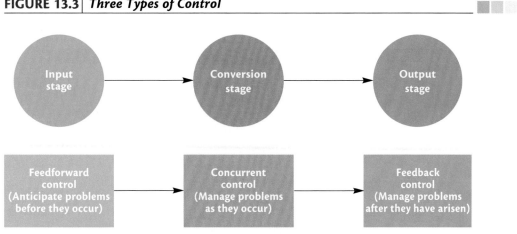

FIGURE 13.4 | *Three Organizational Control Systems*

Type of control	Mechanisms of control
Output control	Financial measures of performance Organizational goals Operating budgets
Behaviour control	Direct supervision Management by objectives Rules and standard operating procedures
Clan control	Values Norms Socialization

quick reaction to the source of the problem, be it a defective batch of inputs, a machine that is out of alignment, or an employee who lacks the skills necessary to perform a task efficiently. Concurrent control is at the heart of total quality management programs, in which employees are expected to constantly monitor the quality of the goods or services they provide at every step of the production process and inform managers as soon as they discover problems. One of the strengths of Toyota's production system, for example, is that individual employees are given the authority to push a button to stop the assembly line whenever they discover a quality problem. When all problems have been corrected, the result is a finished product that is much more reliable.

Feedback Control

Once the work is completed, managers use **feedback control** to provide information about customers' reactions to goods and services so that corrective action can be taken if necessary. For example, a feedback control system that monitors the number of customer returns alerts managers when defective products are being produced, and a system that measures increases or decreases in product sales alerts managers to changes in customer tastes so they can increase or reduce the production of specific products.

feedback control
Control that gives managers information about customers' reactions to goods and services so that corrective action can be taken if necessary.

Styles of Control

Managers need to determine internal control systems that will motivate employees and ensure that they perform effectively. In the following sections, we consider the three most important styles of control that managers use to coordinate and motivate employees: *output control, behaviour control,* and *clan control* (see Figure 13.4). Managers use all three to govern and regulate organizational activities, no matter what specific organizational structure is in place.

Output Control

Control, Accountability, and Corporate Governance[20]

The marketplace over the past few years has experienced much corporate scandal. The question many have been asking is, "Where were the controls?" The answer that often emerged was that "there was no accountability." Hence, the issue of corporate governance looms large on the business horizon.

Many realize today that Canada's corporate governance laws have been inadequate. Joel Rochon, a litigator at Rochon Genova LLP in Toronto,[21] says," Regulators can put in laws and regulations, but unless they're followed and unless corporations really understand that investors are not to be disadvantaged by their actions, the message is not going to get to them. I think any law the regulator is planning to pass in Ontario is hugely inadequate."

Company directors are getting the message as well because Canadian stock market regulators are demanding more accountability. In some cases boards of directors have had to dump executives linked to accounting scandals. For example,

- Nortel Network's chief executive officer Frank Dunn, chief financial officer Douglas Beatty, and controller Michael Gollogly were all fired over accountability for financial reporting.
- Mississauga-based technology firm Hip Interactive Corp. followed by firing a senior vice-president of finance after the firm revised earnings guidance downward due to accounting errors.
- Descartes Systems Group Inc. fired Manuel Pietra, the chief executive and president, after announcing revenue and losses would be materially below expectations announced in a press release two months before.

In March 2004, the Canadian Securities Administrators passed a slate of new rules, which included shorter filing deadlines for financial information, chief executive and chief financial officer certification of financial statements, and rules on audit committee independence. Barry Reiter, a corporate lawyer and chairman of the technology group at Torys LLP, says the new Canadian rules "are going to make a difference." In fact, Mr. Reiter, who serves as a director on a number of companies, says he has already noticed changes at least in the boardroom at the director level. "Directors are much more aware that they have responsibility and need to take their jobs more seriously and spend more time trying to do their jobs. There's a level of carelessness and complacency that might have existed before that doesn't exist as much now."

Again, the issue is as we discussed it above: balancing too much control vs. too little. The challenge for market regulators is finding the right balance and creating a regulatory environment that cracks down on malfeasance without stifling the ability of small companies to tap the capital markets and spend time growing their businesses—rather than focusing their efforts on filing paper. How to do precisely this task is one of the most important new challenges in organizational control. Balance is everything. Doug Hyndman, chair of the British Columbia Securities Commission, says, "Shareholders ultimately pay for the cost of all these governance processes. It's our duty to make sure shareholders get value for their money."

All managers, such as Paul Madden of The Spa at the Monastery in St. John's and Robert Schad of Husky Injection Mouldings of Aurora, Ontario (profiled in the *Management Snapshot* and *Think About It*, "A Husky Solution for Organizational Control"), develop a system of output control for their organizations. First, they choose the goals or output performance standards or targets that they think will best measure factors such as efficiency, quality, innovation, and responsiveness to customers. Then they measure to see whether the performance goals and standards are being achieved at the corporate, divisional or functional, and individual levels of the organization. If the goals are being met, usually organizations give rewards to employees and managers. If goals are not being met, senior management needs to evaluate the reasons why performance standards are missed. Scotia McLeod had been measuring the number of trades that brokers made, and commissions were used as rewards for all trades. The company became concerned, however, that brokers were carrying out too many trades.

Financial Measures of Performance

Top managers are most concerned with overall organizational performance and use various financial measures to evaluate performance. The most common are *profit ratios*, *liquidity ratios*, *leverage ratios*, and *activity ratios*. They are discussed below and summarized in Table 13.1.[22]

Profit Ratios
Profit ratios measure how efficiently managers are using the organization's resources to generate profits. *Return on investment (ROI)*, an organization's net income before taxes divided by its total assets, is the most commonly used financial performance measure because it allows managers of one organization to compare performance with that of other organizations. ROI allows managers to assess an organization's competitive advantage. *Gross profit margin* is the difference between the amount of revenue generated by a product and the resources used to produce the product. This measure provides managers with information about how efficiently an organization is using its resources and about how attractive customers find the product. It also provides managers with a way to assess how well an organization is building a competitive advantage.

Liquidity Ratios
Liquidity ratios measure how well managers have protected organizational resources so as to be able to meet short-term obligations. The *current ratio* (current assets divided by current liabilities) tells managers whether they have the resources available to meet the claims of short-term creditors. The *quick ratio* tells whether they can pay these claims without selling inventory.

Leverage Ratios
Leverage ratios such as the *debt-to-assets ratio* and the *times-covered ratio* measure the degree to which managers use debt (borrow money) or equity (issue new shares) to finance ongoing operations. An organization is highly leveraged if it uses more

TABLE 13.1 | *Four Measures of Financial Performance*

Profit Ratios			
Return on investment	=	$\dfrac{\text{Net profit before taxes}}{\text{Total assets}}$	Measures how well managers are using the organization's resources to generate profits.
Gross profit margin	=	$\dfrac{\text{Sales revenue} - \text{cost of goods sold}}{\text{Sales revenue}}$	The difference between the amount of revenue generated from the product and the resources used to produce the product.
Liquidity Ratios			
Current ratio	=	$\dfrac{\text{Current assets}}{\text{Current liabilities}}$	Do managers have resources available to meet claims of short-term creditors?
Quick ratio	=	$\dfrac{\text{Current assets} - \text{Inventory}}{\text{Current liabilities}}$	Can managers pay off claims of short-term creditors without selling inventory?
Leverage Ratios			
Debt-to-assets ratio	=	$\dfrac{\text{Total debt}}{\text{Total assets}}$	To what extent have managers used borrowed funds to finance investments?
Times-covered ratio	=	$\dfrac{\text{Profit before interest and taxes}}{\text{Total interest charges}}$	Measures how far profits can decline before managers cannot meet interest charges. If ratio declines to less than 1, the organization is technically insolvent.
Activity Ratios			
Inventory turnover	=	$\dfrac{\text{Cost of goods sold}}{\text{Inventory}}$	Measures how efficiently managers are turning inventory over so excess inventory is not carried.
Days sales outstanding	=	$\dfrac{\text{Accounts receivable}}{\dfrac{\text{Total Sales}}{360}}$	Measures how efficiently managers are collecting revenues from customers to pay expenses.

debt than equity. Debt can be very risky when profits fail to cover the interest on the debt.

Activity Ratios

Activity ratios provide measures of how well managers are creating value from organizational assets. *Inventory turnover* measures how efficiently managers are turning inventory over so that excess inventory is not carried. *Days sales outstanding* provides information on how efficiently managers are collecting revenue from customers to pay expenses.

The objectivity of financial measures of performance is the reason why so many managers use them to assess the efficiency and effectiveness of their organizations. When an organization fails to meet performance standards such as ROI, revenue, or stock price targets, managers know that they must take corrective action. Thus, financial controls tell managers when a corporate reorganization might be necessary, when they should sell off divisions and exit from businesses, or when they should rethink their corporate-level strategies.[23] For example, Nortel Networks, JDS Uniphase Corp., and Lucent Technologies had to rethink corporate strategies in the spring and summer of 2001 after their stock prices plummeted.

While financial information is an important output control, on its own it does not provide managers with all the information they need about whether the plans they have made are being met. Financial results inform managers about the results of decisions they have already made; they do not tell managers how to find new opportunities to build competitive advantage in the future. To encourage a future-oriented approach, top managers, in their planning function, establish organizational goals that provide direction to middle and first-line managers. As part of the control function, managers evaluate whether those goals are being met.

Organizational Goals

Once top managers, in consultation with lower-level managers, have set the organization's overall goals, they then establish performance standards for the divisions and functions. These standards specify for divisional and functional managers the level at which their units must perform if the organization is to reach its overall goals.[24] For instance, if the goals for the year include improved sales, quality, and innovation, sales managers might be evaluated for their ability to increase sales, materials management managers for their ability to increase the quality of inputs or lower their costs, and R&D managers for the number of products they innovate or the number of patents they receive. By evaluating how well performance matches up to the goals set, managers at all levels can determine whether the plans they had made are being met, or whether adjustments need to be made in either the plans or the behaviours of managers and employees. Thus goals can be a form of control by providing the framework for what is evaluated and assessed.

Operating Budgets

Once managers at each level have been given a goal or target to achieve, the next step in developing an output control system is to establish operating budgets that regulate how managers and employees reach those goals. An **operating budget** is a blueprint that states how managers intend to use organizational resources to achieve organizational goals efficiently. Typically, managers at one level allocate to subordinate managers a specific amount of resources to use to produce goods and services. Once they have been given a budget, these lower-level managers must decide how to allocate resources for different organizational activities. They are then evaluated for their ability to stay within the budget and to make the best use of available resources. The failure of many dot-com companies illustrates what happens when organizations do not emphasize control. It would appear that many dot-com companies focused more on spending whatever money came in (i.e., had a high "burn rate") without consideration of developing and then staying within a budget. This practice proved to be disastrous when investors decided to stop pouring money into these companies after they had little in the way of performance that they could show investors.

Large organizations often treat each division as a singular or stand-alone responsibility centre. Corporate managers then evaluate each division's contribution to corporate performance. Managers of a division may be given a fixed budget for resources and evaluated for the amount of goods or services they can produce using those resources (this is a *cost* or *expense* budget approach). Or managers may be asked to maximize the revenues from the sales of goods and services produced (a *revenue* budget approach). Or managers may be evaluated on the difference between the revenues generated by the sales of goods and services and the budgeted cost of making those goods and services (a *profit* budget approach). Japanese companies' use of operating budgets and challenging goals to increase efficiency is instructive in this context.

In summary, three components—objective financial measures, performance standards derived from goals, and appropriate operating budgets—are the essence of effective output control. Most organizations develop sophisticated output control systems to allow managers at all levels to maintain an accurate picture of the organization so that they can move quickly to take corrective action as needed.[25] Output control is an essential part of management.

operating budget
A budget that states how managers intend to use organizational resources to achieve organizational goals.

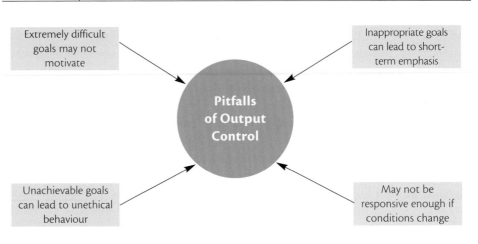

Problems with Output Control

As we saw in *Think About It* and the corporate governance challenge, boards of directors have to adopt new organizational output accounting control systems with managers and executives in order to reduce potential ethical conflicts. When designing an output control system, managers must be careful to avoid some pitfalls, as shown in Figure 13.5. First, they must be sure that their output standards motivate managers at all levels and do not cause managers to behave in inappropriate ways to achieve organizational goals. ScotiaMcLeod's system of rewarding for each individual trade ended up creating "churning." Brokers advised clients to trade too much, and this led to investigations by regulatory bodies, as well as fines and discipline against the brokerages and individual brokers.

Problems can also occur if the standards that are set turn out to be unrealistic. Suppose that top managers give divisional managers the goal of doubling profits over a three-year period. This goal seems challenging and reachable when it is jointly agreed upon, and in the first two years profits go up by 70 percent. In the third year, however, an economic recession hits and sales plummet. Divisional managers think it is increasingly unlikely that they will meet their profit goal. Failure will mean losing the substantial monetary bonus tied to achieving the goal. How might managers behave to try to preserve their bonus?

One course of action they might take is to find ways to reduce costs, since profit can be increased either by raising revenues or by reducing costs. Thus, divisional managers might cut back on expensive research and development activities, delay maintenance on machinery, reduce marketing expenditures, and lay off middle managers and employees to reduce costs so that at the end of the year they will make their target of doubling profits and will receive their bonus. This tactic might help them achieve a short-run goal—doubling profits—but such actions could hurt long-term profitability or ROI (because a cutback in R&D can reduce the rate of product innovation, a cutback in marketing will lead to the loss of customers, and so on).

The long term is what corporate managers should be most concerned about. Thus, top managers must consider carefully how flexible they should be when using output control. If conditions change (as they will because of uncertainty in the task and general environments), it is probably better for top managers to communicate to managers lower in the hierarchy that they are aware of the changes taking place and are willing to revise and lower goals and standards. Indeed, most organizations schedule yearly revisions of their five-year plan and goals.

Second, the inappropriate use of output control systems can lead lower-level managers and employees to behave unethically. If goals are too challenging, employees may be motivated to behave unethically toward customers, as sometimes happens in brokerage firms. ScotiaMcLeod has moved to a fee-based system to change the way in which its brokers are rewarded in order to reduce potential ethical conflicts.

The message is clear: Although output control is a useful tool for keeping managers and employees at all levels motivated and the organization on track, it is only a guide to appropriate action. Output controls need to be flexible enough to accommodate changes in the organization's environment. Therefore, managers must be sensitive to how they use output control and constantly monitor its effects at all levels in the organization.

Behaviour Control

THINK ABOUT IT

Control and the Call Centre: Convergys Corp.[26]

The average Canadian would probably cringe at wanting to be one of the roughly 500 000 Canadians in full-time and part-time work at a call centre with its image in the public's mind of annoying telephone calls during dinner. There are high turnover rates in this industry; there is an obvious recruitment challenge for the industry; and yet, there is increasing demand, as more businesses outsource their customer service functions. "It really is a sales job, to constantly find the people we need to fuel the growth," said Curtis Stoll, vice-president of international human resources with Convergys Corp., a global company that employs almost 15 000 Canadians in call centres in British Columbia, Alberta, Manitoba, Ontario, Nova Scotia, and Newfoundland.

Wayne Fraser, Ontario and Atlantic director of the United Steelworkers of America, said that working conditions in the estimated 14 000 call centres operating in Canada range from good to "sweatshop." In Ontario, his union represents 4500 call-centre employees. Stress levels are particularly high among employees hired to place outbound, telemarketing calls, he said. "It's very regimented and controlled by automation. They have automatic dialers, so when you are finished one call, within a very few seconds you are on another call with another person."

However, a company such as Convergys and some of the other large call centre employers in Canada pride themselves on maintaining lower-than-average turnover rates by offering competitive pay, benefits, training, and promotion opportunities.

You Be the Manager

1. What factors have to be controlled in call centres?

Organizational structure is often viewed as a way of achieving control by designating who reports to whom, and what the responsibilities of each individual are. However, structure by itself does not provide any mechanism that motivates managers and non-managerial employees to behave in ways that make the structure work or even improve the way it works—hence the need for control. Output control is one way to motivate employees; behaviour control is another. In this section, we examine three mechanisms of behaviour control that managers can use to keep subordinates on track and make organizational structures work as they are designed to work: *direct supervision, management by objectives,* and *rules and standard operating procedures* (see Figure 13.4).

Direct Supervision

The most immediate and potent form of behaviour control is direct supervision by managers who actively monitor and observe the behaviour of their subordinates, teach subordinates the behaviours that are appropriate and inappropriate, and intervene to take corrective action as needed. When managers personally supervise subordinates, they lead by example and in this way can help subordinates develop and increase their own skill levels (leadership is the subject of Chapter 9). Thus, control through personal supervision can be a very effective way of motivating employees and promoting behaviours that increase efficiency and effectiveness.[27]

Nevertheless, certain problems are associated with direct supervision.

- It is very expensive. A manager can personally manage only a small number of subordinates effectively. Therefore, direct supervision requires a lot of managers and this will raise costs.

- It can demotivate subordinates if they feel that they are not free to make their own decisions. Subordinates may avoid responsibility if they feel that their manager is waiting to reprimand anyone who makes the slightest error.

- For many jobs, direct supervision is simply not feasible. The more complex a job is, the more difficult it is for a manager to evaluate how well a subordinate is performing.

For all of these reasons, output control is usually preferred to behaviour control. Indeed, output control tends to be the first type of control that managers at all levels use to evaluate performance.

Management by Objectives

To provide a framework within which to evaluate subordinates' behaviour and, in particular, to allow managers to monitor progress toward achieving goals, many organizations implement some version of management by objectives (MBO), which we described in Chapter 5.

From a control perspective, the important element of MBO is that managers and their subordinates need to periodically review the subordinates' progress toward meeting goals. Normally, salary raises and promotions are linked to the goal-setting process, and managers who achieve their goals receive greater rewards than those who fall short. (The issue of how to design reward systems to motivate managers and other organizational employees is discussed in Chapter 8.)

In companies that decentralize responsibility for the production of goods and services to empowered teams and cross-functional teams, management would review the accomplishments of the team, and then the rewards would be linked to team performance, not to the performance of any one team member. For either the individual or team situation, MBO creates the conditions for providing standards that are evaluated.

Bureaucratic Control

bureaucratic control
Control of behaviour by means of a comprehensive system of rules and standard operating procedures.

When direct supervision is too expensive and management by objectives is inappropriate, managers might turn to another mechanism to shape and motivate employee behaviour: bureaucratic control. **Bureaucratic control** is control by means of a comprehensive system of rules and standard operating procedures (SOPs) that shape and regulate the behaviour of divisions, functions, and individuals. In the appendix to Chapter 1, we discussed Max Weber's theory of bureaucracy and noted that all organizations use bureaucratic rules and procedures but some use them more than others.[28]

Rules and SOPs guide behaviour and specify what employees are to do when they confront a problem that needs a solution. It is the responsibility of a manager to develop rules that allow employees to perform their activities efficiently and effectively. When employees follow the rules that managers have developed, their behaviour is *standardized*—actions are performed in the same way time and time again—and the outcomes of their work are predictable. In addition, to the degree that managers can make employees' behaviour predictable, there is no need to monitor the outputs of behaviour because standardized behaviour leads to standardized outputs.

Suppose a worker at Toyota comes up with a way to attach exhaust pipes that reduces the number of steps in the assembly process and increases efficiency. Always on the lookout for ways to standardize procedures, managers make this idea the basis of a new rule: "From now on, the procedure for attaching the exhaust pipe to the car is as follows . . ." If all workers followed the rule to the letter, every car would come off the assembly line with its exhaust pipe attached in the new way, and there would be no need to check exhaust pipes at the end of the line. In practice, mistakes and lapses of attention do happen, so output control is used at the end of the line, and each car's exhaust system is given a routine inspection. However, the number of quality problems with the exhaust system is minimized because the rule (bureaucratic control) is being followed.

Service organizations such as retail stores and fast-food restaurants try to standardize the behaviour of employees by instructing them on the correct way to greet customers or the appropriate way to serve and bag food. Employees are trained to follow the rules that have proven to be most effective in a particular situation. The better trained the employees are, the more standardized is their behaviour, and the more trust managers can have that outputs (such as food quality) will be consistent.

Problems with Bureaucratic Control

All organizations make extensive use of bureaucratic control because rules and SOPs effectively control routine organizational activities. With a bureaucratic control system in place, managers can manage by exception and intervene and take corrective action only when necessary. However, managers need to be aware of a number of problems associated with bureaucratic control, because they can reduce organizational effectiveness.[29]

First, establishing rules is always easier than discarding them. Organizations tend to become overly bureaucratic over time if managers do everything according to the rule book. When the amount of "red tape" becomes too great, decision making slows and managers react slowly to changing conditions. This slowness can harm an organization's survival if quicker new competitors emerge.

Second, because rules constrain and standardize behaviour and lead people to behave in predictable ways, people may become so used to automatically following rules that they stop thinking for themselves. By definition, new ideas do not come from blindly following standardized procedures. Similarly, the pursuit of innovation implies a commitment by managers to discover new ways of doing things; innovation, however, is incompatible with the use of extensive bureaucratic control.

Managers must therefore be sensitive about the way they use bureaucratic control. It is most useful when organizational activities are routine and well understood and employees are making programmed decisions such as in mass-production settings or in a routine service setting, for example such restaurants and stores as Tim Hortons, Canadian Tire, and Midas Muffler. Bureaucratic control is not nearly as useful in situations where nonprogrammed decisions have to be made and managers have to react quickly to changes in the organizational environment.

To use output control and behaviour control, managers must be able to identify the outcomes they want to achieve and the behaviours they want employees to perform to achieve these outcomes.

> ## ✓ Tips for Managers
> ### CONTROL
>
> 1. Make a list of "must-do" items that need to be accomplished to get the job done (an efficiency task).
> 2. Make another list of "must-do" items that need to be accomplished that takes into consideration the people who complete the work (an effectiveness task).
> 3. Involve employees in training programs that will help not only themselves do a better job but will meet your control targets (e.g., safety, better financial reporting, etc.).
> 4. List the different ways you feel you can balance the challenge of too much control vs. too little.

Clan Control

>
> ## THINK ABOUT IT
> ### "Scotiabank," not "Brian Toda"[30]
>
> Mr. Toda's willingness to share his office space reflects Scotiabank's team-oriented culture. "People who want to be part of a team do well here," says Brian Toda, vice-president of human resources for Scotiabank's compensation group. He has a huge office with upscale cherry wood furniture and a view. What makes Toda different from many other executives is that he invites his employees to use his office when he's not there with such activities as making conference calls from his comfortable, black leather chair or holding small meetings at a round table.
>
> His objective: he wants the office to communicate "Scotiabank" rather than "Brian Toda." Because he has built such a strong organizational culture, staff are able to continue without him when he is not there. "It's not like employees are coming into my space. It's their space, too," he explains. He has built such a culture because his aim has always been to deliver "the best employment experience."
>
> ### *You Be the Manager*
>
> 1. What is Brian Toda doing to build an employee self-responsibility and clan control culture?

For many of the most important organizational activities, output control and behaviour control are inappropriate for several reasons:

- Not all employees can be observed on a day-to-day basis.

- Rules and SOPs are of little use in either crisis situations or situations requiring innovation.

- Output controls can be a very crude measure of the quality of performance, and could in fact harm performance, in some instances.

Professionals such as scientists, engineers, doctors, and professors often have jobs that are relatively ambiguous in terms of standard operating procedures, and which may require individualized response based on the situation.

How can managers try to control and regulate the behaviour of their subordinates when personal supervision is of little use, when rules cannot be developed to tell employees what to do, and when outputs and goals cannot be measured at all or can be measured usefully only over long periods? One source of control increasingly being used by organizations is clan control, which relies on a strong organizational culture. This form of control is also increasingly being used in organizations that value innovation, and want to empower their employees.

How Clan Control Works

William Ouchi used the term **clan control** to describe the control exerted on individuals and groups in an organization by shared values, norms, standards of behaviour, and expectations. The control arising from clan control is not an externally imposed system of constraints, such as direct supervision or rules and procedures, but constraints that come from organizational culture (discussed in Chapter 7).

Clan control is an important source of control for two reasons. First, it makes control possible in situations where managers cannot use output or behaviour control. Second and more important, when a strong and cohesive set of organizational values and norms is in place, employees focus on thinking about what is best for the organization in the long run—all their decisions and actions become oriented toward helping the organization perform well. For example, a teacher spends personal time after school coaching and counselling students; an R&D scientist works 80 hours a week, evenings and weekends, to help speed up a late project; a sales clerk at a department store runs after a customer who left a credit card at the cash register. Many researchers and managers believe that employees of some organizations go out of their way to help their organization because the organization has a strong and cohesive organizational culture—a culture that controls employee attitudes and behaviours. Strong bureaucratic control is less likely to foster positive attitudes and behaviours that encourage employees to go above and beyond. Brian Toda and Scotiabank are examples of how effective clan culture can be in encouraging effective behaviour from all employees. As Toda says, his objective is to deliver "the best employment experience."[31]

clan control
Control exerted on individuals and groups in an organization by shared values, norms, standards of behaviour, and expectations.

How Culture Controls Managerial Action

The way in which organizational culture shapes and controls behaviour is evident in the way managers perform their four main functions—planning, organizing, leading, and controlling—when they work in different types of organizations (see Table 13.2). As we consider these functions, we continue to distinguish between two kinds of top managers: those who create organizational values and norms that encourage creative, *innovative* behaviour, and those who encourage a *conservative*, cautious approach by their subordinates. We noted earlier that both kinds of values and norms may be appropriate in different situations.

Planning

Top managers in an organization with an *innovative* culture are likely to encourage lower-level managers to take part in the planning process and develop a flexible approach to planning. They are likely to be willing to listen to new ideas and to take risks involving the development of new products.

TABLE 13.2 | *How Culture Controls Action*

Managerial Function	Type of Organization	
	Conservative	**Innovative**
Planning	Formal, top-down planning	All managers encouraged to participate in decision making
Organizing	Well-defined hierarchy of authority and clear reporting relationships	Organic, flexible structure
Leading	Rigid MBO and constant monitoring	Managers lead by example, encourage risk-taking
Controlling	Bureaucratic control	Clan control

In contrast, top managers in an organization with *conservative* values are likely to emphasize formal top-down planning. Suggestions from lower-level managers are likely to be subjected to a formal review, which can significantly slow decision making. Although this deliberate approach may improve the quality of decision making in a nuclear power plant, it also can have unintended consequences. At conservative IBM, for example, before its more recent turnaround, the planning process became so formalized that managers spent most of their time assembling complex slide shows and overheads to defend their current positions rather than thinking about what they should be doing to keep IBM abreast of the changes taking place in the computer industry.

Organizing

Valuing creativity, managers in an *innovative* culture are likely to try to create an organic structure, one that is flat, with few levels in the hierarchy, and in which authority is decentralized so that employees are encouraged to work together to find solutions to ongoing problems. A product team structure may be very suitable for an organization with an innovative culture.

In contrast, managers in a *conservative* culture are likely to create a well-defined hierarchy of authority and establish clear reporting relationships so that employees know exactly to whom to report, and how to react to any problems that arise.

Leading

In an *innovative* culture, managers are likely to lead by example, encouraging employees to take risks and experiment. They are supportive regardless of whether employees succeed or fail.

In contrast, managers in a conservative culture are likely to develop a rigid management by objectives system and to constantly monitor subordinates' progress toward goals, overseeing their every move.

Controlling

As this chapter makes clear, there are many control systems that managers can adopt to shape and influence employee behaviour. The control systems managers choose reflect a choice about how they want to motivate organizational members and keep them focused on organizational goals. Managers who want to encourage the development of *innovative* values and norms that encourage risk-taking choose output and behaviour controls that match this objective. They are likely to choose output controls that measure performance over the long run and develop a flexible MBO system suited to the long and uncertain process of innovation.

In contrast, managers who want to encourage the development of conservative values choose the opposite combination of output and behaviour controls. They develop specific, difficult goals for subordinates, frequently monitor progress toward these goals, and develop a clear set of rules that subordinates are expected to adhere to. Sometimes managers who are hired by a company do not fit into the existing culture. Calgary-based WestJet fired CEO Steve Smith, who was far more controlling than the rest of the company's culture. WestJet's founders sent a strong message to the employees by firing Smith in a year when the company had done very well financially.

The values and norms of an organization's culture strongly affect the way managers perform their management functions. The extent to which managers buy into the values and norms of their organization shapes their view of the world and their actions and decisions in particular circumstances.[32] In turn, the actions that managers take can have an impact on the performance of the organization. Thus, organizational culture, managerial action, and organizational performance are linked together. Geoffrey Relph, interviewed as IBM's director of services marketing, notes that his previous company (GE Appliances in Louisville, Kentucky) had a very different set of expectations than IBM Canada. "The priorities in GE are: 'Make the financial commitments. Make the financial commitments. Make the financial commitments.' At IBM, the company's attention is divided among customer satisfaction, employee morale, and positive financial results."[33] GE Appliances' focus on financial commitments may deter employees from also looking at customer satisfaction. Relph's experience at GE Appliances may also suggest that managers need to be concerned with employee morale.

GE Appliances Company
www.geappliances.com

Although organizational culture can give rise to managerial actions that ultimately benefit the organization, this is not always the case. Sometimes culture can become so much a part of the organization that it becomes difficult to improve performance.[34] For example, Wayne Sales, the new president and CEO of Canadian Tire, is trying desperately to revitalize customer service in the company's stores. Canadians have become so used to poor service that employees don't necessarily see the need to change. However, with alternatives such as Home Hardware, Revy Home Centres, and Home Depot Canada, lack of customer service is likely to become an increasing issue as Sales sets out to "drive away the chain's 'crappy tire' image."[35] He will need to change the control system to encourage employees to be more customer-focused.

Summary and Review

1. **WHAT IS ORGANIZATIONAL CONTROL?** Controlling is the process that managers use to monitor and regulate how efficiently and effectively an organization and its members are performing the activities necessary to reach organizational goals. Controlling is a four-step process: (1) establishing performance standards, (2) measuring actual performance, (3) comparing actual performance against performance standards, and (4) evaluating the results and taking corrective action if needed.

2. **OUTPUT CONTROL** To monitor output or performance, managers choose goals or performance standards that they think will best measure efficiency, quality, innovation, and responsiveness to customers at the corporate, divisional, departmental or functional, and individual levels. The main mechanisms that managers use to monitor output are financial measures of performance, organizational goals, and operating budgets.

3. **BEHAVIOUR CONTROL** In an attempt to shape behaviour and induce employees to work toward achieving organizational goals, managers use direct supervision, management by objectives, and bureaucratic control by means of rules and standard operating procedures.

4. **CLAN CONTROL** *Clan control* operates on individuals and groups through shared values, norms, standards of behaviour, and expectations. The way managers perform their management functions influences the kind of culture that develops in an organization.

Key Terms

bureaucratic control, p. 382
clan control, p. 385
concurrent control, p. 374
control systems, p. 374

feedback control, p. 375
feedforward control, p. 374
operating budget, p. 379

SO WHERE DO YOU STAND?

Wrap-Up to Opening Case

We began this chapter with a discussion of The Spa at the Monastery in St. John's, Nfld. John Madden's business grew by over 350 percent in the space of four years. The issue at hand was how companies such as his, which offer stress-reducing personal services for staff can go a long way to embed effective controls in an organization. Dr. Gabor Maté, a Vancouver, B.C. physician, author, and stress expert reminded us that as employees are more able to cope with their stressors, the more contributory they can be for the organization. Wendy Poirier of Towers Perrin in Calgary said that this is the key to improved productivity, especially for today's younger employees who want a better work/life balance in their lives.

It's obvious that when we get stressed we are often less capable to perform at optimum levels. This, in turn, affects employee motivation and, if the stress levels increase too much, can result in employees feeling "out of control." A survey of 114 chief executive officers by Ipsos-Reid in 2004 found that 66 percent of them said that the biggest drain on productivity for Canadian corporations wasn't bad bosses or lazy employees, or even inadequate training; it was stress. The report stated that "stress, burnout or other physical and mental health issues" are having a negative impact on work force productivity—and the problem had escalated to the extent that they were worrying about their ability to pay future disability claims.[36]

FGIworld CEO Allon Bross,[37] whose firm commissioned the Ipsos-Reid poll, said, "Companies are still trying to be more competitive by doing more with less." He was concerned because, for him, in 10 years time, serious problems caused by employee stress and lack of control are developing now. The editor of *Fast Company* magazine[38] reminds us that even though companies in the future will have to be "fast" in order to compete and survive, other realities must also be kept in check:

These days, building companies that win big in the marketplace, that create value for their customers and shareholders, and that operate in ways that bring out the best in employees and executives is not just smart business—it's also an obligation of leadership. Fast companies prosper by meeting that obligation. They compete on the originality of their ideas. They embrace the disruptive power of technology but understand that cutting-edge technology is most powerful when it's used in the service of age-old virtues: delighted customers, engaged employees, and productive operations. Fast companies know the value of values—the proposition that what a company stands for is just as important as what it sells.

This chapter's opening scenario has been part of the *Management Snapshot* scenarios for the beginning of each chapter in this book. In late March 2005 when Bank of Canada governor David Dodge was speaking at Humber College Institute of Technology and Advanced Learning on the importance of Canadian competitiveness, he told the audience that putting people first was the best way to ensure a prosperous Canadian future. He acknowledged

the realities of rapid technological change, globalization, and an aging population. But he also said that in order to assure a future worth going to, Canada needed to do a much better job of improving productivity. Dodge put it this way, "While we're talking the talk on productivity, we are not doing a good job of walking the walk."[39]

As we saw in this chapter, when there is an appropriate balance between too much control and not enough control, then the vision that Governor Dodge speaks about can become a reality. Change is good when employees have a sense of control and everyone is involved.[40]

After studying the preceding material, be sure to check out our Online Learning Centre at
www.mcgrawhill.ca/olc/jones
for more in-depth information and interactivities that correspond to this chapter.

Management in Action

Topics for Discussion and Action

1. What is the relationship between organizing and controlling?
2. How do output control and behaviour control differ?
3. Ask a manager to list the main performance measures that he or she uses to evaluate how well the organization is achieving its goals.
4. Ask the same or a different manager to list the main forms of output control and behaviour control that he or she uses to monitor and evaluate employee behaviour.
5. Why is it important for managers to involve subordinates in the control process?
6. What is clan control, and how does it affect the way employees behave?
7. What kind of controls would you expect to find most used in (a) a hospital, (b) the Armed Forces, (c) a city police force. Why?

Building Management Skills

UNDERSTANDING CONTROLLING

For this exercise, you will analyze the control systems used by a real organization such as a department store, restaurant, hospital, police department, or small business. It can be the organization that you investigated for previous *Building Management Skills* exercises or a different one. Your objective is to uncover all the different ways in which managers monitor and evaluate the performance of the organization and employees.

1. At what levels does control take place in this organization?
2. Which output performance standards (such as financial measures and organizational goals) do managers use most often to evaluate performance at each level?
3. Does the organization have a management by objectives system in place? If it does, describe it. If it does not, speculate about why not.
4. How important is behaviour control in this organization? For example, how much of managers' time is spent directly supervising employees? How formal is the organization? Do employees receive a book of rules to instruct them about how to perform their jobs?
5. To what extent does clan control have an impact on the organization? What is its relative importance compared with output and behaviour control?
6. Based on this analysis, do you think there is a fit between the organization's control systems and its culture? What is the nature of this fit? How could it be improved?

Management for You

Your parents have let you know that they are expecting a big party for their 25th wedding anniversary, and that you are in charge of planning it. Develop a timeline for carrying out the project, and then identify ways to monitor progress toward getting the party planned. How will you know that your plans have been successful? At what critical points do you need to examine your plans to make sure that everything is on track?

Small Group Breakout Exercise

HOW BEST TO CONTROL THE SALES FORCE?

Form groups of three or four people, and appoint one member as the spokesperson who will communicate your findings to the whole class when called on by the instructor. Then discuss the following scenario.

You are the regional sales managers of an organization that supplies high quality windows and doors to building supply centres nationwide. Over the last three years, the rate of sales growth has slackened. There is increasing evidence that, to make their jobs easier, salespeople are primarily servicing large customer accounts and ignoring small accounts. In addition, the salespeople are not dealing promptly with customer questions and complaints, and this inattention has resulted in a drop in after-sales service. You have talked about these problems, and you are meeting to design a control system to increase both the amount of sales and the quality of customer service.

1. Design the control system that you think will best motivate salespeople to achieve these goals.

2. What relative importance do you put on (a) output control, (b) behaviour control, and (c) organizational culture in this design?

Managing Ethically

You are a manager of a group of 10 employees in their 20s. They are very innovative and are not accustomed to tight rules and regulations. Managers at the company want order and control on every front. Your team is fighting the rules and regulations, which is creating an ethical dilemma. They are being very productive and innovative but clearly not in the way the top management wants things run. You have been asked to bring more order to your team. You really like your team and think they are effective and will leave if they are forced to conform. And the company needs their expertise and energy to remain competitive in the high-tech world. What would you do?

Exploring the World Wide Web

SPECIFIC ASSIGNMENT

Review the "Sustainable Competitive Advantage" website (www.1000ventures.com/business_guide/crosscuttings/sca_main.html). Read what the page says on the relationship between corporate culture and building a sustainable competitive advantage in business. Then on the left side of the screen, in a boxed area, click on "Organizational Culture" (www.1000ventures.com/business_guide/crosscuttings/culture_corporate.html) and read what's on this screen.

1. What are the key factors in corporate culture?
2. What is the relationship between corporate culture and building a sustainable competitive advantage in business?

GENERAL ASSIGNMENT

Search for the website of a company that actively uses organizational culture (or one of the other types of control) to build competitive advantage. What kind of values and norms is the culture based on? How does it affect employee behaviour?

Developing a Business Plan

(APPENDIX B, PAGE 405)

Go to www.mcgrawhill.ca/olc/jones/13 for online exercises.

Be the Manager

SAVE THE CHILDREN PROJECT

Assume your professor has asked you to consult and manage the design of a special "Save the Children" innovative program that 10 teams of five students in your course will be working on. Save the Children Canada will be acting as final judge on the winning program submitted by different colleges and universities. While there are 10 teams you must manage, because of the shortness of time for this request, the innovative program will need aspects designed by each team because no one team can do it all. Hence, all 10 teams will have contributed to the finished product. Your professor will be grading you on how well you actually manage, motivate, and put into action controls to help each team function at optimal levels.

Questions

1. What will be your "control plan" for the teams to function optimally?
2. What are key factors from this chapter that you intend to utilize to accomplish your mandate?
3. How will the key factors you have chosen work to facilitate the teams to function optimally *as a team* as well as function optimally *between teams*?

Video Management Case

McDonald's Everywhere

A powerhouse of international expansion, McDonald's has half of its total (over 13 000) restaurants located outside of the US. It prides its success on a consistent quality of food and service and a commitment to developing partnerships with local infrastructure.

Questions to Consider

1. How does McDonald's facilitate its penetration of the local marketplace while maintaining its global standard?
2. What are the implications of corporate development at the local level; of getting a country "up to standard" so that it can accommodate McDonald's needs, while also adapting to the country's culture, as in the case of India?

Part 6: Integrated Case

Dell's New Business Model: Redemption[41]

The PC maker, which lost market share in the past quarter to archrival Hewlett-Packard, is fighting back with millions of dollars' worth of improvements

ROUND ROCK, TEX.—Ask Michael Dell what went wrong with his company over the past year and he will tell you the world's largest PC maker grew faster than the industry.

Ask him a second time and he will tell you that Dell Inc. is more profitable than all the other major players combined.

Ask him a third time and he will pause, suppressing some frustration. In the 22 years since he started the

company in his dorm room at the University of Texas, Mr. Dell has rarely had to respond to anything but good news.

The 41-year-old multibillionaire is considered one of the world's most respected executives running one of its best companies. Using a special model that involves selling directly to customers via the Internet or telephone, Dell has grown tenfold in 10 years. In the process, it has also helped make computer technology less expensive and more widely available.

But something has gone wrong in the past year. Despite the advantage of almost instant market feedback through its direct sales model, Dell executives have made uncharacteristic, critical errors that have sent the stock down 46 percent and caused it to lose market share to archrival Hewlett-Packard Co.

"We believe we understand the things that have happened that caused that to occur and we've taken a number of steps to address those," Mr. Dell, the company's chairman, finally responds. "I'm not going to give you the dirty laundry about that."

Other executives are a little less reluctant to reach into the hamper. They offer more details of what's gone wrong. Kevin Rollins, chief executive officer since 2004, admits he and his team have recently made mistakes. They underestimated competitors, failed to see trends in market data, and let customer service slip. "Why would Dell, the perfect company, ever have a mistake? We did. Right now we're not dwelling on that. We're going to dwell on what we're doing to fix it," he says.

The repair list includes removing US$3 billion of costs this year from an already lean machine, pouring resources into customer care, pushing further into overseas markets, and jazzing up Dell's traditional black-box designs.

But some analysts and investors think the problems run deeper. They believe Dell is selling to an increasingly saturated market and, even more disturbing, that its renowned direct sales model has lost much of its advantage.

"We think Dell's key selling points have historically been lower prices and superior customer service and believe it has largely lost its advantage in these areas," Cindy Shaw, an analyst at Moors & Cabot Inc., told clients this week as she cut her expectations for the stock.

Two days later, Benjamin Reitzes, an analyst at UBS AG, trimmed his profit forecast for Dell and warned that competition may continue to bite into sales.

The reports added to one of the worst weeks in the past year for Dell shares, which hit a 52-week low on Thursday of $21.67, off their high of $41.99 last July.

The past year has brought big changes to the landscape, says Momin Khan, an analyst with Technology Business Research Inc. "Before, Dell had the wind to its back. Going forward it's a strong headwind."

Dell's sprawling headquarters in Round Rock, Texas, are devoid of almost any art or aesthetic touch. The walls bear some of the company's 1581 patents and notices prohibiting weapons on company property.

The spartan executive building has added few, if any, luxuries in the past six years, despite management's success during that period at more than doubling sales, which hit $55.9 billion last year.

The surroundings suggest a practical, no-nonsense culture rather than a corporate environment where employees can get fat and comfortable. "Anyone inside the company would laugh at the complacency charge," Mr. Dell says.

During two days of briefings with a group of reporters recently, executives made it clear that the company has plotted a course that they say will keep it the undisputed leader in the PC industry.

Things are clearly already in motion. During the past few days, Dell has launched an advertising campaign, simplified its pricing, and ventured into the world of blogging to improve its image with individual consumers, who represent about 15 percent of sales.

The advertising campaign, called "Purely You," stresses that Dell PCs are built to order rather than mass produced in batches. The pricing revamp will reduce the plethora of promotions on its site by as much as 80 percent, making the net price more transparent to buyers.

The blog, at one2one.dell.com, is a pioneering attempt by a corporation to use the new interactive nature of the Web to its advantage. The site features product information, edited comments from customers, and some straight talking from customer service staff, such as Laura Bosworth, who wrote on the blog this week: "Like the proverbial frog in the pot of water that slowly starts to boil, we didn't realize that many of our problem resolution processes were no longer designed from a customer's perspective."

The blog edits consumer complaints, but it does link to some of its biggest critics, including the US journalist Jeff Jarvis, whose blog, buzzmachine.com, has become a cauldron of unsatisfied customers' hostility. "You'd better be prepared for a mob," Mr. Jarvis wrote on Thursday.

Longer term, Dell is investing $100 million to improve customer care, which includes hiring more than 2000 staff and retraining another 5000. It is adding or expanding 10 call centres around the world, including one in Edmonton and another in Ottawa.

Another way the company is trying to improve efficiency using the Internet is with a new tool called DellConnect that lets a Dell technician access a customer's computer over a broadband connection and conduct repairs remotely. The satisfaction rate has been almost 95 percent among the first 750 000 customers, Mr. Rollins says.

Dell's website, which is doing $16-billion worth of business in 12 months, is conducting an overhaul that includes adding more multimedia features aimed at giving products a sense of touch and feel.

Dell's products themselves are getting a facelift, as design has become an important part of consumers' buying decisions during the past couple of years. Quoting material from the research firm International Data Corp., Dell executives say design is now the second most important criteria for consumers buying technology, behind improved features. The company says it will add at least 20 people to its design team of 50 in the next couple of years. "We feel we have the strongest product line now than we've had since Dell has been around," says Kevin Kettler, the chief technology officer.

One thing that the company is not willing to change, however, is its direct-sales business model.

None of Dell's eight manufacturing plants around the world begins assembling a computer until it has been ordered. The system allows Dell to keep its supply of raw materials to just a few days and its finished inventory to a minimum. In comparison, it's not unusual for rivals to have several weeks' worth of inventory of both raw materials and finished goods. In addition, prices aren't marked up by a retailer and customers are buying machines made with the latest components on the market.

The direct contact and exchange of information with customers is "the life flow" of the company, Mr. Dell says. "Our business model really gives us very fresh input every single day from our customers who tell us what they like or don't like, and that allows us to grow very consistently."

It also works universally, he adds. Dell has gained market share in each of its top 15 countries every year since 1995.

But the Dell model is under fierce attack as changes hit the industry. Competitors, particularly HP, have streamlined their manufacturing and distribution operations. At the same time, prices of components such as chips and memory boards are not falling as fast as they used to.

Five years ago, Dell was able to undersell rival PC manufacturers by between 15 and 20 percent. Today, however, that price advantage has shrunk to just 5 percent, according to estimates by Richard Gardner, an analyst at Citigroup Global Markets Inc.

"It would be presumptuous of me to say we have totally eliminated the advantages that they have with their direct business. I think I could say that we have negated the advantage such that it is no longer a huge strategic advantage," says David Booth, US country manager and senior vice-president of HP. "We feel we've blunted any advantage that our competitors have had."

Some analysts and industry executives also question whether direct selling is as appropriate today, when international markets account for more growth and technology products carry richer features.

Mr. Khan expects HP and China's Lenovo Group Ltd. to keep gaining on Dell, especially in Europe and Asia, where retailers are more important. "Anyone in India who buys anything, they always sit down and have a cup of tea with the store owner first. Dell is not set up to drink tea," he says.

In North America, the savings from using Dell's direct model are no longer worth it for many buyers. "As long as [Dell] could undercut the competition, they could expand market share. But what's happened now is Dell has reached the floor," Mr. Khan says. "When the spread has narrowed to less than $50, it then matters how the PC is bought. Buying direct doesn't necessarily provide the type of rewards that it used to bring."

Milko Van Duijl, president of Lenovo's operations in Europe, the Middle East and Africa, says the company is able to get hour-by-hour market information through its established relationships with IT services companies and resellers.

More than three-quarters of Lenovo's $13 billion of sales is done through direct channels, he says. "Customers want to see it and feel and touch the machine. And after paying for it, they want to walk away with the machine."

Dell remains No. 1 in worldwide PC shipments, according to the research firm Gartner Inc. But its market share slipped in the quarter to 16.5 percent from 16.9 percent, while HP's share rose to 14.9 percent from 13.8 percent. "At the end of the day, you don't take market share to the bank. You take profit to the bank," Mr. Rollins says. "We love market share. We want to grow. Don't get me wrong. But at the end of the day you have to win by having excellent profitability."

There is a religion-like faith in Round Rock that Dell can sell technology and services more efficiently than anyone else. In addition to the $3 billion in savings the company aims to find this year, it cut $2.2 billion last year and $1.8 billion the year before that.

From inside its five command centres worldwide, which monitor large corporate clients' computer systems, repair technicians aren't just dispatched with driving directions, but with local weather and traffic reports to save time.

Mr. Dell is unwavering in his belief that the direct-relationship model he launched from his dorm room with a $1000 investment will keep powering the company's growth beyond $80-billion in sales.

Those recent market share gains made by his competitors are so far limited to just one quarter over the past 10 years, he says. "So okay, the score is 39 to 1."

THE DELL STORY

Chapter 1: The model
Build computers to order and sell directly to customers. By cutting out the retailer, Dell eliminated time and cost and created a direct relationship with customers.

Chapter 2: The breakout
The direct-sales model was well-suited for the Internet. Dell turbocharged sales when it began taking orders online in 1996. It became the first company to record online daily sales of $1 million in 1997. Today it does $16 billion of its $56 billion of annual sales directly online.

Chapter 3: The fall
Recently revealed that it has grown more slowly than the rest of the PC market. Failed to see that rivals were

closing the gap on Dell's price advantage. Failed to move quickly enough into fast-growing markets such as China, India, Brazil and Russia. Let customer satisfaction slide.

Chapter 4: The fix?
Step up international expansion, build more computers overseas, poor resources into customer service, form new alliances that include Google's software and AMD's chips, and find $3-billion worth of cuts this year.

Our business model really gives us very fresh input every single day from our customers who tell us what they like or don't like, and that allows us to grow very consistently.

MICHAEL DELL

Discussion Questions

1. What control failed at Dell Inc.?
2. How would you design control systems to prevent what happened at Dell Inc.?

The Evolution of Management Theory

Management theory concerning appropriate management practices has evolved in modern times. The so-called classical management theories emerged around the start of the 20th century. These include scientific management, which focuses on matching people and tasks to maximize efficiency, and administrative management, which focuses on identifying the principles that will lead to the creation of the most efficient system of organization and management. Behavioural management theories, developed both before and after the Second World War, focus on how managers should lead and control their workforces to increase performance. Management science theory, developed during the Second World War, has become more important as researchers have developed rigorous analytical and quantitative techniques to help managers measure and control organizational performance. Finally, theories were developed during the 1960s and 1970s to help explain how the external environment affects the way organizations and managers operate.

Scientific Management Theory

The evolution of modern management began in the closing decades of the 19th century, after the Industrial Revolution had swept through Europe, Canada, and the United States. Small workshops run by skilled workers who produced hand-manufactured products (a system called crafts production) were replaced by large factories. In these factories, hundreds or even thousands of unskilled or semi-skilled employees controlled the sophisticated machines that made products.

Many of the managers and supervisors had only technical knowledge, and were unprepared for the social problems that occur when people work together in large groups (as in a factory or shop system). Managers began to search for new ways to manage their organizations' resources, and soon they began to focus on how to increase the efficiency of the employee-task mix.

Job Specialization and the Division of Labour

The Adam Smith Institute
www.adamsmith.org

The famous Scottish economist Adam Smith was one of the first to look at the effects of different manufacturing systems.[1] He compared the relative performance of two different manufacturing methods. The first was similar to crafts-style production, in which each employee was responsible for all of the 18 tasks involved in producing a pin. The other had each employee performing only one or a few of the 18 tasks that go into making a completed pin.

Smith found that factories in which employees specialized in only one or a few tasks had greater performance than factories in which each employee performed all 18 pin-making

FIGURE A.1 | *The Evolution of Management Theory*

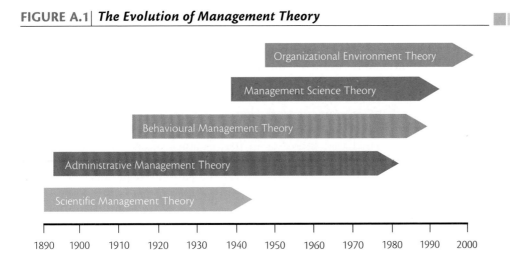

tasks. In fact, Smith found that 10 employees specializing in a particular task could, between them, make 48 000 pins a day, whereas those employees who performed all the tasks could make only a few thousand at most.[2] Smith reasoned that this difference in performance was due to the fact that the employees who specialized became much more skilled at their specific tasks, and, as a group, were thus able to produce a product faster than the group of employees in which everyone had to perform many tasks. Smith concluded that increasing the level of **job specialization**—the process by which a division of labour occurs as different employees specialize in different tasks over time—increases efficiency and leads to higher organizational performance.[3]

Based on Adam Smith's observations, early management practitioners and theorists focused on how managers should organize and control the work process to maximize the advantages of job specialization and the division of labour.

job specialization
The process by which a division of labour occurs as different employees specialize in different tasks over time.

F.W. Taylor and Scientific Management

Frederick W. Taylor (1856–1915) is best known for defining the techniques of **scientific management**, the systematic study of relationships between people and tasks for the purpose of redesigning the work process to increase efficiency. Taylor believed that the production process would become more efficient if the amount of time and effort that each employee spent to produce a unit of output (a finished good or service) could be reduced. He noted that increased specialization and the division of labour could increase efficiency. Taylor believed that the way to create the most efficient division of labour could best be determined by means of scientific management techniques, rather than intuitive or informal rule-of-thumb knowledge. Based on his experiments and observations as a manufacturing manager in a variety of settings, he developed four principles to increase efficiency in the workplace:[4]

scientific management
The systematic study of relationships between people and tasks for the purpose of redesigning the work process to increase efficiency.

The F.W. Taylor Project
attila.stevens-tech.edu/~rdowns/

- Principle 1. *Study the way workers perform their tasks, gather all the informal job knowledge that workers possess, and experiment with ways of improving the way tasks are performed.*

- Principle 2. *Codify the new methods of performing tasks into written rules and standard operating procedures.*

- Principle 3. *Carefully select workers so that they possess skills and abilities that match the needs of the task, and train them to perform the task according to the established rules and procedures.*

- Principle 4. *Establish a fair or acceptable level of performance for a task, and then develop a pay system that provides a reward for performance above the acceptable level.*

By 1910, Taylor's system of scientific management had become known and, in many instances, faithfully and fully practised.[5] However, managers in many organizations chose to use the new principles of scientific management selectively. This decision ultimately resulted in problems. For example, some managers using scientific management saw increases in performance, but rather than sharing performance gains with employees through bonuses as Taylor had advocated, they simply increased the amount of work that each employee was expected to do. Thus, employees found they were required to do more work for the same pay. Employees also learned that increases in performance often resulted in layoffs, because fewer employees were needed. In addition, the specialized, simplified jobs were often monotonous and repetitive, and many employees became dissatisfied with their jobs.

Scientific management brought many employees more hardship than gain, and left them with a distrust of managers who did not seem to care about their well-being.[6] These dissatisfied employees resisted attempts to use the new scientific management techniques and at times even withheld their job knowledge from managers to protect their jobs and pay.

Taylor's work has had an enduring effect on the management of production systems. Managers in every organization, whether it produces goods or services, now carefully analyze the basic tasks that must be performed and try to create work systems that will allow their organizations to operate most efficiently.

The Gilbreths

The Gilbreth Network
gilbrethnetwork.
tripod.com

Two prominent followers of Taylor were Frank Gilbreth (1868–1924) and Lillian Gilbreth (1878–1972), who refined Taylor's analysis of work movements and made many contributions to time-and-motion study.[7] Their aims were to (1) break up a particular task into individual actions, and analyze each step needed to perform the task, (2) find better ways to perform each step, and (3) reorganize each of the steps so that the action as a whole could be performed more efficiently—at less cost in time and effort.

The Gilbreths often filmed an employee performing a particular task and then separated the task actions, frame by frame, into their component movements. Their goal was to maximize the efficiency with which each individual task was performed so that gains across tasks would add up to enormous savings of time and effort.

In workshops and factories, the work of the Gilbreths, Taylor, and many others had a major effect on the practice of management. In comparison with the old crafts system, jobs in the new system were more repetitive, boring, and monotonous as a result of the application of scientific management principles. Employees became more dissatisfied. Frequently, the management of work settings became a game between employees and managers: Managers tried to introduce work practices to increase performance, and employees tried to hide the true potential efficiency of the work setting in order to protect their own well-being.[8]

Administrative Management Theory

administrative management
The study of how to create an organizational structure that leads to high efficiency and effectiveness.

Side by side with scientific managers studying the person-task mix to increase efficiency, other researchers were focusing on **administrative management**—the study of how to create an organizational structure that leads to high efficiency and effectiveness. Organizational structure is the system of task and authority relationships that control how employees use resources to achieve the organization's goals. Two of the most influential views regarding the creation of efficient systems of organizational administration were developed in Europe. Max Weber, a German professor of sociology, developed one theory. Henri Fayol, the French manager, developed the other.

The Theory of Bureaucracy

Max Weber (1864–1920) wrote at the start of the 20th century, when Germany was undergoing its Industrial Revolution.[9] To help Germany manage its growing industrial enterprises at a time when it was striving to become a world power, Weber developed the principles of **bureaucracy**—a formal system of organization and administration designed to ensure efficiency and effectiveness.

- Principle 1. *In a bureaucracy, a manager's formal authority derives from the position he or she holds in the organization.*

  In a bureaucratic system of administration, obedience is owed to a manager, not because of any personal qualities that he or she might possess—such as personality, wealth, or social status—but because the manager occupies a position that is associated with a certain level of authority and responsibility.[10]

- Principle 2. *In a bureaucracy, people should occupy positions because of their performance, not because of their social standing or personal contacts.*

  This principle was not always followed in Weber's time and is often ignored today. Some organizations and industries are still affected by social networks in which personal contacts and relations, not job-related skills, influence hiring and promotional decisions.

- Principle 3. *The extent of each position's formal authority and task responsibilities, and its relationship to other positions in an organization, should be clearly specified.*

  When the tasks and **authority** associated with various positions in the organization are clearly specified, managers and employees know what is expected of them and what to expect from each other. Moreover, an organization can hold all its employees strictly accountable for their actions when each person is completely familiar with his or her responsibilities.

- Principle 4. *For authority to be exercised effectively in an organization, positions should be arranged hierarchically. This helps employees know whom to report to and who reports to them.*[11]

  Managers must create an organizational hierarchy of authority that makes it clear (a) who reports to whom and (b) to whom managers and employees should go if conflicts or problems arise. This principle is especially important in the Armed Forces, Canadian Security Intelligence Service (CSIS), Royal Canadian Mounted Police (RCMP), and other organizations that deal with sensitive issues where there could be major repercussions.

- Principle 5. *Managers must create a well-defined system of rules, standard operating procedures (SOPs), and norms so that they can effectively control behaviour within an organization.*

  Rules, SOPs, and norms provide behavioural guidelines that improve the performance of a bureaucratic system because they specify the best ways to accomplish organizational tasks. **Rules** are formal written instructions that specify actions to be taken under different situations to achieve specific goals. **SOPs** are specific sets of written instructions on how to perform a certain aspect of a task. **Norms** are unwritten rules and informal codes of conduct on how to act in particular situations. Companies such as McDonald's and Wal-Mart have developed extensive rules and procedures to specify the types of behaviours that are required of their employees, such as, "Always greet the customer with a smile."

bureaucracy
A formal system of organization and administration designed to ensure efficiency and effectiveness.

authority
The power to hold people accountable for their actions and to make decisions concerning the use of organizational resources.

rules
Formal written instructions that specify actions to be taken under different circumstances to achieve specific goals.

standard operating procedures (SOPs)
Specific sets of written instructions about how to perform a certain aspect of a task.

norms
Unwritten rules and informal codes of conduct that prescribe how people should act in particular situations.

TABLE A.1 | *Fayol's 14 Principles of Management*　　　■ ■ ■

Division of Labour　Job specialization and the division of labour should increase efficiency, especially if managers take steps to lessen employees' boredom.

Authority and Responsibility　Managers have the right to give orders and the power to exhort subordinates for obedience.

Unity of Command　An employee should receive orders from only one superior.

Line of Authority　The length of the chain of command that extends from the top to the bottom of an organization should be limited.

Centralization　Authority should not be concentrated at the top of the chain of command.

Unity of Direction　The organization should have a single plan of action to guide managers and employees.

Equity　All organizational members are entitled to be treated with justice and respect.

Order　The arrangement of organizational positions should maximize organizational efficiency and provide employees with satisfying career opportunities.

Initiative　Managers should allow employees to be innovative and creative.

Discipline　Managers need to create a workforce that strives to achieve organizational goals.

Remuneration of Personnel　The system that managers use to reward employees should be equitable for both employees and the organization.

Stability of Tenure of Personnel　Long-term employees develop skills that can improve organizational efficiency.

Subordination of Individual Interests to the Common Interest　Employees should understand how their performance affects the performance of the whole organization.

Esprit de Corps　Managers should encourage the development of shared feelings of comradeship, enthusiasm, or devotion to a common cause.

Weber believed that organizations that implement all five principles will establish a bureaucratic system that will improve organizational performance. The specification of positions and the use of rules and SOPs to regulate how tasks are performed make it easier for managers to organize and control the work of subordinates. Similarly, fair and equitable selection and promotion systems improve managers' feelings of security, reduce stress, and encourage organizational members to act ethically and further promote the interests of the organization.[12]

If bureaucracies are not managed well, however, many problems can result. Sometimes, managers allow rules and SOPs—"bureaucratic red tape"—to become so cumbersome that decision making becomes slow and inefficient and organizations are unable to change. When managers rely too much on rules to solve problems and not enough on their own skills and judgment, their behaviour becomes inflexible. A key challenge for managers is to use bureaucratic principles to benefit, rather than harm, an organization.

Fayol's Principles of Management

Working at the same time as Weber but independently of him, Frenchman Henri Fayol (1841–1925), the CEO of Comambault Mining, identified 14 principles (summarized in Table A.1) that he believed to be essential to increasing the efficiency of the management process.[13] Some of the principles that Fayol outlined have faded from contemporary management practices, but most have endured.

The principles that Fayol and Weber set forth still provide a clear and appropriate set of guidelines that managers can use to create a work setting that makes efficient and effective use of organizational resources. These principles remain the foundation of modern management theory; recent researchers have refined or developed them to suit modern conditions. For example, Weber's and Fayol's concerns for equity and for establishing appropriate links between performance and reward are central themes in contemporary theories of motivation and leadership.

Behavioural Management Theory

The **behavioural management** theorists writing in the first half of the 20th century all chose a theme that focused on how managers should personally behave in order to motivate employees and encourage them to perform at high levels and be committed to the achievement of organizational goals.

The Work of Mary Parker Follett

If F.W. Taylor is considered to be the father of management thought, Mary Parker Follett (1868–1933) serves as its mother.[14] Much of her writing about management and about the way managers should behave toward employees was a response to her concern that Taylor was ignoring the human side of organization. Follett also proposed that knowledge and expertise, and not managers' formal authority deriving from their position in the hierarchy, should decide who would lead at any particular moment. She believed, as do many management theorists today, that power is fluid and should flow to the person who can best help the organization achieve its goals. Follett took a horizontal view of power and authority, in contrast to Fayol, who saw the formal line of authority and vertical chain of command as being most essential to effective management. Follett's behavioural approach to management was radical for its time.

The Hawthorne Studies and Human Relations

Probably because of its radical nature, Follett's work was unappreciated by managers and researchers until quite recently. Instead, researchers continued to follow in the footsteps of Taylor and the Gilbreths. One focus was on how efficiency might be increased through improving various characteristics of the work setting, such as job specialization or the kinds of tools employees used. One series of studies was conducted from 1924 to 1932 at the Hawthorne Works of the Western Electric Company.[15] This research, now known as the Hawthorne studies, began as an attempt to investigate how characteristics of the work setting—specifically the level of lighting or illumination—affect employee fatigue and performance. The researchers conducted an experiment in which they systematically measured employee productivity at various levels of illumination.

One of the main implications of the Hawthorne studies was that the behaviour of managers and employees in the work setting is as important in explaining the level of performance as the technical aspects of the task. Managers must understand the workings of the **informal organization**, the system of behavioural rules and norms that emerge in a group, when they try to manage or change behaviour in organizations. Many studies have found that, as time passes, groups often develop elaborate procedures and norms that bond members together, allowing unified action either to cooperate with management in order to raise performance or to restrict output and undermine organizational goals.[16] The Hawthorne studies demonstrated the importance of understanding how the feelings, thoughts, and behaviour of work-group members and managers affect performance. It was becoming increasingly clear to researchers that understanding behaviour in organizations is a complex process that is critical to increasing performance.[17] Indeed, the increasing interest in the area of management known as **organizational behaviour**—the study of the factors that have an impact on how individuals and groups respond to and act in organizations—dates from these early studies.

behavioural management
The study of how managers should behave in order to motivate employees and encourage them to perform at high levels and be committed to achieving organizational goals.

Mary Parker Follett Foundation
www.follettfoundation.org

Hawthorne Studies
www.wikipedia.org/wiki/Hawthorne_studies

informal organization
The system of behavioural rules and norms that emerge in a group.

organizational behaviour
The study of the factors that have an impact on how individuals and groups respond to and act in organizations.

Douglas McGregor
www.lib.uwo.ca/busines/
dougmcgregor.html

Theory X
Negative assumptions about employees that lead to the conclusion that a manager's task is to supervise them closely and control their behaviour.

Theory Y
Positive assumptions about employees that lead to the conclusion that a manager's task is to create a work setting that encourages commitment to organizational goals and provides opportunities for imagination, initiative, and self-direction.

Theory X and Theory Y

Several studies after the Second World War revealed how assumptions about employees' attitudes and behaviour affect managers' behaviour. Perhaps the most influential approach was developed by Douglas McGregor. He proposed that two different sets of assumptions about work attitudes and behaviours dominate the way managers think and affect how they behave in organizations. McGregor named these two contrasting sets of assumptions *Theory X* and *Theory Y*.[18]

According to the assumptions of **Theory X**, the average employee is lazy, dislikes work, and will try to do as little as possible. Moreover, employees have little ambition and wish to avoid responsibility. Thus, the manager's task is to counteract employees' natural tendencies to avoid work. To keep employees' performance at a high level, the manager must supervise them closely and control their behaviour by means of rewards and punishments.

Theory Y assumes that employees are not inherently lazy, do not naturally dislike work, and, if given the opportunity, will do what is good for the organization. According to Theory Y, the characteristics of the work setting determine whether employees consider work to be a source of satisfaction or punishment; and managers do not need to control employees' behaviour closely in order to make them perform at a high level, because employees will exercise self-control when they are committed to organizational goals. It is the manager's task to create a work setting that encourages commitment to organizational goals and provides opportunities for employees to be imaginative and to exercise initiative and self-direction.

management science theory
An approach to management that uses rigorous quantitative techniques to help managers make full use of organizational resources.

Management Science Theory

Management science theory is a contemporary approach to management that focuses on the use of rigorous quantitative techniques to help managers make maximum use of organizational resources to produce goods and services. In essence, management science theory is a contemporary extension of scientific management. There are many branches of management science, each of which deals with a specific set of concerns:

- *Quantitative management* uses mathematical techniques—such as linear and nonlinear programming, modelling, simulation, queuing theory, and chaos theory—to help managers decide, for example, how much inventory to hold at different times of the year, where to build a new factory, and how best to invest an organization's financial capital.

- *Operations management (or operations research)* provides managers with a set of techniques that they can use to analyze any aspect of an organization's production system to increase efficiency.

- *Total quality management (TQM)* focuses on analyzing an organization's input, conversion, and output activities to increase product quality.[19]

- *Management information systems (MIS)* help managers design information systems that provide information about events occurring inside the organization as well as in its external environment—information that is vital for effective decision making.

All these subfields of management science provide tools and techniques that managers can use to help improve the quality of their decision making and increase efficiency and effectiveness.

Organizational Environment Theory

An important milestone in the history of management thought occurred when researchers went beyond the study of how managers can influence behaviour within organizations to consider how managers control the organization's relationship with its external environment, or **organizational environment**—the set of forces and conditions that operate beyond an organization's boundaries but affect a manager's ability to acquire and use resources. Resources in the organizational environment include the raw materials and skilled people that an organization needs to produce goods and services, as well as the support of groups—such as customers who buy these goods and services—that provide the organization with financial resources. The importance of studying the environment became clear after the development of open-systems theory and contingency theory during the 1960s.

The Open-Systems View

One of the most influential views of how an organization is affected by its external environment was developed by Daniel Katz, Robert Kahn, and James Thompson in the 1960s.[20] These theorists viewed the organization as an **open system**—a system that takes in resources from its external environment and converts or transforms them into goods and services that are then sent back to that environment, where they are bought by customers.

The system is said to be "open" because the organization draws from and interacts with the external environment in order to survive; in other words, the organization is open to its environment. A **closed system**, in contrast, is a self-contained system that is not affected by changes that occur in its external environment. Organizations that operate as closed systems, that ignore the external environment and that fail to acquire inputs, are likely to experience **entropy**, the tendency of a system to dissolve and disintegrate because it loses the ability to control itself.

Researchers using the open-systems view are interested in how the various parts of a system work together to promote efficiency and effectiveness. Systems theorists like to argue that "the parts are more than the sum of the whole"; they mean that an organization performs at a higher level when its departments work together rather than separately. **Synergy**, the performance gains that result when individuals and departments coordinate their actions, is possible only in an organized system. The recent interest in using teams comprising people from different departments reflects systems theorists' interest in designing organizational systems to create synergy and thus increase efficiency and effectiveness.

Contingency Theory

Another milestone in management theory was the development of **contingency theory** in the 1960s by Tom Burns and G.M. Stalker in the United Kingdom and Paul Lawrence and Jay Lorsch in the United States.[21] Recognizing that organizations need to acquire valuable resources, the crucial message of contingency theory is that there is no one best way to organize: The organizational structures and the control systems that managers choose depend on—are contingent on—characteristics of the external environment in which the organization operates.

An important characteristic of the external environment that affects an organization's ability to obtain resources is the degree to which the environment is changing. Changes in the organizational environment include: changes in technology, which can lead to the creation of new products (such as compact discs) and result in the disappearance of existing products (eight-track tapes); the entry of new competitors (such as foreign organizations that compete for available

organizational environment
The set of forces and conditions that operate beyond an organization's boundaries but affect a manager's ability to acquire and use resources.

open system
A system that takes in resources from its external environment and converts them into goods and services that are then sent back to that environment for purchase by customers.

closed system
A system that is self-contained and thus not affected by changes that occur in its external environment.

entropy
The tendency of a system to dissolve and disintegrate because it loses the ability to control itself.

synergy
Performance gains that result when individuals and departments coordinate their actions.

contingency theory
The idea that managers' choice of organizational structures and control systems depends on—is contingent on—characteristics of the external environment in which the organization operates.

resources); and unstable economic conditions. In general, the more quickly the organizational environment is changing, the greater are the problems associated with gaining access to resources and the greater is the manager's need to find ways to coordinate the activities of people in different departments in order to respond to the environment quickly and effectively.

The basic idea behind contingency theory—that there is no one best way to design or lead an organization—has been incorporated into other areas of management theory, including leadership theories.

Key Terms

administrative management, p. 398

authority, p. 399

behavioural management, p. 401

bureaucracy, p. 399

closed system, p. 403

contingency theory, p. 403

entropy, p. 403

informal organization, p. 401

job specialization, p. 397

management science theory, p. 402

norms, p. 399

open system, p. 403

organizational behaviour, p. 401

organizational environment, p. 403

rules, p. 399

scientific management, p. 397

standard operating procedures (SOPs), p. 399

synergy, p. 403

Theory X, p. 402

Theory Y, p. 402

Developing a Business Plan

The Business Plan as an Exercise in the Processes of Management[1]

Writing a business plan may never be a more important exercise than in the context of today's rapidly changing environment. Even if you are not an entrepreneur and do not wish to develop a new original idea and bring it to market, developing a business plan is still a valuable exercise in practising the management processes. It provides a crucial foundation for managing an organization. In this section of the text, we will treat developing a business plan as an exercise in the management processes of planning, organizing, leading, and controlling. By doing the exercises at the end of each chapter, you will have the foundation to put together a plan that will help you develop as a manager. The experience you will gain is valid for profit and not-for-profit organizations as well as new and existing ventures. Writing a business plan gives you practice in thinking about managing activities such as:

- Developing an idea to solve a problem
- Tapping into opportunities and countering threats in competitive conditions
- How to organize resources to achieve goals
- How to target potential customers with promotional opportunities
- How to design an effective organizational structure
- How to secure sources of finance
- How to control for risk

What Is a Business Plan?

A business plan is a recognized management tool used to document the organization's objectives and to set out how these objectives will be achieved within a specific timeframe. It is a written document that describes who you are, what you intend to accomplish, how you will organize resources to attain your goals, and how you will overcome the risks involved to provide the anticipated returns. In general, a business plan is comprised of several elements, each gives the reader a piece of the overall picture of the project you are undertaking and provide convincing reasons why you will be successful in this undertaking. Managers and entrepreneurs use a business plan to seek support and financing to expand an existing business or to finance a new venture.

Putting it All Together

Throughout this course you have been completing the end-of-chapter exercises on developing a business plan. Now is the time to start to put all the pieces together to create your comprehensive plan. Draw on the work that you have already done to write the major components of the business plan.

At this point, you should familiarize yourself with Business Plan writer software. There are several on the market. Your professor will instruct you as to which is appropriate for your course.[2] The software will help you compile the main elements in your plan and calculate the financial statements.

TABLE B.1 | *Major Business Plan Components*

	Check off and date when completed and add any notes of interest
1. **Non-Disclosure Statement**	❑
2. **Executive Summary**	❑
3. **Profile of the Organization**	❑
4. **Profile of the Industry or Sector**	❑
5. **Profile of the Product or Service**	❑
6. **Marketing Plan**	❑
7. **Organization Plan**	❑
8. **Operating and Control Systems Plan**	❑
9. **Financial Plan**	❑
10. **Appendices**	❑

1. Non-Disclosure Statement

A non-disclosure agreement is optional in a business plan. When used, it usually states that the information in the plan is proprietary and not to be shared, copied, or disclosed. The agreement should have a unique "copy number" that is the same as a number on the title page of the plan and a place for the recipient's signature. The agreement should be either a loose-leaf page or a page that can be torn out of the plan and retained by you. See the following example:[3]

Copy Number _____ 123 _____

FFP Consulting, Inc.'s business plan is confidential, containing information proprietary to FFP Consulting, Inc. None of the information contained in this plan may be reproduced or disclosed to any person under any circumstances without express written permission of FFP Consulting, Inc. I have accepted and will protect the confidentiality of this business plan.

_____
Recipient's signature

---

2. Executive Summary

The executive summary is the first thing, besides the Table of Contents and Title page, that the reader will view, but it is generally the last thing the writer creates. The executive summary is a maximum one-page précis of your business plan. It is probably the most important part of your plan because readers will make a judgment as to whether or not they want to continue to examine your plan based on this summary. The executive summary tells the reader the following information:

- Who you are and what your company/organization does

- The products and/or services that you provide or intend to provide

- Your target markets; i.e., who are or will be your customers

- How you will promote your product/service to your customers

- What your financial projections are for a given period of time

- How you will achieve your goals, i.e., your strategy for gaining a competitive advantage

- The strengths of your management team and why the reader should believe you can do what you are proposing

Write the Executive Summary last. Input your summary into the Business Plan Software.

3. Profile of the Organization

This section of the business plan tells the reader your vision, mission, and goals for the organization.

Consider the following questions when preparing this section.

- What is the name of your company/organization?

- What is the legal structure and form of ownership?

- What are your reasons for going into business?

- What problem or needs gap does your product or service provide?

- What experience do you have that would enable you to pursue this venture successfully?

- Who makes up your management team and what roles and responsibilities will the personnel have?

Vision Statement

The vision for your company/organization is set out in a written statement telling the reader what direction or dream you wish your company to pursue for the next three to five years. Write this statement in the future tense. As stated in Chapter 5, Bill Gate's vision for Microsoft when it first began was to have "a computer on every desk, in every home and in every office." The vision of the TD Bank is simply, "To be the better bank."[4] The Australian company, The Body Shop's vision is "to be operating and recognised as the benchmark Company for the integration of Economic Success, Stakeholder Fulfillment and Social and Environmental Change."[5] Cara Operations Ltd., founded by the Phelan family in 1883, is a privately owned Canadian company and the largest operator of full service restaurants and the leading caterer to the travel industry in Canada. Cara's vision is "to be Canada's leading integrated restaurant company."[6] The vision of Renée's, a Canadian gourmet food products company, is "To be the market leader in developing and delivering superior quality, innovative fresh food products."[7]

For additional examples, refer to Chapter 5: The Manager as a Planner and Strategist.

Refer to the exercise you did for Chapter 5: The Manager as a Planner and Strategist. Revise your vision statement now that you have finished all the exercises.

Input your vision statement into the Business Plan Software. Keep it to approximately 150 words.

Mission Statement

The mission statement tells the reader what the purpose of your company/organization is. Refer to the mission statement of The Body Shop outlined below.[8] Ask yourself what the essence of your business is. What will the business really be doing? Why does it exist? What values is it premised on? Every noun, adjective, and verb in the statement is important and should explain the problem that will be solved or the need that will be fulfilled. Your mission statement should reflect your basic beliefs, values, and principles.

TABLE B.2 | *Mission Statement of The Body Shop*

Our reason for being is to:

- Dedicate our business to the pursuit of social and environmental change.

- Creatively balance the financial and human needs of our stakeholders: employees, customers, franchisees, suppliers, and shareholders.

- Courageously ensure that our business is ecologically sustainable, meeting the needs of the present without compromising the future.

- Meaningfully contribute to local, national, and international communities in which we trade, by adopting a code of conduct, which ensures care, honesty, fairness, and respect.

- Passionately campaign for the protection of the environment, human and civil rights, and against animal testing within the cosmetics and toiletries industry.

- Tirelessly work to narrow the gap between principle and practice, whilst making fun, passion, and care part of our daily lives.

- Refer to the value statement and code of ethics you created for the exercise you did for Chapter 3: Managing Ethics, Social Responsibility, and Diversity. Incorporate these values and principles in your mission statement.

- Refer to the mission statement you wrote for the exercise you did for Chapter 5: The Manager as a Planner and Strategist. Revise your mission statement now that you have finished all the exercises.

Write the revised version of your Mission Statement for your venture in the present tense, in the Business Plan Software. Keep it to approximately 150 words.

Organizational Goals

Organizational goals must be made for the business as a whole and for each functional area. Organization-wide goals are longer term and are strategic in nature, while functional level goals are shorter term and are more operational in nature. For example, functional level goals can be made in the areas of market share, efficiency, profitability, and finance. The objectives of the organization aim to realize the vision and mission statements. Goals and objectives are statements of the level of performance desired within a certain timeframe. Goals must be S.M.A.R.T. They must be formulated so that they are:

- **S**pecific

- **M**easurable

- **A**ttainable

- **R**ealistic within a

- **T**imeframe

An example of a smart goal relating to market share might look like the following:

> *"By the end of the first year of operation, ABC company will have a 20% market share for its product XYZ."*

The Body Shop might formulate the goal of …

> *"giving 5% of gross profits to the major charitable organizations in the environmental movement by the year 2010."*

This goal is consistent with the company's mission and strategic vision as stated above. Once goals are developed, plans must be formulated to achieve the objectives. These plans are generally referred to as strategies. The formulation of strategy depends upon the opportunities and threats facing your company from the forces in the organizational environment. You will formulate your strategy after doing an analysis of the current situation. The competitive analysis and strategy is analyzed in the context of the industry as a whole and detailed in Section 4, The Market.

Formulate two smart goals for each of the following areas using a one- and two-year timeframe:

Functional Area	Goals	Rank the importance of each goal to fulfilling the mission of the venture
Finance and/or Debt Repayment	1. 2.	
Sales	1. 2.	
Marketing	1. 2.	
Research and Development	1. 2.	
Quality	1. 2.	
Corporate Culture	1. 2.	
Planning	1. 2.	
Organizing	1. 2.	
Controlling	1. 2.	
Leading	1. 2.	
Production	1. 2.	
Other (specify)	1. 2.	

Summarize the primary business goals of your organization in this section. Refer to the exercise you did for Chapter 13: Organizational Control.

State what control measures you will use for each business goal or standard.

Enter the highest-ranking business goals as part of your Executive Summary.

Form of Ownership

Refer to the Developing a Business Plan exercise for Chapter 1: Managers and Managing. You were asked to scan the environment in which your business/company/organization will be operating. One of the questions asked you to think about what type of legal form would be appropriate for your organization. Will you need a partner? Should you incorporate or simply operate as a sole proprietor? What advantages, if any, would there be in forming a cooperative structure? Refresh your memory about the advantages and disadvantages of each legal structure by reviewing an introductory business textbook. Now that you have developed your ideas and business plan up to this point, describe the legal form of your organization.

Which legal structure do you think is most appropriate and why?

Describe the legal form of ownership in the Business Plan Software.

Authority of Principals

At the beginning of a new venture, the principal person who writes the Business Plan generally has overriding authority over other members of the management team, if a team exists at all. In the case that several people are involved in the management team, the positions they will hold and roles they will play should be described and justified based on their experience and expertise.

Who are the members of the management team? Describe their experience and expertise in this section of your Business Plan.

List the roles and responsibilities of each member of the management team. Include who has cheque-signing authority.

- *A description of the management team and their roles should be included in the Executive Summary. The résumés of the management team should be included in the Appendices.*

4. Profile of the Industry or Sector

This part of the business plan reviews industry trends and competitive strategies. It is based on a detailed analysis of the forces in the organizational environment that may impact the new venture. Refer to the preliminary research you did in the Developing a Business Plan exercise in Chapter 2: Managing the Organizational Environment. Use this research to support the opportunities and strategy of your organization. You may have to do further research now that your ideas have solidified somewhat.

Future Outlook and Trends Within the Industry

In this subsection tell the reader what your research suggests about demand within the industry. Refer to the data you gathered for the Developing a Business Plan exercise in Chapter 2: Managing the Organizational Environment. Answer the following questions:

- What are the major economic, technological, legal, and political trends on a national and local level?

- Is the market growing or declining?
- What are the numbers of competitors operating in this sector?
- Are the numbers of competitors increasing or decreasing?
- How many new firms entered this industry in the past three years?
- Are consumers' needs changing? What is the trend?

  Describe the environmental and industry analysis.

- *Make sure you reference the source of all the information used.*

5. Profile of the Product/Service

This part of the business plan provides the reader with a complete overview of all products, services, and operations of the venture. It answers questions such as:

- What are your products and/or services?
- Describe the products and/or services, including whether or not any trademarks, patents, copyright, or licensing must be dealt with.
- To date, what development work has been completed?
- Where will the venture be located? Why? Consider traffic patterns, supply of labour, local taxes etc.
- Will the building be leased or purchased? State the terms.
- What office equipment will be needed? Will this be leased or purchased?
- Will the facility have room for expansion, adequate parking, hydro and sewage, correct zoning, etc?

Product or Service Description

Describe with as much detail as you can, the product or service you will be providing. If you have a sample of the product, a photograph should become part of the Appendix. If you have developed a prototype of an original product or a modification of an existing product, you should apply for a patent and/or protection of your intellectual property. This can be done online:

- http://strategis.ic.gc.ca/sc_mrksv/cipo/welcome/welcom-e.html

  Tell the reader where you are in the development process at the time of writing this business plan and when you expect the process to be completed.

Size and Location of the Organization

In this subsection, consider how to decide on an appropriate location for your venture. Consider the criteria below for each potential site. Assign a weight to each criterion in order of importance from 1 (lowest) to 10 (highest) and apply the weighted criteria to each site to come up with a rank ordering of the most desirable to the least desirable.

- How much space will you need for your operation?
- How much will that space and location cost per square foot?
- Do any restrictions exist for parking?

- Is it zoned for commercial use?
- Is the building in need of renovation?
- Is there potential for expansion at this location?
- Can the building be leased or purchased?
- How many competitors exist in the area?

Criteria	Site X	Site Y	Site Z
Cost per square foot			
Parking			
Accessibility			
History of the building			
Number of competitors in the area			
Zoning laws			
Potential for expansion			
Features of the area: specify			
Other (specify)			

Describe the size and location of your venture.

Office Equipment and Personnel

Tell the reader what office equipment, such as phone/fax, computer and printer, cartridges, desks, lamps, chairs, paper, pens, paper clips, etc. will be needed and what the cost of those items will be. These costs will be documented in the Financial Plan but should be discussed here. Also describe the personnel needed to staff the office. A detailed plan on managing human resources will be constructed in Section 8.0, Development.

Describe the office equipment and personnel required by your venture in the first year of operation.

History of the Venture

End this subsection with a note on the evolution of the venture and the background of yourself and any other people who are involved.

Describe your experience with the product/service and/or the demographic market you are seeking to tap in this location.

6. Marketing Plan

This part of the business plan describes how the product or service will be distributed, priced, and promoted. Detailed research must be gathered on who will buy the product or service; what the potential size of the market is and whether there is potential for growth; the prices that should be charged; the distribution channel and the most effective promotion strategy to reach the target market. Analysis of current and future trends, market conditions, and the competitive analysis you completed in the previous section, will inform your marketing plan. The importance of this section of the Business Plan cannot be underestimated. Marketing textbooks should be consulted and reviewed to be able to fully articulate the steps involved in the Marketing Plan, however, the following captures the essential principles that must be incorporated.

Market Segment

Which segment of the market will buy your product or service? Demographic characteristics like age, income, geographic location, and buyer behaviour need to be researched and documented. This is usually done through conducting focus groups, giving surveys, interviewing potential market segments, and through observing and recording pre- and post-purchase behavioural habits of customers.

For each market segment, create a customer profile by researching the following:

- Demographic questions

- Customer attitudes on price and quality

- Where customers currently buy the product/service

- Where customers wish to buy the product/service

- What is the influence of advertising

- How much of the product/service does the customer buy and how often

- Why does the customer buy this product/service

Characteristics of the Customer	Customer Profile for Your Venture's Product/ Service/Offering	Potential for Growth/Trends	Source
Demographic information			
Frequency of purchase			
No. of units purchased yearly			
Price sensitivity			
Lifestyle/personality			
Advertising influences			
Motivation			
Buying decisions based on:			
Other			

Use this information to describe who the prospective buyer is, why they want an offering like yours, what needs they are having met by using your product/service, and why they would buy yours over the competition.

Pricing

Before setting the price of your product or service, you must evaluate your costs per unit, what the markup should be and what the competition charges for a similar product/service. Cost of goods should include material and labour (if manufacturing a product), overhead (utilities, rent, insurance, salaries), and costs from suppliers. You must add up the costs based on an estimate of the volume of sales. Markups or margins in your industry can be found by reading a trade journal or by asking the suppliers. The markup usually includes a degree of profit that represents the industry standard.

- If you plan to increase market penetration by using pricing specials or volume discounts, you should describe them. Before discounting to undercut the competition and gain market share, you should consider that the competition could also lower its prices and therefore reduce the profit margins for everyone.

- If you adopt a differentiation business level strategy for your product/service, you may be able to justify charging more than the competition. To do this, you will offer customers a product or service that is unique and/or better quality such that people will pay the higher price relative to the competition.

   Describe your pricing strategy in terms of dollars per unit and how that compares to the competition.

Distribution

How will you make it convenient for your customers to access your product/service? The market conditions, attributes of the product/service cost benefits, and characteristics of the venture should all be considered when deciding on a channel of distribution. It may be appropriate to sell directly to the customer or to a retailer if the target market is concentrated in a particular geographical area. If not, it may be appropriate to use a distributor or wholesaler. If the product is large, bulky, perishable, hazardous, or expensive, the rule of thumb is to channel the product through direct sales. If the cost of indirect sales (using a middle person such as a retailer or wholesaler) is minimal and the benefit is great in terms of reaching a dispersed market, it may be more appropriate to channel indirectly. And finally, if the venture has great financial strength, multiple channels may be considered.

If you intend to use dealers or distributors, discounts or commissions will be required, and should be described.

   Describe your distribution strategy.

Promotion

The success of your venture will largely depend on your promotional plan. Advertising, public relations, and Internet marketing are common ways of promoting your organization to your target market. Consider that each market segment may require different promotional activities. Also consider the degree to which your target market is influenced by advertising. Would a slogan be appropriate to capture the vision of your organization or capitalize on the uniqueness of your product/service?

   Develop a slogan and/or logo that promotes the image you want to project about your organization/product/service.

   Decide whether you will "Pull" or "Push" your promotions. Things to consider include:

- The Pull strategy requires direct contact with the customer. This requires a major commitment to advertising. The objective is to attract the customers to every channel outlet for your product/service. If enough customers demand your product, the channels will want to carry it. The price and quality of your product is important here.

- The Push strategy requires less investment in advertising. The Push strategy maximizes the use of all available channels of distribution to "push" the offering into the marketplace, usually by giving large discounts or commissions as incentives to the channels to promote the offering. Research must be done into the channel discount requirements and the relationship the competition has with the channel.

Create a list of public relations, Internet activities, and types of advertising that you can undertake to generate awareness of your venture in your target market(s). Expected returns include the audience reached and how this exposure will benefit you.

Promotional Activity	Date and Contact Person	Cost and Length of Run	Expected Returns
Send a press kit with your company's profile, pictures, and press releases to newspapers and trade journals			
Host an open house			
Go to a trade show			
Write letters to the editor of various papers			
Develop a company website			
Blog			
Register with search engines			
Banner ads			
Billboard ads			
Radio/TV ads			
Other			

Write your promotional strategy for each market segment.

- *Keep in mind the image you want others to perceive about your offering.*

Competitive Analysis

Tell the reader what strategies you intend to pursue to develop the product or service and achieve your business goals. Analyze the potential threats your venture will face from businesses in the same industry. The more you know about the strengths and weaknesses of your competitors, the more effective your Business Plan is likely to be. Most competitors can be identified from websites, trade journal articles, advertisements, the Yellow pages, and experience.

Summarize the Competitive Analysis you conducted to determine the feasibility of your project, from Chapter 5: The Manager as a Planner and Strategist.

Evaluate the Weaknesses of the Organization

Tell the reader what you see as your venture's weakest link in successfully achieving the vision, mission, and business goals you have set out above and how you will counter any threats.

Assessment of Risk

Use the five forces analysis you did in the Developing a Business Plan exercise for Chapter 5 to summarize the main threats facing your venture and how you will assume the risk. Refer to an introductory business textbook for information on ways to manage risks.

Growth Strategy

In discussing your business strategy, be sure to answer the following questions:

- How will you take advantage of your competitors' weaknesses to gain an advantage?
- What will you do differently?
- How is your model unique?

Describe the business level strategy you intend to use.

Ending the Venture

What are your long-term exit strategies? Give the reader a sense of how you will end the venture. Do you intend to sell the venture, transform the business in the maturity phase of development, franchise, or dissolve the company? *Include your long-term exit strategies in the Executive Summary.*

7. Organization Plan

This section addresses the engineering and development activities within your enterprise. It also provides a description of the organizational structure, current and projected size, personnel requirements, and the human resources management plan.

Things to consider:

- What are the roles and responsibilities of personnel and how might these change after the first year?

- Is your product/service ready to go to market immediately?

- What cultural and technological considerations do you need to address in the production or delivery?

- What is your human resources management plan?

Roles and Responsibilities of Members of the Organization

The relationships that jobs have with one another are depicted in an Organizational Chart. The Organizational Chart shows the roles and responsibilities of all members within the organization. Refer to the Building a Business Plan exercise you did for Chapter 6, Managing Organizational Structure.

Recreate the Organizational Chart for year one.

Describe how you anticipate the design of the organization to change in year two if your revenue forecasts are correct. You may have to add a layer of management as the organization/company grows. How will you assemble the right mix of people?

Building Organizational Culture

The organizational structure creates the foundation for the coordination of work that needs to be done. But finding the right mix of people to assume the responsibilities outlined in the structure is just as critical to the success of the organization as having a marketable product.

Revisit the value statement you wrote for the Developing a Business Plan exercise in Chapter 3, Managing Ethics, Social Responsibility, and Diversity. The management team will foster the values and principles embodied in your vision and mission statements. The desired culture must be consistently role modelled for employees. It must be deliberately embodied in the symbols and practices of the organization if it is to be successful.

Refer to your own leadership style as assessed in the Developing a Business Plan Exercise, Chapter 9: Leadership.

Write a statement telling the reader what type of characteristics (personalities, attitudes, behaviours, dress, communication styles) they would find in your management team.

Refer to the exercise you did for Chapter 7: Organizational Culture and Change.

> **What set of values and principles do you want to form the basis of your new organization/company's culture?**

> **Make a list of what you need to consider in terms of technology utilization requirements to service customers effectively.**

HR Management Plan

The principal people involved in the management of the venture must make a plan to deal with recruiting and selecting, training and developing, appraising, and compensating employees as the organizational design evolves and grows. The objective of human resources planning is to match the right people to the right job at the right time. All jobs should have a job description and set of job specifications.

Refer to the exercises you did for Chapter 11: Managing Human Resources and Chapter 8: Motivation.

> **Include all job descriptions you have developed in the Appendices to your Business Plan.**

Consider the degree of responsibility and autonomy you build into a job as a motivating factor.

> **Make a list of the external sources of potential applicants.**

> **What selection criteria will you use to hire new employees? Describe why they are valid and reliable.**

Research some organizations that share your values and look up their employment policies on their website. Use these to develop your company policies (on things like sick leave and other benefits).

> **Include your company policies as Appendices to your Business Plan.**

- Make sure you build the perception of equity in all policies.

> **Use the chart you developed in the Business Plan exercise for Chapter 11: Managing Human Resources to help you anticipate your personnel needs and costs. Describe your human resource plan.**

- Consider the type of rewards you will give employees for high performance.

- Make sure you build in measures, such as training and development, which will strengthen your employee's levels of expectancy.

8. Operating and Control Systems Plan

This section of the Business Plan describes the flow of goods and services from production to the customer. Even if your venture does not manufacture goods, you still need to tell the reader how your business transactions will occur. For example, if your venture is a retail-clothing store, you must describe who will supply the clothing you sell, how you will store and control the inventory, and how you will sell the goods to the customer (store front operation or Internet?). What type of technology will you utilize to serve customers efficiently? Describe your suppliers, their financial stability, how they will deliver your orders (logistics), their reputation, and whether they in any way, might be a competitor. Indicate whether you have a second source for each of the suppliers and what the impact would be on your operation if the original supplier failed to meet their commitments and you had to resort to the second source.

Retail Operation or Service Provider

If your venture is a retail operation or a service provider, you should consider the following questions:

1. From whom will merchandise be purchased?
   - Consider the supplier's reputation, past record, prices versus other suppliers, delivery methods, whether or not they supply your competitors, and how important your business is to them.

2. How will the inventory and quality control system operate?
   - Consider how you will inspect the goods received and what you will do if materials are defective.
   - What are the storage and processing space needs?
   - What is your ordering materials process?

3. How will the goods flow to the customer?
   - What steps are involved in a business transaction?
   - What technology (debit machines, scanners) will you need to service customers effectively?

Manufacturing Operation

If your venture is a manufacturing operation, you should describe the complete process. How much, if any, of the manufacturing processes will be subcontracted? What kind of physical plant does the operation require? What type of specialized machinery or equipment is needed to perform the manufacturing operations? Who will supply the raw materials and at what terms? Will any capital expenditures be necessary?

1. If subcontractors are used, give the names and addresses and tell the reader why they were selected. Include the costs of subcontracting and copies of any contracts that have been signed.
2. What will be the layout of the production process?
   - Illustrate the steps if possible.
3. What equipment and raw materials will be needed?
4. Who are the suppliers and what are the costs?
   - Describe why you chose these suppliers.
5. What are the future capital equipment needs of the venture?

Enter your answers to the above questions in your Business Plan.

9. Financial Plan

The Financial Plan tells the reader what the level of potential investment commitment is needed and whether or not the business plan is feasible. It details the needed capital requirements for starting the venture, the forecasted sales, and the expenses incurred in selling the product/service over a number of months and years.

Anyone reading your financial projections will want to know what assumptions went into the creation of the projections. This includes assumptions about for example, the size of the market and your ability to penetrate it, staffing plans, management salaries, inventory turnover, receivables and payables periods, and expectations for investment or loans.

Refer to the exercise you did for Chapter 13: Organizational Control and an accounting textbook to help you calculate the financial statements for your venture for a period of two years. Or simply follow the instructions in the Business Plan software program. This will create the spreadsheets for your plan.

When you are ready to enter the data for the financial plan in your Business Plan, the software program will guide you through questions and assumptions about all the financial variables needed to accurately project your cash flow and income statements.[9]

For up-to-date tax rates, refer to www.deloitte.com/dtt/newsletter/0,1012,sid%253D3634%2526cid%253D86099,00.html

Pro Forma Income Statement

The Income Statement subtracts all the costs incurred to operate your enterprise from the amounts received from selling goods and services. The result is a net income or a net loss for the year. You will be asked to enter revenue and expenses for each month of the first year, for each quarter of the second year.

Cash Flow Projections

The Cash Flow Statement will show the amount of cash you have available at any given time during your business plan. If a negative cash balance occurs you will have to examine your revenue and expense projections. To address the negative cash balance you will have to increase revenues, decrease expenses, or arrange to get cash through a loan or capital investment. Cash flow is projected for each month of the first year, for each quarter of the second year.

Pro Forma Balance Sheet

The balance sheet is divided into two sections: assets and liabilities plus shareholders' equity. The two sections must always be in balance. A dollar amount or a "balance" represents each asset, liability, and component of shareholders' equity reported in the balance sheet. The balance sheet is projected for each month of the first year, for each quarter of the second year.

Alternative Scenarios

When presenting your business plan to an investor or to your management it is of value to show projections for revenues and expenses that represent the best possible case and the worst possible case. It is recommended you provide some explanation for the circumstances that might precipitate either the best or worst case in the financial assumptions section.

Break-Even Analysis

The projection of when the revenue will surpass the expenses of the venture is called the Break-even point and will be depicted graphically by the software.

Enter the financial data in the software for your Business Plan.

10. Appendices

The appendix of the Business Plan generally contains all the documents that are referenced in the plan itself and any backup material that is not necessary in the text of the document. You might consider including the following:

- Product/service samples
- Market research data
- Legal forms and documents
- Leases or contracts
- Price lists from suppliers, if applicable
- Promotional material examples
- Résumés of the management team
- Other back up material

Glossary

ACCOMMODATIVE APPROACH Moderate commitment to social responsibility; willingness to do more than the law requires if asked.

ADMINISTRATIVE MANAGEMENT The study of how to create an organizational structure that leads to high efficiency and effectiveness.

ADMINISTRATIVE MODEL An approach to decision making that explains why decision making is basically uncertain and risky and why managers usually make satisficing rather than optimum decisions.

AMBIGUOUS INFORMATION Information that can be interpreted in multiple and often conflicting ways.

ARTIFACTS Aspects of an organization's culture that one sees, hears, and feels.

ASSUMPTIONS The taken-for-granted notions of how something should be in an organization.

AUTHORITY The power to hold people accountable for their actions and to make decisions concerning the use of organizational resources.

BARRIERS TO ENTRY Factors that make it difficult and costly for an organization to enter a particular task environment or industry.

BEHAVIOURAL MANAGEMENT The study of how managers should behave in order to motivate employees and encourage them to perform at high levels and be committed to achieving organizational goals.

BELIEFS The understandings of how objects and ideas relate to each other.

BENCHMARKING Comparing performance on specific dimensions with the performance of high-performing organizations.

BIAS The systematic tendency to use information about others in ways that result in inaccurate perceptions.

BOTTOM-UP CHANGE Change that is introduced gradually and involves managers and employees at all levels of an organization.

BOUNDARYLESS ORGANIZATION An organization whose members are linked by computers, faxes, computer-aided design systems, and video teleconferencing, and who rarely, if ever, see one another face to face.

BOUNDED RATIONALITY Cognitive limitations that constrain one's ability to interpret, process, and act on information.

BRAINSTORMING A group problem-solving technique in which individuals meet face to face to generate and debate a wide variety of alternatives from which to make a decision.

BRAND LOYALTY Customers' preference for the products of organizations that currently exist in the task environment.

BUREAUCRACY A formal system of organization and administration designed to ensure efficiency and effectiveness.

BUREAUCRATIC CONTROL Control of behaviour by means of a comprehensive system of rules and standard operating procedures.

BUSINESS-LEVEL PLAN Divisional managers' decisions relating to divisions' long-term goals, overall strategy, and structure.

BUSINESS-LEVEL STRATEGY A plan that indicates how a division intends to compete against its rivals in an industry.

BUSINESS-TO-BUSINESS (B2B) NETWORKS A group of organizations that join together and use software to link themselves to potential global suppliers to increase efficiency and effectiveness.

CAFETERIA-STYLE BENEFIT PLAN A plan from which employees can choose the benefits that they want.

CHARISMATIC LEADER An enthusiastic, self-confident leader able to communicate clearly his or her vision of how good things could be.

CLAN CONTROL Control exerted on individuals and groups in an organization by shared values, norms, standards of behaviour, and expectations.

CLOSED SYSTEM A system that is self-contained and thus not affected by changes that occur in its external environment.

CODES OF ETHICS Formal standards and rules, based on beliefs about right or wrong, that managers can use to help themselves make appropriate decisions with regard to the interests of their stakeholders.

COERCIVE POWER The ability of a manager to punish others.

COLLECTIVE BARGAINING Negotiation between labour unions and managers to resolve conflicts and disputes about issues such as working hours, wages, benefits, working conditions, and job security.

COMMAND ECONOMY An economic system in which the government owns all businesses and specifies which and how many goods and services are produced and the prices at which they are sold.

COMMAND GROUP A group composed of subordinates who report to the same supervisor; also called a department or unit.

COMMUNICATION The sharing of information between two or more individuals or groups to reach a common understanding.

COMPETITIVE ADVANTAGE The ability of one organization to outperform other organizations because it produces desired goods or services more efficiently and effectively than competitors do.

COMPETITORS Organizations that produce goods and services that are similar to a particular organization's goods and services.

CONCEPTUAL SKILLS The ability to analyze and diagnose a situation and to distinguish between cause and effect.

CONCURRENT CONTROL Control that gives managers immediate feedback on how efficiently inputs are being transformed into outputs so that managers can correct problems as they arise.

CONTINGENCY THEORY The idea that managers' choice of organizational structures and control systems depends on—is contingent on—characteristics of the external environment in which the organization operates.

CONTROL SYSTEMS Formal target-setting, monitoring, evaluation, and feedback systems that provide managers with information about how well the organization's strategy and structure are working.

CONTROLLING Evaluating how well an organization is achieving its goals and taking action to maintain or improve performance; one of the four principal functions of management.

CORPORATE-LEVEL PLAN Top management's decisions relating to the organization's mission, overall strategy, and structure.

CORPORATE-LEVEL STRATEGY A plan that indicates the industries and national markets in which an organization intends to compete.

COST-LEADERSHIP STRATEGY Driving the organization's costs down below the costs of its rivals.

CREATIVITY A decision maker's ability to discover original and novel ideas that lead to feasible alternative courses of action.

CROSS-FUNCTIONAL TEAM A group of individuals from different departments brought together to perform organizational tasks.

CUSTOMERS Individuals and groups that buy the goods and services that an organization produces.

DATA Raw, unsummarized, and unanalyzed facts.

DECISION MAKING The process by which managers analyze the options facing them and make decisions about specific organizational goals and courses of action.

DECODING Interpreting and trying to make sense of a message.

DEFENSIVE APPROACH Minimal commitment to social responsibility; willingness to do what the law requires and no more.

DELPHI TECHNIQUE A decision-making technique in which group members do not meet face to face but respond in writing to questions posed by the group leader.

DEMOGRAPHIC FORCES Outcomes of changes in, or changing attitudes toward, the characteristics of a population, such as age, gender, ethnic origin, race, sexual orientation, and social class.

DEPARTMENT A group of people who work together and possess similar skills or use the same knowledge, tools, or techniques to perform their jobs.

DEVELOPMENT Building the knowledge and skills of organizational members so that they will be prepared to take on new responsibilities and challenges.

DEVELOPMENTAL CONSIDERATION Behaviour a leader engages in to support and encourage followers and help them develop and grow on the job.

DEVIL'S ADVOCACY Critical analysis of a preferred alternative, made by a group member who plays the role of devil's advocate to defend unpopular or opposing alternatives for the sake of argument.

DIFFERENTIATION STRATEGY Distinguishing an organization's products from the products of competitors in dimensions such as product design, quality, or after-sales service.

DIGITAL CAPITAL Intellectual capital consisting of three elements: people's brains or "human capital," organizational knowledge, and customer, brand and market share capital.

DISTRIBUTIVE JUSTICE A moral principle calling for the distribution of pay raises, promotions, and other organizational resources to be based on meaningful contributions that individuals have made and not on personal characteristics over which they have no control.

DISTRIBUTIVE NEGOTIATION Adversarial negotiation in which the parties in conflict compete to win the most resources while conceding as little as possible.

DISTRIBUTORS Organizations that help other organizations sell their goods or services to customers.

DIVERSIFICATION Expanding operations into a new business or industry and producing new goods or services.

DIVERSITY Differences among people in age, gender, race, ethnicity, religion, sexual orientation, socio-economic background, and capabilities or disabilities.

DIVISION A business unit that has its own set of managers and functions or departments and competes in a distinct industry.

DIVISION OF LABOUR Splitting the work to be performed into particular tasks and assigning tasks to individual workers.

DIVISIONAL MANAGERS Managers who control the various divisions of an organization.

DIVISIONAL STRUCTURE An organizational structure composed of separate business units within which are the functions that work together to produce a specific product for a specific customer.

DRIVING FORCES Forces that direct behaviour away from the status quo.

ECONOMIC FORCES Interest rates, inflation, unemployment, economic growth, and other factors that affect the general health and well-being of a nation or the regional economy of an organization.

ECONOMIES OF SCALE Cost advantages associated with large operations.

EFFECTIVENESS A measure of the appropriateness of the goals an organization is pursuing and of the degree to which the organization achieves those goals.

EFFICIENCY A measure of how well or productively resources are used to achieve a goal.

EMOTIONAL INTELLIGENCE The ability to understand and manage one's own moods and emotions and the moods and emotions of other people.

EMPLOYEE-CENTRED BEHAVIOUR Behaviour indicating that a manager trusts, respects, and cares about subordinates.

EMPOWERMENT Expanding employees' tasks and responsibilities.

ENCODING Translating a message into understandable symbols or language.

ENTROPY The tendency of a system to dissolve and disintegrate because it loses the ability to control itself.

ENVIRONMENTAL CHANGE The degree to which forces in the task and general environments change and evolve over time.

EQUITY The justice, impartiality, and fairness to which all organizational members are entitled.

EQUITY THEORY A theory of motivation that focuses on people's perceptions of the fairness of their work outcomes relative to their work inputs.

ESCALATING COMMITMENT A source of cognitive bias resulting from the tendency to commit additional resources to a project even if evidence shows that the project is failing.

ETHICAL DECISION A decision that reasonable or typical stakeholders would find acceptable because it aids stakeholders, the organization, or society.

ETHICS Moral principles or beliefs about what is right or wrong.

ETHICS OMBUDSPERSON An ethics officer who monitors an organization's practices and procedures to be sure they are ethical.

EXPECTANCY In expectancy theory, a perception about the extent to which effort will result in a certain level of performance.

EXPECTANCY THEORY The theory that motivation will be high when employees believe that high levels of effort will lead to high performance, and high performance will lead to the attainment of desired outcomes.

EXPERT POWER Power that is based in the special knowledge, skills, and expertise that a leader possesses.

EXTERNAL ENVIRONMENT The forces operating outside an organization that affect how the organization functions.

EXTINCTION Stopping the performance of dysfunctional behaviours by eliminating whatever is reinforcing them.

EXTRINSICALLY MOTIVATED BEHAVIOUR Behaviour that is performed to acquire material or social rewards or to avoid punishment.

FEEDBACK CONTROL Control that gives managers information about customers' reactions to goods and services so that corrective action can be taken if necessary.

FEEDFORWARD CONTROL Control that allows managers to anticipate and deal with potential problems.

FILTERING Withholding part of a message out of the mistaken belief that the receiver does not need or will not want the information.

FIRST-LINE MANAGERS Managers who are responsible for the daily supervision and coordination of nonmanagerial employees.

FOCUSED DIFFERENTIA-TION STRATEGY Serving only one segment of the overall market and trying to be the most differentiated organization serving that segment.

FOCUSED LOW-COST STRATEGY Serving only one segment of the overall market and being the lowest-cost organization serving that segment.

FORMAL APPRAISAL An appraisal conducted at a set time during the year and based on performance dimensions and measures that were specified in advance.

FREE-MARKET ECONOMY An economic system in which private enterprise controls production, and the interaction of supply and demand determines which and how many goods and services are produced and how much consumers pay for them.

FUNCTION A unit or department in which people have the same skills or use the same resources to perform their jobs.

FUNCTIONAL MANAGERS Managers who supervise the various functions—such as manufacturing, accounting, and sales—within a division.

FUNCTIONAL STRUCTURE An organizational structure composed of all the departments that an organization requires to produce its goods or services.

FUNCTIONAL-LEVEL PLAN Functional managers' decisions relating to the goals that functional managers propose to pursue to help the division reach its business-level goals.

FUNCTIONAL-LEVEL STRAT-EGY A plan that indicates how a function intends to achieve its goals.

GENERAL ENVIRONMENT The economic, technological, socio-cultural, demographic, political and legal, and global forces that affect an organization and its task environment.

GEOGRAPHIC STRUCTURE An organizational structure in which each region of a country or area of the world is served by a self-contained division.

GLOBAL FORCES Outcomes of changes in international relationships; changes in nations' economic, political, and legal systems; and changes in technology—such as falling trade barriers, the growth of representative democracies, and reliable and instantaneous communication.

GLOBAL ORGANIZATIONS Organizations that operate and compete in more than one country.

GLOBAL STRATEGY Selling the same standardized product and using the same basic marketing approach in each national market.

GOAL A desired future outcome that an organization strives to achieve.

GOAL-SETTING THEORY A theory that focuses on identifying the types of goals that are most effective in producing high levels of motivation and performance and explaining why goals have these effects.

GROUP Two or more people who interact with each other to reach certain goals or meet certain needs.

GROUP COHESIVENESS The degree to which members are attracted or loyal to a group.

GROUP NORMS Shared guidelines or rules for behaviour that most group members follow.

GROUP ROLE A set of behaviours and tasks that a member of a group is expected to perform because of his or her position in the group.

GROUPTHINK A pattern of faulty and biased decision making that occurs in groups whose members strive for agreement among themselves at the expense of accurately assessing information relevant to a decision.

HERZBERG'S MOTIVATOR-HYGIENE THEORY A needs theory that distinguishes between motivator needs (related to the nature of the work itself) and hygiene needs (related to the physical and psychological context in which the work is performed). Herzberg proposed that motivator needs must be met in order for motivation and job satisfaction to be high.

HEURISTICS Rules of thumb that simplify decision making.

HIERARCHY OF AUTHOR-ITY An organization's chain of command, specifying the relative authority of each manager.

HOSTILE WORK ENVIRON-MENT SEXUAL HARASS-MENT Telling lewd jokes, displaying pornography, making sexually oriented remarks about someone's personal appearance, and other sex-related actions that make the work environment unpleasant.

HUMAN RESOURCE MAN-AGEMENT (HRM) Activities that managers engage in to attract and retain employees and to ensure that they perform at a high level and contribute to the accomplishment of organizational goals.

HUMAN RESOURCE PLAN-NING Activities that managers use to forecast their current and future needs for human resources.

HUMAN SKILLS The ability to understand, alter, lead, and control the behaviour of other individuals and groups.

ILLUSION OF CONTROL A source of cognitive bias resulting from the tendency to overestimate one's own ability to control activities and events.

INDIVIDUAL ETHICS Personal standards that govern how individuals interact with other people.

INEQUITY Lack of fairness.

INFORMAL APPRAISAL An unscheduled appraisal of ongoing progress and areas for improvement.

INFORMAL ORGANIZATION The system of behavioural rules and norms that emerge in a group.

INFORMATION Data that are organized in a meaningful fashion.

INFORMATION DISTOR-TION Changes in the meaning of a message as the message passes through a series of senders and receivers.

INFORMATION RICHNESS The amount of information that a communication medium can carry and the extent to which the medium enables sender and receiver to reach a common understanding.

INFORMATION TECHNOL-OGY The means by which information is acquired, organized, stored, manipulated, and transmitted.

INNOVATION The process of creating new goods and services or developing better ways to produce or provide goods and services.

INSTRUMENTALITY In expectancy theory, a perception about the extent to which performance will result in the attainment of outcomes.

INTEGRATIVE BARGAINING Cooperative negotiation in which the parties in conflict work together to achieve a resolution that is good for them all.

INTELLECTUAL STIMULA-TION Behaviour a leader engages in to make followers aware of problems and view these problems in new ways, consistent with the leader's vision.

INTERNAL ENVIRONMENT The forces operating within an organization and stemming from the organization's structure and culture.

INTRINSICALLY MOTIVATED BEHAVIOUR Behaviour that is performed for its own sake.

INTUITION Ability to make sound decisions based on past experience and immediate feelings about the information at hand.

JARGON Specialized language that members of an occupation, group, or organization develop to facilitate communication among themselves.

JOB ANALYSIS Identifying the tasks, duties, and responsibilities that make up a job and the knowledge, skills, and abilities needed to perform the job.

JOB DESIGN The process by which managers decide how to divide tasks into specific jobs.

JOB ENLARGEMENT Increasing the number of different tasks in a given job by changing the division of labour.

JOB ENRICHMENT Increasing the degree of responsibility a worker has over his or her job.

JOB SIMPLIFICATION Reducing the number of tasks that each worker performs.

JOB SPECIALIZATION The process by which a division of labour occurs as different employees specialize in different tasks over time.

JOB-ORIENTED BEHAV-IOURS Behaviours that managers engage in to ensure that work gets done, subordinates

perform their jobs acceptably, and the organization is efficient and effective.

JOINT VENTURE A strategic alliance among two or more companies that agree to establish jointly and share the ownership of a new business.

JUDGMENT Ability to develop a sound opinion based on one's evaluation of the importance of the information at hand.

LABOUR RELATIONS The activities that managers engage in to ensure that they have effective working relationships with the labour unions that represent their employees' interests.

LATERAL MOVE A job change that entails no major changes in responsibility or authority levels.

LEADER An individual who is able to exert influence over other people to help achieve group or organizational goals.

LEADER SUBSTITUTE Characteristics of subordinates or characteristics of a situation or context that act in place of the influence of a leader and make leadership unnecessary.

LEADERSHIP The process by which an individual exerts influence over other people and inspires, motivates, and directs their activities to help achieve group or organizational goals.

LEADING Articulating a clear vision and energizing and empowering organizational members so that everyone understands their individual roles in achieving organizational goals; one of the four principal functions of management.

LEARNING ORGANIZATION An organization in which managers try to maximize the ability of individuals and groups to think and behave creatively and thus maximize the potential for organizational learning to take place.

LEGITIMATE POWER The authority that a manager has by virtue of his or her position in an organization's hierarchy.

LINGUISTIC STYLE A person's characteristic way of speaking.

MAINTENANCE ROLES Roles performed by group members to make sure there are good relations among group members.

MANAGEMENT The planning, organizing, leading, and controlling of resources to achieve organizational goals effectively and efficiently.

MANAGEMENT BY OBJEC-TIVES A system of evaluating subordinates for their ability to achieve specific organizational goals or performance standards.

MANAGEMENT SCIENCE THEORY An approach to management that uses rigorous quantitative techniques to help managers make full use of organizational resources.

MANAGER A person who is responsible for supervising the use of an organization's resources to achieve its goals.

MARKET STRUCTURE An organizational structure in which each kind of customer is served by a self-contained division; also called *customer structure*.

MASLOW'S HIERARCHY OF NEEDS An arrangement of five basic needs that, according to Maslow, motivate behaviour. Maslow proposed that the lowest level of unmet needs is the prime motivator and that only one level of needs is motivational at a time.

MATRIX STRUCTURE An organizational structure that simultaneously groups people and resources by function and by product.

MECHANISTIC STRUCTURE An organizational structure in which authority is centralized at the top of the hierarchy, tasks and roles are clearly specified, and employees are closely supervised.

MEDIUM The pathway through which an encoded message is transmitted to a receiver.

MESSAGE The information that a sender wants to share.

MIDDLE MANAGERS Managers who supervise first-line managers and are responsible for finding the best way to use resources to achieve organizational goals.

MISSION STATEMENT A broad declaration of an organization's purpose that identifies the organization's products and customers, and distinguishes the organization from its competitors.

MIXED ECONOMY An economic system in which some sectors of the economy are left to private ownership and free-market mechanisms and others are owned by the government and subject to government planning.

MOTIVATION Psychological forces that determine the direction of a person's behaviour in an organization, a person's level of effort, and a person's level of persistence.

MULTIDOMESTIC STRATEGY Customizing products and marketing strategies to specific national conditions.

NEED A requirement or necessity for survival and well-being.

NEEDS ASSESSMENT An assessment of which employees need training or development and what type of skills or knowledge they need to acquire.

NEEDS THEORIES Theories of motivation that focus on what needs people are trying to satisfy at work and what outcomes will satisfy those needs.

NEGATIVE REINFORCEMENT Eliminating or removing un-desired outcomes once people have performed organizationally functional behaviours.

NEGOTIATION A method of conflict resolution in which the parties in conflict consider various alternative ways to allocate resources to each other in order to come up with a solution acceptable to them all.

NETWORK STRUCTURE A series of strategic alliances that an organization creates with suppliers, manufacturers, and distributors to produce and market a product.

NOISE Anything that hampers any stage of the communication process.

NOMINAL GROUP TECHNIQUE A decision-making technique in which group members write down ideas and solutions, read their suggestions to the whole group, and discuss and then rank the alternatives.

NONPROGRAMMED DECISION MAKING Nonroutine decision making that occurs in response to unusual, unpredictable opportunities and threats.

NONVERBAL COMMUNICATION The encoding of messages by means of facial expressions, body language, and styles of dress.

NORMS Unwritten rules or guidelines for appropriate behaviour in particular situations.

OBSTRUCTIONIST APPROACH Disregard for social responsibility; willingness to engage in and cover up unethical and illegal behaviour.

OPEN SYSTEM A system that takes in resources from its external environment and converts them into goods and services that are then sent back to that environment for purchase by customers.

OPERATING BUDGET A budget that states how managers intend to use organizational resources to achieve organizational goals.

OPTIMUM DECISION The best decision in light of what managers believe to be the most desirable future consequences for their organization.

ORGANIC STRUCTURE An organizational structure in which authority is decentralized to middle and first-line managers and tasks and roles are left ambiguous to encourage employees to cooperate and respond quickly to the unexpected.

ORGANIZATIONAL BEHAVIOUR The study of the factors that have an impact on how individuals and groups respond to and act in organizations.

ORGANIZATIONAL BEHAVIOUR MODIFICATION (OB MOD) The systematic application of operant conditioning techniques to promote the performance of organizationally functional behaviours and discourage the performance of dysfunctional behaviours.

ORGANIZATIONAL CONFLICT The discord that arises when the goals, interest, or values of different individuals or groups are incompatible and those individuals or groups block or thwart each other's attempts to achieve their objectives.

ORGANIZATIONAL CULTURE A system of shared meaning, held by organization members, that distinguishes the organization from other organizations.

ORGANIZATIONAL DESIGN The process by which managers make specific organizing choices that result in a particular kind of organizational structure.

ORGANIZATIONAL ENVIRONMENT The set of forces and conditions that operate beyond an organization's boundaries but affect a manager's ability to acquire and use resources.

ORGANIZATIONAL LEARNING The process through which managers seek to improve employees' desire and ability to understand and manage the organization and its task environment.

ORGANIZATIONAL PERFORMANCE A measure of how efficiently and effectively a manager uses resources to satisfy customers and achieve organizational goals.

ORGANIZATIONAL SOCIALIZATION The process by which newcomers learn an organization's values and norms and acquire the work behaviours necessary to perform jobs effectively.

ORGANIZATIONAL STAKEHOLDERS Shareholders, employees, customers, suppliers, and others who have an interest, claim, or stake in an organization and in what it does.

ORGANIZATIONAL STRUCTURE A formal system of both task and reporting relationships that coordinates and motivates organizational members so that they work together to reach organizational goals.

ORGANIZATIONS Collections of people who work together and coordinate their actions to achieve goals.

ORGANIZING Structuring workplace relationships in a way that allows members of an organization to work together to achieve organizational goals; one of the four principal functions of management.

OUTSOURCING Using outside suppliers and manufacturers to produce goods and services.

OVERPAYMENT INEQUITY Inequity that exists when a person perceives that his or her own outcome/input ratio is greater than the ratio of a referent.

OVERT DISCRIMINATION Knowingly and willingly denying diverse individuals access to opportunities and outcomes in an organization.

PATH-GOAL THEORY A contingency model of leadership proposing that leaders can motivate subordinates by identifying their desired outcomes, rewarding them for high performance and the attainment of work goals with these desired outcomes, and clarifying for them the paths leading to the attainment of work goals.

PAY LEVEL The relative position of an organization's pay incentives in comparison with those of other organizations in the same industry employing similar kinds of workers.

PAY STRUCTURE The arrangement of jobs into categories that reflect their relative importance to the organization and its goals, levels of skill required, and other characteristics.

PERCEPTION The process through which people select, organize, and interpret sensory input to give meaning and order to the world around them.

PERFORMANCE APPRAISAL The evaluation of employees' job performance and contributions to their organization.

PERFORMANCE FEEDBACK The process through which managers share performance appraisal information with subordinates, give subordinates an opportunity to reflect on their own performance, and develop, with subordinates, plans for the future.

PLANNING Identifying and selecting appropriate goals and courses of action; one of the four principal functions of management.

POLICY A general guide to action.

POLITICAL AND LEGAL FORCES Outcomes of changes in laws and regulations, such as the deregulation of industries, the privatization of organizations, and increased emphasis on environmental protection.

POSITION POWER The amount of legitimate, reward, and coercive power that a leader has by virtue of his or her position in an organization; a determinant of how favourable a situation is for leading.

POSITIVE REINFORCEMENT Giving people outcomes they desire when they perform organizationally functional behaviours well.

PRIOR HYPOTHESIS BIAS A cognitive bias resulting from the tendency to base decisions on strong prior beliefs even if evidence shows that those beliefs are wrong.

PRIVATELY HELD ORGANIZATIONS Companies whose shares are not available on the stock exchange but are privately held.

PROACTIVE APPROACH Strong commitment to social responsibility; eagerness to do more than the law requires and to use organizational resources to promote the interests of all organizational stakeholders.

PROCEDURAL JUSTICE A moral principle calling for the use of fair procedures to determine how to distribute outcomes to organizational members.

PROCESS THEORIES Theories of motivation that explore how one actually motivates someone.

PRODUCT STRUCTURE An organizational structure in which each product line or business is handled by a self-contained division.

PRODUCT TEAM STRUCTURE An organizational structure in which employees are permanently assigned to a cross-functional team and report only to the product team manager or to one of his or her direct subordinates.

PRODUCTION BLOCKING A loss of productivity in brainstorming sessions due to the unstructured nature of brainstorming.

PROFESSIONAL ETHICS Standards that govern how members of a profession are to make decisions when the way they should behave is not clear-cut.

PROGRAMMED DECISION MAKING Routine, virtually automatic decision making that follows established rules or guidelines.

PUBLICLY HELD ORGANIZATIONS Companies whose shares are available on the stock exchange for public trading by brokers or dealers.

PUNISHMENT Administering an undesired or negative consequence when dysfunctional behaviour occurs.

QUID PRO QUO SEXUAL HARASSMENT Asking or forcing an employee to perform sexual favours in exchange for some reward or to avoid negative consequences.

RATIONAL DECISION-MAKING MODEL A prescriptive approach to decision making based on the idea that the decision maker can identify and evaluate all possible alternatives and their consequences and rationally choose the most suitable course of action.

REAL-TIME INFORMATION Frequently updated information that reflects current conditions.

RECEIVER The person or group for which a message is intended.

RECRUITMENT Activities that managers use to develop a pool of qualified candidates for open positions.

REFERENT POWER Power that comes from subordinates' and co-workers' respect, admiration, and loyalty.

REINFORCEMENT Anything that causes a given behaviour to be repeated or stopped.

REINFORCEMENT THEORY A motivation theory based on the relationship between a given behaviour and its consequence.

RELATED DIVERSIFICATION Entering a new business or industry to create a competitive advantage in one or more of an organization's existing divisions or businesses.

REPRESENTATIVE DEMOCRACY A political system in which representatives elected by citizens and legally accountable to the electorate form a government whose function is to make decisions on behalf of the electorate.

REPRESENTATIVENESS BIAS A cognitive bias resulting from the tendency to generalize inappropriately from a small sample or from a single vivid case or episode.

REPUTATION The esteem or high repute that individuals or organizations gain when they behave ethically.

RESEARCH AND DEVELOPMENT TEAM A team whose members have the expertise and experience needed to develop new products.

RESOURCES Assets such as people, machinery, raw materials, information, skills, and financial capital.

RESTRAINING FORCES Forces that prevent movement away from the status quo.

RESTRUCTURING Downsizing an organization by eliminating the jobs of large numbers of top, middle, and first-line managers and nonmanagerial employees.

REWARD POWER The ability of a manager to give or withhold tangible and intangible rewards.

ROLE The specific tasks that a person is expected to perform because of the position he or she holds in an organization.

ROLE MAKING Taking the initiative to modify an assigned role by taking on extra responsibilities.

RULES Formal written instructions that specify actions to be taken under different circumstances to achieve specific goals.

RUMOURS Unofficial pieces of information of interest to organizational members but with no identifiable source.

SATISFICING Searching for and choosing acceptable, or satisfactory, ways to respond to problems and opportunities, rather than trying to make the best decision.

SCENARIO PLANNING The generation of multiple forecasts of future conditions followed by an analysis of how to respond effectively to each of those conditions; also called *contingency planning.*

SCIENTIFIC MANAGEMENT The systematic study of relationships between people and tasks for the purpose of redesigning the work process to increase efficiency.

SELECTION The process that managers use to determine the relative qualifications of job applicants and the individuals' potential for performing well in a particular job.

SELF-MANAGED (OR SELF-DIRECTED) WORK TEAMS Groups of employees who supervise their own activities and monitor the quality of the goods and services they provide.

SELF-MANAGED TEAMS Groups of employees who supervise their own activities and monitor the quality of the goods and services they provide.

SENDER The person or group wishing to share information.

SEXUAL HARASSMENT Unwelcome behaviour of a sexual nature in the workplace that negatively affects the work environment or leads to adverse job-related consequences for the employee.

SITUATIONAL LEADERSHIP THEORY (SLT) A contingency model of leadership that focuses on the followers' readiness.

SOCIAL AUDIT A tool that allows managers to analyze the profitability and social returns of socially responsible actions.

SOCIAL LOAFING The tendency of individuals to put forth less effort when they work in groups than when they work alone.

SOCIAL RESPONSIBILITY A manager's duty or obligation to make decisions that promote the well-being of stakeholders and society as a whole.

SOCIETAL ETHICS Standards that govern how members of a society are to deal with each other on issues such as fairness, justice, poverty, and the rights of the individual.

SPAN OF CONTROL The number of subordinates who report directly to a manager.

STANDARD OPERATING PROCEDURES (SOPs) Specific sets of written instructions about how to perform a certain aspect of a task.

STEREOTYPE Simplistic and often inaccurate beliefs about the typical characteristics of particular groups of people.

STRATEGIC ALLIANCE An agreement in which managers pool or share their organization's resources and know-how with a foreign company, and the two organizations share the rewards and risks of starting a new venture.

STRATEGIC HUMAN RESOURCE MANAGEMENT The process by which managers design the components of a human resource management system to be consistent with each other, with other elements of organizational architecture, and with the organization's strategy and goals.

STRATEGY A cluster of decisions about what goals to pursue, what actions to take, and how to use resources to achieve goals.

STRATEGY FORMULATION Analysis of an organization's current situation followed by the development of strategies to accomplish the organization's mission and achieve its goals.

SUPPLIERS Individuals and organizations that provide an organization with the input resources that it needs to produce goods and services.

SWOT ANALYSIS A planning exercise in which managers identify organizational strengths (S) and weaknesses (W), and environmental opportunities (O) and threats (T).

SYNERGY Performance gains that result when individuals and departments coordinate their actions.

SYSTEMATIC ERRORS Errors that people make over and over again and that result in poor decision making.

TASK ENVIRONMENT The set of forces and conditions that start with suppliers, distributors, customers, and competitors and affect an organization's ability to obtain inputs and dispose of its outputs, because they influence managers on a daily basis.

TASK FORCE A committee of managers or nonmanagerial employees from various departments or divisions who meet to solve a specific, mutual problem; also called an *ad hoc committee*.

TASK STRUCTURE The extent to which the work to be performed is clear-cut so that a leader's subordinates know what needs to be accomplished and how to go about doing it; a determinant of how favourable a situation is for leading.

TASK-ORIENTED ROLES Roles performed by group members to make sure the task gets done.

TEAM A group whose members work intensely with each other to achieve a specific common goal or objective.

TECHNICAL SKILLS Job-specific knowledge and techniques that are required to perform an organizational role.

TECHNOLOGICAL FORCES Outcomes of changes in the technology that managers use to design, produce, or distribute goods and services.

TECHNOLOGY The combination of skills and equipment that managers use in the design, production, and distribution of goods and services.

THEORY X Negative assumptions about employees that lead to the conclusion that a manager's task is to supervise them closely and control their behaviour.

THEORY Y Positive assumptions about employees that lead to the conclusion that a manager's task is to create a work setting that encourages commitment to organizational goals and provides opportunities for imagination, initiative, and self-direction.

360-DEGREE APPRAISAL A performance appraisal by peers, subordinates, superiors, and sometimes clients who are in a position to evaluate a manager's performance.

TIME HORIZON The intended duration of a plan.

TOP MANAGERS Managers who establish organizational goals, decide how departments should interact, and monitor the performance of middle managers.

TOP-DOWN CHANGE Change that is introduced quickly throughout an organization by upper-level managers.

TOP-MANAGEMENT TEAM A group composed of the CEO, the president, and the heads of the most important departments.

TOTALITARIAN REGIME A political system in which a single party, individual, or group holds all political power and neither recognizes nor permits opposition.

TRAINING Teaching organizational members how to perform their current jobs and helping them acquire the knowledge and skills they need to be effective performers.

TRANSACTIONAL LEADERSHIP Leaders who guide their subordinates toward expected goals with no expectation of exceeding expected behaviour.

TRANSFORMATIONAL LEADERSHIP Leadership that makes subordinates aware of the importance of their jobs and performance to the organization and aware of their own needs for personal growth, and that motivates subordinates to work for the good of the organization.

UNCERTAINTY Unpredictability.

UNDERPAYMENT INEQUITY Inequity that exists when a person perceives that his or her own outcome/input ratio is less than the ratio of a referent.

UNETHICAL DECISION A decision that a manager would prefer to disguise or hide from other people because it enables a company or a particular individual to gain at the expense of society or other stakeholders.

UNRELATED DIVERSIFICATION Entering a new industry or buying a company in a new industry that is not related in any way to an organization's current businesses or industries.

VALENCE In expectancy theory, how desirable each of the outcomes available from a job or organization is to a person.

VALUES The stable, long-lasting beliefs about what is important.

VERBAL COMMUNICATION The encoding of messages into words, either written or spoken.

VERTICAL INTEGRATION A strategy that allows an organization to create value by producing its own inputs or distributing and selling its own outputs.

VIRTUAL TEAM A team whose members rarely or never meet face to face and interact by using various forms of information technology such as email, computer networks, telephones, faxes, and videoconferences.

VISION STATEMENT A broad declaration of the big picture of the organization and/or a statement of its dreams for the future.

Endnotes

Chapter 1

1. Adapted from Virginia Galt, "Managers on Fast Track Try Out the Hot Seat," *The Globe and Mail*, Wednesday, June 29, 2005, pp. C1, 5.

2. "People are living longer and healthier lives. A Canadian woman who is 40 today can expect to live to 85.4, a man to 82.1, according to Canada Pension Plan actuarial estimates. Currently, the average Canadian working male retires at 62.5, females at 60.5, according to 2004 CPP statistics." Quoted in Steven Theobald and Sharda Prashad, "Rethinking Retirement," *Toronto Star*, Saturday, March 19, 2005, pp. D1, 4.

3. William Byham, Audrey Smith, and Matthew Paese in *Grow Your Own Leaders: How to Identify, Develop and Retain Leadership Talent*. Toronto: *Financial Times* Prentice Hall, 2002, 416 pages. Referenced in Virginia Galt, "Managers on Fast Track Try Out the Hot Seat," *The Globe and Mail*, Wednesday, June 29, 2005, pp. C1, 5.

4. G.R. Jones, *Organizational Theory* (Reading, MA: Addison-Wesley, 1995).

5. J.P. Campbell, "On the Nature of Organizational Effectiveness," in P.S. Goodman, J.M. Pennings, and Associates, *New Perspectives on Organizational Effectiveness* (San Francisco: Jossey-Bass, 1977).

6. P. Drucker, *Management: Tasks, Responsibilities, Practices* (New York: Harper and Row, 1974).

7. Adapted from Sinclair Stewart, "Cult of Ed," *Report on Business Magazine, The Globe and Mail*, July 2005, pp. 12–16, 18, 20.

8. H. Fayol, *General and Industrial Management* (New York: IEEE Press, 1984). Fayol's work was first published in 1916. Fayol actually identified five different managerial functions but most scholars today believe these four capture the essence of Fayol's ideas.

9. P.F. Drucker, *Management Tasks, Responsibilities, and Practices* (New York: Harper and Row, 1974).

10. G. Dixon, "Clock Ticking for New CEOs," *The Globe and Mail*, May 8, 2001.

11. Adapted from John Greenwood, "Selling Books Online: Chapter 2," *National Post*, Monday, June 20, 2005, pp. FP1, 5.

12. J. Kotter, *The General Managers* (New York: Free Press, 1992).

13. C.P. Hales, "What Do Managers Do? A Critical Review of the Evidence," *Journal of Management Studies*, January 1986, pp. 88–115; A.I. Kraul, P.R. Pedigo, D.D. McKenna, and M.D. Dunnette, "The Role of the Manager: What's Really Important in Different Management Jobs," *Academy of Management Executive*, November 1989, pp. 286–293.

14. A.K. Gupta, "Contingency Perspectives on Strategic Leadership," in D.C. Hambrick (ed.), *The Executive Effect: Concepts and Methods for Studying Top Managers* (Greenwich, CT: JAI Press, 1988), pp.147–178.

15. D.G. Ancona, "Top Management Teams: Preparing for the Revolution," in J.S. Carroll (ed.), *Applied Social Psychology and Organizational Settings* (Hillsdale, NJ: Erlbaum, 1990); D.C. Hambrick and P.A. Mason, "Upper Echelons: The Organization as a Reflection of Its Top Managers," *Academy of Management Journal*, 9, 1984, pp. 193–206.

16. T.A. Mahony, T.H. Jerdee, and S.J. Carroll, "The Jobs of Management," *Industrial Relations*, 4, 1965, pp. 97–110; L. Gomez-Mejia, J. McCann, and R.C. Page, "The Structure of Managerial Behaviours and Rewards," *Industrial Relations*, 24, 1985, pp. 147–154.

17. Deena Waisberg, "Bank Executive Proves He's a Stand-up Guy," *National Post*, Saturday, May 28, 2005, p. FW9.

18. K. Labich, "Making Over Middle Managers," *Fortune*, May 8, 1989, pp. 58–64.

19. "'Haves & Have-Nots': Canadians Look for Corporate Conscience," *Maclean's*, December 30, 1996/January 6, 1997, pp. 26, 37.

20. Ibid.

21. Ibid.

22. W.F. Cascio, "Downsizing: What Do We Know? What Have We Learned?" *Academy of Management Executive*, 7, 1993, p. 100.

23. T.H. Wagar, "Exploring the Consequences of Workforce Reduction," *Canadian Journal of Administrative Sciences*, December 1998, pp. 300–309.

24. S.R. Parker, T.D. Wall, and P.R. Jackson, "That's Not My Job: Developing Flexible Work Orientations," *Academy of Management Journal*, 40, 1997, pp. 899–929.

25. B. Dumaine, "The New Non-Manager," *Fortune*, February 22, 1993, pp. 80–84.

26. Scott Peterson, "Good Leaders Empower People," *National Post*, Wednesday, May 18, 2005, p. FP9.

27. See James Collins, Ph.D. *Good to Great: Why Some Companies Make the Leap... and Others Don't*. New York: Harper Collins, 2001.

28. Adapted from Harvey Schachter, "Being an MBA Doesn't Mean You Can Manage," *The Globe and Mail*, Wednesday, June 2, 2004, p. C6. See also Henry Mintzberg, "Forget Heroes: What We Really Need Are 'Engaging' Managers," *The Globe and Mail*, Friday, May 28, 2004, pp. C1, 4; also Henry Mintzberg. *Managers Not MBAs: A Hard Look at the Soft Practice of Managing and Management Development*. San Francisco: Berrett-Koehler Publishers, 2004.

29. R.H. Guest, "Of Time and the Foreman," *Personnel*, 32, 1955, pp. 478–486.

30. C.W.L. Hill, *Becoming a Manager: Mastery of a New Identity* (Boston: Harvard Business School Press, 1992).

31. H. Mintzberg, "The Manager's Job: Folklore and Fact," *Harvard Business Review*, July–August 1975, pp. 56–62.

32. H. Mintzberg, *The Nature of Managerial Work* (New York: Harper and Row, 1973).

33. Ibid.

34. R.L. Katz, "Skills of an Effective Administrator," *Harvard Business Review*, September–October 1974, pp. 90–102.

35. Ibid.

36. Quoted in Michael Adams, "Whose Conventional Wisdom?" *The Globe and Mail*, Monday, May 16, 2005, p. A15.

37. Gordon Nixon, "Unleashing Canada's People Power," *National Post*, Tuesday, June 21, 2005, p. A16.

38. Data on manufacturing, public sector, and service sector employment for July 2003. Statistics Canada, "Latest Release From the Labour Force Survey," August 8, 2003, www.statcan.ca/english/Subjects/Labour/LFS/lfs-en.htm.

39. Statistics Canada, "Establishments by Industry," www.statcan.ca/english/Pgdb/econ18.htm.

40. C. Harris, "Prime Numbers: A Statistical Look at the Trends and Issues That Will Dominate Our Future," *The Financial Post*, November 15/17, 1997, p. P13.

41. Statistics Canada, "Latest Release From the Labour Force Survey," August 8, 2003, www.statcan.ca/english/Subjects/Labour/LFS/lfs-en.htm.

42. J.A. Brander, *Government Policy Toward Business*, 3rd ed. (Toronto: John Wiley and Sons, 2000), p. 380.

43. D. Jamieson and J. O'Mara, *Managing Workforce 2000: Gaining a Diversity Advantage* (San Francisco: Jossey-Bass, 1991).

44. T.H. Cox and S. Blake, "Managing Cultural Diversity: Implications for Organizational Competitiveness," *Academy of Management Executive*, August 1991, pp. 49–52.

45. Adapted from Gordon Pitts, "Search for Talent Tougher Than Drilling for Oil," *The Globe and Mail*, Monday, July 18, 2005, p. B8.

46. A. Shama, "Management Under Fire: The Transformation of Management in the Soviet Union and Eastern Europe," *Academy of Management Executive*, 1993, pp. 22–35.

47. "Radio Canada and Montreal La Presse Sign Partnership Agreement," Canadian Press Newswire, January 20, 2001.

48. Michael Rachlis, "Medicare Made Easy," *The Globe and Mail*, Monday, April 26, 2004, p. A13.

49. K. Seiders and L.L. Berry, "Service Fairness: What It Is and Why It Matters," *Academy of Management Executive*, 12, 1998, pp. 8–20.

50. C. Anderson, "Values-Based Management," *Academy of Management Executive*, 11, 1997, pp. 25–46.

51. W.H. Shaw and V. Barry, *Moral Issues in Business*, 6th ed. (Belmont, CA: Wadsworth, 1995); and T. Donaldson, *Corporations and Morality* (Englewood Cliffs, NJ: Prentice-Hall, 1982).

52. T. Tedesci, "Nesbitt Burns Procedures Investigated," *The Vancouver Sun*, April 7, 2001, pp. A1, A4; and D. DeCloet, "Industry Owes a Duty of Care," *The Vancouver Sun*, April 7, 2001, pp. D1, D6.

53. D.R. Tobin, *The Knowledge Enabled Organization* (New York: AMACOM, 1998).

54. "Canadian Productivity Rising Because of High Tech Investment, Says Conference Board," Canadian Press Newswire, November 30, 2000.

55. Adapted from Virginia Galt, "Managers on Fast Track Try Out the Hot Seat," *The Globe and Mail*, Wednesday, June 29, 2005, pp. C1, 5.

56. Adapted from: Mark Kozak-Holland, "Plan for the Unthinkable," *Financial Post*, Monday, October 18, 2004, p. FE9.

57. The official Titanic site by Paramount Pictures and Twentieth Century Fox: www.titanicmovie.com.

58. Marcy Zitz, "The Anniversary of the Titanic Disaster: The Date the Titanic Sank," website: http://familyinternet.about.com/cs/entertainment/a/aatitanic.htm.

Chapter 2

1. Adapted from Tony Keller, "Reinventing the Firm," *National Post Business*, June 2000, pp. 68–70, 72, 74, 76, 78, 81; see also Don Tapscott and David Agnew, "Governance in the Digital Economy The Importance of Human Development," *International Monetary Fund (IMF) Finance & Development*, December 1999, Volume 36, Number 4, 9 printed pages. Website: www.imf.org/external/pubs/ft/fandd/1999/12/tapscott.htm.

2. For more information, see the website: http://en.wikipedia.org/wiki/Eatons.

3. L.J. Bourgeois, "Strategy and Environment: A Conceptual Integration," Academy of Management Review, 5, 1985, pp. 25–39.

4. Adapted from Jacqueline Thorpe, "Mauled by China Inc.," *Financial Post*, Saturday, April 23, 2005, pp. FP1, 6.

5. Don Tapscott and David Agnew, "Governance in the Digital Economy The Importance of Human Development," International Monetary Fund (IMF) Finance & Development, December 1999, Volume 36, Number 4, 9 printed pages. Website: www.imf.org/external/pubs/ft/fandd/1999/12/tapscott.htm.

6. Jacqueline Thorpe, "Mauled by China Inc.," *Financial Post*, Saturday, April 23, 2005, pp. FP1, 6.

7. M.E. Porter, *Competitive Strategy* (New York: Free Press, 1980).

8. Hollier Shaw, "Bowrings Files for Bankruptcy," *Financial Post*, Thursday, August 25, 2005, pp. FP1, 4. See also www.dnb.ca/news/2005-08-26.htm.

9. M.E. Porter, *Competitive Advantage* (New York: Free Press, 1985).

10. For views on barriers to entry from an economics perspective, see M.E. Porter, *Competitive Strategy* (New York: Free Press, 1980). For the sociological perspective, see J. Pfeffer and G.R. Salancik, *The External Control of Organization: A Resource Dependence Perspective* (New York: Harper and Row, 1978).

11. M.E. Porter, *Competitive Strategy* (New York: Free Press, 1980); J.E. Bain, *Barriers to New Competition* (Cambridge, MA: Harvard University Press, 1956); R.J. Gilbert, "Mobility Barriers and the Value of Incumbency," in R. Schmalensee and R.D. Willig (eds.), *Handbook of Industrial Organization*, vol. 1 (Amsterdam: North Holland, 1989).

12. Brent Jang, "Leblanc on Sorrow, Remorse and His Little 'White Lie'" *The Globe and Mail*, Friday, March 18, 2005, pp. B1, 2.

13. C.W.L. Hill, "The Computer Industry: The New Industry of Industries," in C.W.L. Hill and G.R. Jones, *Strategic Management: An Integrated Approach*, 3rd ed. (Boston: Houghton Mifflin, 1995).

14. "Western Glove Works Ltd.," ENTREPRENEUR: Special Feature to National Post, *Financial Post*, Friday, June 10, 2005, p. FP20.

15. Martin Slofstra, "Collaborate or Die," *EDGE*, March 2005, Vol. 3 No. 3, pp. 18–19.

16. J. Schumpeter, *Capitalism, Socialism and Democracy* (London: Macmillan, 1950), p. 68. Also see R.R. Winter and S.G. Winter, *An Evolutionary Theory of Economic Change* (Cambridge, MA: Harvard University Press, 1982).

17. Margaret Wente, "It's Manly at the Top," *The Globe and Mail*, Saturday, May 7, 2005, p. A21.

18. Ibid.

19. For a detailed discussion of the importance of the structure of law as a factor explaining economic change and growth, see D.C. North, *Institutions, Institutional Change and Economic Performance* (Cambridge: Cambridge University Press, 1990).

20. Barbara Shecter, "Cineplex Snaps Up Rival," *Financial Post*, Tuesday, June 14, 2005, pp. FP1, 6. See also Richard Blackwell, "Movie

Marriage Promises Blockbuster Savings," *The Globe and Mail*, Wednesday, June 22, 2005, p. B3; Gayle MacDonald, "Movie Boss Has Best Seat in the House," *The Globe and Mail*, Wednesday, June 15, 2005, pp. B1, 4.

21. Marina Strauss, "Tribunal Rules Sears Broke Law by Inflating Tire Savings," *The Globe and Mail*, Tuesday, January 25, 2005, pp. B1, 8.

22. R.B. Reich, *The Work of Nations* (New York: Knopf, 1991).

23. Jagdish Bhagwati, *Protectionism* (Cambridge, MA: MIT Press, 1988).

24. P.M. Sweezy and H. Magdoff, *The Dynamics of US Capitalism* (New York: Monthly Review Press, 1972).

25. Peter Foster, "Vlad the Great," *Financial Post*, Friday, November 5, 2004, p. FP15.

26. The ideology is that of individualism, which dates back to Adam Smith, John Stuart Mill, and the like. See H.W. Spiegel, *The Growth of Economic Thought* (Durham, NC: Duke University Press, 1991).

27. M. Magnier, "Chiquita Bets Czechoslovakia Can Produce Banana Bonanza," *Journal of Commerce*, August 29, 1991, pp. 1, 3.

28. George Bragues, "The Capitalist Pope," *Financial Post*, Tuesday, April 5, 2005, p. FP23.

29. Michael Rock, Ed.D. and Laurent Leduc, Ph.D., "Ethics of the *Worth*place," in *Ethics: To Live By, to Work By*. Toronto: McGraw-Hill Ryerson, 2005, pp. 95–112.

30. "Roll-up-Rim Contest Wasteful, Critics Say," *The London Free Press*, March 2, 2005. Website: www.canoe.ca/NewsStand/ LondonFreePress/News/2005/03/02/946850-sun.html

31. Bill Mah, "Tim Hortons Contest a Litterbug, Critics Say: Roll Up the Rim Begins," *National Post*, March 1, 2005.

32. R.B. Duncan, "Characteristics of Organization Environment and Perceived Environment," *Administrative Science Quarterly*, 17, 1972, pp. 313–327.

33. See "McDonald's USA Food Allergens and Sensitivities Listing," Website: www.mcdonalds.com/app_controller. nutrition.categories.allergens.index.html.

34. "Former McDonald's CEO Charlie Bell Dies of Cancer," *USA Today*, Monday, January 17, 2005.

35. Mike Adams, "Former CEO of McDonald's Dies of Colon Cancer at Age of 44," *News Target*, January 16, 2005. Website: www.newstatget.com/003232.html.

36. Not everyone agrees with this assessment. Some argue that organizations and individual managers have little impact on the environment. See M.T. Hannan and J. Freeman, "Structural Inertia and Organizational Change," *American Sociological Review*, 49, 1984, pp. 149–164.

37. Bill Sweetman, "Career Reboot: Reconfigure Your Professional Self," *The Globe and Mail*, Friday, May 7, 2004, pp. C1, 4.

38. Cited in Harvey Schachter, "Google and Your 'Personal Brand'," *The Globe and Mail*, Friday, May 14, 2004, pp. C1, 5.

39. Ron McGowan, "Forget a Job: Grads Must Sell Selves to New World of Work," *The Globe and Mail*, Wednesday, May 5, 2004, pp. C1, 2.

40. Cited in Michael Kesterton, "Social Studies," *The Globe and Mail*, January 14, 2005, p. A16. See also Daniel H. Pink. *Free Agent Nation: The Future of Working for Yourself*. New York: Time Warner, 2002.

41. Geof Wheelwright, "'Two in a Box' Leadership," FP EDGE, Special Report, *Financial Post*, Monday, April 19, 2004, pp. FE1, 2.

42. Cited in Margaret Wente, "Why I'll Never Be CEO," *The Globe and Mail*, Saturday, October 25, 1997, p. D7.

43. Lee Hawkins Jr., "GM Set to Slash Non-Union Work Force," *The Globe and Mail*, Monday, March 21, 2005, pp. B1, 12.

44. Paul Lima, "Visualize Success," *National Post*, FP ENTREPRENEUR, Strategies for Small and Mid-Size Businesses, Monday, March 14, 2005, p. FP8.

45. Adapted from Paul Lima, "E-mail Is No substitute for Face-to-Face Contact," *National Post*, Wednesday, June 15, 2005, p. FP9.

46. D. Olive, "In Beermaking, Two's a Crowd," *Financial Post (National Post)*, January 10, 2001, p. C2.

47. "Sleeman Poised for US Moves After Building Beer Company with Crafty Deals," *Canadian Press Newswire*, December 28, 2000.

48. Ibid.

49. Ibid.

50. "Smaller Brewers Want to Face Smaller Excise Tax Than Labatt and Molson," *Canadian Press Newswire*, September 19, 2000.

51. Ibid.

52. Ibid.

Chapter 3

1. Based on Richard Bloom, "How Parmalat Juggled the Struggle," *The Globe and Mail*, Monday, May 23, 2005, p. B3; "Spilled milk—Parmalat Finanziaria SpA—brief article," Latin Trade, March, 2004, 2 pages. Website: www.findarticles.com/p/articles/mi_m0BEK/ is_3_12/ai_114366804.

2. Jennifer Wells, "'Aw Shucks' Defence Fails," *Toronto Star*, Wednesday, March 16, 2005, pp. A1, 15.

3. Adapted from Tu Thanh Ha, "Ad Executive Pays Back $1-Million," *The Globe and Mail*, Wednesday, August 17, 2005, p. A4.

4. On September 19, 2005 Paul Coffin was sentenced to a conditional sentence of two years less a day, to be served in the community. In sentencing him Justice Jean-Guy Boilard of Quebec Superior Court said, "Mr. Coffin is genuinely contrite but unfortunately he cannot turn the clock back. In my view the risk of reoffending is extremely minimal, I would dare say inexistent." Les Perreaux, "Paul Coffin Avoids Prison Over Sponsorship Fraud," *The Globe and Mail*, Monday, September 19, 2005, p. 1.

5. T.L. Beauchamp and N.E. Bowie (eds.), *Ethical Theory and Business* (Englewood Cliffs, NJ: Prentice-Hall, 1979); and A. Macintyre, *After Virtue* (South Bend, IN: University of Notre Dame Press, 1981).

6. R.E. Goodin, "How to Determine Who Should Get What," *Ethics*, July 1975, pp. 310–321.

7. T.M. Jones, "Ethical Decision Making by Individuals in Organizations: An Issue Contingent Model," *Academy of Management Journal*, 16, 1991, pp. 366–395; and G.F. Cavanaugh, D.J. Moberg, and M. Velasquez, "The Ethics of Organizational Politics," *Academy of Management Review*, 6, 1981, pp. 363–374.

8. L.K. Trevino, "Ethical Decision Making in Organizations: A Person–Situation Interactionist Model," *Academy of Management Review*, 11, 1986, pp. 601–617; and W.H. Shaw and V. Barry, *Moral Issues in Business*, 6th ed. (Belmont, CA: Wadsworth, 1995).

9. A.S. Waterman, "On the Uses of Psychological Theory and Research in the Process of Ethical Inquiry," *Psychological Bulletin*, 103, no. 3, 1988, pp. 283–298.

10. www.shell.ca/code/values/ethics/ ethics.html.

11. J.A. Pearce, "The Company Mission as a Strategic Tool," *Sloan Management Review*, Spring 1982, pp. 15–24.

12. C.I. Barnard, *The Functions of the Executive* (Cambridge, MA: Harvard University Press, 1948).

13. R.E. Freeman, *Strategic Management: A Stakeholder Approach* (Marshfield, MA: Pitman, 1984).

14. Diane Francis, "Mining's New Frontier," *National Post*, Saturday, July 30, 2005, pp. FP1, 5.

15. M. McClearn, "African Adventure," *Canadian Business*, September 1, 2003.

16. "Corruption Still Tainting Asian Financial Picture, Study Says," *The Vancouver Sun*, March 20, 2001, p. D18.

17. "Canadian Firms Ink New Ethics Code [for International Operations]," *Plant*, October 6, 1997, p. 4.

18. Vern Krishna, "When Does Grease Become a Bribe?" *National Post*, Wednesday, February 2, 2005, p. FP9.

19. B. Victor and J.B. Cullen, "The Organizational Bases of Ethical Work Climates," *Administrative Science Quarterly*, 33, 1988, pp. 101–125.

20. H. Demsetz, "Towards a Theory of Property Rights," *American Economic Review*, 57, 1967, pp. 347–359.

21. Kevin Cox, "Irving Oil Fuels Its Leaders," *The Globe and Mail*, Wednesday, April 21, 2004, pp. C1, 3.

22. Website summary: "Hart Energy Publishing, LP is one of the world's largest energy industry publishers, with a diverse array of informational products and services. Since 1973, Hart has been recognized for its expert coverage of the global energy industry through its highly respected, award-winning magazines, newsletters and directories, conferences, consulting services and online resources." Website: www.hartenergy.com/about.html.

23. D. Hasselback, "BC Hydro Overcharging California Utilities, Report Says," *Financial Post (National Post)*, April 12, 2001, p. C4.

24. D. Baines, "BC Hydro Unit Cited for Blame in California's Electricity Crisis," *The Vancouver Sun*, April 12, 2001, pp. F1, F5.

25. C. Howes, "Ethics as More Than Just a Course: More Companies Are Promoting Ethical Practices in Work," *National Post*, October 28, 2000, p. D4.

26. Erin McClam, "Eight Former KPMG Executives Indicted," *The Globe and Mail*, Tuesday, August 30, 2005, p. B9.

27. C. Howes, "Ethics as More Than Just a Course: More Companies Are Promoting Ethical Practices in Work," *National Post*, October 28, 2000, p. D4.

28. Ibid.

29. P.E. Murphy, "Creating Ethical Corporate Structure," *Sloan Management Review*, Winter 1989, pp. 81–87.

30. G.R. Jones, *Organizational Theory: Text and Cases* (Reading, MA: Addison-Wesley, 1997).

31. "When It Comes to Ethics, Canadian Companies Are All Talk and Little Action, a Survey Shows," Canadian Press Newswire, February 17, 2000.

32. Catherine McLean, "Nortel's New Ethics Officer Eligible for Bonus," *The Globe and Mail*, Saturday, January 15, 2005, p. B2.

33. Jeff Bell, "Bus Driver Buys Lemonade for All His Passengers," *National Post*, Friday, August 12, 2005, p. A2.

34. E. Gatewood and A.B. Carroll, "The Anatomy of Corporate Social Response," *Business Horizons*, September–October 1981, pp. 9–16.

35. M. Friedman, "A Friedman Doctrine: The Social Responsibility of Business Is to Increase Its Profits," *New York Times Magazine*, September 13, 1970, p. 33.

36. "Wal-Mart Canada Says Imports From Myanmar Ended in Spring," Canadian Press Newswire, July 18, 2000.

37. "What," *National Post*, Saturday, June 11, 2005, p. WP3.

38. Paul Tsaparis, "This Quarter's Profit Isn't All There Is to Life," *National Post*, Monday, February 21, 2005, p. FP19.

39. W.G. Ouchi, *Theory Z: How American Business Can Meet the Japanese Challenge* (Reading, MA: Addison-Wesley, 1981).

40. J.B. McGuire, A. Sundgren, and T. Schneewis, "Corporate Social Responsibility and Firm Financial Performance," *Academy of Management Review*, 31, 1988, pp. 854–872.

41. J. Jedras, "Social Workers," *Silicon Valley NORTH*, July 30, 2001, p. 1.

42. M. Friedman, "A Friedman Doctrine: The Social Responsibility of Business Is to Increase Its Profits," *New York Times Magazine*, September 13, 1970, pp. 32, 33, 122, 124, 126.

43. E.D. Bowman, "Corporate Social Responsibility and the Investor," *Journal of Contemporary Business*, Winter 1973, pp. 49–58.

44. Prithi Yelaja, "Business With an Indian Twist," *Toronto Star*, Sunday, May 22, 2005, p. A19.

45. Information for this paragraph was based on Canada's Ethnocultural Portrait: The Changing Mosaic, January 2003, www12.statcan.ca/english/census01/products/analytic/companion/etoimm/provs.cfm (accessed May 16, 2003).

46. Mary Teresa Bitti, "The New Face of Canadian Business," FP ENTREPRENEUR: Strategies for Small and Mid-Size Businesses, *National Post*, Monday, May 2, 2005, pp. FP110.

47. R. Folger and M.A. Konovsky, "Effects of Procedural and Distributive Justice on Reactions to Pay Raise Decisions," *Academy of Management Journal*, 32, 1989, pp. 115–130; and J. Greenberg, "Organizational Justice: Yesterday, Today, and Tomorrow," *Journal of Management*, 16, 1990, pp. 399–402.

48. G. Glynn, "Bank of Montreal Invests in Its Workers," *Workforce*, December 1997, pp. 30–38.

49. D. Calleja, "Equity or Else: Employment Equity Has Been Around for a Long Time With No One to Enforce It," *Canadian Business*, March 19, 2001, pp. 29–30+.

50. J. Greenberg, "Organizational Justice: Yesterday, Today, and Tomorrow," *Journal of Management*, 16, 1990, pp. 399–402.

51. D. Calleja, "Equity or Else," *Canadian Business*, March 19, 2001, p. 31.

52. G. Robinson and K. Dechant, "Building a Case for Business Diversity," *Academy of Management Executive*, 1997, pp. 3, 32–47.

53. K. Kalawsky, "US Group Wants Royal's Centura Buy Delayed: Alleges Takeover Target Discriminates Against Minorities," *Financial Post (National Post)*, April 10, 2001, p. C4.

54. H. Branswell, "When Nestlé Canada Said Last Month It Would No Longer Be Making Chocolate Bars in a Nut-Free Facility, Thousands Wrote in to Protest," Canadian Press Newswire, May 14, 2001.

55. Ibid.

56. A.P. Carnevale and S.C. Stone, "Diversity: Beyond the Golden Rule," *Training & Development*, October 1994, pp. 22–39.

57. Website: www.rcmp-grc.gc.ca/clet/cletweb/mssn_e.htm.

58. Website: www.rcmp-grc.gc.ca/clet/cletweb/orntn/ornt_40_e.htm.

59. "Selling Equity," *Financial Post Magazine*, September 1994, pp. 20–25.

60. "Study Shows Women Who Are Unhappy with Corporate Life Plan to Start Own Businesses," *Women in Management*, December–January 1999, pp. 1–3.

61. Judith Timson, "The Cold-Blooded Balance of Workplace Power," *The Globe*

and Mail, Wednesday, September 8, 2004, pp. C1, 7.

62. Wallace Immen, "The Plague That Haunts Us Still," *The Globe and Mail*, Wednesday, September 8, 2004, pp. C1, 3.

63. "Eight in 10 Women Claim Sex Discrimination," *hrlook.com*, Monday, August 9, 2004.

64. J. Goddu, "Sexual Harassment Complaints Rise Dramatically," Canadian Press Newswire, March 6, 1998.

65. B. Carton, "Muscled Out? At Jenny Craig, Men Are Ones Who Claim Sex Discrimination," *The Wall Street Journal*, November 29, 1994, pp. A1, A7.

66. R.L. Paetzold and A.M. O'Leary-Kelly, "Organizational Communication and the Legal Dimensions of Hostile Work Environment Sexual Harassment," in G.L. Kreps (ed.), *Sexual Harassment: Communication Implications* (Cresskill, NJ: Hampton Press, 1993).

67. M. Galen, J. Weber, and A.Z. Cuneo, "Sexual Harassment: Out of the Shadows," *Fortune*, October 28, 1991, pp. 30–31.

68. "Employers Underestimate Extent of Sexual Harassment, Report Says," *The Vancouver Sun*, March 8, 2001, p. D6.

69. A.M. O'Leary-Kelly, R.L. Paetzold, and R.W. Griffin, "Sexual Harassment as Aggressive Action: A Framework for Understanding Sexual Harassment," paper presented at the annual meeting of the Academy of Management, Vancouver, August 1995.

70. "Employers Underestimate Extent of Sexual Harassment, Report Says," *The Vancouver Sun*, March 8, 2001, p. D6.

71. Information in this paragraph based on Ian Jack, "Magna Suit Spotlights Auto Industry Practices," *The Financial Post Daily*, September 10, 1997, p. 1.

72. I. Jack, "Magna Suit Spotlights Auto Industry Practices," *The Financial Post Daily*, September 10, 1997, p. 1.

73. S.J. Bresler and R. Thacker, "Four-Point Plan Helps Solve Harassment Problems," *HR Magazine*, May 1993, pp. 117–124.

74. Adrian Michaels, "Milan Judge Sentences 11 in Parmalat Case," *Financial Times*, Tuesday, June 27 2005. Website for picture: http://news.ft.com/cms/s/9453527a-e6a7-11d9-b6bc-00000e2511c8,dwp_uuid=f88742da-d1d4-11d8-85fc-00000e2511c8.html.

75. Michael Rock and Laurent Leduc. *Ethics: To Live By, To Work By*. Toronto: McGraw-Hill Ryerson, 2005, 51. ISBN 007-097-554X.

76. Adapted from Howard Levitt, "Spurning Lover or Workplace Harasser?" *National Post*, Wednesday, March 9, 2005, p. FP10.

77. George Abraham, "2005 Looking Good for Newcomers," *Toronto Star*, Monday, July 4, 2005, p. A17. *Italics* added.

78. Kathryn May, "PS Faces Critical Loss of Workers," *The Ottawa Citizen*, Monday, June 26, 2006, pp. A1, 7.

Chapter 4

1. Adapted from Donald Sull, "Managing by Commitments," *Harvard Business Review*, June 2003, Product Number: R0306E; (HBR OnPoint Enhanced Edition), 12 pages.

2. Bill Breen, "The Three Ways of Great Leaders," *Fast Company*, Issue 98, September 2005, 50ff. Website: www.fastcompany.com/magazine/98.

3. Pete DeLisi and Ron Danielson, "'I Think I am, Therefore ......': An Inquiry into the Thinking Styles of IT Executives and Professionals," *Organizational Synergies*, Website: www.org-synergies.com/ThinkingStyles.htm; posted in *Sloan Management Review*, August 2002. Full-Text Article: Reprint 4341, Summer 2002, Volume 43, Number 4, p. 13.

4. Adapted from Michael Roberto. *Why Great Leaders Don't Take Yes For An Answer: Managing for Conflict and Consensus*. Boston: Wharton School Publishing, 2005, 278 pages. ISBN 0131454390. Reported in Harvey Schachter, "Why Banning Yes Men—Or Women—Can Improve Decisions," *The Globe and Mail*, Wednesday, August 10, 2005, p. C3.

5. Website: www.encyclopedia.com/html/B/BayP1igsI1.asp.

6. Website: www.jfklancer.com/jfk1bop.html.

7. Laurence Chang and Peter Kornbluh, Foreword by Robert S. McNamara. *A National Security Archive Documents Reader*, 2nd Edition. New York: The New Press, 1998. Website: www.gwu.edu/~nsarchiv/nsa/cuba_mis_cri/declass.htm.

8. H.A. Simon, *The New Science of Management* (Englewood Cliffs, NJ: Prentice-Hall, 1977).

9. Michael Kesterton, "Social Studies," *The Globe and Mail*, Monday, August 29, 2005, p. A14.

10. Sandra E. Martin, "Staff Stay at Companies With Heart," *Financial Post*, Monday, August 16, 2004, p. FP10.

11. Robert Burns writes, "The best laid schemes o' mice an' men / Gang aft a-gley." E.D. Hirsch, Jr., Joseph F. Kett, and James

Trefil (Eds.). *The New Dictionary of Cultural Literacy*. Third Edition. Houghton Mifflin Company, 2002. Website: www.bartleby.com/59/3/bestlaidplan.html.

12. Risha Gottlieb, "Is Collaboration the Next Big Web Thing?" *Backbone*, July/August 2004, pp. 20–21.

13. H.A. Simon, *Administrative Behavior* (New York: Macmillan, 1947), p. 79.

14. H.A. Simon, *Models of Man* (New York: Wiley, 1957).

15. K.J. Arrow, *Aspects of the Theory of Risk Bearing* (Helsinki: Yrjo Johnssonis Saatio, 1965).

16. R.L. Daft and R.H. Lengel, "Organizational Information Requirements, Media Richness and Structural Design," *Management Science*, 32, 1986, pp. 554–571.

17. R. Cyert and J. March, *Behavioral Theory of the Firm* (Englewood Cliffs, NJ: Prentice-Hall, 1963).

18. Alan Kearns, "The Big Career Decisions," *National Post*, Wednesday, May 4, 2005, p. FP9. See also the website: www.econlib.org/library/Enc/bios/Simon.html.

19. J.G. March and H.A. Simon, Organizations (New York: Wiley, 1958).

20. H.A. Simon, "Making Management Decisions: The Role of Intuition and Emotion," *Academy of Management Executive*, 1, 1987, pp. 57–64.

21. M.H. Bazerman, *Judgment in Managerial Decision Making* (New York: Wiley, 1986); G.P. Huber, *Managerial Decision Making* (Glenview, IL: Scott, Foresman, 1993); and J.E. Russo and P.J. Schoemaker, *Decision Traps* (New York: Simon and Schuster, 1989).

22. M.D. Cohen, J.G. March, and J.P. Olsen, "A Garbage Can Model of Organizational Choice," *Administrative Science Quarterly*, 17, 1972, pp. 1–25.

23. P.C. Nutt, *Why Decisions Fail: Avoiding the Blunders and Traps That Lead to Debacles* (San Francisco: Berrett-Koehler Publishers, 2002); and M.H. Bazerman, *Judgment in Managerial Decision Making* (New York: Wiley, 1986).

24. www.perceptivesciences.-com/

25. Victor Godinez, "Usability Pro Thinks Outside the Box," *Financial Post*, Wednesday, September 8, 2004, p. FP13.

26. J.E. Russo and P.J. Schoemaker, *Decision Traps* (New York: Simon and Schuster, 1989).

27. M.H. Bazerman, *Judgment in Managerial Decision Making* (New York: Wiley, 1986).

28. Janis Foord Kirk, "Unfair Rule Destroys Productivity," *Toronto Star*, Saturday, March 12, 2005, pp. D1, 13.

29. Pete DeLisi and Ron Danielson, "'I Think I am, Therefore ......': An Inquiry into the Thinking Styles of IT Executives and Professionals," *Organizational Synergies*, Website: www.org-synergies.com/ ThinkingStyles.htm; posted in *Sloan Management Review*, August 2002.

30. P.C. Nutt, *Why Decisions Fail: Avoiding the Blunders and Traps That Lead to Debacles* (San Francisco: Berrett-Koehler Publishers, 2002).

31. Ibid.

32. J.E. Russo and P.J. Schoemaker, *Decision Traps* (New York: Simon and Schuster, 1989).

33. Connie Guglielmo and Dina Bass, "The HP Way Revival," *National Post*, Thursday, March 31, 2005, p. FP8.

34. Daniel Goleman, Richard Boyatzis and Annie McKee. Boston: *Primal Leadership: Realizing the Power of Emotional Intelligence*, Harvard Business School Press, 2002. ISBN: 1-57851-486-X.

35. Eric Bonabeau, Dan Lovallo, Daniel Kahneman, John S. Hammond III, Ralph L. Keeney, and Howard Raiffa, "Make Better Decisions—Faster," (HBR OnPoint Enhanced Edition) *Harvard Business Review*, July 2003, 35 pages. Product Number: 3582.

36. Gordon Pitts, "'No Ultimatum ... I Resigned'," *The Globe and Mail*, Monday, July 18, 2005, pp. B1, 13; "The Story Behind the Nortel Divorce," *The Globe and Mail*, Monday, June 20, 2005, pp. B1, 12.

37. D. Kahneman and A. Tversky, "Judgment Under Uncertainty: Heuristics and Biases," *Science*, 185, 1974, pp. 1124–1131.

38. C.R. Schwenk, "Cognitive Simplification Processes in Strategic Decision Making," *Strategic Management Journal*, 5, 1984, pp. 111–128.

39. Gordon Pitts, "The Story Behind the Nortel Divorce," *The Globe and Mail*, Monday, June 20, 2005, pp. B1, 12.

40. An interesting example of the illusion of control is Richard Roll's hubris hypothesis of takeovers. See R. Roll, "The Hubris Hypothesis of Corporate Takeovers," *Journal of Business*, 59, 1986, pp. 197–216.

41. B.M. Staw, "The Escalation of Commitment to a Course of Action," *Academy of Management Review*, 6, 1981, pp. 577–587.

42. J.E. Russo and P.J. Schoemaker, *Decision Traps* (New York: Simon and Schuster, 1989).

43. Ibid.

44. Christine A. Yost and Mary L. Source, "Are Effective Teams More Emotionally Intelligent? Confirming the Importance of Effective Communication in Teams," *Delta Pi Epsilon Journal*, Vol. 42, No. 2, Spring 2000, 101–09. ISSN: 0011-8052. Number: BEDI01001013.

45. Williams, W., & Sternberg, R., "Group Intelligence: Why Some Groups Are Better Than Others," *Intelligence*, 1988, Vol. 12, No. 4, 351–377.

46. S.R. Covey, S. R. "Unstoppable Teams," *Executive Excellence*, July 1996, Vol. 13, pp. 7–9. Website: http://proquest.umi.com/pqdlink.

47. I.L. Janis, *Groupthink: Psychological Studies of Policy Decisions and Fiascoes*, 2nd ed. (Boston: Houghton Mifflin, 1982).

48. Ibid.

49. Robert Pear, "He Wrote the Book on Intelligence," *The New York Times*, Sunday, July 11, 2004, p. WK12.

50. J.N. Choi and M.U. Kim, "The Organizational Application of Groupthink and Its Limitations in Organizations," *Journal of Applied Psychology*, 84, 1999, pp. 297–306.

51. C. McCauley, "The Nature of Social Influence in Groupthink: Compliance and Internalization," *Journal of Personality and Social Psychology*, 57, 1989, pp. 250–260; P.E. Tetlock, R.S. Peterson, C. McGuire, S. Chang, and P. Feld, "Assessing Political Group Dynamics: A Test of the Groupthink Model," *Journal of Personality and Social Psychology*, 63, 1992, pp. 781–796; S. Graham, "A Review of Attribution Theory in Achievement Contexts," *Educational Psychology Review*, 3, 1991, pp. 5–39; and G. Moorhead and J.R. Montanari, "An Empirical Investigation of the Groupthink Phenomenon," *Human Relations*, 39, 1986, pp. 399–410.

52. J. Longley and D.G. Pruitt, "Groupthink: A Critique of Janis' Theory," in L. Wheeler (ed.), *Review of Personality and Social Psychology* (Newbury Park, CA: Sage, 1980), pp. 507–513; and J.A. Sniezek, "Groups Under Uncertainty: An Examination of Confidence in Group Decision Making," *Organizational Behavior and Human Decision Processes*, 52, 1992, pp. 124–155.

53. J.N. Choi and M.U. Kim, "The Organizational Application of Groupthink and Its Limitations in Organizations," *Journal of Applied Psychology*, 84, 1999, pp. 297–306.

54. See N.R.F. Maier, *Principles of Human Relations* (New York: Wiley, 1952); I.L. Janis, *Groupthink: Psychological Studies of Policy Decisions and Fiascoes*, 2nd ed. (Boston: Houghton Mifflin, 1982); and C.R. Leana,

"A Partial Test of Janis' Groupthink Model: Effects of Group Cohesiveness and Leader Behavior on Defective Decision Making," *Journal of Management*, Spring 1985, pp. 5–17.

55. See R.O. Mason, "A Dialectic Approach to Strategic Planning," *Management Science*, 13, 1969, pp. 403–414; R.A. Cosier and J.C. Aplin, "A Critical View of Dialectic Inquiry in Strategic Planning," *Strategic Management Journal*, 1, 1980, pp. 343–356; I.I. Mitroff and R.O. Mason, "Structuring III—Structured Policy Issues: Further Explorations in a Methodology for Messy Problems," *Strategic Management Journal*, 1, 1980, pp. 331–342.

56. Mary C. Gentile, *Differences That Work: Organizational Excellence Through Diversity* (Boston: Harvard Business School Press, 1994).

57. Richard Saul Wurman, in *Information Anxiety* in Ian Mitroff, Ph.D. *Smart Thinking for Crazy Times. The Art of Solving the Right Problems*. San Francisco: Berrett-Koehler Publishers, Inc., 1998, vi. 1-57675-020-5.

58. Quoted in Chris Young, "Copy Rights and Copy Wrongs," *Toronto Star*, Sunday, May 22, 2005, pp. D1, 10.

59. Arthur H. Bell and Dayle M. Smith. *Developing Leadership Abilities*. Upper Saddle River, New Jersey: Prentice Hall, 2002, p. 127. ISBN 0-13-091758-3

60. Wynn Quon, "Music Loss Leader," *National Post*, Friday, July 29, 2005, p. FP17.

61. Lynn Moore, "Corporate Fool Too Funny for Workplace Fired," *National Post*, Saturday, February 19, 2005, p. FW5.

62. B. Hedberg, "How Organizations Learn and Unlearn," in W.H. Starbuck and P.C. Nystrom (eds.), *Handbook of Organizational Design*, vol. 1 (New York: Oxford University Press, 1981), pp. 1–27.

63. See P. Senge, The *Fifth Discipline: The Art and Practice of the Learning Organization* (New York: Doubleday, 1990).

64. T.A. Stewart, "3M Fights Back," *Fortune*, February 5, 1996, pp. 94–99; and T.D. Schellhardt, "David in Goliath," *The Wall Street Journal*, May 23, 1996, p. R14.

65. R.W. Woodman, J.E. Sawyer, and R.W. Griffin, "Towards a Theory of Organizational Creativity," *Academy of Management Review*, 18, 1993, pp. 293–321.

66. M. Ullmann, "Creativity Cubed: Burntsand Has Found a Novel Program to Motivate Its Most Creative Employees. Can It Work for You?" SVN Canada, February 2001, pp. B22–B23+.

67. T.J. Bouchard Jr., J. Barsaloux, and G. Drauden, "Brainstorming Procedure, Group Size, and Sex as Determinants of Problem Solving Effectiveness of Individuals and Groups," *Journal of Applied Psychology,* 59, 1974, pp. 135–138.

68. L. Thompson and L.F. Brajkovich, "Improving the Creativity of Organizational Work Groups," *Academy of Management Executive,* 17, no. 1, 2003, pp. 96–111; B. Mullen, C. Johnson, and E. Salas, "Productivity Loss in Brainstorming Groups: A Meta-Analytic Integration," *Basic and Applied Social Psychology,* 12, no. 1, 1991, pp. 3–23; and M. Diehl and W. Stroebe, "Productivity Loss in Brainstorming Groups: Towards the Solution of a Riddle," *Journal of Personality and Social Psychology,* 53, 1987, pp. 497–509.

69. D.H. Gustafson, R.K. Shulka, A. Delbecq, and W.G. Walster, "A Comparative Study of Differences in Subjective Likelihood Estimates Made by Individuals, Interacting Groups, Delphi Groups, and Nominal Groups," *Organizational Behavior and Human Performance,* 9, 1973, pp. 280–291.

70. N. Dalkey, *The Delphi Method: An Experimental Study of Group Decision Making* (Santa Monica, CA: Rand Corp., 1989).

71. William M. Bulkeley, "Women the Focus of Kodak's Digital Moment," *The Globe and Mail,* Saturday, July 9, 2005, B13. The quote is originally from William M. Bulkeley, "Kodak Sharpens Digital Focus on Female Customers," *The Wall Street Journal,* Wednesday, July 06, 2005, 6 printed ages. Alternate website: www.post-gazette.com/pg/05187/533671.stm.

72. Cover Story: "Special Report: The Art of Foresight: Preparing For a Changing World," *The Futurist,* May–June 2004, Volume 38, No. 3, 31–38.

73. N.B. Macintosh, *The Social Software of Accounting Information Systems* (New York: Wiley, 1995).

74. R.I. Benjamin and J. Blunt, "Critical IT Issues: The Next Ten Years," *Sloan Management Review,* Summer 1992, pp. 7–19; W.H. Davidow and M.S. Malone, The Virtual Corporation (New York: Harper Business, 1992).

75. C.A. O'Reilly, "Variations in Decision Makers' Use of Information: The Impact of Quality and Accessibility," *Academy of Management Journal,* 25, 1982, pp. 756–771.

76. G. Stalk and T.H. Hout, *Competing Against Time* (New York: Free Press, 1990).

77. R. Cyert and J. March, *Behavioral Theory of the Firm* (Englewood Cliffs, NJ: Prentice-Hall, 1963).

78. Harriet Rubin, "The Power of Words," *Fast Company,* Issue 21, January 1999, 142ff.

79. Bert Hill, "Nortel's New CTO Roese Vows to 'Wake Up the Industry,'" *The Ottawa Citizen,* Friday, June 23, 2006, p. A1.

80. News release: "Nortel Appoints John J. Roese as Chief Technology Officer," Nortel website: www2.nortel.com/go/news_detail.jsp?cat_id=-8055&oid=100202457.

81. Adapted from Keith Damsell, "Vulcan of Bay Street Refuses to Let Emotion Get in the Way," *The Globe and Mail,* Thursday, October 7, 2004, p. B21.

82. Adapted from: "Case Study: Overnight Opportunities with Geology Office and LiveQuest," website: www.slb.com/content/services/resources/casestudies/software/cs_overnight_opp.asp.

83. Website: www.huskyenergy.ca/.

Chapter 5

1. Adapted from John Greenwood, "His Big, Fat Military Coup," *National Post,* Monday, June 27, 2005, pp. FP1, 18.

2. Laura Fowlie, "The Ultimate Test," SPECIAL REPORT: FP EDGE, *Financial Post,* Monday, May 3, 2004, p. FE4.

3. A. Chandler, *Strategy and Structure: Chapters in the History of the American Enterprise* (Cambridge, MA: MIT Press, 1962).

4. M. Ingram, "Our Job Is to Be Better," *The Globe and Mail,* May 12, 2001, p. F3.

5. A. Chandler, *Strategy and Structure: Chapters in the History of the American Enterprise* (Cambridge, MA: MIT Press, 1962).

6. V. Pilieci, "The Lost Generation of Business Talent," *The Vancouver Sun,* May 2, 2001, pp. D1, D9.

7. F.J. Aguilar, "General Electric: Reg Jones and Jack Welch," in *General Managers in Action* (Oxford: Oxford University Press, 1992).

8. Ibid.

9. Ibid.

10. www.ge.com, 2001.

11. C.W. Hofer and D. Schendel, *Strategy Formulation: Analytical Concepts* (St. Paul, MN: West, 1978).

12. H. Fayol, *General and Industrial Management* (New York: IEEE Press, 1984). Fayol's work was first published in 1916.

13. H. Fayol, *General and Industrial Management* (1916; New York: IEEE Press, 1984), p. 18.

14. R. Phelps, C. Chan, S.C. Kapsalis, "Does Scenario Planning Affect Firm Performance?" *Journal of Business Research,* March 2001, pp. 223–232.

15. Adapted from Gordon Pitts, "After the Fall: Oliphant Now Calling His Own Shots," *The Globe and Mail,* Monday, June 13, 2005, p. B10.

16. Mark Kozak-Holland, "Plan for the Unthinkable," *Financial Post,* Monday, October 18, 2004, p. FE9.

17. J.A. Pearce, "The Company Mission as a Strategic Tool," *Sloan Management Review,* Spring 1992, pp. 15–24.

18. P.C. Nutt and R.W. Backoff, "Crafting Vision," *Journal of Management Inquiry,* December 1997, p. 309.

19. D.F. Abell, *Defining the Business: The Starting Point of Strategic Planning* (Englewood Cliffs, NJ: Prentice-Hall, 1980).

20. www.worksafebc.com/corporate/about/goals/default.asp.

21. G. Hamel and C.K. Prahalad, "Strategic Intent," *Harvard Business Review,* May–June 1989, pp. 63–73.

22. E.A. Locke, G.P. Latham, and M. Erez, "The Determinants of Goal Commitment," *Academy of Management Review,* 13, 1988, pp. 23–39.

23. P.F. Drucker, *The Practice of Management* (New York: Harper and Row, 1954).

24. S.J. Carroll and H.L. Tosi, *Management by Objectives: Applications and Research* (New York: Macmillan, 1973).

25. R. Rodgers and J.E. Hunter, "Impact of Management by Objectives on Organizational Productivity," *Journal of Applied Psychology,* 76, 1991, pp. 322–326.

26. M.B. Gavin, S.G. Green, and G.T. Fairhurst, "Managerial Control Strategies for Poor Performance Over Time and the Impact on Subordinate Reactions," *Organizational Behaviour and Human Decision Processes,* 63, 1995, pp. 207–221.

27. Adapted from Bertrand Marotte, "Vidéotron Takes the Lead in Residential VoIP Service," *The Globe and Mail,* Tuesday, January 25, 2005, p. B6.

28. K.R. Andrews, *The Concept of Corporate Strategy* (Homewood, IL: Irwin, 1971).

29. Denisa Georgescu, Canadian Tourism Commission and Per Nilsen, Parks Canada, "A Canadian Study of Indicators Relating to Sustainable Tourism and Ecotourism: The Case Study of Northern Cape Breton," The 7th International Forum on Tourism Statistics, Stockholm, June 9–11, 2004, Tourism Commission, website: www.tourism-forum.scb.se/presentations/SDTheme9June/

Canada/Stockholm_Presentation.ppt; see also Business to Business website: www.canadatourism.com and Consumer website: www.travelcanada.ca.

30. Based on G. Pitts, "Tide Turns for P&G Canada President," *The Globe and Mail,* October 14, 2002, p. B3.

31. Adapted from Harvey Schachter, "Challenging the Conventions of Strategy One Bite at a Time," *The Globe and Mail,* Wednesday, April 13, 2005, C4 and Editorial Review—*From the Inside Flap,* Amazon.ca. Website: www.amazon.ca/exec/obidos/ tg/detail/-/books/0273693468/reviews/ ref=cm_rev_more_2/702-7104076-7622461.

32. John Kotter. *The Heart of Change.* Boston, Mass.: Harvard Business School Press, 2002, p. x. Note: This was an interesting observation by one of the world's most noted scholars of organizational behaviour and corporate culture. He had originally written John Kotter. *Leading Change.* Cambridge, MA.: Harvard University Press, 1996, 187 pages. ISBN 0875847471 and realized its incompleteness.

33. M. McNeill, "Peak of the Market Buys Competitor," *Winnipeg Free Press,* June 2001, pp. B1, B3.

34. Catherine McLean and Gordon Pitts, "Bell Adopts a New Party Line," *The Globe and Mail,* Saturday, May 14, 2005, p. B4.

35. E. Penrose, *The Theory of the Growth of the Firm* (Oxford: Oxford University Press, 1959).

36. M.E. Porter, "From Competitive Advantage to Corporate Strategy," *Harvard Business Review,* 65, 1987, pp. 43–59.

37. Website: http://web.linix.ca/pedia/index. php/E.D._Smith.

38. "Jam Today: Imperial Capital Merchant Bank Takes Over E.D. Smith," Canadian Press Newswire, January 28, 2002.

39. Website: Report on Business Company, www.globeinvestor.com/snapshots/B0003334. htm.

40. Website: www.brascancorp.com/ AboutBrascan/BoardofDirectors.html.

41. G. Pitts, "Small Is Beautiful, Conglomerates Signal," *The Globe and Mail,* April 1, 2002, pp. B1, B4.

42. For a review of the evidence, see C.W.L. Hill and G.R. Jones, *Strategic Management: An Integrated Approach,* 3rd ed. (Boston: Houghton Mifflin, 2000), Ch. 10.

43. V. Ramanujam and P. Varadarajan, "Research on Corporate Diversification: A Synthesis," *Strategic Management Journal,* 10, 1989, pp. 523–551. Also see A. Shleifer

and R.W. Vishny, "Takeovers in the 1960s and 1980s: Evidence and Implications," in R.P. Rumelt, D.E. Schendel, and D.J. Teece, *Fundamental Issues in Strategy* (Boston: Harvard Business School Press, 1994).

44. J.R. Williams, B.L. Paez, and L. Sanders, "Conglomerates Revisited," *Strategic Management Journal,* 9, 1988, pp. 403–414.

45. H. Shaw, "Fish, Dairy Units Sacrificed to Help Raise Cash for Baked Goods: Bestfoods Deal," *Financial Post (National Post),* February 20, 2001, pp. C1, C6.

46. Website: Doug Krumrei, "Corporate Profiles: George Weston Bakeries, Inc.," *Milling & Baking News,* December 1, 2001.

47. C.A. Bartlett and S. Ghoshal, *Managing Across Borders* (Boston: Harvard Business School Press, 1989).

48. C.K. Prahalad and Y.L. Doz, *The Multinational Mission* (New York: Free Press, 1987).

49. M.K. Perry, "Vertical Integration: Determinants and Effects," in R. Schmalensee and R.D. Willig, *Handbook of Industrial Organization,* vol. 1 (New York: Elsevier Science Publishing, 1989).

50. Tony Keller, "Reinventing the Firm," *National Post Business,* June 2000, pp. 68–70, 72, 74, 76, 78, 81.

51. T. Muris, D. Scheffman, and P. Spiller, "Strategy and Transaction Costs: The Organization of Distribution in the Carbonated Soft Drink Industry," *Journal of Economics and Management Strategy,* 1, 1992, pp. 77–97.

52. "Matsushita Electric Industrial (MEI) in 1987," Harvard Business School Case #388-144.

53. P. Ghemawat, *Commitment: The Dynamic of Strategy* (New York: Free Press, 1991).

54. D. McMurdy, "The Human Cost of Mergers," *Maclean's,* November 20, 2000, p. 128.

55. Hollie Shaw, "Metro's Lessard Will Stick to Grocer's Recipe for Success," *Financial Post,* Friday, August 19, 2005, p. FP3.

56. M.E. Porter, *Competitive Strategy* (New York: Free Press, 1980).

57. Gordon Pitts, "Ganong Boss Aims for Sweet Spot," *The Globe and Mail,* March 3, 2003, p. B4.

58. Marina Strauss, "Watt to Light Up Wal-Mart Private Label," *The Globe and Mail,* Tuesday, April 19, 2005, pp. B1, 22.

59. Carolyn Leitch, "Best Buy's Secret: Sales Staff," *The Globe and Mail,* Friday, June 17, 2005, p. B12.

60. C.W.L. Hill, "Differentiation Versus Low Cost or Differentiation and Low Cost: A Contingency Framework," *Academy of Management Review,* 13, 1988, pp. 401–412.

61. For details see J.P. Womack, D.T. Jones, and D. Roos, *The Machine That Changed the World* (New York: Rawson Associates, 1990).

62. M.E. Porter, *Competitive Strategy* (New York: Free Press, 1980).

63. C.W.L. Hill and G.R. Jones, *Strategic Management: An Integrated Approach,* 3rd ed. (Boston: Houghton Mifflin, 2000).

64. See D. Garvin, "What Does Product Quality Really Mean?" *Sloan Management Review,* 26, Fall 1984, pp. 25–44; P.B. Crosby, *Quality Is Free* (New York: Mentor Books, 1980); and A. Gabor, *The Man Who Discovered Quality* (New York: Times Books, 1990).

65. Website: www.camh.net/pdf/camh_ strategicplan2003.pdf.

66. Adapted partly from Greg Fjetland, "Allied Wings Takes Off," *Canadian Business,* April 25, 2005. Website: www. canadianbusiness.com/companies/article.jsp? content=20050425_66939_66939#.

67. Website: www.thegreendoor.ca/.

68. Website: http://web.ustpaul.uottawa.ca/en/.

69. Website: www.ottawaplus.ca/portal/ profile.do?profileID=45275.

70. Terrence Belford, "Trusted Gatekeeper," FP ENTREPRENEUR, *National Post,* Monday, November 22, 2004, pp. FP8, 9.

71. Danny Bradbury, "Window of Opportunity," *National Post,* Friday, May 20, 2005, p. FP9.

Chapter 6

1. Dee Hock. *Birth of the Chaordic Age.* San Francisco: Berrett-Koehler Publishers, Inc., 1999, 146. ISBN 1-57675-074-4.

2. "Value-Based Management Thought Leader: Art Kleiner Biography—Core Group Theory of Power, Privilege and Success," website: www.valuebasedmanagement. net/leaders_kleiner.html.

3. Adapted from Art Kleiner, "Elliott Jaques Levels With You," *strategy + business,* 1st Quarter, 2001. Website: www.well.com/~art/ s+b12001cm.html.

4. Websites: www.ci.austin.tx.us/police/ default.htm; www.houstontx.gov/police/.

5. In the U.S., website: www.shell.com/home/ Framework?siteId=us-en&FC2=/ us-en/html/iwgen/leftnavs/zzz_lhn1_0_0. html&FC3=/us-en/html/iwgen/welcome.html; in Canada, website: www.shell.ca/.

6. Website: www.unitedstationers.com/home/index.asp.

7. www4.bmo.com/.

8. www.hydroone.com/.

9. Adapted from M. Mitchell Waldrop, "The Trillion-Dollar Vision of Dee Hock," *Fast Company*, Issue 5, October–November, 1996, 75ff. Website: www.fastcompany.com/fastco/5/well/deehock.htm.

10. Harvey Schachter, "Business Embarks on Design Revolution," *The Globe and Mail*, Friday, March 19, 2004, p. C1.

11. William Thorsell, "A Little Less Adam Smith, a Lot More William Shakespeare," *The Globe and Mail*, Saturday, October 22, 1994, p. D6.

12. For a discussion of this notion in relation to Canadian cities, see Gilles Paquet and Jeffrey Roy, "Smarter Cities in Canada Through E-Governance," *Journal of Canadian Studies*, December 2002. Website: www.smartcapital.ca/aboutsmartcapital/smartresults/SmarterCitiesinCanada2003.pdf. See also their home page website: www.ffcf.bc.ca/.

13. Linda Rising, "Chaordic Organizations," DDC-I Online News, August, 2004. Website: www.ddci.com/news_vol3num8.shtml. According to this website, "Linda Rising has a Ph.D. from Arizona State University in the area of object-based design metrics. Her background includes university teaching as well as work in industry in telecommunications, avionics, and strategic weapons systems. She is the author of numerous articles and has published three books: *Design Patterns in Communications*, *The Pattern Almanac 2000*, and *A Patterns Handbook*. She is currently writing a book with Mary Lynn Manns: *Introducing Patterns (or any Innovation) into Organizations*, to appear in Fall 2002." See also www.lindarising.org.

14. M. Mitchell Waldrop, "Dee Hock on Organizations," *Fast Company*, Issue 05, October/November 1996, p. 84.

15. "Who We Are," website: www.ffcf.bc.ca/DETAILS.HTM.

16. Seven Years of FarmFolk/CityFolk: A Summary of Past and Current Endeavours, August 2000. Website: www.ffcf.bc.ca/seven.html. See also the Organization Forum, Conference 2001. Website: www.organizationdesignforum.org/conference/2001.asp.

17. G.R. Jones, *Organizational Theory: Text and Cases* (Reading, MA: Addison-Wesley, 1995).

18. J. Child, *Organization: A Guide for Managers and Administrators* (New York: Harper and Row, 1977).

19. Bill Breen, "Soundoff," *Fast Company*, Issue 85, August 2004, 10. Website: http://pf.fastcompany.com/magazine/83/mod.html.

20. F.W. Taylor, *The Principles of Scientific Management* (New York: Harper, 1911).

21. R.W. Griffin, *Task Design: An Integrative Approach* (Glenview, IL: Scott, Foresman, 1982).

22. Ibid.

23. Emily Chung, "Dream Jobs—in Hell," *Toronto Star*, Monday, August 15, 2005, pp. C1, 5.

24. Roger Martin, "The Design of Business," *Rotman Management*, Winter 2004, 7–10. Website: www.rotman.utoronto.ca/roger-martin/DesignofBusiness.pdf.

25. Roger Martin, "The Design of Business," *Rotman Management*, Winter 2004, 9. Website: www.rotman.utoronto.ca/rogermartin/DesignofBusiness.pdf.

26. J.R. Galbraith and R.K. Kazanjian, *Strategy Implementation: Structure, System, and Process*, 2nd ed. (St. Paul, MN: West, 1986).

27. P.R. Lawrence and J.W. Lorsch, *Organization and Environment* (Boston: Graduate School of Business Administration, Harvard University, 1967).

28. G.R. Jones, *Organizational Theory: Text and Cases* (Reading, MA: Addison-Wesley, 1995).

29. P.R. Lawrence and J.W. Lorsch, *Organization and Environment* (Boston: Graduate School of Business Administration, Harvard University, 1967).

30. R.H. Hall, *Organizations: Structure and Process* (Englewood Cliffs, NJ: Prentice-Hall, 1972); and R. Miles, *Macro Organizational Behaviour* (Santa Monica, CA: Goodyear, 1980).

31. A.D. Chandler, *Strategy and Structure* (Cambridge, MA: MIT Press, 1962).

32. G.R. Jones and C.W.L. Hill, "Transaction Cost Analysis of Strategy–Structure Choice," *Strategic Management Journal*, 9, 1988, pp. 159–172.

33. Michael Maccoby, "Knowledge Workers Need New Structures," *Research Technology Management*, Vol. 30, No. 3 January–February 1996, pp. 56–58. Website: www.maccoby.com/Articles/KnowledgeWorkers.html.

34. "Toronto Charges to the Top: The City Of Toronto Works Best Practices Program,"

website: www.ema-inc.com/canada/canada_case_studies.htm.

35. S.M. Davis and P.R. Lawrence, *Matrix* (Reading, MA: Addison-Wesley, 1977); and J.R. Galbraith, "Matrix Organization Designs: How to Combine Functional and Project Forms," *Business Horizons*, 14, 1971, pp. 29–40.

36. L.R. Burns, "Matrix Management in Hospitals: Testing Theories of Matrix Structure and Development," *Administrative Science Quarterly*, 34, 1989, pp. 349–368.

37. C.W.L. Hill, *International Business* (Homewood, IL: Irwin, 1997).

38. C.A. Bartlett and S. Ghoshal, *Transnational Management* (Homewood, IL: Irwin, 1992).

39. G.R. Jones, *Organizational Theory: Text and Cases* (Reading, MA: Addison-Wesley, 1995).

40. Adapted from Paul Vieira, "Bureaucracy's Radical Reno," *National Post*, Thursday, March 3, 2005, p. FP3.

41. P. Blau, "A Formal Theory of Differentiation in Organizations," *American Sociological Review*, 35, 1970, pp. 684–695.

42. J. Child, *Organization: A Guide for Managers and Administrators* (New York: Harper and Row, 1977).

43. Information about Ducks Unlimited from "Salute! Celebrating the Progressive Employer," advertising supplement, *Benefits Canada*, March 1999, p. Insert 1–23; and www.ducksunlimited.ca.

44. P.M. Blau and R.A. Schoenherr, *The Structure of Organizations* (New York: Basic Books, 1971).

45. G.R. Jones, *Organizational Theory: Text and Cases* (Reading, MA: Addison-Wesley, 1995).

46. Adapted from Sharda Prashad, "Law Firms Urged to Balance Work, Family Life," *Toronto Star*, Thursday, March 17, 2005, pp. C1, 5.

47. T. Burns and G.M. Stalker, *The Management of Innovation* (London: Tavistock, 1961).

48. L.A. Perlow, G.A. Okhuysen, and N.P. Repenning, "The Speed Trap: Exploring the Relationship Between Decision Making and Temporal Context, *Academy of Management Journal*, 45, 2002, pp. 931–955.

49. P.R. Lawrence and J.W. Lorsch, *Organization and Environment* (Boston: Graduate School of Business Administration, Harvard University, 1967).

50. R. Duncan, "What Is the Right Organizational Design?" *Organizational Dynamics*, Winter 1979, pp. 59–80.

51. T. Burns and G.R. Stalker, *The Management of Innovation* (London: Tavistock, 1966).

52. Scott Peterson, "Good Leaders Empower People," *National Post,* Wednesday, May 18, 2005, p. FP9.

53. D. Miller, "Strategy Making and Structure: Analysis and Implications for Performance," *Academy of Management Journal,* 30, 1987, pp. 7–32.

54. A.D. Chandler, *Strategy and Structure* (Cambridge, MA: MIT Press, 1962).

55. J. Stopford and L. Wells, *Managing the Multinational Enterprise* (London: Longman, 1972).

56. J. Woodward, *Management and Technology* (London: Her Majesty's Stationery Office, 1958).

57. Barbara Shecter, "Banking on Bands," *National Post,* Tuesday, August 23, 2005, pp. FP1, 3.

58. B. Kogut, "Joint Ventures: Theoretical and Empirical Perspectives," *Strategic Management Journal,* 9, 1988, pp. 319–332.

59. See, for example, B. Hedberg, G. Dahlgren, J. Hansson, and N.-G. Olve, *Virtual Organizations and Beyond: Discovering Imaginary Systems* (New York: Wiley, 2001); N.A. Wishart, J.J. Elam, and D. Robey, "Redrawing the Portrait of a Learning Organization Inside Knight-Ridder, Inc.," *Academy of Management Executive,* 10, no. 1 (1996), pp. 7–20; G.G. Dess, A.M.A. Rasheeed, K.J. McLaughlin, and R.L. Priem, "The New Corporate Architecture," *Academy of Management Executive,* 9, no. 3 (1995), p. 720; and R. Keidel, "Rethinking Organizational Design," *Academy of Management Executive,* November 1994, pp. 12–27.

60. B. Hedberg, G. Dahlgren, J. Hansson, and N.-G. Olve, *Virtual Organizations and Beyond: Discovering Imaginary Systems* (New York: Wiley, 2001).

61. "Outsourcing," advertising supplement in *Purchasing B2B,* October 2000, pp. Insert 1–12.

62. Poonam Khanna, "CP Rail Jumps Aboard Outsourcing Train," *Computing Canada,* December 10, 2004, p. 30. For more on outsourcing, visit www.ezgoal.com/outsourcing/c.asp?a=Canada&outsourcing.

63. Grant Buckler, "Economies Of Scale A Big Hit For IT Managers," *Computing Canada,* February 15, 2002. Website: www.findarticles.com/p/articles/mi_m0CGC/is_4_28/ai_83056527#continue.

64. J. Barthelemy and D. Adsit, "The Seven Deadly Sins of Outsourcing," *Academy of Management Executive,* 17, no. 2, 2003, pp. 87–100.

65. Adapted partly from Greg Fjetland, "Allied Wings Takes Off," *Canadian Business,* April 25, 2005. Website: www.canadianbusiness.com/companies/article.jsp?content=20050425_66939_66939#.

66. © 1996, Gareth R. Jones.

67. Website: www.onex.com/index.taf?pid=49&_UserReference=DC9773E6122AC2DA44A1B665.

68. George Day and Paul Schoemaker. *Peripheral Vision.* Cambridge, Mass.: Harvard Business School Press, 248 pages. ISBN: 1422101541.

69. Editorial review, amazon.ca. Website: www.amazon.ca/exec/obidos/ASIN/1422101541/sr=8-1/qid=1151507093/ref=sr_1_1/701-8310829-0022710?%5Fencoding=UTF8&s=gateway&v=glance.

70. Harvey Schacter, "Strategy Gleaning from the Corner of Your Eye," *The Globe and Mail,* Wednesday, June 28, 2005, p. C3.

71. Slightly adapted from Kali Saposnick, "The People Who Really Shape Our Organizations: An Interview with Art Kleiner," *Leverage Points Newsletter,* July 24, 2003, Issue 40. Website: www.pegasuscom.com/levpoints/kleinerint.html.

72. *Italics* added. This is the opening paragraph of the article.

Chapter 7

1. Samy Chong, "Crystal Clear Need to Respect Employees," FP ENTREPRENEUR: Strategies for Small and Mid-Size Businesses, *Financial Post,* Monday, February 21, 2005, p. FP11.

2. Website: http://whatthebleep.com/.

3. Gordon Pitts, "It Boiled Down to a Culture Clash," *The Globe and Mail,* Saturday, June 11, 2005, p. B5.

4. "NASA Culture Blamed for Shuttle Disaster," *National Post,* Tuesday, August 26, 2003.

5. John Kotter and James L. Heskett. *Corporate Culture and Performance.* New York: Simon and Schuster, 1992, 224 pages. ISBN: 0029184673.

6. Marilyn Linton, "The 'New Worker' Needs New Employer," FP EDGE, *Financial Post,* Monday, April 13, 2004, pp. FP1, 10.

7. See, for example, H.S. Becker, "Culture: A Sociological View," *Yale Review,* Summer 1982, pp. 513–527; and E.H. Schein, *Organizational Culture and Leadership* (San Francisco: Jossey-Bass, 1985), p. 168.

8. T.E. Deal and A.A. Kennedy, "Culture: A New Look Through Old Lenses," *Journal of Applied Behavioral Science,* November 1983, p. 501.

9. M. Rokeach, *The Nature of Human Values* (New York: Free Press, 1973).

10. D. Yedlin, "Entwistle Faces Potholes at Telus," *The Globe and Mail,* March 17, 2003, p. B2.

11. Catherine McLean, "Free MP3s? For Some at Telus, It's the Sound of Crossing the Line," *The Globe and Mail,* Thursday, August 25, 2005, pp. B1, 6.

12. E.H. Schein, "Leadership and Organizational Culture," in F. Hesselbein, M. Goldsmith, and R. Beckhard (eds.), *The Leader of the Future* (San Francisco: Jossey-Bass, 1996), pp. 61–62.

13. J.B. Sorensen, "The Strength of Corporate Culture and the Reliability of Firm Performance," *Administrative Science Quarterly,* 47, no. 1, 2002, pp. 70–91.

14. D.C. Feldman, "The Development and Enforcement of Group Norms," *Academy of Management Review,* 9, 1984, pp. 47–53.

15. Paul Brent, "Culture Shock May Be Brewing," *National Post,* Saturday, February 5, 2005, pp. FP1, 5.

16. D. Yedlin, "Merging Corporate Cultures Not Always Easy," *Calgary Herald,* June 2, 2001, p. E1.

17. G.R. Jones, *Organizational Theory: Text and Cases* (Reading, MA: Addison-Wesley, 1995).

18. H. Schein, "The Role of the Founder in Creating Organizational Culture," *Organizational Dynamics,* 12, 1983, pp. 13–28.

19. J.M. George, "Personality, Affect, and Behaviour in Groups," *Journal of Applied Psychology,* 75, 1990, pp. 107–116.

20. J. Van Maanen, "Police Socialization: A Longitudinal Examination of Job Attitudes in an Urban Police Department," *Administrative Science Quarterly,* 20, 1975, pp. 207–228.

21. P.L. Berger and T. Luckman, *The Social Construction of Reality* (Garden City, NY: Anchor Books, 1967).

22. H.M. Trice and J.M. Beyer, "Studying Organizational Culture Through Rites and Ceremonials," *Academy of Management Review,* 9, 1984, pp. 653–669.

23. "Bonding and Brutality: Hazing Survives as a Way of Forging Loyalty to Groups," *Maclean's,* January 30, 1995, p. 18.

24. "Employer, Directors Held Liable for Workplace Assault," *hrreporter.com,* May 11, 2004.

25. B. Ortega, "Wal-Mart's Meeting Is a Reason to Party," *The Wall Street Journal,* June 3, 1994, p. A1.

26. Website: www.senecac.on.ca/.

27. C. Stephenson, "Corporate Values Drive Global Success at Lucent Technologies," *Canadian Speeches,* November/December 1999, pp. 23–27.

28. A. Rafaeli and M.G. Pratt, "Tailored Meanings: On the Meaning and Impact of Organizational Dress," *Academy of Management Review,* January 1993, pp. 32–55.

29. J. Greenwood, "Job One: When Bobbie Gaunt Became Ford of Canada President Earlier This Year, the Appointment Put a Spotlight on the New Rules of the Auto Industry: It's Less About Manufacturing These Days Than About Marketing and Sales," *Financial Post Magazine,* June 1997, pp. 18–22.

30. D. Akin, "Big Blue Chills Out: A Canadian Executive Leads the Campaign to Turn IBM into Cool Blue," *Financial Post (National Post),* October 11, 1999, pp. C1, C6.

31. Adapted from Susan Bourette, "10 Dirty Secrets of a Bay Street Temp," *Report on Business Magazine,* September 2005, pp. 28–29, 31, 33–34, 36.

32. J. Lee, "Canadian Businesses Not Good at Adjusting, Survey Says," *The Vancouver Sun,* December 14, 1998, pp. C1–2.

33. Sean Silcoff, "Shermag: Evolving and Surviving," *Financial Post,* Friday, August 12, 2005, p. FP3.

34. E. Schein, *Organizational Culture and Leadership* (San Francisco, Jossey-Bass, 1985).

35. Michael Hepworth, "Who Do You Think You Are?" *The Globe and Mail,* Wednesday, May 4, 2005, p. B4.

36. Jason Keller, "A Shoe Named Chuck," *National Post,* Saturday, July 16, 2005, p. WP5.

37. Website: www.buildingbrands.com/didyouknow/08_new_coke.shtml.

38. L. Brown, "Research Action: Organizational Feedback, Understanding and Change," *Journal of Applied Behavioral Research,* 8, 1972, pp. 697–711; P.A. Clark, *Action Research and Organizational Change* (New York: Harper and Row, 1972); and N. Margulies and A.P. Raia (eds.), *Conceptual Foundations of Organizational Development* (New York: McGraw-Hill, 1978).

39. Sean Silcoff, "Shermag: Evolving and Surviving," *Financial Post,* Friday, August 12, 2005, p. FP3.

40. W.L. French and C.H. Bell, *Organizational Development* (Englewood Cliffs, NJ: Prentice-Hall, 1990).

41. K. Lewin, *Field Theory in Social Science* (New York: Harper and Row, 1951).

42. W.L. French, "A Checklist for Organizing and Implementing an OD Effort," in W.L. French, C.H. Bell, and R.A. Zawacki (eds.), *Organizational Development and Transformation* (Homewood, IL: Irwin, 1994), 484–495.

43. Sean Silcoff, "Shermag: Evolving and Surviving," *Financial Post,* Friday, August 12, 2005, p. FP3.

44. Robert Townsend. *Up the Organization.* New York: Knopf, 1970, 93. *Italics* added for emphasis.

45. Website: www.answers.com/topic/featherbedding.

46. Colby Cosh, "Do Unions Still Matter?" *National Post,* Wednesday, August 3, 2005, p. A16.

47. Workplace Information Directorate. Website: www.hrsdc.gc.ca/en/lp/wid/union_membership.shtml.

48. Paul Vieira, "Canada Faces Productivity Crisis: Professor," *Financial Post,* Monday, April 11, 2005, p. FP4. See also Gilles Paquet, "Productivity and Innovation in Canada: A Case of Governance Failure," *Policy Options,* March–April 2005. Download .pdf document. Website: www.irpp.org/po/. The summary at the website reads: *While there is broad agreement on the benefits of productivity growth and innovation, Canada has not done very well on these fronts, trailing behind all its major trading partners. This, says Gilles Paquet, has to do with the fact that Canada is a risk-averse society "plagued by social rigidities that prevent it from adapting to the evolving context." Despite efforts to put these issues on the public agenda, Canadians have remained largely unconcerned, due to three mental blocks: the very little knowledge we have about the sources and causes of productivity gains and innovation, the growing anti-economic-growth sentiment, and the lack of leadership of public officials in educating individuals about their central importance. Paquet reviews the steps that Canada has to take in order to rise to the challenge of innovation and productivity and capture the accruing benefits: "This will entail a major reframing of Canadian perspectives, much restructuring and a fair bit of retooling,"* he says.

49. J.R. Stepp and T.J. Schneider, "Fostering Change in a Unionized Environment," *Canadian Business Review,* Summer 1995, pp. 13–16.

50. Ibid.

51. Susan Bourette, "10 Dirty Secrets of a Bay Street Temp," *Report on Business Magazine,* September 2005, pp. 28–29, 31, 33–34, 36.

52. Jim Collins, "Level 5 Leadership: The Triumph of Humility and Fierce Resolve," *Harvard Business Review,* HBR OnPoint, 15 pages. Product No. 5831.

53. Adapted from "Impersonal Approach Hurts Business, Study Says," *The Globe and Mail,* Wednesday, August 20, 2003, p. C3.

54. Slightly adapted from Marilyn Linton, "The 'New Worker' Needs New Employer," FP EDGE, *Financial Post,* Monday, April 13, 2004, pp. FP1, 10.

55. Slightly adapted from Barbara Moses, "Who Wants to Work for a 'Stinky' Employer?" *The Globe and Mail,* Wednesday, June 9, 2004, p. C3.

Chapter 8

1. Wallace Immen, "Managers Hold Key to Keep Staff Happy," *The Globe and Mail,* Wednesday, June 16, 2004, C3.

2. See www.keepem.com.

3. www.cohnwolfe.ca/.

4. "Management Tip From the Top," *FP EDGE, Financial Post,* Monday, May 10, 2004, FE2.

5. R. Kanfer, "Motivation Theory and Industrial and Organizational Psychology," in M.D. Dunnette and L.M. Hough (eds.), *Handbook of Industrial and Organizational Psychology,* 2nd ed., vol. 1 (Palo Alto, CA: Consulting Psychologists Press, 1990), pp. 75–170.

6. Based on Barbara Moses, "Coddled, Confident and Cocky: The Challenges of Managing Gen Y," *The Globe and Mail,* Friday, March 11, 2005, C1, 2.

7. A.H. Maslow, *Motivation and Personality* (New York: Harper and Row, 1954); and J.P. Campbell and R.D. Pritchard, "Motivation Theory in Industrial and Organizational Psychology," in M.D. Dunnette (ed.), *Handbook of Industrial and Organizational Psychology* (Chicago: Rand McNally, 1976), pp. 63–130.

8. R. Kanfer, "Motivation Theory and Industrial and Organizational Psychology," in M.D. Dunnette and L.M. Hough (eds.), *Handbook of Industrial and Organizational Psychology,* 2nd ed., vol. 1 (Palo Alto, CA: Consulting Psychologists Press, 1990), pp. 75–170.

9. S. Ronen, "An Underlying Structure of Motivational Need Taxonomies: A Cross-Cultural Confirmation," in H.C. Triandis, M.D. Dunnette, and L.M. Hough (eds.),

Handbook of Industrial and Organizational Psychology, vol. 4 (Palo Alto, CA: Consulting Psychologists Press, 1994), pp. 241–269.

10. N.J. Adler, *International Dimensions of Organizational Behavior,* 2nd ed. (Boston: P.W.S.-Kent, 1991); G. Hofstede, "Motivation, Leadership and Organization: Do American Theories Apply Abroad?" *Organizational Dynamics,* Summer 1980, pp. 42–63.

11. F. Herzberg, *Work and the Nature of Man* (Cleveland: World, 1966).

12. N. King, "Clarification and Evaluation of the Two-Factor Theory of Job Satisfaction," *Psychological Bulletin,* 74, 1970, pp. 18–31; and E.A. Locke, "The Nature and Causes of Job Satisfaction," in M.D. Dunnette (ed.), *Handbook of Industrial and Organizational Psychology* (Chicago: Rand McNally, 1976), pp. 1297–1349.

13. R.A. Clay, "Green Is Good for You," *Monitor on Psychology,* April 2001, pp. 40–42.

14. Adapted from Virginia Galt, "Kid-Glove Approach Woos New Grads," *The Globe and Mail,* Wednesday, March 9, 2005, C1, 3.

15. T.R. Mitchell, "Expectancy-Value Models in Organizational Psychology," in N.T. Feather (ed.), *Expectations and Actions: Expectancy-Value Models in Psychology* (Hillsdale, NJ: Erlbaum, 1982), pp. 293–312; V.H. Vroom, *Work and Motivation* (New York: Wiley, 1964).

16. Kevin Cox, "Irving Oil Fuels Its Leaders," *The Globe and Mail,* Wednesday, April 21, 2004, C1, 3.

17. P. Engardio and G. DeGeorge, "Importing Enthusiasm," *Business Week/21st Century Capitalism,* 1994, pp. 122–123.

18. Quoted in Michael Kesterton, "Social Studies," *The Globe and Mail,* Wednesday, May 19, 2004, A22.

19. E.A. Locke and G.P. Latham, *A Theory of Goal Setting and Task Performance* (Englewood Cliffs, NJ: Prentice-Hall, 1990).

20. Barbara Moses, "Make Sure Goals Really Do Serve You," *The Globe and Mail,* Friday, October 15, 2004, C1.

21. E.A. Locke and G.P. Latham, *A Theory of Goal Setting and Task Performance* (Englewood Cliffs, NJ: Prentice-Hall, 1990); J.J. Donovan and D.J. Radosevich, "The Moderating Role of Goal Commitment on the Goal Difficulty–Performance Relationship: A Meta-Analytic Review and Critical Analysis," *Journal of Applied Psychology,* 83, 1998, pp. 308–315; and M.E. Tubbs, "Goal Setting: A Meta-Analytic Examination of the Empirical Evidence,"

Journal of Applied Psychology, 71, 1986, pp. 474–483.

22. Charles Mitchell, "A Night in the Life of 'Graveyard Shift' Workers," *Toronto Star,* Saturday, March 12, 2005, D1, 15. The picture is the second image at www2.lut.fi/~garrido/unpleasant_jobs.htm.

23. F. Luthans and R. Kreitner, *Organizational Behavior Modification and Beyond* (Glenview, IL: Scott, Foresman, 1985); A.D. Stajkovic and F. Luthans, "A Meta-Analysis of the Effects of Organizational Behavior Modification on Task Performance, 1975–95," *Academy of Management Journal,* 40, 1997, pp. 1122–1149.

24. "Despite Progress, N.S. Women Face Wage Gap," *The Globe and Mail,* Wednesday, June 16, 2004, C8.

25. Wayne F. Cascio, "Human Resources Systems in an International Alliance: The Undoing of a Done Deal?" Vol. 20, *Organizational Dynamics,* January 1, 1991, pp. 63ff.

26. J.S. Adams, "Toward an Understanding of Inequity," *Journal of Abnormal and Social Psychology,* 67, 1963, pp. 422–436; J. Greenberg, "Approaching Equity and Avoiding Inequity in Groups and Organizations," in J. Greenberg and R.L. Cohen (eds.), *Equity and Justice in Social Behavior* (New York: Academic Press, 1982), pp. 389–435; J. Greenberg, "Equity and Workplace Status: A Field Experiment," *Journal of Applied Psychology,* 73, 1988, pp. 606–613; and R.T. Mowday, "Equity Theory Predictions of Behavior in Organizations," in R.M. Steers and L.W. Porter, (eds.), *Motivation and Work Behavior* (New York: McGraw-Hill, 1987), pp. 89–110.

27. Katherine Harding, "Your New Best Friend," *The Globe and Mail,* Wednesday, March 12, 2003, C1, 10.

28. Katherine Harding, "Once and Future Kings," *The Globe and Mail,* Wednesday, April 9, 2003, C1, 6.

29. Based on Suzanne Wintrob, "Reward a Job Well Done," *FP EDGE, Financial Post,* Monday, May 10, 2004, FE7 and Janis Foord Kirk, "Unfair Rule Destroys Productivity," *Toronto Star,* Sunday, March 12, 2005, D1, 13.

30. *Creating Healthy Workplaces,* IAPA, November 2004. Website: www.iapa.ca/resources/resources_downloads.asp#healthy.

31. E.E. Lawler III, *Pay and Organization Development* (Reading, MA: Addison-Wesley, 1981).

32. Based on S.E. Gross and J.P. Bacher, "The New Variable Pay Programs: How Some

Succeed, Why Some Don't," *Compensation & Benefits Review,* January–February 1993, p. 51; and J.R. Schuster and P.K. Zingheim, "The New Variable Pay: Key Design Issues," *Compensation & Benefits Review,* March–April 1993, p. 28.

33. Peter Brieger, "Variable Pay Packages Gain Favour: Signing Bonuses, Profit Sharing Taking Place of Salary Hikes," *Financial Post (National Post),* September 13, 2002, p. FP5.

34. E. Beauchesne, "Pay Bonuses Improve Productivity, Study Shows," *The Vancouver Sun,* September 13, 2002, p. D5.

35. "Hope for Higher Pay: The Squeeze on Incomes Is Gradually Easing Up," *Maclean's,* November 25, 1996, pp. 100–101.

36. www.keepem.com. Also, Beverly Kaye with Sharon Jordan-Evans. *Love 'em or Lose 'em: Getting Good People to Stay.* San Francisco, CA: Berrett-Koehler, 2002, 244 pages. ISBN: 1576751406.

37. Adapted from "Case Studies: Motivating Your Team," website: www.cokepubandbar.co.uk/lic_casestudy_07.html.

Chapter 9

1. Adapted from Gabriel Draven, "Leadership and The Duty to The Seventh Generation," *hr.com,* Sunday, September 20, 2004. Website: www.hr.com.

2. Gabriel Draven is a Canadian-based thinker who works with clients to improve their organizational effectiveness by helping them align their people with organizational purpose. He conducts his work amidst a community of practice comprised of senior experts in the disciplines of marketing, strategy, technology, innovation, organizational behaviour, organizational design, and change management.

3. See www.chaordic.org/.

4. Director of the Trudeau Centre for Peace and Conflict Studies at the University of Toronto, and Associate Professor in the Department of Political Science at the University of Toronto, author of *The Ingenuity Gap* (Knopf, 2000), which won the 2001 Governor General's Non-fiction Award, and *Environment, Scarcity, and Violence* (Princeton University Press, 1999). Website: www.homerdixon.com/index.html.

5. Virginia Galt, "Disengagement Said 'Common' in Workplace," *The Globe and Mail,* Saturday, July 31, 2004, B7.

6. Janis Foord-Kirk, "Showing Up to Work, But Not Really There," *Toronto Star,* Saturday, February 12, 2005, D1, 11.

7. Paul Hemp, "Presenteeism: At Work-But Out of It," *Harvard Business Review*, October 2004, 49–58. Product Number: R0410B.

8. Bryony Gordon, "Slacking Off Can Be Such Hard Work," *National Post*, Tuesday, November 9, 2004, A1, 2.

9. See www.phd.antioch.edu/Pages/APhDWeb_Program/bennis.

10. Website: www.greenleaf.org/.

11. Visit the website: www.seventhgeneration.com/site/pp.asp?c=coIHKTMHF&b=90085.

12. Based on Margaret Wheatley. *Finding Our Way: Leadership For An Uncertain Time*. San Francisco: Berrett-Koehler, 2005, 300 pages. ISBN: 1576753174 See also Harvey Schachter, "Command and Control Mentality Hurts Living Organizations," *The Globe and Mail*, Wednesday, May 18, 2005, C3.

13. G. Yukl, *Leadership in Organizations*, 2nd ed. (New York: Academic Press, 1989); and R.M. Stogdill, *Handbook of Leadership: A Survey of the Literature* (New York: Free Press, 1974).

14. "Leadership and The Duty to The Seventh Generation," *hr.com*, Sunday, September 20, 2004. Website: www.hr.com.

15. "Dee Hock on Management," *Fast Company*, Issue 5, October/November 1996, 79. Website: www.fastcompany.com/online/05/dee2.html.

16. J. Fierman, "Winning Ideas From Maverick Managers," *Fortune*, February 6, 1995, p. 70.

17. H. Mintzberg, *Power in and Around Organizations* (Englewood Cliffs, NJ: Prentice-Hall, 1983); and J. Pfeffer, *Power in Organizations* (Marshfield, MA: Pitman, 1981).

18. R.P. French Jr. and B. Raven, "The Bases of Social Power," in D. Cartwright and A.F. Zander (eds.), *Group Dynamics* (Evanston, IL: Row, Peterson, 1960), pp. 607–623.

19. Ken Petress, Ph.D., "Power: Definition, Typology, Description, Examples, and Implications," Website: http://bliss.umpi.maine.edu/~petress/power.pdf.

20. Rob Shaw, "Reward Employee Ideas–Literally," *The Globe and Mail*, Friday, August 19, 2005, C1, 2.

21. Glen L. Urban, "The Elements of Customer Advocacy," Part 2 of 3, *FP EDGE*, *Financial Post*, Monday, March 8, 2004, FE2.

22. Wolf J. Rinke, Ph.D., *Don't Oil the Squeaky Wheel and 19 Other Contrarian Ways to Improve Your Leadership Effectiveness*, New York: McGraw-Hill, 2004, 224 pages. ISBN: 007142993X. See also Wolf J. Rinke, "The Squeaky Wheels Deserve No Oil," *The Globe and Mail*, Friday, August 13, 2004, C1, 5.

23. "Meeting the Challenges of Tomorrow's Workplace," *Chief Executive Perspectives*, August/September 2002.

24. Sharda Prashad, "Fill Your Power Gap," *The Globe and Mail*, Wednesday, July 23, 2003, C3.

25. Mario F. Heilmann, "Social Evolution and Social Influence: Selfishness, Deception, Self-deception," from "V. Some Aspects of Raven's Power Interaction Model Under an Evolutionary Point of View, p. 28," Website: www.a3.com/myself/ravenpap.htm.

26. T.M. Burton, "Visionary's Reward: Combine 'Simple Ideas' and Some Failures; Result: Sweet Revenge," *The Wall Street Journal*, February 3, 1995, pp. A1, A5.

27. L. Nakarmi, "A Flying Leap Toward the 21st Century? Pressure From Competitors and Seoul May Transform the Chaebol," *Business Week*, March 20, 1995, pp. 78–80.

28. J. Schaubroeck, J.R. Jones, and J.L. Xie, "Individual Differences in Utilizing Control to Cope With Job Demands: Effects on Susceptibility to Infectious Disease," *Journal of Applied Psychology*, 86, no. 2, 2001, pp. 265–278; and A.M. Owens, "Empowerment Can Make You Ill, Study Says," *National Post*, April 30, 2001, pp. A1, A8.

29. "Delta Promotes Empowerment," *The Globe and Mail*, May 31, 1999, advertising supplement, p. C5.

30. J.P. Kotter, "What Leaders Really Do," *Harvard Business Review*, May–June 1990, pp. 103–111.

31. R.N. Kanungo, "Leadership in Organizations: Looking Ahead to the 21st Century," *Canadian Psychology*, 39, no. 1–2, 1998, p. 77. For more evidence of this consensus, see N. Adler, *International Dimensions of Organizational Behavior*, 3rd ed., (Cincinnati, OH: South Western College Publishing), 1997; R.J. House, "Leadership in the Twenty-First Century," in A. Howard (ed.), *The Changing Nature of Work* (San Francisco: Jossey-Bass), 1995, pp. 411–450; R.N. Kanungo and M. Mendonca, *Ethical Dimensions of Leadership* (Thousand Oaks, CA: Sage Publications, 1996); and A. Zaleznik, "The Leadership Gap," *Academy of Management Executive*, 4, no. 1, 1990, pp. 7–22.

32. Gordon Pitts, "Invisible Billionaire Casts a Huge Shadow," *The Globe and Mail*, Monday, April 18, 2004, JB3.

33. Website: www.jimpattison.com/.

34. B.M. Bass, Bass and Stogdill's *Handbook of Leadership: Theory, Research, and Managerial Applications*, 3rd ed. (New York: Free Press, 1990); R.J. House and M.L. Baetz, "Leadership: Some Empirical Generalizations and New Research Directions," in B.M. Staw and L.L. Cummings (eds.), *Research in Organizational Behavior*, vol. 1 (Greenwich, CT: JAI Press, 1979), pp. 341–423; S.A. Kirpatrick and E.A. Locke, "Leadership: Do Traits Matter?" *Academy of Management Executive*, 5, no. 2, 1991, pp. 48–60; and G. Yukl, *Leadership in Organizations*, 2nd ed. (New York: Academic Press, 1989); and G. Yukl and D.D. Van Fleet, "Theory and Research on Leadership in Organizations," in M.D. Dunnette and L.M. Hough (eds.), *Handbook of Industrial and Organizational Psychology*, 2nd ed., vol. 3 (Palo Alto, CA: Consulting Psychologists Press, 1992), pp. 147–197.

35. E.A. Fleishman, "Performance Assessment Based on an Empirically Derived Task Taxonomy," *Human Factors*, 9, 1967, pp. 349–366; E.A. Fleishman, "The Description of Supervisory Behavior," *Personnel Psychology*, 37, 1953, pp. 1–6; A.W. Halpin and B.J. Winer, "A Factorial Study of the Leader Behavior Descriptions," in R.M. Stogdill and A.I. Coons (eds.), *Leader Behavior: Its Description and Measurement* (Columbus Bureau of Business Research, Ohio State University, 1957); and D. Tscheulin, "Leader Behavior Measurement in German Industry," *Journal of Applied Psychology*, 56, 1971, pp. 28–31.

36. R. Likert, *New Patterns of Management* (New York: McGraw-Hill, 1961); and N.C. Morse and E. Reimer, "The Experimental Change of a Major Organizational Variable," *Journal of Abnormal and Social Psychology*, 52, 1956, pp. 120–129.

37. R.R. Blake and J.S. Mouton, *The New Managerial Grid* (Houston: Gulf, 1978).

38. David Sirota, Louis A. Mischkind, and Michael Irwin Meltzer, "Nothing Beats an Enthusiastic Employee," *The Globe and Mail*, Friday, July 29, 2005, C1.

39. Edited slightly from "Diversity Lies in Workplace Environment Not People Selection," Website: www.personnelzone.com/WebSite/WebWatch.nsf/ArticleListHTML/02548FEC0EAE4D63802570970037DE87.

40. E.A. Fleishman and E.F. Harris, "Patterns of Leadership Behavior Related to Employee Grievances and Turnover," *Personnel Psychology*, 15, 1962, pp. 43–56.

41. F.E. Fiedler, *A Theory of Leadership Effectiveness* (New York: McGraw-Hill, 1967); and F.E. Fiedler, "The Contingency Model and the Dynamics of the Leadership Process," in L. Berkowitz (ed.), *Advances in Experimental*

Social Psychology (New York: Academic Press, 1978).

42. R.J. House and M.L. Baetz, "Leadership: Some Empirical Generalizations and New Research Directions," in B.M. Staw and L.L. Cummings (eds.), *Research in Organizational Behavior,* vol. 1 (Greenwich, CT: JAI Press, 1979), pp. 341–423; L.H. Peters, D.D. Hartke, and J.T. Pohlmann, "Fiedler's Contingency Theory of Leadership: An Application of the Meta-Analysis Procedures of Schmidt and Hunter," *Psychological Bulletin,* 97, 1985, pp. 274–285; and C.A. Schriesheim, B.J. Tepper, and L.A. Tetrault, "Least Preferred Co-Worker Score, Situational Control, and Leadership Effectiveness: A Meta-Analysis of Contingency Model Performance Predictions," *Journal of Applied Psychology,* 79, 1994, pp. 561–573.

43. P. Hersey and K.H. Blanchard, "So You Want to Know Your Leadership Style?" *Training and Development Journal,* February 1974, pp. 1–15; and P. Hersey and K.H. Blanchard, *Management of Organizational Behavior: Utilizing Human Resources,* 6th ed. (Englewood Cliffs, NJ: Prentice-Hall, 1993).

44. Cited in C.F. Fernandez and R.P. Vecchio, "Situational Leadership Theory Revisited: A Test of an Across-Jobs Perspective," *Leadership Quarterly,* 8, no. 1, 1997, p. 67.

45. M.G. Evans, "The Effects of Supervisory Behavior on the Path–Goal Relationship," Organizational Behavior and Human Performance," 5, 1970, pp. 277–298; M.G. Evans, "Leadership and Motivation: A Core Concept," *Academy of Management Journal,* 13, 1970, pp. 91–102; R.J. House, "A Path–Goal Theory of Leader Effectiveness," *Administrative Science Quarterly,* September 1971, pp. 321–338; R.J. House and T.R. Mitchell, "Path–Goal Theory of Leadership," *Journal of Contemporary Business,* Autumn 1974, p. 86; M.G. Evans, "Leadership," in S. Kerr (ed.), *Organizational Behavior* (Columbus, OH: Grid Publishing, 1979); R.J. House, "Retrospective Comment," in L.E. Boone and D.D. Bowen (eds.), *The Great Writings in Management and Organizational Behavior,* 2nd ed. (New York: Random House, 1987), pp. 354–364; M.G. Evans, "Fuhrungstheorien, Weg-ziel-theorie" (trans. G. Reber), in A. Kieser, G. Reber, and R. Wunderer (eds). *Handworterbuch Der Fuhrung,* 2nd ed. (Stuttgart, Germany: Schaffer Poeschal Verlag, 1995), pp. 1075–1091; and J.C. Wofford and L.Z. Liska, "Path–Goal Theories of Leadership: A Meta-Analysis," *Journal of Management,* 19, 1993, pp. 857–876.

46. R. McQueen, "The Long Shadow of Tom Stephens: He Branded MacBlo's Crew as Losers, Then Made Them into Winners," *Financial Post (National Post),* June 22, 1999, pp. C1, C5.

47. S. Kerr and J.M. Jermier, "Substitutes for Leadership: Their Meaning and Measurement," *Organizational Behavior and Human Performance,* 22, 1978, pp. 375–403; P.M. Podsakoff, B.P. Niehoff, S.B. MacKenzie, and M.L. Williams, "Do Substitutes for Leadership Really Substitute for Leadership? An Empirical Examination of Kerr and Jermier's Situational Leadership Model," *Organizational Behavior and Human Decision Processes,* 54, 1993, pp. 1–44.

48. S. Kerr and J.M. Jermier, "Substitutes for Leadership: Their Meaning and Measurement," *Organizational Behavior and Human Performance,* 22, 1978, pp. 375–403; and P.M. Podsakoff, B.P. Niehoff, S.B. MacKenzie, and M.L. Williams, "Do Substitutes for Leadership Really Substitute for Leadership? An Empirical Examination of Kerr and Jermier's Situational Leadership Model," *Organizational Behavior and Human Decision Processes,* 54, 1993, pp. 1–44.

49. Adapted from David Rooke and William R. Torbert, "Transformations of Leadership," *Harvard Business Review,* April 2005, 66–76. Reprint R0504D. *Italics* added to opening quote.

50. See also Bill Torbert. *Action Inquiry: The Secret of Timely and Transforming Leadership.* San Francisco: Berrett-Koehler, 2004, 300 pages. ISBN: 157675264X—CDN$ 29.37. Also, "WEB Links To Participatory Action Research Sites: An Action-Research Resource for Both Students and Practitioners," Website: www.goshen.edu/soan/soan96p.htm.

51. J.M. Howell and B.J. Avolio, "The Leverage of Leadership," in *Leadership: Achieving Exceptional Performance,* supplement prepared by the Richard Ivey School of Business, *The Globe and Mail,* May 15, 1998, pp. C1, C2.

52. Ibid.

53. V. Smith, "Leading Us On," *Report on Business Magazine,* April 1999, pp. 91–96.

54. A. Bryman, "Leadership in Organizations," in S.R. Clegg, C. Hardy, and W.R. Nord (eds.), *Handbook of Organization Studies* (London: Sage Publications, 1996), pp. 276–292.

55. B.M. Bass, *Leadership and Performance Beyond Expectations* (New York: Free Press, 1985); B.M. Bass, Bass and Stogdill's *Handbook of Leadership: Theory, Research, and Managerial Applications,* 3rd ed. (New York: Free Press, 1990); and G. Yukl and

D.D. Van Fleet, "Theory and Research on Leadership in Organizations," in M.D. Dunnette and L.M. Hough (eds.), *Handbook of Industrial and Organizational Psychology,* 2nd ed., vol. 3 (Palo Alto, CA: Consulting Psychologists Press, 1992), pp. 147–97.

56. L. Nakarmi, "Goldstar is Burning Bright," *Business Week,* September 26, 1994, p. 129.

57. J.A. Conger and R.N. Kanungo, "Behavioral Dimensions of Charismatic Leadership," in J.A. Conger, R.N. Kanungo, and Associates, *Charismatic Leadership* (San Francisco: Jossey-Bass, 1988).

58. J.A. Conger and R.N. Kanungo, *Charismatic Leadership in Organizations* (Thousand Oaks, CA: Sage, 1998).

59. "Building a Better Boss," *Maclean's,* September 30, 1996, p. 41.

60. T. Dvir, D. Eden, B.J. Avolio, and B. Shamir, "Impact of Transformational Leadership on Follower Development and Performance: A Field Experiment," *Academy of Management Journal,* 45, no. 4, 2002, pp. 735–744; R.J. House, J. Woycke, and E.M. Fodor, "Charismatic and Noncharismatic Leaders: Differences in Behavior and Effectiveness," in J.A. Conger and R.N. Kanungo, *Charismatic Leadership in Organizations,* (Thousand Oaks, CA: Sage, 1998), pp. 103–104; D.A. Waldman, B.M. Bass, and F.J. Yammarino, "Adding to Contingent-Reward Behavior: The Augmenting Effect of Charismatic Leadership," *Group & Organization Studies,* December 1990, pp. 381–394; S.A. Kirkpatrick and E.A. Locke, "Direct and Indirect Effects of Three Core Charismatic Leadership Components on Performance and Attitudes," *Journal of Applied Psychology,* February 1996, pp. 36–51; and J.A. Conger, R.N. Kanungo, and S.T. Menon, "Charismatic Leadership and Follower Outcome Effects," paper presented at the 58th Annual Academy of Management Meetings, San Diego, CA, August 1998.

61. J.M. Howell and P.J. Frost, "A Laboratory Study of Charismatic Leadership," *Organizational Behavior & Human Decision Processes,* 43, no. 2, April 1989, pp. 243–269.

62. "Building a Better Boss," *Maclean's,* September 30, 1996, p. 41.

63. A. Elsner, "The Era of CEO as Superhero Ends Amid Corporate Scandals," globeandmail.com, July 10, 2002.

64. B.M. Bass, *Leadership and Performance Beyond Expectations* (New York: Free Press, 1985); B.M. Bass, Bass and Stogdill's *Handbook of Leadership: Theory, Research, and Managerial Applications,* 3rd ed. (New York: Free Press, 1990); and G. Yukl and

D.D. Van Fleet, "Theory and Research on Leadership in Organizations," in M.D. Dunnette and L.M. Hough (eds.), *Handbook of Industrial and Organizational Psychology,* 2nd ed., vol. 3 (Palo Alto, CA: Consulting Psychologists Press, 1992), pp. 147–197.

65. Ibid.

66. Cited in B.M. Bass and B.J. Avolio, "Developing Transformational Leadership: 1992 and Beyond," *Journal of European Industrial Training,* January 1990, p. 23.

67. J.M. Howell and B.J. Avolio, "The Leverage of Leadership," in *Leadership: Achieving Exceptional Performance,* supplement prepared by the Richard Ivey School of Business, *The Globe and Mail,* May 15, 1998, p. C2.

68. B.M. Bass, Bass and Stogdill's *Handbook of Leadership*; B.M. Bass and B.J. Avolio, "Transformational Leadership: A Response to Critiques," in M.M. Chemers and R. Ayman (eds.), *Leadership Theory and Research: Perspectives and Directions* (San Diego: Academic Press, 1993), pp. 49–80; B.M. Bass, B.J. Avolio, and L. Goodheim, "Biography and the Assessment of Transformational Leadership at the World Class Level," *Journal of Management,* 13, 1987, pp. 7–20; J.J. Hater and B.M. Bass, "Supervisors' Evaluations and Subordinates' Perceptions of Transformational and Transactional Leadership," *Journal of Applied Psychology,* 73, 1988, pp. 695–702; R. Pillai, "Crisis and Emergence of Charismatic Leadership in Groups: An Experimental Investigation," *Journal of Applied Psychology,* 26, 1996, pp. 543–562; J. Seltzer and B.M. Bass, "Transformational Leadership: Beyond Initiation and Consideration," *Journal of Management,* 16, 1990, pp. 693–703; and D.A. Waldman, B.M. Bass, and W.O. Einstein, "Effort, Performance, Transformational Leadership in Industrial and Military Service," *Journal of Occupation Psychology,* 60, 1987, pp. 1–10.

69. R. Pillai, C.A. Schriesheim, and E.S. Williams, "Fairness Perceptions and Trust as Mediators of Transformational and Transactional Leadership: A Two-Sample Study," *Journal of Management,* 25, 1999, pp. 897–933.

70. Mary Teresa Bitti, "If You Play the Game to Get Rich Quickly, You Will Lose," *National Post,* Monday, December 13, 2004, FP10. See also Anne Cummings, "The 'Masculine' and 'Feminine' Sides of Leadership and Culture: Perception vs. Reality Workers," *Knowledge@Wharton,* September 21–October 4, 2005.

71. David Olive, "Wrong Person for the Job," *Toronto Star,* Sunday, February 13, 2005, A20.

72. R. McQueen, "Glitter Girls No More," *National Post Business,* March 2001, p. 68; and J. McFarland, "Women Still Find Slow Rise to Power Positions," *The Globe and Mail,* March 13, 2003, pp. B1, B7.

73. L. Ramsay, "A League of Their Own," *The Globe and Mail,* November 23, 2002, p. B11.

74. A.H. Eagly and B.T. Johnson, "Gender and Leadership Style: A Meta-Analysis," *Psychological Bulletin,* 108, 1990, pp. 233–256.

75. Ibid.

76. Ibid.

77. A.H. Eagly and B.T. Johnson, "Gender and Leadership Style: A Meta-Analysis," *Psychological Bulletin,* 108, 1990, pp. 233–256.

78. Ibid.

79. A.H. Eagly, S.J. Karau, and M.G. Makhijani, "Gender and the Effectiveness of Leaders: A Meta-Analysis," *Psychological Bulletin,* 117, 1995, pp. 125–145.

80. Ibid.

81. R. Calori and B. Dufour, "Management European Style," *Academy of Management Executive,* 9, no. 3, 1995, pp. 61–70.

82. Ibid.

83. J.M. George and K. Bettenhausen, "Understanding Prosocial Behavior, Sales Performance, and Turnover: A Group-Level Analysis in a Service Context," *Journal of Applied Psychology,* 75, 1990, pp. 698–709.

84. N.M. Ashkanasy and C.S. Daus, "Emotion in the Workplace: The New Challenge for Managers," *Academy of Management Executive,* 16, no. 1, 2002, pp. 76–86; and J.M. George, "Emotions and Leadership: The Role of Emotional Intelligence," *Human Relations,* 53, 2002, pp. 1027–1055.

85. J.M. George, "Emotions and Leadership: The Role of Emotional Intelligence," *Human Relations,* 53, 2000, pp. 1027–1055.

86. Harvard Business School professor. Website: www.johnkotter.com/bio.html.

87. Gabriel Draven, "Leadership and The Duty to The Seventh Generation," *hr.com,* Sunday, October 17, 2004.

88. Keith Kalawsky, "Trash a Fallen Star," *The Globe and Mail Report on Business Magazine,* April 2005, 21–22.

89. Joshua Chaffin, "Vanishing Imperial CEOs," *Financial Post,* Monday, March 21, 2005, FP20.

90. Brian Banks, "Life Wish," *National Post Business Magazine,* August 2005, 30–34, 36, 38, 40.

91. Adapted from: Gyle Konotopetz, "Smed Boss Climbed Ladder to Success," *Business Edge,* Volume 4, Number 16, April 22, 2004.

92. Adapted from: Harvey Schachter, "Monday Morning Manager," *The Globe and Mail,* Monday, July 3, 2006, p. B2 and Amazon.com website: www.amazon.com/gp/product/078521285X/002-5716207-3409632?v=glance&n=283155.

93. Jerry Manas. *Napoleon on Project Management: Timeless Lessons in Planning, Execution, and Leadership.* Toronto: Nelson Business, 2006, 288 pages. ISBN (hardback): 078521285X.

94. Adapted from Gabriel Draven, "Leadership and The Duty to The Seventh Generation," *hr.com,* Sunday, October 17, 2004. Website: www.hr.com/servlets/sfs;jsessionid=16DD76DFE8F4F1A1954FEF8BD11F2D73?s=GDpdoD1wICmIkSP9y&t=/contentManager/onStory&i=1116423256281&b=1116423256281&l=0&e=UTF-8&StoryID=1119654493515.

Chapter 10

1. Slighted adapted from Suzanne Wintrob, "Drum Circles Encourage Rhythm in Companies," *National Post,* Saturday, July 30, 2005, FW3.

2. Website: www.corporatedrumcircles.com/.

3. W.R. Coradetti, "Teamwork Takes Time and a Lot of Energy," *HR Magazine,* June 1994, pp. 74–77; and D. Fenn, "Service Teams That Work," Inc., August 1995, p. 99; "Team Selling Catches on, but Is Sales Really a Team Sport?" *The Wall Street Journal,* March 29, 1994, p. A1.

4. Slightly adapted from M.B. Owens, "Teamwork Tips: Make the Most of Group Dynamics," *The Globe and Mail,* Friday, December 17, 2004, C3.

5. P. Booth, Challenge and Change: Embracing the Team Concept, Report 123-94, Conference Board of Canada, 1994.

6. Cited in C. Joinson, "Teams at Work," *HRMagazine,* May 1999, p. 30; and P. Strozniak, "Teams at Work," *Industry Week,* September 18, 2000, p. 47.

7. Reuven Bar-On. EQ-i. *BarOn Emotional Quotient Inventory. A Measure of Emotional Intelligence. Technical Manual.* Toronto: Multi-Health Systems Inc., 1997.

8. Pamela R. Johnson and Julie Indvik, "Organizational Benefits of Having Emotionally Intelligent Managers and

Employees," *Journal of Workplace Learning,* Vol. 11, Issue 3, 1999, 84ff.

9. Website: www.leadershipadvantage.com/ emotionalIntelligence.shtml.

10. For additional information and ideas, see the following website: www.elsevier.com/wps/ find/bookdescription.cws_home/680342/ description#description.

11. T.M. Mills, *The Sociology of Small Groups* (Englewood Cliffs, NJ: Prentice-Hall, 1967); M.E. Shaw, *Group Dynamics* (New York: McGraw-Hill, 1981).

12. P. Willcocks, "Yours and Mine? Can the New Owner of the Once-Troubled Myra Falls Copper and Zinc Mine Near Campbell River Forge a New Relationship With Workers and Their Union to Create a True Partnership?" *BCBusiness Magazine,* September 2000, pp. 114–120.

13. For additional research and papers on the top of self-managed work teams, see *Conference Proceedings: Anniversary Collection: The Best of 1990–1994.* Center for Collaborative Organizations (Center for the Study of Work Teams, University of North Texas, Denton, Texas. Website: www. workteams.unt.edu/old/literature/ proceedings/Anver-contents.htm.

14. J.A. Pearce II and E.C. Ravlin, "The Design and Activation of Self-Regulating Work Groups," Human Relations, 11, 1987, pp. 751–782.

15. P. Booth, *Challenge and Change: Embracing the Team Concept,* Report 123–94, Conference Board of Canada, 1994.

16. B. Dumaine, "Who Needs a Boss?" *Fortune,* May 7, 1990, pp. 52–60; and J.A. Pearce II and E.C. Ravlin, "The Design and Activation of Self-Regulating Work Groups," *Human Relations,* 11, 1987, pp. 751–782.

17. B. Dumaine, "Who Needs a Boss?" *Fortune,* May 7, 1990, pp. 52–60; and A.R. Montebello and V.R. Buzzotta, "Work Teams That Work," *Training & Development,* March 1993, pp. 59–64.

18. T.D. Wall, N.J. Kemp, P.R. Jackson, and C.W. Clegg, "Outcomes of Autonomous Work Groups: A Long-Term Field Experiment," *Academy of Management Journal,* 29, 1986, pp. 280–304.

19. W.R. Pape, "Group Insurance," Inc. (Inc. Technology Supplement), June 17, 1997, pp. 29–31; A.M. Townsend, S.M. DeMarie, and A.R. Hendrickson, "Are You Ready for Virtual Teams?" *HRMagazine,* September 1996, pp. 122–126; and A.M. Townsend,

S.M. DeMarie, and A.M. Hendrickson, "Virtual Teams: Technology and the Workplace of the Future," *Academy of Management Executive,* 12, no. 3, 1998, pp. 17–29.

20. A.M. Townsend, S.M. DeMarie, and A.R. Hendrickson, "Are You Ready for Virtual Teams?" *HRMagazine,* September 1996, pp. 122–126.

21. W.R. Pape, "Group Insurance," Inc. (Inc. Technology Supplement), June 17, 1997, pp. 29–31; and A.M. Townsend, S.M. DeMarie, and A.R. Hendrickson, "Are You Ready for Virtual Teams?" *HRMagazine,* September 1996, pp. 122–126.

22. A.B. Drexler and R. Forrester, "Teamwork—Not Necessarily the Answer," *HRMagazine,* January 1998, pp. 55–58.

23. R. Forrester and A.B. Drexler, "A Model for Team-Based Organization Performance," *Academy of Management Executive,* August 1999, p. 47. See also S.A. Mohrman, with S.G. Cohen and A.M. Mohrman Jr., *Designing Team-Based Organizations* (San Francisco: Jossey-Bass, 1995); and J.H. Shonk, *Team-Based Organizations* (Homewood, IL: Business One Irwin, 1992).

24. Claire Sookman, "Building Your Virtual Team," *ITWorldCanada,* March 2004. Website: www.itworldcanada.com/a/search/55dd71fe-030c-4487-8d27-e0e237b9ec49.html. *Claire Sookman specializes in 'virtual team' building, helping project managers who work remotely to collaborate more effectively to increase productivity and efficiency. She can be reached at csookman@sympatico.ca.*

25. A. Deutschman, "The Managing Wisdom of High-Tech Superstars," *Fortune,* October 17, 1994, pp. 197–206.

26. Ibid.

27. J.S. Lublin, "My Colleague, My Boss," *The Wall Street Journal,* April 12, 1995, pp. R4, R12.

28. B.W. Tuckman, "Developmental Sequences in Small Groups," *Psychological Bulletin,* 63, 1965, pp. 384–399; and B.W. Tuckman and M.C. Jensen, "Stages of Small Group Development," *Group and Organizational Studies,* 2, 1977, pp. 419–427.

29. C.J.G. Gersick, "Time and Transition in Work Teams: Toward a New Model of Group Development," *Academy of Management Journal,* 31, March 1988, pp. 9–41; C.J.G. Gersick, "Marking Time: Predictable Transitions in Task Groups," *Academy of Management Journal,* 32, June 1989, pp. 274–309.

30. J.R. Hackman, "Group Influences on Individuals in Organizations," in M.D. Dunnette and L.M. Hough (eds.), *Handbook of Industrial and Organizational Psychology,*

2nd ed., vol. 3 (Palo Alto, CA: Consulting Psychologists Press, 1992), pp. 199–267.

31. Ibid.

32. Ibid.

33. L. Festinger, "Informal Social Communication," *Psychological Review,* 57, 1950, pp. 271–282; and M.E. Shaw, *Group Dynamics* (New York: McGraw-Hill, 1981).

34. J.R. Hackman, "Group Influences on Individuals in Organizations," in M.D. Dunnette and L.M. Hough (eds.), *Handbook of Industrial and Organizational Psychology,* 2nd ed., vol. 3 (Palo Alto, CA: Consulting Psychologists Press, 1992), pp. 199–267; and M.E. Shaw, *Group Dynamics* (New York: McGraw-Hill, 1981).

35. Richard Bloom, "FedEx Set for a Parcel Invasion as Industry's D-Day Arrives," *The Globe and Mail,* Monday, December 20, 2004, B1, 10.

36. I.L. Janis, Groupthink (Boston: Houghton Mifflin, 1982); W. Park, "A Review of Research on Groupthink," *Journal of Behavioral Decision Making,* July 1990, pp. 229–245; C.P. Neck and G. Moorhead, "Groupthink Remodeled: The Importance of Leadership, Time Pressure, and Methodical Decision Making Procedures," *Human Relations,* May 1995, pp. 537–558; and J.N. Choi and M.U. Kim, "The Organizational Application of Groupthink and Its Limits in Organizations," *Journal of Applied Psychology,* April 1999, pp. 297–306.

37. M.E. Turner and A.R. Pratkanis, "Mitigating Groupthink by Stimulating Constructive Conflict," in C. De Dreu and E. Van de Vliert (eds.), *Using Conflict in Organizations* (London: Sage, 1997), pp. 53–71.

38. See N.R.F. Maier, *Principles of Human Relations* (New York: Wiley, 1952); I.L. Janis, *Groupthink: Psychological Studies of Policy Decisions and Fiascoes,* 2nd ed. (Boston: Houghton Mifflin, 1982); and C.R. Leana, "A Partial Test of Janis' Groupthink Model: Effects of Group Cohesiveness and Leader Behavior on Defective Decision Making," *Journal of Management,* Spring 1985, pp. 5–17.

39. P.C. Earley, "Social Loafing and Collectivism: A Comparison of the United States and the People's Republic of China," *Administrative Science Quarterly,* 34, 1989, pp. 565–581; J.M. George, "Extrinsic and Intrinsic Origins of Perceived Social Loafing in Organizations," *Academy of Management Journal,* 35, 1992, pp. 191–202; S.G. Harkins, B. Latane, and K. Williams, "Social Loafing: Allocating Effort or Taking it Easy," *Journal of Experimental Social Psychology,* 16, 1980,

pp. 457–465; B. Latane, K.D. Williams, and S. Harkins, "Many Hands Make Light the Work: The Causes and Consequences of Social Loafing," *Journal of Personality and Social Psychology,* 37, 1979, pp. 822–832; and J.A. Shepperd, "Productivity Loss in Performance Groups: A Motivation Analysis," *Psychological Bulletin,* 113, 1993, pp. 67–81.

40. Adapted from the American Management Association, "How to Build High-Performance Teams," Self-Study Course. Website: www.amanet.org/selfstudy/b13759.htm.

41. Adapted from Andy Georgiades, "Business Heeds the Beat," *Toronto Star,* August 4, 1999. Website: www.souldrums.com/star.html.

42. Adapted from Jim Clemmer, "Team Spirit Built From the Top," *The Globe and Mail,* Friday, November 26, 2004, C1.

43. Sharda Prashad, "Transparency Is the Ticket," *Toronto Star,* Sunday, April 24, 2005, A21.

Chapter 11

1. Adapted from Grant Buckler, "Squeezing Returns From Training Investments," *Computing Canada,* April 22, 2005, 24 and www.opels.ca/index.html.

2. www.opels.ca/learnPerform.html.

3. www.shrc.ca/.

4. The SHRC, a non-profit council that represents software professionals, is offering OPELS to its members as part of a Human Resources Toolkit that the Ottawa-based council is developing. For a limited time, the SHRC is offering a one-year licence to use OPELS and an SHRC membership for $995.

5. www.opels.ca/.

6. www.opels.ca/largeDiagram.html.

7. www.opels.ca/slides/slide12.pdf; www.opels.ca/slides/slide14.pdf.

8. http://strategis.ic.gc.ca/app/ccc/search/navigate.do?language=eng&portal=1&estblmntNo=123456226188&profile=completeProfile.

9. Adapted from Joan Ransberry, "Farming in Suburbia's Shadow," *The Markham Economist & Sun,* Tuesday, August 9, 2005, 3.

10. J.E. Butler, G.R. Ferris, and N.K. Napier, *Strategy and Human Resource Management* (Cincinnati, OH: South Western, 1991); P.M. Wright and G.C. McMahan, "Theoretical Perspectives for Strategic Human Resource Management," *Journal of Management,* 18, 1992, pp. 295–320.

11. Joan Ransberry, "Farming in Suburbia's Shadow," *The Markham Economist & Sun,* Tuesday, August 9, 2005, 3.

12. C.D. Fisher, L.F. Schoenfeldt, and J.B. Shaw, *Human Resource Management* (Boston: Houghton Mifflin, 1990).

13. P.M. Wright and G.C. McMahan, "Theoretical Perspectives for Strategic Human Resource Management," *Journal of Management,* 18, 1992, pp. 295–320.

14. L. Baird and I. Meshoulam, "Managing Two Fits for Strategic Human Resource Management," *Academy of Management Review,* 14, 1989, pp. 116–128; J. Milliman, M. Von Glinow, and M. Nathan, "Organizational Life Cycles and Strategic International Human Resource Management in Multinational Companies: Implications for Congruence Theory," *Academy of Management Review,* 16, 1991, pp. 318–339; R.S. Schuler and S.E. Jackson, "Linking Competitive Strategies With Human Resource Management Practices," *Academy of Management Executive,* 1, 1987, pp. 207–219; P.M. Wright and S.A. Snell, "Toward an Integrative View of Strategic Human Resource Management," *Human Resource Management Review,* 1, 1991, pp. 203–225.

15. Derek Sankey, "Boomers Aim to fill the Gaps in Management Expertise," *FP EDGE, Financial Post,* Monday, May 10, 2004, FE3.

16. http://greyfox.ca/.

17. S.L. Rynes, "Recruitment, Job Choice, and Post-Hire Consequences: A Call for New Research Directions," in M.D. Dunnette and L.M. Hough (eds.), *Handbook of Industrial and Organizational Psychology,* vol. 2 (Palo Alto, CA: Consulting Psychologists Press, 1991), pp. 399–444.

18. Rosemary McCracken, "No Time to Retire," *FP EDGE, Financial Post,* Monday, March 8, 2004, FE1, 4.

19. M. Lewis, "BCE Appoints Alcan Recruit 'Chief Talent Officer,'" *Financial Post (National Post),* May 24, 2001, p. C11.

20. R.J. Harvey, "Job Analysis," in M.D. Dunnette and L.M. Hough (eds.), *Handbook of Industrial and Organizational Psychology,* vol. 2 (Palo Alto, CA: Consulting Psychologists Press, 1991), pp. 71–163.

21. E.L. Levine, *Everything You Always Wanted to Know About Job Analysis: A Job Analysis Primer* (Tampa, FL: Mariner, 1983).

22. R.L. Mathis and J.H. Jackson, *Human Resource Management,* 7th ed. (St. Paul, MN: West, 1994).

23. S.L. Rynes, "Recruitment, Job Choice, and Post-Hire Consequences: A Call for New Research Directions," in M.D. Dunnette and L.M. Hough (eds.), *Handbook of Industrial and Organizational Psychology,* vol. 2 (Palo Alto, CA: Consulting Psychologists Press, 1991), pp. 399–444.

24. R.M. Guion, "Personnel Assessment, Selection, and Placement," in M.D. Dunnette and L.M. Hough (eds.), *Handbook of Industrial and Organizational Psychology,* vol. 2 (Palo Alto, CA: Consulting Psychologists Press, 1991), pp. 327–397.

25. R.A. Noe, J.R. Hollenbeck, B. Gerhart, and P.M. Wright, *Human Resource Management: Gaining a Competitive Advantage* (Burr Ridge, IL: Irwin, 1994); J.A. Wheeler and J.A. Gier, "Reliability and Validity of the Situational Interview for a Sales Position," *Journal of Applied Psychology,* 2, 1987, pp. 484–487.

26. R.A. Noe, J.R. Hollenbeck, B. Gerhart, and P.M. Wright, *Human Resource Management: Gaining a Competitive Advantage* (Burr Ridge, IL: Irwin, 1994).

27. "Wanted: Middle Managers, Audition Required," *The Wall Street Journal,* December 28, 1995, p. A1.

28. Terrence Belford, "Strategy for the New Economy," *National Post,* FP ENTREPRENEUR, Strategies for Small and Mid-Size Businesses, Monday, March 14, 2005, FP9.

29. I.L. Goldstein, "Training in Work Organizations," in M.D. Dunnette and L.M. Hough (eds.), *Handbook of Industrial and Organizational Psychology,* vol. 2 (Palo Alto, CA: Consulting Psychologists Press, 1991), pp. 507–619.

30. M.B. Arthur, D.T. Hall, and B.S. Lawrence (eds.), *Handbook of Career Theory* (Cambridge: Cambridge University Press, 1989), p. 8.

31. S.L. McShane, *Canadian Organizational Behaviour,* 4th ed. (Whitby, ON: McGraw-Hill Ryerson, 2001), p. 548.

32. L. Chwialkowska, "Ottawa Plan Targets Jobs Crisis," *National Post,* June 18, 2001, p. A1.

33. See, for example, P.O. Benham Jr., "Developing Organizational Talent: The Key to Performance and Productivity," *SAM Advanced Management Journal,* January 1993, pp. 34–39.

34. Information about Alcan and Hewlett-Packard based on L. Duxbury, L. Dyke, and N. Lam, "Career Development in the Federal Public Service: Building a World-Class

Workforce," Treasury Board of Canada, January 1999.

35. S.P. Robbins and N. Langton, *Organizational Behaviour: Concepts, Controversies, Applications,* 3rd Canadian ed. (Toronto: Pearson Education Canada, 2003), pp. 512–513.

36. L. Chwialkowska, "Ottawa Plan Targets Jobs Crisis," *National Post,* June 18, 2001, p. A1.

37. For further elaboration of these points see B. Moses, *Career Intelligence: Mastering the New Work and Personal Realities,* (Toronto: Stoddart, 1997).

38. Sanjiv Purba, "When Reviews Deserve a Failing Grade," *The Globe and Mail,* Friday, June 11, 2004, C1.

39. Sources on the Internet that offer useful performance review forms, tools and human resource-related best practices: www.opm.gov/perform/monitor.asp; www.hr.com; www.businesstown.com/people/reviews-overview.asp; www.toolpack.com/performance.html; www.workplacetoolbox.com/index.jsp.

40. C.D. Fisher, L.F. Schoenfeldt, and J.B. Shaw, *Human Resource Management* (Boston: Houghton Mifflin, 1990).

41. M.A. Peiperl, "Getting 360° Feedback Right," *Harvard Business Review,* January 2001, pp. 142–147.

42. T. Davis and M.J. Landa, "A Contrary Look at Employee Performance Appraisal," *Canadian Manager,* Fall 1999, pp. 18–19+.

43. Adapted from the American Management Association, "How to Build High-Performance Teams," Self-Study Course. Website: www.amanet.org/selfstudy/b13759.htm.

44. "Employers Moving to Strategic Compensation," *The Globe and Mail,* Tuesday, January 12, 2005, C9.

45. www.watsonwyatt.com/canada-english/news/press.asp?ID=14103.

46. L. Duxbury, L. Dyke, and N. Lam, "Career Development in the Federal Public Service: Building a World-Class Workforce," Treasury Board of Canada, January 1999.

47. Adapted from Deborah Yedlin, "Not a Lot of Love for Unionization in the Wild West," *The Globe and Mail,* Tuesday, August 2, 2005, B2.

48. Colby Cosh, "Do Unions Still Matter?" *National Post,* Wednesday, August 3, 2005, A16.

49. See http://socserv.socsci.mcmaster.ca/fun/.

50. S. Premack and J.E. Hunter, "Individual Unionization Decisions," *Psychological Bulletin,* 103, 1988, pp. 223–234.

51. *The Daily* (Statistics Canada), "Fact-Sheet on Unionization in Canada," August 28, 2003.

52. F. Milhar, "Leaders out of Step With Members," *Financial Post (National Post),* September 2, 2003, pp. FP1, FP4.

53. S. Greenhouse, "Unions to Push to Make Organizing Easier," *NYTimes.com,* August 31, 2003, www.nytimes.com/2003/08/31/national/31SWEE.html.

54. The SHRC, a non-profit council that represents software professionals, is offering OPELS to its members as part of a Human Resources Toolkit that the Ottawa-based council is developing. For a limited time, the SHRC is offering a one-year licence to use OPELS and an SHRC membership for $995.

55. Peter B. Vaill, Ph.D. *Learning as a Way of Being. Strategies for Survival in a World of Permanent White Water.* San Francisco: Jossey-Bass Publishers, 1966, 4, 14. See also http://gseweb.harvard.edu/~hepg/HER-BookRev/Articles/1997/1-Spring/Vaill.html.

56. Ibid. See also J.Z. Young. *Doubt and Certainty in Science.* New York: Oxford University Press, 1960.

57. Daniel H. Kim and Eileen Mullen, "The Spirit of the Learning Organization," LEVERAGE POINTS for a New Workplace, New World, August 26, 2004, Issue 53. This article, excerpted from *The Systems Thinker Newsletter,* appears in the Pegasus anthology, "Reflections on Creating Learning Organizations." Website: www.pegasuscom.com/levpoints/spiritlearn.html, or see *The Systems Thinker,* Vol. 4, No. 4, May 1993. Also, www.pegasuscom.com/levpoints/lp53.html.

58. Peter Brieger, "From Health to Wealth," *National Post,* Tuesday, May 17, 2005, FP6.

59. Brian Stanfield, " Editorial: Learning a Living," *Edges,* Volume 6, Number 1, Winter 1994, 3–4.

60. Adapted from: Greg Keenan, "Toyota to Build Parts Plant in Ontario," *The Globe and Mail,* Monday, July 109, 2006 and "New Toyota Plant for Woodstock," *Toronto Star,* Monday, July 10, 2006.

61. Adapted from Michael Stern, "Expanding Role for HR Executives," *Financial Post,* August 1, 2004, FP10.

62. M. Conlin, "Job Security, No. Tall Latte, Yes," *Business Week,* April 2, 2001, pp. 62, 64.

Chapter 12

1. Adapted from Alexandra Edmiston, "Conduct Yourself as a Communications Leader," *The Globe and Mail,* Friday, June 24, 2005, C1; Janis Foord Kirk, "Unfair Rule Destroys Productivity," *Toronto Star,* Saturday, March 12, 2005, D1, 13; IN BRIEF, "Impersonal Approach Hurts Business, Study Says," *The Globe and Mail,* Wednesday, August 20, 2003, C3.

2. Quoted in Michael Kesterton, "Social Studies," *The Globe and Mail,* Wednesday, May 19, 2004, A22.

3. "LEVERAGE POINTS for a New Workplace, New World," *Electronic Newsletter,* August 26, 2004, Issue 53.

4. Wendy Stueck, "Wanted: Mining Executives With 'Soft Skills'," *The Globe and Mail,* Monday, January 31, 2005, B3.

5. Writing in the August 2003 issue of the *Journal of Personality and Social Psychology,* Sanchez-Burks said he traded notes with colleagues at the University of Michigan, Seoul National University in Korea and the International Business University in Nanjing, China. *Source:* IN BRIEF, "Impersonal Approach Hurts Business, Study Says," *The Globe and Mail,* Wednesday, August 20, 2003, C3.

6. Adapted from Wallace Immen, "CFOs Want Employees Who Think on Their Feet, Survey Says," *The Globe and Mail,* Saturday, October 30, 2004, B10.

7. C.A. O'Reilly and L.R. Pondy, "Organizational Communication," in S. Kerr (ed.), *Organizational Behavior* (Columbus, OH: Grid, 1979).

8. Richard Bloom, "How Parmalat Juggled the Struggle," *The Globe and Mail,* Monday, May 23, 2005, B3.

9. D.A. Adams, P.A. Todd, and R.R. Nelson, "A Comparative Evaluation of the Impact of Electronic and Voice Mail on Organizational Communication," *Information & Management,* 24, 1993, pp. 9–21.

10. E.M. Rogers and R. Agarwala-Rogers, *Communication in Organizations* (New York: Free Press, 1976).

11. Deena Waisberg, "Dress Code Still in Force Though It's Stinking Hot," *National Post,* Saturday, August 6, 2005, FW3.

12. Mary Teresa Bitti, "The New Face of Canadian Business," FP ENTREPRENEUR: Strategies for Small and Mid-Size Businesses, *National Post,* Monday, May 2, 2005, FP110.

13. Paul Lima, "E-mail Is No substitute for Face-to-Face Contact," *National Post*, Wednesday, June 15, 2005, FP9. See also IN BRIEF, "Tech Worse Than Talk in Resolving Conflicts," *The Globe and Mail*, Friday, July 29, 2005, C1.

14. R.L. Daft, R.H. Lengel, and L.K. Trevino, "Message Equivocality, Media Selection, and Manager Performance: Implications for Information Systems," *MIS Quarterly*, 11, 1987, pp. 355–366; R.L. Daft and R.H. Lengel, "Information Richness: A New Approach to Managerial Behavior and Organization Design," in B.M. Staw and L.L. Cummings (eds.), *Research in Organizational Behavior* (Greenwich, CT: JAI Press, 1984).

15. R.L. Daft, *Organization Theory and Design* (St. Paul, MN: West, 1992).

16. Ibid.

17. "Lights, Camera, Meeting: Teleconferencing Becomes a Time-Saving Tool," *The Wall Street Journal*, February 21, 1995, p. A1.

18. "E-Mail Abuse: Workers Discover High-Tech Ways to Cause Trouble in the Office," *The Wall Street Journal*, November 22, 1994, p. A1; and "E-Mail Alert: Companies Lag in Devising Policies on How It Should Be Used," *The Wall Street Journal*, December 29, 1994, p. A1.

19. J. Kay, "Someone Will Watch Over Me: Think Your Office E-Mails are Private? Think Again," *National Post Business*, January 2001, pp. 59–64.

20. "Office Workers Urged to Go 'Email Free,'" *Health & Beauty: News*, Monday, 17th October 2005. Website: www.manchesteronline.co.uk/healthandbeauty/news/s/178/178139_office_workers_urged_to_go_email_free.html.

21. "Fact Sheet: Privacy in the Workplace," Office of the Privacy Commissioner of Canada. Website: www.privcom.gc.ca/fs-fi/02_05_d_17_e.asp.

22. Wallace Immen, "'C-Suite' Coaching Losing Its Stigma," *The Globe and Mail*, Wednesday, March 30, 2005, C1, 2.

23. Personal communication, November 28, 2005.

24. Daniel Goleman, Richard Boyatzis and Annie McKee. *Primal Leadership: Realizing the Power of Emotional Intelligence*. Boston: Harvard Business School Press, 2002. See also Mary Pearson, "Don't Play the Blame Game at Work," *The Globe and Mail*, Friday, June 25, 2004, C1, 8.

25. "On the Road," *Newsweek*, June 6, 1994, p. 8.

26. C.R. Mill, "Feedback: The Art of Giving and Receiving Help," in L. Porter and

C.R. Mill (eds), *The Reading Book for Human Relations Training* (Bethel, ME: NTL Institute of Applied Behavioral Science, 1976), pp. 18–19.

27. Based on S.P. Robbins and P.L. Hunsaker, *Training in Interpersonal Skills: TIPS for Managing People at Work*, 2nd ed. (Upper Saddle River, NJ: Prentice-Hall, 1996), Ch 3.

28. D. Tannen, "The Power of Talk," *Harvard Business Review*, September–October 1995, pp. 138–148; D. Tannen, *Talking from 9 to 5* (New York: Avon Books, 1995).

29. Ibid.

30. D. Tannen, *Talking from 9 to 5* (New York: Avon Books, 1995).

31. Ibid.

32. D. Tannen, "The Power of Talk," *Harvard Business Review*, September–October 1995, pp. 138–148; and D. Tannen, *Talking from 9 to 5* (New York: Avon Books, 1995).

33. Ibid.

34. Ibid.

35. Susan Dunn, "Multicultural Differences in Greetings You Need to Be Aware of," Website: www.bpic.co.uk/articles/greetings.htm.

36. Ron Csillag, "Obituraries: Peter Frost, Psychologist and Teacher, 1939–2004," *The Globe and Mail*, Thursday, December 16, 2004, S7.

37. Gillian Shaw, "Emotionally 'Toxic Offices' Sicken Staff and Bleed Bottom Lines," *Business Edge, Financial Post*, Monday, April 28, 2003, BE2.

38. Gabriel Draven, "Leadership and The Duty to The Seventh Generation," *hr.com*, Sunday, October 17, 2004.

39. Peter Frost. *Toxic Emotions at Work: How Compassionate Managers Handle Pain and Conflict*. Cambridge, Mass.: Harvard Business Review, 2003, 256 pages. ISBN: 1578512573

40. J.A. Litterer, "Conflict in Organizations: A Reexamination," *Academy of Management Journal*, 9, 1966, pp. 178–186; S.M. Schmidt and T.A. Kochan, "Conflict: Towards Conceptual Clarity," *Administrative Science Quarterly*, 13, 1972, pp. 359–370; and R.H. Miles, *Macro Organizational Behavior* (Santa Monica, CA: Goodyear, 1980).

41. S.P. Robbins, *Managing Organizational Conflict: A Nontraditional Approach* (Englewood Cliffs, NJ: Prentice-Hall, 1974); and L. Coser, *The Functions of Social Conflict* (New York: Free Press, 1956).

42. L.R. Pondy, "Organizational Conflict: Concepts and Models," *Administrative Science*

Quarterly, 2, 1967, pp. 296–320; and R.E. Walton and J.M. Dutton, "The Management of Interdepartmental Conflict: A Model and Review," *Administrative Science Quarterly*, 14, 1969, pp. 62–73.

43. K.W. Thomas, "Conflict and Negotiation Processes in Organizations," in M.D. Dunnette and L.M. Hough (eds.), *Handbook of Industrial and Organizational Psychology*, 2nd ed., vol. 3 (Palo Alto, CA: Consulting Psychologists Press, 1992), pp. 651–717.

44. P.R. Lawrence, L.B. Barnes, and J.W. Lorsch, *Organizational Behavior and Administration* (Homewood, IL: Irwin, 1976).

45. Adapted from the American Management Association, "How to Build High-Performance Teams," Self-Study Course. Website: www.amanet.org/selfstudy/b13759.htm.

46. Ingrid Peritz, "Labour Strige Disrupts Classes of 65,000 Quebec College Students," *The Globe and Mail*, Monday, August 22, 2005, A4.

47. Quoted in Michael Kesterton, "Social Studies," *The Globe and Mail*, Wednesday, May 19, 2004, A22.

48. R.J. Lewicki and J.R. Litterer, *Negotiation* (Homewood, IL: Irwin, 1985); G.B. Northcraft and M.A. Neale, *Organizational Behavior* (Fort Worth, TX: Dryden, 1994); J.Z. Rubin and B.R. Brown, *The Social Psychology of Bargaining and Negotiation* (New York: Academic Press, 1975).

49. L. Thompson and R. Hastie, "Social Perception in Negotiation," *Organizational Behavior and Human Decision Processes*, 47, 1990, pp. 98–123.

50. K.W. Thomas, "Conflict and Negotiation Processes in Organizations," in M.D. Dunnette and L.M. Hough (eds.), *Handbook of Industrial and Organizational Psychology*, 2nd ed., vol. 3 (Palo Alto, CA: Consulting Psychologists Press, 1992), pp. 651–717.

51. R.J. Lewicki, S.E. Weiss, and D. Lewin, "Models of Conflict, Negotiation and Third Party Intervention: A Review and Synthesis," *Journal of Organizational Behavior*, 13, 1992, pp. 209–252.

52. G.B. Northcraft and M.A. Neale, *Organizational Behavior* (Fort Worth, TX: Dryden, 1994).

53. R.J. Lewicki, S.E. Weiss, and D. Lewin, "Models of Conflict, Negotiation and Third Party Intervention"; G.B. Northcraft and M.A. Neale, *Organizational Behavior* (Fort Worth, TX: Dryden, 1994); and D.G. Pruitt, "Integrative Agreements: Nature and Consequences," in M.H. Bazerman and

R.J. Lewicki (eds.), *Negotiating in Organizations* (Beverly Hills, CA: Sage, 1983).

54. R. Fischer and W. Ury, *Getting to Yes* (Boston: Houghton Mifflin, 1981); and G.B. Northcraft and M.A. Neale, *Organizational Behavior* (Fort Worth, TX: Dryden, 1994).

55. P.J. Carnevale and D.G. Pruitt, "Negotiation and Mediation," *Annual Review of Psychology,* 43, 1992, pp. 531–582.

56. Adapted from "Negotiation," *Negotiation Strategies,* International Online Training Program On Intractable Conflict, Conflict Research Consortium, University of Colorado, Copyright ©1998. Website: www.colorado.edu/conflict/peace/treatment/negotn.htm.

57. Gerry Blackwell, "The Same Team," *EDGE,* March 2005, Vol. 3 No. 3, 10–12.

58. Adapted from "Impersonal Approach Hurts Business, Study Says," *The Globe and Mail,* Wednesday, August 20, 2003, C3.

59. Slightly adapted from: Karl Moore, "CEO in Waiting Keeps the Engine Running," *The Globe and Mail,* Monday, July 10, 2006, B10.

Chapter 13

1. Slightly adapted Diedre McMurdy, "People Get Stress Relief Express-Style," *Financial Post,* Saturday, January 15, 2005, IN1, 2.

2. Website: www.monastery-spa.com/welcome.htm.

3. Website: www.elibay.com/.

4. Gabor Mate M.D. *When the Body Says No: the Cost of Hidden Stress.* Toronto: Vintage Canada, 2004, 320 pages. ISBN: 0676973124

5. Website: www.uccm.net/.

6. Website: www.pureyoga.ca/. See also the website for chair massage for workplaces: www.infinitemassage.com/.

7. W.G. Ouchi, "Markets, Bureaucracies, and Clans," *Administrative Science Quarterly,* 25, 1980, pp. 129–141.

8. Slightly adapted from Diedre McMurdy, "People Get Stress Relief Express-Style," *Financial Post,* Saturday, January 15, 2005, IN1, 2.

9. A. Kinicki and B.K. Williams, Management: A Practical Introduction" (Boston: McGraw-Hill Irwin, 2003).

10. E.E. Lawler III and J.G. Rhode, *Information and Control in Organizations* (Pacific Palisades, CA: Goodyear, 1976).

11. C.W.L. Hill and G.R. Jones, *Strategic Management: An Integrated Approach,* 4th ed. (Boston: Houghton Mifflin, 1997).

12. W.G. Ouchi, "The Transmission of Control Through Organizational Hierarchy," *Academy of Management Journal,* 21, 1978, pp. 173–192.

13. W.G. Ouchi, "The Relationship Between Organizational Structure and Organizational Control," *Administrative Science Quarterly,* 22, 1977, pp. 95–113.

14. W.G. Ouchi, "Markets, Bureaucracies, and Clans," *Administrative Science Quarterly,* 25, 1980, pp. 129–141.

15. W.H. Newman, *Constructive Control* (Englewood Cliffs, NJ: Prentice-Hall, 1975).

16. J.D. Thompson, *Organizations in Action* (New York: McGraw-Hill, 1967).

17. R.N. Anthony, *The Management Control Function* (Boston: Harvard Business School Press, 1988).

18. P. Lorange, M. Morton, and S. Ghoshal, *Strategic Control* (St. Paul, MN: West, 1986).

19. H. Koontz and R.W. Bradspies, "Managing Through Feedforward Control," *Business Horizons,* June 1972, pp. 25–36.

20. Adapted from Jim Middlemiss, "New Rules Tough on Smaller Firms," *Financial Post FP EDGE,* Monday, July 26, 2004, FP9; Canada's CFO of the Year, "Peter Rubenovitch: Integrity, Vision Key to Financial Leadership," *The Globe and Mail,* Friday, May 7, 2004, P1.

21. Website: www.rochongenova.com/.

22. W.G. Ouchi, "Markets, Bureaucracies, and Clans," *Administrative Science Quarterly,* 25, 1980, pp. 129–141.

23. C.W.L. Hill and G.R. Jones, *Strategic Management: An Integrated Approach,* 4th ed. (Boston: Houghton Mifflin, 1997).

24. R. Simons, "Strategic Orientation and Top Management Attention to Control Systems," *Strategic Management Journal,* 12, 1991, pp. 49–62.

25. J.A. Alexander, "Adaptive Changes in Corporate Control Practices," *Academy of Management Journal,* 34, 1991, pp. 162–193.

26. Virginia Galt, "Industry Buffs Its Image as Demand for Staff Soars," *The Globe and Mail,* Monday, November 15, 2004, B4.

27. G.H.B. Ross, "Revolution in Management Control," *Management Accounting,* 72, 1992, pp. 23–27.

28. D.S. Pugh, D.J. Hickson, C.R. Hinings, and C. Turner, "Dimensions of Organizational Structure," *Administrative Science Quarterly,* 13, 1968, pp. 65–91.

29. P.M. Blau, *The Dynamics of Bureaucracy* (Chicago: University of Chicago Press, 1955).

30. Adapted from Deena Waisberg, "Bank Executive Proves He's a Stand-up Guy," *Financial Post,* Saturday, May 28, 2005, FW9.

31. Ibid.

32. S. Mcgee, "Garish Jackets Add to Clamor of Chicago Pits," *The Wall Street Journal,* July 31, 1995, p. C1.

33. T. Cole, "How to Stay Hired," *Report on Business Magazine,* March 1995, pp. 46–48.

34. K.E. Weick, *The Social Psychology of Organization* (Reading, MA: Addison-Wesley, 1979).

35. J. McCann, "Cutting the Crap," *National Post Business,* March 2001, pp. 47–57.

36. Virginia Galt, "Productivity Buckling Under the Strain of Stress, CEOs say," *The Globe and Mail,* Thursday, June 9, 2005, A1, 15.

37. Website: www.fgiworld.com/.

38. Editorial, "From the Founders: How Fast Is Your Company?" *Fast Company,* June 2003, Issue 71, 18.

39. David Crane, "Upgrading Skills Should Be Priority," *Toronto Star,* Friday, April 1, 2005, F2.

40. Virginia Galt, "Change Is a Good Thing When Everyone Is Involved," *The Globe and Mail,* Saturday, June 25, 2005, B11.

41. Simon Avery, "Dell's New Business Model: Redemption," *The Globe and Mail,* Sunday, July 16, 2007.

Appendix A

1. A. Smith, *The Wealth of Nations* (London: Penguin, 1982).

2. Ibid., p. 110.

3. J.G. March and H.A. Simon, *Organizations* (New York: Wiley, 1958).

4. F.W. Taylor, *Shop Management* (New York: Harper, 1903); F.W. Taylor, *The Principles of Scientific Management* (New York: Harper, 1911).

5. J.A. Litterer, *The Emergence of Systematic Management as Shown by the Literature from 1870–1900* (New York: Garland, 1986).

6. H.R. Pollard, *Developments in Management Thought* (New York: Crane, 1974).

7. F.B. Gilbreth, *Primer of Scientific Management* (New York: Van Nostrand Reinhold, 1912).

8. D. Roy, "Efficiency and the Fix: Informal Intergroup Relations in a Piece Work Setting," *American Journal of Sociology,* 60, 1954, pp. 255–266.

9. M. Weber, in H.H. Gerth and C.W. Mills (eds.), *From Max Weber: Essays in Sociology*

(New York: Oxford University Press, 1946); M. Weber, in G. Roth and C. Wittich (eds.), *Economy and Society* (Berkeley: University of California Press, 1978).

10. C. Perrow, *Complex Organizations,* 2nd ed. (Glenview IL: Scott, Foresman, 1979).

11. M. Weber in H.H. Gerth and C.W. Mills (eds.), *From Max Weber: Essays in Sociology* (New York: Oxford University Press, 1946), p. 331.

12. See C. Perrow, *Complex Organizations,* 2nd ed. (Glenview IL: Scott, Foresman, 1979), Ch. 1, for a detailed discussion of these issues.

13. H. Fayol, *General and Industrial Management* (New York: IEEE Press, 1984).

14. L.D. Parker, "Control in Organizational Life: The Contribution of Mary Parker Follett," *Academy of Management Review,* 9, 1984, pp. 736–745.

15. E. Mayo, *The Human Problems of Industrial Civilization* (New York: Macmillan, 1933); F.J. Roethlisberger and W.J. Dickson, *Management and the Worker* (Cambridge, MA: Harvard University Press, 1947).

16. D. Roy, "Banana Time: Job Satisfaction and Informal Interaction," *Human Organization,* 18, 1960, pp. 158–161.

17. For an analysis of the problems in determining cause from effect in the Hawthorne studies and in social settings in general, see A. Carey, "The Hawthorne Studies: A Radical Criticism," *American Sociological Review,* 33, 1967, pp. 403–416.

18. D. McGregor, *The Human Side of Enterprise* (New York: McGraw-Hill, 1960).

19. W.E. Deming, *Out of the Crisis* (Cambridge, MA: MIT Press, 1986).

20. D. Katz and R.L. Kahn, *The Social Psychology of Organizations* (New York: Wiley, 1966); J.D. Thompson, *Organizations in Action* (New York: McGraw-Hill, 1967).

21. T. Burns and G.M. Stalker, *The Management of Innovation* (London: Tavistock, 1961); P.R. Lawrence and J.R. Lorsch, *Organization and Environment* (Boston: Graduate School of Business Administration, Harvard University, 1967).

Appendix B

1. Written by J.W. Haddad, Professor, School of Business Management, Seneca College of Applied Arts and Technology, Toronto, Canada.

2. I suggest using *PlanWrite Business Plan Writer Deluxe 2006,* McGraw-Hill Irwin, ISBN-13: 978-0-07-328146-9, ISBN-10: 0-07-328146-8.

3. *PlanWrite Business Plan Writer Deluxe.*

4. TD Bank Financial Group, 150th Annual Report 2005, p. 4.

5. www.thebodyshop.com.au/infopage. cfm?topicID=20

6. www.cara.com

7. www.renees.com/vision.asp

8. www.thebodyshop.com.au/infopage. cfm?pageID=53

9. Based on *PlanWrite,* op. cit.

Photo Credits

CHAPTER 1

Page 3: image 100/PunchStock; Page 13: Ray Reiss Photography; Page 25: Monty Rakusen/Getty Images.

CHAPTER 2

Page 37: CP; Page 43: CP; Page 46: Digital Vision.

CHAPTER 3

Page 61: Corbis; Page 68: The McGraw-Hill Companies/John A. Karachewski, photographer; Page 74: Spike Mafford/ Getty Images; Page 79: AP/Brian Branch-Price; Page 81: CP.

CHAPTER 4

Page 93: Digital Vision; Page 97: CP; Page 102: Photo Link/Getty Images.

CHAPTER 5

Page 121: CP; Page 125: CP; Page 142: Peter Blakely/SABA.

CHAPTER 6

Page 161: Digital Vision/Getty Images; Page 167: John A. Rizzo/Getty Images; Page 168: CP; Page 180: Photodisc Collection/Getty Images.

CHAPTER 7

Page 195: Photo Link/Getty Images; Page 198: CP; Page 205: Royalty-free/Corbis.

CHAPTER 8

Page 221: CP; Page 224: Tomi/PhotoLink/Getty Images; Page 299: Courtesy of Inco Ltd.

CHAPTER 9

Page 247: Comstock/Punch Stock; Page 253: The McGraw-Hill Companies, Inc./Gary He, photographer; Page 268: CP.

CHAPTER 10

Page 279: Lyle Stafford; Page 289: Royalty-free/Corbis; Page 295: CP.

CHAPTER 11

Page 305: Adam Crowley/Getty Images; Page 307: CP; Page 311: Royalty-free/Corbis.

CHAPTER 12

Page 335: Ilya Rozhdestvensky/Getty Images; Page 351: Getty Images (photo of girls) Page Source/Picture Quest (photo of boys); Page 344: Ryan McVay/Getty Images.

CHAPTER 13

Page 367: Ryan McVay/Getty Images; Page 370: Scala/Art Resource, NY.

Name/Company/URL Index

Subject Index